Materia Magica

NEW TEXTS FROM ANCIENT CULTURES

Edited by

Traianos Gagos†
James G. Keenan, Loyola University of Chicago
Terry Wilfong, University of Michigan

Settling a Dispute: Toward a Legal Anthropology of Late Antique Egypt
by Traianos Gagos and Peter van Minnen

Women of Jeme: Lives in a Coptic Town in Late Antique Egypt
by T. G. Wilfong

Wine, Wealth, and the State in Late Antique Egypt:
The House of Apion at Oxyrhynchus
by T. M. Hickey

New Literary Papyri from the Michigan Collection:
Mythographic Lyric and a Catalogue of Poetic First Lines
by Cassandra Borges and C. Michael Sampson

Materia Magica:
The Archaeology of Magic in Roman Egypt, Cyprus, and Spain
by Andrew T. Wilburn

Materia Magica

---

*The Archaeology of Magic in
Roman Egypt, Cyprus, and Spain*

Andrew T. Wilburn

The University of Michigan Press
Ann Arbor

Copyright © by the University of Michigan 2012
All rights reserved

This book may not be reproduced, in whole or in part, including illustrations, in any form (beyond that copying permitted by Sections 107 and 108 of the U.S. Copyright Law and except by reviewers for the public press), without written permission from the publisher.

Published in the United States of America by
The University of Michigan Press
Manufactured in the United States of America
⊗ Printed on acid-free paper

2015   2014   2013   2012   4   3   2   1

A CIP catalog record for this book is available from the British Library.

Library of Congress Cataloging-in-Publication Data

Wilburn, Andrew T., 1974–
Materia magica : the archaeology of magic in Roman Egypt, Cyprus, and Spain / Andrew T. Wilburn.
   pages cm. — (New texts from ancient cultures)
Includes bibliographical references and index.
ISBN 978-0-472-11779-6 (cloth : alkaline paper) — ISBN 978-0-472-02868-9 (e-book)
1. Magic, Ancient—History. 2. Magic, Roman—History. 3. Magic—Egypt—History—To 1500. 4. Magic—Cyprus—History—To 1500. 5. Magic—Spain—History—To 1500. 6. Egypt—Antiquities, Roman. 7. Cyprus—Antiquities, Roman. 8. Spain—Antiquities, Roman. I. Title.
BF1591.W55 2012

133.4'3093—dc23   2012047393

Dedicated to the memory of
Traianos Gagos
1960–2010

Foreword

This book began as a seminar paper investigating the context and function of some curious bones from the Kelsey Museum of Archaeology at the University of Michigan. I wrote the paper for a class taught by Traianos Gagos, taken as part of my training as a graduate student in the Interdepartmental Program in Classical Art and Archaeology. Traianos was an amazing teacher and mentor, and working with him on this project sparked a fascination that led directly to this book. Over the years, I learned much through our conversations on antiquity, academia, and life; Traianos was not only a teacher and adviser, but also a dear and dearly missed friend.

I am indebted to Oberlin College and the Loeb Classical Library Foundation for the financial support needed to bring the work to completion. An Oberlin College Grant-in-Aid and the Thomas Cooper Fund for Faculty Research provided funding for production costs. During earlier stages of this book, I benefited from funding provided by the Rackham School of Graduate Studies at the University of Michigan (2000), the American Institute of Archaeology (2002), and the Cyprus Fulbright Commission (2003). I produced the maps of Karanis through a grant from the University of Michigan Collaborative for the Advancement of Research and Technology (2004).

This book would not have been possible without the assistance, advice, and encouragement of Terry Wilfong and David Frankfurter. I also owe thanks to numerous friends and colleagues from whom I have received assistance. Christopher Faraone and Jacco Dieleman read and provided insightful comments on the opening and closing chapters. The anonymous readers of my initial manuscript supplied important guidance. Ellen Bauerle, my editor, as well as Alexa Ducsay at the University of Michigan Press have been instrumental in helping me bring the project to completion. My dissertation committee, includ-

viii   Foreword

ing Susan Alcock, Janet Richards, Derek Collins, and Stuart Kirsch, provided much-needed guidance and direction. Many others provided thoughts, bibliography, and encouragement along the way: Björn Anderson, Pierre Aupert, Roger Bagnall, Nancy Bookidis, Del Chrol, James Cook, Gregory Daugherty, Paola Davoli, Smadar Gabrelli, Jennifer Gates-Foster, Michael Given, Carla Goodnoh, Alison Griffith, Todd Hickey, David Jordan, Thomas Landvatter, Nikos Litinas, Daniel McCaffrey, John Pedley, C. H. Peters, Adam Rabinowitz, Margaret Root, Guy Sanders, J. J. Shirley, Jim Sickinger, Gina Soter, Stephen Tracy, and Philip Ventricinque. The support of my colleagues in the Oberlin College Department of Classics, Thomas Van Nortwick, Kirk Ormand, Benjamin Lee, and Christopher Trinacty, has been invaluable. John Harwood and Amy Margaris, colleagues in art history and anthropology, as well as the Friday working group at the Feve, provided cross-disciplinary direction. At Oberlin College, I have benefited from the assistance of a number of talented and dedicated undergraduate students, Gabe Baker, Ploy Keener, Christopher Motz, Eush Tayco, Lauren Clark, Laura Wilke, and Emily Thaisrivongs.

My research required significant assistance with museum collections, and I am grateful to the many people who helped me with archival materials and images. The Kelsey Museum of Archaeology in Ann Arbor has been instrumental in my work, and I wish to thank Sharon Herbert, the director, Elaine Gazda, curator of Hellenistic and Roman antiquities, as well as Robin Meador-Woodruff, the former registrar. Sebastían Encina and Michelle Fontenot, collections managers, and Suzanne Davis and Claudia Chemello, the conservators at the Kelsey, provided valuable assistance in locating objects and supplying illustrations for the Karanis artifacts. I owe thanks as well to Adam Hyatt and Arthur Verhoogt of the University of Michigan Papyrus Collection for images of the papyrus and ostracon from Karanis. I am greatly indebted to Dr. David S. Reese of the Peabody Museum of Natural History, Yale University, who performed faunal analysis on the bones and identified the joins. Scott Swann of the Center for Statistical Consultation and Research and Karl Longstreth of the University of Michigan Map Library provided important assistance. I am grateful to Zahi Hawass and the Supreme Council of Antiquities who granted permission to study artifacts in the Egyptian Museum in Cairo and to visit the sites of Karanis and Soknopaiou Nesos. I also owe thanks to Madam Amira Khattab at the American Research Center in Egypt, Ann Radwan at the Egyptian Fulbright Commission, Mr. Adel Mahmoud, the curator of the New Kingdom at the Egyptian Museum, and Mr. Lotfy Abed Elhamid, who provided me with access to Karanis objects in the museum and in the storerooms. At the British Museum, I am grateful to J. Leslie Fitton, Keeper of Greece and Rome, and to Thomas Kiely who provided assistance with the material from Amathous as well as the correspondence related to the acquisition of the tablets. The Trustees of the British Museum kindly provided permission to print images of the tablets. On Cyprus, I benefited from the resources of the Cyprus American Archaeological Research Institute, and wish to thank Tom Davis, the director, Vathoulla Moustoukki, the executive assistant, and Diana Constantides, the former librarian. In the Cyprus Department of Antiquities, I am greatly indebted to Sophocles Hadjisavvas and Pavlos Floruentzos, directors of the department, as well as to Depso Pilidou and Yiannis Violitis in Nicosia and Eleni Procopiou in Limassol. In Spain I benefited from the assistance of Xavier Aquilué Abadias, of the Museu d'Arqueologia de Catalunya, as well as Marta Santos Retolaza and Joaquim Tremoleda Trilla at the Empúries museum. I am grateful for their permission to reprint the map from Empúries as well as images of the curse tablets and their ceramic vessels. The Museo Nazionale Romano kindly provided an image of the curse tablet from the cache found near the San Sebastiano gate. I also thank Anne-Laure Ranoux and the Musée du Louvre for providing the image of the pierced female doll. Robert Daniel of the Cologne Papyrus Collection kindly provided access to the wax figurines from north of Assiut.

My sincere thanks are due to my parents, Aaron and Nancy Wilburn, aunts Annette Wilburn and Janice McCouch, and to my sister and brother in-law, Robin and Ravic Nijbroek, for years of support. I truly owe the completion of this manuscript, however, to my loving wife, Maureen Peters, for her tireless patience, assistance, and encouragement.

July 2011

Contents

List of Abbreviations	xiii
Introduction	1
Chapter 1. Finding Magic in the Archaeological Record	12
Chapter 2. *Materia Magica*	54
Chapter 3. Identifying the Remains of Magic in the Village of Karanis	95
Chapter 4. Practitioners and Craft at Amathous, Cyprus	169
Chapter 5. Three Curses from Empúries and Their Social Implications	219
Chapter 6. The Archaeology of Magic	254
Appendixes	273
Appendix 1. The Excavations at Karanis	275
Appendix 2. Bones from Karanis Areas 262 and 265	284
Bibliography	287
Index	327

Plates follow page 272

Abbreviations

ABSA	*Annual of the British School at Athens*
ACM	M. Meyer and R. Smith, *Ancient Christian magic: Coptic texts of ritual power* (San Francisco, 1994)
AD	*Archaiologikon Deltion*
AfR	*Archiv für Religionsgeschichte*
AJA	*American Journal of Archaeology*

Almagro Basch, *Inscripciones* M. Almagro Basch, *Las Inscripciones Ampuritanas Griegas, Ibéricas y Latinas* (Barcelona, 1952)

Almagro Basch, "Plomos" M. Almagro Basch, "Plomos con inscripción del Museo de Ampurias," *Memorias de los Museos Arqueológicos Provinciales* 8 (1947)

ANRW	*Aufstieg und Niedergang der römischen Welt: Geschichte und Kultur Roms im Spiegel der neuren Forschung,* ed. H. Temporini (New York, 1972–)
AncSoc	*Ancient Society*
APapyrol	*Analecta Papyrologica*
A&R	*Atene e Roma*
AR	*Archaeological Reports*
ArchClass	*Archeologia classica*
ARW	*Archiv für Religionswissenschaft*
BASP	*Bulletin of the American Society of Papyrologists*
BCH	*Bulletin de correspondance hellénique*
BGU	*Aegyptische Urkunden aus den Königlichen* (later *Staatlichen*) *Museen zu Berlin, Griechische Urkunden*
BIFAO	*Bulletin de l'Institut français d'archéologie orientale de Caire*
BIWK	*Die Beichtinschriften Westkleinasiens,* ed. Petzl (Bonn, 1994)

xiv   Abbreviations

BM	British Museum
BMCRev	*Bryn Mawr Classical Review*
BSRAA	*Bulletin de le Société royale d'archéologie d'Alexandrie*
Bull épigr	*Bulletin épigraphique*
CAJ	*Cambridge Archaeological Journal*
CdE	*Chronique d'Égypte*
CIL	*Corpus inscriptionum latinarum*
ClAnt	*Classical Antiquity*
CPh	*Classical Philology*
CPR	*Corpus Papyrorum Raineri*
CQ	*Classical Quarterly*
CR	*Classical Review*
CT	J. G. Gager, *Curse tablets and binding spells from the ancient world* (New York, 1992)
DT	A. Audollent, *Defixionum Tabellae* (Paris, 1904)
DTA	R. Wünsch, *Defixionum Tabellae Atticae,* Inscriptiones Graecae 3.3 (Berlin, 1897)
EVO	*Egitto e Vicino Oriente*
GMP	*The Greek magical papyri in translation,* ed. H. D. Betz (Chicago, 1992)
GRBS	*Greek, Roman, and Byzantine Studies*
HR	*History of Religions*
HSPh	*Harvard Studies in Classical Philology*
HThR	*Harvard Theological Review*
ICS	*Illinois Classical Studies*
IGFayyum	E. Bernand, *Recueil des inscriptions grecques du Fayoum,* 3 vols. (Leiden, 1975)
IRC	G. Fabre, M. Mayer, and I. Rodà, *Inscriptions romaines de Catalogne* (Paris, 1984)
JARCE	*Journal of the American Research Center in Egypt*
JEA	*Journal of Egyptian Archaeology*
JHS	*Journal of Hellenic Studies*
JJurP	*Journal of Juristic Papyrology*
JNES	*Journal of Near Eastern Studies*
JRA	*Journal of Roman Archaeology*
JRS	*Journal of Roman Studies*
JS	*Journal des Savants*

Abbreviations xv

JWarb	*Journal of the Warburg and Courtauld Institutes*
K.M. inv.	Kelsey Museum of Archaeology inventory number, Kelsey Museum of Archaeology, Ann Arbor, MI
LÄ	*Lexikon der Ägyptologie,* 7 vols., ed. W. Helck and E. Otto (Wiesbaden, 1972)
LF	A. Kropp, *Defixiones: ein aktuelles Corpus lateinischer Fluchtafeln* (Speyer, 2008)
MHNH	*MHNH: revista internacional de investigación sobre magia y astrología antiguas*
MonAL	*Monumenti antichi, pubblicati dall'Accademia dei Lincei*
NGD	D. R. Jordan, "New Greek curse tablets (1985–2000)," *Greek, Roman and Byzantine Studies* 41 (2000)
O.Ashm.Shelt.	*Greek Ostraca in the Ashmolean Museum from Oxyrhynchus and other sites,* ed. J. C. Shelton (Florence, 1988)
O.Bodl.	*Greek Ostraca in the Bodleian Library at Oxford and various other collections*
O.Edfou	*Tell Edfou I–III* (Cairo: Institut Français d'Archéologie Orientale du Caire, 1937–50)
O.Köln	*Greek Ostraca in the Kölner Papyrus-Sammlung* (Cologne, Germany)
O.Mich.	*Greek Ostraca in the University of Michigan Collection*
P.Cair.Zen	*Zenon Papyri, Catalogue général des antiquités égyptiennes du Musée du Caire,* ed. C. C. Edgar (Cairo, 1925–40)
P.Col.	*Columbia Papyri*
PDM xiv, lxi	*Papyri Demoticae Magicae*
PG	*Patrologia Graeca,* ed. J. P. Migne (Paris, 1857–66)
PGM I–CXXX	*Papyri Graecae Magicae* (I–LXXI), ed. K. Preisendanz (Stuttgart, 1973–74); *The Greek Magical Papyri in translation* (I–CXXX), ed. H. D. Betz (Chicago, 1986).
P.Haun.	*Papyri Graecae Haunienses*
P.Köln	*Kölner Papyri*
PL	*Patrologia Latina,* ed. J. P. Migne (Paris, 1841–64)
P.Mich.	*Michigan Papyri*
P.Mil.Vogl.	*Papiri della R. Università di Milano,* ed. A. Vogliano.
P.Oslo	*Papyri Osloenses*
PSBA	*Proceedings of the Society of Biblical Archaeology*
RAC	*Rivista di archeologia cristiana*

SGD	D. R. Jordan, "A survey of Greek *defixiones* not included in the special corpora," *Greek, Roman and Byzantine Studies* 26 (1985)
SMSR	*Studi e materiali di storia delle religioni*
SO	*Symbolae Osloenses*
Suppl. Mag.	*Supplementum Magicum,* ed. R. Daniel and F. Maltomini (Opladen, 1990–92)
Tab. Sulis	R. S. O. Tomlin, *Tabellae sulis: Roman inscribed tablets of tin and lead from the sacred spring at Bath* (Oxford, 1988)
TAM	*Tituli Asiae Minoris*
TAPA	*Transactions of the American Philological Association*
VD	C. A. Faraone, "Binding and burying the forces of evil: The defensive use of 'voodoo' dolls in ancient Greece," *Classical Antiquity* 10, no. 2 (1991)
W.Chr.	L. Mitteis and U. Wilcken, *Grundzüge und Chrestomathie der Papyruskunde* (Leipzig/Berlin, 1912)
ZPE	*Zeitschrift für Papyrologie und Epigraphik*

Introduction

Cursing on the Via Appia, Rome

Sometime around 1850, a certain Mr. Jacobini conducted excavations in the Marini vineyard, which was located along the Via Appia, just outside of the San Sebastiano gate in the Aurelian Wall at Rome. Over the course of the work, he came upon a badly disturbed tomb, which was, in all likelihood, a columbarium, a building that housed a large number of cremation burials, likely arranged in rows of alcoves.[1] The tomb was decorated with a mosaic of a woman and child, and contained both a large, perfectly preserved sarcophagus and sizable number of smaller urns, made of both terra-cotta and marble. When the ceramic urns were opened, excavators discovered an even more remarkable find inside: approximately fifty-six small sheets of lead were deposited in the cinerary chests.[2] Most of the lead sheets had been rolled up and pierced with one or more nails. Preservation of the tablets was varied. Of the fifty-six, thirty-

---

1. J. Matter, *Une excursion gnostique en Italie* (Strasbourg: Berger-Levrault, 1852), 28–36, plates X–XII. Giovanni Battista de Rossi identified the tombs as a columbarium. "Adunanza dell'Istituto," *Bullettino dell'Istituto di Corrispondenza Archeologica* (1880).

2. R. Wünsch, *Sethianische verfluchungstafeln aus Rom* (Leipzig: B. G. Teubner, 1898) *DT* nos. 140–87, pp. 198–246. Wünsch, *Sethianische verfluchungstafeln aus Rom* 1; F. Heintz, "Agonistic magic in the Late Antique circus" (Harvard University, 1999), 197; see also the discussion in A. Mastrocinque, "Le 'defixiones' di Porta San Sebastiano," *MHNH* 5 (2005), and M. Bailliot, *Magie et sortilèges dans l'Antiquité romaine* (Paris: Hermann éditeurs, 2010), 117–20. Audollent's publication, which is the standard reference, supplies almost no archaeological data and no images, but instead describes the condition of the tablets and provides only transcriptions. Many of the publication choices reflect the conventions of scholarship at the time, and similar presentations of material are evident in contemporary papyrological research. T. Gagos, J. Gates, and A. Wilburn, "Material culture and texts of Graeco-Roman Egypt: Creating context, debating meaning," *BASP* 42, no. 1–4 (2005): 178.

2   Materia Magica

four essentially were whole, and twenty-two were very fragmentary.[3] Each of
the tablets differed in shape, size, and inscription, although some elements
suggest that the practitioner had access to a template or formulary.[4] Even the
lead of the tablets varied significantly, with some exhibiting a darker color or
a greater thickness than others. Greek, Latin, and a variety of nonsense words
and mystical symbols were scratched into the surfaces. Lurid and nightmarish
drawings also were emblazoned on the lead tablets—mummies, horse-headed
divinities, threatening serpents, and other uncertain depictions embellish and
enhance the arcane texts.

On one tablet (*DT* no. 155, *CT* no. 13, plate 2), the inscription calls upon
various deities to restrain and bind a man named Kardelos, the son of Pholgentia, so that he suffers torments and dies within five days. Kardelos was
a charioteer in the Roman circus, and the tablet was intended to prevent the
victim and his horses from racing effectively.[5] An inscribed spell and drawings
decorate the face of the lead sheet; both the text and its accompanying illustrations are necessary to comprehend its function. The text occupies the upper
right-hand corner, the left side, and the bottom of the tablet. The inscription
was written so that every other line is upside down and backward, suggesting
that the practitioner turned the tablet while inscribing the spell. The repetition
in the text suggests that the practitioner wrote out Section 3, but ran out of

---

3. The tablets have decayed further and are now housed in the Museo Nazionale Archeologico
    Romano. R. Friggeri, *La collezione epigrafica del Museo nazionale romano alle Terme di
    Diocleziano* (Milan: Electa, 2001), 178.
4. Other large caches of tablets that used a formulary are also known. Carthage, from a cem-
    etery: *DT* nos. 213–62; D. R. Jordan, "New defixiones from Carthage," in *The circus and a
    Byzantine cemetery at Carthage,* ed. J. H. Humphrey (Ann Arbor: University of Michigan
    Press, 1988); Hadrumentum: *DT* nos. 263–98; Amathous/Agios Tychonas: *DT* nos. 22–37,
    discussed at length in chapter 4. Almost all of the tablets from Hadrumentum, Carthage, and
    the Porta San Sebastiano are concerned with chariot racing. On the use of spell books, see
    W. Brashear, "Hocus Pocus, Verbatim," *Language Quarterly* 29, no. 1 (1992); W. Brashear,
    "Magical papyri: Magic in book form," in *Das Buch als magisches und als Repräsentation-
    sobjekt,* ed. P. Ganz (Wiesbaden: Otto Harrassowitz, 1992); D. R. Jordan, "Inscribed lead
    tablets from the games in the sanctuary of Poseidon," *Hesperia* 63, no. 1 (1994): 123–25;
    C. A. Faraone, "Handbooks and anthologies: The collection of Greek and Egyptian incanta-
    tions in late Hellenistic Egypt," *Archiv für Religionsgeschichte* 2, no. 2 (2000); D. R. Jordan,
    "Defixiones from a well near the southwest corner of the Athenian Agora," *Hesperia* 54, no.
    3 (1985): 211, 33–36; C. A. Faraone, *Ancient Greek love magic* (Cambridge: Harvard Univer-
    sity Press, 1999), 32–34; D. R. Jordan, "Magia nilotica sulle rive del Tevere," *Mediterraneo
    antico: economie, società, culture* 7, no. 2 (2004). C. A. Faraone, "A Greek magical gemstone
    from the Black Sea: Amulet or miniature handbook?" *Kernos* 23 (2010).
5. Charioteers were often associated with magic: P. Lee-Stecum, "Dangerous reputations: Chari-
    oteers and magic in fourth-century Rome," *Greece & Rome* 53, no. 2 (2006).

Introduction   3

room; Section 1 appears to be a continuation of the spell, squeezed in at the top above magical symbols. Although lengthy, it is useful to quote the entirety of the text, as it includes many of the features that typify Late Antique magic:[6]

(Section 1)
and archangels, and archangels, by the one beneath the earth, just as I hand this one over to you, the impious and accursed and ill fated Kardelos, whom the mother Pholgentia bore, thus, make him to pay a penalty on a bed of punishment to die by means of an evil death within five days. Quickly! Quickly!

(Section 2)
EULAMŌN restrain
X OUSIRI OUSIRI
Z APHI OUSIRI
    MNE
(magical symbols) PHRI

(Section 3)
The spell: You, Phrygian goddess, Nymph goddess EIDŌNEA, NEOIE KATOIKOUSE, I invoke you by your [power], cooperate, and together bind down and restrain and make him being punished by an evil death on a bed of punishment, and to come into an evil condition, Kardelos, whom the mother Pholgentia bore, and you, holy EULAMŌN and you, holy Kharaktēres, and holy magical assistants, those on the right and left, and holy holy Symphonia. Those things which I have written on this

(Section 4)
EULAMŌN restrain
OUSIRI OUSIRI API

(Section 5)
AAAAAAA
EEEEEEE
ĒĒĒĒĒĒĒ
ĒĒĒĒĒĒĒ

---

6. This translation is dependent on a number of emendations and assumptions that I have made working from the text given in *DT* 155. For a commentary on side A, line 1–45, see *CT* 70–71.

IIIIIII
OOOOOOO
UUUUUUU
ŌŌŌŌŌŌŌ

(Section 6)
OUSIRI MNE PHRI

(Section 3, continued) sheet, a cold water pipe, just as I give over this one
to you, impious and accursed and ill fated, Kardelos, whom the mother
Phōlgentia bore, bound, bound hand and foot, bound down, Kardelos, whom
the mother Phōlgentia bore, thus, bind down this one and make him to be suffering vengeance on a bed of vengeance, dying an evil death, Kardelos, whom
the mother Pholgentia bore, within five days. This I command you according to
the one who becomes young again under the earth, the one that binds down the
(zodiacal) circles and OIMĒNEBENCHUCH BACHUCH BACHACHUCH
BAZACHUCH BACHAZACHUCH BACHAXICHUCH BADĒTOPHŌTH
PHTHŌSIRO, and I command you holy angels

(Section 7)
You, Phrygian goddess, and you, nymph goddess EIDŌEA VEOIKOUSE
KATAKOUSE, I command you according to your power, and according to
your holy infernal spirits, just as I place this one beside you, this impious and
accursed and ill-fated Kardelos, whom the mother Pholgentia bore, bound,
bound hand and foot, bound down, this one, cooperate and bind down and
give him over to the one beneath the earth, in the infernal house of those in
Tartaros, this impious and accursed and ill-fated Kardelos, whom the mother
Pholgentia bore and just as this is ŌPIONEPI cold, make very cold, melt
down again, make wither, make waste away, melt down again, SUNZARI
KATARAZI the being and the life and the bones and the marrow and the sinews and the flesh and the power of Kardelos, whom the mother Pholgentia
bore, within five days from the very hour and day of Ares. This I command
you by the power that renews itself under the earth and restrains the (zodiacal) circles, OIMĒNEBECHUCH BACHUCH BACHACHUCH BAZU-
CHUCH BACHAZACHUCH BAENCHAZICHUCH BADĒTOPHTHŌTH
PHTHŌSISIRŌ CHRE. I command you holy angels and archangels and holy
EULAMONAN and holy magical assistants and holy SUNPHŌNIA and holy

Kharaktêres which I have written on this sheet, a cold water pipe, together bind down and bind hand and foot and work together and chill the strength, the marrow, the sinews, the flesh, and the power in his prime of life, Kardelos, whom the mother Pholgentia bore . . . and the prime of life . . . Kardelos, whom the mother Pholgentia bore, from this day of Ares . . . the seventh . . . Quickly! Quickly!

Invocations and nonsensical passages are sprinkled throughout, including garbled phrases borrowed from other languages, and special symbols, the *kharaktêres,* or "ring-letters."

With one exception, the images on the tablet are not integrated into the inscription but are typically surrounded by blank space, perhaps resulting from the addition of these drawings by a second individual. Moving around the tablet in a clockwise direction, in the upper left-hand corner, a figure with four antennae emerges from a rectangle that may represent a tomb. This individual's body is decorated with a crosshatch pattern; the rectangle from which the figure emerges has a similar design, but each of the squares formed by the pattern surrounds a dot. The central figure shows a horse-headed man dressed in Roman military garb—identifiable by the pteryges at the lower hem—and holding a whip in one hand and a round object in the other. The feet of this figure are oddly shaped. Above the figure and beneath its left arm are mystical symbols, including *kharaktêres* and Greek vowels. On either side of the horse-headed man are two additional representations: human busts surmount trapezoids, where the upper, left, and right edges are composed of crosshatched lines. The Greek vowels, each repeated seven times, with both uppercase and lowercase etas, appear above the rightmost figure; below the figure is a line of omegas. These figures may represent the assistants (*paredroi*) mentioned in the text or, alternatively, other charioteers. The horse-headed figure is positioned above an image of a mummified individual around which wrap two snakes, shown bearded with forked tongues. The mummy is decorated in the same fashion as the figure in the upper left-hand corner, with a crosshatched pattern. This likely is the putative target of the spell, dead and buried.

The lead sheets from the Via Appia are known as *defixiones* in Latin or *katadesmoi* in Greek.[7] They are part of a long tradition of cursing that employed

---

7.   Curse tablets from antiquity are collected in a number of specialized corpora: R. Wünsch, *Defixionum Tabellae Atticae* (Berlin: G. Reimer, 1897); A. M. H. Audollent, *Defixionum Tabellae* (Paris: Fontemoing, 1904); H. Solin, "Eine Neue Fluchtafel aus Ostia," *Commenta-*

6   Materia Magica

small tablets, a phenomenon that began in the fifth century BCE, if not earlier, and continued through the Roman period. These curse tablets are incontrovertible examples of what we customarily call *magic*.[8] The term *magic* has been debated extensively in studies of the classical world, as in other fields, and indeed, isolating a universally accepted definition for the phenomenon has proved an impossible task. Scholars are in general agreement about the spaces that magic may occupy: the phenomenon is often marked by mechanistic gestures and speech, which sometimes compel supernatural or divine forces, in order to achieve a particular, personal goal. Other members of society often consider acts of magic antisocial or unacceptable. We will return to the definition of magic and its accompanying problems in the next chapter.

It is unlikely that Jacobini recorded much information about the tablets beyond a general description of the tomb and its location. The objects were discovered outside of the Porta Appia, along the Via Appia. Other tablets from the cache target charioteers who would compete in both the "Racetrack of Rome" (the Circus Maximus) and the "Circus of New Babylon" (an otherwise unattested hippodrome). The Vigna Marini, where the tablets were discovered, is very near to the Circus Maximus, which lies to the northwest, and not far from the Circus of Maxentius, which lies about two and half kilometers further along the Via Appia to the southeast and could be the Circus of New Babylon. Proximity to the potential targets of the spell was likely an important factor in determining where the artifacts were deposited.[9] The practitioners responsible for the tablets employed a funerary space that was currently in ruins; cremation

---

tiones humanarum litterarum, Societas scientiarum Fennica 42, no. 3 (1968); D. R. Jordan, "A survey of Greek defixiones not included in the special corpora," *GRBS* 26 (1985); D. R. Jordan, "New Greek curse tablets (1985–2000)," *GRBS* 41 (2000); A. Kropp, *Defixiones: ein aktuelles corpus lateinischer Fluchtafeln* (Speyer: Kartoffeldruck-Verlag Kai Brodersen, 2008). For a general introduction to curse tablets and a brief survey of some of the relevant questions, see C. A. Faraone, "The agonistic context of early Greek binding-spells," in *Magika hiera: Ancient Greek magic and religion,* ed. C. A. Faraone and D. Obbink (New York: Oxford University Press, 1991); D. Ogden, "Binding spells: Curse tablets and voodoo dolls in the Greek and Roman worlds," in *Witchcraft and magic in Europe: Ancient Greece and Rome,* ed. B. Ankarloo and S. Clark (Philadelphia: University of Pennsylvania Press, 1999); D. Collins, *Magic in the ancient Greek world* (Malden, MA: Blackwell, 2008), 64–103; Bailliot, *Magie et sortilèges dans l'Antiquité romaine,* 71–132.

8.   On the problems with the overrepresentation of lead tablets from Attica in the corpus, see C. Faraone, "The problem of dense concentrations of data for cartographers (and chronographers) of ancient Mediterranean magic: Some illustrative case studies from the East," in *Contextos màgicos/Contesti magici,* ed. M. Piranomonte (Rome: forthcoming).

9.   F. Heintz, "Circus curses and their archaeological contexts," *JRA* 11 (1998): 338–39.

Introduction 7

burials effectively had ceased when the tablets were created, suggesting that the columbarium was no longer being used or frequented.[10]

For a moment, we can imagine the tablet cursing Kardelos, without this archaeological context, and divorced from the additional lead tablets and other associated artifacts. If this artifact had appeared on the antiquities market, either the contemporary one or the market of one hundred years ago, we might know nothing of its provenance, and even less about the physical and contextual circumstances of its discovery. Reading only the text, we note that the names of the victim and his mother are Roman names, Cardelus and Fulgentia, that have been transliterated into Greek, the language in which the curse has been written. The text invokes Egyptian divinities, which could lead us to wrongly conclude that it was produced in Egypt. In our tablet, there is no mention of a racetrack, horses, chariots, or competition—that information derives from other objects within the cache—so the purpose for which the tablet was composed also would be lost. The lead sheet cursing Kardelos was one of fifty-six recovered—an enormous find, and a veritable archive of magical objects, but all of this accompanying data would be inaccessible.

The tablets from the Via Appia also exemplify many of the problems that are inherent in an investigation of the archaeology of magic in the Roman Mediterranean. Early investigations such as those that produced the tablets were not conducted scientifically. Record keeping was virtually non-existent, and excavators often wrote memoirs of their work, rather than precisely recording findspots while in the field. Even so, early excavations did recognize the coherence of a cache such as this one; all of the tablets were kept together and could be used to interpret their associates. In the intervening years between the discovery of the tablets around 1850 and R. Wünsch's publication in 1898, much of the archaeological data about the find had been lost or deemed irrelevant. Notably, Wünsch was able more easily to discuss the peregrinations of the tablets (from museum to storeroom, and then to another museum) than to describe the tomb in which they were found, or even to provide the dimensions of the smaller urns.[11] For many early excavators, the process of discovery was less important than the object that had been found. The extensive length of

---

10. Heintz, "Agonistic magic in the Late Antique circus," 197.

11. Following their discovery, the artifacts were taken to the Ministry of Public Works and Antiquities and subsequently moved to the storage area of the Nuevo Museo Vittorio Emmanuel, where they languished for a number of years. Thirty-eight years after their discovery, de Rossi discussed the tablets at a meeting of the German Archaeological Institute in Rome (above, n. 1).

8 Materia Magica

time between when the tablets were first unearthed and their eventual publication also meant that little was known about the precise circumstances of the discovery.

Despite the limited information about archaeological context, the artifacts have much to tell us about the process of doing magic. Indeed, the tablet from the Via Appia even comments on its own creation, stating that it has been "made from a cold water pipe." Lead water pipes, commonplace in Roman cities, would have provided a source for raw material for the practitioner, perhaps prized because they carried cold water. Removing part of a public water pipe, however, may have been difficult or dangerous, thus increasing its value as a forbidden or extraordinary material, worthy of mention in the inscription.[12] The assertion of its origin, found within the text of the tablet, also points us to the important role played by physicality—magic frequently involved objects in order to accomplish its protective and aggressive goals.

The written texts of spell instructions, preserved on papyri from Roman Egypt and roughly contemporary with the tablets, similarly iterate that ancient magic was constantly entangled with *things:* strange parts of animals, limbs or hair from the dead or the living, foodstuffs, blood, milk, metal, clay and wax, all appear within instructions for magical rites.[13] Words that were spoken or written during the enactment of a particular ritual provided direction for the powers invoked by the practitioner, but most magical acts were fundamentally grounded in both the incantation and physical actions. This book will focus on this intersection of physicality, materiality, and magic, and will employ archaeology to illuminate the central role that artifacts and their contexts played in ancient ritual practice. In part, this involves tracing magic from its physical manifestation in the artifact back to the process of production. In these pages, we will take a comprehensive approach that analyzes Latin and Greek inscriptions in tandem with the artifacts on which they were written, and addresses the text as a key component of the object. This will allow us to draw new meaning

---

12. Ogden, "Binding spells," 12. Compare the instructions that require the use of a cold water pipe: PGM VII.396–404; XXXVI.1–34; from the *Sepher ha-Razim,* Second firmament, lines 60–65 = *CT* no. 114 = *Sepher ha-razim* = *the book of the mysteries,* trans. M. A. Morgan (Chico, CA: Scholars Press, 1983), 49.

13. Fourth-century Christianity reveals a comparable interest in materiality. See P. C. Miller, *The corporeal imagination: Signifying the holy in late ancient Christianity* (Philadelphia: University of Pennsylvania Press, 2009), esp. 3–7, 131–78; and compare W. J. T. Mitchell, *Picture theory: Essays on verbal and visual representation* (Chicago: University of Chicago Press, 1994).

from the depositional context of magical objects and their associated finds, which in turn permits a fuller reconstruction of a ritual occasion and its social repercussions. Over the course of this study, the archaeological analysis of magic will take us in two complementary directions—first locating and identifying magical artifacts and then using the objects to reconstruct how magic was practiced within the local environment.

The Scope of This Book

This book explores magical practice at three different locations in the Roman empire: Karanis in the Fayum region of Egypt, Amathous, located on the southern coast of Cyprus, and Empúries, a Greek colonial settlement on the eastern coast of Spain (see plate 1). These areas are separated by both geography and cultural traditions. Because of the objects discovered at each and their respective archaeological histories, the three sites supply particularly good evidence for case studies that will articulate the manifold ways in which artifacts and deposition can contribute to our understanding of local forms of magical practice.

Chapter 1 will lay the groundwork for the study by proposing an etic definition of the term *magic* that focuses on identifiable, empirical markers: the phenomenon makes use of mechanistic ritual to achieve its ends, it adopts elements of religious practices broadly understood in order to lend legitimacy or exoticism, and it frequently is performed in private rather than public, serving personal rather than community ends. The first chapter also delineates a methodology for finding magic in the archaeological record. Magical practice can be identified and understood by adopting an object-centered approach that traces the life history of artifacts. This material must then be contextualized, that is, studied in tandem with its findspot and other associated finds. Through this sort of an investigation, it is possible to identify how an artifact or group of artifacts entered the archaeological record, and whether ritual activity led to the deposit.

The second chapter continues the work of framing the study by proposing a series of categories through which the materials of magic can be investigated. Although much of the evidence that is used in the chapter is drawn from the Greek and Demotic Magical Papyri, other data from diverse regions of the Roman empire indicate that these categories are appropriate for the Mediterranean as a whole. I suggest that there are four classes of materials that can be incorporated into the physical enactment of a magical event: (1) inscribed language, (2) figurines and other representations, (3) naturally occurring flora, fauna, and minerals, including *exuviae* or material gathered from the victim, and (4) objects that have been repurposed for magical use. Often, a practitioner would combine items drawn from these classes of materials within the performance, or a single artifact may be classed within multiple categories. Contextual investigation of archaeological data allows us to consider the interaction of magical materials and may permit us to reconstruct the rituals that were employed during a magical event.

Chapter 3 applies the methodology established in the introductory chapters to archaeological evidence from Karanis. Using the ritual framework suggested by the Greek and Demotic Magical Papyri, I analyze a number of archaeological contexts in an attempt to find evidence of ritual activity. The chapter begins by investigating each of the known magical artifacts from the site and determines whether archaeological context can add to our understanding of how these artifacts were utilized. From that point, we move to two other contexts at the site: a small figurine of a woman and a large cache of painted bones. Although they have not been identified previously as magical, close investigation of the objects and their depositions suggests that each group of artifacts was used in a rite.

From Egypt, the book next moves to areas in which the traditions of magic are less well known, beginning with Cyprus. Named by Pliny the Elder as one of the centers of ancient magical knowledge, the identified examples of magical practice on the island are limited in geographic extent, if not in the size of the corpus. In the late nineteenth century, local residents uncovered a huge cache of more than 200 tablets inscribed with magical imprecations. My focus in this chapter is on the production of magical artifacts within a single location. The majority of the tablets relied on a single spell, but multiple individuals were responsible for the creation of the artifacts. One of the texts, however, uses a different model that can be related to a spell recorded in the magical papyri. This prompts a discussion of the relationship between the spell instructions from Egypt and magical artifacts discovered at other sites.

In chapter 5, I use material from the site of Empúries to discuss the social place of magical practice within a local community. The chapter focuses on three curse tablets, each discovered within a roughly made jug and found in one of the cemeteries around the site. Archaeological analysis demonstrates

Introduction 11

that each of the tablets was deposited intentionally at the same time as the burial of the cinerary urn, perhaps by members of the family of the deceased. The tablets target administrators of the provincial government of Hispania, suggesting that local individuals may have employed magic as a means of covert resistance.

In the concluding chapter, I reflect critically on the methodology developed in the study and suggest ways in which current and future excavations can lay the groundwork for finding and interpreting magic within the archaeological record. Finally, I situate the case studies within the larger context of magic in the ancient world and briefly touch on three general topics that the materiality of magic urges us to consider: the place of secrecy in magic, the local identity of the practitioner, and the spread of magical technology.

Chapter 1

Finding Magic in the Archaeological Record

Looking at Magic

Excavating at the site of Karanis in the Egyptian Fayum in 1924, the team from the University of Michigan uncovered a cache of more than eighty animal and human bones, all of which had been decorated with red paint (plate 3). The substance had been applied in one or more of three designs—dots, straight lines arranged in a horizontal row and bisected by a perpendicular line, and undulating lines that curve or form other sinuous shapes. The bones are strange to look at—worn by time, with the red colorant fading to brown in places, the symbols, although repeated, seem random and inexplicable. In a word, the objects and their accompanying markings are "weird." Does this strangeness, however, require that they must be magical?

In discussing the role of speech in magical practice, Malinowski has suggested that words of spells are distinct from the speech of every day according to what he has called the "coefficient of weirdness." This variation can be tied to the irregularity of magical speech; some words may be incomprehensible, while others may be variations from normal, understandable terminology. Furthermore, magical language is situated within ritual and is intoned in a manner different from regular speech—the context of the spell also marks it as unusual.[1] Anthropologists have attempted to resolve this "coefficient of weirdness" by understanding language or speech within its cultural context, potentially revealing that only the observer infers the oddity of certain words or actions. But in the examples from the Trobriand Islands, the informants agree that mag-

---

1. B. Malinowski, *Coral gardens and their magic: A study of the methods of tilling the soil and of agricultural rites in the Trobriand Islands,* 2 vols. (London: G. Allen & Unwin, 1935), II. 218–25.

ical words are specialized and are used appropriately by the practitioner alone. What is most striking, however, is that magical speech integrates both unusual and special words with more common language; the strangeness of magical speech derives, in part, from the juxtaposition of comprehensible material with unintelligible words and phrases.

Malinowski's concept of the "coefficient of weirdness" can be applied productively to objects as well as words, an approach recently taken by David Frankfurter.[2] Those who engaged in magic often sought out raw materials for ritual acts from among exotic or mysterious items, and, conversely, the products of magic may have been constructed in order to look unusual or strange. Indeed, magic often derives its efficacy from this strangeness. The decoration and appearance of certain artifacts incorporated into magic is frequently off-putting or unusual. As is the case with magical texts, magical artifacts typically juxtapose objects or images that are strange with the mundane, so that, as on the curse tablets from the Via Appia, a representation may combine an image of a man with the head of a rooster. This juxtaposition of weird and commonplace can cause problems of interpretation for the modern viewer, and it is necessary to make a distinction between objects with odd or inexplicable elements that were designed to be magical, and those that were not. An object with unusual elements may be considered magical because of those elements, but it may just as easily have been a commonplace object in the ancient world that looks strange to the modern viewer. Therefore, the context in which an object was used and found, as well as the other materials associated with the object, can provide essential evidence of that artifact's nature, whether magical or not.[3]

Before embarking on a search to find and interpret magic as it appears in the archaeological record, it is useful to define what is meant by the term. There has been extensive debate on this topic, and no single definition has met with the approval of the academic community at large. Some scholars have chosen to discard the term altogether. One alternative, for example, has been to refer to discrete practices, such as cursing, rather than magic as a whole.[4]

---

2. D. Frankfurter, "Fetus magic and sorcery fears in Roman Egypt," *GRBS* 46 (2006): 15–19.

3. A. Gell, "The technology of enchantment and the enchantment of technology," in *Anthropology, art, and aesthetics,* ed. J. Coote and A. Shelton (New York: Oxford University Press, 1992), 40–66. G. Lewis, *Day of shining red: an essay on understanding ritual* (New York: Cambridge University Press, 1980).

4. M. Meyer and R. Smith, *Ancient Christian magic: Coptic texts of ritual power* (San Francisco: HarperSanFrancisco, 1994), 1–6; J. Z. Smith, "Trading places," in *Ancient magic and ritual power,* ed. M. W. Meyer and P. A. Mirecki (New York: Brill, 1995), 16–17; C. A. Hoff-

14   Materia Magica

Such attempts often result in substituting other, equally problematic labels in the place of the contested word. As Gideon Bohak points out, the term magic is productive, particularly when used as a heuristic label to refer to a group of practices that share broad similarities.[5]

Other researchers have chosen to use literary and textual evidence from antiquity to suggest the sorts of practices that the Greeks and Romans considered magical. This can permit us to understand the phenomena through indigenous cultural concepts (the emic approach). In recent years, a number of scholars have grappled with the conflicting terminology used by Greeks and Romans that may relate to our term magic.[6] Often, such investigations result in stripping meaning from the word except within its immediate cultural context. "Magic" could be used as a term of approbation, employed for personal or political ends in order to exclude, demean, or debase an opponent. In short, magic referred to rituals that the speaker did not approve of, including the religious practices of other cultures.[7] There was no "magic" except in reference

man, "Fiat Magia," in *Magic and ritual in the ancient world,* ed. P. A. Mirecki and M. Meyer (Leiden: Brill, 2002), 192–93.

5.   G. Bohak, *Ancient Jewish magic: A history* (New York: Cambridge University Press, 2008), 62. H. Versnel sums up the conundrum: "one problem is that you cannot talk about magic without using the term 'magic.'" "Some reflections on the relationship magic-religion," *Numen* 38, no. 2 (1991): 181.

6.   See, for example, among recent publications: K. B. Stratton, *Naming the witch: Magic, ideology, & stereotype in the ancient world* (New York: Columbia University Press, 2007); Collins, *Magic in the ancient Greek world.* On the Greek term *magos,* see A. D. Nock, "Paul and the magus," in *Essays on religion and the ancient world,* ed. Z. Stewart (Cambridge: Harvard University Press, 1972), 308–24; J. N. Bremmer, "The birth of the term 'magic,'" *ZPE* 126 (1999): 1–9; J. N. Bremmer and J. R. Veenstra, eds., *The metamorphosis of magic from Late Antiquity to the early modern period,* vol. 1 (Leuven: Peeters, 2002), 1–11; J. N. Bremmer, *Greek religion and culture, the Bible, and the ancient Near East* (Leiden: Brill, 2008), 235–47; on the Latin term *magus,* see F. Graf, *Magic in the ancient world,* trans. P. Franklin (Cambridge: Harvard University Press, 1997), 36–41; J. B. Rives, "*Magus* and its cognates in Classical Latin," in *Magical practice in the Latin West: Papers from the international conference held at the University of Zaragoza, 30 Sept.–1 Oct. 2005,* ed. R. L. Gordon and F. Marco Simón (Leiden: Brill, 2010).

7.   P. Brown, "Sorcery, demons and the rise of Christianity from Late Antiquity into the middle ages," in *Witchcraft: Confessions and accusations,* ed. M. Douglas (New York: Tavistock, 1970); D. E. Aune, "Magic in early Christianity," *ANRW* II 23, no. 2 (1980); A. F. Segal, "Hellenistic magic: Some questions of definition," in *Studies in Gnosticism and Hellenistic religions,* ed. R. Van Den Broek and M. J. Vermaseren, *Études préliminares aux religions orientales dans l'Empire romain* (Leiden: Brill, 1981); N. Janowitz, *Magic in the Roman world: Pagans, Jews, and Christians* (New York: Routledge, 2001). Compare H. Geertz: "Whether or not a particular idea or attitude was said to be magical . . . depended mainly on who said it, and the persuasiveness of the label depended mainly on the weight of authority behind it." "An anthropology of religion and magic I," *Journal of Interdisciplinary History* 6, no. 1 (1975): 75.

Finding Magic in the Archaeological Record 15

to the "other." This assessment, however, does not fit the archaeological evidence; material culture indicates that magic was an actual practice. We possess curse tablets such as those discovered on the Via Appia as well as long papyrus rolls of spell instructions, in which the scribes proudly proclaim that they are *magoi,* magicians.[8]

The emic approach, with its preference for identifying the mental constructions that give meaning to a term within a society, cannot provide the necessary tools to explore the archaeology of magic. To accurately articulate and identify which archaeological objects are magical, we must rely instead on a working definition that can accommodate empirical markers, evidence that we can see, or at least infer, from an object. The etic approach reverses the method employed by the emic mode of inquiry; rather than rely on the ancient sources to define magic, the investigator proposes a working definition for the term that is subsequently used to discuss the data.[9] I would propose the following working definition of magic:

1. Magic was firmly grounded in ritual actions, including spoken or written words and the manipulation of objects. These rituals typically are performed with the expectation of a particular result.
2. Magic may draw on religious traditions for both efficacy and exoticism.
3. Magic is frequently a private or personal activity, although certain practices might be undertaken in the public sphere.

These characteristics can help us pinpoint which phenomena should be considered magic and establish a framework within which magic can be discussed. It should be noted that the end goal of this work is neither to determine a universal definition for magic nor even to find one that is always applicable to

---

8. J. Braarvig, "Magic: Reconsidering the grand dichotomy," in *The world of ancient magic: Papers from the first international Samson Eitrem seminar at the Norwegian Institute at Athens, 4–8 May 1997,* ed. D. R. Jordan, H. Montgomery, and E. Thomassen (Bergen: Norwegian Institute at Athens, 1999), 51; Segal, "Hellenistic magic: Some questions of definition," 350, n. 8–9. Compare PGM I.127, 331; IV.210, 243, 2081, 2289, 2319, 2449, 2453. The individuals who used these texts were Egyptian priests, and the papyri represent compendia collected for ritual needs; the priests were experts for hire. For further discussion, see below, ch. 2 nn. 12, 13.
9. As S. I. Johnston notes, research within the Mediterranean basin requires the ability to talk across cultures; only etic categories can provide the terminology necessary to conduct such a conversation. "Review: Describing the undefinable: New books on magic and old problems of definition," *HR* 43, no. 1 (2003): 54.

16   Materia Magica

phenomena in the Classical world. Rather, it is necessary to isolate the sorts of practices that fit into the category of magic and to determine whether, and by what means, they may be detectable within the archaeological record.

Magic was firmly grounded in ritual actions. The belief that magic was a mechanistic process has a long history in scholarly thought and can be traced back to James Frazer and Edward Tylor, both working in the nineteenth century. Tylor believed that the magician's fallacy lay in the belief that mechanistic action could change the world through a belief in underlying analogies: observing that the sun rose at the same time as the rooster crowed, ancient peoples believed that forcing a rooster to crow would cause the sun to come up also.[10] Frazer likewise viewed action as endemic to magical practice—by performing a rite in a specific way, without variation, the practitioner ensured that the expected result would come to pass.[11] Although much of Tylor's and Frazer's work has been dismissed as colonialist, the focus on ritual as an essential feature of magic continues to have resonance. The concept underlying magic may rely on the idea of instrumental control; as human beings are able to control nature or the environment through their actions, so also might they control other domains through magical action.[12] Ritual, as a performative event, is embodied within the actor or actors who move through space and enact a given rite.[13] In Stanley Tambiah's conception of magic, for example, practice is comprised of two elements: the word, or *logos,* and the deed, or *praxis.* These components are combined within ritual action; magic may be

---

10. E. B. Tylor, *Primitive culture: Researches into the development of mythology, philosophy, religion, language, art, and custom,* 2 vols. (London: J. Murray, 1929), 116. On Tylor and Frazer, see the Graf, *Magic in the ancient world,* 14; Hoffman, "Fiat Magia," 182–86.

11. J. G. Frazer, *The golden bough: A study in magic and religion,* 3rd ed. (New York: Collier Books, 1985), 56, 58. The importance of precisely following the components of a ritual varies between cultures; in some societies, deviation would result in failure, while others allowed for invention. E. E. Evans-Pritchard, "The morphology and function of magic," *American Anthropologist* 31, no. 4 (1929): 623–24, 32. Compare the claims made for necessity of precise enactment in the magical papyri: PGM XIII.343–646, PDM xiv.574–85 and discussion at W. Brashear, "The Greek magical papyri: An introduction and survey; annotated bibliography (1928–1994)," *ANRW* II 18, no. 5 (1995): 3414.

12. W. van Binsbergen and F. Wiggermann, "Magic in history: A theoretical perspective, and its application to ancient Mesopotamia," in *Mesopotamian magic: Textual, historical and interpretive perspectives,* ed. T. Abusch and K. van der Toorn (Groningen: Styx, 1999), 12, 16.

13. E. Thomassen, "Is magic a subclass of ritual?" in *The world of ancient magic,* ed. D. R. Jordan, H. Montgomery, and E. Thomassen (Norwegian Institute at Athens: Bergen, 1999), 58, 60–61; C. M. Bell, *Ritual theory, ritual practice* (New York: Oxford University Press, 1992), 98; P. Bourdieu, *Outline of a theory of practice,* trans. R. Nice (New York: Cambridge University Press, 1977), 89.

given direction by a spoken incantation, but objects often convey the force and power of spell.[14] Specialized speech, locations, and objects—brought together through performance—signal to those undertaking a magical rite that these actions stand outside of typical, everyday events.[15]

Magic may leave traces in the archaeological record through material objects. Although spoken words are ephemeral, the process of inscribing an incantation can transfer the spoken spell to a more permanent form.[16] Similarly, the material components of a ritual may be visible in the archaeological record.[17] Even so, finding such objects may be difficult, as the vagaries of preservation often result in the decay of organic materials, and many items that were once components of rites do not survive. Additionally, the physical location in which a rite occurred may be altered. Repeated activities, undertaken in the same location, can result in changes within the landscape.[18]

Magic may draw on religious traditions for both efficacy and exoticism. A significant degree of fluidity existed between magic and religion during antiquity, and finding clear-cut distinctions between these two poles of ritual practice is nearly impossible.[19] Indeed, magic often adopted and employed many of the formal and informal characteristics of religious practice, including prayer and sacrifice.[20] These shared features should not be surprising, as magic

---

14. S. J. Tambiah, "The magical power of words," *Man* 3, no. 2 (1968): 188–90; Malinowski, *Coral gardens and their magic,* 231–39. On the social function of objects as vehicles for ritual speech, see A. B. Weiner, "From words to objects to magic: Hard words and the boundaries of social interaction," *Man* 18, no. 4 (1983).

15. R. Grimes, *Beginnings in ritual studies* (Washington, DC: University Press of America, 1982), 57–60; R. Bauman, "Verbal art as performance," *American Anthropologist* 77, no. 2 (1975): 275; Malinowski, *Coral gardens and their magic,* 231–39.

16. Smith, "Trading places," 15, 26.

17. W. H. Walker, "Where are the witches of prehistory?" *Journal of Archaeological Method and Theory* 5, no. 3 (1998): 246.

18. J. P. Mitchell, "Performance," in *Handbook of material culture,* ed. C. Tilley et al. (Thousand Oaks, CA: Sage, 2006), 394; C. Malone, D. A. Barrowclough, and S. Stoddart, "Introduction: Cult in context," in *Cult in context: Reconsidering ritual in archaeology,* ed. D. A. Barrowclough and C. Malone (Oxford: Oxbow, 2007), 2.

19. Versnel rightly summarizes the conundrum: "What is important is to make a distinction between magic and non-magic, and it will be impossible—and if, possible, utterly impractical—to completely eliminate religion as one obvious model of contrast." "Some reflections on the relationship magic-religion," 187. The distinction between magic and religion is an intellectual development of the Victorian age; the ancients were only concerned with the distinction between proper and improper ritual practices. Bremmer, "The birth of the term 'magic,'" 11–12.

20. On these topics, see F. Graf, "Prayer in magic and religious ritual," in *Magika hiera,* ed. C. A. Faraone and D. Obbink (New York: Oxford University Press, 1991); S. I. Johnston, "Sacrifice

18   Materia Magica

and religion were both the products of the same culture. As Einar Thomassen states, "Magic depends on normal ritual and relates dialectically to it, by combining features which are the same as the ones performed in normal rituals—hymns, prayers, invocations, sacrifices, etc.—with features that are deliberately different from it."[21] The practitioner may incorporate features of religious ritual but intentionally alter these same characteristics, often through inversion.[22] Practitioners also might adopt features from foreign religious traditions, believing that these rites had power or would lend an air of exoticism to their own practice. Indeed, the power of foreign gods is often something to be feared, and the appropriation of such wild and undomesticated forces could provide the practitioner with significant power. Conversely, the implementation of foreign names, words, and imagery increased the weirdness of a given ritual process, even when the practitioner did not (or could not) understand the meaning or original context of the alien element.[23]

Magic is frequently a private activity. Both Émile Durkheim and Marcel Mauss defined magic, in part, by its apparent opposition to public enactment and to society at large. Durkheim famously stated that the magician possessed a client rather than a church, and this idea, of the separateness of the magician from community rites, has remained a central tenet in differentiating magic from religious practice.[24] Indeed, Augustine cited the private performance of rites as symptomatic of the illegitimacy of pagan ritual.[25] Scholars have frequently suggested that magic is undertaken alone, without social approval; its practitioners often are associated with the margins of society.[26]

---

in the Greek magical papyri," in *Magic and ritual in the ancient world,* ed. P. A. Mirecki and M. Meyer (Leiden: Brill, 2002).

21. Thomassen, "Is magic a subclass of ritual?" 65.

22. Ibid., 64.

23. Y. Koenig, "La Nubie dans les textes magiques: 'l'inquiétante étrangeté'," *Revue d'Égyptologie* 38 (1987); Brashear, "The Greek Magical Papyri," 3434; H. S. Versnel, "The poetics of the magical charm: An essay on the power of words," in *Magic and ritual in the ancient world,* ed. P. A. Mirecki and M. Meyer (Leiden: Brill, 2002), 144–47; J. Dieleman, *Priests, tongues, and rites: The London-Leiden magical manuscripts and translation in Egyptian ritual (100– 300 CE)* (Leiden: Brill, 2005), 71–75; Bohak, *Ancient Jewish magic,* 258–64, 274–76.

24. É. Durkheim, *The elementary forms of the religious life,* trans. J. W. Swain (New York: Macmillan, 1915), 44; M. Mauss, *A general theory of magic* (London: Routledge and K. Paul, 1972), 18–24.

25. Augustine, *Div. quaest.* 79.1; F. Graf, "Theories of magic in antiquity," in *Magic and ritual in the ancient world,* ed. P. A. Mirecki and M. Meyer (Leiden: Brill, 2002), 99–100.

26. R. L. Fowler, "Greek magic, Greek religion," *ICS* 20 (1995): 341; Thomassen, "Is magic a subclass of ritual?" 57; M. W. Dickie, *Magic and magicians in the Greco-Roman world* (New York: Routledge, 2001), 41.

Finding Magic in the Archaeological Record   19

Some aspects of magic, however, are clearly public, or at least presented a public face. Amulets, which were used for protection, could be worn on the body, and homes were often decorated with publicly visible inscriptions to ward off evil or avert the evil eye. Even certain acts of magic, such as an aggressive act of throwing a fetus at an enemy, discussed in chapter 3, could be publicly performed. Rather than distinguishing the performance of magic by the space in which actions occur, the divide between public and private might be better understood through the goals of the ritual act. The performance of magical rites is often guided by private gain, and it is for this reason, the privileging of the individual over society, that such acts are sometimes viewed as asocial.[27] This reorientation, however, brings new difficulties, as it may become impossible, or nearly so, to differentiate magic from other household or private ritual activities. Often, household rites echoed many of the performances undertaken by the polis or state, and features of domestic architecture frequently were doubled within civic spaces.[28] The home possessed a hearth that was paralleled, in larger form, by a civic hearth, housed in Rome at the Temple of Vesta. Indeed, many of the protective functions of rituals that were undertaken in the domestic sphere blur any distinction between magic and religion.[29]

The markers of magic that have been delineated—mechanistic ritual, appeals or references to religion, and private performance—are not intended to encompass all of the potential features of the phenomenon. When looking for magic in the archaeological record, we seldom possess the testimony of ancient witnesses; objects too often are silent. In order to locate magic, we must delineate the phenomenon through characteristics that also are identifiable within the material record. In other words, our definition of magic must be predicated on empirical markers that can be located through artifacts, including traces of production, use and consumption, physical decoration, and depositional context. As we will see in the next section, magical practice often was deliberately obscure. Finding magic, and determining that we are correct in our

---

27. Thomassen, "Is magic a subclass of ritual?" 63.
28. C. A. Faraone, "Household religion in ancient Greece," in *Household and family religion in antiquity,* ed. J. Bodel and S. M. Olyan (Malden, MA: Blackwell, 2008), 213–17, but compare J. Bodel, "Cicero's Minerva, *Penates,* and the Mother of the *Lares:* An outline of Roman domestic religion," in *Household and family religion in antiquity,* 264–68.
29. J. Z. Smith, "Here, there, and anywhere," in *Relating religion: Essays in the study of religion,* ed. J. Z. Smith (Chicago: University of Chicago, 2004); R. K. Ritner, "Household religion in ancient Egypt," in *Household and family religion in antiquity,* 184–86; Faraone, "Household religion in ancient Greece," 218–24; D. Boedeker, "Family matters: Domestic religion in classical Greece," in *Household and family religion in antiquity,* 239–44.

identification, involves balancing our expectations of what the practice should look like with the evidence that we discover in the ground.

The Elusiveness of Magical Practice in the Roman Period

Magical practice appears to have been commonplace during antiquity, and the phenomenon was a frequent subject in poetry and the ancient novel. Cases of amulets visible in museums and the lengthy catalogs of spells preserved on Egyptian papyri reinforce the idea of the prevalence of ancient practice.[30] Even the encyclopedist Pliny the Elder, who scoffs at some superstitious beliefs, states that nearly everyone feared the power of magic.[31] Archaeologically, however, the preserved evidence of enacted magic such as curse tablets is comparatively small when juxtaposed with other corpora of textual artifacts such as public inscriptions or ostraca. The number of published curse tablets stands at approximately 1,600, which derive from over a period of approximately one thousand years and the full geographic extent of the Roman empire. In contrast, over one thousand ostraca have been published from the University of Michigan excavations at the site of Karanis alone.[32]

There are multiple causes for the discrepancy between our expectations that magic will be visible at every turn, and the reality that magic is difficult to find and equally hard to prove conclusively. One factor in this disjunction is survival. Many magical artifacts may have been made of organic material that has decomposed in the intervening centuries. Simaetha, in Theocritus's second *Idyll,* uses a variety of organic materials to recall her lover, including bay leaves, bran, cloth from his cloak, and a potion made from a powdered lizard. In the novelist and orator Apulieus's second century CE *Apology,* which records the author's defense against a charge of magic, the evidence for nocturnal sacrifices was similarly transient.[33] Smoke marks preserved on the wall could have been washed away, and the feathers swept up, with no evidence of magic left for anyone, let alone an archaeologist, to discover. Even the corpus of curse tablets may be woefully underrepresented; we know from the magi-

---

30. Graf, *Magic in the ancient world,* 1. Compare the discussion in Fowler, "Greek magic, Greek religion," 317–21.
31. Plin. *HN* XXX.2.
32. *P.Mich.* VI; *P.Mich.* VIII.
33. Apul. *Apol.* 57–60.

Finding Magic in the Archaeological Record   21

cal papyri that curses could be written on a variety of materials such as wax tablets or papyrus that ordinarily would not have survived outside of Egypt.[34] Moreover, magical materials may have been destroyed or used up as part of the rite. The victims of a spell typically ingested *pharmaka,* or drugs, and rituals such as the oath ceremony known from Cyrene melted the wax figurines that represented the participants, effectively destroying the evidence of the rite.[35]

Furthermore, magic may be difficult to find because practitioners wanted it to be that way. Throughout the empire, professionals employed a patois of concealment, secrecy, and misdirection. Literary sources record that spells were intoned using low voices to maintain secrecy and to avoid angering the infernal powers that were necessary for magic.[36] This obfuscation served a variety of purposes for the local practitioner, reasons that may have differed according to the community and the needs of the individual. Knowledge of how to perform spells was specialized and closely guarded. The texts of the magical recipe books frequently require that the practitioner keep the contents of rituals secret or perform the rites away from witnesses.[37] Control of this information would have played a significant role in assuring the reputation of individual practitioners.[38] Moreover, the rituals may have required that the practitioner hide the materials that are used in the rite. Artifacts are frequently buried, placed in graves, dropped down wells, burned up, or hidden in someone's home. This would also conceal a ritual act from the victim, preventing him or her from negating the spell.

Modern investigators, too, may not initially recognize an artifact as magi-

---

34. I.e., PGM V.304–69 specifies either a hieratic papyrus or a lead lamella. On the problem of survival and the overrepresentation of lead tablets, see Faraone, "The problem of dense concentrations of data for cartographers (and chronographers) of ancient Mediterranean magic: Some illustrative case studies from the East."

35. R. Meiggs and D. M. Lewis, eds., *A selection of Greek historical inscriptions to the end of the fifth century B.C.* (Oxford: Clarendon Press, 1969), no. 5, pp. 5–9; cf. Hdt IV 145–59. For discussion, see C. A. Faraone, "Molten wax, spilt wine, and mutilated animals: Sympathetic magic in Near Eastern and early Greek oath ceremonies," *JHS* 113 (1993).

36. Ogden, "Binding spells," 82. A. S. F. Gow, *Theocritus,* 2 vols. (Cambridge: Cambridge University Press, 1950), vol. 2, 38, 43.

37. In general on secrecy in the papyri, see H. D. Betz, "Secrecy in the Greek magical papyri," in *Secrecy and concealment: Studies in the history of Mediterranean and Near Eastern religions,* ed. H. G. Kippenberg and G. G. Stroumsa (Leiden: Brill, 1995). On the importance of secrecy in the Demotic Magical Papyri, see Dieleman, *Priests, tongues, and rites,* 80–87, 276, and n. 51.

38. R. L. Gordon, "Aelian's peony: The location of magic in Graeco-Roman tradition," in *Comparative criticism 9,* ed. E. Shaffer (Cambridge: Cambridge University Press, 1987), 64; Dieleman, *Priests, tongues, and rites,* 83.

22   Materia Magica

cal, although they may consider it to be odd or weird. The problem of identifying magic may be related to the focal range of most inquiries. Scholars
typically look at single artifacts rather than groups of associated finds, while
magic may be best identified through the analysis of combinations of multiple
objects, some of which may be utilitarian, in conjunction with archaeological
context.[39]

We often attribute secrecy to magical performance because ancient evidence suggests that the practice was illegal under the Roman Empire. Imperial law codes attest to the frequent condemnation of magical acts, a tradition
that has its origins in Republican laws, perhaps as early as the archaic XII
Tables.[40] Closer to our period of interest, the *Lex Cornelia de sicariis et veneficiis,* passed in 81 BCE under L. Cornelius Sulla, focused on cases of murder
and included both traditional killing as well as death that occurred through
hidden or unknown means, including magic or poisoning.[41] Outside of murder, an undated (though likely first or second century CE) *senatus consultum*
condemned those undertaking *mala sacrificia,* wicked or harmful sacrifices,
which presumably included religious deviance and aggressive magical rites,
and linked these practices with the *Lex Cornelia.*[42] By the third century, curse
tablets are explicitly included among the methods of homicide associated with
the Sullan law: Tertullian lists *ferrum* (iron), *venenum* (poison), and *magicae
devinctiones* (magical curses).[43] Late Antique legal texts reinforce the illegality
of magic. So, among the laws under the heading of *de maleficis et mathema-
ticis et ceteris similibus,* "on magicians, astrologers and the like," dated to
either 317–19 or 321–24 CE, we find the requirement, "Punishment must be
meted out and deservedly; by the severest laws must vengeance be taken on
the science of those who gird themselves with magic arts and attempt anything
against the life or person of anyone, or on those who are found guilty of influ-

---

39. Walker, "Where are the witches of prehistory?" 259.
40. See J. B. Rives, "Magic in the XII Tables revisited," *CQ* 52, no. 1 (2002).
41. J. B. Rives, "Magic in Roman law: The reconstruction of a crime," *ClAnt* 22, no. 2 (2003):
    320; J. B. Rives, "Magic, religion and law: The case of the *Lex Cornelia de sicariis et venefi-
    ciis,*" in *Religion and law in classical and Christian Rome,* ed. C. Ando and J. Rüpke (Stutt-
    gart: Steiner, 2006), suggests that the Sullan law remained focused on murder.
42. Modestinus (3rd century) D. 48.8.13; Graf, *Magic in the ancient world,* 47; R. L. Gordon,
    "Imagining Greek and Roman magic," in *Witchcraft and magic in Europe: Ancient Greece
    and Rome,* ed. B. Ankarloo and S. Clark (Philadelphia: University of Pennsylvania Press,
    1999), 260; Rives, "Magic, religion and law: The case of the *Lex Cornelia de sicariis et ven-
    eficiis,*" 64–67.
43. Tertullian, *Spect.* 2. See further discussion at Rives, "Magic in Roman law: The reconstruction
    of a crime," 321 n. 24.

Finding Magic in the Archaeological Record   23

encing chaste minds to lust."[44] Although the legal texts focus on harmful acts
as examples of magic, the individual bringing the case determined whether a
particular action could be tried as magic. Such an interpretative disjunction is
apparent in the *Apology* of Apuleius, where the author reconfigures magical
misconduct as harmless philosophical inquiry.

The impact of the laws against magic are more difficult to gauge.[45] We
possess few historically attested cases of trials of magic, but a woman named
Numantina under the reign of Tiberius in 23/24 CE was prosecuted on a charge
of driving her ex-husband insane by means of incantations and poison/magic
(*carminibus et veneficiis*).[46] Numantina was acquitted, but other evidence suggests that those found guilty of magic in the second century were ordinarily
burned alive.[47] Apuleius's *Apology* likewise was written as a defense against
an accusation of magic. M. Dickie has suggested that the prevalence of accusations of magic in the Late Antique horoscopes of Firmicus Maternus reflects
a social reality.[48] Maternus was a fourth-century senator who composed a
lengthy treatise on astrology, the *Metheseos;* the brief life spans of sorcerers
are the result of legal condemnations. This suggests an ancient world filled not
just with magic but with trials of practitioners.

Outside of legal proceedings, magicians and other suspicious individuals
also might be expelled from cities, towns, or villages. Cassius Dio informs us
that Agrippa, Augustus's right-hand man, expelled all astrologers and sorcerers from the city.[49] This is not an isolated incident, and the historical sources
record numerous occasions on which the emperor or other governmental bodies ordered the removal of soothsayers, magicians, or foreign priests from the
city of Rome; expulsions are recorded under Tiberius (16 CE), Claudius (52
CE), Nero (66 and perhaps 68 CE), Vitellius (69 CE), Vespasian (70 and 71

---

44. *Cod. Just.* IX.18; *Cod. Theod.* IX.16. Translation from C. Pharr, "The interdiction of magic
    in Roman law," *Transactions and Proceedings of the American Philological Association* 63
    (1932): 283.

45. The charge of magic often masked political intrigue from as early as the Julio-Claudian
    period, and scholars have rightly isolated the myriad political and strategic uses that it served.
    By the Late Antique period, accusations of magic were regularly used as a pretense for purges
    of enemies and even former political allies, and reflected contemporary tensions among the
    governing classes. See Brown, "Sorcery, demons and the rise of Christianity from Late Antiq-
    uity into the middle ages," 23–24.

46. Tac. *Ann.* 4.22.

47. P. Garnsey, *Social status and legal privilege in the Roman Empire* (Oxford: Clarendon, 1970),
    110–11.

48. Dickie, *Magic and magicians in the Greco-Roman world,* 150–51.

49. Dio Cass. 49.43.5. Josephus (*AJ* xviii. 65) records that Tiberius persecuted the devotees of Isis
    in 19 CE. The altars to Egyptian gods were destroyed in 59, 58, 53, and 48 BCE.

24   Materia Magica

CE), Domitian (89/90 and 93/94 CE), and Marcus Aurelius (175 CE).[50] Other communities also may have ousted magicians and wonder-workers, but our evidence for this is largely circumstantial. After the Apostle Paul gained popularity by performing exorcisms in the name of Jesus, one of the leaders of the local silversmiths, Demetrius, roused the townspeople against Paul and his assistants, and dragged Gaius and Aristarchus into the theater. A riot nearly erupted but was narrowly averted by the local magistrate.[51] In the *Metamorphosis,* Apuleius depicts a similar situation. A local community in Thessaly held a meeting in which they decided to stone to death the witch Meroe, who according to the narrator, had been terrorizing the community. The powers of the witch exceeded those of the townspeople, and through divine means, she confined the residents to their homes until they swore not to harm her.[52]

We should not, however, make too much of the illegality of magic. Some forms of magic, as we have defined the practice, were never illegal, and in fact, exceptions are made in the legal codes for beneficial rites, such as healing or preventing hailstorms.[53] Amulets were worn publicly, and houses might be adorned with incantations to ward off misfortune. In villages and towns throughout the empire, local herbalists, wise women, or even religious specialists likely dabbled in magic. Of course, practice typically was not grounds for expulsion. Rather it is likely that some unexplained event may have led to such extreme responses. The illegality of some forms of magic, coupled with local reactions to misfortune, must have played a role in marginalizing certain kinds of ritual practices but it does not follow that illegality diminished magical activity. C. Faraone, for example, has demonstrated that some Late Antique divinatory practices that used skull cups may represent the transformation of necromantic rituals.[54]

---

50. Tiberius: Tac. *Ann.* 2.32; Suet. *Tib.* 36; Ulpian *De off. procons.* 7 (in *Leg. mos. et rom.* coll. 15.2.1); Dio Cassius 57.15.8–9; Claudius: Tac. *Ann.* 12. 52; Dio Cass. 60 (61) 33.36; Nero: *Cat. cod. astrol. graec.* 8:4.100; Vitellius: Tac. *Hist.* 2.62; Dio Cassius 64 (65). 1–4; Suet. *Vit.* 14.4; Xonaras 11.6; Vespasian: Dio Cassius 65 (66).9.2; 12.2–3; 13.1; Suet. *Vesp.* 13 and 15; Domitian: Dio Cassius 67.13.2–3; Suet. *Dom.* 10.3; Pliny. *Ep.* 3.11; Suidas s.v. Δομετιανός; Philostratus *VApol.* 7.3; Jerome, *Chron.* Ad A.D. 89/90 and 93/94; M. Aurelius: Ulpian *De off. procons.* 7 (in *Leg. mos. et rom.* coll. 15.2.6). See as well Tertullian *De idol.* 9, with commentary at F. H. Cramer, *Astrology in Roman law and politics* (Philadelphia: American Philosophical Society, 1954).
51. *Acts* 19.23–41.
52. Apul. *Met.* 1.10.
53. *Cod. Just.* IX.18: *Cod. Theod.* IX.16; Pharr, "The Interdiction of magic in Roman law," 283.
54. C. A. Faraone, "Necromancy goes underground: The disguise of skull- and corpse-divination in the Paris magical papyri," in *Mantikê: Studies in ancient divination,* ed. S. I. Johnston and P. T. Struck (Leiden: Brill, 2005).

Finding Magic in the Archaeological Record 25

Our inability to square the frequent testimony of magic with the appearance of the phenomenon in the archaeological record has numerous causes: the vagaries of preservation, a desire for secrecy on the part of the practitioner, and the tendency of rituals to destroy or use up the material components of a spell. Part of the problem of finding magic also is related to our inability to accurately recognize it in the archaeological record: we lack the appropriate criteria for identifying and evaluating the material residue of magical rites.

Ritual and Magic in the Archaeological Record

Magical practice is grounded in ritual acts, often utilizing material culture, that are undertaken to achieve a desired effect. Therefore, to locate magic in the archaeological record requires us to find material evidence that these rituals have occurred. Literary and documentary sources, such as accounts of folklore or spell manuals, can provide insight into the physical processes of ritual activity, supplying lists of materials that are employed as well as recounting actions that the practitioner is supposed to take. In recent years, a number of American scholars have undertaken productive work linking documentary sources and the archaeological remains of magic. Working in the domestic spaces of African American slaves and their descendants, Mark Leone and Gladys-Marie Fry have suggested that discrete deposits of coins, beads, pins, quartz, pebbles, and potsherds can be read as evidence of "conjure."[55] "Conjure," "rootwork," and "Hoodoo" are all terms given to ritual practices undertaken by enslaved Africans or enslaved Americans of African descent to control spirits, divine the future, or ward off malign spiritual intervention. Leone, Fry, and Tim Ruppel cataloged all references to material objects that were recorded in the autobiographies of formerly enslaved Africans and African Americans; these documentary sources provided a listing of material that

---

55. M. P. Leone and G.-M. Fry, "Conjuring in the big house kitchen: An interpretation of African American belief systems based on the uses of archaeology and folklore sources," *Journal of American Folklore* 112, no. 445 (1999); M. P. Leone, G.-M. Fry, and T. Ruppel, "Spirit management among Americans of African descent," in *Race and the archaeology of identity,* ed. Charles E. Orser Jr. (Salt Lake City: University of Utah Press, 2001); T. Ruppel et al., "Hidden in view: African spiritual spaces in North American landscapes," *Antiquity* 77, no. 296 (2003); L. A. Wilkie, "Secret and sacred: Contextualizing the artifacts of African-American magic and religion," *Historical Archaeology* 31, no. 4 (1997); C. C. Fennell suggests that similar material also could be the product of European-American traditions. "Conjuring boundaries: Inferring past identities from religious artifacts," *International Journal of Historical Archaeology* 4, no. 4 (2000).

could be used in ritual practices.[56] For Fry and Leone, archaeology uncovered discrete instances of the practice of conjure, but the phenomenon could only be understood by applying information gathered through the documentary sources.[57]

It is possible to develop a similar methodology for antiquity, where literary and documentary evidence can suggest the sorts of materials that frequently were employed in magical rites. A survey of the ancient sources suggests four classes of materials: (1) written or inscribed objects, (2) figurines and representations, (3) naturally occurring plants and animals, including parts of bodies, often employed to establish a connection to the victim, and (4) household objects that have been repurposed for magical use. These four categories will be discussed at greater length in the following chapter. Identifying ritual practice in the archaeological record also requires us to know how these items were utilized and where they might appear. Without such information, it may be difficult to distinguish between artifacts employed in ritual and those that were discarded as trash.[58]

Precise information about *materia magica* as well as the performance of magic in Greek and Roman antiquity can be found in the corpora of ritual manuals composed in Greek and Demotic Egyptian. In antiquity, the compilation of magical spells in Greek can likely be traced to the Hellenistic period.[59] This tradition continued well into the Roman period, resulting in the production of numerous small collections of model texts and a smaller number of larger handbooks, some as long as thousands of lines. Both the manuals written in Greek and those composed in Demotic are likely the products of Egyptian priests.[60]

In the modern period, the spell manuals have been cataloged as the Greek and Demotic Magical Papyri, or PGM and PDM, respectively, a system of indexing the texts that is dependent on the language in which they were written. For the initial compilation and publication of the *Papyri Graecae Magicae* in 1928 and 1931, Karl Preisendanz cataloged only the Greek spells, leaving

---

56. Leone, Fry, and Ruppel, "Spirit management among Americans of African descent," 152.
57. Leone and Fry, "Conjuring in the big house kitchen," 375–77.
58. Leone, Fry, and Ruppel, "Spirit management among Americans of African descent," 147.
59. Faraone, "Handbooks and anthologies: The collection of Greek and Egyptian incantations in late Hellenistic Egypt," 209–13.
60. J. Dieleman has argued recently that the Demotic spell books were written against the backdrop of the Greek manuals that preceded them. *Priests, tongues, and rites,* 288–94.

out the Demotic spells and even neglecting to mention their existence.[61] The Demotic spells, in contrast, when originally composed as part of a roll with Greek spells, such as PGM XII, were not given a PDM number until 1986.[62] This process divorced both the Greek and Demotic spells from their proper, shared context. Throughout this book, the spells of the magical handbooks will be referenced according to their PGM and PDM numbers, although it is important to recall that these designations may not, in fact, reflect differences in cultural context or even different papyrus rolls. The modern process of compilation juxtaposes texts that were not originally on the same roll, of the same date, or written by the same individual. Furthermore, as the PGM incorporates all documents related to magic, it includes both the instructions for the performance of rites and the results of magical acts, such as curse tablets and fever amulets discovered in Egypt. An activated love spell from Hawara (PGM XXXIIa) may be followed by a fever amulet spell from Tebtunis (PGM XXXIII), then a literary piece from the Fayum (PGM XXXIV), a charm for favor from Oxyrhynchus (PGM XXV), and finally a formulary associated with the Fayum (PGM XXXVI).

Many of the texts cataloged in the PGM and PDM are instructional and contain directives for the performance of rituals. These texts may leave spaces for the names of victims or clients, often indicated in translations by "NN" or "so and so." An instructional text also may include a model or template that the practitioner should copy or repeat. An individual papyrus in the PGM or PDM might include only a single instructional spell, or it may group together multiple spells into a single roll, such as we find in PGM XXXVI or PGM IV.

The Greek and Demotic magical papyri are incredibly detailed, listing the material components of a rite, indicating how these components are to be

---

61. For an extensive bibliography on the PGM, see Brashear, "The Greek Magical Papyri." The original volume of the PGM began the numbering system that has been maintained in subsequent volumes and editions, including the second volume, K. Preisendanz, E. Diehl, and S. Eitrem, *Papyri graecae magicae: die griechischen Zauberpapyri* (Leipzig: B. G. Teubner, 1941), a translation of the Greek and Demotic texts, H. D. Betz, *The Greek magical papyri in translation,* 2nd ed. (Chicago: University of Chicago Press, 1992), the Christian texts, M. Meyer and R. Smith, *Ancient Christian magic: Coptic texts of ritual power* (San Francisco: HarperSanFrancisco, 1994), and a compilation of magical texts not included in the original PGM, R. W. Daniel and F. Maltomini, *Supplementum magicum* (Opladen: Westdeutscher Verlag, 1990). The Magical Papyri are discussed further in Chapter 2.

62. See Johnson, "Introduction to the Demotic Magical Papyri," in *GMP*, lv; R. K. Ritner, "Egyptian magical practice under the Roman empire: The Demotic spells and their religious context," *ANRW* II 18, no. 5 (1995): 3358–61; Dieleman, *Priests, tongues, and rites,* 11–17 and nos. 47 and 48.

28   Materia Magica

treated, and supplying the invocations that the practitioner should intone. Most of these documents, however, reflect the process of production, compilation, redaction, and interpretation by priests associated with traditional Egyptian temples.[63] It is necessary to keep in mind that these documents are artifacts, used in a particular place and time and employed by inhabitants of that geographic and temporal space; the texts of the papyrus rolls possess an archaeological context and pedigree, even if we cannot reconstruct it. Employing the PGM and PDM documents across the Mediterranean basin, as a template for local religious practice, presents numerous problems, as it unlikely that these texts circulated extensively outside of the province. Rather, these documents provide a detailed prospectus on ritual practice in Egypt during the period in which they were composed and utilized.

Using this rich body of material for the study of Graeco-Roman Egypt is not without its own problems, particularly when scholars have attempted to match the spell instructions known from the magical papyri to archaeological data. Many of the artifacts that have been identified as magical are concerned with amatory magic. This may be due equally to the popularity of this kind of spell and our ability to recognize figurines as evidence of magical practice. The most spectacular instance of parallelism between the text of a magical papyrus and material artifacts came to light in the early 1970s somewhere in Middle Egypt (plate 4). Inside a ceramic vessel, looters discovered a lead tablet and a clay figurine of a kneeling woman, who was depicted with her arms bound behind her back, and pierced in various parts of her body by thirteen nails.[64]

---

63. On the production of the PGM and PDM rolls, see G. Fowden, *The Egyptian Hermes: A historical approach to the late pagan mind* (New York: Cambridge University Press, 1986), 168–76; R. K. Ritner, *The mechanics of ancient Egyptian magical practice* (Chicago: Oriental Institute of the University of Chicago, 1993), 204–14, 220–33; Ritner, "Egyptian magical practice under the Roman empire," 3361–71; D. Frankfurter, *Religion in Roman Egypt: Assimilation and resistance* (Princeton: Princeton University Press, 1998), 228–33, 57–64; Dieleman, *Priests, tongues, and rites,* 280–94.

64. P. du Bourguet, "Ensemble magique de la période romaine en Égypte," *Revue du Louvre* 25 (1975). For further discussion, see S. Kambitsis, "Une nouvelle tablette magique d'Égypte, Musée du Louvre Inv. E27145, 3e/4e siècle," *BIFAO* 76 (1976); D. G. Martinez, *Michigan Papyri XVI: A Greek love charm from Egypt (P.Mich. 757)* (Atlanta: Scholars Press, 1991); Ritner, *The mechanics of ancient Egyptian magical practice,* 112–13; Faraone, *Ancient Greek love magic,* esp. chap. 2; and C. A. Faraone, "The ethnic origins of a Roman-era *Philtrokatadesmos* (*PGM* IV.296–434)," in *Magic and ritual in the ancient world,* ed. P. A. Mirecki and M. Meyer (Leiden: Brill, 2002). More limited discussions occur within J. J. Winkler, *The constraints of desire: The anthropology of sex and gender in ancient Greece* (New York: Routledge, 1990); M. W. Dickie, "Who practiced love-magic in classical antiquity and in the late Roman world?" *CQ* 50, no. 2 (2000). Generally, on binding figurines, C. A. Faraone, "Binding and burying the forces of evil: The defensive use of 'voodoo' dolls in ancient

Finding Magic in the Archaeological Record   29

This small statuette was purchased subsequently by the Louvre and will be referred to as the "Louvre figurine."

The text, inscribed on the lead sheet, which curses a woman named Ptolemais, the daughter of Aias and Horigenes, can be compared to a spell found in PGM IV, the longest roll found within the cache of magical papyri at Thebes. "A Wonderful Love Charm," at lines 296–466, includes specific directives for the creation of two figures of clay or wax, and requires that the magician

> make the male in the form of Ares fully armed, holding a sword in his left hand and threatening to plunge it into the right side of her neck. And make her with her arms behind her back and down on her knees. And you are to fasten the magical material on her head or neck . . . [the magician is then instructed to write magical words on various parts of her body] . . . And take thirteen copper needles and stick 1 in the brain while saying "I am piercing your brain, NN"; and stick 2 in the ears and 2 in the eyes and 1 in the mouth and 2 in the midriff and 1 in the hands and 2 in the pudenda and 2 in the soles, saying each time, "I am piercing such and such member of her, NN, so that she may remember no one but me, NN, alone."[65]

In this translation, "NN" indicates the target of the spell; the practitioner would fill in the name of the victim. Although the figurine largely complies with the prescriptions recorded within the PGM, a number of differences can be detected between the instructions and the archaeological object. Most notably, the text instructs the creation of two figures that enact the spell in tandem; the Ares figure, which symbolically represented the commissioner of the spell, is absent. The placement of the nails also is slightly different from that prescribed in the text, and the Louvre figurine lacks inscriptions required by the PGM text.[66] The spell instructions from Thebes require that the practitioner

> tie the lead leaf to the figures with thread from the loom after making 365 knots while saying as you have learned, "ABRASAX, hold her fast!" You place it, as the sun is setting, beside the grave of one who has died untimely or violently, placing beside it also the seasonal flowers.

Greece," *ClAnt* 10, no. 2 (1991). The provenance of the objects was originally given as Antinoopolis, in part because of an invocation in the text to the ghost of Antinoüs.

65. Trans. E. N. O'Neil in *GMP*, 44.

66. Faraone, "The ethnic origins of a Roman-era *Philtrokatadesmos* (*PGM* IV.296–434)," 320; Brashear, "The Greek Magical Papyri," 3417, n.152.

30   Materia Magica

As a purchase from the art market, the Louvre assemblage possesses no provenance, external clues for dating, or archaeological context. Scholars have suggested that the entire group may derive from a funerary context, but that is largely based on evidence from the text of the tablet.[67] The artifacts indicate that the ensemble resulted from an altogether different process of deposition than that required in the PGM instructions. The bound, pierced figurine and the tablet are placed in a jar, perhaps with the intention of enclosing and therefore binding together victim and spell. This process of burial within a jar is common in earlier, Pharaonic execration rituals, which often involved depositing figurines in vessels.[68] This evidence may suggest that the practitioner responsible for the Louvre ensemble drew upon native Egyptian traditions in enacting the love spell and did not rely solely on a spell closely comparable to the PGM text.

Five other Egyptian tablets and artifacts have been associated with the directions found in PGM IV, but none precisely corresponds to the assemblage—figurines of a bound woman and Ares, tied to a lead tablet—that we expect from reading the instructional text.[69] Only one of these artifacts could be asso-

---

67. Faraone, *Ancient Greek love magic,* 42 n. 3; Martinez, *Michigan Papyri XVI: A Greek love charm from Egypt (P.Mich. 757),* 18.

68. Ritner, *The mechanics of ancient Egyptian magical practice,* 175. Spell 1016 from the Coffin Texts reads, "Oh you who are hateful . . . I put my hands on the jar in the bounds of which you sit, it descends before you." For a New Kingdom parallel, see G. Poesner, "Les empreintes magiques de Gizeh et les morts dangereux," *Mitteilungen des Deutschen Archäologischen Instituts, Athenische Abteilung* 16 (1958).

69. These texts are discussed at length in Martinez, *Michigan Papyri XVI: A Greek love charm from Egypt (P.Mich. 757).* The artifacts include:
    (1) A lead tablet from Hawara in the Fayum, *Suppl. Mag.* I. 46 = Cairo Museum Journal d'Entrée 48217 (2nd or 3rd CE) = *SB* IV. 7425 = *SEG* 8 [1937] 574. Bibliography: C. C. Edgar, "A love charm from the Fayoum," *Bulletin de la Société royale d'archéologie d'Alexandrie* 21 (1925); D. R. Jordan, "A love charm with verses," *ZPE* 72 (1988), 247–48 and n. 4.
    (2) A lead tablet of unknown provenance, *Suppl. Mag.* I. no. 48 (2nd–3rd CE) = P.Mich. inv. 757 (2nd–4th CE); Bibliography: Martinez, *Michigan Papyri XVI: A Greek love charm from Egypt (P.Mich. 757)* (3rd–4th CE).
    (3) A group of three artifacts found together at Oxyrhynchus, which each preserve a variation of the PGM spell (2nd–4th CE) Bibliography: D. Wortmann, "Neue magische texte," *Bonner Jahrbücher* 168 (1968) 56–80 (3rd–4th CE), Corrections in *SGD* nos. 155–56; Jordan, "A love charm with verses."
      (3a) A lead tablet, *Suppl. Mag.* I. no. 49 = P. Köln Inv. T. 1 = Wortmann "Neue magische texte," no. 1.
      (3b) A lead tablet, *Suppl. Mag.* I. no. 50 = P. Köln Inv. T. 2 = Wortmann "Neue magische texte," no. 2.
      (3c) An inscribed ceramic vessel, *Suppl. Mag.* I. no. 51 = P. Köln inv. O. 409 = Wortmann "Neue magische texte," no. 3; tablets (3a) and (3b) were discovered inside.

Finding Magic in the Archaeological Record 31

ciated with figurines: a lead tablet from Hawara, discovered in the cemetery, possessed two holes that might have been used for suspending figurines, but no images were discovered with the tablet. Edgar notes that small wax images, one of an ass-headed man, likely Set, and another of a bound woman, are in the collection of the Egyptian Museum, but these were not found in association with the tablet. The text inscribed on the tablet, while very close to the instructional text, is significantly shorter.

Two lead tablets and an associated ceramic vessel from Oxyrhynchus, each inscribed with a version of the PGM instructional text, present a different arrangement of object and text. Like the Louvre assemblage, the Oxyrhynchus artifacts were purchased, and our knowledge about their archaeological context is limited. The same hand wrote all three objects, and the spell urges a woman named Matrona to love a man named Theodoros. The longest of the three inscriptions, *Suppl. Mag.* I 49, consisting of eighty-four lines written on one of the lead tablets, is closely related to the PGM text but it contains an extensive verse invocation to Artemis Hekate that is not paralleled.[70] The other lead sheet, *Suppl. Mag.* I 50, lacks this invocation, and where the sense of the text overlaps with the longer version, the shorter inscription does not precisely replicate it. Finally, the third text, *Suppl. Mag.* I 51, written on the exterior of the clay vessel in which the two tablets were interred, preserves a greatly abbreviated version of the invocation, combining elements of the other two inscriptions. It functions much like the brief summaries that are known from the verso of some papyri, inscriptions that would be visible when the document was rolled up.

Another text related to the PGM spell, now in the University of Michigan Collection (*P.Mich. inv.* 757) is a long iteration of an incantation similar to that preserved in PGM IV, inscribed on a lead sheet. Neither the three artifacts from Oxyrhynchus, nor the Michigan tablet, preserve any indications that the artifacts were once associated with figurines. Lacking any information about the findspots or artifacts associated with these objects, very little can be said about the ritual that produced these inscribed pieces.

The "Wonderful Love Charm" recorded in PGM IV and the associated artifacts attest to the popularity of this ritual enactment in Graeco-Roman Egypt, as the spell appears in multiple permutations and was discovered in multiple localities. At the same time, these examples highlight the disjunctions between the preserved spell books and the archaeological examples of magic,

---

70. Wortmann, "Neue magische texte," 59; Jordan, "A love charm with verses," 248–59.

32   Materia Magica

and suggest that a one-to-one correlation between spell book instructions and the magical product is largely illusory. It seems likely that the ritual experts of Graeco-Roman Egypt took some liberties with the spells they enacted, changing materials and language to suit circumstance. These texts functioned more like cookbooks, albeit complex documents that only an experienced cook could use.[71] Later spell books written in Coptic provide another example of this junction between the authoritative text and a more fluid ritual enactment.[72] In London Hay 10391, spell-texts that may have been recited orally are followed by brief lists of ingredients, suggesting that the individual performing the spells possessed sufficient knowledge to enact the spell without instructions. For example, a spell that is enacted so that "I may accomplish the things of my mouth and you may fulfill the things of my hand" precedes the ingredient list, "mastic, censer of bronze, vine wood, virgin radish oil."[73]

The investigation of the archaeology of magic in Egypt can neither rely solely on the PGM for identifying magic nor expect the archaeological evidence of magic to directly match a particular spell recorded in the compendia. Fry and Leone, working on material from early American history, reached comparable conclusions, noting that while oral testimony of conjure may overlap the archaeological evidence, there are significant discrepancies that also warrant explanation.[74] For the material from Egypt, many of the correspondences that have been noted between instructional manuals and archaeological evidence have relied on the inscribed texts as an indicator of formulary usage. Less attention has been paid to the form of the artifact, its associated finds, or its findspot. Magic must be understood contextually, on a local level, using the PGM as a guide, rather than as a sourcebook. Indeed, this is how ancient practitioners appear to have used the ancient collections of spells as they served the local population.

The Greek and Demotic Magical Papyri can offer a framework through which we can identify and evaluate ritual practices in Graeco-Roman Egypt.[75] There, as elsewhere, magical practice operates within a set range of parameters that define what might be viewed as both efficacious and acceptable ritual activity. A set of shared beliefs and principles that underpin and structure

---

71. M. Smith, *Jesus the magician* (San Francisco: Harper & Row, 1978), 114.
72. *ACM*, pp. 259–62.
73. *ACM* no. 127, pp. 265–66, trans. D. Frankfurter and M. Meyer.
74. Leone, Fry, and Ruppel, "Spirit management among Americans of African descent," 147.
75. Compare the discussion on classifying Jewish magic at Bohak, *Ancient Jewish magic,* 67–69.

Finding Magic in the Archaeological Record   33

the actions of individuals within a society, termed the *habitus* by P. Bourdieu, establishes a framework within which society functions and material culture is produced, employed, and consumed.[76] As we investigate the archaeological remains of magical practice, it is important to recall that the rituals prescribed by the spell manuals as well as individual variation and invention were circumscribed by the cultural structures within which the practitioner operated.[77] In other words, the papyri can provide us with a rough outline of what practice should look like, but the documents are best at showing us the sorts of rituals that we might expect to find rather than the precise form and appearance of the material residue of those rites. What we uncover from the ground can, in turn, be evaluated through comparison with other forms of material culture from the community, including the physical manifestations of religious practice.

Within other regions of the Roman empire, such as Cyprus and Spain, we lack descriptive material that can provide a comparable guide to ritual practice, encompassing both the breadth of rites as well as the details of performance. The papyri include instructions for the performance of rituals that are attested archaeologically in other regions, most notably the production of curse tablets or the manufacture of figurines. The Egyptian material, however, encapsulates one local manifestation of these practices, and it is difficult to know how applicable the PGM instructions might be for investigations in other vicinities. So, for example, in PDM xiv 675–94 one finds a spell to cause "evil sleep." According to the text, the practitioner should place a donkey's head between his feet at dawn and dusk, and recite a lengthy invocation that is given in the text. The discovery of a donkey head at a site in Germany could be related to magic, but it would be difficult to associate this find with the spell provided in the papyrus. Even when we encounter texts that show clear similarities, as is the case with an artifact known from Amathous and discussed in chapter 4, such textual congruencies may not be indicative of the same ritual enactment. As we will see, the text is the same, but its function and the ritual in which the text is used show sharp divergences. Outside of Egypt, magic was likely characterized by a comparable range and variety of practices to which the papyri attest, but the task of identifying these rituals is more difficult.

---

76. P. Bourdieu, "The Berber house or the world reversed," in *Interpretive archaeology: A reader,* ed. J. Thomas (New York: Leicester University Press, 2000), 496–97; Bourdieu, *Outline of a theory of practice,* 73, 79–82, 89–91. Bourdieu writes, "The mental structures which construct the world of objects are constructed in the practice of a world of objects constructed according to the same structures." Ibid., 91.

77. Ibid., 95.

34   Materia Magica

Throughout the Mediterranean, inscriptions that include magical words and phrases, as well as representations of the victim of the spell or of demons and other supernatural figures, can point to ritual enactment. Magical objects were specialized, because they were intended to convey ideas or perform functions that were not easily expressed.[78] Such specialization can provide indicators by which magical objects may be identified accurately in the absence of detailed descriptions like those found in the PGM. The texts and images of magic are often strange, and, as was discussed above, this weirdness may be suggestive of a magical purpose for an object. Common features of objects used in magic will be discussed at length in the succeeding chapter. Coupled with the archaeological context of a find, magical artifacts can allow us to explore the physical and material processes that are involved in ritual enactment, and to locate these activities in specific times and places.

Object-Specific Inquiry

Investigating an object through its biography can highlight the spaces in which ritual and artifacts intersected.[79] The material record of the past, as it is preserved in the soil, is a testament to what the residents of a particular place did at a particular time. Indeed, objects were often integral to human actions and occupy an important place within the workings of a given city, town, or village.[80] Created by a specific society, the material world gives physical form to societal ideas, so that artifacts, architecture, dress, and other products reflect their makers' ideas about form, appearance, and arrangement. Moreover, objects condition and affect the human beings that live among them, structuring the way in which individuals understand their community and its values; as Bourdieu notes, objects and spaces can reproduce and replicate society. Artifacts, architecture, and dress (the *habitus*) can allow us to reconstruct the societal structures that resulted in these physical reflections.[81] As artifacts reinforce and lend fixity to the social world, however, they require human interlocutors, actors who produce, engage with, and even destroy the material culture that surrounds them.[82] Human actors created or manufactured, subsequently used,

---

78. D. Miller, *Material culture and mass consumption* (New York: B. Blackwell, 1987), 28.
79. Walker, "Where are the witches of prehistory?" 249–58.
80. C. Gosden and Y. Marshall, "The cultural biography of objects," *World Archaeology* 31, no. 2 (1999): 169.
81. Bourdieu, *Outline of a theory of practice,* 81–91.
82. D. Pels, K. Hetherington, and F. Vandenberghe, "The status of the object: Performances,

reused, recycled, and eventually consumed, artifacts, and it is this series of events, this life history, that archaeology can reconstruct.[83] Within the span of its existence, an individual artifact may be exchanged or given as a gift, passing from the hand of its creator into that of another.[84] An artifact also may remain in an individual's possession for a long period of time as an item of display, or as a memento, recalling an important event in the owner's life.[85] As artifacts make their way along the path from origination to consumption, each of these actions has the potential to leave traces within the material record.[86]

This object-centered approach has proved an effective and informative means by which archaeologists can study the use and reuse of artifacts. Often, however, the life history of an artifact charts its importance as an item of exchange or trade, where the object serves a clear economic purpose, such as the transport of a commodity. The path and function of an amphora, for example, can be charted with some degree of surety.[87] After manufacture, the amphora is used to move a commodity, often from the locale in which it was produced, to another market. The amphora may then be repaired and reused, perhaps to transport another item or as packing material for a different good. Alternatively, the amphora or its component parts may have been used for a variety of different applications, from a container for foodstuffs in the domestic sphere, to use as an incense burner or a gaming piece. The success or failure of the transport of goods, for example, is visible and occurs in the world; one can chart the movement of an amphora and the sale of its contents in a subsequent market.

Ritual objects frequently stand outside of the process of exchange, and their value and function may be determined differently from traditionally

---

mediations, and techniques," *Theory, Culture and Society* 19, no. 5–6 (2002): 11.

83. J. T. Peña, *Roman pottery in the archaeological record* (Cambridge: Cambridge University Press, 2007), 6–16; I. Kopytoff, "The cultural biography of things: Commoditization as process," in *The social life of things: Commodities in cultural perspective,* ed. A. Appadurai (Cambridge: Cambridge University Press, 1986), 66–68; J. Hoskins, "Agency, biography and objects," in *Handbook of material culture,* ed. C. Tilley et al. (Thousand Oaks, CA: Sage, 2006), 75; M. B. Schiffer, "Archaeological context and systemic context," *American Antiquity* 37, no. 2 (1972): 157–60.

84. A. Appadurai, "Introduction: Commodities and the politics of value," in *The social life of things: Commodities in cultural perspective,* ed. A. Appadurai (Cambridge: Cambridge University Press, 1986), 9, 15.

85. Miller, *Material culture and mass consumption,* 191.

86. W. H. Walker and L. J. Lucero, "The depositional history of ritual and power," in *Agency in archaeology,* ed. M.-A. Dobres and J. E. Robb (New York: Routledge, 2000), 133.

87. The discussion of the life cycle of amphorae is adapted from Peña, *Roman pottery in the archaeological record,* 325–27 and fig. 11.2. On the reuse of amphorae, see ibid., 119–92.

36   Materia Magica

traded commodities.[88] The efficacy of a magical artifact—its primary use and subsequent reuse—cannot be gauged in the same manner as that of an amphora because the purpose for which a magical artifact was created may be ephemeral. The goal of a curse is to bind an opponent through the intercession of supernatural powers, and neither the act of binding nor the intervention of a divine force can be measurable. Despite these discrepancies between ritual objects and everyday items, the life-history approach still can provide a constructive critical lens through which the material culture of magic may be viewed.

The investigation of an object's biography can permit us to engage with different kinds of magical artifacts, both those that entered the archaeological record as a direct result of ritual enactment as well as objects that were deposited through nonmagical processes such as loss or disposal as trash. In the study of conjure among Americans of African descent, Leone and Fry note that their documentary sources identified the physical remains of conjure within items that were buried intentionally in significant spaces as well as objects that were worn on the body.[89] These two groups of materials would not enter the archaeological record in the same way, and while we may be able to identify that an object served a ritual function, it may not have been deposited as part of a ritual. As an example, we can compare two common magical items, a binding figurine, such as the clay doll from Egypt discussed above, and a protective amulet that was worn on the body. The figurine is consistently engaged in ritual up to and even after its deposition—the practitioner creates it and subsequently buries it in order to have an effect on the world. He or she may believe that the figurine continued to act on its target, but the interaction between the individual and the object is unlikely to occur after the completion of the rite, unless the artifact needs to be removed for some reason. The amulet, on the other hand, is endowed initially with power through a ritual, but then protects its bearer passively. It leaves the circumscribed, special realm of ritual that accompanied its creation and is subsequently used by an individual in daily, nonritual activities. While it may enter the archaeological record through ritual, it may also be lost or discarded. Reconstructing the biography of magical objects permits us to identify important moments when the artifact was incorporated into a ritual

---

88. Kopytoff, "The cultural biography of things: Commoditization as process," 75; but on the exchange of ritual technology see S. Harrison, "The commerce of cultures in Melanesia," *Man* 28, no. 1 (1993).

89. Leone, Fry, and Ruppel, "Spirit management among Americans of African descent," 153.

Finding Magic in the Archaeological Record   37

activity: at the moment of creation, during a period of active use, and at the final consumption of the artifact.

Material culture results from the transmutation of raw materials into things of value, and indeed, it may be possible to read the creation of an object from its final form. The physicality of an artifact's origination cannot be separated from the process of production.[90] In the case of a magical artifact, the raw materials required for production may be related to the task that an object was intended to perform. A sympathetic relationship, perhaps expressed as an analogy where like affects like, or in which the image was believed to affect its antecedent, may provide the reason for which a particular substance or material was used.[91]

Ritual often played an active role in the transformation of raw materials into efficacious magical objects that possessed the ability to act on the world.[92] A ritual specialist may have been responsible for the acquisition of raw materials, their transformation in to things of value, and the initial (and perhaps final) use of a magical object.[93] Examining a carved amulet in a museum case, for example, allows us to suggest parts of its creation: the practitioner acquired a stone, perhaps roughly carved in the desired shape. He or she subsequently worked the stone, and the same individual, or perhaps a different specialist, performed a ritual that endowed the newly made object with its protective or other powers.[94] The representation that appears on the stone can suggest a model or prototype that was used in its creation, and indeed, the image may allow us to consider how magic was believed to have functioned. Other fea-

---

90. A. Gell, *Art and agency: An anthropological theory* (New York: Oxford University Press, 1998), 67; Miller, *Material culture and mass consumption,* 114–15; L. Meskell, *Object worlds in ancient Egypt: Material biographies past and present* (New York: Berg, 2004), 19; A. Gell, "The technology of enchantment and the enchantment of technology," in *Anthropology, art, and aesthetics,* ed. J. Coote and A. Shelton (New York: Oxford University Press, 1992).

91. Mauss, *A general theory of magic,* 102–3; Frazer, *The golden bough: A study in magic and religion,* 12; M. Taussig, *Mimesis and alterity: A particular history of the senses* (New York: Routledge, 1993), 55–56; W. MacGaffey, "Complexity, astonishment and power: The visual vocabulary of Kongo minkisi," *Journal of Southern African Studies* 14, no. 2 (1988): 192–96.

92. Walker and Lucero, "The depositional history of ritual and power," 130; Meskell, *Object worlds in ancient Egypt: Material biographies past and present,* 38; Gell, *Art and agency,* 18; Pels, Hetherington, and Vandenberghe, "The status of the object: Performances, mediations, and techniques," 8.

93. Dieleman, *Priests, tongues, and rites,* 174 and n. 78; Mitchell, "Performance," 392; J. P. Mitchell, "Towards an archaeology of performance," in *Cult in context: Reconsidering ritual in archaeology,* ed. D. A. Barrowclough and C. Malone (Oxford: Oxbow, 2007), 336.

94. A. D. Nock, "Magical notes," *JEA* 11, no. 3–4 (1925): 154–55.

38   Materia Magica

tures of the stone, such as an inscription, may imply the words that were spoken as part of a rite. Some elements of the creative process, however, will remain obscure or unknowable. In PGM III.410–23, for example, the practitioner is told to place silver lamella beneath a clean bowl, and then make bread in the bowl using barley meal. Only after shaping the bread into twelve rolls in female forms, eating these, and incanting a specific spell, can the practitioner inscribe the tablet.[95] It is unlikely that the investigator could reconstruct the act of making or eating bread, or even the fact that the uninscribed amulet was placed under a bowl. While some aspects of creation may not be recoverable, the consideration of beginnings prompts us to view ritual as a creative act, necessary for the generation of material culture that served a magical function.

As we consider the material remains of magic, it is also necessary to engage with the question of equifinality, that is, whether different processes could have resulted in the production of the same material artifact.[96] Any attempt to identify the archaeological remains of magical practice must struggle with the uncertainties related to the production and distribution of material culture. In each of the case studies addressed within this book, comparative data can provide some assurances about the readings of the material, as we attempt to position ritual events within local, regional, and Mediterranean-wide frameworks. As scholars, we can and must consider and address alternative possibilities for how artifacts may have been created and deposited.[97]

---

95. In Egypt, the process of endowing amulets with magical force sometimes relied on rites of "opening the mouth," a quintessentially Egyptian rite that brought divine force into statues and other inanimate objects. See Dieleman, *Priests, tongues, and rites,* 171–75; I. Moyer and J. Dieleman, "Miniaturization and the opening of the mouth in a Greek magical text (PGM XII.270–350)" *Journal of Ancient Near Eastern Religions* 3 (2003).

96. On the theoretical question of equifinality, see the discussions in J. G. Enloe, "Theory, method and the archaeological study of occupation surfaces and activities," in *Archaeological concepts for the study of the cultural past,* ed. A. P. Sullivan (Salt Lake City: University of Utah Press, 2008); J. M. Skibo, M. W. Graves, and M. T. Stark, eds., *Archaeological anthropology: Perspectives on method and theory* (Tucson: University of Arizona Press, 2007), 49–52; B. G. Trigger, *A history of archaeological thought,* 2nd ed. (Cambridge: Cambridge University Press, 2006), 440; J. G. Enloe, "Equifinality, assemblage integrity and behavioral inferences at Verberie," *Journal of Taphonomy* 2, no. 3 (2004); D. F. Dincauze, *Environmental archaeology: Principles and practice* (New York: Cambridge University Press, 2000), 31–35; A. R. Rogers, "On equifinality in faunal analysis," *American Antiquity* 65, no. 4 (2000): 721–22; M. Johnson, *Archaeological theory: An introduction* (Malden, MA: Blackwell, 1999), 100–108; O. de Montmollin, *The archaeology of political structure: Settlement analysis in a classic Maya polity* (New York: Cambridge University Press, 1989), 67.

97. Enloe, "Theory, method and the archaeological study of occupation surfaces and activities," 126; M. Deal, "Abandonment patterning at archaeological settlements," in *Archaeological concepts for the study of the cultural past,* ed. A. P. Sullivan (Salt Lake City: University of

Finding Magic in the Archaeological Record   39

Artifacts produced through magical rites subsequently may follow different paths. Some may be commoditized—exchanged, sold, bartered, or given as a gift. The historical sources document the sale and exchange of magical goods and services during all periods of Classical antiquity. Plato, for example, rails against mendicant priests who traffic in ritual purifications and curse tablets.[98] In the Late Antique period, charioteers are mentioned in legal texts as particularly likely to consort with magicians, presumably for the purpose of purchasing charms or curses.[99] The amulet provides a useful example of a magical object that was also a commercial good. Although created through a ritual, amulets could become important accessories for their owners, worn as jewelry or otherwise kept close to the body to provide protection. The amulet's meaning was derived from its possession, and the way in which the possessor employed the object.[100] Some traces of this usage of the piece even may be visible in its physical form, such as wear marks, or a suspension chain that allowed an amulet to be worn as a necklace or ring.

The terminus of an object's life history occurs when it is taken out of circulation. Artifacts can decay or deteriorate and be discarded, or they may be lost or forgotten. Some objects may be deposited in a hoard along with other similar pieces and stored away due to fears of economic or political upheaval.[101] Other artifacts may have had limited life spans as objects of exchange; ritual objects or offerings given to the gods, for example, do not move beyond the ceremony in which they were used or the sanctuary in which they were dedicated.[102] Magical artifacts offer a specialized form of consumption, as a ritual might require that an object be burned, shattered, buried, or otherwise disposed of in a specific way. Removing an object from the active world was often necessary for the item to have an effect—this displacement also pre-

---

Utah Press, 2008), 151; M. B. Schiffer, "Foreword," in *The Archaeology of settlement abandonment in Middle America,* ed. T. Inomata and R. W. Webb, *Foundations of archaeological inquiry* (Salt Lake City: University of Utah Press, 2003), xii.

98. Plato, *Rep.* 2.364b–c.

99. *Cod. Theod.* 9.16.11 (August 389). See discussion in Lee-Stecum, "Dangerous reputations: Charioteers and magic in fourth-century Rome," 227–28; Heintz, "Agonistic magic in the Late Antique circus," 15–16.

100. Appadurai, "Introduction: Commodities and the politics of value," 16; Gosden and Marshall, "The cultural biography of objects," 174; W. H. Walker, "Ritual technology in an extranatural world," in *Anthropological perspectives on technology,* ed. M. B. Schiffer, Amerind Foundation New World studies (Albuquerque: University of New Mexico Press, 2001), 92.

101. R. Bradley, *The passage of arms: An archaeological analysis of prehistoric hoards and votive deposits,* 2nd ed. (Oxford: Oxbow Books, 1998), 10–14.

102. Kopytoff, "The cultural biography of things: Commoditization as process," 75.

vented others from counteracting the spell and ensured that the outcome of the rite would be permanent or continual. Indeed, curses would have had little or no value if they remained in circulation, and it was only through burial or otherwise sequestering the item that it could have an effect. Understanding where and how an object's "life" was terminated can inform us about its social role and how human beings interact with the artifact.[103] It is at this last moment in an object's biography that archaeology is the most informative, as excavation uncovers artifacts that have been consumed.

Locating Ritual Events Through Archaeological Contexts

The close analysis of archaeological contexts can suggest the ways in which objects were employed in rituals. Contemporary excavation focuses on deposition, by which I mean the process by which an artifact enters the archaeological record and becomes a part of the past. Reading its deposition can tell us how an object was used and what happened to it at the end of its life cycle, when the object moved from active use (or reuse) and into the archaeological record. Like other excavated artifacts, magical artifacts may be discovered in place, that is, in the space in which the rite or part of the rite occurred; discarded because the object was no longer useful or was lost; or displaced, that is, moved from its appropriate ritual space through postdepositional processes.[104] Of these three possibilities, the discovery of objects in situ, that is, in the same space as the occurrence of the ritual, offers the greatest potential for interpretation and reconstruction, and will occupy the bulk of our discussion. As we will see, deposition was often a necessary component of the ritual process that completed or perfected a spell. Moreover, the discovery of potentially magical artifacts in telling locations, such as spaces associated with the underworld, the gods, or the victim of the spell, may be significant.

Deposition can be recovered and inferred through the use of archaeological context, a series of interlocking spatial and geographic loci.[105] The study of

---

103. D. Miller, "Consumption," in *Handbook of material culture,* ed. C. Tilley et al. (Thousand Oaks, CA: Sage, 2006), 341.

104. Walker and Lucero, "The depositional history of ritual and power," 135; M. B. Schiffer, *Formation processes of the archaeological record* (Albuquerque: University of New Mexico Press, 1987), 47–98; Peña, *Roman pottery in the archaeological record,* 272–318.

105. I. Hodder and S. Hutson, *Reading the past: Current approaches to interpretation in archaeology,* 3rd ed. (Cambridge: Cambridge University Press, 2003), 171–72.

Finding Magic in the Archaeological Record   41

context is valuable for the interpretation of both artifacts, the traditional focus of archaeological inquiry, and papyrological texts such as the PGM, which also derive from controlled or illicit excavations.[106] Context can include the physical findspot of the object, the architecture in which the artifact was unearthed, and other associated finds, in short, the totality of the immediate unit of discovery. An artifact's location is described and understood through physical features in the landscape, such as houses, pits, or buildings, and stratigraphy, the layers of soil that correspond to periods of occupation or activity. Similarly, archaeological context must be understood within ever-widening circles of spatial or temporal relationships: an individual excavation unit is part of a larger site and is uncovered relative to earlier and later deposits, while the site must be placed within its region and its historical circumstances.

Context can expand our understanding of the role that an artifact served in society by suggesting how an individual object was used and indicating the other artifacts with which a given object was deposited.[107] Moreover, the final space of deposition can potentially illuminate the practices that employed the object by looking back to how the object was created and perhaps exchanged.[108] An artifact may be discovered along with the tools that were used in its construction, or it may be clear that the raw materials employed in the creation of an object could have derived from a significant distance away. Object-specific inquiry can provide access to the rites that may have led to the creation of the artifact, while the analysis of archaeological context can illuminate rituals that may have been occurred during deposition, when the object was consumed. Furthermore, context can allow us to chart distinctions between objects that may be identical in form, by allowing us to determine the function of a specific artifact.[109]

Ancient literature and the magical papyri all stress the importance of deposition as a key feature of ritual—only by putting the magical artifact in a specific place, sometimes in conjunction with other materials, would the spell be effective. In certain cases, the instructions are detailed, laying out specif-

---

106. Gagos, Gates, and Wilburn, "Material culture and texts of Graeco-Roman Egypt: Creating context, debating meaning," 185.
107. J. Thomas, *Time, culture and identity: An interpretive archaeology* (London: Routledge, 1996), 159–64; C. Tilley, *An ethnography of the Neolithic: Early prehistoric societies in southern Scandinavia* (Cambridge: Cambridge University Press, 1996), 316–22; Peña, *Roman pottery in the archaeological record,* 18–20.
108. Walker and Lucero, "The depositional history of ritual and power," 130.
109. Walker, "Where are the witches of prehistory?" 247.

42   Materia Magica

ics regarding where the magical artifacts should be buried or placed. In PGM XXXVI.69–101, for example, the practitioner is instructed to inscribe a papyrus with a love spell and then glue it to the vaulted vapor room of a bath.[110] The grave of one recently dead appears frequently among the instructions, particularly with regard to the placement of curse tablets.[111] PDM lxi.112–127 instructs the practitioner to bury an image of Osiris made of wax along with the hair and wool of a donkey and the bone of a lizard beneath the doorsill of the desired woman.[112] Other spells provide fewer details, presumably because the practitioner could judge the precise location from the circumstances of the rite. In a spell to induce illness, the practitioner is told to bury an inscribed potsherd in the house, presumably the residence of the victim.[113] Using textual and archaeological evidence, we can identify specific locations that were significant for ritual activities related to aggressive or protective acts: mortuary spaces, areas associated with divinities, and locations pertinent to the goals of the rite. Often, these areas were liminal zones that stood between the places of the living and those of the dead or the divine, or between private and public. Such areas, which lack fixity because they are neither within nor without, positioned magical activity between worlds, permitting the practitioner to engage with supernatural forces.[114]

Graves and cemeteries were commonly used as spaces for deposition, as they were viewed as conduits to the underworld, or a means to contact and harness the power of the entombed individual. Mortuary spaces likely were important to magic for a variety of reasons. Physical contact between the dead and a curse tablet or figurine may have been connected with the idea of ritual pollution, so that miasma was conveyed from the deceased individual to the target of the spell.[115] The tomb also could house spirits that were deemed par-

---

110. Compare PGM II.51, where the practitioner is told to throw a figurine into the furnace of the bath.

111. I.e. PGM IV.296–466; PGM IV.2145–2240; PGM VII.396–404; PGM LVIII.1–14.

112. The spell uses what Faraone has termed erotic attraction magic, and the house door provides the physical location where the spell was enacted as well as the intended destination of the victim. Faraone, *Ancient Greek love magic,* 56.

113. PGM CXXIV.1–43.

114. A. van Gennep, *The rites of passage,* trans. M. B. Vizedom and G. L. Caffee (Chicago: University of Chicago Press, 1960), 15–25; V. Turner, "Betwixt and between: The liminal period in rites de passage," in *Symposium on new approaches to the study of religion: Proceedings of the 1964 annual spring meeting of the American Ethnological Society,* ed. J. Helm (Seattle: University of Washington Press, 1964); E. Turner, "Liminality," in *Encyclopedia of religion,* ed. L. Jones (Detroit: Macmillan Reference USA, 2005), 5460.

115. M. H. Jameson, D. R. Jordan, and R. Kotansky, *A 'lex sacra' from Selinous* (Durham, NC, 1993), 129; Parker, *Miasma: Pollution and purification in early Greek religion,* 198.

Finding Magic in the Archaeological Record   43

ticularly appropriate because they harbored anger against the living.[116] Those who had died before their time—individuals killed by violence, and young, unwed men and women—were considered restless, and were appropriate for ritual exploitation.[117] These dead, who may have desired revenge against those who had killed them, or were bitter because they could not partake of the joys of life, could be directed against a victim through spells.[118] Most often, graves were used as magical conduits only after the rituals of burial had been completed; the material from Empúries, however, suggests that extenuating circumstances may have led to the deposition of a tablet with the body. Wells and bodies of water were frequent depositories for curse tablets, as these locations were seen also as connected with the underworld and the dead.[119] Caches of tablets were deposited in wells in Athens, Caesarea, and (perhaps) Amathous, among other locations, suggesting that these spaces were used over a period of time for magical activity.[120]

Other areas were viewed as significant locations for enacting magic because of associations with the supernatural. In some ways, this use of religious spaces echoed dedications made to a divinity in order to convey a message or otherwise interact with the numinous.[121] Dedication at a shrine or in some other location that was consciously chosen removed the item from the world of human experience and transmitted it to the realm of the supernatural.[122] Such objects were intended as part of an exchange and communication between the dedicator and the divine, and were gifts given as thanks for or in the expectation of a good return.[123] Deposition of the object initiates and

---

116. Tertullian, *De anima,* 56–57.

117. Pl. *Phd.*81cd; Hippoc. 1.38 cf. S. I. Johnston, *Restless dead: Encounters between the living and the dead in ancient Greece* (Berkeley: University of California Press, 1999), esp. 71–80; Ogden, "Binding spells," 16; D. R. Jordan, "Two inscribed lead tablets from a well in the Athenian Kerameikos," *Mitteilungen des Deutschen Archäologischen Instituts, Athenische Abteilung* 95 (1980): 234. For the suggestion that early curse tablets only invoke the dead as a persuasive metaphor for the curse, see E. Eidinow, *Oracles, curses, and risk among the ancient Greeks* (Oxford: Oxford University Press, 2007), 148–50.

118. A. Bernand, *Sorciers grecs* (Paris: Fayard, 1991), 131–55; D. R. Jordan, "New archaeological evidence for the practice of magic in classical Athens," *Praktika tou XII Diethnous Synedriou Klasikes Archaiologias* IV (1988): 273–75.

119. Ogden suggests that this practice developed during the imperial period. "Binding spells," 13.

120. Athens: Jordan, "Defixiones from a well near the southwest corner of the Athenian Agora"; Caesarea: B. Burrell, "'Curse tablets' from Caesarea," *Near Eastern Archaeology* 61, no. 2 (1998). The tablets from Amathous are discussed in chapter 5.

121. R. Osborne, "Hoards, votives, offerings: The archaeology of the dedicated object," *World Archaeology* 36, no. 1 (2004): 1.

122. G. Bataille, *Theory of religion,* trans. R. Hurley (New York: Zone Books, 1989), 49.

123. Osborne, "Hoards, votives, offerings: The archaeology of the dedicated object," 2–3.

44   Materia Magica

perpetuates the relationship between human and supernatural actors. Binding tablets and figurines have been discovered along the exterior of temples, suggesting that practitioners deposited these items in order to secretly appropriate the power of the divinity. So, for example, four first-century BCE figurines from Delos, each carved from a piece of lead, were discovered within the outer retaining walls of the temple of Zeus Hypsistos.[124] Iron nails pierced the eyes, ears, and mouth of the male figurines, while collars bound the female figurines. The fountain of Anna Perenna in Rome, where the enshrined divinity was associated with a watery feature, recently has produced a stunning corpus of curses and small figurines made of organic materials, each of which was sealed in a lead tube.[125] Other locations that were associated with chthonic deities, such as the crossroads, which was significant to Hekate, might be chosen as suitable spaces for magic.[126] Plato suggests that Athenian practitioners placed wax figurines at the crossroads, and two separate spells from the magical papyri specify this location for ritual activity.[127] Magic might be enacted at a temple to a divinity, appropriating this religious space, or occur within other areas marked as significant because of an association with the supernatural.

Of equal importance were locations related to the goals of a magical performance. Proximity to the victim or placement in a location that was significant to the intention of the spell could also ensure its efficacy. In the passage

---

M. Mauss, *The gift: The form and reason for exchange in archaic societies* (London: Routledge, 1990), 41–44.

124. Musée du Délos inv. nos. 3787–3790. A. Plassart, *Les sanctuaires et les cultes du Mont Cynthe* (Paris: E. de Boccard, 1928), 292–93; *VD* no. 12.

125. Anna Perenna: M. Piranomonte, *Il santuario della musica e il bosco sacro di Anna Perenna* (Milan: Electa, 2002), 37; M. Piranomonte, "Religion and magic at Rome: The fountain of Anna Perenna," in *Magical practice in the Latin West: Papers from the international conference held at the University of Zaragoza, 30 Sept.–1 Oct. 2005*, ed. R. L. Gordon and F. Marco Simón (Leiden: Brill, 2010), esp. 204–31. The discovery of the tablets has produced a flurry of scholarly excitement: C. A. Faraone, "When spells worked magic," *Archaeology* 56, no. 2 (2003); M. Piranomonte, "La fontana sacra di Anna Perenna a Piazza Euclide tra religione e magia," *MHNH* 5 (2005); A. Mastrocinque, "Late Antique lamps with defixiones," *GRBS* 47 (2007); J. Blänsdorf, "The texts from the Fons Annae Perennae," in *Magical practice in the Latin West: Papers from the international conference held at the University of Zaragoza, 30 Sept.–1 Oct. 2005*, ed. R. L. Gordon and F. Marco Simón (Leiden: Brill, 2010); J. Blänsdorf, "Dal segno alla scrittura. Le defixiones della fontana di Anna Perenna," *SMSR* 76 (2010); C. A. Faraone, "A blinding curse from the fountain of Anna Perenna in Rome," *SMSR* 76 (2010); M. Piranomonte, "I contenitori di piombo dalla fontana di Anna Perenna e la loro valenza magica," *SMSR* 76 (2010). A further study is in preparation; M. Piranomonte, "The fountain of Anna Perenna in Rome, magical ritual connected to the water," in *Atti del Convegno "Rituelle Deponierung," Mainz, april 2008* (Forthcoming).

126. S. I. Johnston, "Crossroads," *ZPE* 88 (1991): 223.

127. Plato *Laws* 933b. PGM IV 2943–66; PGM LXX 4–25.

Finding Magic in the Archaeological Record   45

detailing the death of Germanicus, the nephew of Augustus, in 19 CE, Tacitus attributes his demise to an illness brought about by poisoning, an accusation that carried overtones of sorcery. Tacitus relates that

> there were discovered, unearthed from the ground and the walls, the remains of human bodies, spells and curses (*devotiones*), and the name "Germanicus" etched on lead tablets, half burned ashes smeared with putrid matter, and other malefic devices by which it is believed that souls are consecrated to the infernal divinities.[128]

The historian's description provides a fascinating list of items that may have been employed in aggressive magic—materials that were considered powerful because they were strange, associated with supernatural forces, or part of the typical tool kit of the ritual practitioner. In this account, the mere existence of magical items was not sufficient to cause harm to Germanicus. Rather, the placement of objects beneath the floors and in the walls of his living space is fundamental to the rite's efficacy. This belief can be paralleled in other authors. Pliny suggests that close physical proximity can ensure that magic will have an effect on its intended victim: "So too, as Orpheus and Archelaus write, arrows drawn out of a body and not allowed to touch the ground act as a love-charm upon those under whom when in bed they have been placed."[129] The spells of the magical papyri instruct the practitioner to place artifacts in locations that are frequented by the target; five related spells in PGM XII/PDM xii require the practitioner to inscribe a curse on a potsherd or papyrus and bury the item in a space that the victims visit or pass.[130] Curses that targeted the charioteers of the circus, too, were placed at the racetrack. Tablets have been discovered in the spina, at the starting gates, and at particularly difficult turns, where the tablet might cause the victim to lose control of his chariot.[131]

---

128. Tacitus *Ann.* 2.69, "The Annals," trans. A. Woodman (Indianapolis: Hackett, 2004), 75. See the similar descriptions provided in Suet. *Calig.* 1–3; Dio 57.18.9; Josephus *AJ* 18.54. For discussion, see Rives, "Magic, religion and law: The case of the *Lex Cornelia de sicariis et veneficiis*," 55–58; on magic in Tacitus, see M. W. Dickie, "Magic in the Roman historians," in *Magical practice in the Latin West: Papers from the international conference held at the University of Zaragoza, 30 Sept.–1 Oct. 2005*, ed. R. L. Gordon and F. Marco Simón (Leiden: Brill, 2010).

129. Pliny, *HN* XXVIII.34. Trans. W. H. S. Jones in the Loeb Classical Library (Cambridge: Harvard University Press, 2000), 27.

130. PGM XII.365–75; PDM xii.50–61; 62–75; 76–107; 108–18. See discussion in Dieleman, *Priests, tongues, and rites,* 136–38.

131. Heintz, "Circus curses and their archaeological contexts," 339–40. Carthage, arena floor and

46   Materia Magica

Later Christian sources attest to the continued importance of nearness to the victim: in Jerome's *Life of Saint Hilarion the Hermit,* a virgin is driven mad by a love spell placed underneath the threshold of her door by an amorous pagan suitor.[132] Although close proximity of the target was desired, the practitioner would not have needed direct access to the bedroom or even the interior of the house, as the liminal space where the home meets the outside world would have been sufficient. Because it was positioned in-between, the object could affect both inside and outside. The magical potential of an object may have been activated when the target was in the vicinity of the enchanted item; when the abbot Shenoute was due to arrive in the village of Pleuit, local residents buried magical potions along the road to the town, presumably in an effort to prevent him from entering.[133]

Practitioners were aware of the importance of spatial location and physical deposition, and a number of magical artifacts illustrate and comment upon this fact. A tablet that likely derives from a tomb at Megara in Greece invokes the occupant, and reads, "But just as you, O Pasianax, lie here idle, so let Neophanes be idle and do nothing."[134] Rites such as this one made use of depositional context in two ways. The grave or other underground location served as a conduit to the netherworld, and permitted the practitioner to directly communicate with the spirits of dead and with gods and spirits who inhabited infernal regions. This spell also invokes the resident of the grave directly, calling on the corpse as an accomplice in the ritual. Pasianax must aid the magician and serve as an example that Neophanes should follow.

Further support to our argument that placement is important to efficacy is provided by references to negating spells that are found in literature and in the magical papyri, where the removal of the ritual object would negate the curse

---

starting gates: Jordan, "New defixiones from Carthage"; L. Pintozzi and N. Norman, "The lead curse tablets from the Carthage circus," *ArchN* 17 (1992); Lepcis Magna, starting gates: J. Rea, "Aspects of the circus at Leptis Magna, appendix: The lead curse tablet," *Libya Antiqua* 9–10 (1972–73); Antioch, in the drains near the turning posts: *SGD* no. 167; W. A. Campbell, "The third season of excavation at Antioch-on-the-Orontes," *AJA* 40, no. 1 (1936): 2; J. H. Humphrey, *Roman circuses: Arenas for chariot racing* (London: B. T. Batsford, 1986), 455. Corinth, *meta* of the hippodrome: *SGD* no. 166; J. Wiseman, "Excavations in Corinth, the gymnasium area, 1967–1968," *Hesperia* 38, no. 1 (1969): 70; D. G. Romano, "A Roman circus in Corinth," *Hesperia* 74, no. 4 (2005): 594.

132. *PL* vol. 23, col. 38.

133. Besa, *Vita Shenoute* 83–84; D. Frankfurter, "Ritual expertise in Roman Egypt and the problem of the category 'magician,'" in *Envisioning magic: A Princeton seminar and symposium,* ed. P. Schäfer and H. G. Kippenberg (Leiden: Brill, 1997), 125–26.

134. *DT* no. 43–44 = *CT* no. 43; trans. *CT*, p. 131.

and free the victim. In one of his orations, the fourth-century orator Libanius reports that at the age of seventy, he was struck by fierce headaches that prevented him from lecturing, reading, writing, or performing any necessary tasks.[135] Doctors were unable to aid him, and, by means of a dream, he deduced that he was the victim of witchcraft. Soon after, Libanius found a chameleon in his lecture room, one that had been twisted and mutilated; with its removal, his symptoms abated. A similar case is attested at the site of Tuder, where an inscription gives thanks to Jupiter Optimus Maximus for uncovering curses that had been directed at local *decuriones*. Presumably, the elimination of the tablets permitted the curses to be lifted.[136] Within the spell instructions, too, removing the artifact could negate the magical act, suggesting that the same remedy was acknowledged in Graeco-Roman Egypt. In PGM IV 2943–66, after making a little dog out of clay, the practitioner is told to "deposit it at a crossroad after you have marked the spot, so that if you wish to recover it, you can find it."[137] Presumably, the practitioner would only take away the dog if he wished to counteract the spell. An artifact might be left in place for a number of reasons: the practitioner wished the object to continue its work; he or she forgot about or could not access the artifact; or, the practitioner deemed the object worthless because the magical act was unsuccessful.

In these literary, subliterary, and epigraphic accounts, significant attention has been paid to deposition, which was an integral component of the rite. Acts of magic are not realized fully until the materials created or transformed through the rite have been appropriately deposited, and it is often through deposition that the magical artifact is activated. Because archaeology encounters artifacts at the point of deposition, the discipline is in the unique position to examine how an object was removed from circulation and employed at this last stage of the ritual process.

Finding artifacts in such significant locations—graves, spaces with religious importance, or domestic structures—may indicate that a particular area was used for a ritual, but this information must be considered in conjunction with the analysis of specific artifacts, their associated finds, and the method by

---

135. Libanius, *Or.* I, 9–10. Cf. C. Bonner, "Witchcraft in the lecture room of Libanius," *TAPA* 63 (1932).

136. CIL 11.2.4639; G. Luck, *Arcana mundi: Magic and the occult in the Greek and Roman worlds: A collection of ancient texts* (Baltimore: Johns Hopkins University Press, 1985), 90–91; *CT* no. 135; Ogden, "Binding spells," 69–70.

137. Trans. E. N. O'Neil in *GMP,* 94.

48   Materia Magica

which the artifacts were deposited.[138] The rite may have resulted in the consumption of material culture in this space, as this would have taken the objects out of circulation and removed them from the realm of human interactions. Indeed, the space where a magical object is discovered may preserve traces of the entire life cycle of a magical artifact, particularly if the item were created or manipulated in the same geographic and temporal space as part of the ritual. So, for example, in the love spell cited above, the practitioner is told to make two figurines out of wax or clay, an Ares and a bound woman. The entirety of the rite may have taken place at graveside, where the practitioner would have tied the figurines with thread, and placed (or buried?) the artifacts by the tomb of an untimely dead individual. We must be cognizant, however, of the potential for a circular argument, in which we assume an object is magical because it is found within a significant space. It is necessary to closely examine the finds and the entirety of the archaeological context, and to analyze the material with reference to other comparable examples or textual accounts.

Discovery of a magical object within a mortuary space also may be tied to rituals related to the burial of the dead, and the artifact may have been intended to protect or otherwise serve the deceased individual. In societies where formal burial was practiced, artifacts were placed within the grave as a deliberate choice on the part of those who undertook the funerary rites, and expressed the expenditure made by members of society.[139] Amulets offer an informative illustration of the variety of reasons for which the living might deposit an artifact with the dead. A protective amulet may have been owned by the deceased, and buried with him or her because this was an important personal possession. Amulets might show wear, or were perhaps placed in a setting for use as personal adornment. Alternatively, an artifact such as an amulet could have been

---

138. Walker, "Where are the witches of prehistory?" 256.
139. Schiffer, *Formation processes of the archaeological record,* 85–89; J. E. Richards, *Society and death in ancient Egypt: Mortuary landscapes of the Middle Kingdom* (Cambridge: Cambridge University Press, 2005), 55–56; on social stratification, see L. R. Binford, "Mortuary practices: Their study and potential," in *Approaches to the social dimensions of mortuary practices,* ed. J. A. Brown (Washington, DC: Society for American Archaeology, 1971); J. Brown, "Charnel houses and mortuary crypts: Disposal of the dead in the Middle Woodland period," in *Hopewell archaeology: The Chillicothe conference,* ed. D. S. Brose and N. Greber (Kent, OH: Kent State University Press, 1979); J. M. O'Shea, *Mortuary variability: An archaeological investigation* (Orlando: Academic Press, 1984); K. M. Trinkhaus, "Mortuary behavior, labor organization, and social rank," in *Regional approaches to mortuary analysis,* ed. L. A. Beck (New York: Plenum Press, 1995); but compare the critiques and relevant bibliography at Richards, *Society and death in ancient Egypt,* 57–58.

Finding Magic in the Archaeological Record 49

specifically manufactured for use in burial in order to protect the dead on their journey to the underworld.[140] Because funerary rituals are often undertaken publicly, and can entail conspicuous consumption of resources, appropriately contextualizing magical artifacts as intentional grave gifts may help us to understand of the role of magic within a local community.

Finally, a magical artifact may be discovered in a space that is not related to its use as a power object; it may have been discarded or lost, or its findspot may have been compromised through events that occurred after it was ritually deposited. When objects or structures were past their period of usefulness, human actors either threw these items out or abandoned them.[141] For example, an inscription to ward off fever may have had a limited window of usefulness; once the danger of illness had passed, the owner may have tossed it onto a nearby trash heap. As buildings or other structures were damaged through natural or human causes, residents may have completed the destruction, filled in soil to raise the ground level, and rebuilt. Magical artifacts, like other household materials, may have been included within this sequence of abandonment and reoccupation.[142] Similarly, objects could be lost.[143] Coins provide a commonplace example, as individuals in antiquity, as now, seemed to have constantly dropped small—and large—denominations, sometimes in opportune locations, such as foundation trenches. Amulets or other small magical items could have met their ends in a similar manner. Artifacts could also be hidden away for safekeeping and their locations subsequently forgotten, or the

---

140. Peña refers to this latter usage as *depositional use. Roman pottery in the archaeological record,* 10. See further R. Gilchrist, "Magic for the dead? The archaeology of magic in later medieval burials," *Medieval Archaeology* 52 (2008): esp. 123–35, 147–53; on Egyptian amulets and the dead, see S. Ikram and A. Dodson, *The mummy in ancient Egypt: Equipping the dead for eternity* (New York: Thames & Hudson, 1998), 137–46; Y. Koenig, *Magie et magiciens dans l'Egypte ancienne* (Paris: Pygmalion/Gérard Watelet, 1994), 245–50; G. Pinch, *Magic in ancient Egypt* (Austin: University of Texas Press, 1995), 104–19.

141. M. B. Schiffer, *Behavioral archaeology* (New York: Academic Press, 1976), 30–34. Items abandoned in the area in which they were used are referred to as "primary refuse." Conversely, items that are taken to a new location and discarded are "secondary refuse." See Schiffer, *Formation processes of the archaeological record,* 58–64; M. Deal, "Household pottery disposal in the Maya highlands: An ethnoarchaeological interpretation," *Journal of Anthropological Archaeology* 4 (1985).

142. On the abandonment of sites, see A. Joyce and S. Johannessen, "Abandonment and the production of archaeological variability at domestic sites," in *Abandonment of settlements and regions: Ethnoarchaeological and archaeological approaches,* ed. C. M. Cameron and S. A. Tomka (Cambridge: Cambridge University Press, 1993).

143. M. B. Schiffer, *Behavioral archaeology: First principles* (Salt Lake City: University of Utah Press, 1995), 29–30; Peña, *Roman pottery in the archaeological record,* 13.

individual may have been unable to retrieve a sequestered object for another reason, such as death.[144] When the analysis of archaeological context indicates that an object was lost or discarded, the materials discovered with the artifact can tell us little of the process of doing magic. Rather, the artifact itself must serve as the starting point of our investigation, pointing back to its creation or its use.

A variety of natural and human activities may have altered the final resting place of a magical object, and decay may have eliminated the traces of other associated materials. Pits dug into the soil, or robbed-out walls, may have disturbed a ritual location. These postdepositional processes have the potential to radically alter or skew what the material record looks like, shifting materials from their original resting places to new stratigraphic homes, mixing up levels, and making a muddle of the archaeological record.[145] With time and patience, the archaeological record can (sometimes) be un-muddled. Moreover, organic materials may decay over time—spells inscribed on wood, hide, papyrus, or wax will not survive, except in climatic extremes, such as bogs, deserts, or wells.[146] These caveats suggest some of the limits of our evidence, and indeed, archaeological data are often fragmentary, incomplete, and subject to multiple interpretations.

Magical activity in the Roman period was a process that entailed many elements, from a spoken incantation to the manipulation of raw materials and the creation of something that was believed to have the potential to act in the world. Although greater attention has been paid to the words written on curse tablets, the act of ritually binding another person involved the creation of the artifact, inscribing the text upon it, perhaps performing other rites involving additional materials, and finally depositing the object in a significant space. In this chapter, we have suggested a method by which the process of creation and deposition can be understood within the archaeological record. While the question of which objects are magical will be taken up in the next chapter, textual sources such as the PGM can indicate the kinds of materials that were utilized in rites. Once an object has been recognized as a potential component of magic, the scholar must first consider the artifact's life history, beginning with its generation, continuing through its use and exchange as a commodity,

---

144. Bradley, *The passage of arms: An archaeological analysis of prehistoric hoards and votive deposits,* 11–29; Schiffer, *Formation processes of the archaeological record,* 78–80.
145. Schiffer, *Formation processes of the archaeological record,* 121–40.
146. Ibid., 143–98.

and ending at its final consumption. Facets of this process may be suggested through the analysis of the item, although we must recognize that not all stages of an object's production and use can be recovered. As a snapshot of the final phase of magic—the burial or consumption of a power object—the artifact and its depositional context look back to each previous step and ask us to consider how the ritual occurred. The space of deposition often was significant for the purpose of the rite, and other finds that can be associated with the magical object may hint at additional components of a ritual enactment. Artifacts and contexts also permit us to look further than the single artifact, outward to the community and individuals that were engaged in magic as practitioners, consumers, and victims.

Mediterranean Magic and Local Magic

This study takes as its premise that the idea of magic was loosely constructed across the Mediterranean basin. Within individual villages and towns, a shared conceptualization of magic existed—practitioners and their audiences each understood that magic utilized a range of signs and symbols. The distribution of curse tablets and magical gems suggest the existence of a shared vocabulary or *koine* of magical practice; similar stock phrases, names of divinities, and symbols appear throughout the Mediterranean. In part, this may be due to the increased presence and proliferation of professional practitioners, a development that some scholars have placed around the second century CE.[147] At the village or even regional level, magic depended on the local ritual specialist, who practiced his craft in the service of neighborhood problems.[148] Literature played a role in creating the idea of magic by reinforcing and formalizing many of the global signifiers, and textual representations of magicians,

---

147. Jordan, "Inscribed lead tablets from the games in the sanctuary of Poseidon," 123–25; D. R. Jordan, "Notes from Carthage," *ZPE* 111 (1996): 119; Faraone, *Ancient Greek love magic,* 32–33; Jordan, "Magia nilotica sulle rive del Tevere," 698; R. A. Gordon, "Competence and 'felicity conditions' in two sets of North African curse-tablets (*DT* nos. 275–85; 286–98)," *MHNH* 5 (2005): 62–65.

148. W. Burkert, "Itinerant diviners and magicians: A neglected element in cultural contacts," in *The Greek Renaissance of the eighth century B.C.: Tradition and innovation: Proceedings of the second international symposium at the Swedish Institute in Athens, 1–5 June 1981,* ed. R. Hägg (Stockholm: Svenska institutet i Athen; Distributor P. Åströms förlag, 1983),118–19; D. Frankfurter, "The consequences of Hellenism in Late Antique Egypt," *Archiv für Religionsgeschichte* 2, no. 2 (2000): 173; Dieleman, *Priests, tongues, and rites,* 71.

sorcerers, and witches affected how practitioners presented themselves on a local level, as they adopted and internalized the culturally recognized markers of magical practice.[149] Ancient magic was not a centralized endeavor, with authoritative texts that were widely distributed, but, as Gideon Bohak notes, the process of exchange, transmission, and "naturalization" was uneven. The appearance of similar elements in different traditions and at variant locations may have resulted from multiple means, including independent development as well as the direct appropriation of ritual technology. In the case of the latter, the direction of exchange may not be immediately evident. Furthermore, borrowed practices underwent varying degrees of integration within their new environment; some foreign rites might be classified as anomalous insertions, while others were provided with false genealogies, belying the belief that they were originally part of the host culture.[150] In Egyptian magical texts, there is evidence that Demotic words were transliterated into Greek characters and subsequently reappropriated by Demotic scribes as *voces magicae*.[151] As Bohak cautions, however, it is necessary to investigate the local meanings of these foreign imports, as the reception of a symbol, artifact, or even an entire rite is determined by those who appropriated the ritual element, and symbols, words, and representations may acquire new significance within their adoptive homes.[152]

Magical practice at the local level can be constructed from individual archaeological sites. Field archaeology, as a discipline, is concentrated on the small scale—the site or, in the case of survey archaeology, the region—and its focal range is limited by the landscape and its ancient occupation. Artifacts discovered in a particular geographic space are tied to that place; residents imported, produced, or discarded the material culture that is found on a site, and the archaeological findspot—its context—can tell us about how the object was used and by whom. Through artifacts, domestic assemblages, and household refuse, the close study of archaeological remains has the potential to illuminate the lives of those residents within the ancient world who employed magic, and to examine the problems they faced, their responses, and how they viewed their place within the cosmos with relation to nature and the divine.

---

149. Frankfurter, *Religion in Roman Egypt,* 225–33.
150. Bohak, *Ancient Jewish magic,* 229–30. Compare Harrison, "The commerce of cultures in Melanesia."
151. Dieleman, *Priests, tongues, and rites,* 72–76.
152. Bohak, *Ancient Jewish magic,* 230.

Finding Magic in the Archaeological Record   53

The vagaries of preservation and the difficulties inherent in interpretation constantly impact the conclusions that can be drawn from the material remains. Therefore, an awareness of the evidential constraints is necessary, particularly for understanding archaeological material that was discovered in the latter part of the nineteenth and early twentieth centuries. Despite these potential problems, the development of an approach to the material remains of magic, such as that outlined above, can suggest the myriad ways in which contemporary excavations can better assess the presence of this and other obscure cultural practices.

Chapter 2

Materia Magica

In 1933, with excavation moving along at a swift pace, the University of Michigan team began digging under a house in the top layer of occupation. There was little that was notable about the house, which the excavators designated as number 165, and, in later reports, it is not singled out for any special treatment. Nor was it architecturally remarkable: its contents did not contain material more striking than typical domestic debris, the sorts of things that might be found among the other hundreds of houses cleared at the site. As excavation continued, the workmen came upon a variety of materials beneath the floor of the structure, in what must have been a basement area that was used for storage: an assortment of papyri and ostraca, a small unbaked mud figurine, a piece of lead wrapped around a cord, beads, a cloth bag, and a few bone pins, among other materials. Most of this material did not appear to be out of the ordinary, and the marginalia in the massive Record of Objects for 1933 only make a few brief notes: certain objects were found low in the fill, others were found in the same general vicinity. Reanalysis of this material, however, leads us to a different conclusion altogether—parts of this deposit, most notably the small figurine and the bone pins, are the remains of a ritual act, perhaps undertaken to compel the erotic affection of an resident of the house.

On the other side of the Mediterranean, approximately twenty years later, excavation in the necropoleis at the site of Empúries, which had been a prosperous trading center in antiquity, was similarly moving along at a productive rate. Graves were being excavated in the Ballesta cemetery, and work, at least among some of the excavators, was concentrating on a moderate-sized stone enclosure that likely distinguished an intentional group of graves. Eight separate cremations had been buried in the enclosure, and many of these were fairly rich, with ceramic and glass unguentaria and other small grave goods. Placed against one corner of the rectangular wall was a group of three coarseware jugs that had been used as the receptacles for the human remains. These were simple vessels, but they contained surprising finds in addition to the ashes— three lead sheets that had been inscribed with curses targeting some of the senior administrators of the province. In contrast to the finds at Karanis, these pieces were immediately identified as magical and soon were published; great interest in the scholarly community followed.

All of these artifacts were uncovered in controlled excavations and provide data that will allow us to investigate the materials within their cultural contexts. A larger question is raised when we ask why these items can be identified as components of magical practice. As was discussed in the last chapter, American archaeologists were able to identify the remains of conjure by contextualizing finds from domestic spaces and reading the associated artifacts against folklore accounts of ritual practices. For Greek and Roman antiquity, we can locate magic in the archaeological record by evaluating potentially magical artifacts with reference to their archaeological contexts and associated finds. The ancient sources can provide guidance by suggesting the different classes of materials that might be used in ritual activity. We can arrive at such a list by consulting two groups of documents: "outsider" evidence, including literature, inscriptions, and historical documents written about magic, and "insider" evidence, the spell manuals and other primary sources employed by practitioners in the service of their craft.[1] These sources suggest that magic employed (1) inscribed objects that convey a spell or use language; (2) images or figurines that utilize mimesis and representation to achieve the desired effect; (3) natural ingredients, including plants and animals sacrificed or harvested for component parts, as well as *ousia,* the cast-off or collected body parts of the victim; and (4) household objects that have been repurposed for magical use. As was discussed in the preceding chapter, such materials may suggest magical activity, but ritual performance was required to transform these items into power objects that could have an effect on the world.

Outsider evidence was written by poets, historians, and philosophers, and often reflects a common consensus as to what sorts of materials might be employed in magic. The geographic and temporal environment in which the document was written determines the picture of the materials of magic that is presented in each work. Literary and historical authors were not active par-

---

1. On this distinction see Bohak, *Ancient Jewish magic,* 70; insider evidence may also be called *primary documentation,* and outsider, *secondary.*

56   Materia Magica

ticipants in magical rites but, rather, described the actions and events that they perceived as magical. For example, in the *Apology,* the author, Apuleius, is accused of *magica maleficia* (Apol. 1.3), magical crimes. The charges brought against the defendant may have been stock accusations, similar to those used against countless others in sham trials that often disguised political persecution.[2] In order to convict the defendant, the specific practices charged by the prosecution must have been credible as a list of magical acts that an individual could perform. Therefore, the objects that Apuleius is accused of possessing or employing in magic were believable components of the practitioner's tool kit. According to the prosecution, Apuleius (1) sought out a particular kind of fish that would have been used in an erotic magical rite to bewitch Pudentilla, a woman ten years his senior, (2) caused a young boy to fall down using incantations, (3) kept a secret object among the household goods of his friend Potianus, (4) performed nocturnal sacrifices that included the sacrifice of birds, and (5) possessed a suspicious wooden figurine that he worshipped.[3] Leaving aside the question of guilt or Apuleius' knowledge of magic, the alleged rituals incorporate commonplace as well as strange and wondrous ingredients for purposes ranging from divination to erotic attraction: an unusual fish, birds, incantations, an unknown object, and a statuette. Apuleius tells us almost nothing about how these objects would have been used, and it is unclear whether the artifacts had inherent magical force or if the prosecution suggested that he manipulated them in some fashion.

Other authors provide meaningful glimpses into the materials that are associated with magic. In his *Laws,* Plato famously singles out certain practices of magic for condemnation, including sorceries (*manganeiai*), incantations (*epaoidai*), and bindings (*katadeseis*); the latter term has been interpreted as referring to curse tablets. In the same passage, Plato also stresses that "it is not worthwhile for us to try to tell the souls of men who mistrust each other, if ever they see molded wax figurines at doors or at crossroads, or sometimes

---

2. Gordon, "Imagining Greek and Roman magic," 263; Rives, "Magic in Roman law: The reconstruction of a crime," 322–28; H. G. Kippenberg, "Magic in Roman civil discourse: Why rituals should be illegal," in *Envisioning magic: A Princeton seminar and symposium,* ed. P. Schäfer and H. G. Kippenberg, *Studies in the history of religions* (Leiden: Brill, 1997), 140.

3. On the charges, see, among others, A. Abt, *Die Apologie des Apuleius von Madaura und die antike Zauberei* (Gießen: A. Töpelmann, 1908); F. Nordén, *Apulejus von Madaura und das römische privatrecht* (Leipzig: B. G. Teubner, 1912); B. L. Hijmans, "Apuleius Orator: 'Pro se de Magia' and 'Florida,'" *ANRW* II 34, no. 2 (1994), and V. Hunink, *Apuleius of Madauros: Pro se de magia (Apologia),* 2 vols. (Amsterdam: Gieben, 1997).

Materia Magica   57

on the tombs of their ancestors, to ignore all such things."[4] For Plato, the presence of small figurines, presumably shaped like human beings, provide clear evidence that magic has been enacted when they are discovered in specific locations. Molded representations also appear as implements of magical practice in a variety of authors; in Horace's *Satires* I.8, for example, the witches Canidia and Sagana manipulate two figurines, one made of wool and the other of wax. At the close of the rite, the two witches bury naturally occurring but weird materials, in this case, a wolf's beard and a snake's tooth in the ground. Theocritus's famed depiction of Simaetha (*Idyll* 2) similarly provides a litany of materials that might be employed in a magical rite. In the opening lines, she asks her companion, Thestylis, to bring her bay leaves, love potions, a bowl, and crimson sheep's wool; later in the poem she melts a wax doll, whirls around an unusual tool (a *rhombos*), employs strange substances, such as *hippomanes,* burns a fragment of her lover's cloak, and concocts a drink using a powdered lizard.[5] This list of ingredients demonstrates the variability and versatility present in magical performance, which often combined the mundane with the unusual. Indeed, as discussed in the previous chapter, Malinowski's emphasis on "weirdness" provides an apt characterization for the picture of magic that can be drawn from the literary sources.

A comparable roster of *materia magica* appears within the documents that were written by "insiders." Insider evidence was composed or recorded by those who were actively engaged in ritual practices that we can identify as magic. These sources—such as spell manuals composed on papyri or inscriptions that record public rites—are also archaeological artifacts, with precise findspots and contextual histories. In contrast to literary documents that may have been widely circulated and read again and again after publication, archaeological evidence tells us about rituals that were undertaken in a specific time and place. For example, we can find a description of magical materials within a fourth-century BCE inscription from Cyrene that details instructions for dealing with troublesome "visitors" or ghosts.[6] The document collates ritual proce-

---

4.   Plato *Leg.* 933 a–b.
5.   On the magical practices in Idyll 2, see Gow's commentary, *Theocritus,* 35–36; C. A. Faraone, "The 'performative future' in three Hellenistic incantations and Theocritus' second Idyll," *CPh* 90, no. 1 (1995); Graf, *Magic in the ancient world,* 176–84.
6.   SEG 9.72.111–121. For translation and commentary, see Parker, *Miasma: Pollution and purification in early Greek religion,* 347. On the term *hikesios,* see C. A. Faraone, "Talismans and Trojan horses: Guardian statues in ancient Greek myth and ritual" (Oxford University Press, 1992), 91, n. 60.

dures, presumably from archaic sources, and includes instructions for dealing with unwelcome spirits. The inscription relates that:

> if [in either case?] he does not know his name [he shall address him]: "O human being (*anthropos*) whether you are a man or woman," and having made male and female figurines (*kolossoi*) either from wood or earth he shall entertain them and set beside them a portion of everything. When you have done the customary things, take the figurines (*kolossoi*) and [their] portions and deposit them in an unworked glen.[7]

The significance of these figurines will be discussed at length below, but it is important to note the components of magic that the document articulates: the practitioner must make multiple representations from wood or clay, and then provide these figurines with food and drink. Public documents like this inscription are admittedly brief and pointed—they may only address a single issue, or record a specific response undertaken by a community. A much richer and detailed corpus of insider evidence can be found in the manuals of magic that we possess from antiquity, but these, too, possess their own evidential problems.

The dry, desert conditions of Egypt have preserved more than one hundred papyrus rolls, codices, and fragments that reference magical spells, some of which possess a known or surmised archaeological context. These papyri, written in Greek, Demotic, Coptic, Aramaic, Hebrew, and Arabic, among other languages, range in date from the second or first centuries BCE down into the Arabic period and offer tantalizing clues to the nature of magical practice in the Imperial and Late Antique periods. The Cairo Genizah, for example, a massive collection of documents written in Hebrew, Aramaic, and Judeo-Arabic, was discovered in the storeroom of the Ben Ezra synagogue in Old Cairo. Only certain of the texts from the Genizah are related to magic, and a smaller number of these might be appropriate for the period under study in this volume. Among the documents from the Genizah were fragments of the Sepher ha-Razim, or "Book of the Mysteries," a volume that has been painstakingly reconstructed by Mordecai Margalioth from these sources, as well as later frag-

---

7.   Translation adapted from Faraone, "Talismans and Trojan horses: Guardian statues in ancient Greek myth and ritual," 82. On other instances of public rites of magic, see ibid., 36–93, but see also 114–17 on the role of secrecy.

ments in Hebrew, Arabic, and even Latin.[8] The Sepher ha-Razim provides a mystical map of the heavens, detailing the angels that are resident in each zone and the means by which these forces may be manipulated. This and other Hebrew and Aramaic texts were written for and used by Jewish practitioners, and while there is some overlap between these traditions and those of Graeco-Roman Egypt, most of the spells reflect a specifically Jewish cultural context.[9]

Of greater relevance for the current study are the papyrus documents written in Greek and Demotic, nearly all of which date from the fourth or fifth centuries CE. Although the majority of the spells in the magical papyri were written in Greek, the presence of spells in the Egyptian languages, including Demotic, Hieratic, Old Coptic, and ciphers of the Egyptian language, which were seldom used outside of the religious sphere in the fourth century CE, strongly suggests that the longer rolls of the magical papyri, such as those discovered at Thebes, were compiled by members of the Egyptian priesthood.[10] Scholarship has held that spell manuals were produced in the context of the temple scriptoria. A number of Egyptian temples included small rooms that have been identified as libraries because of the presence of lists of books preserved on the walls of some of these chambers.[11] Either under the direction and control of the temple, or acting as private operators, priests in the Roman periods who were conversant in Greek as well as Demotic and the priestly languages, were in the unique position to compile and edit collections of spells.[12]

---

8. M. Margalioth, *Sefer ha-Razim: A newly recovered book of magic from the Talmudic period* (Tel Aviv: Yediot Acharonot, 1966).

9. On the connections between "insider" Jewish documents and Greek and Roman magic, see Bohak, *Ancient Jewish magic,* 143–226, esp. 169–75, 201–9, 215–21.

10. On the production of formularies in antiquity, see bibliography listed above, Introduction n. 4 and ch.1, n. 147. On the structure of individual rolls, see L. R. LiDonnici, "Compositional patterns in *PGM* IV (=*P.Bibl.Nat.Suppl.* gr. no. 574)," *BASP* 40 (2003); Dieleman, *Priests, tongues, and rites,* 26–45.

11. Ritner, *The mechanics of ancient Egyptian magical practice,* 206 and n. 952. Ritner, "Egyptian magical practice under the Roman empire," 3345–46, 54; A. H. Gardiner, "The House of Life," *Journal of Egyptian Archaeology* 24, no. 2 (1938). For the evidence from the temple at Edfu, see É. Chassinat and M. d. Rochemonteix, *Le temple d'Edfou,* vol. 3 (Paris: Leroux, 1928), 351; B. Porter and R. L. B. Moss, *Topographical bibliography of ancient Egyptian hieroglyphic texts, reliefs, and paintings* (Oxford: Clarendon Press, 1927), 135.

12. Frankfurter, *Religion in Roman Egypt,* 250. While we can say with certainty that priests were responsible for the production of the formularies, whether these texts were being produced under the aegis of the temple is less clear (T. Wilfong, personal communication). Many of the magical texts related to the needs of private individuals were not discovered in temples. The Roman period temple library at Tebtynis has yielded few magical texts, and of these, none are concerned with aggressive spells or with the sorts of privately oriented magical rites that appear most frequently in the PGM spells. K. Ryholt, "On the contents and nature

60   Materia Magica

It follows that priests were responsible for the compilation of the Greek and
Demotic magical papyri as a by-product of priestly interest in preserving the
king and cosmos and ministering to the needs of the local population. Ritual
expertise was necessary for various activities, such as cursing the enemies of
the state through the manipulation of figurines and dolls, in the former, and, in
the case of the latter, healing and the creation of amulets.[13] The large library
from Thebes, consisting of both Demotic and Greek rolls, was produced and
copied by priests, who were also the intended audience of these texts. While
some of the papyri, such as P.London-Leiden and P.Leiden I 384 appear to be
the products of a single workshop, other spell manuals from Thebes show evi-

---

of the Tebtunis Temple Library: A status report," in *Tebtynis und Soknopaiu Nesos: Leben im
römerzeitlichen Fajum,* ed. S. Lippert and M. Schentuleit (Wiesbaden: Harrassowitz, 2005),
151. On the nature of the Tebtynis Temple Library, with a discussion of its archaeological
context, see ibid., 157–62. For the view that this cache does not derive from a temple, see W.
J. Tait, "Demotic literature and Egyptian society," in *Life in a multi-cultural society: Egypt
from Cambyses to Constantine and beyond,* ed. J. H. Johnson (Chicago: Oriental Institute,
1992), 306–7. Earlier spell texts were often found in private contexts. The library of Qenherkhepshef, dating to the thirteenth century, included material related to dreams and lucky
and unlucky days as well as magical spells. A late eighteenth / early seventeenth century
BCE tomb discovered beneath the Ramasseum at Thebes included magical papyri as well as
artifacts related to magical performance; the tomb may have been used to store this material,
or it could have been the final resting place of a priest. Pinch, *Magic in ancient Egypt,* 64–65,
131; Ritner, *The mechanics of ancient Egyptian magical practice,* 222–32. Likewise, papyri
from the Chester Beatty collection, which includes spells against demons, were the personal
property of two scribes, Amennakhte and Keniherkhepeshef, and magical texts were in the
possession of workmen at Deir el-Medineh. Ritner, *The mechanics of ancient Egyptian magical practice,* 206, n.954. The conspirators involved in the Harim Conspiracy under Ramses II
took ritual material, including instructions for execration spells, from the palace library. Ritner, *The mechanics of ancient Egyptian magical practice,* 232. A critical question is whether
the spells contained in the formularies represent ritual practices directly sanctioned by the
temple authorities. Priests who were working outside of the temple proper, moonlighting as
ritual specialists for hire and redeploying traditionally sanctioned technologies in private contexts, may have produced some of the PGM and PDM texts. Families of priests or even loose
associations of independent operators could have maintained and recopied the texts that we
now possess. This is an area that urges further study, including detailed work on the precise
findspots of the PGM and PDM texts, where they are known.

13. Frankfurter, "The consequences of Hellenism in Late Antique Egypt," 166. Overlap sometimes occurred within the rituals in these two areas. On the role of the traditional Egyptian
priesthood in the practice of domestic and personal religion, see J. Baines, "Society, morality,
and religious practice," in *Religion in ancient Egypt: Gods, myths and personal practice,*
ed. B. E. Shafer (Ithaca: Cornell University Press, 1991); J. Baines, "Practical religion and
piety," *JEA* 73 (1987); Ritner, *The mechanics of ancient Egyptian magical practice,* 204–5;
Frankfurter, *Religion in Roman Egypt,* 211; D. Frankfurter, "Dynamics of ritual expertise in
antiquity and beyond: Towards a new taxonomy of 'magicians,'" in *Magic and ritual in the
ancient world,* ed. P. A. Mirecki and M. Meyer (Leiden: Brill, 2002).

dence of multiple hands, suggesting that more than one individual was responsible for the texts that make up the large hoard.[14] Moreover, the texts of some of these documents appear to have resulted from more than one hundered years of compilation and editing, suggesting the involvement of numerous individuals.

Priests only served part of the year in the temple and were free to engage in private practice during the remainder, and may have borrowed copies of temple texts or been in possession of private copies.[15] There is evidence for the exchange of magical instructions between priests in different areas, suggesting an active and flourishing network of practitioners throughout the countryside. In a Demotic letter dated to the Ptolemaic period, Miysis, who is presumably a priest as well, writes to a priest of Thoth, requesting the return of a medical text.[16] Moreover, it is clear that following the collapse of the temple scriptoria in or around the fourth century CE, Egyptian priests became independent ritual specialists, either by removing the spell manuals from the temple libraries or utilizing compilations of spells already in their possession.[17]

Although many of the published texts lack specific archaeological provenance, papyri containing spell instructions have been discovered in numerous contexts—in temples, houses, and graves, and in cities, towns, and villages throughout Egypt. Plate 5 illustrates the known locations where magical texts have been discovered. As each of the magical papyri is an artifact in its own right, the archaeological and geographic context of an individual roll can suggest that it was in use in a particular place at a particular time. Such information can be useful for recovering and identifying archaeological examples of magic that may have been produced with reference to these formularies.

The spells included within the PGM provide detailed instructions that are to be followed in the performance of a rite. We can cite one example from the

---

14. Dieleman, *Priests, tongues, and rites,* 22, 28 and nn.12–13.

15. Ritner, *The mechanics of ancient Egyptian magical practice,* 232.

16. P. Carlsberg 21. (K.-T. Zauzich, "Zwei Briefe von Bücherfreunden," in *The Carlsberg Papyri 3* [Copenhagen: 2000]); Dieleman, *Priests, tongues, and rites,* 265–66. Compare the exchange related to a love spell from Coptic Kellis, discussed on, p. 164–65, 267. Likewise, there are two citations in PGM V.372–75 and PGM V.383 in which the writer claims to have received information from "a man from Herakleopolis." For discussion, see Dieleman, *Priests, tongues, and rites,* 266.

17. D. Frankfurter, *Elijah in Upper Egypt: The apocalypse of Elijah and early Egyptian Christianity* (Minneapolis: Fortress Press, 1993), 233–36; Frankfurter, *Religion in Roman Egypt,* 230–32, 57. Coptic priests were forbidden from consulting books of magic, which presumably would have been privately held. Indeed, a substantial spell manual was discovered in the cell of a monk at the monastery of Epiphanius of Thebes. See Frankfurter, *Religion in Roman Egypt,* 258, with references.

Great Magical Papyrus of Paris (PGM IV), a compendium of spells discovered in the mid-nineteenth century, probably in the vicinity of Thebes. The magical act was performed in order to induce love through sleeplessness, and instructs the practitioner to

> Take the eyes of a bat and release it alive, and take a piece of unbaked dough or unmelted wax and mold a little dog; put the right eye of the bat into the right eye of the little dog, implanting also in the same way the left one in the left. And take a needle, thread it with the magical material (*ousia*) and stick it through the eyes of the little dog, so that the magical material is visible. And put the dog in a new drinking vessel, attach a papyrus strip to it, and seal it with your own ring which has crocodiles with the backs of their heads attached, and deposit it at a crossroad after you have marked the spot, so that if you wish to recover it, you can find it.
>
> Spell written on the papyrus strip: "I adjure you three times by Hekate PHORPHORBA BAIBŌ PHŌRBŌRBA, that she NN, lose the fire in her eye, or even lie awake with nothing on her mind except me, NN, alone. I adjure by Kore, who has become the Goddess of Three roads, and who is the true mother of . . . (whom you wish), PHORBEA BRIMŌ NĒRĒATO DAMŌN BRIMŌN SEDNA DARDAR, All-seeing one, IOPE, make her, NN, lie awake for me through all [eternity].[18]

The spell is intended to transfer the sleeplessness of the bat, a nocturnal creature, to the victim, who is associated with the little dog. Beyond the grotesque extraction of the bat eyes, the remainder of the spell requires commonplace ingredients that have been altered through the ritual process: dough or wax, a needle, a ring, and a strip of papyrus. In addition, the spell calls for the use of magical material, or *ousia* in Greek. This term, which can be roughly translated as substance or stuff, refers either to some special material from a sacrificed animal or to substances that derive from the victim, either a possession or some form of bodily detritus, such as hair or fingernails that have been discarded. All of these materials are manipulated in order to create the small figurine, and this object is subsequently buried as part of the rite.

We also may encounter references to materials of magic that accompanied a rite within the texts inscribed on magical artifacts. These documents attest

---

18. PGM IV.2943–66, trans. adapted from E. N. O'Neil in *GMP*, 94.

Materia Magica 63

to the elements of rituals that are lost or are no longer recoverable. So, for example, a curse tablet from Aquitania discovered in a grave states, "just as this puppy harmed no one, so [may they harm no one] and may they not be able to win this suit; just as the mother of this puppy cannot defend it, so may their lawyers be unable to defend them."[19] Although the original report about the tablet does not indicate the presence of animal remains, the inscribed text makes it likely that the sacrifice of the puppy was part of the rite.

Both the insider sources and the outsider documents point to the same sorts of materials that could be incorporated into magical practice—incantations or other instances of writing inscribed onto various materials, figurines and visual representations, naturally occurring plants and animals, including strange and weird substances, and commonplace household objects that have been appropriated for magical use. The agreement between these two classes of source material is striking, although it should not be surprising, given that both sorts of evidence derive from the same cultural environment. In antiquity, the interplay between those who wrote about magic and practitioners could take many forms, suggesting a complex dialectical relationship between local rites and a general *koine* of magical practice. Our outsider sources may have been familiar with magic as it was practiced within their own communities, and some authors even could have sought the services of a ritual professional. Furthermore, the inscription from Cyrene suggests that ritual events that we have classed as magical might have been public, or the procedures for undertaking private rites may have been well known.

Conversely, local practitioners may have incorporated popular conceptions of what magic should look like into their own ritual techniques. David Frankfurter, in his analysis of Roman Egypt, has termed this process "stereotype appropriation."[20] Throughout the period of the *Pax Romana,* travelers came to Egypt for many reasons, seeking wisdom, secret knowledge, and the wonders of the past. In the area of magic-working, additions and changes to the spell

---

19. *DT* nos. 111–12; R. Wünsch, "Neue Fluchtafeln," *Rheinisches Museum* 55 (1900), no. 9; *CT* no. 53, translation from *CT*, p. 144.

20. Frankfurter, *Religion in Roman Egypt,* 224–37; Frankfurter, "The consequences of Hellenism in Late Antique Egypt," 168–83. With reference to the Demotic spells, see Dieleman, *Priests, tongues, and rites,* 9–10. For a critique of this concept, see R. L. Gordon, "Shaping the text: Innovation and authority in Graeco-Egyptian malign magic," in *Kykeon: Studies in honour of H. S. Versnel,* ed. H. F. J. Horstmanshoff et al., Religions in the Graeco-Roman world (Leiden: Brill, 2002), 71–76. On tourism to Egypt, see V. A. Foertmeyer, "Tourism in Graeco-Roman Egypt" (PhD diss., Princeton University, 1989).

books themselves attest a reorientation of traditional Egyptian magic for the tourist audience. Prior to the Hellenistic period, there is little evidence of erotic or necromantic magic, but spells for both appear frequently in the corpus of the PGM. This may suggest a conscious effort by those using the spell books to conform to Greek and Roman conceptions of magic and magic-working by focusing on spells that would satisfy the desires of both a tourist audience and an increasingly Hellenized Egyptian population, desirous of similar magical aids.[21] As Frankfurter states:

> For financial interest, for the intrinsic benefits of operating in an urban, ecumenical milieu, out of a desire to promote traditional religious ideas in the new idioms of Hellenism, or simply to answer foreigner's requests to "translate" ritual traditions, Egyptian priests sought to reframe their traditions and charismatic appeal according to Greco-Roman stereotypes of the "Oriental wizard," capitalizing on the talents, wisdom and skills for which they were avidly sought by spiritual tourists.[22]

The formularies of Late Antiquity, although composed by and for different audiences (i.e., Jews, Egyptians, and tourists), often integrated and reinterpreted general ideas about magic as well as specific cultural practices, sometimes adopted from other Mediterranean cultures. In all areas of the Roman Empire, we might expect to find similar processes of appropriation, as local practitioners attempted to make their own craft appear more like the expectations of their clients. Although we might note that similar objects and substances appear in all of our sources, a more compelling question lies in determining how these materials were employed, combined, and consumed in the local context.[23] Before turning to that question, which occupies the succeeding chapters, it is necessary to consider in detail each of the four categories of *materia magica* in order to articulate the different sorts of materials that make up each category and to consider how best to approach the archaeological evidence.

---

21. Frankfurter, "The consequences of Hellenism in Late Antique Egypt," 177. Earlier, Pharaonic spell books, such as Papyrus Harris, and P. Chester Beatty VII are largely concerned with medicinal and apotropaic spells.
22. Ibid., 183.
23. Bohak, *Ancient Jewish magic,* 229–31.

Inscribed Objects

Raw materials such as lead, papyrus, and semiprecious stones were often employed as media for magic. The written word and the rituals that surround the process of scratching, drawing, or incising letters and other signs could transform a simple item into a magical artifact. Often, items that have been inscribed explicitly tell the investigator about their function through language, and most of the objects currently identified as magical include a written or inscribed text. Many were created to communicate with supernatural forces, but modern scholars have benefited as the unintended recipients of these objects' narratives. Text may indicate a magical function through three mechanisms: the meaning of the inscribed words, the presence of special signs and symbols that are typically associated with magic, and the arrangement of words or letters to form pictures.

In a well-known example from Tacitus's *Annals,* quoted above in chapter 1, the death of Augustus's nephew Germanicus is attributed to sorcery, in part because his name was found inscribed on tablets. The practice of cursing using small lead sheets or other materials, such as potsherds or papyrus, is documented at least as early as the fifth century BCE, when, in Athens and Sicily, tablets inscribed with brief snippets of text were intended to bind a victim.[24] Curse tablets, often demonstrating greater complexity over time, continued to be employed through the Late Antique period and even beyond, with the tablets from the Via Appia, discussed at the beginning of this book, but one example among many. Numerous other classes of objects also employ texts as means of magical efficacy; amulets, magical gems, and texts that address divinities all incorporate the written word. In the instructional text from the PGM discussed above, the practitioner is enjoined to write a lengthy incantation on a papyrus strip that he attaches to the little dog. The model spell includes invocations to divinities, and strange words that resist translation.

Some scholars have suggested that the Late Antique period witnessed a dramatic increase in the importance of writing in magical practice, as the spell instructions frequently request that the practitioner both speak and write a spell.[25] Indeed, this process—the technical act of inscribing an incantation or

---

24. For bibliography on the curse tablets, see above, Introduction, n. 7.
25. Bohak, *Ancient Jewish magic,* 283–85; Johnston, *Restless dead,* 76.

other words—was a vital and significant component of ritual activity. Written inscriptions on amulets appear with greater frequency during the Roman period, perhaps suggesting a greater reverence for the power of the written word as opposed to the spoken.[26] Such prophylactics could take many forms, from silver and gold lamellae to folded pieces of papyrus or strips of lead encased in tubes.[27] The texts that appear on these objects were often (although not always) brief and included *historiolae* in which the goal of the spell is likened to a mythological or historical story, injunctions that ills or evils flee, invocations to divinities for protection, and prayers for salvation.[28] Magical gemstones, serving a similar purpose, were decorated with either images or inscriptions, or a combination of the two.[29]

The mere presence of writing on an artifact is not sufficient to indicate a ritual function, and indeed, commonly identified magical objects share both material and form with other artifacts that are not magical. For example, lead could be used for water pipes, a function that was cited in the San Sebastiano tablets from the Via Appia, and the material also was employed for a variety of civic documents. The Athenian Kerameikos yielded 574 lead sheets that assess the horses employed by the Athenian cavalry; two curse tablets were discovered within this larger cache of public documents.[30] Gemstones frequently were used for seals and signet rings; many may not have possessed a magical function. So too, papyrus, the ubiquitous writing material of ancient world, was

---

26. R. Kotansky, "Incantations and prayers for salvation on inscribed Greek amulets," in *Magika hiera,* ed. C. A. Faraone and D. Obbink (New York: Oxford University Press, 1991), 114.

27. R. Kotansky, *Greek magical amulets: The inscribed gold, silver, copper, and bronze "Lamellae": Text and commentary* (Opladen: Westdeutscher Verlag, 1994).

28. For discussion, see D. Frankfurter, "Narrating power: The theory and practice of the magical historiola in ritual spells," in *Ancient magic and ritual power,* ed. M. W. Meyer and P. A. Mirecki, *Religions in the Graeco-Roman world* (New York: Brill, 1995).

29. The bibliography on inscribed gems is substantial. See, recently, A. Nagy, "Ancient magical gems," in *Greek magic: Ancient, medieval, and modern,* ed. J. C. B. Petropoulos (New York: Routledge, 2008); C. A. Faraone, "Notes on four inscribed magical gemstones," *ZPE* 160 (2007); S. Michel, *Die Magischen Gemmen: zu Bildern und Zauberformeln auf geschnittenen Steinen der Antike und Neuzeit* (Berlin: Akademie Verlag, 2004); S. Michel, "(Re)Interpreting magical gems, ancient and modern," in *Officina magica: Essays on the practice of magic in antiquity,* ed. S. Shaked, Institute of Jewish studies: Studies in Judaica vol. 4 (Leiden: Brill, 2005); M. Eiland, "Bright stones, dark images: Magic gems," *Minerva* 13, no. 6 (2002); S. Michel, *Bunte Steine—Dunkle Bilder: "Magische Gemmen"* (Munich: Biering & Brinkmann, 2001); S. Michel, P. Zazoff, and H. Zazoff, *Die magischen Gemmen im Britischen Museum,* 2 vols. (London: British Museum Press, 2001).

30. Jordan, "Two inscribed lead tablets from a well in the Athenian Kerameikos," 225; K. Braun, "Der Dipylon-Brunnen B1, Die Funde," *Mitteilungen des Deutschen Archäologischen Instituts, Athenische Abteilung* 85 (1970); on the archaeological context, see J. H. Kroll, "An archive of the Athenian cavalry," *Hesperia* 46, no. 2 (1977).

Materia Magica 67

hardly reserved for magical use; small papyrus chits were employed for oracle questions as well as protective amulets.[31] Certain features of these objects, rather than the form of writing or medium, demonstrate that the artifact was created through or employed within a ritual.

Most often, the meaning of the words inscribed on an artifact can secure its identification as magical. A lead sheet from Attica, dated to the fourth century, is inscribed on both sides, with the first side reading only "Hermes of the underworld and Hekate of the underworld." This address to the chthonic or underworld deities is reminiscent of a private letter, with the names of the addressees on one side and the main body of the text written on the opposite side. The reverse of the tablet includes a much longer inscription that begins

> Let Pherenikos be bound before Hermes of the underworld and Hekate of the underworld. I bind Pherenikos's (girl) Galene to Hermes of the underworld and Hekate of the underworld I bind (her). And just as this lead is worthless and cold, so let that man and his property be worthless and cold, and those who are with him who have spoken and counseled concerning me . . . [32]

In a later portion of the spell, the text urges, "also Pherenikos's soul and mind and tongue and plans and the things that he is doing and the things that he is planning concerning me. May everything be contrary for him . . ."[33] Not only is Pherenikos bound, but so also are those things that might oppose the commissioner of the tablet—his mind, his tongue, and his plans. The tablet is also careful to account for any other potential actions or anatomical elements that he did not list in detail, asking that all things should be against the victim of the spell. Moreover, it is important to note the conscious recognition of the medium on which the spell is written—the practitioner asks that the victim become cold and worthless just as the lead tablet. Individuals who performed

---

31. Compare, for example, the oracle questions from Soknopaiou Nesos with the magical drawings discovered at the same site. Oracle questions: *W.Chr.* 122, *SB* XVIII.14043, *P.Vindob.G.* 298; see L. Papini, "Struttura e prassi delle domande oracolari in greco su papiro," *APapyrol* 2 (1990); L. Papini, "Domande oracolari: elenco delle attestazioni in greco ed in copto," *APapyrol* 4 (1992). Magical drawings on papyrus: M. Capasso, "Alcuni papiri figurati magici recentemente trovati a Soknopaiou Nesos," in *New archaeological and papyrological researches on the Fayyum: Proceedings of the international meeting of Egyptology and papyrology, Lecce 8th–10th June 2005*, ed. M. Capasso and P. Davoli, *Papyrologica Lupiensia 14/2005* (Galatina [Lecce]: Congedo, 2007).
32. *DTA* no. 107 = *CT* no. 40, translation, *CT*, p. 127. On this tablet, see Faraone, "The agonistic context of early Greek binding-spells," 15.
33. Translation, *CT*, p. 127

68 Materia Magica

magic exploited the material culture that they employed in order to increase the efficacy of a rite. Comparison can be made with a gold lamella from the J. Paul Getty Museum that is inscribed, "The God of Abraham, the God of Isaac, the God of Jacob, our God, deliver Aurelia from every evil spirit and from every epileptic fit and seizure, I implore you Lord, Iao, Sabaoth, Eloaion (names of divinities and *voces magicae*) protect Aurelia from every evil spirit and from every epileptic fit and seizure."[34] The precious metal employed for the amulet may be related to its protective powers. The meaning of the inscribed text, with references to ritual binding or invocations to divinities for protection, indicates that the practitioner believed mechanistic action would result in a particular outcome, achieved through the material medium of the artifact.

Much as the meaning of a text may allow us to differentiate between magical and nonmagical objects, so certain words and phrases can indicate a particular ritual use. The inscriptions preserved on a number of lead sheets, largely from England but also from Corinth, Cnidus, and other areas of the Mediterranean, suggest a function that was distinct from the curses that we have encountered in Rome, Athens, and elsewhere.[35] Indeed, Henk Vernsel has suggested that these artifacts, previously identified as curse tablets, are a separate class of ritual object that he has termed "Prayers for Justice." Rather than intended to bind an enemy in anticipation of a coming event, the prayer for justice often responds to something that has already occurred. Versnel identifies the main markers of prayers for justice as follows:

1. the principal states his or her name
2. some grounds for the appeal are offered; this statement may be reduced to a single word, or may be enlarged upon
3. the principal requests that the act be excused or that he be spared the possible adverse effects

---

34. R. Kotansky, "Two amulets in the Getty Museum," *J. Paul Getty Museum Journal* 8 (1980): 181.
35. Bath, England: R. S. O. Tomlin, *Tabellae Sulis: Roman inscribed tablets of tin and lead from the sacred spring at Bath* (Oxford: Oxford University Committee for Archaeology, 1988); Uley, England: A. Woodward, P. Leach, and J. Bayley, eds., *The Uley shrines: Excavation of a ritual complex on West Hill, Uley, Gloucestershire, 1977–9* (London: English Heritage in association with British Museum Press, 1993), 113–30; Cnidus: *DT* nos. 1–13 = C. T. Newton, *A History of discoveries at Halicarnassus, Cnidus, and Branchidae* (London: Day & Son, 1863), II 719–45 = W. Blümel, *Die Inschriften von Knidos* (Bonn: R. Habelt, 1992), nos. 147–59, pp. 85–103. Corinth: R. S. Stroud, *The sanctuary of Demeter and Kore: The inscriptions* (Princeton, NJ: American School of Classical Studies at Athens, forthcoming).

Materia Magica 69

4. gods other than the usual chthonic deities are often invoked
5. these gods, either because of their superior character, or as an emollient gesture, may be awarded a flattering epithet (e.g. φίλη) or a superior title (e.g. κύριος, κύρια, or δέσποινα)
6. words expressing supplication (ἱκετεύω, βοήθει μοι, βοήθησον αὐτῷ) are employed as well as direct, personal invocations of the deity
7. use of terms and names referring to (in)justice and punishment (e.g. Praxidike, Dike, ἐκδικέω, ἀδικέω, κολάζω, and κόλασις).[36]

Other scholars have proposed additional features that might indicate prayers for justice, including the lack of knowledge of the identity of the victim, the absence of binding language and magical terminology such as *voces magicae,* and a clear condition for the curse and its removal.[37] There are cases, however, in which an artifact may demonstrate features that are similar to both traditional aggressive binding curses and prayers for justice.[38] Indeed, the tablets discussed in this volume from Empúries and Amathous highlight some of the overlap between these two classes of artifact.

The inscriptions found on magical artifacts often replicated and gave physical form to oral spells. The Greeks had long possessed an ambivalent relationship with writing, frequently viewing the written word as prone to decep-

---

36. H. S. Versnel, "Prayers for justice, east and west: Recent finds and publications since 1990," in *Magical practice in the Latin West: Papers from the international conference held at the University of Zaragoza, 30 Sept.–1 Oct. 2005,* ed. R. L. Gordon and F. Marco Simón (Leiden: Brill, 2010), 279–80. This list summarizes the characteristics found in H. S. Versnel, "Beyond cursing: The appeal for justice in judicial prayers," in *Magika hiera,* ed. C. A. Faraone and D. Obbink (New York: Oxford University Press, 1991), passim, but esp. 75–80, 90–91. On the topic of judicial prayers, see also H. S. Versnel, "καὶ εἴ λ[οιπὸν] τῶν μερ[ῶ]ν [ἔσ]ται τοῦ σώματος ὅλ[ο]υ[.. (. . . and any other part of the entire body there may be . . .). An essay on anatomical curses," in *Ansichten griechischer Rituale: Geburtstags-Symposium für Walter Burkert,* ed. F. Graf (Stuttgart: B. G. Teubner, 1998); H. S. Versnel, "ΚΟΛΑΣΑΙ ΤΟΥΣ ΗΜΑΣ ΤΟΙΟΥΤΟΥΣ ΗΔΕΩΣ ΒΛΕΠΟΝΤΕΣ: "Punish those who rejoice in our misery": On curse texts and *Schadenfreude,*" in *The world of ancient magic,* ed. D. R. Jordan, H. Montgomery, and E. Thomassen (Bergen: Norwegian Institute at Athens, 1999); H. S. Versnel, "Writing mortals and reading gods: Appeal to the gods as a dual strategy in social control," in *Demokratie, Recht und soziale Kontrolle im klassischen Athen,* ed. D. Cohen and E. Müller-Luckner (Munich: Oldenbourg, 2002); A. Chaniotis, "Under the watchful eyes of the gods: Divine justice in Hellenistic and Roman Asia Minor," in *The Greco-Roman East: Politics, culture, society,* ed. S. Colvin, Yale Classical Studies (New York: Cambridge University Press, 2004).
37. Ogden, "Binding spells," 279–80.
38. See, for example, the cases adduced at Versnel, "Beyond cursing," 64–68; Versnel, "Prayers for justice, east and west," 322–42.

70 Materia Magica

tion. For Plato, the invention of writing discouraged the use of memory and led to a decline in true wisdom, and even as late as the fourth century BCE, writing was still viewed with skepticism, with oral transactions and testimony typically preferred to written ones.[39] The Greeks did not believe that inscribed language was inherently magical; writing was viewed as stemming from, and subservient to, the spoken word. In contrast, the Egyptian conceptualization of the power of text, which is also crucial for understanding Roman period magic in Egypt, viewed the written or inscribed word as powerful in and of itself. Hieroglyphic writing conveyed magical force, so much so that pouring water over the characters inscribed on stele or other religious documents would effectively transfer this power to the liquid, allowing magical language to be ingested or otherwise employed by suppliants.[40]

Following the Greek preference for oral expression in ritual, writing in the Greek world typically served to record all or part of the spoken spell.[41] John Petropoulos has suggested that the erotic spells were likely an oral medium before the Roman period; even afterward, the spells continue to read like speech.[42] The lesser role attributed to writing in magic, however, does not mean that the inscribed word served no function beyond the replication of speech. Through writing, the spell was continually reiterated, maintaining the words and phrases of the rite in perpetuity. Because the ancients read aloud, writing served not only to record the spell but to ensure that its efficacy would continue unabated, reenacting the spell each time another individual—whether human or divine—encountered the text.[43]

The preserved inscription may record only part of the oral spell.[44] Many of the earliest curse tablets, and even a significant number of later examples,

---

39. Plato, *Phaedrus* 275 A-B; W. V. Harris, *Ancient literacy* (Cambridge: Harvard University Press, 1989), 72–73.
40. D. Frankfurter, "The magic of writing and the writing of magic: The power of the word in Egyptian and Greek traditions," *Helios* 21, no. 2 (1994): 192–96.
41. C. A. Faraone, "Aeschylus' *hymnos desmios* (Eum 306) and Attic judicial curse tablets," *JHS* 105 (1985): 153 and n. 21.
42. J. C. B. Petropoulos, "The erotic magical papyri," in *Proceedings of the XVIII international congress of papyrology, Athens, 25–31 May 1986*, ed. B. G. Mandilaras (Athens: Greek Papyrological Society, 1988), 215, 21.
43. J. Svenbro, *Phrasikleia: An anthropology of reading in ancient Greece,* trans. J. Lloyd (Ithaca: Cornell University Press, 1993), 18, 23, 35–36; R. Thomas, *Literacy and orality in Ancient Greece* (Cambridge: Cambridge University Press, 1992), 62–65; B. M. W. Knox, "Silent reading in antiquity," *GRBS* 9 (1968); Frankfurter, "The magic of writing and the writing of magic," 195.
44. Bailliot, *Magie et sortilèges dans l'Antiquité romaine,* 174–75.

Materia Magica   71

list only the names of the victims. A late sixth- or early fifth-century tablet from an unknown location in Athens reads, "Nereides, Demosthenes, Sokles, Lukourgos, Euthukrates, Epikles, Charisios, Boethos, Poluokos, and all the others who are accusers of Nereides."[45] The inscription provides neither explicit instruction regarding what should happen to these individuals nor does it invoke a deity or other force for assistance. In this spell, the written word does not merely transcribe the spoken incantation. As in others, the use of the nominative suggests a degree of independence from the incantation, where the accusative would have indicated that the victim was the target of the binding.[46] Oral spells would have directed the force of the magical act, but because speech is ephemeral, the precise language of the curse must remain unknown. This example urges a recognition that magical acts may have included additional features that are now lost.

The text may highlight important parts of the spoken spell or completely diverge from it. In the instructions of the Greek Magical Papyri, there are numerous instances in which the practitioner is instructed to intone one spell but write something different on the object. So, in PGM XXXVI.161–77, a charm to restrain anger, the practitioner is told to repeat seven times "ERMALLOTH ARCHIMALLOTH stop the mouths that speak against me, because I glorify your sacred and honored names which are in heaven" but to inscribe a separate spell on papyrus that included many more divine names and invocations to angels.[47]

Written, comprehensible text also could be used for purposes other than incantations that were necessary for the efficacy of the magical act. For example, an inscription could associate a physical artifact with a target; figurines may have included the name of the intended victim in order to assure that the spell worked properly. Although the name may have been intoned as part of a spoken spell, its appearance on the artifact would not have repeated the incantation. Rather, writing particularized the object, specifying who would be affected by the ritual through the practitioner's manipulation of the figurine.

Inscribed letters and signs without clear meaning may suggest that a particular object was used for ritual purposes. We encountered strange names of gods and other magical phrases, known as *voces magicae,* on the gold lamella from the J. Paul Getty Museum, but such magical phrases may occur alone. For

---

45. Wünsch, "Neue Fluchtafeln," 63; *DT* no. 60; *CT* no. 42; translation, *CT*, p. 130.
46. Ogden, "Binding spells," 9.
47. Trans. R. F. Hock in *GMP,* 273.

72 Materia Magica

example, the appearance of the name Chnoubis, or the presence of a magical phrase such as SESENGEN BARPHARANGES on a gemstone may suggest that the artifact was employed for a ritual purpose.[48] The *Ephesia Grammata,* or Ephesian letters, a series of six special characters—*askion, kataskion, lix, tetrax, damnameneus,* and *aision* (or *aisia)*—are found on curses from the first century CE onward, appearing as well in the magical papyri and in later Jewish magic.[49] Moreover, some ritual writing is completely incomprehensible, as it employs symbols that are not drawn from any alphabet but instead are specialized for magical use. The *kharaktêres,* a set of mystical letterforms, are inscribed on curse tablets and even invoked on their own, suggesting some form of inherent power.[50] In form, some *kharaktêres* appear similar to Greek script but possess rounded bulbs at the ends of the strokes. Other *kharaktêres* are more unusual, appearing similar to starbursts or suns with radiating arms. As Frankfurter has argued, these symbolic images were not cryptographs but instead represented a sacred script.[51] We know little about how, or even if, the *kharaktêres* were pronounced, suggesting that they served as a visual means of communication with the divine.

Beyond its precise meaning or letterforms, an inscription may be indicative of magic through the arrangement of the words and signs. Writing could be used to produce images, the so-called *carmina figurata,* where letters, particularly vowels, were arranged in triangles, squares, or wing patterns.[52]

---

48. On *voces magicae* in general, see D. Porreca, "Divine names: A cross-cultural comparison (Papyri Graecae Magicae, Picatrix, Munich handbook)," *Magic, Ritual, and Witchcraft* 5, no. 1 (2010); Bohak, *Ancient Jewish magic,* 258–64; G. Bohak, "Hebrew, Hebrew everywhere? Notes on the interpretation of *voces magicae,*" in *Prayer, magic, and the stars in the ancient and Late Antique world,* ed. S. B. Noegel, J. T. Walker, and B. M. Wheeler (University Park: Pennsylvania State University Press, 2003); Brashear, "The Greek magical papyri," 3429–38.

49. C. C. McCown, "The Ephesia Grammata in popular belief," *Transactions and Proceedings of the American Philological Association* 54 (1923); K. Preisendanz, "Ephesia grammata," *Reallexikon für Antike und Christentum* 5 (1961); Kotansky, "Incantations and prayers for salvation on inscribed Greek amulets," 111–12; *CT,* p. 5–6; Bohak, *Ancient Jewish magic,* 267–70. Earlier iterations of the Ephesian letters: inscription from near Mycenae: L. H. Jeffery, "Further comments on archaic Greek inscriptions," *ABSA* 50 (1955): 69–76; text from Selinus: Jordan, "A love charm with verses."

50. On the *kharaktêres,* see discussion and bibliography at Brashear, "The Greek magical papyri," 3441–43; Frankfurter, "The magic of writing and the writing of magic," 206–10; Frankfurter, *Religion in Roman Egypt,* 255–56; Dieleman, *Priests, tongues, and rites,* 97–101; Bohak, *Ancient Jewish magic,* 270–74.

51. Frankfurter, "The magic of writing and the writing of magic," 207.

52. F. Dornseiff, *Das alphabet in mystik und magie* (Leipzig: B. G. Teubner, 1925), 58–60, 63–67; C. Lenz, "Carmina figurata," *RAC* 2 (1952); Martinez, *Michigan Papyri XVI: A Greek love charm from Egypt (P.Mich. 757),* 105–11. Frankfurter, "The magic of writing and the writ-

Materia Magica 73

Some fifth- and fourth-century tablets employ boustrophedon, a contemporary recording style in which text was written going left to right in one line, then right to left, and so on, as if following the path of an ox through a field. While this manner fell out of style shortly after the archaic period, curse tablets continued to use it. There may be an element of conservatism in the retention of this practice, but twisted writing also replicated the goals of the tablet by using the inscription to bind the victim.[53] In other texts, the entirety of the inscription is written backward, with the letters facing the wrong way.[54] Some tablets focus this manipulation on the names of the victims, ensuring that targets of the spell will be twisted and bound through the magical act.[55] The tablet may make reference to the method of binding that is conveyed by the inscription, as a fourth-century Attic tablet declares, "just as these words are cold and right to left, so too may the words of Crates be cold and backwards."[56] The text that has been inscribed onto the tablet is an important component of magic both through its meaning—the words convey instructions to divinities, or enforce the binding of an enemy—but also because of its appearance, as this too could be an effective means of control or manipulation of the victim. Reading the inscribed text and visually inspecting its form each contribute to our identification of a particular artifact as magical and can aid us in our interpretation of the function of the object and the ritual process that generated it. Inscribed language moves beyond merely conveying meaning or replicating the spoken incantation; letters and symbols carried magical force that was employed in the service of the ritual.

The physical and material form of the artifact often contributed to the goals of the inscribed spell; numerous inscriptions comment upon or make use of the physical object on which the incantation has been inscribed. Moreover, analysis of the magical artifact that served as a writing surface can provide vital information about the performance of the spell. For example, many of the curse tablets that we possess were created solely for the rite in which they were used and were cut to a size appropriate for the text that they would receive. Chemical analysis of the large cache of curses from Bath, in England, has

---

ing of magic," 199–200; A. Mastrocinque, "Le pouvoir de l'écriture dans la magie," *Cahiers Mondes Anciens* 1 (2009).

53. Conservatism in curses: Faraone, "The agonistic context of early Greek binding-spells," 8 and n. 35. On twistedness as a means of binding: Ogden, "Binding spells," 29.

54. *DTA* nos. 24, 86; *Tab. Sulis,* no. 61.

55. *CT,* p. 5. Cf. *DT* no. 60; *DTA* no. 95; *SGD* no. 105.

56. *DTA* no. 67, cited in Ogden, "Binding spells," 30.

revealed that each of the tablets was composed of a different ratio of tin to lead.[57] The practitioner may have manipulated the tablet by rolling it or piercing it with a nail, acts that would have employed the physical form of the artifact for magical efficacy in order to bind down or constrain the victim.[58] Using nails to secure curse tablets is a common occurrence, one that continues well into the Late Antique period, as attested by the tablets from the Via Appia described in the introduction. In some cases, the presence of a nailed tablet may be the only indicator that the artifact was used in magic. A cache of uninscribed sheets of lead tablets from Rom in modern France, varying in size from 150 g to more than 2 kg, was identified as a group of curses because they had been pierced with nails.[59] This final example can point toward another class of magical material—artifacts that were intended to affect a target by representing the victim or some other entity.

Images and Figurines

Images and other representations, in two- or three-dimensional form, pervade magic in the ancient world. At Karanis, the presence of a small figurine made of unbaked clay, with primary and secondary sexual characteristics, was likely an important feature within an erotic ritual. In the spell from the Greek Magical Papyri, translated on p. 62, the practitioner is enjoined to make a figurine of a small dog for use in the rite; the dog's eyes are the eyes of a bat, and magical material, presumably from the target of the spell, is affixed to the figurine. Images used in magic may also consist of drawings and pictures: the curse tablets from the Via Appia with which this book began included a monstrous central figure with a horse head, as well as a mummy, entwined by snakes, and smaller images of magical assistants. Representations may be intended to depict a variety of actors within a particular magical rite, from the target of the spell to the divinities called upon to enact the will of the practitioner, or they may fulfill some other function altogether, as may be the case for the figurine of the dog in the PGM spell. In this discussion, plastic images and drawings will be treated as alternative but comparable manifestations of the

---

57. *Tab. Sulis,* 82.
58. Bailliot, *Magie et sortilèges dans l'Antiquité romaine,* 72–76.
59. C. Jullian, "Les fouilles de M. Blumereau à Rom (Deux Sèvres)," *Mémoires de la Société nationale des Antiquaires de France* LVIII (1897): no. 1 = *DT* no. 109.

Materia Magica 75

same desire—to physically represent another entity. While figurines and other three-dimensional representations offered the practitioner a way to affect a target through tactile manipulation, a flat image could be inscribed, pierced or drawn in a specific position. Indeed, it could be argued that two- and three-dimensional representations occupied the same conceptual space within magical practice.

The process of creating a figurine or image and subsequently manipulating it may have resulted in cathartic release for the practitioner or client, allowing him or her to act upon the target.[60] But such actions were also believed to have an effect on the person, divinity, or thing represented. Indeed, the idea of imitation as a means of effecting change in the world can be observed in many cultural groups, and the role of correspondences in magic has long been established.[61] There are multiple ways by which two distinct entities—the human victim and an object that can be manipulated by the practitioner—might be associated. Primarily, one may consider the linkages created through visual or tactile similarity, where a representation is intended to physically mimic its human or divine antecedent. As well, an object may be metaphorically associated with the target of the spell, as the practitioner, often by means of performative utterance, links the victim and another item. Finally, objects may be joined through their component parts, where specific ingredients associated with the victim, such as a cloak or nail clippings, are employed as a metonymic stand-in for the target. This final mechanism will be explored in the succeeding section, as the practitioner does not create an artifact but instead employs preexisting materials or *exuviae* to establish a link with the target.

A representation ideally can copy something else, permitting the viewer or creator to grasp (both physically and intellectually) that which is represented through its double.[62] True reproduction would replicate every aspect of the original object, effectively cloning a person or thing into two- or three-

---

60. B. Malinowski, *Magic, science and religion, and other essays* (Garden City, NY: Doubleday, 1954), 79–81; G. E. R. Lloyd, *Magic, reason and experience* (New York: Cambridge University Press, 1979), 47–48; Frankfurter, "Fetus magic and sorcery fears in Roman Egypt," 4.

61. Frazer: "The magician infers that he can produce any effect he desires merely by imitating it." *The golden bough: A study in magic and religion,* 12. Compare S. J. Tambiah, "Form and meaning of magical acts: a point of view," in *Modes of thought,* ed. R. Horton and R. Finnegan (London: Faber & Faber, 1973), 67, citing G. E. R. Lloyd, *Polarity and analogy: Two types of argumentation in early Greek thought* (Cambridge: Cambridge University Press, 1966), 160.

62. W. Benjamin, "The work of art in the age of mechanical reproduction," in *Illuminations,* ed. H. Arendt (New York: Schocken Books, 1969), 223; Taussig, *Mimesis and alterity,* 32.

dimensional form. The Greeks and Romans understood this well; the highest skill in art, according to Pliny, was to recreate nature in such a way as to fool the eye. Zeuxis is credited with painting a bowl of fruit that a bird tried to eat, while Parrhasius, his better, produced an image of a curtain that Zeuxis asked to be pulled back.[63] Indeed, mimesis collapses the distance between the object and the viewer, and provides a tactile and sensual understanding of the thing portrayed.[64] Through the act of creating, the artist experiences the individual lines and shapes of that which is being portrayed, so that the completed artifact records the artist's understanding of his or her subject.[65] Thus, the newly created object, outside of its faithfulness to the original, is more a testament to how the artist understood and interacted with his or her subject than it is to the nature or form of the original object.

The artist, as creator, is able to determine the form and shape of the object that he or she has made; in a similar fashion, the artist also controls the fate of that object—how it is manipulated, and whether it might be consumed or destroyed. The visual and tactile linkage between the object and the thing represented permits a slippage of boundaries, as the representation is elided into its antecedent. Indeed, in the mind of the artist, the artifact may become the thing that it supposedly represents; no longer is the object merely a sign or symbol of something else, but instead the object is something else.[66] Statuary, and in particular representations of divinities, can operate in this fashion. Although the god was believed to be present in his or her image, worshippers did not think that supernatural force moved or directed an inanimate object; those cases in which statues did things, such as weeping or bleeding, were highly unusual and warranted special comment.[67] Rather, the god, resident in the representation,

---

63. Pliny, *HN* XXXV.36.

64. Taussig, *Mimesis and alterity,* 35; Mitchell, *Picture theory: Essays on verbal and visual representation,* 420–21.

65. M. Taussig, "What do drawings want?" *Culture, Theory and Critique* 50, nos. 2 & 3 (2009): 269.

66. E. H. Gombrich, *Art and illusion: A study in the psychology of pictorial representation,* 6th ed. (New York: Phaidon, 2002), 85.

67. Miller, *The corporeal imagination: Signifying the holy in late ancient Christianity,* 136–39; Gell, *Art and agency,* 122. Speaking statues, however, may have been commonplace. Compare the examples known from Egypt, in which priests hid inside the statues or spoke through a tube: Theodoret, *Historia Ecclesiastica* 5.22. See discussion in Frankfurter, *Religion in Roman Egypt,* 150–51, and D. Frankfurter, "Voices, books, and dreams: The diversification of divination media in Late Antique Egypt," in *Mantikê: Studies in ancient divination,* ed. S. I. Johnston and P. T. Struck (Leiden: Brill, 2005). Evidence from Kom el-Wist: L. Habachi, "Finds at Kôm el-Wist," *Annales du service des Antiquités de l'Égypte* 47 (1947); G. Brunton,

Materia Magica 77

was able to hear the prayers of suppliants, receive food offerings, and effect change in the world. By providing an idol with a sacred meal, or dressing it in a newly made peplos, the priest could engage in real, rather than merely symbolic, activities with the god. What was done to the image of the god was also done to the god.[68] This slippage of boundaries between image and that which the image represented permits the practitioner, who is also the creator of the image, to control and determine the fate of both object, and through extension, its double, the victim of the spell.[69] The representation can have an effect on reality, as the practitioner mimes or mimics an ideal reality—a reality that he or she has determined—into being.[70]

The figurine of the woman pierced with pins that is now in the Louvre (plate 4) and discussed in chapter 1, points us to the important role played by mimesis in magical practice. The statuette, which depicts the woman nude, on her knees, and bound, has been modeled with great care. The hair is plaited in an apparent attempt to mimic a specific hairstyle, and the figurine is endowed with both earrings and a necklace.[71] The face is rounded, with wide-set eyes, traces of thick eyebrows may be visible above, and the mouth is cut deeply. The magical doll can compared to the famed depiction of Julia Domna, the wife of the emperor Septimius Severus (193–211 CE), on the "Severan Family Portrait," a painted wooden roundel discovered in Fayum and now housed in Berlin. In particular, the hairstyle, roundness of the face, and jewelry demonstrate close similarities. A number of details in the modeling are also significant: the shoulders are wide, the breasts are relatively small with large nipples, the stomach protrudes slightly, and the pubis is marked by a deep incision. Some of these features are expected in the creation of an erotic figurine, particularly the emphasis placed on the sexual organs, but the attention paid to the hairstyle and the jewelry, as well as the care taken in the modeling of the body, may suggest an attempt at portraiture, so that the figurine specifically references the victim of the spell, Ptolemais. The pins are intended to cause pain in the specific body parts that they pierce, suggested that the mimetic similarities

---

"The oracle of Kôm el-Wist," *Annales du service des antiquités de l'Égypte* 47 (1947).

68. Gell, *Art and agency,* 121–26, 33–35.

69. Taussig, *Mimesis and alterity,* 113, 271; Gell, *Art and agency,* 107.

70. Taussig, *Mimesis and alterity,* 30, 106–8.

71. For the hairstyle, also compare the later portrait types of Julia Domna, with the so-called helmet hairstyle. Cf. D. E. E. Kleiner, *Roman sculpture* (New Haven: Yale University Press, 1992), 326–27; F. Ghedini, *Giulia Domna tra oriente e occidente: le fonti archeologiche* (Rome: "L'Erma" di Bretschneider, 1984).

78   Materia Magica

between the modeled features of the doll closely corresponded to the appendages and organs of the target of the spell.

While we might imagine that greater accuracy and adherence to the
original would have a corroborative influence on the efficacy of a magical
act, this does not seem to be the case. Indeed, magic seems to function most
often through imperfect or defective copies.[72] The image frequently mimics
those features that are significant to the spell or that can permit identification
between object and victim. In an inscription from Cyrene, quoted in the beginning of this chapter, figurines are employed to control hostile ghosts that are
tormenting the residents. When the ghost's identity is unknown, the person
undertaking the rite is instructed to create male and female figurines (*kolossoi*)
from either wood or earth, entertain the dolls by offering them food and other
gifts, and then deposit them in a secluded natural setting.[73] An accurate physical representation is impossible because the residents do not know who the
ghost is. Care is taken to ensure that some features of the object, specifically
its sexual characteristics, might be associated with the deceased individual.
Two separate figurines are created, despite the fact that only a single ghost
was the probable culprit. In this instance, sex differentiation and human form
are viewed as important components of mimetic duplication, and only these
limited characteristics were deemed necessary to ensure the removal of the
offending spirit. The images are representations of the dead individual, created
in order to appease the ghost through sympathetic burial rites: offerings given
to the image would be likewise shared by the figurine's double, and the ghost
would be removed from the community.[74]

Much like the process of miniaturization, imperfect representation stresses
certain features that are relevant or viewed as important by the creator of the
object.[75] In a late fifth-century (ca. 400 BCE) grave from the Kerameikos cem-

---

72. Mauss, *A general theory of magic,* 68.
73. On the word *kolossos,* see É. Benveniste, "Le sens du mot KOLOSSOS et les noms grecs de la
    statue," *Rev. de phil.* 58 (1932); C. Picard, "Le rite magique des εἴδολα de cire brûlés, attesté
    sur trois stèles araméennes de Sfiré," *Revue archeologique* 3 (1961); M. W. Dickie, "What is
    a *kolossos* and how were *kolossoi* made in the Hellenistic period?" *GRBS* 37, no. 3 (1996).
74. Faraone, "Talismans and Trojan horses: Guardian statues in ancient Greek myth and ritual,"
    82; W. Burkert, *Die orientalisierende Epoche in der griechischen Religion und Literatur* (Hei-
    delberg: Winter, 1984), 68–71. For Near Eastern parallels for this practice, see J. A. Scurlock,
    Magico-medical means of treating ghost-induced illnesses in ancient Mesopotamia (Leiden:
    Brill / Styx, 2006), 50. On offerings, see Scurlock, *Magico-medical means of treating ghost-
    induced illnesses in ancient Mesopotamia,* nos. 12, 13, 220, 25, 26, 30. On burial, see nos. 11,
    18, 26, 30.
75. S. Stewart, *On longing: Narratives of the miniature, the gigantic, the souvenir, the collection*
    (Baltimore: Johns Hopkins University Press, 1984), 44, 54.

Materia Magica   79

etery on the outskirts of Athens, excavators discovered a lead figurine with
exaggerated male genitals, his hands twisted behind his back, and the name
Mnesimachos inscribed on its right leg. The image, however, is only remotely
human in form; the representation does not accurately copy the target of the
spell. Instead, by naming the image through an inscription, a link is created
between artifact and antecedent. The importance of the image to the rite relies
not on mimetic accuracy but instead on how the form relates to the goals of the
ritual act.[76] The head of the figurine is barely differentiated from the body and
lacks indications of features, such as eyes, ears, or hair. Care has been taken to
accurately depict the arms and legs, which have been elongated for emphasis.
These appendages have been twisted behind the body to indicate binding. The
exaggerated genitals ensure that the target is identified as male but may also
have served a ritual purpose.[77] The object was placed inside a roughly made
coffin, constructed of two inscribed lead sheets that curse multiple individuals,
including Mnesimachos.[78] The object was intended to restrain the named individual in two ways: the practitioner bound the hands of the statuette behind its
back and deposited it within a makeshift coffin, effecting a double burial that
would prevent Mnesimachos as well as the other associates named within the
text from undertaking some action.

Danger may lie in mimesis, as the creator may elide with his or her creation and suffer the fate intended for the victim.[79] In order to ensure that the
representation is not confused with the practitioner, the image may be marked
in some way that determines its identity. The practitioner might be instructed
to inscribe the name of the victim on the figurine, or material from the victim
(*ousia,* see below) may be attached to the creation, denoting that it is the target

---

76. Gombrich, *Art and illusion: A study in the psychology of pictorial representation,* 94.

77. It is not certain whether the exaggerated genitals are an intentional and important part of the
figurine or merely out of proportion due to its small size. In Greek art, exaggerated genitals
often mark wild and bestial creatures, such as satyrs. Collins has suggested that the prevalence
of genitals may be related to the use of the phallus in apotropaic magic. *Magic in the ancient
Greek world,* 93 and n. 140. It seems more likely that the representation was intended to
establish a parallel between the victim and the monstrous, as the figurines were meant to harm
or at least restrain their victims.

78. *SGD* no. 9; J. Trumpf, "Fluchtafel und Rachepuppe," *Mitteilungen des Deutschen Archäologischen Instituts, Athenische Abteilung* 73 (1958) 71.3–4, 72.1–2; Jordan, "New archaeological evidence for the practice of magic in classical Athens"; *VD* no. 5; F. Constabile,
"Καταδεσμοι," *Mitteilungen des Deutschen Archäologischen Instituts, Athenische Abteilung*
114 (1999): 87–91, no. 1; F. Constabile, "Defixiones dal Kerameikos di Atene, II. maledizioni
processuali," *Minima epigraphica et papyrologica* 4 (2000).

79. W. J. T. Mitchell, *What do pictures want? The lives and loves of images* (Chicago: University
of Chicago Press, 2005), 25.

of the spell. Alternatively, the practitioner might create a double of himself or herself, or of the client, to perform a role in the spell. In Horace's *Satires* I.8, the two witches create two figurines; one may be the target of the spell while the other could be the practitioner or client. This duplication is also apparent in the famous love spell from Egypt (PGM IV.296–466), in which the practitioner is instructed to create two figurines, one of a bound woman and the other of Ares. The female figurine is associated with the target through the attachment of magical material taken from the victim. According to the PGM text, the male figurine should threaten the female with a sword, symbolically forcing her to submit to his will. The magician is able to effect change by occupying both roles concurrently—he is the figure of Ares, exerting control, and, concurrently, he mimes submission to the desire of the commissioner through the figurine of the woman. At the same time, the practitioner stands outside of the two figurines and inserts bronze needles into the doll in order to control the sexual activities of the victim. Performative speech acts, too, may associate the representation with its prototype, as a declarative statement can ritually transform an image into its mimetic antecedent.

In the absence of visual or tactile fidelity to a prototype, an artifact may serve as a representation through metaphoric similarities. As a counterpoint to mimesis, we can consider how representation functions in Minkisi (sing. Nkisi) figurines, containers that housed powerful medicines, which are known from the BaKongo people of central Africa. Minkisi could take many forms, ranging from the jarring "nail fetishes" common to museum collections to simple cloth bags.[80] The outermost form of the Nkisi may be a statue or other representation, frequently made of wood, into which the medicines have been placed; the statue, lacking the medicines, is ineffectual.[81] Although associated with the dead, this outer shell is not intended to represent the spirit that inhabited it. Rather, the appearance of the object is a physical translation of

---

80. On the Minkisi, see Z. Volavkova, "Nkisi figures of the lower Congo," *African Arts* 5, no. 2 (1972); W. MacGaffey and J. M. Janzen, "Nkisi figures of the Bakongo," *African Arts* 7, no. 3 (1974); W. MacGaffey, "Fetishism revisited: Kongo 'nkisi' in sociological perspective," *Africa: Journal of the International African Institute* 47, no. 2 (1977); MacGaffey, "Complexity, astonishment and power: The visual vocabulary of Kongo minkisi"; W. MacGaffey, "The eyes of understanding: Kongo minkisi," in *Astonishment and power,* ed. W. MacGaffey et al. (Washington, DC: Smithsonian Institution Press, 1993); J. Mack, "Fetish? Magic figures in central Africa," in *Fetishism: Visualising power and desire,* ed. A. Shelton (London: South Bank Centre, 1995).

81. MacGaffey, "Fetishism revisited: Kongo 'nkisi' in sociological perspective," 173; Mac-Gaffey, "The eyes of understanding: Kongo minkisi," 43.

Materia Magica   81

the intended effect of the Minkisi.[82] Some Minkisi may be images of dogs, monkeys, or other animals, even though the nkisi was associated with a human ancestor. The animating force of the Minkisi, and the source of its efficacy, did not lie in mimetic correspondence between the artifact and an intended target, but instead in the power of the medicines that were placed inside the image. These medicines were selected because of both physical characteristics and metaphorical concepts. So, dirt from a grave could link the Minkisi with the ancestors and the dead, but the name of a particular item also might lead to its inclusion, or an object might be incorporated because it is remarkable.[83] The Minkisi figurines are not intended to effect change through the creation of a visually similar double. Rather, metaphor, expressed through the will of the practitioner and embodied in speech, establishes a conceptual linkage between the object and the desired outcome. The magical object does not represent the victim; rather the artifact embodies the ideal, intended result.

The example of the Minkisi figurines urges us to consider the multiple ways that we might interpret a representation. For some images, function does not rely on mimetic similarities between the artifact and its prototype, and the purpose of a particular representation cannot be derived solely from its form and appearance. We can return to one of the examples cited above, the PGM spell in which the practitioner is instructed to mold a figurine of a dog out of clay. The figurine has been threaded with *ousia,* which suggests that the dog should be associated with the woman. The statuette, however, is not a representation of the victim but is instead a duplicate of one of the hounds of Hekate. The practitioner addresses the statuette in the guise of goddess, taking on a divine role in order to give directions to the image.[84] The image is supposed to perform a particular function that establishes a relationship between its component parts, the eyes of the bat, a sleepless animal, and the victim. The magician proclaims that the desired lover will be unable to sleep until she comes to the commissioner. The figurine, then, is a vehicle that translates the desires of the practitioner into physical form; its appearance is dependent on a metaphorical

---

82. See, for example, the image of Nkondi: MacGaffey, "The eyes of understanding: Kongo minkisi," 84, 90–93; for a description of Nkisi Lunkanka, see ibid., 80–86.

83. MacGaffey, "Complexity, astonishment and power," 190–92, 96; MacGaffey, "The eyes of understanding: Kongo minkisi," 62–68.

84. S. I. Johnston, *Hekate soteira: A study of Hekate's roles in the Chaldean oracles and related literature* (Atlanta: Scholars Press, 1990), 140. Compare the Eros image created as part of the Sword of Dardanos, PGM IV.1716–1820 and PGM XII (*P.Lug.Bat.* J384), in which the doll is instructed to send dreams to the beloved until she appears at the house of the commissioner.

82   Materia Magica

relationship between Hekate and the hounds that she controls. The victim is the hound, and able to be controlled because the practitioner has become like Hekate. Curse tablets, too, may work through a metaphoric congruence between object and victim, as the lead sheet shares no physical similarities with the target of the spell. The act of piercing the lead with a nail implies that the tablet was seen as a stand-in, an an-iconic copy of the individual or individuals who were cursed in the spell. The relationship between the tablet and the target was established by writing the name on the lead sheet. By puncturing the tablet, the practitioner would transfix the artifact and concurrently bind the victim.[85] A similar process was at work in Late Antique, Coptic, and even Arabic magic, where a variety of non-figurative objects, such as a potsherd, a jar, a piece of copper, or even a frog might represent the target of a spell.[86] The chosen item often engenders a metaphorical relationship between the target and the intended effect of the rite.

Both metaphor and mimesis may be at work within the same representation. In an inscribed text from Cyrene that purports to be a fourth-century copy of a sixth-century oath, the new colonial residents of Cyrene swear an vow while burning wax images in a fire, declaring, "May he who does not abide by this agreement but transgresses it melt away and dissolve like the images, himself, his seed and his property."[87] The inscription does not mention how many figurines were employed in the ritual, but it seems unlikely that each colonist was represented by a separate doll. Mimetic similarity between the images and the putative targets, the colonists, may have been limited to the rough approximation of a human form. The union between image and human counterpart is achieved through performative speech: by swearing the oath, each colonist identifies himself and his descendants with the melting image. But the outcome of the transference is integral to the functioning of the rite,

---

85. Gell, *Art and agency,* 102. For a discussion of *defixiones* and *Minkisi,* see D. Dungworth, "Mystifying Roman nails: *Clavus annalis, defixiones* and *minkisi,*" in *TRAC 97: Proceedings of the seventh annual theoretical Roman archaeology conference, which formed part of the second international Roman archaeology conference, University of Nottingham, April 1997,* ed. C. Forcey, J. Hawthorne, and R. Witcher (Oakville, CT: Oxbow Books, 1998).

86. A. Karivieri, "Magic and syncretic religious culture in the East," in *Religious diversity in Late Antiquity,* ed. D. M. Gwynn and S. Bangert, *Late Antique Archaeology 6* (Leiden: Brill, 2010), 412; N. B. Hansen, "Ancient execration magic in Coptic and Islamic Egypt," in *Magic and ritual in the ancient world,* ed. P. A. Mirecki and M. Meyer (Leiden: Brill, 2002), 432–36.

87. Meiggs and Lewis, eds., *A selection of Greek historical inscriptions to the end of the fifth century B.C.,* 5–9, no. 5; cf. Herodotus iv. 145–59. Trans. A. J. Graham, *Colony and mother city in ancient Greece,* 2nd ed. (Chicago: Ares, 1983), 226.

Materia Magica   83

as the colonists employ the images to mime what will occur if they break the oath. The residents of Cyrene are embodied within the wax images, and as they manipulate the representations, they similarly enact a horrible fate on themselves. The ritual is not intended to immediately affect those undertaking the spell; rather the rite includes a "trigger" that will only enact the punishment should they break the agreement.[88]

A single image may function on multiple levels, and it may not be clear immediately whether a representation is intended to be a mimetic copy or to serve another purpose. Moreover, the same figurine or statuette may have fulfilled multiple roles at various stages of its life history, as the function assigned to an image may change depending upon the viewer or possessor. Meticulous analysis of the artifact and its component parts can suggest a likely interpretation, and archaeological context can provide important clues for isolating why a particular figurine or statuette might be employed. In the third chapter of this book, we will encounter multiple images and representations that may have played a role in magic. A statuette of the god Harpocrates, for example, was discovered in conjunction with an ostracon that likely preserves spell instructions. It is unlikely that the figurine, which was probably mold-made, was created for use in the spell. Rather, in the course of the ritual act, the practitioner could have assigned a particular role to this image, one that was likely connected with both the mimetic character of the figurine as well as its metaphorical use, which may have brought about divine protection from the god's mother, Isis.

Plants, Animals, and Natural Ingredients

Magic could incorporate organic materials that might be manipulated or combined to produce some effect. Our knowledge of the herbs, plants, and ani-

---

88. On the Cyrene decree, see Faraone, "Molten wax, spilt wine, and mutilated animals," esp. 60–65. Similar practices can also be adduced from the Near East, as is the case in the Vassal Treaties of Esarhaddon, where the subjects of the king invoke the destruction of the gods in the case of oath-breaking. See D. J. Wiseman, "The vassal-treaties of Esarhaddon," *Iraq* 20, no. 1 (1958): 534–40; S. Parpola and K. Watanabe, *Neo-Assyrian treaties and loyalty oaths* (Helsinki: Helsinki University Press, 1988), 28–58; compare the Sefire Inscription, a mid-eighth-century Aramaic text discovered near Aleppo. Pritchard, *Ancient Near Eastern texts relating to the Old Testament,* 660, discussed in Faraone, "Molten wax, spilt wine, and mutilated animals," 63.

mals used in potions or other magical concoctions derives from a variety of sources, including Theophrastus and other authors concerned with herbal lore, encyclopedic compilers like Pliny the Elder, and magical handbooks including the Greek and Demotic Magical Papyri. Animals might be sacrificed as part of a rite to make a specific offering to a divinity or in order to harvest some body part or fluid. Plants were pounded, stewed, roasted, and even burned in their entirety. The range of organic materials that appear in the Greek Magical Papyri, for example, is astounding, and almost any naturally occurring substance seems to have been used for magic. Magic employed substances that had medicinal value; sacrifice, incense, or other inedibles typically associated with religious rituals; obscure or strange materials that were difficult to acquire; and *exuviae,* parts of human beings or their possessions that form a tangible link to the target of the spell.

Natural substances could be used medicinally when ingested or applied to the body, and Pliny frequently uses the term *magicus* to refer to plants, animals, and minerals that can affect human beings.[89] Some plants and herbs may have had pharmacological or medicinal value that was exploited, perhaps unknowingly, by the practitioner. There has been extensive research on these substances, particularly with reference to the medical function of plants and fungi.[90] Combined with other "inactive" ingredients, or employed in conjunction with incantations, petitions to divinities, or figurines and amulets, drug lore had the potential to cause actual change in the target of the spell. Finding traces of these curative or psychotropic substances in the archaeological record may be suggestive of ritual connected with medical or magical practice.[91]

Often, however, the organic materials employed in magic caused no physical change in either client or practitioner. The linkages that existed between such materials and the ritual ends to which they were put may be more difficult to grasp, as these correspondences might have existed only within the

---

89. Rives, "*Magus* and its cognates in Classical Latin," 62 and n. 28.

90. On the use of effective drugs and substances in magic, see J. Stannard, "Medicinal plants and folk remedies in Pliny, *Historia Naturalis,*" *History and Philosophy of the Life Sciences* 4, no. 1 (1982); J. Scarborough, "The pharmacology of sacred plants, herbs and roots," in *Magika hiera,* ed. C. A. Faraone and D. Obbink (New York: Oxford University Press, 1991); on herbals, see W. R. Dawson, "Studies in medical history: (a) the origin of the herbal. (b) castor-oil in antiquity," *Aegyptus* 10 (1929); L. Manniche, *An ancient Egyptian herbal* (Austin: University of Texas Press, 1989); Dieleman, *Priests, tongues, and rites,* 195–98.

91. L. R. LiDonnici, "Beans, fleawort, and the blood of a hamadryas baboon: recipe ingredients in Greco-Roman magical materials," in *Magic and ritual in the ancient world,* ed. P. A. Mirecki and M. Meyer (Leiden: Brill, 2002), 357–63.

Materia Magica 85

mind of the practitioner. Some plants or natural items may have been associated with divinities, or chosen because of similarities between the substance and its desired effect. This process can be seen in the Minkisi figurines from the BaKongo, discussed above. Metaphor often linked the medicines that animated the figurines with their intended functions. A cord, talons from a bird, or the head of a poisonous snake might be included in an Nkisi figurine that was employed to attack a victim or seek revenge, transferring the power of these animals to the object.[92] The spells of the magical papyri similarly employed metaphoric or linguistic play for magical efficacy. PGM I.262–347 instructs its user to hold a laurel sprig with seven leaves that has been inscribed with special characters before summoning a god, likely Apollo, for divinatory purposes.[93] Substances such as laurel leaves, however, present a complex problem of interpretation. Identifying a connection between these materials and ritual activity may only be possible if we possess texts that speak directly about a specific natural material, or if we can posit an association based on our knowledge of its name or other characteristics.

Perhaps due to the propensity of magic to adopt and transform the trappings of religious practice, one commonly finds reference in the papyri to offerings for divinities or the incorporation of other religious items, such as incense or an altar. The sacrifice of animals and the extraction of animal parts play a frequent role in magical activity, but the scale of sacrifice, its function, and the animals selected as gifts to the gods diverged from traditional religious observation; there is little evidence, for example, that the sacrifice of an animal in a magic rite was followed by a meal.[94] Most often, one finds the practitioner in the papyri offering a small animal or, alternatively, dedicating a part of the animal to the god. In PGM IV 2891–2942, the celebrant offers Aphrodite pellets made of fat and dove's blood.[95] Practitioners also dedicated animals that were not traditional offerings in Graeco-Roman cults, including cats, dogs, mice, lizards, or bats. It is important to note that some of these animals were sacred to Egyptian divinities and typically were mummified and offered as dedica-

---

92. MacGaffey, "Complexity, astonishment and power: The visual vocabulary of Kongo minkisi," 192.
93. Compare PGM IV.3172–3208, and discussion in LiDonnici, "Beans, fleawort, and the blood of a hamadryas baboon: Recipe ingredients in Greco-Roman magical materials," 371.
94. Johnston, "Sacrifice in the Greek magical papyri," 347; Petropoulos, "The erotic magical papyri," 34–35.
95. Johnston, "Sacrifice in the Greek magical papyri," 349.

tions to the gods at prominent shrines.[96] In PGM III 1–164, the practitioner is instructed to "make a cat divine" by drowning it in water and reciting a spell. Outside of Egypt, associations with a divinity, such as Hekate, may have led to the incorporation of an unusual sacrifice into the rite. The joined curse tablets from Aquitania, mentioned above, presumably were deposited in association with a puppy that may have been sacrificed as part of the rite.[97] At Dorchester, England (ancient Durnovaria), excavators discovered a series of nineteen pits with layers of whole ceramic vessels, personal items, and animal bones, including remains from dogs, puppies, sheep, and birds, particularly ravens, crows, and jackdaws. The pits may have been used for foundation rites that were associated with the goddess Hekate and the appeasement of the dead.[98] The discovery of animal remains in archaeological contexts may suggest a variety of proximate causes—that the animal was eaten as part of a meal, that its body parts were used for some utilitarian purpose, or that it was employed in a rite. Much as in the case of artifacts, close analysis of faunal remains may permit the investigator to determine, for example, if the animal was butchered or deposited whole.

Other artifacts and substances traditionally associated with religious expression find their way into magical practices, although these may occur in miniaturized or contracted form.[99] Frankincense, myrrh, and aromatics were burned as part of magical rites, particularly those associated with the visitations of deities.[100] In the spells of the magical papyri, however, the rituals often require only a small amount of the substance, such as a lump of incense or a

---

96. Individual animals and their roles in magic and religion have been the subject of articles and monographs: H. H. Scholz, *Der Hund in der griechisch-römischen Magie und Religion* (Berlin: Triltsch & Huther, 1937); W. R. Dawson, "The mouse in Egyptian and later medicine," *JEA* 10, no. 2 (1924); A. D. Nock, "The lizard in magic and religion," in *Essays on religion and the ancient world,* ed. Z. Stewart (Cambridge: Harvard University Press, 1972). On animal mummification, see S. Ikram, *Divine creatures: Animal mummies in ancient Egypt* (Cairo: American University in Cairo Press, 2004); D. Kessler, *Die Heiligen Tiere und der König* (Wiesbaden: Otto Harrassowitz, 1989).

97. Bailliot suggests that sacrifice may have been a common element in cursing. *Magie et sortilèges dans l'Antiquité romaine,* 98–101.

98. P. Woodward and A. Woodward, "Dedicating the town: Urban foundation deposits in Roman Britain," *World Archaeology* 36, no. 1 (2004): 72–77, 83–84 and figs. 2 and 3; J. Rykwert, *The idea of a town: The anthropology of urban form in Rome, Italy and the ancient world* (Princeton: Princeton University Press, 1976), 66.

99. Smith, "Trading places," 23–25.

100. LiDonnici, "Beans, fleawort, and the blood of a hamadryas baboon: Recipe ingredients in Greco-Roman magical materials," 362.

Materia Magica 87

part of the animal. The miniaturization of religious materials also could take the form of small altars on which sacrifices were made, as well as little shrines or statuettes of divinities.[101] Small size does not, however, imply that the rites were any less potent, and indeed, as S. Stewart notes, reduction in size is often accompanied by a sharpening of certain details, as choices are made regarding which features might encapsulate the larger idea.[102] Religious elements effectively brought interaction with divinities out of the temple—where the access of the layperson was sharply limited—and into the domestic sphere, where the majority of magical activities took place.[103] This appropriation of religious features, including the sacrifice or dedication of animals, was not intended to reverse or distort traditional religious practices but was the result of extrapolation or modification on the part of the practitioner. Magical offerings may isolate important elements of a sacrifice, perhaps through miniaturization, or they may adapt the tenets of sacrificial practice to a new situation.[104] Such mainstays of traditional religion were appropriated by magical practice to lend a patina of sanctification to rite.[105] Perhaps of equal importance, incense, sacrifice, and other religious trappings were part of the socially determined structures within which humans contacted the supernatural; practitioners, like priests, may have chosen to address the divine by means of well-established pathways.

Beyond the realm of recognizable and relatively commonplace objects and materials, one moves into the category of the truly "weird"—strange substances that were obscure, difficult to acquire, and often repulsive. In PGM IV. 2943–66, the practitioner is told to insert the eyes of a bat, extracted from the living animal, into the figurine of the dog. Strange materials are a key element of magic, and literary references are filled with allusions to unusual plants, animal parts, and bodily products. In Horace's *Epodes* and *Satires,* the witches Canidia and Sagana employ a wolf's beard and a tooth from a variegated snake (1.8), and burn "wild fig trees, funereal cypresses, eggs pasted with the blood of a foul frog, a feather of the nocturnal screech owl, herbs which Iolchus and Iberia, fertile in poisons, export, and bones snatched from the mouth of a

---

101. Smith, "Trading places," 24.
102. Stewart, *On longing: Narratives of the miniature, the gigantic, the souvenir, the collection,* 44, 54. Frankfurter, *Religion in Roman Egypt.* 140–42.
103. Graf, "Prayer in magic and religious ritual," 195.
104. Johnston, "Sacrifice in the Greek magical papyri," 347–48. Inversion was certainly important to magical practice, but defamation was not the primary goal of such rites.
105. Ibid., 347; LiDonnici, "Beans, fleawort, and the blood of a hamadryas baboon: Recipe ingredients in Greco-Roman magical materials," 362.

ravening dog" (*Epodes* 5).[106] Apuleius, in the *Apology*, is accused of seeking out a rare kind of fish that was not available at the local market, and it is the distinctiveness of his shopping list that is cause for the accusation of magic. The magical papyri specify a wide variety of extraordinary goods, sometimes requesting materials from specific geographic regions.[107] Even normal substances and objects can be weird because they have been displaced and taken out of their appropriate spaces; bones removed from a grave, for example, arouse a sense of wrongness.[108] Indeed, in some cases, commonplace items could be made unusual through performative utterances that expressed the practitioner's understanding of an object. The Minkisi figurines mentioned above provide a cross-cultural example of this, but we can see a similar process of alteration at work in the magical papyri. According to PGM IV.2967–3006, when acquiring herbs, Egyptians invoke the name of the god to whom the plant will be dedicated, thereby increasing the efficacy of the object in the later rite; an all-purpose invocation then follows.

The PGM IV text involving the creation of a figurine of a dog also contains a curious feature: the practitioner is instructed to thread a needle with *ousia* (l. 2949) and stick it into the eye of the dog. *Ousia* is translated as "magical material," and the term is often used to refer to cast-off parts of a human body— hair, nails, or other corporeal parts, but also clothing or personal effects.[109] In the context of magic, *ousia* could be used to direct the force of a spell against a particular individual, affecting them at a distance through the use of a nearby fragment of their personhood.[110] Parts of a victim, like a representation, can establish a connection with the real individual or object, distributed in the world and separate from the original owner.[111] Indeed, this appears to be how

---

106. Trans. D. Ogden, *Magic, witchcraft, and ghosts in the Greek and Roman worlds: A sourcebook* (Oxford: Oxford University Press, 2002), 117.
107. LiDonnici, "Beans, fleawort, and the blood of a hamadryas baboon: Recipe ingredients in Greco-Roman magical materials," 363–64.
108. Frankfurter, "Fetus magic and sorcery fears in Roman Egypt," 14–18.
109. On *ousia*, see T. Hopfner, *Griechisch-ägyptischer Offenbarungszauber. Mit einer eingehenden Darstellung des griechisch-synkretistischen Daemonenglaubens und der Voraussetzungen und Mittel des Zaubers überhaupt und der magischen Divination im besonderen* (Amsterdam: A. M. Hakkert, 1921), 401–8; Jordan, "Defixiones from a well near the southwest corner of the Athenian Agora," 251.
110. Compare Frazer's concept of contagion: Frazer, *The golden bough: A study in magic and religion*, 12. In each of Frazer's examples, however, *exuviae* are used in connection with images or other representations, so that magical material acts to cement the correspondence between the imperfect copy and the victim of the spell. Taussig, *Mimesis and alterity*, 55.
111. Gell, *Art and agency*, 104.

exuviae are conceptualized in the ancient world, as another means by which the practitioner might control or affect the victim; a part stands in for the whole.

Often used in conjunction with other ingredients, *ousia* appear frequently in literary portrayals of magic as a vital component in assuring the affections of a victim. Lucian, in the *Dialogues of the Courtesans* 4, for example, includes a witch who, when asked about retrieving an errant lover, requires "one of the man's possessions, clothes, boots, some hairs, or some such thing."[112] Simaetha, in Theocritus's *Idyll* II, written centuries earlier, anticipates Lucian's instructions, as she burns part of the cloak of her lover, Delphis, in order to draw her lover home. The use of such cast-off leavings of potential lovers does appear to have been practiced in antiquity, as a number of curse tablets attest. D. Jordan reports damage caused by human hair, as well as a few remaining strands, on the interior of a lead tablet deposited in a well in the Athenian Agora; he suggests that the tablet was a love spell.[113] Human hair also was discovered in PGM XVI, an enacted erotic spell on papyrus that had been folded up into a small packet. *Suppl. Mag.* I 49, one of the lead tablets from Oxyrhynchus related to the Wonderful Love Spell discussed in chapter 1 refers to *ousia* that was included with the artifacts (l. 4).[114]

Even cursory examination of ancient records of magical practice in literature and the papyri reveals that almost any organic material could be employed in a rite. Finding these naturally occurring ingredients in the archaeological record, and associating them with magic, however, is a complicated endeavor. Organic matter decays quickly in the soil, and it is highly unlikely that this material would survive from antiquity in any but the most arid or wet conditions, as one might encounter in the desert regions of Egypt or a British bog. For the majority of the Roman Mediterranean—even if we could determine which materials might be included in magic—it may be nearly impossible to reconstruct the presence of such items in the archaeological record. There are a number of welcome exceptions, and in some cases, ritual activity may act to preserve material that would otherwise be lost. For example, organic material that has been burned may survive as carbonized remains. Advances in recovery techniques such as soil flotation have permitted archaeologists to discover

---

112. Trans. K. Sidwell in *Chattering courtesans and other sardonic sketches* (London: Penguin Books, 2004), 163.
113. For discussion, see Jordan, "Defixiones from a well near the southwest corner of the Athenian Agora," 251.
114. See above, ch. 1 n. 67, for full citation and discussion.

90 Materia Magica

many more seeds, pollen, and other organic traces. The discovery of these kinds of remains in contemporary fieldwork can allow scholars to reconstruct the presence of organic materials that may have been incorporated into ancient rites. In the recent excavations at the Sanctuary of Isis and Magna Mater at Mainz, for example, a small clay figurine was found in association with an oil lamp, a lead curse tablet, fruit pips, and a miniature pot; the fruit pips may indicate that organic matter was deposited with the material or consumed in this space as part of the rite.[115] While there are a number of categories that may suggest magical activity—religious materials, substances with pharmacological value, and certain sacrificed animals—the mere presence of such items in isolation is not sufficient to deduce the existence of magic. Rather, only the amalgamation of such organic matter and other materials, discovered in the same archaeological context, can permit us to suggest that magic has occurred.

Household Objects Repurposed for Magical Use

The instructions from the Greek Magical Papyri for the creation of the little dog require that the practitioner use a number of household items in the performance of the rite. The magician should thread the magical material onto a needle, he is told to tie a strip of papyrus to the dog, and he should place the figurine in a new drinking vessel. Each of these objects is innocuous and could be found in almost any home in Graeco-Roman Egypt. Although the cup may have been purchased for use in the rite (the instructions specify that the vessel be new), there is no indication that any of these materials would have been specifically made for the ritual. Rather, these are all commonplace items that have been repurposed for the magical act. At the conclusion of the rite, the dog, the cup, and the papyrus are buried at a crossroads. The needle, however, may return to normal use, as there is nothing in the spell instructions that specifies that it should be discarded or buried with the other objects. Each of these items moves into and out of ritual space.[116] Ritual empowers normal objects, transforming them into powerful artifacts. This use of everyday items is not limited

---

115. M. Witteyer, "Curse tablets and voodoo dolls from Mainz: The archaeological evidence for magical practices in the Sanctuary of Isis and Magna Mater," *MHNH* 5 (2005): 111.
116. Durkheim, *The elementary forms of the religious life,* 261; Walker and Lucero, "The depositional history of ritual and power," 133; Walker, "Ritual technology in an extranatural world," 88.

Materia Magica   91

to this spell, as literary portrayals of magicians as well as the instructions of the PGM include instances where commonplace artifacts are bent to the service of magic. A comparable example again can be found among the Minkisi figurines, where the Nkisi is only a statue until it has been empowered by medicines.[117] Indeed, household objects often find a role in magic cross-culturally, as items that are close at hand frequently become endowed with ritual potential or power by practitioners.[118]

One of the most common objects required by the spells of the Greek Magical Papyri is a lamp, and often, particularly in the case of beneficial spells, the instructions specify "a lamp, not painted red."[119] In the Egyptian context, this requirement is likely due to negative associations between the color red and evil, particularly with respect to the god Seth.[120] In a divination spell at PGM VII.540–78, for example, a lamp that is not colored red is used to request the presence of a divinity. The lamps used in the rites could be purchased or made for the occasion, or part of the accoutrements of the household. In order to appear to someone in their dreams, the text at PGM VIII.407–10 requires a lamp that is in daily use.[121] In these spells, lamps may serve to light the way for the divinity, and the movement of the flame may indicate when the god is present. What is important to note, however, is that there is little to distinguish the lamps that might be used in a magic ritual from other lamps sold at a local emporium.

Outside of Egypt, lamps frequently appear in ritual contexts, where they were deposited as votives in sanctuaries or employed in funerary rites. Perhaps not surprisingly, we also find lamps used in magic. The fountain of Anna Perenna in Rome, excavated between 1999 and 2000, provides a recently discovered group of artifacts that have been repurposed for use in magic. In the late Republic, the fountain served as a shrine to Anna Perenna, a goddess associated with early Roman religion. The shrine appears to have gone out of use by the reign of Theodosius I, but in the final years of pagan activity at the site, it served as a space for the deposition of curse tablets and binding figurines that had been enclosed in small, round canisters similar to miniatur-

---

117. MacGaffey, "The eyes of understanding: Kongo minkisi," 90–98.
118. Walker, "Where are the witches of prehistory?" 246–51.
119. S.v. "Lamps, not painted red," in *GMP*, 336.
120. Ritner, *The mechanics of ancient Egyptian magical practice,* 147 and n. 663; compare F. L. Griffith and H. Thompson, *The demotic magical papyrus of London and Leiden* (Milan: Istituto editoriale Cisalpino-La goliardica, 1976), 44–45, note to l. 4.
121. The language might suggest that the spell should be undertaken daily. *GMP*, 128 n. 54.

ized funerary urns.[122] The majority of the curse tablets—there were twenty-two in all—were discovered in the basin, but six were found placed within the nozzle of an unused lamp, as if it were the wick.[123] While lamps occasionally may have been used as a surface for inscribing a curse, the presence of these artifacts as vehicles for the tablets suggests that they served an important function within the spell. As Attilo Mastrocinque notes, even some of the lamps that lack associated tablets may have been used as curses, even though these were uninscribed. In the Athenian Agora, as well, lamps and curse tablets were discovered in pits, suggesting that at these locations, the lamps may have been used to bind an enemy.[124] In each of these examples, the lamps were new, or only used once, as they show few traces of burning.

Like the organic materials discussed above, artifacts intended for another use but repurposed for magic do not, on their own, indicate that a magical rite has occurred. If discovered in the course of an excavation, these objects would be regarded as typical domestic items and would not be identified as components of a ritual. An investigator could only suggest an association with magical practice if these objects had been manipulated in some way, perhaps by an inscription, or through intentional breakage. Almost any commonplace item, from cookpots to lamps or needles, however, may be suborned into magical use, and this is particularly the case when the practitioner required objects or artifacts to achieve a relatively mundane task as part of the rite. In the example from the Greek Magical Papyri, the practitioner was instructed to place the magical material within the eye of the bat, and a logical way to do this might be to thread it through the eye using a needle. The practitioner may have had a needle in his tool kit, but it is just as likely that a commonplace domestic item would have been appropriated for use in the spell. Such an object may not have had an intrinsic ritual character, but for the duration of the rite, the needle would have been an accoutrement of magic. The brief period in which the needle was employed in the rite may not have left traces on the artifact; follow-

---

122. For the bibliography on Anna Perenna, see above, ch. 1 n. 125.

123. Mastrocinque, "Late Antique lamps with defixiones," 87–88. Piranomonte, "Religion and magic at Rome: The fountain of Anna Perenna," 203–4.

124. H. A. Thompson, "Activities in the Athenian Agora: 1959," *Hesperia* 29, no. 4 (1960): 159. Mastrocinque, "Late Antique lamps with defixiones," 91–93, 96. Wells associated with curse tablets are listed in Jordan, "Defixiones from a well near the southwest corner of the Athenian Agora," 209–10. Most notable is Agora Well IV, which contained two lamps and forty-four *defixiones*: J. Perlzweig, *Lamps of the Roman period, first to seventh century after Christ* (Princeton, NJ: American School of Classical Studies at Athens, 1961), J 12.2, IL 64-IL 107.

ing the rite, this object may have returned to its customary use. And indeed, if such an object were discovered, it might not be possible to determine from the artifact if it had been used in such a manner. Rather, it is only through association with other objects that the needle might be seen as magical.

Context and Magic

This chapter has suggested that a variety of materials could be employed in a magical act: inscribed objects, figurines and other representations, *exuviae,* naturally occurring materials, and household or domestic items. The categories of *materia magica* often overlap, as the practitioner might write on bay leaves as part of the spell or place *ousia* within a three-dimensional image in order to associate it with the victim of the spell. Indeed, a ritual enactment may have incorporated a variety of substances in order to produce the desired outcome. The spell from the PGM, for example, required additional materials in addition to a representation of a dog, and the spell was only effective through the combination of organic substances, household objects, and the statuette. Although the identification of magic may be predicated on a single, unusual object, it is necessary to analyze and study other associated materials, as these also may have been integral to the performance. Investigators can identify and reconstruct ritual activity through a close analysis of archaeological context, which encompasses potentially magical artifacts, their associated finds, and the circumstances of deposition.

Archaeological context—that is, the physical space in which objects are found—can tell us about how an object was used, and suggest which artifacts might be related. Leone and Fry were able to identify groups of artifacts as conjure rather than debris because the archaeological context indicated intentional deposition. The question of intentionality, however, is difficult to answer with certainty. Close analysis of stratigraphy can permit the investigator to reconstruct the way artifacts entered the soil. As was discussed in the previous chapter, finding items in significant locations, including graves, sacred spaces, or places pertinent to a potential victim, may increase the likelihood that an artifact has been placed in a location intentionally. Textual sources, either those that are inscribed on the artifact itself or ones associated with the local geographic context, such as the Greek and Demotic Magical Papyri, can provide further evidence that an accretion of material was not random, but rather was deliberate. By fully assessing the material evidence within its local and regional environment, it is possible to reconstruct the most likely scenario by which a group of associated finds entered the archaeological record, and to determine whether a magical performance was the reason for deposition.

At each site under investigation in this book, reconstructing the archaeological context of artifacts associated with magic permits a fuller analysis of both the role of the individual item within its excavation unit and of magical activity in its broader social environment. The next chapter will turn to the first of three case studies, the material from the site of Karanis in the Egyptian Fayum. The investigation of magic at Karanis is dependent on the Greek and Demotic Magical Papyri, a body of evidence that is specific to Graeco-Roman Egypt. This textual material provides a framework within which the excavation data from the site can be investigated and reinterpreted. Unusual material and inscribed artifacts can point us toward the practice of magic at the local level, as we assess the finds that were associated with individual rooms or areas on the site. By closely analyzing the archaeological context of these objects, we can determine first whether these artifacts reveal the existence of ritual activity and second how the enactment of ritual fits into and was received by the community at large. Karanis offers an opportunity to identify magic, given the settlement's rich archaeological heritage and its place within the textually rich environment of Egypt. The other two focal points of this book, Amathous and Empúries, present different cultural frameworks and distinct sources of data, but the investigative method with which we will approach the Egyptian material also may be applied to questions asked of other regions of the Mediterranean.

Chapter 3

Identifying the Remains of Magic in the Village of Karanis

An Official Accusation of Magic

Magic was alive and well in the villages of the Roman empire. Our sources point to the rural town as a place where spells and curses lurked around every corner. We can well imagine village grandmothers curling fingers around thumbs to avoid the evil eye or swarthy foreigners enchanting young women by more than their good looks. For Egypt and rest of the Mediterranean, there are a few tantalizing anecdotes about magic at the village level, such as the fantastic (yet fictional) tales preserved in Apuleius's *Metamorphosis* or the inscription that thanks Jupiter Optimus Maximus for his assistance in locating the curses that had been cast against local officials. Surprisingly, we possess one documented case of magical attack against a local man from the village of Karanis.

Sometime in the spring of 197 CE, Gemellus, who is also known as Horion and Gaius Julius Horigenes, ran into trouble with one Sotas and his brother Julius, two sons of Eudas.[1] Gemellus possessed only one eye and saw poorly

---

1. *P.Mich.* VI 422 and *P.Mich.* VI 423–24 (duplicates). Original publication: *P.Mich.* VI pp.117–25. Discussion: H. I. Bell, review of *Papyri and Ostraca from Karanis* by Herbert C. Youtie and Orsamus M. Pearl, *JRS* 35 (1945): 40; N. Lewis, *Life in Egypt under Roman rule* (Oxford: Clarendon Press, 1983), 78–79; J.-J. Aubert, "Threatened wombs: Aspects of ancient uterine magic," *GRBS* 30, no. 3 (1989): 437–38; *Women and society in Greek and Roman Egypt: A sourcebook,* ed. J. Rowlandson (New York: Cambridge University Press, 1998), 141–43; T. Derda, *Arsinoites nomos: Administration of the Fayum under Roman rule* (Warsaw: Faculty of Law and Administration of Warsaw University, 2006), 208; Frankfurter, "Fetus magic and sorcery fears in Roman Egypt"; A. Z. Bryen and A. Wypustek, "Gemellus' evil eyes (*P.Mich.* VI 423–24)," *GRBS* 49, no. 4 (2009). The archive of Gaius Apolinarius

out of the other; he often made reference to his disability in his correspondence with the authorities.[2] It was during the sowing season that the initial conflict transpired. The brothers entered Gemellus's property and, according to the text, hindered him through the power that they exercised in the vicinity. The conflict was presumably over landownership, as Gemellus is careful to inform the prefect to whom the petition is addressed that he had inherited the property of his father and uncle without "opposition from anyone" (ll. 12–13; 19–20).

We do not know the outcome of this initial petition, but Sotas soon died (presumably an unrelated event), and Julius, his brother, continued the family feud. During the harvest season, Julius forcibly entered Gemellus's fields and took the agricultural produce that was awaiting collection. In a petition to the local authorities, Gemellus records what followed:

> To Hierax also called Nemesion, strategos of the division of Herakleides of the Arsinoite nome, from Gemellus also called Horion, son of Gaius Apolinarius, Antinoite. I appealed, my lord, by petition to the most illustrious prefect, Aemilius Saturninus, informing him of the attack made upon me by a certain Sotas, who held me in contempt because of my weak vision and wished himself to get possession of my property with violence and arrogance, and I received his sacred subscription authorizing me to appeal to his excellency the epistrategos. Then Sotas died and his brother Julius, also acting with the violence characteristic of them, entered the fields that I had sown and carried away a substantial quantity of hay; not only that, but he also cut dried olive shoots and heath plants from my olive grove near the village of Kerkesoucha. When I came there at the time of the harvest, I learned that he had committed these transgressions. In addition, not content, he again trespassed with his wife and a certain Zenas, having with them a *brephos* (βρέφος), intending to hem in my cultivator with malice (βουλόμενοι τὸν γεωργόν μου φθώνῳ περικλῖσαι) so that he should abandon his labor after having harvested in part from another

---

Niger is discussed in I. Biezunska-Malowist, "La famille du vétéran romain C. Iulius Niger de Karanis," *Eos* 49 (1957); R. Alston, *Soldier and society in Roman Egypt: A social history* (New York: Routledge, 1995), 129–32.

2. In *P.Mich.* VI 425, Gemellus claims that he was the victim of violence by a tax collector because of his impaired vision; the man, Kastor, destroyed the doors to Gemellus's home and beat both him and his mother. This loss of sight may have affected Gemellus's ability to write; although his father and grandfather were literate, a number of the documents related to Gemellus are signed by another on his behalf. *P.Mich.* VI 423 and 424, copies of the petition regarding the *brephos* and dated to 197 CE, are signed by Gemellus; SB IV 7360 (214 CE); *P.Mich.* VI 422 (also 197 CE) and 425 (198) are signed by another.

Identifying the Remains of Magic in the Village of Karanis   97

allotment of mine, and they themselves gathered in the crops. When this happened, I went to Julius in the company of officials, in order that these matters might be witnessed. Again, in the same manner, they threw the same *brephos* toward me, intending to hem me in also with malice (βουλόμενοι καί με φθώνῳ περικλῖσαι), in the presence of Petesouchos and Ptollas, elders of the village of Karanis who are exercising also the functions of the village secretary, and of Sokras the assistant, and while the officials were there, Julius, after he had gathered in the remaining crops from the fields, took the *brephos* away to his house. These acts I made matters of public record through the same officials and the collectors of grain taxes of the same village. Wherefore of necessity I submit this petition and request that it be kept on file so that I may retain the right to plead against them before his excellency the epistrategos concerning the outrages perpetrated by them and the public rents of the fields due to the imperial fiscus because they wrongfully did the harvesting.

(2nd hand) Gemellus also called Horion, about 26 years of age, whose vision is impaired.

(3rd hand) The 5th year of Lucius Septimius Severus Pius Pertinax Augustus, Pachon 27.[3]

We cannot be certain where the fields were located, although some were presumably the same holdings that were disputed in *P.Mich.* VI 422, in which Gemellus lists the theft of grain from a field and separately mentions damage to his olive groves near Kerkesoucha. The village elders who accompany Gemellus during a later incident are all from Karanis, where the papyri were found. Although the opening of the passage seems rather ordinary—a dispute over land with overtones of violence—the text quickly veers into the realm of the unusual. We learn that Julius, his wife, and a man named Zenas had brought a curious object that is described as a *brephos* in the petition. This *brephos* was intended to "hem in (Gemellus's) cultivator with malice." When used, this object somehow forced the cultivator to abandon his work, although the exact mechanism is not stated. Julius, his wife, and Zenas were able to collect the newly harvested grain and abscond with it. Gemellus heard of these events and promptly rushed to the scene along with three village officials, the elders Petesouhos and Ptollas and their assistant Sokras, all of whom could act as witnesses. Julius appeared not to be perturbed by the appearance of the

---

3.   Trans. Youtie and Pearl, *P.Mich.* VI, pp. 125–26.

98   Materia Magica

authorities, and, as Gemellus tells it, threw the *brephos* again. Once more, the object was intended to prevent and did successfully prevent Gemellus and the authorities from halting the theft; the three perpetrators were able to gather up the grain and flee. According to the report, Julius picked up the *brephos* and took it back to his house, presumably to be used another time. Here the petition ends; Gemellus states that he wishes to enter these events into the public record so that he can plead against them and be exempted from the rents that are due on the property. We do not know the final result of the complaint, but in a later document, dated to 207 CE, Julius appears as a tenant farmer on Gemellus's land, suggesting that some sort of resolution had occurred.[4]

The term chosen by Gemellus to describe the object—a *brephos*—is significant, as it provides a relatively precise description of what was shown to and subsequently cast at Gemellus and his companions. An uncommon word in Greek, *brephos* can refer to a fetus or baby, or the offspring of an animal. We should not assume that Gemellus, whose poor eyesight is well documented, misidentified the object, as both the cultivator and his companions agreed with this characterization. While Gemellus may have used the term *brephos* to refer to another object, such as a doll or a small statuette, this seems less likely since *brephos* is such an uncommon word. Alternatively, Gemellus may have misidentified something that Julius carried—perhaps a doll or another wrapped item—as a fetus. If so, this does not have a sizable effect on how we are to read the incident, as Gemellus understood the object carried by Julius, regardless of what it might have been, to act just as a fetus would have with the result that he and his companions were bound.

There are no other attested cases of fetus-throwing in the documentary record of Karanis or any other town in Egypt, and locating references to the use of fetuses in sorcery is equally problematic. The spell texts of the PGM, which are not averse to requiring practitioners to use strange or macabre materials, contain no overt references to employing a fetus or a young animal in a magical rite. A fetus appears as part of a slander spell, PGM IV.2441–2621, which charges a victim with having burned the magical material of a dog and a woman's embryo as a sacrifice, but this is a spurious accusation, rather than an actual ingredient list. Its purpose is to draw the anger of the goddess Selene against the victim, to whom it imputes these forbidden and grotesque actions.[5]

---

4.   PGM VI.398, with discussion at Bryen and Wypustek, "Gemellus' evil eyes (*P.Mich.* VI 423–24)," 554–55.

5.   Frankfurter, "Fetus magic and sorcery fears in Roman Egypt," 53–54.

Identifying the Remains of Magic in the Village of Karanis 99

Outside of the magical papyri, Pliny the Elder (28.20.1) includes an obscure reference to cutting up stillborn babies or aborted fetuses for malicious purposes, but characteristically does not explain what these rites might entail, or for what purposes they were enacted.[6]

The text is striking because neither Gemellus, nor his cultivator, nor the elders of Karanis hesitate to recognize the *brephos* as an object of power or to know how this object was supposed to work. The text does not specify whether the *brephos* was marked with sorcerous symbols that would permit the victims to recognize its magical nature. We know that the item was small: it could be carried, thrown, and then picked up again, and it was sufficiently visible to be identified as a *brephos* rather than some other small object. The sight of the *brephos,* or being in close physical proximity to it, was enough to cause a malign reaction. It is unclear whether throwing the object was necessary to its efficacy, but this was surely perceived as an aggressive act.[7] Casting the *brephos* would have brought the object closer to the victims, permitting them to see it clearly and allowing the object to exert its power through proximity. Moreover, the complaint does not relate to the possession of such an object—Gemellus does not ask the authorities to seize the *brephos* as an illegal and inappropriate possession—but instead on the manner in which this artifact was used. Julius had acted with violence and arrogance when he brandished and threw the *brephos.*

In each instance, the object produced an effect similar that of a curse tablet, binding the victim and preventing him or her from halting the theft.[8] This

---

6. W. B. McDaniel, "The medical and magical significance in ancient medicine of things connected with reproduction and its organs," *JHM* 3, no. 4 (1948): 531–32.

7. A possible parallel for throwing the *brephos,* cited by Bryen and Wapustek, is PDM xiv.451–58 / PGM XIVb.12–15, in which the practitioner states that he is carrying the mummy of Osiris to Abydos. He threatens that he will (προσ<τ>ρέψω) throw the mummy of Osiris at or turn it toward his adversary, who is a superior. In the Egyptian text, however, the practitioner threatens to discard the mummy, rather than throw it. Dieleman (127–30) notes that the text demonstrates a clear understanding of Egyptian religious topography, most notably at Abydos. Despite this cultural familiarity with Egypt, which would suggest that the Demotic text takes precedence, Dieleman demonstrates that the Greek version was the original one. In this context, the act of throwing or showing an object may be significant, but it seems that the Demotic spell, as it is preserved, was spoken only, as instructions are included to speak the spell seven times; no indication of an accompanying action is recorded, but the injunction that the spell is to be spoken is also absent from the Greek version. Throwing is attested in love magic, where apples (and pomegranates) are tossed at prospective victims; these were intended to strike the target and induce erotic attraction. See *Suppl. Mag.* no. 72, col. 8. 5–14; Faraone, *Ancient Greek love magic,* 69–78.

8. Frankfurter, "Fetus magic and sorcery fears in Roman Egypt," 40.

100   Materia Magica

result—binding—is familiar, and frequently associated with magic, but the method by which the power object was utilized, as well as its public display, diverges sharply from our expectations. Gemellus, in describing the effect of the *brephos,* twice uses the same phrase: φθόνῳ περικλῖσαι, it enclosed or confined (περικλῖσαι) the victims through (or with) envy, spite, or malice (φθόνῳ). Pharaonic magic often incorporated encircling as a means of gaining power over a target, sometimes for aggressive ends.[9] In the Graeco-Roman context, *phthonos* is a significant term, as it is used often in conjunction with harmful or malicious envy, particularly that associated with the evil eye.[10] Bryen and Wypustek have suggested that Julius, the putative aggressor, believes that Gemellus possesses the evil eye, and therefore, the fetus is intended to avert the power of Gemellus's one-eyed gaze, while also publicly challenging his social better in the ongoing conflict over land rights.[11] While this is a compelling suggestion, the document that we possess has been composed for Gemellus and presumably reflects his interpretation of events. Gemellus's identification of the effect of the *brephos*—that it hemmed in both himself and his companions with *phthonos*—would be disadvantageous; the implication would be that Gemellus possessed the power of the evil eye, which would make Julius's actions necessary. Rather, we should understand *phthonos* as Gemellus's interpretation of Julius's motivation: Julius had entered Gemellus's fields and revealed a grotesque and powerful object on account of his (Julius's) violent envy, a jealousy that had a magical effect on his adversaries.

The efficacy of the *brephos* is tied to its appearance, both through its physical form and its revelation. Images that are used for apotropaic purposes often incorporate the shocking or grotesque in order to both repulse and attract,

---

9. Ritner, *The mechanics of ancient Egyptian magical practice,* 57–67, esp. 64–66.

10. On *phthonos,* see P. Walcot, *Envy and the Greeks: A study of human behavior* (Warminster: Aris & Phillips, 1978); M. W. Dickie, "Lo φθόνος degli dei nella letteratura greca del quinto secolo avanti Christo," *A&R* 32, no. 113–25 (1987); M. W. Dickie, "Heliodorus and Plutarch on the evil eye," *CPh* 86, no. 1 (1991); Y. Yatromanolakis, "*Baskanos eros:* Love and the evil eye in Heliodorus' *Aethiopica*," in *The Greek novel, AD 1–1985,* ed. R. Beaton (London: Croom Helm, 1988); K. M. D. Dunbabin and M. W. Dickie, "Invidia rumpantur pectora: The iconography of phthonos/invidia in Graeco-Roman Art," *Jahrbuch für Antike und Christentum* 26 (1983); C. A. Barton, *The sorrows of the ancient Romans: The gladiator and the monster* (Princeton: Princeton University Press, 1993), 91–95; R. Schlesier, "Zauber und Neid: Zum Problem des bösen Blicks in der antiken griechischen Tradition," in *Tradition und Translation: zum Problem der interkulturellen Übersetzbarkeit religiöser Phänomene: Festschrift für Carsten Colpe zum 65. Geburtstag,* ed. C. Elsas and C. Colpe (New York: De Gruyter, 1994).

11. Bryen and Wypustek, "Gemellus' evil eyes (*P.Mich.* VI 423–24)," 551–55.

Identifying the Remains of Magic in the Village of Karanis   101

and to cause fascination in the viewer.[12] The target of the apotropaic image—
the threatening force—might be threatened in turn by a representation that
is frightening to the image's creator, or the possession of such a comparably
threatening image might put the threat to flight.[13] The effect on the targets of
the *brephos* is just this—first the cultivator, and subsequently Gemellus and the
elders of Karanis, are entranced and turned away from their intended actions.

While investigations at Karanis have not (yet) uncovered fetal remains—
whether from the home of Julius or not—archaeological excavation has found
a fetus that may have been employed in a ritual act. In 1993, excavation at
the site of Kellis, located in the Dakleh oasis to the west of the Nile Valley,
revealed a tightly wrapped fetus that was found in the collapsed debris of a
house. David Frankfurter, who published this artifact, has suggested that it
was used as a power object, deriving its force though removal from its right-
ful place in a garbage dump and its subsequent linkage with impurity through
this displacement.[14] The manner in which the artifact was constructed—tightly
wrapped in linen bandages in a haphazard function and subsequently encircled
multiple times with a length of twine—differs from the traditional manner in
which mummified remains, even those of fetuses or infants, are prepared for
burial. This special treatment suggests that it was intended to bind or otherwise
bewitch the structure and its inhabitants.[15]

Magical practice at Karanis, as at Kellis, involved the production of objects
that reflect a local conception of how magic should look. This is not, however, a ritual creation *ex nihilo,* in which Julius, or some practitioner working
on his behalf, decided that a *brephos* would be an appropriate tool in magic.
Rather, the *brephos* represents a form of adaptation and innovation within
the set parameters of magic as it was understood in each community. The

---

12. Mitchell, *Picture theory: Essays on verbal and visual representation,* 82.

13. Faraone, "Talismans and Trojan horses: Guardian statues in ancient Greek myth and ritual,"
    36–48; E. H. Gombrich, *The sense of order: A study in the psychology of decorative art,* 2nd
    ed. (Oxford: Phaidon Press, 1984), 261. The gorgon's head was one of the most common apo-
    tropaic images in ancient Greece and can serve as a basic example of the type. On gorgoneia
    as apotropaic images, see Bailliot, *Magie et sortilèges dans l'Antiquité romaine,* 50–53; J. D.
    Belson, "The gorgoneion in Greek architecture" (PhD diss., Bryn Mawr College, 1981), 217;
    B. S. Ridgway, *The archaic style in Greek sculpture* (Princeton: Princeton University Press,
    1977), 193.

14. Frankfurter, "Fetus magic and sorcery fears in Roman Egypt," 51, 54. On impurity, see R.
    Parker, *Miasma: Pollution and purification in early Greek religion* (Oxford: Oxford Univer-
    sity Press, 1983), 60, n. 67.

15. Frankfurter, "Fetus magic and sorcery fears in Roman Egypt," 43–45.

brephos, because it had been removed from its appropriate place, was considered impure, grotesque, and, counterintuitively, powerful. Its force lies within the way in which such impure and grotesque objects could function in magic, as either components within compounds meant to draw the ire of divinities through their inappropriateness, or as apotropaic mechanisms, intended to avert or repel a perceived threat. Gemellus, his cultivator, and his companions react to this *brephos* in a prescriptive way—they are bound and deprived of individual agency. Furthermore, the effect of the *brephos* is described in terms that are related to magic—the power object is like the evil eye. While it is possible that a spell from a now-lost papyrus required the practitioner to employ a fetus for malign magic, the existence of such a text is not necessary to classify this event as magical. Rather, local evidence (the petition) informs us that a fetus could be used for aggressive magic in the village of Karanis. The Gemellus papyrus tells us that magic was negotiated on the local level and understood within preexisting notions of what magic should look like and what its effect should be.

As was discussed in the previous chapter, the papyri can help us to understand the artifacts that we discover in the soil and to determine whether they were utilized for a magical purpose. We do not possess every papyrus that recorded spell instructions, nor were all spell variations necessarily written down; only those of some experts have survived to us.[16] We cannot expect a one-to-one correspondence between finds made in the soil and the instructional handbooks, as variation existed in ritual enactment. We have already noted permutations in the texts and objects that are related to PGM IV.296–466 (the bound figurine of the woman), and the papyri frequently make reference to alternate rituals, even including multiple iterations of a single spell. But these texts can provide a sense of what was appropriate within—or recognized as—magic in Egyptian society during the Late Antique period. As we will see, magic in Roman Egypt could be created and employed at the local level, as priests and other ritual experts negotiated the desires of local residents and the materials on hand with which they could perform magical acts.

In addition to revealing a hidden world of magical activity that may have pervaded village life, the Gemellus papyrus also points us to some of the benefits and problems related to using a site like Karanis to understand the practices of ancient magic. Excavation records from Karanis allow us to pinpoint

_____

16. Ibid., 55.

the building in which the papyrus was discovered, and we can even relate this document to other texts to construct a life story for our protagonist, Gemellus. The two copies of the complaint as well as the earlier petition are part of a larger cache excavated during the initial 1924 season of the University of Michigan excavations at Karanis.[17] From the texts, we learn that the family of Gaius Julius Niger was relatively wealthy, and its members owned a significant number of houses and agricultural property in Karanis and the surrounding villages; Gemellus Horion and his sister were the heirs of these substantial holdings.[18] As Byren and Wypustek convincingly argue, Gemellus Horion emerges as the scion of this well-off family, who maintains a relatively high social rank in the village but also submits numerous complaints to the authorities about mistreatment at the hands of others. Maps of the 1924 excavation season, how-

---

17. Investigators found 105 fragments of papyrus; the archive was discovered in a subterranean storage chamber beneath room A of House 5006 during the first season of excavation (Record of Objects, Karanis 1924–25: 8–13). This house was situated along the west side of the Street of Salim M (identified as locus 5000) as part of an insula block or group of multiple residences that shared party walls. Many of these buildings possessed two stories (stairs are present in at least one of the excavated rooms), as well as storage areas beneath the ground level. The street and the buildings along it were all covered by a substantial layer of wind-blown sand, which suggests that the last phase of occupation ended in abandonment of the area. The latest dated material includes coins and papyrus documents from the end of the third or the beginning of the fourth century CE, but much of this material comes from the upper layer of sand (e.g., K.M. inv. 50856: coin of Numerianus, 283 CE). Building 5006, where the cache of documents was discovered, was a relatively simple structure and consisted of six rooms, including two subterranean storage chambers, each constructed in two levels (Rooms E and F). Room A produced a large amount of material, most of it typical domestic debris, including ceramics, wooden items, and a few fragments of figurines. This material dates from the late third century, which was probably the period in which the house was abandoned. The papyri, which predate the material on the floor above, were all discovered beneath the house, within the subterranean storage chamber 5006 E 2. The dates of the documents range from the reign of Claudius or Nero (41–68 CE, *P.Mich.* VI 421) in a petition related to the theft of a donkey, down to 214 CE, when a man named Horion son of Simourk received a receipt for the payment of money tax to the collectors of the annona of cheap wine of Karanis (*P.Mich.* VI 390). It is unclear why the two documents related to Horion son of Simourk (*P.Mich.* VI 390 and SB XVI 12593) are in the archive. Gemellus Horion was the son of Tasoucharion and Gaius Apolinarius Niger, and I was not able to find another reference to Horion son of Simourk. Many of the documents are related to the family of a Roman cavalry veteran named Gaius Julius Niger, who had been discharged honorably from the army sometime before 154 CE, when he purchased a house from Valeria Diadora (*P.Mich.* VI 428). Gaius Julius Niger had two sons, Gaius Julius Longinus (154–189) and Gaius Apoliniarius Niger (died before March 186); the latter's son was named Gemellus, who is also known as Horion. Horion was likely the final possessor of the archive. Although the earlier documents cannot be easily associated with his family, the circumstances of their discovery—in an underground chamber with little other material—suggests that the papyri were placed there intentionally.

18. *P.Mich.* VI 370; VI 422.

ever, do not show a house 5006. Record keeping during the first season of work at the site was not as precise as in later years, and this is particularly apparent in areas that were badly damaged by land reclamation. The 5000 series of buildings, all from the top layer and excavated on the western side of the mound, was only briefly described in excavation diaries, allowing us to know how many rooms house 5006 included, and what items were found in those rooms, but not how space was organized or the exact findspot of the artifacts. Even if we were able to rediscover house 5006, it is not clear that the archaeological data would contribute further to our understanding of magic at the site.[19] Gemellus was the victim of an aggressive rite, and the papyrus records Gemellus's interpretation of the event; the document did not play a role in this act or in any other. Its archaeological context, therefore, cannot tell us more about the mechanisms of magic.

In order to better understand the processes of enacting magic on the local level, we must turn to the archaeological evidence of the phenomenon. This chapter will attempt to discover instances of magic that are revealed in artifacts and their contexts, as they can be reconstructed from excavation records and field notes. Necessarily, this process will entail navigating some of the problems associated with early fieldwork. Although record keeping at the Karanis lacked the precision and attention to stratigraphy that is commonplace in contemporary archaeological investigations, the University of Michigan expedition moved a massive amount of dirt. The scale of the excavation permits us to explore a sizable number of archaeological contexts, but some of these are better recorded than others. This chapter will survey four archaeological contexts from Karanis, positing that each can be identified as magic through the methodology outlined in the previous chapters. The available evidence suggests that magicians did not lurk around every corner; rather, rituals for personal gain may have been relatively open or available procedures as part of the toolbox of a temple priest. These potentially magical happenings stray beyond acts that are canonically recognizable, such as curse tablets, and our identification relies on comparative material from Egypt. Whenever possible, texts and artifacts from the Fayum will be employed to better understand local manifes-

---

19. On the problem of relating papyri to associated finds, see E. M. Husselman, *Papyri from Karanis, third series* (Cleveland: Case Western Reserve University Press, 1971), 1, 8–9; on papyri and the occupants of houses, see P. van Minnen, "House-to-house enquiries: An interdisciplinary approach to Roman Karanis," *ZPE* 100 (1994); P. van Minnen, "Boorish or bookish? Literature in Egyptian villages in the Fayum in the Graeco-Roman period," *JJurP* 28 (1998). On this topic, see also appendix 1.

Identifying the Remains of Magic in the Village of Karanis 105

tations of magic (plate 5). It seems likely that these materials may have been in circulation in the region or known to residents. We have noted that ancient practitioners may have been itinerant visitors to multiple villages or could have exchanged ritual technologies. Of particular note is an illustrated formulary associated with the Fayum, PGM XXXVI (*P. Oslo* I), which has been attributed to the region, although it was not found through stratigraphic excavation. By surveying the four contexts at Karanis, we can begin to get a sense of what magic looked like on the local level. At the same time, we will test our methodology for finding magic against archaeological data that was acquired in the early part of the twentieth century. Before turning to the archaeological material, however, this chapter will first sketch a picture of Karanis from the archaeological record, drawing on both preserved texts and the rich corpus of artifacts uncovered by the University of Michigan excavations.

Situating the Village

At the time when Gemellus filed his petition, in 197 CE, Karanis was nearing a period of significant prosperity in the third century CE. The site had been established in the northeast corner of the Fayum region, a large fertile depression to the west of the Nile valley. Although largely untouched by the invasion of Alexander in 332–331 BCE, the Fayum became a focal point in the land reclamation projects of the newly established Ptolemaic kingdom. Like the Middle Kingdom Pharaohs before him, Ptolemy II Philadelphus (285–246) targeted the region for intensive agricultural development in order to increase its productivity.[20] Karanis was one of a number of new colonial foundations, established as a settlement for Greek and Macedonian veterans of the Alexandrian and Ptolemaic wars.[21] The earliest area of habitation has been hypothesized to be between the southern temple to Pnepheros and Petesouchos and

---

20. For the Ptolemaic period reclamation in the Fayum: W. L. Westermann, "Land reclamation in the Fayum under Ptolemies Philadelphus and Euergetes I," *CPh* 12, no. 4 (1917); G. Hölbl, *A history of the Ptolemaic empire,* trans. T. Saavedra (London: Routledge, 2001), 62–63.

21. E. K. Gazda and T. G. Wilfong, *Karanis, an Egyptian town in Roman times: Discoveries of the University of Michigan expedition to Egypt (1924–1935)* (Ann Arbor: Kelsey Museum of Archaeology, 2004), 8. The earliest papyrus from Karanis is *P.Cair.Zen* 3.38, dated to 242 BCE; Caton and Thompson report coins of Ptolemy II Philadelphus from a basin located to the north of Karanis. G. Caton-Thompson and E. W. Gardner, *The desert Fayum* (London: Royal Anthropological Institute of Great Britain and Ireland, 1934), 149–51. This reference was kindly supplied by R. J. Cook.

106   Materia Magica

the southernmost irrigation canal.[22] The settlement grew northward, and, after a brief decline, perhaps associated with the Antonine plague, the site reached its greatest geographic extent in the third century. This floruit appears to have been short-lived; the fourth century ushered in a period of contraction, and outskirts of the site appear to have been abandoned. When the town recovered in the fifth century CE, new constructions were erected on top of a layer of sand that covered the earlier foundations. The site was abandoned in the sixth or seventh century, when the Fayum region as a whole witnessed significant depopulation.[23] It was never reoccupied, and Karanis suffered little damage in the intervening centuries, up until the end of the nineteenth century. The occupation of the site thus encompasses more than seven hundred years, a lifespan documented by papyri and other records that attest to vibrant interactions with the larger Fayum region.

Archaeological exploration of the site was initiated in the late nineteenth century through the work of Flinders Petrie (1890) and Bernard Grenfell, Arthur Hunt, and D.G. Hogarth (1895/6 and 1900). Around this same time, mining for nitrogen-rich fertilizer (*sebbakh*) damaged much of the center of the settlement, which likely included the administrative buildings for the village. The University of Michigan excavations (plate 6), undertaken from 1924 to 1935, employed new field methodologies that were aimed at total recovery of all aspects of habitation at the site, rather than acquiring museum-quality

22. This area was largely destroyed by the sebbakhim, who mined it for fertilizer, leaving no recoverable traces of occupation: E. M. Husselman, *Karanis excavations of the University of Michigan in Egypt 1928–1935: Topography and architecture: A summary of the reports of the director, Enoch E. Peterson* (Ann Arbor: University of Michigan Press, 1979), 8; E. Peterson, "The architecture and topography of Karanis" (Kelsey Museum Archives, Ann Arbor Michigan, 1973), 1; on the canals and settlement history of the site, see now R. J. Cook, "Economy, society and irrigation at a Graeco-Roman site in Egypt: the Karanis canal system" (PhD diss., University of Michigan, 2011).

23. The latest dated documents from Karanis are SB XIV 12109 (377 CE), *P.Haun* III 58 (439 CE) and *P.Col.* VIII 242 (fifth century). See D. Bonneau, "Un réglement de l'usage de l'eau au Ve siècle de notre ère. Commentaire de P. Haun. inv. 318," in *Hommages à la mémoire de Serge Sauneron, 1927–1976* (Cairo: Institut français d'archéologie orientale, 1979); J. R. Rea, "*P.Haun.* III 58: Caranis in the fifth century," *ZPE* 99 (1993); J. R. Rea, "*P.Col.* VIII 242: Caranis in the fifth century," in *Proceedings of the 20th International Congress of Papyrologists, Copenhagen, 23–29 August, 1992*, ed. A. Bülow-Jacobsen (Copenhagen: Museum Tusculanum Press, 1994); J. G. Keenan, "Deserted villages: From the ancient to the medieval Fayyūm," *BASP* 40 (2003): 125–29. None of these documents was found at Karanis, but they probably come from the 1877–78 excavations at Kiman Faris, near Medinet el-Fayum (ancient Arsinoe / Krokodilopolis). Keenan, "Byzantine Egyptian villages," 228. The Arab writer al Nabulsi mentions a "Washeem" as deserted in the thirteenth century, but it is unlikely that this is a reference to Karanis (J. Keenan, personal communication).

Identifying the Remains of Magic in the Village of Karanis 107

artifacts and finding papyri. A discussion of the excavation history, as well as an analysis of the recording methods employed during the Michigan seasons, is included in appendix 1.

Each artifact, as it was unearthed, was listed in the Record of Objects for the appropriate year of excavation under the heading of the structure and room in which it was found. This material can be cross-referenced with the maps and plans of the site, which record excavation squares and individual insula blocks, in order to precisely locate in which building the artifacts were discovered. Photographs of many of the objects, some taken during excavation, complement the textual record. Although the Michigan team employed techniques that were revolutionary for the early twentieth century, for the modern investigator the methodological problems associated with the Karanis excavations are multiple. The excavators did not differentiate between individual soil layers that may have existed within a single house or room, and thus it cannot be determined whether fill within a building was deposited over time. As houses were excavated, they were given a layer designation based on visible changes in architecture, such as the addition of walls or, in some cases, a layer of clean sand between architectural features. Houses in an area that were assigned to the same layer were believed to represent an occupation phase, and the excavators began to speak of "A" or "B" periods of occupation. Initially, the excavators recognized that the layer designations assigned in one part of the mound did not fully correspond to the layer designation in another part of the mound.[24] Later publications suggest that the layer designations, once applied only to specific parts of the site, were soon viewed as applicable across the site, so that a B-Layer house in a southern sector should be dated to the same period as a B-Layer house in a northern sector, even though the layer designations were assigned relative to houses above and below in the southern and northern sectors respectively. Broad dates were assigned to these levels according to the artifacts recovered within each. Preference was given to dates associated with papyri and coins, rather than chronologies derived from ceramic or lamp seriation.[25] E-Level structures were dated to the second century BCE, D-Level to the first century BCE, C-Level between the first century and mid-second century CE, B-Level from the mid-second to the early third century, and A-Level construction to the late third and fourth centuries.

---

24. A. E. R. Boak and E. E. Peterson, *Karanis: Topographical and architectural report of excavations during the seasons 1924–28* (Ann Arbor: University of Michigan Press, 1931), 9.

25. Peterson, "The architecture and topography of Karanis," 863.

More recent studies of material from Karanis have reassessed the dating of the site and, in particular, have pushed the final period of occupation into the Byzantine period. Pollard's study of the ceramics from the site has convincingly demonstrated that Karanis was inhabited well into the late fifth and early sixth centuries, and may have been occupied as late as the seventh or eighth century.[26] The apparent absence of material datable to the latest periods of occupation can be attributed to the low levels of coin production in the sixth century as well as the probable destruction of papyri in the upper stratigraphic levels.[27] Furthermore, as much of the Roman period documentation relates to the interaction between the small village and the larger city, changes in administrative structures during the Byzantine period that may have resulted in the production of fewer documents.[28] This redating brings the abandonment of Karanis in line with the broader decline among the villages of the Fayum in the sixth century, a collapse that perhaps may be associated with the neglect of the canals in the region.[29] Archaeological fieldwork at the site is ongoing under the direction of W. Wendrich, and her research will provide a much-needed reassessment of the site's chronology and its place in the larger region.[30]

Any attempt to use the material from Karanis for a study such as the current one must first wrestle with the problems associated with the excavation methodology, most notably the difficulties in establishing archaeological contexts within a particular unit. Occasional notations in the Record of Objects provide descriptive details about findspots of individual objects or groups of objects, which can be helpful in untangling which objects belong with one another

---

26. N. Pollard, "The chronology and economic condition of late Roman Karanis: An archaeological reassessment," *JARCE* 35 (1998): 155–56; T. G. Wilfong, "Fayum, Graeco-Roman sites," in *Encyclopedia of the archaeology of Ancient Egypt,* ed. K. A. Bard and S. B. Shubert (New York: Routledge, 1999), 13. J. Keenan notes that Karanis is likely named in *BGU* II 608, an Arabic period document that lists villages and their populations. "Deserted villages: From the ancient to the medieval Fayyūm," 129. On this topic, see also P. van Minnen, "Deserted villages: Two Late Antique town sites in Egypt," *BASP* 32, no. 1–2 (1995); J. G. Keenan, "Byzantine Egyptian villages," in *Egypt in the Byzantine world, 300–700,* ed. R. S. Bagnall (New York: Cambridge University Press, 2007).

27. Pollard, "The chronology and economic condition of late Roman Karanis," 160–61.

28. Keenan, "Byzantine Egyptian villages," 241; R. S. Bagnall, *Egypt in Late Antiquity* (Princeton: Princeton University Press, 1993), 5. On the latest dated documents at Karanis, see above n. 23.

29. D. Rathbone, "Towards a historical topography of the Fayum," in *Archaeological research in Roman Egypt,* ed. D. M. Bailey (Ann Arbor: Thomson-Shore, 1996), 52.

30. Wendrich's preliminary reports can be accessed online at http://www.archbase.com/fayum/project.htm.

Identifying the Remains of Magic in the Village of Karanis 109

and, at times, where in the fill the objects were discovered. The published and unpublished reports—including E. Peterson's unpublished final report and E. Husselman's published summary of this final report—describe important finds as well as the fill of rooms or buildings that are of typological value.[31] George Swain, the site photographer, recorded the field units in the process of excavation as well as after the sand and debris had been cleared. Furthermore, the photographic archive from Karanis includes images of artifacts that were retained by the Cairo Museum or left in the field.

The individual room—through both the objects discovered in its fill and its architectural form—provides the rudimentary unit for reassessing any archaeological context at the site. Careful reading of the artifacts, the reports, and the photographic archive can aid in determining the function of a room and subsequently the building in which it is located. The room also can offer a means to redate buildings and insula blocks. The layers that were initially assigned to architecture and fills at Karanis can be adjusted for individual structures through the critical analysis of datable materials such as ceramics or lamps. The site cannot be completely rehabilitated—gaps in the data will continue to exist, and there will be many questions that the excavation materials cannot answer—but the records left by the Michigan team can be reinterpreted to produce a better understanding of life at Karanis.

A Fever Amulet beneath House 242

Among the numerous artifacts discovered in the excavations at Karanis, a small inscribed piece of papyrus intended for use as an amulet, *P.Mich.* XVIII 768 (plate 7), is clearly magical.[32] The papyrus is relatively small, and measures 10 cm by 7.5 cm. It is inscribed with the following text:

> Iao, Sabaoth, Adonai! I beseech Anatiel, Raphael, Gabriel, Suriel, Azariel, Uriel, -aubrael, Ablanathanalba, Sesengembarpharanges. These are the Potentates of God and (the) Powers of the cure. Cure Sarapion, whom Allous bore,

---

31. For bibliography, see above, n. 22.
32. P.Mich. inv. 5302a. *editio princeps:* W. Brashear, *P.Mich.* XVIII 768; W. Brashear, "'Botokudenphilologie' vindicated," review of *The Greek magical papyri in translation, including the demotic spells, volume I: Texts* by Hans Dieter Betz, *International Journal of the Classical Tradition* 5, no. 1 (1998): 78.

110   Materia Magica

from every three-day fever-chill, every-other-day (fever-chill), quotidian (fever-chill) and from every sickness every day(?) . . . (Now, now! Quickly, quickly!)[33]

The initial three names, Iao, Sabaoth, Adonai, invoked in the papyrus are associated with the Hebrew god and frequently appear in the spells of the magical papyri and on inscribed gems, but seldom as a recognizable triad.[34] The next seven names can be associated with archangels, although the first name, Anatiel, is otherwise unattested (Brashear suggests a misreading of Ananael).[35] The names of the seven angels are followed by two *voces magicae* that are relatively common in magical texts and often found together, the palindrome ABLANATHANALBA and the magical word SESENGEMBARPHARANG-ES.[36] Sarapion, the person for whom the amulet is intended, is identified by his mother's name, as the son of Allous. This, too, is conventional, both for Egyptian texts in general and magical texts specifically, as spells, most notably curses, frequently cite maternal lineage rather than paternal.[37] The amulet iter-

---

33. Trans. Brashear, *P.Mich.* XVIII 768, p. 81.
34. R. Kotansky, "Kronos and a new magical inscription formula on a gem in the J. P. Getty Museum," *Ancient World* 3 (1980): 29.
35. Brashear, *P.Mich.* XVIII 768, pp. 82–83. On the importance of the number seven, see A. Y. Collins, "Numerical symbolism in Jewish and early Christian apocalyptic literature," *ANRW* II 21, no. 2 (1984), as well as the bibliography cited at W. Brashear, *Magica Varia,* ed. J. N. G. Bingen (Brussels: Fondation Egyptologique Reine Elisabeth, 1991), 69–70. Notable for its absence is the name of the archangel Michael. On the archangels Michael, Gabriel, Raphael, and Uriel, see Kotansky, *Greek magical amulets: The inscribed gold, silver, copper, and bronze "Lamellae": Text and commentary,* no. 26, pp. 104–6, and M. Meyer, *The magical book of Mary and the angels (P.Heid. Inv. Kopt. 685): Text, translation and commentary* (Heidelberg: Universitätsverlag C. Winter, 1996), 70–73. On Souriel, see E. Peterson, "Engel- und Damonennamen. Nomina barbara," *Rheinisches Museum für Philologie* 75 (1926): 418; H. J. Polotsky, "Suriel der Trompeter," *Muséon* 49 (1936). Azariel is mentioned in PGM I.8. Brashear notes that the incomplete name -aubrael is similar to Sopheriel and Scopheriel, attested in J. Michl, "Engelnamen," *RAC* 5 (1962): 235. *P.Mich.* XVIII 768, p. 83.
36. A. M. Kropp, *Ausgewählte koptische zaubertexte* (Brussels: Édition de la Fondation égyptologique reine Élisabeth, 1930), 3. 126 § 211. On the palindrome ABLANATHANALBA, see *Suppl. Mag.* I no. 9; W. Brashear, "Zwei Zauberformulare," *Archiv für Papyrusforschung und verwandte Gebiete* 38 (Jan. 1992): 21; Brashear, "The Greek magical papyri," 3577; for bibliography on SESENGEMBARPHARANGES, normally spelled SESENGENBAR-PHARANGES see Brashear, "The Greek magical papyri," 3598; *Suppl. Mag.* I. no. 10 line 2. Bohak argues that this is not a Jewish magical word, despite some scholarly claims to the contrary. *Ancient Jewish magic,* 209.
37. The use of the metronymic has a long history in Egyptian magical texts and was commonplace in the Roman era. M. Depauw, "Do mothers matter? The emergence of metronymics in early Roman Egypt," in *The language of the papyri,* ed. T. V. Evans and D. D. Obbink (New

Identifying the Remains of Magic in the Village of Karanis   111

ates a variety of illnesses, asking the invoked divinities to cure Sarapion not only of these specific fevers but indeed of every potential medical threat.[38] The verso of the papyrus preserves traces of writing, but these may be offsets.

The artifact was discovered in 1928 as part of the fill beneath house 242.[39] This building was located in the northern part of the site, to the northeast of the destroyed area. Excavators indicate, however, that they found the object beneath the top layer, that is, in unit 242*, where the asterisk indicates that the excavation unit was dug beneath house 242. This is a large archaeological area, measuring nineteen meters by twelve meters, and, as notation in the Record of Objects indicates, it was a very deep stratum. Material from the fill beneath the house suggests that the structure was built during or after the fourth century and likely went out of use when the site was abandoned. The findspot of the fever amulet is given with a fair degree of specificity: "about on level with top of C 65," presumably at the same elevation as the highest preserved course of C65.[40] Other artifacts found with the fever amulet are listed as being "very low, just above C walls," and "three meters down," presumably a distance measured from the structure above, building 242.[41] The depth of the deposit, well below house 242, suggests that the amulet not be associated with the occupation period of that structure. Rather, the fever amulet was likely deposited prior to the construction of House 242.

The area in which the fever amulet was discovered likely was in use at the same time as the nearby granary, C65, in which case it may have served as a courtyard. Many of the ostraca found in the unit were receipts for grain transport, liturgical work, or lists of donkey drivers, all dating to the late third or

---

York: Oxford University Press, 2010). In part, this usage may be due to the belief that the descent from the mother was certain, while that of the father was uncertain, an idea initially proposed by Wünsch. *DTA*, xxiii; cf. R. Wünsch, *Antike fluchtafeln* (Bonn: A. Marcus und E. Weber, 1907), 9; *DT* li–lii. On metronymy in magical texts, see D. R. Jordan, "CIL VIII 19525 (B).2 QPVVLVA = q(uem) p(eperit) vulva," *Philologus* 120 (1976): 128–32; J. B. Curbera, "Maternal lineage in Greek magical texts," in *The world of ancient magic,* ed. D. R. Jordan, H. Montgomery, and E. Thomassen (Bergen: Norwegian Institute of Athens, 1999), esp. 199–201.

38. On listing in magical texts, see R. L. Gordon, "'What's in a list?' Listing in Greek and Graeco-Roman malign magical texts," in *The world of ancient magic,* ed. D. R. Jordan, H. Montgomery, and E. Thomassen (Bergen: Norwegian Institute at Athens, 1999), esp. 241–42.

39. Brashear erroneously lists the findspot of the artifact as house 242, room P. The field number for the artifact was 1928-242*-P, where P indicated the object number. *P.Mich.* XVIII 768, p. 78, n. 13.

40. Record of Objects, Karanis 1928: 102*-242*, B108-B172, CS23-CS130, 242*.

41. *O.Mich.* I 438 and *O.Mich.* I 365, respectively.

112   Materia Magica

early fourth century CE.[42] The majority of this material probably accumulated in this area as a result of abandonment; individuals who received small receipts on ostraca from the granary may have tossed them aside soon after leaving the building. A variety of objects were associated with the fever amulet as part of the same stratigraphic unit, including a gaming piece, a fragment of bronze that may have resembled a human figure (it was not retained), clay stoppers, combs, a kohl stick, a miniature hammer, and the ostraca discussed above. The varied nature of these objects suggests that some of this material may have been lost or discarded in this space. Before the construction of building 242, the level of the courtyard had risen substantially either through general occupation and the accumulation of debris and windblown sand, or by the active importation of fill material. These associated artifacts can tell us little about the amulet's use. As the fever amulet was discovered among this occupational debris, it should likely be seen as a similarly discarded or lost object.

Brashear suggests a fourth century date, presumably on the basis of the hand, and this accords with the data derived from the archaeological locus. The unit contained coins of Maximianus Heraclius (286–305 CE) as well as an ostracon that was dated to 311 CE, discovered very low in the fill.[43] Material from the structures above, houses 241 and 242, suggests a similar date, the late third or early fourth century CE. The fourth century represents the date by which this deposit was established; material could have entered this unit at an earlier point, and indeed, the fever amulet was discovered low in the unit. Given the problems associated with the stratigraphy and recording, we

---

42. *O.Mich.* I 159: 287/288 CE (receipt for delivery in kind); *O.Mich.* I 183: 301 CE (delivery of chaff); *O.Mich.* I 220: 4th (receipt for delivery in kind); *O.Mich.* I 228: early 4th CE (receipt for delivery in kind); *O.Mich.* I 267: late 3rd (grain transport); *O.Mich.* I 365: late 3rd (grain transport); *O.Mich.* I 376: late 3rd (grain transport); *O.Mich.* I 438: 290 (receipt for transport); *O.Mich.* I 442: 3rd CE (grain receipt); *O.Mich.* I 450: 294 CE (fragmentary text); *O.Mich.* I 490: February 13, 290 CE (grain receipt); *O.Mich.* I 504: November 12, 302 CE (grain receipt); *O.Mich.* I 514: 307/308 CE (grain receipt); *O.Mich.* I 522: 311 CE (grain receipt); *O.Mich.* I 562: late 3rd / early 4th (grain transport); *O.Mich.* I 579: late 3rd / early 4th (list of names); *O.Mich.* I 699: late 3rd CE (fragmentary text). A few of the items found in the unit were not associated with grain transport; *O.Mich.* I. 663, records an acclamation, and reads "All victories to the Romans! Success . . . for our Lords! . . ." (trans. L. Amundsen). This text has been associated with the imperial cult and perhaps was associated with one of the temples or a procession at the site. Traianos Gagos and Paul Heilporn had been working on this document at the time of Dr. Gagos's untimely death.

43. Coins: 28-242*-AI, K.M. inv. 64757; Ostracon: 28-242*-N, Receipt for transport of grain, *O.Mich.* I 522.

Identifying the Remains of Magic in the Village of Karanis   113

must accept this date with a degree of caution, but the evidence at our disposal strongly suggests the fourth century.

It is highly probable that the fever amulet was lost or discarded. While it is tempting to read the text's injunction that the amulet should "cure Sarapion" as directly leading to the disposal of the object—because it either worked or failed to—there is little secondary evidence that would support such a premise. The fever amulet cannot be connected securely to other finds associated with its archaeological context, or even other material from the site. Other ostraca found in the same excavation unit refer to individuals named Sarapion: *O.Mich.* I 522, dated to February 6, 311 CE, records that Ptollas, the son of Sarapion, transported grain from Karanis to the harbor at Kerke, while *O.Mich.* I 579 numbers a Sarapion among a list of liturgical workers. Sarapion, however, was a common name among the residents of Karanis, and no other documents from the site refer to a Sarapion as the son of Allous.

But the artifact can tell us more about how it was used and what purpose such objects served within a village such as Karanis. The papyrus on which the spell was written was folded multiple times; creases are visible running vertically down the document at approximately 1.5 cm intervals. This suggests that the artifact had been folded from the right side to the left. No comparable areas of damage are visible to indicate whether the document was also folded from top to bottom to form a small rectangle. The small size of the folded amulet suggests that it was highly portable and could have been carried around by Sarapion. There are no further indications of wear, such as traces of damage from a suspension cord or holes to indicate that it was affixed in some manner. This may indicate that it was enclosed in an amulet case, which would have protected the document and allowed Sarapion to wear the amulet on his body.

Fever amulets were common in antiquity, as a variety of illnesses that could be accompanied by a febrile distress beset ancient individuals.[44] In some cases, magic may have been the best solution. While Pliny discusses potential medicinal and magical cures for fever at length, he concedes that traditional medicines were nearly useless for combating quartans fever (malaria).[45] Common among magical responses were inscribed incantations aimed at relieving

---

44. On the various kinds of fevers associated with malaria, see M. D. Grmek, *Diseases in the ancient Greek world,* trans. M. Muellner and L. Muellner (Baltimore: Johns Hopkins University Press, 1989), 281.

45. Pliny *HN* XXX.30.98.

the symptoms, if not curing the disease. A large number of such amulets are known from Egypt from as early as the Pharaonic period; the corpus includes examples in Hieratic, Demotic, Greek, Coptic, Hebrew, and Arabic.[46] It is therefore not surprising to discover an example at Karanis, but its presence raises more important questions, particularly with regard to the production of this object.

The artifact includes a number of features that suggest the use of a model text or *Vorlage* in the production of the artifact. Brashear notes the abrupt shifts in syntax, particularly apparent in lines 4–5, where the text shifts from a general invocation to a description of these figures.[47] Furthermore, mistakes in copying (or, more accurately, copying a defective prototype) are apparent in missing letters, erasures, and grammatical errors.[48] It is likely that a professional scribe who had access to a handbook produced the amulet. The invocation refers to a series of Jewish or Christian divinities and angels, as well as the pair of *voces magicae* that are typical of Mediterranean magic in this period. Furthermore, the text may show signs of Gnostic influence, as twelve separate individuals are named, divided into a group of seven (the angels) and a grouping of five (Iao, Sabaoth, Adonai, Ablanathanalba and Sesengembarpharanges).[49] More important, however, is the fact that all of these individuals are addressed as the "Dynamerai of God and (the) Dynameis of the Healing." This particular form of address is also found in Coptic documents, most notably P.Köln inv. 20826, which invokes the twelve powers in a similar fashion.[50] Notable is the absence of invocations to traditional Egyptian divinities. This is not definitive evidence that a Jewish or Christian priest, rather than an Egyptian or pagan individual, produced the amulet, but the spell appears to be reflect a Christian, rather than pagan, conceptualization of the cosmos. It therefore prompts the question of who wrote out the amulet and in what context this magical object was created.

---

46. For a partial list of fever amulets in Hieratic, Demotic, Coptic, Aramaic, and Hebrew, see Brashear, *P.Mich.* XVIII 768, pp. 77–78, nn.6–10; for Greek fever amulets, see Brashear, "The Greek magical papyri," 3500; Kotansky, *Greek magical amulets: The inscribed gold, silver, copper, and bronze "Lamellae": Text and commentary.*
47. Brashear, *P.Mich.* XVIII 768, commentary on lines 4–5, pp. 79, 84.
48. Note particularly the use of the singular aorist imperative θεράπευσον (line 6, read by Brashear for θεράπευσαν) rather than the plural θεραπεύσατε. Ibid., 84–85.
49. Ibid., 79, citing a suggestion by R. Kotansky. This proposed division, however, elides the three initial names and the *voces magicae* at the end of the invocation into a single group of "other" as distinguished from the angels.
50. Ibid., 80; C. Römer and H. J. Thissen, "Eine magische Anrufung in koptischer Sprache," *ZPE* 84 (1990); *ACM* no. 59.

Identifying the Remains of Magic in the Village of Karanis 115

It seems most likely that a literate individual, working from a handbook, produced the fever amulet. The identity of this individual, however, is more difficult to pin down. During the first few centuries of the Common Era, literate priests, working outside of the temple, were responsible for the creation of most magical objects created from formularies. In the period under discussion, however, it is more difficult to find these priests still active at Karanis. The traditional dating of the site suggests that the two temples were in decline during the fourth century. According to Boak and Peterson, the northern temple was abandoned by the mid-third century, while the southern temple to Pnepheros and Petesouchos survived into the late third or early fourth centuries.[51] The excavators suggested that a period of economic depression affected Karanis in the late C period (ca. 250 CE), leading to widespread abandonment of parts of the town; the temples were one casualty of the downturn. More important, Boak and Peterson proposed that the triumph of Christianity, which they believed had been fully accomplished by the fourth century, meant that there were no pagans left to worship at the temples, which subsequently went out of use.[52] Indeed, Roger Bagnall has argued that the fourth century marked a period of substantial decline for traditional Egyptian religion, as there is limited papyrological evidence for activities of the temples or of Egyptian priests.[53] At Karanis, individuals associated with the temple are mentioned only in a handful of late third- or early fourth-century ostraca.[54] Household objects also appear to corroborate this conversion sequence, as there is substantial evidence for the incorporation of Christian motifs into lamps, textiles, and ceramics, and a variety of crosses, some strung on suspension chains, can be found in the houses of the later periods.[55]

This model of Christian triumph might suggest that a monk, working for a

---

51. Northern Temple: A. E. R. Boak, *Karanis: The temples, coin hoards, botanical and zoölogical reports, seasons 1924–31* (Ann Arbor: University of Michigan Press, 1933), 14–15; Southern Temple: Boak, *Karanis: The temples, coin hoards, botanical and zoölogical reports, seasons 1924–31*, 19–20. Inscriptional evidence indicates that the Southern temple was rebuilt substantially in 180 CE, probably through the combined efforts of many of the townspeople; a local benefactor, Apollonios, restored the temple ten years later. *IGFayyum* 1.88–89.

52. Boak, *Karanis: The temples, coin hoards, botanical and zoölogical reports, seasons 1924–31*, 20.

53. Bagnall, *Egypt in Late Antiquity*, 261–68, but compare D. Frankfurter, review of *Egypt in Late Antiquity*, by R. S. Bagnall, *BMCRev*, no. 5 (1994).

54. *O.Mich.* 1.248; I.586; I.344; *P.Col.* VII.138 is a document is written by Aurelius Eudaimon, former chief priest and *epimeletes* of gold, to Aurelius Isodorus.

55. Gazda and Wilfong, *Karanis, an Egyptian town in Roman times*, 44.

116   Materia Magica

Christian at the site, created the amulet, but scholars in recent years have questioned the narrative of large-scale conversion. David Frankfurter has proposed that conversion occurred at the level of the community, as local individuals collectively chose to embrace the new faith. This transformation of the religious landscape occasionally brought upheaval and social discord; we can witness vividly the forced destruction of pagan holy sites in hagiographies from the period, and see the results of angry Christian mobs in the hacked-out faces of Egyptian divinities still visible in the temples that were left standing.[56] If we are to situate the fever amulet and other artifacts related to magic in the late fourth century, the story of the decline of the two temples at Karanis and the corresponding conversion of the residents of the town to Christianity requires reassessment and more detailed nuance.

Unlike many of the temples of Egypt, neither the southern nor northern temple at Karanis was transformed into a church.[57] Christianity, however, had certainly taken hold among the administrators of the town by the fifth century. *P.Haun.* III 58, a declaration about water rights, provides evidence for the existence of two priests and five deacons, perhaps indicating that a number of churches were active in the village.[58] No evidence for these structures survives.

---

56. Frankfurter, *Religion in Roman Egypt,* 267, 77–83. Compare Bagnall, *Egypt in Late Antiquity,* 260–68, and Frankfurter, review of *Egypt in Late Antiquity.*

57. On the transformation of Egyptian temples, see J.-P. Caillet, "La transformation en église d'édifices publics et de temples à la fin de l'antiquité," in *La fin de la cité antique et le début de la cité médiévale: de la fin du IIIe siècle à l'avènement de Charlemagne: actes du colloque tenu à l'Université de Paris X-Nanterre, les 1, 2 et 3 avril 1993,* ed. C. Lepelley (Bari: Edipuglia, 1996), 196–99; B. Warde-Perkins, "Re-using the Architectural Legacy of the Past, *entre idéologie et pragmatisme,"* in *The idea and ideal of the town between Late Antiquity and the Middle Ages,* ed. G. P. Brogiolo and B. Warde-Perkins (Boston: Brill, 1999), 234; L. Forschia, "La reutilization des sanctuaires paiens par les chretiens en Grece continentale," *Revue des études grecques* 113 (2000); J. H. F. Dijkstra, *Philae and the end of ancient Egyptian religion: A regional study of religious transformation (298–642 CE)* (Leuven: Peeters, 2008); S. Emmel, U. Gotter, and J. Hahn, "'From temple to church': Analyzing a Late Antique phenomenon of transformation," in *From temple to church: Destruction and renewal of local cultic topography in Late Antiquity,* ed. S. Emmel, U. Gotter, and J. Hahn (Leiden: Brill, 2008); D. Brakke, "From temple to cell, from gods to demons: Pagan temples in the monastic topography of fourth century Egypt," in *From temple to church: Destruction and renewal of local cultic topography in Late Antiquity,* ed. S. Emmel, U. Gotter, and J. Hahn (Leiden: Brill, 2008); A. Chaniotis, "The conversion of the temple of Aphrodite at Aphrodisias in context," in *From temple to church: Destruction and renewal of local cultic topography in Late Antiquity,* ed. S. Emmel, U. Gotter, and J. Hahn (Leiden: Brill, 2008).

58. J. G. Keenan, "Egypt," in *The Cambridge ancient history, vol. XIV: Late Antiquity: Empire and successors, A.D. 425–600,* ed. A. Cameron, B. Ward-Perkins, and M. Whitby (Cambridge: Cambridge University Press, 2000), 619–20; Keenan, "Deserted villages: From the

Identifying the Remains of Magic in the Village of Karanis 117

This may be due to the excavation history of the site, as the central part of the village was completely destroyed by the depredations of the sebbakhim.[59] A church or another Christian religious structure may have been located in the middle of the town, but its existence is no longer recoverable.

At the end of the fourth century, the Christian population of the village was surely increasing, but it does not follow that paganism, or pagan priests, had been eradicated or silenced. At Philae in Late Antiquity, Christians were progressively integrated into society, while paganism held on but was increasingly isolated. There, the last attestation of pagan cultic activity can be dated to 456/457, and in the following century, Christians began to assert their own identity against the now-vacant temple of Isis and the ghosts of a pagan past.[60] Our material, however, predates this by a considerable margin, and the fourth century was a period of transition in which pagans and Christians likely lived together peaceably.[61] Through this period of religious transformation and coexistence, individuals continued to require the services of ritual professionals. Magic, in particular, was suited to fulfill the needs of both Christians and pagans, or those somewhere in between, as ritual techniques associated with Late Antique practice drew on multiple traditions, including deities and spirits that were associated with Jews, Christians, and pagan cults. One could well imagine a charismatic individual, trained in the Egyptian temple and familiar with traditional ritual practices, might easily apply these same skills in the increasingly Christian society.[62] The identity of this individual must remain uncertain, but another artifact, discovered in a nearby structure, indicates the continuing influence of literate magic in the village and points to a contemporary rite that was likely undertaken by a pagan priest. As an addition to scattered artifacts bearing Christian iconography and a few late papyri that mention elders, the fever amulet provides further evidence of a growing community of Christians at the site.

---

ancient to the medieval Fayyūm," 126; Bagnall, *Egypt in Late Antiquity,* 283–84; D. Bonneau suggests that the text names twelve priests and five deacons. Bonneau, "Un réglement de l'usage de l'eau au Ve siècle de notre ère. Commentaire de P.Haun. inv. 318," 5–6. This number seems overly high given the likely size of the settlement at this date.

59. Traianos Gagos believed that the Christian structures may have been located in the center of the settlement, an area that was robbed out by the sebbhakim (personal communication).

60. Dijkstra, *Philae and the end of ancient Egyptian religion: A regional study of religious transformation (298–642 CE)*, 343–44.

61. Ibid., 348.

62. Frankfurter, *Religion in Roman Egypt,* 222.

118   Materia Magica

A Magical Ostracon in Structure C403

On the other side of the site and north of the temple of Pnepheros and Pete-souchos lies house C403,[63] excavated during the 1933 season. This building was a small, two-room structure with a central staircase that likely led to an upper floor or a rooftop (plate 8). C403 was part of a large insula block bounded by street CS400 on the east and street CS405 on the north. The block contains a number of smaller houses that often share walls, and the entire group of build-ings appears to have functioned as a single structure. A large granary, C404, and its subsidiary structure, C406, located to the east, dominate the insula. Two alleyways cut into the block, permitting access to some of the interior rooms and buildings. Excavators associated the block with the C-Layer of occupa-tion, although a number of earlier walls are visible in the construction. Mate-rial found in the fill suggests that it was last occupied in the late third or early fourth century.[64]

Discovered in room J, the space to the north of the central staircase of C403, O.Mich. inv. 9883 (plate 9) is a small ostracon, or inscribed potsherd, that likely served a magical function. As pieces of broken pottery from all sorts of ceramic vessels, ostraca were the ubiquitous scrap paper of the ancient world, used for receipts, drawings, or notes. The ostracon measures 8.5 cm across and is roughly triangular in shape. It has been inscribed on its convex side. The ceramic vessel from which the potsherd derives was thick-walled and may have been an amphora; the ostracon was therefore sturdy and would not have been easily broken or damaged. The text of this ostracon includes a number of features that can be paralleled among the ritual texts from both the Fayum and Graeco-Roman Egypt. The evidence suggests that the object was a copy of an instructional text, transferred to an ostracon for use by a practitio-ner. Three very brief lines of text are preserved:

] ως ζῴδια
ϙοοοοϙεεεεεε
γυνή παιδίν

---

63. Publication history: H. C. Youtie, "Ostraca from Karanis," *ZPE* 16 (1975); *Suppl. Mag.* no. 68.

64. Ostracon, C403: *O.Mich.* II 902 (297 CE); Coins in C401: K.M. inv. 45776, 5th yr. Probus (279 CE); in C404, K.M. inv. 64746; R. A. Haatvedt, E. E. Peterson, and E. Husselman. *Coins from Karanis: The University of Michigan excavations, 1924–1935* (Ann Arbor: University of Michigan Press, 1964), no. 1455 (Diocletian 284–305 CE).

Identifying the Remains of Magic in the Village of Karanis 119

[. . . image

oooooo eeeeee

woman (or mother) child]

Although the text is very short, unpacking its meaning and analyzing the artifact in its depositional context can articulate a clear function for this item and for the structure in which it was found. These data suggest that the artifact provided protection for grain or for the grain processing that likely occurred in the room. This hypothesis is supported by additional evidence from the site; a large image of the god, enthroned on a chair, appears in one of the major public granaries. At Karanis, Horus may have lent special protection to agricultural produce. Like the fever amulet that was discussed in the previous section, the inscribed ostracon is dated to the end of the fourth century and raises further questions about the activities of ritual practitioners at the site.

The word *zōdia,* which appears in the first line, is found frequently in the magical papyri, where it precedes small illustrations in some of the spell recipes.[65] These drawings, or *figurae magicae,* were intended to be copied by the practitioner onto another medium, such as an amulet or a curse. PGM XXXVI (*P.Oslo* I), the formulary attributed to the Fayum, contains a series of drawings that are to be reproduced; line 234, for example, instructs the practitioner to "take a lead lamella and inscribe with a bronze stylus the following names and the figure (τὸ ζῴδιον), and after smearing it with blood from a bat, roll up the lamella in the usual fashion . . ."[66] The instructions are followed by an image of a rooster-headed, anthropomorphic figure in military garb that holds a sword in one hand and a decapitated head in the other. Other texts lack such models but provide written directions for the creation of images. So, PGM IV reads, "And this is the figure written on the hide: (ἔστι δὲ τὸ εἰς τὸν ὑμένα γραφόμενον

---

65. Parallels for the use of this term include PGM XXXVI 2: γράφε χαλκῷ γραφίῳ τὸ ὑποκίμενον ζῴδιο[ν. Similar terms appear in numerous other magical papyri. On the images from magical papyri, see A. Delatte, "Études sur la magie greque 5: *Akephalos Theos,*" *BCH* 38 (1914); A. Procopé-Walter, "Iao und Set," *ARW* 30 (1933); H. Seyrig, "Invidiae Medici," *Berytus* 1 (1934); A. A. Barb, "Diva matrix," *JWarb* 16, no. 3–4 (1953); A. A. Barb, "The mermaid and the devil's grandmother," *JWarb* 29 (1966); I. Grumach, "On the history of a Coptic Figura Magica," in *Proceedings of the 12th international congress of papyrology* (Toronto, 1970); Brashear, "The Greek magical papyri," 3443; Brashear, *Magica Varia,* 74–79; Capasso, "Alcuni papiri figurati magici recentemente trovati a Soknopaiou Nesos"; A. T. Wilburn, "Representations and images in magical practice," in *The Brill guide to ancient magic,* ed. D. Frankfurter and H. S. Versnel (Leiden: Brill, forthcoming). The appearance of model drawings in the Egyptian spell instructions has a long history, and some of the images first appear during the Pharaonic period. See Dieleman, *Priests, tongues, and rites,* 33–34 and n. 38.

66. Trans. R. F. Hock in *GMP,* 274–75.

ζῴδιον) a lion faced form of a man wearing a sash, holding in his right hand a staff, and let there be a serpent. / And around all his left hand let an asp be entwined, and from the mouth of the lion let fire breath forth."[67] The Karanis ostracon does not include a drawing, but rather instructs the practitioner as to what images are to be represented; the final line includes the words *woman child.*

The second line consists of a string of six omicrons followed by six epsilons. The use of strings of vowels or other incomprehensible words is similarly a common feature of magical documents, appearing on amulets and curse tablets and as part of spell instructions.[68] Often, however, texts incorporate all eight of the vowels, frequently with ascending repetition, so that the practitioner might be instructed to write out one alpha, two epsilons, and so on, in the order in which the vowels appear in the alphabet. Our text contains only omicrons and epsilons, and these are not in alphabetical order. A similar text can be found on an ostracon from Oxyrhynchus, published by Priesendanz.[69] The inscription, which is preserved on both sides side of the potsherd, begins with a long iteration of *voces magicae.* Lines 18–19 of the text, on the exterior, convex side, read:

ααααα οοοοοο υυυυυυ
εεεεε ωωωωωωωωωωωωω

The ostracon from Oxyrhynchus was intended to separate a woman named Allous from her husband Apollonios, perhaps by being placed in a significant location. The vowels on the Karanis ostracon suggest that magic was being employed, but on their own, they do not provide sufficient context to indicate how the artifact was being used. Vowels are frequently employed as an element of a magical rite, but their use is not limited to one kind of spell or another.

The final two words on the ostracon, *woman child* or, as is more likely,

---

67. Trans. E. N. O'Neil, in *GMP*, 75. Images may have been added by separate professional artists: LiDonnici, "Compositional patterns in *PGM* IV (=*P.Bibl.Nat.Suppl.* gr. no. 574)," 170.

68. Similar vowel strings are present in PGM XXXVI.187–210, the magical compendium from the Fayum. Compare PGM II.97; PGM XIII.734–1077, and *CPR* 3/Preisendanz *Christ.* 11. In general, see Brashear, "The Greek magical papyri," 3430–34; Frankfurter, "The magic of writing and the writing of magic."

69. PGM O 2 (II:233); *CT* no. 35; L. Amundsen, "Magical text on an Oslo ostracon," *SO* 7, no. 1 (1928).

mother child, likely refer to Isis and Horus/Harpocrates.[70] It is less probable that these terms refer to the Virgin Mary and her child Jesus, although such a possibility cannot be ruled out completely and is addressed below. The archaeological context of the find suggests that we should interpret the ostracon as referring to Isis, as a number of Horus statuettes in the room suggest a pagan space. In the Egyptian tradition, Isis was closely associated with magical power and was invoked frequently in conjunction with her child Horus, or Harpocrates, to provide protection for the commissioner of the spell.[71] The role of Isis as protector was well established in the Pharaonic period. At the temple of Edfu, for example, an inscription invokes the goddess as "Isis the enchanter who knows her spell, who protects Horus with her effective word" and later as "Isis the mother who enchanted Horus in his nest."[72]

Most relevant to the Karanis ostracon, however, are the invocations to Isis and Horus that are preserved on the Horus cippi, stone stelai that are first attested in the Rammeside period and produced well into the Roman period. These objects were set up in Egyptian temples and homes, and employed for protection and healing.[73] A Horus cippus was discovered at Karanis, although it was a surface find and therefore lacks significant information about its context.[74] These monuments typically show an image of the young god Harpocrates, facing outward and identified by the lock of youth on the right side of his head. The god holds a wild animal in each hand, personifications of chaos, and stands on top of two crocodiles. Hieroglyphs decorate the front and rear of the stele; the reverse often contains a number of standardized texts that associate the suppliant with the god Horus. Through persuasive analogy, the texts drive off dangerous scorpions, snakes, and other creatures, and provide healing for the patient. Suppliants would pour water over the stele, or submerge smaller examples in basins, and subsequently drink the empowered liquid.[75]

---

70. Youtie, "Ostraca from Karanis," 274.
71. Dieleman, *Priests, tongues, and rites,* 142; M. Münster, *Untersuchungen zur Göttin Isis* (Berlin: B. Hessling, 1968), 192–96; J. Bergman, *Ich bin Isis. Studien zum memphitischen Hintergrund der griechischen Isisaretalogien* (Stockholm: Almqvist & Wiksell, 1968), 286–89.
72. Ritner, *The mechanics of ancient Egyptian magical practice,* 45, n.209; cf. M. Rochemonteix et al., *Le temple d'Edfou* (Cairo: Institut français d'archéologie orientale du Caire, 1897), 233.
73. On the Horus cippi, see the recent catalogs: H. Sternberg-El Hotabi, *Untersuchungen zur Überlieferungsgeschichte der Horusstelen: ein Beitrag zur Religionsgeschichte Ägyptens im 1. Jahrtausend v. Chr,* 2 vols. (Wiesbaden: Harrassowitz, 1999), and A. Gasse and C. Ziegler, *Les stèles d'Horus sur les crocodiles* (Paris: Réunion des Musées Nationaux, 2004).
74. K.M. inv. 25755; a Horus cippus was also discovered at Soknopaiou Nesos, K.M. inv. 29770.
75. R. K. Ritner, "Horus on the crocodiles: A juncture of religion and magic," in *Religion and*

122   Materia Magica

In the inscribed text, Isis is identified as a powerful enchantress credited with repelling powerful sorceries: a New Kingdom spell names "Isis who repels the deeds of the enchanters by the spells of her mouth."[76] A Horus cippus from the Museum of Seized Antiquities in Cairo contains the following inscription:

> Words spoken by Isis, the Great, mother of God, Mistress of magic, mistress of the book(s). She protects her [brother?] Osiris and fights for her son. She defeats those who rebel [against] Wenennofer in her name of [Seshat] mistress of writing . . . She seals the mouth of all reptiles which bite with their [mouths] and sting with their tails . . . [77]

The power of the goddess is instrumental to both protecting and healing her son, and, through analogy, the suppliant. Horus cippi are, at times, created as a feature of statuettes that show Isis holding or breastfeeding her child, further illustrating the close connection between mother, child, and healing or protection.[78]

Like their three-dimensional counterparts, drawings of the goddess and her son also could serve a protective or healing function. These images typically were dissolved in fluids. The Rammeside Papyrus Turin 1993, an anti-scorpion spell, instructs the practitioner to recite words over images of Atum, Horus-of-Praise, Isis, and Horus (named a second time, perhaps here as the young god) that have been drawn onto the hand of the patient; this image is then licked off.[79] The invocation that should be recited appears in four other enacted examples, including an ostracon from Deir el-Medineh.[80] In each of

---

philosophy in ancient Egypt, ed. W. K. Simpson (New Haven: Yale Egyptological Seminar, 1989), 105–7. On drinking the words of spells to activate them, see Ritner, *The mechanics of ancient Egyptian magical practice,* 102–11; L. Kákosy, *Egyptian healing statues in three Museums in Italy: Turin, Florence, Naples* (Torino: Ministero per i beni e le attività culturali, Soprintendenza al Museo delle antichità egizie, 1999), 16–17.

76. M. Lichtheim, *Ancient Egyptian literature: A book of readings,* 3 vols. (Berkeley: University of California Press, 1973), 2:83.

77. Trans. L. Kákosy and A. M. Moussa, "A Horus stela with Meret goddesses," *Studien zur Altägyptischen Kultur* 25 (1998): 150.

78. E. Bresciani, "Isis lactans et Horus sur les crocodiles," in *Egyptian religion: The last thousand years; Studies dedicated to the memory of Jan Quaegebeur,* ed. W. Clarysse et al. (Leuven: Peeters, 1998), 59.

79. Ritner, *The mechanics of ancient Egyptian magical practice,* 95; F. Rossi, *Papyrus de Turin* (Wiesbaden: LTR Verlag, 1981), 114–15, plates LXXVII, XXXI.

80. *O. Deir el-Medineh* 1263, part of Legend of Isis and Re, found on P.Turin. Ritner, *The mechanics of ancient Egyptian magical practice,* 95 n.466; G. Posener, *Catalogue des ostraca*

Identifying the Remains of Magic in the Village of Karanis 123

these spells, the patient is associated with Harpocrates and healed through the power of Isis.

The brevity of the text suggests that it was a practice model, perhaps a partial copy of a longer text that the practitioner would use in the field. The inscription appears to be nearly complete, although there are traces of letters to the left of the word *zodion*. All around the inscription, there is a significant amount of blank space, suggesting that we are not missing any other lines or an image. The space beneath these final two words shows no traces of ink, and this absence of a drawing makes it unlikely that the scribe mistakenly copied the instructions onto a power object. The strings of vowels, too, fit a model. They may indicate part of spell to be spoken by the practitioner, or this could be an inscription that was to be written along with the images. If the text was a model to be copied, the practitioner even may have arranged the letters into a triangular pattern, a form that was significant for *voces magicae;* the six letters could yield a one row of one, another of two, and a third of three.

While most ostraca were employed in ritual practice as components of an enacted spell,[81] comparative evidence from other sites indicates that potsherds—the ubiquitous scrap paper of antiquity—could be used as a mnemonic device. An ostracon would provide a highly portable, inexpensive medium for the itinerant or even local priest to write down a few notes about the intended rite or other instructions for ritual activities such as the locations where rites should be undertaken. In 1938, 1,555 ostraca were discovered within the enclosure of the temple to Renenutet at the site of Narmouthis.[82] The ostraca, written in both

---

 hiératiques littéraires de Deir el Médineh (Cairo: Impr. de l'Institut français d'archéologie orientale, 1934), 42 and plate 69.

81. PGM O 1 = *CT* no. 111; PGM O 2 = *CT* no. 35; PGM O 4; PGM O 5; *Medinet Madi* No. 16 (A. Vogliano, *Secondo rapporto degli scavi condotti dalla Missione archeologica d'Egitto della R. Università di Milano nella zona di Madinet Madi* [Cairo: Institut français d'archéologie orientale, 1937]) O. Köln inv. 409 = Wortmann, "Neue magische texte," 80 = *CT* no. 29 = *Suppl. Mag.* no. 51, found with two lead tablets; *O. Ashm.Shelt.* 194; *O. Bodl.* 2180 = *Suppl. Mag.* no 58; *O. Antinoe* 121–22; *O. Edfou* 1 227–28. In the formularies, ostraca are mentioned among the materials that could be used for written incantations. In PGM XXXVI.256–64, an inscribed potsherd will counteract the magic of others and "dissolve every enchantment against (the practitioner)." Trans. M. Smith *GMP*, 275. Fragments of pottery are also used as ingredients for rituals intended to attract lovers (PDM xii.62–75, where the sherd is placed in the home of the target, PDM xii.76–107, CXIXa 4–6), to silence enemies (PGM XLVI.4–8), and to inflict illness (PGM CXXIV.1–43). The Karanis example varies from these, as the text is not a record of a performed spell.

82. P. Gallo, "The wandering personnel of the temple of Narmuthis in the Faiyum and some toponyms of the Meris of Polemon," in *Life in a multi-cultural society: Egypt from Cambyses to Constantine and beyond,* ed. J. Johnson (Chicago: Oriental Institute of the University of

Demotic and Greek, were composed for various purposes and include school exercises, receipts, lists of objects, and medical prescriptions. Many of the texts are problematic and have proven to be difficult to interpret. Some seem to record instructions for the priests of the temple, with itineraries of villages that the priests are instructed to visit. Often, the priests are told to carry certain materials to the villages for use in the local temple and perhaps to perform ritual acts for the local populace.[83]

Another ostracon from Narmouthis, not found with the others, brings us closer to our Karanis artifact, as it appears to preserve both *voces magicae* and ritual materials. The convex side of Vogliano 15 contains a magical phrase, written in a triangular pattern, with each line diminishing the word ALBANATHANABLA by a single letter. The other side of the object lists ingredients including herbs, myrrh, dried figs, and white pennyroyal.[84] Although publications of this object have suggested that the latter side is a medical prescription, these materials are also common in the spell papyri. The two sides of the Narmouthis ostracon should be understood together, as different portions of the same spell. The use of abbreviated spell instructions is paralleled in many of the Coptic ritual texts, which are made up only of lists of ingredients; a practitioner in the later period presumably would have known what to do with such concise instructions.[85] A gem from Anapa on the Black Sea may provide another example of a portable object that was used as a model for magical production. One side of the gem has been inscribed with a brief statement of purpose, that the gem will be used to send away dangerous spells. This is followed by a magical phrase and the word DAMNAMENEUS in a descending *figura magica,* in which one letter is dropped in each line. The other side of the gem includes lists of body parts, such as "for the ears" followed by magical symbols. Christopher Faraone recently has suggested that the gem functioned as a miniature handbook, providing a general all-purpose spell for repelling aggressive magic on one side and context-specific magical

---

Chicago, 1992), 119. Cf. P. Gallo, "Ostraca demotici da Medinet Madi," *EVO* 12 (1989), and P. Gallo, *Ostraca demotici e ieratici dall'archivio bilingue di Narmouthis* (Pisa: ETS, 1997).

83. Gallo, "The wandering personnel of the temple of Narmuthis," 123; A. Vogliano, "Medinet Madi. Fouilles de l'Université Royale de Milan," *CdE* 27 (1939): 88. David Frankfurter has suggested a similar purpose for *BGU* XIII 2215, from Soknopaiou Nesos, which records temples and shrines in the Herakleides and Polemon *merides* (Frankfurter, *Religion in Roman Egypt,* 100).

84. O.Mil.Vogl. inv. 85; Vogliano, *Secondo rapporto degli scavi condotti dalla Missione archeologica d'Egitto della R. Università di Milano nella zona di Madinet Madi,* 49–51, nos. 15–16, *Suppl. Mag.* no. 67.

85. *ACM* pp. 259–62. Compare nos. 127 and 135.

Identifying the Remains of Magic in the Village of Karanis 125

signs used for relieving ailments of the head on the other.[86] At Karanis, the ostracon may have been used in a similar fashion, to preserve a brief summation of the magical act or a portable handbook that could be consulted by the practitioner. We can return to the locus of discovery in order to better understand the purpose this spell may have served.

Although the text of the object is enigmatic, the findspot and archaeological context suggest that the spell was used to protect grain stores against vermin. Finds from the insula block indicate that House 403 was part of a larger complex dedicated to grain processing and storage.[87] The insula block is dominated by two structures, C401, a smaller structure, and C404, a granary outfitted with a variety of rectangular bins for grain storage. House 403 shares a courtyard with the granary, C404, and an access door near C403's interior stairway connects the two structures. Two small alleyways, CS415 and CS410, bisect the block, but these appear to act as passageways within the complex. In C414, C407, and C403, circular bins for grain storage, there are shallow stone mortars and a stone milling pot that may indicate that processing occurred in these spaces. Sometime in the late C period, the doorway to C409A was filled, and a trough was added that may have been used for kneading bread.[88] It seems likely that the insula block was a significant structure on the site, as its wooden door was replaced at some point with a formal stone entranceway.[89] Coin hoards were also discovered beneath the floor of C401, accessible through a trapdoor, perhaps indicating that economic transactions were occurring in the building.[90]

Artifacts discovered in the buildings solidify our interpretation of its function. Grain was discovered still intact within the granary. Receipts for the transport of grain as well as tax payments in kind were discovered in houses 402, 403, and 406, a building directly adjacent to the granary that likely served a subsidiary function. Three ostraca were found in room H of House 403: a list of liturgical workers, a list of donkey drivers that mentions transport to the granary, and a receipt for grain transport by a man named Paesis.[91] These ostraca do not provide sufficient prosopographic details that allow association with

---

86. C. A. Faraone. "A Greek gemstone from the Black Sea: Amulet or miniature handbook?" *Kernos* 23 (2010): 108–11.

87. Peterson, "The architecture and topography of Karanis," 317.

88. Ibid., 319, 327–28.

89. Ibid., 318.

90. Ibid., 223.

91. O.Mich. inv. 9880, list of liturgical workers; *P.Mich.* VI 850, list of donkey drivers; *P.Mich.* VI 902, grain receipt.

126   Materia Magica

an individual known from the site, but this material suggests that the granary was in use when the spell ostracon was deposited. Other finds relate to domestic activities and are typical of household assemblages discovered elsewhere at Karanis. A large number of ceramic vessels and cooking equipment derive from the insula block, and the mortar and milling pots from C403 could be used either for on-site grain processing or food preparation.

We have noted that Horus and Isis, when they appear in magical texts, are invoked for protection. At Karanis, Isis and Horus may have extended their prophylactic powers to inanimate objects, namely, grain. It is not an implausible leap to transfer the idea of divine protection against those creatures capable of killing or harming humans to animals that posed a danger for human sustenance. Granary stores certainly required defensive measures, as pests, including rodents and insects, were a constant threat. Horus and his mother may have prevented vermin from eating or otherwise destroying the agricultural produce that was stored in a building. Moreover, Isis was associated with safeguards against supernatural dangers. The ancient laws of the XII Tables, attributed to fifth-century Rome, vividly illustrate the anxieties that accompanied agricultural production. The laws provide harsh penalties for stealing grain through magical means by chanting out the crops.[92] Indeed, at Karanis, the petition submitted by Gemellus illustrate that such concerns were warranted, and Isis may have lent her protection against malicious magic to agricultural surplus.

A larger pattern associating Horus and grain protection may be detectable at the site. In structure C65, one of the two largest granaries in the village, the central courtyard included a large wall painting that shows Horus seated in a chair and flanked by the god Tutu[93] (plate 10). The painting depicts the god as a youth, as he is shown with the sidelock, and is wearing a bulla. Tutu, painted in maroon with black spots, appears to the god's left as a composite animal, with heads of a jackal and a dog, a long leonine body. Cobras encircle Tutu's legs,

---

92. Plin. *HN* XXVIII.17. On agricultural magic in the XII Tables, see Rives, "Magic in the XII Tables revisited," esp. 277–78; Pharr, "The interdiction of magic in Roman law," 277. The XII tables were presumably the legal basis for the case against C. Furius Cresimus, who was brought to trial because his agricultural return seemed out of proportion with that of his neighbors. Plin. *HN* XVIII.41–3.

93. Husselman, *Karanis topography and architecture,* 61–62. On this wall painting, see A.T. Wilburn "A wall painting at Karanis used for architechtural protection" in *Das Fayum in Hellenismus und Kaiserzeit. Fallstudien zu multikulturellem Leben in der Antike,* ed. C. Arlt and M. A. Stadler (Weisbaden: Harassowitz, forthcoming).

Identifying the Remains of Magic in the Village of Karanis 127

and in each paw, he holds an upright dagger. Both divinities can be associated with protection: Horus on the cippi warded against hostile animals, while Tutu was frequently depicted as a prophylactic against spiritual threats.[94] Few other wall paintings survive from the granary, although a number of bins preserved traces of small vignettes, likely representations of the produce that would be stored within. The wall painting was situated at the main entrance to the granary, and the paired images of Horus and Tutu would have warded off human, animal, and demonic forces that sought to harm the grain stores.

In the same archaeological context as the inscribed potsherd, excavators discovered a headless terra-cotta statuette of the god Harpocrates.[95] It is possible that this image was used in the performance of a rite, as *zodion* can refer to either a small drawing or a three-dimensional representation. A comparable image of Isis, however, was not discovered among the finds. This may be a result of happenstance, as the ritual could have occurred without a depiction of the goddess, or the Isis image may have been removed. Alternatively, the ritual may have employed only a representation of Horus/Harpocrates. Isis is not pictured on the front of the Horus cippi, even though she is frequently invoked. Her depiction sometimes appears on the reverse in two-dimensional form, so it is possible that differing means of representation were employed for mother and son. The text may allude to this possibility, as the word *zodion* is singular, rather than plural; only one image may have been necessary. While the Harpocrates statuette may have been used in conjunction with the instructional ostracon, the evidence for this is not conclusive. The coherence of the deposit, with a large amount of material associated with grain processing, suggests that these rooms and their contents were abandoned, and that the area was not used

---

94. Ritner, "Horus on the crocodiles: A juncture of religion and magic," 111–12; on Tutu see S. Sauneron, "Le nouveau spinx composite du Brooklyn Museum et le rôle du dieu Toutou-Tithoès," *JNES* 19, no. 4 (1960); O. Kaper, *The Egyptian god Tutu: A study of the sphinx-god and master of demons with a corpus of monuments* (Leuven: Peters, 2003).

95. Another statuette of the god was discovered in room J. As the Michigan team often kept single instances of artifact types with the goal of creating a typology, the figurine discovered in the same room as the magical ostracon was not retained. We can note that Harpocrates figurines often were found associated with the granaries at Karanis. Four other statues of Harpocrates were discovered in rooms associated with granary C404, including an additional image of the god in room H of C403 (C403: K.M. inv. 6453, field number 33-C403H-A; C 409: K.M. inv. 6454, field number 33-409J-R; C413: K.M. inv. 6466, field number 33-413K-E). Terracotta statues of the god also were discovered in granaries C65, C113, C121, C123, and C132, sometimes in significant numbers; granary C132 included three images of the god. This may indicate that the god was closely associated with protection at Karanis, but further investigation on this topic is necessary.

128   Materia Magica

as a garbage dump after the building had gone out of use. All of the materials found in the structure should be related to one another, left behind when the insula block was abandoned. Even so, we lack clear evidence such as a pit or niche that would securely place the ostracon and the statuette together yet distinct from the other materials in the room. While it is tempting to read these two objects as the residue of an act of magic, we lack the definitive evidence necessary for such a supposition.

The ostracon, however, still has much to tell us through its archaeological context. The material found in the unit appears to be the result of abandonment; the architectural features related to grain processing align well with the evidence from the ostraca, which concern grain transport. It seems probable that the ostracon was used as a model text by a practitioner who performed a rite in this space related to grain protection. Like the fever amulet discussed above, the ostracon has been dated to the late third or early fourth century CE, the period in which the temples were in decline. The local religious expert continued to be an important individual in village life, where he ministered to personal crises and provided a variety of religious services. This practitioner was a literate individual, as it seems probable that the ostracon was copied from a formulary and served as a mnemonic device. The practitioner likely had access to a privately held ritual text, which may have cobbled together elements of multiple religious traditions.

The ostracon appears to be pagan, although this cannot be said with certainty, as the phrase "woman, child" could equally refer to Isis and Horus as to Mary and Jesus. Isis and Horus are depicted in another wall painting from elsewhere the site in which the child is seated on his mother's lap in a pose that is immediately recognizable through its similarity to depictions of Mary and Jesus.[96] The development of Christian and Coptic magical traditions owes much to its pagan predecessors. A shared Egyptian tradition may have led Jesus and Mary to be associated with the protective power once accorded to Isis and Horus, and we can best understand this artifact through reference to earlier Egyptian and Graeco-Roman magical techniques. A comparable process can be seen in a Coptic lintel now in the collection of Dumbarton Oaks. D. Frankfurter has suggested that the decoration of the lintel appropriated the imagery of the Horus cippus. Where Horus once stood atop the forces of the desert, in the Coptic lintel the Christian cross overcomes paired antelopes, which repre-

---

96. The wall painting is published in Boak and Peterson, *Karanis: Topographical and architectural report of excavations during the seasons 1924–28*, 34 and fig. 49.

sent the desert and chaos. The lintel protects those who lived within the house by asserting the power of Christ over evil, depicted in this case according to traditional Egyptian iconography.[97] Our inability to clearly distinguish a pagan or Christian focus for the ostracon is telling, and reflects the multivalent nature of Late Antique magic. It is altogether possible that the spell instructions could be used for a ritual that would suit either a Christian or a pagan patron, in which the practitioner selected the appropriate mother-child pair according to the religious needs of his audience.

A Love-Inducing Ritual under Structure 165[98]

Structure 165, discovered within the top layer, is located on the eastern side of the large settlement area, close to the destroyed center of the ancient town (plate 11). Among a large number of objects, five artifacts—a lead amulet, a doll, and three hairpins—were excavated from beneath the floor of the house. The close study of the archaeological context, coupled with detailed analysis of the objects, suggests that some of these artifacts represent the residue of magic aimed at fertility or an erotic spell, perhaps deposited in this location in order to target the resident of the house.

Constructed during the last phase of occupation at the site, Structure 165 is made up of eight enclosed rooms, as well as the ruins of two circular bins, probably for the storage of grain. Like many other domestic structures at the site, the house possessed agricultural installations; a mill was built on the outer face of the eastern wall, and residents probably used part of the street directly to the east, AS156, as a courtyard. In the top layer, Street 111 lay to the north, and houses 161 and 162 faced house 165. To the west, house 165 shared a wall with house 164, which consisted of a series of three rooms, likely constructed

---

97. D. Frankfurter, "The binding of antelopes: A Coptic frieze and its Egyptian religious context," *JNES* 63, no. 2 (2004): 108–9.

98. Some of this research was previously published as part of a volume of conference proceedings: A. T. Wilburn, "Excavating love magic at Roman Karanis," in *New archaeological and papyrological researches on the Fayyum: Proceedings of the international meeting of Egyptology and papyrology, Lecce 8th–10th June 2005*, ed. M. Capasso and P. Davoli, *Papyrologica Lupiensia 14/2005* (Galatina [Lecce]: Congedo, 2007). Further information about the archaeological context is included here, as well as a more detailed analysis of the finds with regard to the methodology outlined in chapter 2. I have also benefited from the suggestions proposed by the participants at the Midwestern Consortium on Ancient Magic, held in Ann Arbor, Michigan, on April 10, 2010.

130   Materia Magica

in the top layer of occupation as was house 165. House 166, which may have been constructed slightly earlier than 165, was located to the south; the north wall of house 166 also served as the south wall of house 165.[99]

The artifacts that will be investigated in this section derive from an area designated 165*. References to the findspots of artifacts in the Record of Objects indicate that this excavation unit encompasses the space beneath house 165, house 166, and part of the street AS156. E. E. Peterson's manuscript of the architecture and topography of the site suggests that a significant break existed between the top-layer construction and architecture identified as belonging to an earlier phase: "The floor level of house 166D, which may well have been an open courtyard for the house, was fully four meters above that of the B level Street BS155 and the courtyard B154K."[100] Although the depth of this fill indicates that some of the objects recovered in the excavation of unit 165* were deposited during the period in which the B-layer structures were abandoned, references in the Record of Objects allow the association of other groups of artifacts with the occupation period of house 165. Contemporary site photographs, taken during excavation, document the presence of rubbish holes that were placed beneath the floor.[101] The basement level of the house probably was used for storage, as grain was found within the excavation unit; the discovery of a desiccated, Roman-period rat along with the grain suggests that this area was accessible in antiquity.[102]

Two separate deposits beneath the house provide evidence of magical activity, but while both assemblages relate to the residents of the structure, it seems unlikely that the two groups of artifacts were employed in the same ritual. In an area documented as above the C-level house, excavators found a lead sheet rolled and suspended on a small piece of cording (plate 12), a bronze necklace with a glass bead, a fragment of a red cloth bag, the sole of a sandal, a slipper made of hide, a bronze bracelet, an ankh, grain, coins, beads, and two papyri.[103] A number of these finds may be related to a women's toilette. The

---

99. In the detailed maps and plans of the site, the walls of house 166 are dated to the second layer of occupation. Peterson's unpublished manuscript, however, discusses house 166 as a top-layer construction.

100. Peterson, "The architecture and topography of Karanis," 656.

101. K.M. photograph archive 5.3272; 5.3445.

102. K.M. photograph archive 5.3224.

103. Lead tablet: K.M. inv. 24255; bronze necklace with a glass bead: K.M. inv. 88928; beads: K.M. inv 53095; 53224; 53272; 53445; 53095; papyri: P.Mich. inv. 5278 includes a number of fragments written in a semiliterate hand that was probably part of a private letter, while SB VI. 9246 lists some of the villages in the Fayum in alphabetical order.

Identifying the Remains of Magic in the Village of Karanis   131

lead tablet is likely inscribed but has not been unrolled. The braided cord suggests that this object was meant to be worn; its small size may indicate that it would have adorned the wearer's wrist or the ankle of a child, and probably served as a protective amulet.

This lead tablet may be compared to examples of amulets known from Egypt and the larger Mediterranean world. A fever amulet from Oxyrhynchus, inscribed on a lamella made of a lead-silver alloy, invokes various spirits to protect the bearer from fever and other matters, a broad category that might include not only physical ailments but also other forms of misfortune.[104] Similarly, earlier Egyptian Oracular Amuletic Decrees recorded an oracular pronouncement, attributed to a god, which would protect the bearer against all manner of sickness and hardship.[105] These documents, often intended for children, were inscribed on small pieces of papyrus. The papyrus was subsequently rolled, bound with string, and placed into a cylinder made of bone, ivory, or metal; the person to be protected then wore the cylinder as an amulet. The small size of the Karanis amulet suggests it may have been worn by a child and, like these other examples, perhaps was intended for protection.

A second, curious group of finds was recovered in an area described as "low and to the east of B/C 166," perhaps near the objects associated with the lead amulet. Of particular interest is a small, roughly made mud figurine (K.M. inv. 7525, plate 13). The object is a coarse depiction of a woman—a rectangular shape is indented to indicate a head, the head is topped with a variety of spiky protrusions meant to indicate hair and two pinched knobs represent breasts. Details, including the eyes, nose, a mouth, the nipples, and the genitals, are picked out using a tool. The small object lacks arms, and there is a break at the bottom. In the 1933 excavation notes, the figurine was identified as a toy, but this association seems unlikely given the emphasis placed on the primary and secondary sexual characteristics. The top and back of the head are significantly darker than the front of the torso, and traces of darkened

---

104. Kotansky, *Greek magical amulets: The inscribed gold, silver, copper, and bronze "Lamellae": Text and commentary,* no. 58; on this line, also paralleled in PGM XXXVI.176, see commentary at *Suppl. Mag.* no. 2, p. 9.

105. T. G. Wilfong, *Egyptian anxieties* (in preparation); B. Bohleke, "An oracular amuletic decree of Khonsu in the Cleveland Museum of Art," *JEA* 83 (1997): 155–56. Cf. I. E. S. Edwards, *Hieratic papyri in the British Museum. Fourth series: Oracular amuletic decrees of the late New Kingdom,* 2 vols. (London: Trustees of the British Museum, 1960), and in general on amulets: Pinch, *Magic in ancient Egypt,* 111 and fig. 74; C. Andrews, *Amulets of ancient Egypt,* 1st University of Texas Press ed. (Austin: University of Texas Press, 1994).

132   Materia Magica

discoloration are also visible along the back. This variation in color indicates that the figurine was burned, probably by placing its head into a fire. The small object may have been set on its back in the flames; this would account for the uneven firing of the mud of which it is made. The traces of burning evident on the figurine are striking and significant, as none of the other objects recovered from the excavation locus show similar signs. Rather than suffering damage as part of a larger fire, this object was likely burned intentionally.

The figurine was discovered with a number of other items, including beads, two ostraca, and three bone pins (plate 14).[106] Comparison between the end of one of the bone pins, which measures 3.9 mm, and the right eye of the figurine, which is the same size, suggests that the pin was likely the object used to create the hole. Other holes, such as the left nipple, which is slightly smaller, may reflect the use of a different pin. This forensic match, and the discovery of the two artifacts in close association, may suggest that they were utilized in this space and intentionally deposited here.

Crudely made nude female figurines have been discovered in a variety of earlier, Pharaonic contexts. These artifacts are constructed of multiple materials, including faience, stone, wood, ivory, or clay, with varying degrees of artistic and naturalistic precision.[107] Most often, the figurines are identified by the presence of the pubic triangle. Found in shrines to Hathor, as well as in domestic settings and the graves of women, scholars have associated these objects with the desire for fertility and conception.[108] Sexualized dolls are also found in male graves, which may attest to their use as emblems of male desire for sexual potency in the next world.[109] Some of the figurines are shown with infants, while others are depicted on beds. The dolls may have been intended

---

106. Artifacts discovered in the area with the roughly made mud figurine K.M. inv. 7525: beads, ostraca (*O.Mich.* I 281 and *O.Mich.* I 531), a third-century papyrus (P.Mich. inv. 5282, now in Cairo), a piece of alabaster, three bone pins (K.M. inv. 21776), and a small female figurine. See the discussion in appendix I.

107. Ritner, "Household religion in ancient Egypt," 181–82; G. Pinch, *Votive offerings to Hathor* (Oxford: Griffith Institute, Ashmolean Museum, 1993); G. Pinch, "Childbirth and female figurines at Deir el-Medina and el-'Amarna," *Orientalia* 52 (1983); R. Janssen and J. J. Janssen, *Growing up in ancient Egypt* (London: Rubicon, 1990), 7–8; C. Desroches-Noblecourt, "'Concubines du Mort' et mères de famille au Moyen Empire," *BIFAO* 53 (1953).

108. Pinch, *Votive offerings to Hathor,* 211–25; for Pinch's typology for fertility figurines, see ibid., 198–209.

109. R. K. Ritner, "Des preuves de l'existence d'une nécromancie dans l'Égypte ancienne," in *La magie en Egypte: à la recherche d'une définition: actes du colloque organisé par le Musée du Louvre, les 29 et 30 septembre 2000,* ed. Y. Koenig (Paris: Documentation française: Musée du Louvre, 2002), 291–92.

Identifying the Remains of Magic in the Village of Karanis 133

to promote conception and to provide protection for mother and infant through childbirth and into the first days or weeks of life. Female figurines found in the domestic sphere likely fulfilled this sort of temporary need, while objects with permanent religious importance would have been deposited in temples.[110] Pharaonic figurines sometimes show indications of intentional breakage or damage. Rather than viewing this destruction as an attempt at execration, it is more likely that the owners wished to negate or eliminate the power of the charm. Although the nudity of the Karanis figurine calls to mind fertility and sexuality, the traces of burning as well as the use of the bone pins imply a more malign usage aimed at compelling the affection of a potential lover.

Figurines and other representations are frequently burned in rituals, often with the intent to cause bodily harm or destroy an enemy. In Mesopotamian rituals intended to counteract or dispel witchcraft, known as the Maqlû, or "Burning," wax, dough, wood, and bitumen figurines are destroyed through burning.[111] Likewise, figurines meant to represent the participants in oath ceremonies were melted over a flame in order to call down a conditional curse on the celebrants of rite, should any individual violate the tenets of the agreement. The same principle lies behind an oath ceremony undertaken at Cyrene, discussed above, in which the colonists melted wax figurines as part of a conditional curse against themselves.[112] The Karanis figurine, however, was not destroyed by burning but only was placed over the flame for sufficient time to show traces of damage. Rather than mimed destruction of the target of the spell, this may suggest that a different purpose lay behind the use of flame.

---

110. B. J. Kemp, "How religious were the ancient Egyptians?" *CAJ* 5, no. 1 (1995): 30. Compare the example from Amarna cited in T. E. Peet et al., *The city of Akhenaten* (London: Egypt Exploration Society, 1923), 25; Pinch, "Childbirth and female figurines at Deir el-Medina and el-'Amarna," 414. The artifact was discovered underneath the stairs. For this area as a place for menstruating women, see T. G. Wilfong, "Menstrual synchrony and the 'place of women' in Ancient Egypt," in *Gold of praise: Studies on ancient Egypt in honor of Edward F. Wente,* ed. E. Teeter, J. A. Larson, and E. F. Wente (Chicago: Oriental Institute of the University of Chicago, 1999), 429–30. Three crudely made figurines recently were discovered near the Sanctuary of Isis and Magna Mater in Mainz, Germany, but these likely served a general execratory purpose. See above, ch. 2 n. 115.

111. M.-L. Thomsen, "Witchcraft and magic in ancient Mesopotamia," in *Witchcraft and magic in Europe: Biblical and pagan societies,* ed. B. Ankarloo and S. Clark, *Witchcraft and Magic in Europe* (Philadelphia: University of Pennsylvania Press, 2001), 51–52. In general, on the form and purpose of the Maqlû, see T. Abusch, "Mesopotamian anti-witchcraft literature: Texts and studies part I: The nature of Maqlû: Its character, divisions, and calendrical setting," *JNES* 33, no. 2 (1974).

112. Trans. Graham, *Colony and mother city in ancient Greece,* 226. For bibliography and discussion, see above, ch. 2, n. 88.

Numerous spells preserved from the Fayum region as well as from the broader Nile valley highlight the intersection between fire and erotic magic, often with the goal of causing the victim to feel pain until he or she loves the practitioner. One such instructional text is found in the spell book associated with the Fayum, PGM XXXVI, and called a "love spell of attraction, an excellent enflamer." The practitioner is instructed to glue a papyrus that is inscribed with a series of magical names to the wall of a bath and recite the invocation "TOU SETH, as you are in flames and on fire, so also the soul, the heart of her, NN, whom NN bore, until she comes loving me, NN."[113] As the heat from the bathhouse warmed the image of Seth on the papyrus fragment, the victim would also be burned. In a separate love spell, the practitioner draws an image on a clean sheet of papyrus and writes the words "Attract her to me, NN, her, NN, aflame, on fire, flying through the air . . ."[114] It is possible to note a similar pattern in other love spells from the Fayyum. A papyrus love curse discovered at Hawara begins with the invocation, "As Typhon is the [adversary] of [Helios, so] also inflame [the soul] of Eutyches whom Zosime [bore]."[115]

In each of these spells, fire and flame are used to describe erotic desire metaphorically and to compel passion in reality. Because the body and the psyche were thought to be intertwined, fever or illness could be indicative of the imbalance of the four bodily humors, most notably on account of erotic passion. Conversely, by inflicting an illness on another individual, this could have a complementary effect on their emotional state; the physical symptoms associated with excessive passion may have led the victim to experience desire.[116] The bodily sensations of lovesickness—insomnia, hunger, thirst, lust, fever, and physical pain—may be transferred from the commissioner to his or her beloved, often with the intent that the target of the spell suffer more egregiously than the commissioner.[117] Placing the small statuette above a flame, so that the object was heated but not destroyed, would have had a similar effect on the target of the spell, inducing heat, and thus passionate love, for the client.

---

113. PGM.XXXVI.69–101, trans. E. N. O'Neil in *GMP*, 270. On this spell, see D. Montserrat, *Sex and society in Græco-Roman Egypt* (London: Kegan Paul International, 1996), 191.

114. PGM XXXVI.102–33, trans. E. N. O'Neil in *GMP*, 271.

115. PGM LXVIII.1–20, trans. E. N. O'Neil in *GMP*, 297.

116. Gal. *Anim.mor.corp.* 4–7 (II 45–54 M.); *Mixt.* 2.6 (78 H.), cited in L. R. LiDonnici, "Burning for it: Erotic spells for fever and compulsion in the ancient Mediterranean world," *GRBS* 39 (1998): 83.

117. Winkler, *The constraints of desire: The anthropology of sex and gender in ancient Greece,* 232; LiDonnici, "Burning for it: Erotic spells for fever and compulsion in the ancient Mediterranean world," 96.

Identifying the Remains of Magic in the Village of Karanis 135

Burning also was intended to cause physical pain to the victim, and to act as a goad to convince the beloved to come to the commissioner of the spell.[118] Fire often was employed as one element among other tortures that might induce the affection of the beloved. A spell of unknown provenance, now in Berlin (PGM XIXa), reads:

Aye, lord demon, attract, inflame, destroy, burn, cause her to swoon from love as if she is being burnt, inflamed. Goad the tortured soul, the heart of Karosa, whom Thelo bore, until she leaps forth and comes to Apalos, whom Theonilla bore, out of passion and love.[119]

The application of torture as a means of erotic compulsion has a lengthy history. In Pindar's *Pythian* 4.213–19, Aphrodite instructs Jason in order that he might persuade Medea to love him. She demonstrates the use of the iunx bird, which is strapped to a wheel, and teaches Jason prayers and incantations that are intended to "strip Medea of reverence for her parents, and that desire for Greece might shake her, with the whip of Persuasion as she was burning in her heart."[120] These spells function by torturing the victim with a specific goal in mind—the target will suffer until he or she arrives at the doorstep of the commissioner.

At Karanis, burning the figurine or placing it within a fire would have had a comparable effect on the victim of the spell, causing her head and body to be enflamed, both with passion and as a goad to bring her to the commissioner. It may be possible to note the use of burning a representation to bring about compulsion in a group of objects discovered in a clandestine excavation to the north of Assiut, in Middle Egypt. A clay jar enclosed a papyrus that in turn was wrapped around two crudely shaped wax figurines that were locked in an erotic embrace.[121] These two images mimed the intended result of the spell—that Euphemia would have intercourse with Theon, the commissioner

---

118. Faraone suggests that compulsion by fire is a special subset for *agoge* spells intended to draw the beloved. Faraone, *Ancient Greek love magic,* 26 and n. 115. For further examples of burning as a means of compulsion see ibid., 58–59, n. 81.

119. Trans. O'Neil and Kotansky in *GMP,* 257.

120. Trans. Faraone, *Ancient Greek love magic,* 56. On this passage and the role of torture in love magic, see Faraone, *Ancient Greek love magic,* 56–69; C. A. Faraone, "The wheel, the whip and other implements of torture: Erotic magic in Pindar Pythian 4.213–19," *CJ* 89, no. 1 (1993); for the view of the iunx as a spinning top, see S. I. Johnston, "The song of the iynx: magic and rhetoric in Pythian 4," *TAPA* 125 (1995).

121. Wortmann, "Neue magische texte," esp. 85–102; *Suppl. Mag.* I no. 45; *CT* no. 30: 101–6.

of the assemblage. In the spell for erotic compulsion that had been written on the papyrus, the spirits of the underworld are invoked to bind Euphemia and to "burn her limbs, her liver, her female body . . ." Like the Karanis figurine, these two artifacts were handmade, and the two dolls may preserve some traces of heating. It is difficult to see clear evidence of melting when analyzing the two representations, although the feet of each puppet appear to be curled in an unusual fashion. The warm climate of Egypt likely made the wax malleable, but the practitioner probably warmed the materials prior to modeling the two dolls; this heating may have played a role in the magical act. By wrapping the spell around the two wax puppets, the figurines, like the individuals that they represented, would have been enclosed by the words of the spell and forced to read the text repeatedly, strengthening the rite with each iteration. The ritual may also have intended to bind the victim by trapping the objects within the jar. In the cases of these artifacts, as in many others that fill the collections of museums, illicit excavation has deprived us of the relevant contextual data that surely would have aided our understanding of the ritual and its social setting.[122]

The process of constructing the doll may have also contributed to the efficacy of the magical act. The figurine lacks legs and feet, which may suggest that the practitioner intended to bind or otherwise prevent the target of the spell from moving. A number of magical images have their feet twisted and turned backward in order to constrict and disable the target.[123] A more violent and aggressive process is suggested by the use of the hairpins to add details to the representation. Decorating the figurine and using pins to create the small doll's features may have simulated piercing the woman; with each application of the pin, the woman could have felt pain in her eyes, mouth, breasts, and

---

122. An additional pair of wax figurines, also lacking clear provenance, is housed in the Staatliches Museum Ägyptischer Kunst in Munich. These dolls likewise were discovered inside of an inscribed papyrus that had, in turn, been placed in a ceramic vessel. Some slight discoloration on the shoulders of the figurines could be the remains of heating, but there is little evidence beyond this. The dolls appear to have been pressed together forcibly. On the figurines, see W. Brashear, "Ein neues Zauberensemble in München," *Studien zur altägyptischen Kultur* 19 (1992).

123. *VD* no. 19 is a figurine of Etruscan Heracles with feet and legs intentionally broken off. For representations in which the feet are twisted or turned, see *VD* nos. 3, 7, 8, 10, and 16. In tombs of Pharaonic Egypt, hieroglyphs that depicted dangerous animals were often cut in some way, removing the feet or otherwise rendering the threatening forces ineffectual. On twisting and turning the victim in curse tablets, see C. A. Faraone and A. Kropp, "Inversion, adversion and perversion as strategies in Latin curse-tablets," in *Magical practice in the Latin West: Papers from the international conference held at the University of Zaragoza, 30 Sept.–1 Oct. 2005*, ed. R. L. Gordon and F. Marco Simón (Leiden: Brill, 2010).

Identifying the Remains of Magic in the Village of Karanis   137

pudenda. This use of a hairpin as a weapon, often in the hands of women, is not unattested, although most literary references concern pins used on clothing. So, for example, in Euripides' *Hecuba,* the Phrygian women use the pin of a fibula to blind Polymestor (1170), and the Athenian women were said to have killed the sole survivor of a battle against the Argives and Aeginitans with fibulae pins.[124] Perhaps more relevant in the realm of magic, the hairpins recall the figurine, now in the Louvre, that depicts a bound woman who had been pierced with thirteen copper pins.[125] Needles have been inserted into various parts of her body, including her eyes, ears, mouth, breasts, pubic region, and the soles of her feet. The Louvre figurine and its correlative spell suggest that the act of piercing may have had ritual significance for our Karanis objects. Just as the insertion of the pins into the Louvre figurine was intended to bind the victim's limbs and body parts to the commissioner of the spell, so also the act of creating and piercing the Karanis doll probably played a functional role in the efficacy of the magical act.

The role of the hairpins in the magical rite likely extends beyond their use as a tool to create the artifact. These objects may have been components of the beloved's toilette, as love spells frequently require the inclusion of magical material from the victim. Both literary and archaeological evidence attest to the practice of incorporating *ousia*—hair or items once in contact with the victim—into the rite.[126] A witch in the *Dialogues of the Courtesans* requires either cast-off body parts or clothing for an erotic spell.[127] She places the victim's *ousia* on a peg above burning sulfur, heating or burning the objects in order to draw forth the beloved. *Exuvia* from the victim can cement the analogous association between object and its antecedent; a roughly made figurine currently in the Ashmolean museum contains traces of human hair as well as a papyrus that presumably contains a love spell.[128] The discovery of the hairpins along with the figurine may suggest that these artifacts were intended to bind the beloved through an association between the possessions of the target and

---

124. Sch. in Eur. *Hec.* 934; Hdt. 5.87. Oedipus, too, used the pin of Jocasta's garment to blind himself before taking his own life (Soph. *Oed. Tyr.* 1269).

125. du Bourguet, "Ensemble magique de la période romaine en Égypte," and Kambitsis, "Une nouvelle tablette magique d'Égypte, Musée du Louvre Inv. E27145, 3e/4e siècle," discussed above with bibliography at ch. 1 n. 64.

126. Cf. Apul. *Met.* 2.32 and 3.15–18. On the use of *ousia* in magic, see above, ch. 2, Plants, Animals, and Natural Ingredients.

127. Lucian *Dial. meret* 4.

128. BM EA 37918; discussed in *VD* no. 31; Ogden, "Binding spells," 73.

the magical object. Another possibility, however, can be proposed: that these artifacts, like the other items found in the excavation locus that were associated with a woman's toilette, belonged to the commissioner of the spell. We possess a number of spells written for women who sought the affections of another woman, and a female principal may have employed her own pins as a means to exert power over the potential target.[129] In this case, the spell would have been intended to draw the beloved to the home of the commissioner, employing these feminine items not as *ousia* to connect the victim to the figurine, but rather as implements of torture that would goad the target.

These four objects, the figurine and the three hairpins, highlight the simplicity and mundane nature of the physical components of some magical rites. While other spells may have required obscure ingredients from far-off lands, the remains preserved beneath structure 165 show no signs of the exotic, either because these materials were ephemeral and did not survive or because they were not part of the ritual as it was performed here.

The identification of this small group of objects as magical is dependent on the archaeological context in which they were discovered—these artifacts can be associated with one another through proximity. Numerous houses at Karanis were equipped with underground rooms in which objects were stored, and the discovery of grain in the lower level of structure 165, complementing the grain-processing implements found in the building above, suggests that here, too, the basement was in use during the final occupation phase.[130] At this point, however, the excavation records introduce some uncertainty about the deposition of the figurine and the pins. Marginalia in the Record of Objects may indicate that the group of artifacts was discovered to the east of B/C 166, potentially placing the findspot outside of the house and its basement. During the final use-phase of the building, the residents had installed a milling apparatus along the exterior face of the eastern wall of the building, effectively appropriating part of the street for use as a courtyard. Should we locate the finds

---

129. Four homoerotic attraction spells are known, two of which relate to lesbian attraction: PGM XXXII and *Suppl. Mag.* no. 42. On these spells, see Montserrat, *Sex and society in Græco-Roman Egypt,* 158–59; B. J. Brooten, *Love between women: Early Christian responses to female homoeroticism* (Chicago: University of Chicago Press, 1996), 77–90; Faraone, *Ancient Greek love magic,* 147–48; Dickie, "Who practiced love-magic in classical antiquity and in the late Roman world?" 573. Brooten suggests *Suppl. Mag.* no. 37 should also be read as a homoerotic spell. *Love between women,* 90–96.

130. For a description of underground rooms at Karanis, see Husselman, *Karanis topography and architecture,* 37.

outside of the house, the deposition might suggest that the practitioner surreptitiously buried the charm along the outer wall in order to place it near the target of the spell. The depth of the deposit, however, argues against this scenario, as the find was made at a low level. It seems more likely that the individual who deposited the artifacts did so within the basement level of the structure.

The practitioner may have placed the figurine here in order to draw the target to the home of the commissioner. In PGM XXXVI.134–60, titled "Marvelous love spell of attraction," the text instructs the practitioner to "take myrrh and male frankincense, put them in a drinking-cup and add a (measure) of vinegar, and at the third hour of the night put it into the socket of your door and say the spell seven times." A love spell follows, with injunctions to Isis and Osiris to cause the victim to suffer until she loves the commissioner and attaches her genitals to his. In this spell, the material focus of the spell—the cup—is placed at the home of the commissioner, rather than the target, and a similar process may be at work in the Karanis figurine. The small statuette, which likely caused the victim to burn with love for the commissioner and to feel pain as the image was pierced with needles, may have acted on the target at a distance, compelling her to come to the place where the spell materials were deposited.

Analysis of the archaeological context suggests that this may have been a primary deposit, in which the excavators discovered the artifacts in the same space in which they were abandoned. The other finds discovered beneath the house appear to have been stored there; there is little reason to believe that this area was used as a garbage dump and subsequently filled in prior to the construction of structure 165. The discovery of a rat in one area of the basement, along with unused grain, suggests that agricultural produce may have been kept here. Moreover, the numerous articles associated with a woman's toilette point to the use of this area for storage. The artifacts, too, demonstrate that they were associated in antiquity; we can infer a ritual enactment from the correspondence between the ends of the pins and holes made by piercing the figurine. The fact that that figurine was burned intentionally, while no other objects in the deposit show similar signs of damage, argues that this artifact was either placed over a fire in this location or brought here after being singed. It seems likely, therefore, that the deposit is the residue of a ritual act. Placement underneath the house supports this proposition, as the decision to bury the artifacts in this location would have been significant if the building were the residence of either the commissioner or the target of the spell.

140   Materia Magica

A Large Deposit of Painted Bones

Two excavation units located on the outskirts of the central occupation area at Karanis, areas A262 and A265, yielded a large number of unusual objects that may have been employed for a magical purpose. A total of eighty-four decorated animal and human bones, as well as a small number of bonelike objects similar in appearance and design, were found in this area (plate 3). These artifacts had all been painted with a red substance in one or more of three patterns: dots, straight lines, and undulating lines. Ochre, found nearby and associated with the bones by the original excavators, was probably used in the creation of these objects.[131] This suggests that these artifacts were manufactured and discarded at this location. The analysis of the archaeological context suggests that this corpus of bones represents an instance of ritual practice undertaken away from the main settlement area. The designs that have been painted on the bones can be compared with magical symbols known from other artifacts and from the PGM; moreover, it is possible to demonstrate that bone can be used as a medium for magical practice. There is no clear parallel for the ritual that produced the artifacts, but comparative evidence from the spell instructions suggests that the deposit may have been intended to divine the future, harm an enemy, or protect domesticated animals.

In the top layer of habitation, the excavators cleared the large area A262, which lay to the north of houses A428 and A429, to the west of house A427, and bordered on the western side by an area of sebbakh destruction (plate 15). Area A262 yielded an unusually high quantity of finds, probably due, in part, to the size of the unit. In addition to sherds from ceramic vessels, excavators uncovered a range of objects, including textiles, animal bones, dolls, a libation altar, grain, documents on ostraca, and papyri. Many of these artifacts appear to derive from household assemblages, and the unit extends into areas that may not have been inhabited at the time of deposition.[132] Indeed, the Record of Objects associates some of the material in 262 with rubbish mounds located north of structure 275.[133] A265, located approximately thirteen meters to the south, contained more animal bones with similar decorations. This area is bordered on the north by an insula block containing houses A426 and A424, on

---

131. Red ochre: Field number 25-262-O1, Record of Objects, Karanis 1924–25, 62.
132. Peterson, "The architecture and topography of Karanis," 832.
133. Record of Objects, Karanis 1924–25, A262.

Identifying the Remains of Magic in the Village of Karanis   141

the west by street A267, and on the east and south by two fragmentary walls. The excavators suggested that part of this area, which had been badly damaged by the sebbakhin, possessed some houses in later periods, but few traces were found beyond fragments of walls in excavation square F9.[134] Material from the units suggests that the finds should be dated to the last period of occupation on the site, probably during the fourth or fifth century, if not later.[135] The quantity of finds, as well as the disrepair of many of the artifacts, indicates that this part of the site may have been abandoned when the bones were deposited.

A262 revealed sixteen animal bones, originally accessioned as lot 3504. The bones from A265 were divided into two different excavation lots, 3503 and 10099. A fourth group of bones, accessioned by the Kelsey Museum as lot 3535, is from an unknown area of the site. Physical joins between bone fragments from each of the four lot numbers indicate that the artifacts formed a coherent assemblage at the time of deposition. Bone 81 (Lot 3504) from area 262 joins bone 93 (Lot 3535), linking the undocumented deposit with area 262. Similarly, bone 3503.065 from area 265 joins with 3504.096 from area 265. Finally, bone 10099.070 joins with bone 3503.062, thereby linking the two deposits in area 265 (plate 16). Frequently, the joins between the bones reunite areas of the artifacts that have been painted; this indicates that the bones were decorated prior to being broken.

A number of bones and small fragments of painted plaster are known from other houses. Regrettably, the Michigan team did not keep these artifacts, and only a minute number of the objects were photographed. Site records indicate that bones painted with red dots and similar designs were discovered in houses 161, 181 (K.M. inv. 3492, long bone marked with red splotches), 249, 4006, 4017, B10, and street BS150. Pieces of stone and plaster, similarly with red decoration, were discovered in houses 36, 161, 239 (K.M. inv. 26980, pieces of plaster with red decoration), 244, 312, 5001, and 5022. Photographs suggest that two of these objects were similar to the large deposit of bones from 262/265; it is likely that the remainder of the bones were painted with comparable decorations.[136] Furthermore, a few amphora handles found at the site also

---

134. Peterson, "The architecture and topography of Karanis," 813.
135. L. A. Shier, *Terracotta lamps from Karanis, Egypt: Excavations of the University of Michigan* (Ann Arbor: University of Michigan Press, 1978), 134, no. 388: lamp depicting two heads in relief, dated to late third, early fourth century. The ostraca found in the unit are dated to the late third or early fourth century CE by the hands. The presence of a miniature uninscribed codex, KM inv. 3815, also suggests a late date.
136. Kelsey Museum of Archaeology photograph archive nos. 5.4172; 7.2512.

142   Materia Magica

preserve traces of decoration and may have been used in a similar fashion. If so, it is likely that these artifacts were selected because they mimic the shape of long bones. Almost all of the additional objects were discovered in the early years of excavation and found in the upper strata of the site, suggesting that they date from the last period of occupation. As was also the case with the large deposit, no *in situ* pictures were taken, so it is not possible to know the precise circumstances of discovery for these items. The absence of critical information about the additional finds of painted bones makes it difficult to systematically study the objects. In the case of the pieces that we do possess, however, the quantity of bones discovered in Areas 262 and 265 suggest that those artifacts were significant to the individual that created them and that he or she deposited them in that area. Therefore, it will be productive to initially analyze the artifacts that we can study firsthand, and subsequently consider whether our conclusions might be applied to the additional finds.

The eighty-four bones found in 262 and 265 represent several different species of animals; Dr. David S. Reese undertook analysis of the faunal remains, and tables summarizing these data appear in appendix 2.[137] There are numerous examples of pig, cow, horse, and sheep/goat bones, and medium and large mammals comprise 95.3 percent of the total assemblage. Three of the bones are fragments of human skull, two bones are from fish, and a single bone derives from a dog. A small piece of plaster or chalk, decorated with faint reddish dots on one side, and a fragment of limestone (plate 17), also painted, but with a distinct curve, represent the only decorated artifacts in a medium other than bone that were recovered in these units. The shape of the latter piece resembles one of the skull fragments in the deposit, and both objects may have been included due to their similarity to bone.

The decoration of some of the artifacts continues over what appears to have been preexisting damage. A few of the bones show butchering marks, including a pig scapula (3503.015) and a dog mandible (3503.028). These bones were discarded as domestic or temple refuse after the meat had been consumed. Domesticated animals, which make up the bulk of the deposit, would have been disposed of outside of the settlement area after they had died or were killed, and it seems likely that the practitioner could have recovered these items from the trash heaps or other garbage areas near the village.

---

137. The bones have not been published previously. David Reese, Peabody Museum of Yale University, performed the faunal analysis. One of the artifacts was featured in the Kelsey Museum exhibit "Animals in the Kelsey," spring 2001.

Identifying the Remains of Magic in the Village of Karanis   143

The human bones included in the deposition require a different explanation. The three examples do not demonstrate places where they were originally joined and cannot be definitively ascribed to a single skull. Although it is unlikely that human remains would have been discarded as trash in the desert, this area typically was used for the disposal of the dead, and the cemeteries for Karanis were located not far from areas 262 and 265, to the north of the settlement area. The skull fragments probably derived from a disturbed or robbed grave. There are no indications, however, that the practitioner treated the human specimens differently from others in the deposit, so it is not clear whether these were viewed as significant to the rite or gathered intentionally.

The deposit of bones could derive from either a single occurrence or multiple iterations of the same ritual process undertaken at one location. The decorations on the bones show some variation in color, as the designs on certain bones are browner in hue while others are redder. This may indicate that the bones were painted at different times, using substances of varied composition. Alternatively, the colorant, when applied, may have reacted differently with the bones, or the artifacts may have experienced diverse postdepositional conditions. Chemical testing of the paint on the bones may determine whether all of the artifacts were decorated using the same compound, a fact that would argue for a single ritual incident. As noted above, joins suggest that the bones were all deposited in a single location, but whether this assemblage was formed at a single moment or over time remains uncertain.

The magical nature of the painted bones can be surmised through the analysis of artifacts and the process of production. The designs preserved on the bones can be grouped into three patterns: dots, sinuous lines bisected by an additional line, and undulating lines. These drawings were not intended to be read, although they may mimic writing. Comparison with other magical symbols suggests a range of meanings, from encouraging health to conveying a general idea of mystical efficacy. The dots, which are rounded, vary in size, ranging from relatively small to approximately 2–3 cm in diameter, as on bone K.M. inv. 3503.101 (plate 18). Little patterning is apparent in any of the preserved examples, and the design appears to have been applied in a hurried fashion. The shape, size, and arrangement of the dots may suggest the use of fingertips, rather than a brush, to apply the paint or dye. The sinuous-line pattern consists of a variable number of vertical lines that have been crossed by a single horizontal line. This design typically follows the shape of the inscribed bone, and occasionally, an additional horizontal line is appended to the main stroke, presumably to extend the length of the formal pattern (plate 16). The undulating lines show the greatest amount of variation. Often, a single artifact shows diversity in how this pattern is constructed, both on the level of the individual object and in comparison to other examples. On K.M. inv. 3503.042, these lines may be curved, resembling the lunate sigma, or with loops, similar to the arabic number 3 (plate 19). In other instances, the lines are angled, resembling lambdas or deltas. These marks may be arranged in orderly rows but most frequently appear to have been applied in a random fashion, clumped together or filling one side of a bone. The design may overlap itself, suggesting that the decoration was more important than the construction of a clear image or representation. A single bone may possess only one pattern, or more than one. The amount of painting on either side differs greatly, and the same or a different design might appear on the two sides.

Two bones in particular show notable decoration. On bone 3503.101 (plate 18), excavated as part of Area 265, thirteen medium and large dots are arranged on one half of the obverse of the bone, while a small arrangement of undulating lines appears on the other half; one medium dot is positioned along the lower edge. The undulating lines are grouped together closely and may form some sort of design or figure. Two crossed straight lines bisect a square, and other lines are attached to this representation. A loop extends from the top of the square, and further lines are detected at the bottom. The vertical line that bisects in the interior of the square moves downward from this shape and terminates within the concave side of an inverted omicron. This arrangement is not paralleled on any other bones in the assemblage. On K.M. inv. 10099.070 (plate 16), which is a femur of a cow, the straight-line pattern bisected by a horizontal line runs the length of the bone, following the curve. Directly above it, and running parallel to the other pattern, is a series of undulating lines that appear similar to letters. This may be an attempt to write some form of script, but the pattern is nonsensical. A medium dot is also visible at one end of this bone.

Comparisons between bones within the larger corpus and between the excavator-assigned groups of bones do not reveal consistent patterns that can explain the decoration. None of the four groups is limited in the patterns that it employs, and each grouping shows all three designs. Furthermore, the decoration does not seem to have been dictated by the animal from which a bone was derived; pig bones, for example, are found with all three types of decoration. Nor does the shape of the bone appear to have determined the design applied to it. Rib bone 3503.008 is decorated with lines, while another rib bone of

Identifying the Remains of Magic in the Village of Karanis   145

similar size, 3503.004, is decorated with dots, and a third rib bone, 3503.002, is painted with undulating lines. This suggests that the bones were not decorated according to shape or size, and that the practitioner either was not aware of the species that the bones represented or did not differentiate between the media that he or she adorned.

There is little reason to believe that an ancient individual used these objects for counting or writing exercises, as ostraca, which were plentiful at the site, would have provided a better medium.[138] Writing on the bones, with their curves, indentations, and bumpy surfaces would have been difficult. The designs likewise do not suggest formal use as writing material with the intent of remembering figures or quantities. There is no consistency in the number of strokes used in the patterns. The straight lines, which, to the modern gaze, appear most similar to methods of counting, do not form regular groups. In other words, a single horizontal line crosses no set number of vertical lines. Likewise, the presence of two different patterns on a single artifact does not suggest a form of counting shorthand, as the patterns are not consistent. Finally, the undulating line pattern especially lacks proper articulation, and it would be difficult for the individual using the bones to differentiate the counting marks. If the bones were intended to act as a record of tabulations, rereading the marks would prove as problematic as recounting the quantities.

Known examples of writing exercises from Karanis are markedly different from the appearance of the strokes written on the bones. Often, school exercises focused on perfecting the form of a particular letter or letters, or replicated a passage of a set text, such as a list of divinities.[139] Perhaps most important, the majority of attested examples of writing exercises are composed on papyrus or ostraca, rather than bone.[140] There is not sufficient clarity or coherence of the

---

138. On ostraca as a medium for writing, see U. Wilcken, *Griechische ostraka aus Aegypten und Nubien: ein Beitrag zur antiken Wirtschaftsgeschichte,* 2 vols. (Leipzig: Gieseke & Devrient, 1899), 3–19; P. W. Pestman, *The new papyrological primer* (Leiden: Brill, 1994), 5; Peña, *Roman pottery in the archaeological record,* 160–64.

139. Compare, for example, O.Mich. inv. 9105 (name of pupil and alphabet, written backward); O.Mich. inv. 9598 (alphabet, probably used as model); and P.Mich. inv. 2816 (syllabary). On school texts from Karanis, see R. Cribiore, *Writing, teachers, and students in Graeco-Roman Egypt* (Atlanta: Scholars Press, 1996), nos. 49 (*O.Mich.* I 672); 57 (*O.Mich.* I 659); 81 (P.Mich. inv. 2816; K. McNamee, "Four Michigan Papyri," *ZPE* 46 [1982] 124–26); 108 (*O.Mich.* I 656); 110 (*O.Mich.* I 657); 140 (*O.Mich.* I 661); 143 (*O.Mich.* I 622); 209 (*P.Mich.* VIII 1100); 213 (*O.Mich.* I 693); 214 (*O.Mich.* I 658); 345 (P.Mich. inv. 4832c; T. Renner, "Three new Homerica on papyrus," *HSPh* 83 [1979]: 331–37); 359 (P.Mich. inv. 1588v; Renner, "Three new Homerica on papyrus," 313).

140. Cribiore, *Writing, teachers, and students in Graeco-Roman Egypt,* 63–64, 71–74.

strokes to suggest that the practitioner intended to write in Greek, Demotic, or Coptic. The dots in particular defy explanation as an attempt at letterforms. Only the lines, which could represent an attempt at a lambda, chi, or eta, may suggest letters, but these markings frequently preclude differentiation of the letterforms. Conversely, the patterns evident on the bones argue against mere scribbling, such as one might associate with the doodles of a child. It seems unlikely that the bones were reused as scrap material for writing or for learning to write; the person who inscribed the bones clearly was decorating the artifacts with intention and purpose.

Rather than intelligible script, the practitioner may have intended the painting on the bones to reflect the process of writing. This individual may have been attempting to mimic writing by decorating the artifacts with designs intended to look like letters, words, and phrases. The act of writing is often an important aspect of magical practice, and, as was discussed in the previous chapter, writing transferred the spoken words of a spell into permanent form. In this case, however, the text may preserve the idea of speech, but not the precise words, perhaps because the practitioner was illiterate or chose not to record the incantation. Other magical artifacts show a similar practice at work, where meaningless script composed of loops and squiggles stands in for intelligible words. A number of the Horus cippi are decorated with false writing intended to mimic the spells that normally appear on these stelae. The cippi presumably would have functioned in the same way as their literate counterparts, as suppliants would have poured water over the inscriptions or submerged the artifacts in water and then consumed the liquid that was now infused with the spells.[141] Likewise, a number of magical gems are inscribed with pseudoscript that mimics Greek or Hebrew letters or hieroglyphs. The inscribed signs are not recognizable as *kharaktêres,* or other magical symbols.[142] The Kelsey Museum of Archaeology in Ann Arbor possesses a number of incantation bowls, excavated at Seleucia on the Tigris, that have been inscribed with

---

141. Numerous cippi include false hieroglyphs. See, for example, Alexandria, Graeco-Roman Museum Nr. 642; Baltimore, Walters Art Gallery Nr. 22.333, 22.334, and 22.337; Cairo, Egyptian Museum CG Nr. 9417, 9419, 9420, 9421, 9422, 9423, 9424 (Bibliographic references in Sternberg-El Hotabi, *Untersuchungen zur Überlieferungsgeschichte der Horusstelen: ein Beitrag zur Religionsgeschichte Ägyptens im 1. Jahrtausend v. Chr,* 1, 5–6, 39–40); Ritner, "Horus on the crocodiles: A juncture of religion and magic," 106–7.

142. Michel, Zazoff, and Zazoff, *Die magischen Gemmen im Britischen Museum,* no. 292; Michel, *Die Magischen Gemmen: zu Bildern und Zauberformeln auf geschnittenen Steinen der Antike und Neuzeit,* §28.15.

Identifying the Remains of Magic in the Village of Karanis 147

pseudoscript meant to mimic the texts typically found on other examples of the artifact type.[143] False writing is also found among the curse tablets discovered at the Temple of Sulis Minerva at Bath, and a number of the *defixiones* preserve either squiggles meant to represent writing or repeated signs that are meaningless.[144] The excavators have suggested that these are the attempts of illiterate individuals to compose their own tablets.[145]

The designs that decorate the bones are not common in magical rites, although some examples can be suggested that are similar to each of the three decorative patterns. Significantly earlier than the material under study, a series of graves from Mostagedda in Middle Egypt contained animal bones—typically frontal bones and horns—that had been painted with black and red dots.[146] The painted bones were found in round pits, associated with graves; some bones had been interred with human remains. This material has been associated with mercenary soldiers from Nubia who were interred here during the Second Intermediate Period, and Brunton proposed that these artifacts were indicative of social status for the Pan-Grave people.[147] Important differences between the decorated artifacts at Karanis and Mostagedda are easily identified, most notably in the multiple patterns used at Karanis, whereas only dots were employed at Mostagedda. Egyptians often viewed the religious traditions of other ethnicities as powerful forms of magic, and there is some evidence from the spell texts that Nubian rites were held in high esteem.[148] Although foreign rites likely exerted some allure for village residents, the significant temporal and cultural gap between the Mostagedda remains and the material from

---

143. K.M. inv. 19502 and 19503. Bohak, *Ancient Jewish magic,* 185. On the incantation bowls, see ibid., 183–93; J. A. Montgomery, *Aramaic incantation texts from Nippur* (Philadelphia: University Museum, 1913), 7–116; E. M. Yamauchi, *Mandaic incantation texts* (New Haven: American Oriental Society, 1967); C. D. Isbell, *Corpus of the Aramaic incantation bowls* (Missoula, MT: Society of Biblical Literature and Scholars Press, 1975); D. Levene, *A corpus of magic bowls: Incantation texts in Jewish Aramaic from Late Antiquity* (London: Kegan Paul Limited, 2003); M. G. Morony, "Magic and society in late Sasanian Iraq," in *Prayer, magic, and the stars in the ancient and Late Antique world,* ed. S. B. Noegel, J. T. Walker, and B. M. Wheeler (University Park: Pennsylvania State University Press, 2003).

144. *Tab. Sulis,* nos. 112–16.

145. Ibid., p. 247.

146. G. Brunton and G. M. Morant, *British museum expedition to middle Egypt* (London: B. Quaritch, 1937), 131.

147. I. Shaw, ed., *The Oxford history of ancient Egypt* (Oxford: Oxford University Press, 2000), 202–3; Brunton and Morant, *British museum expedition to middle Egypt,* 115.

148. Dieleman, *Priests, tongues, and rites,* 141–42; Koenig, "La Nubie dans les textes magiques: 'l'inquiétante étrangeté'."

148   Materia Magica

Karanis argues against assuming direct influence between the Nubian artifacts and magic as it was practiced in the Fayum. Furthermore, the Mostagedda remains only relate to the dot pattern and do not account for the other decorative schemes.

Enticing comparative material for the designs painted on the bones can be found in a number of spells of the magical papyri, which contain requirements that the practitioner should draw or inscribe a particular image (a *figura magica*) as part of the ritual act.[149] PGM LXXVIII, for example, instructs practitioner to inscribe a figure onto a piece of tin by using a nail. The illustration depicts a man or, more likely, a demon whose body has been shaded using a series of undulating lines; the lines at the bottom of the figure are similar to those that appear on the bones. In the PGM spell, these looped lines may indicate shading or perhaps were intended to convey material or hair that covered the body of the demon. It is also possible, however, that the lines represent stylized writing on the body of the figure. PGM XXXVI.1–34 includes a large drawing of a god identified as Seth, whose body has been inscribed by magical words, including the names SETH and BRAK. On another spell from PGM XXXVI, the formulary associated with the Fayum (lines 35–68) an anthropomorphic deity identified as IAO holds a snake in his hand; the outline of the snake is likewise filled with crossed and undulating lines. An additional parallel may be present in PGM XXXVI.231–55, an instructional text for a curse. The vignette depicts a rooster-headed, cuirassed divinity, the anguipede, who holds a sword in one hand and a possibly decapitated head in the other. Below, or perhaps a part of the decapitated head, is a series of two sinuous lines, then three lines with an upper loop, and finally four short vertical lines. The first five lines are bisected by a horizontal line, which also caps the final four lines. An additional horizontal line lies beneath all but the first two of the vertical lines. The subject of the representation is unclear, but the markings are similar to the vertical line pattern found on the bones. The examples demonstrate similarities with symbols found in the magical papyri, but none is sufficiently close to imply that the practitioner actually used one of these handbooks as a model. Nor does it seem likely that the drawings on the bones were intended to be illustrations similar to the large-format drawings of demons and spirits in the papyri.

The designs on the bones also show some similarities to symbols that

---

149. On the *figura magica,* see above, n. 65.

Identifying the Remains of Magic in the Village of Karanis 149

appear in the instructional texts, where a model that the practitioner is to copy might incorporate strange symbols or the *kharaktêres*.[150] PGM VII.925–39 lists instructions for writing a curse on a lead tablet; the curse is enclosed in an inscribed box, but various magical symbols are added around it, including *s*-curved undulating lines, figures that look like backward 3's, and Greek consonants. Below the model are further magical symbols, including a series of *s*-curves and lines.[151] Other designs are apparent in PGM XXXV.1–42, a spell to summon a spirit, in which a *figura magica* has been drawn within an oval.[152] This papyrus, which is likely an example of an enacted rite rather than an instructional text, preserves a series of well-attested *kharaktêres* including an asterisk made of eight lines, each of which contains a ball at the end, and a circle inscribed with a variety of crossed lines. Also present are other, less common designs, including a symbol that looks like a 3, and a backward *c*. These representations are placed above three depictions of human busts labeled as Paulus and Julianus. The Fayum instructional text, PGM XXXVI.275–83, provides a model for a charm that is to be inscribed on a silver lamella. Among the series of symbols are a cross, four *s*'s, a box bisected by two crossed lines, and an *x,* all of which can be paralleled in the designs on the bones; many of these are present on bone 3503.101 (plate 18). The bones, however, do not employ a clear pattern in the designs that have been selected—there is little repetition between the artifacts, and often, the symbols are applied in a haphazard manner, where one might expect power signs to demonstrate greater consistency.

Bone 10099.070 (plate 16) provides a useful example in which each of the undulating lines can be paralleled by a pattern found in the magical papyri. Most of the squiggles correspond to the *s* curves and backward 3's discussed above. Moving from left to right, the slanted 2 that appears on the bone is paralleled by a similar symbol on PGM XC.14–18. The backward *c,* which appears twice, is found on PGM XXXVI.178–87, and the curved *t* can be noted on PGM VII.925–39. On the reverse of the bone, the looped curve can be found on PGM II.64–184.

---

150. On the *kharaktêres,* see above, ch. 2, n. 50. The symbols that appear on the bones are not typical magical representations, such as the *kharaktêres,* which often possess rounded circles at the end of each stroke.

151. *GMP*, 143.

152. *GMP*, 268. Compare 10099.070, in which undulating lines are arranged in two rows, directly above and below a pattern of crossed lines.

150   Materia Magica

In contrast to some of the undulating designs, the line pattern, in which straight or sinuous vertical lines are bisected by a horizontal line, shows a greater degree of standardization. It is similar to a design found on a number of magical gems, in which three *s*-shaped lines are bisected by a single horizontal line. Often, this symbol is associated with or appears on the reverse of gems that depict a lion-headed snake, shown with a radiate crown, sometimes identified as Chnoubis.[153] On a small number of gems, this symbol and the lion-headed divinity are connected with the phrase πέσσε πέσσε, "digest," and scholars have suggested that these amulets were used to combat intestinal distress; the symbol has also been connected to difficulties with menstruation and breastfeeding.[154] On PGM CVI.1–10, a fever amulet, it seems to be used as a general charm for health.[155] The bones may also be compared to a series of three crossed *z*'s, a Hebrew symbol that often appears within the encircling snake of the ouroboros.[156] Both of these designs, however, are standardized as three *s*'s or *z*'s bisected by a horizontal line; the Karanis bones demonstrate significantly more lines as a running pattern that often fills the entire surface of the bone and often lacks a sinuous curve.

The decorations that appear on the bones—the bisected straight lines, the dots, and the undulating lines—cannot be mapped precisely to either the instructional texts from the Greek Magical Papyri or other artifacts associated with ritual practice, such as amulets. In other words, we cannot demonstrate that the designs were copied from another source, nor suggest the precise purpose that the designs served. The visual correspondence, however, may imply that the practitioner intended to create magical signs, even if the signs are not precise replicas of other symbols that we possess. The *idea* of magical symbols

---

153. C. Bonner, *Studies in magical amulets, chiefly Graeco-Egyptian* (Ann Arbor: University of Michigan Press, 1950), nos. 83, 86, and 91. Compare also A. Delatte and P. Derchain, *Les intailles magiques gréco-égyptiennes* (Paris: Bibliothèque nationale, 1964), among others, nos. 61, 63–65, 68, 69, and 82; H. Philipp, *Mira et magica: Gemmen im Ägyptischen Museum der Staatlichen Museen Preussischer Kulturbesitz, Berlin-Charlottenburg* (Mainz am Rhein: P. von Zabern, 1986), nos. 126, 27, 28, 31, 33, 34; Michel, Zazoff, and Zazoff, *Die magischen Gemmen im Britischen Museum,* nos. 309, 13–18, 22, and 35.

154. Bonner, *Studies in magical amulets, chiefly Graeco-Egyptian,* 51–62; Michel, Zazoff, and Zazoff, *Die magischen Gemmen im Britischen Museum,* 267–68; A. Mastrocinque, *From Jewish magic to Gnosticism* (Tübingen: Mohr Siebeck, 2005), 63–64.

155. *Suppl. Mag.* no. 10 = *P.Berol.* 21165 = W. Brashear, "Vier Berliner Zaubertexte," *ZPE* 17 (1975): no. 2.

156. Mastrocinque, *From Jewish magic to Gnosticism,* 69; R. Kotansky and J. Spier, "The 'horned hunter' on a lost gnostic gem," *HThR* 88, no. 3 (1995): 324–25. Kotansky suggests that the two symbols had very different meanings.

Identifying the Remains of Magic in the Village of Karanis 151

may have been more important than exact reproduction. A variety of reasons might explain the disjunction: the practitioner may have lacked access to a spell book that would contain the appropriate models, he or she may have worked from memory of the appropriate symbols, or these designs may have been created on the spot for use in this rite. There seems to have been significant fluidity in antiquity regarding magical symbols. Although the most common *kharaktêres* are asterisks and crossed or straight lines that possess round circles at the end of each stroke, the spells of the magical papyri use this word to refer to a wide range of symbols, often instructing the practitioner to copy them precisely. Certain signs, such as the three bisected lines that were linked to Chnoubis, may have been associated with particular effects or spells, but there was no established canon of magical symbols. The designs on the bones may have been considered as efficacious as any other well-known pattern. Indeed, the fact that many of the symbols found on the bones can also be paralleled in the formulary associated with the Fayum, PGM XXXVI, may suggest that the practitioner was drawing upon a vaguely understood or recalled menu-plate of designs that he or she may have encountered in other contexts associated with magical practice.

Like the images preserved on the artifacts, the use of bone as a medium for written spells is found only occasionally in the spell texts, and no spell requires the numbers of bones or the variety of species attested in the Karanis cache. Like the parallels for the inscribed images and symbols, bone was used in the instructional texts for multiple reasons, including harming an enemy, necromancy, inducing erotic attraction, or personal protection. Coffin Text Spell 37, from the Middle Kingdom (ca. 2040–1640 BCE), instructs the practitioner to inscribe a curse on a wax figure using a fish spine.[157] The execration ritual is intended to punish an enemy, and the fish bone serves as a writing implement rather than a feature that is ritually destroyed or otherwise manipulated by the practitioner. A fish or lizard bone is also required in PDM lxi.112–27, a love spell in which an image of the god of Osiris and the animal bone are buried under the threshold of the victim.[158] In PGM IV.1872–1927, another

---

157. R. O. Faulkner, *The ancient Egyptian coffin texts: spells 1-1185 & indexes* (Oxford: Aris & Phillips, 2004), 27–29. On this spell, see H. Willems, "The social and ritual context of a mortuary liturgy of the Middle Kingdom (*CT* Spells 30–41)," in *Social aspects of funerary culture in the Egyptian Old and Middle Kingdoms: Proceedings of the international symposium held at Leiden University, 6–7 June, 1996,* ed. H. Willems (Leuven: Peeters, 2001), 308–24.

158. T. G. Wilfong, review of *Ein neues Archiv koptischer Ostraka,* by M. Hasitzka, *BASP* 35, no. 1–2 (1998): 114.

152   Materia Magica

erotic spell, the practitioner is told to mold a dog with its mouth open, eight fingers high, out of wax, fruit, and manna. The text then reads "and you are to place in the mouth of the dog a bone from the head of a man who has died violently, and inscribe on the sides of the dog these characters: (certain magical symbols follow)."[159] The goal of the spell is to control Cerberus who will be able to attract the woman that the commissioner loves. The fragment of a human skull seems to be an accessory to the rite rather than a means by which the practitioner can access and control the dead. In the invocation to the god, Cerberus is adjured through suicides and those dead by violence, but the text does not mention the skull fragment.

Bone was also used for protection. PGM IV.3086–3124, part of a spell entitled the "Oracle of Kronos," provides instructions for summoning the spirit of the god Kronos using a salt mill. In order to protect himself against misfortune during the rite, the practitioner is told to create a phylactery using an animal bone: "On the rib of a young pig, carve Zeus holding fast a sickle and this name 'CHTHOUMILON' Or let it be the rib of a black, scaly, castrated boar."[160] The shape of a rib bone may also recall earlier Egyptian magic wands.[161] These artifacts, in use during the New Kingdom, were typically made of ivory and inscribed with images of Bes, Taweret, and other apotropaic divinities. Inscriptions suggest that they were used to protect women and young children from dangerous creatures or other misfortune.[162] In some instances, bones were used for a prophylactic shield, perhaps because their association with the underworld would ward off danger from the practitioner.

---

159. Trans. E. N. O'Neil in *GMP*, 71.

160. Trans. W. C. Grese in *GMP*, 98. The Greek in this text is problematic, as the original reading for both references to ribs is σπάθη(v) a word that means a broad blade or the blade of an oar, taken in this instance to refer to the ribs of a pig or boar. Diet suggested an alternative reading of σάθη(v), the penis of the pig (*non vidi,* but see the app. crit. on this passage in Preisendanz, PGM I, p. 175 n. to l. 3115). While Diet's reading recalls the apotropaic uses of the phallus, it would be very difficult to carve or engrave (γλῦψε) the required design on such an object. The original reading seems more likely. On this section of the text, see S. Eitrem, "Kronos in der magie," in *Mélanges Bidez* (Brussels: Secrétariat de l'Institut, 1934); C. A. Faraone, "Kronos and the Titans as powerful ancestors: A case study of the Greek gods in later magical spells," in *The gods of ancient Greece: Identities and transformations,* ed. J. N. Bremmer and A. Erskine (Edinburgh: Edinburgh University Press, 2010), 401–3.

161. Koenig, *Magie et magiciens dans l'Egypte ancienne,* 85–98; H. Altenmüller, "Apotropaikon," in *LÄ,* ed. W. Helck and E. Otto (Wiesbaden: Otto Harrassowitz, 1975). H. Altenmüller, *Die Apotropaia und die Götter Mittelägyptens: Eine typologische und religionsgeschichtliche Untersuchung der sog: "Zaubermesser" des Mittleren Reichs,* 2 vols. (Munich: 1965).

162. Koenig, *Magie et magiciens dans l'Egypte ancienne,* 94–95; Pinch, *Magic in ancient Egypt,* 131–32.

Identifying the Remains of Magic in the Village of Karanis　153

Bones may have been used as a substitute for a corpse, and C. Faraone has argued that in Late Antiquity, necromantic spells sometimes were disguised in the PGM by using code words. In PGM IV, for example, multiple spells use the word *skyphos,* or cup, to refer to a human skull.[163] One of these spells (PGM IV 1928–2005), attributed to King Pitys, requires the practitioner to intone a spell over a skull that will give the practitioner power over the dead individual. At the close of the spell, the practitioner wreathes the skull with ivy and writes an invocation that incorporates a variety of *voces magicae* on its forehead using ink made of serpent's blood and the soot of a goldsmith.[164] Other spells require the practitioner to collect parts of a corpse for use in a rite. So, in PGM IV 296–466, the love spell that requires the bound figurine of the woman and the statuette of Ares, the practitioner refers to holding part of a corpse: "if you go to the depths of the earth and search the regions of the dead, send this daimon, from whose body I hold this remnant in my hand."[165] The erotic rite takes place at graveside, and the practitioner invokes the god to force the dead individual (the daimon) whose body parts (this remnant) the practitioner holds.[166] These spells are all aimed at controlling the ghost from whom the bones derived; by grasping the skull or another body part of the dead individual, the practitioner could instruct the spirit of the dead man or woman to do his bidding. An inscription, either on a separate medium that can touch the corpse, or placed directly onto the bones, secures and formalizes the practitioner's control of the dead.

A number of later instructional texts and artifacts provide clear evidence that bones were incorporated into aggressive rites and used to harness the power of the dead. A human rib bone of unknown date has been inscribed with a Coptic curse against a man named Apollo. The text, which probably was composed in red ink that has now faded to yellow, calls on the spirit of the dead man (the "praised one" of the text) to enflame the victim on behalf of Jacob, son of Euphemia.[167] The rib bone serves as the mechanism by which

---

163. Faraone, "Necromancy goes underground," 257–58.

164. Ibid., 263. The other necromantic spells in this section of the PGM involve bringing elements of a dead body into contact with a written spell, either by placing inscribed leaves on the skull, or inserting a rolled papyrus into the hand of the corpse.

165. Trans. E. N. O'Neil in *GMP*, 46.

166. On the hymn and its relation to Apollonian invocations, see C. A. Faraone, "The collapse of celestial and chthonic realms in a Late Antique 'Apollonian invocation' (*PGM* I 262–347)," in *Heavenly realms and earthly realities in Late Antique religions,* ed. R. S. Boustan and A. Y. Reed (New York: Cambridge University Press, 2004), 229–31.

167. *ACM* no. 97. A. Pellegrini, "Piccoli testi copto-sa'idici del Museo archeologico di Firenze," *Sphinx* 10 (1906); W. E. Crum, "La magie copte: Nouveaux textes," in *Recueil d'études égyp-*

154   Materia Magica

the practitioner gains control over the deceased individual, who is named as a "great force" and associated with "great power." In another example, two separate large camel bones, said to be from Akhmim, serve as the medium for a curse that has been dated to around 900 CE. Three variations of an imprecation are written out on the two bones, and the inscriptions, which are written in red ink, invoke the six powers of death to bear away the soul of and bring suffering upon Aaron son of Tkouikira. The spell addresses a dead individual ("O dead one") and reveals that the camel bone was likely placed beneath the corpse that was invoked in the spell: "at the moment I place this bone under your back, that in the manner (in which) you suffered, you must bring your suffering down upon Aaron."[168] We should understand the dead individual as one who was believed to have suffered an untimely or particularly gruesome demise. The animal bones are not intended to stand in for the dead individual, but rather act as a medium by which a corpse can be contacted and controlled.

The archaeological context of the deposit can not provide much information about the ritual that took place, as many of the associated finds were probably discarded as trash. The practitioner collected the bones that were used in the rite, likely from the desert; the animals associated with the remains were not slaughtered as part of the rite, as many appear to have been bleached and dried by the sun and the desert before being painted. The red ochre found with the bones strongly suggests that the bones were decorated in this space. The practitioner may have used a brush to apply the designs, but he or she also used fingertips, as indicated by the dot pattern. After the completion of the rite, the bones may have been buried, as the designs have been preserved and in many cases are very clear. Had the bones been left on the surface, it seems likely that the paint would have been abraded by the sun and sand.

Although previously thrown away, removing the animal bones from their proper place as waste may have imbued them with ritual power, much as Gemellus's *brephos* was empowered through its displacement. On their own, the animal bones would not have been viewed as bizarre or identified as effica-

---

tologiques dédiées à la mémoire de Jean-François Champollion à l'occasion du centenaire de la lettre à M. Dacier relative à l'alphabet des hiéroglyphes phonétiques (Paris: E. Champion, 1922), 538; Kropp, *Ausgewählte koptische zaubertexte,* 3:111 n.1. Although Ritner identifies this as a spell intended to punish the victim, references to flames and burning may suggest a love spell. *ACM*, pp. 203–4.

168. *ACM* no. 98 trans. R. Ritner, 206. J. Drescher, "A Coptic malediction," *Annales du service des Antiquités de l'Égypte* 48 (1948).

cious through Malinowski's "coefficient of weirdness."[169] It is only by painting and adorning these objects with arcane symbols that they were transformed from jawbones and femurs of domesticated animals into objects of power. The color red, which was used in the decoration of the bones, has strong associations with aggressive magic in the traditions of Pharaonic Egypt.[170] This affiliation continued through the Graeco-Roman period, and red was often connected with demons and the god Seth. Furthermore, numerous spells in the papyri urge practitioners of "positive" magic to use lamps without any red slip, while the practitioner is admonished to write in blood if a harmful or compulsory magic is being performed.[171] It seems most likely, however, that an individual who possessed a rudimentary understanding of the iconography of magic painted the bones and indeed, the absence of inscribed texts on the bones may indicate that the practitioner was illiterate.

The function of the bones is more difficult to ascertain. For the most part, in sharp contrast to the Karanis examples, the instructional texts require human rather than animal remains. The cache does contain three human skull fragments, but these pieces, from the rear of the skull, are not identified easily as human. Indeed, many of the bones clearly are derived from animals, and individuals who lived, worked, and ate in an agricultural community would recognize the canine jaws, as well as some of the larger long bones from domesticated fauna, as nonhuman. Any proposed function for the bones must recognize that these artifacts, while magical, are likely the development of a local tradition. We can venture two hypotheses for the use of the artifacts, dependent upon the nature of the material used to create the objects and the patterns that have been inscribed on the bones. (1) The bones may have been used as substitutes for human bones to contact the underworld or cause harm to a victim. (2) The artifacts may have been used to provide protection for or control local herds.

We might reconstruct a ritual in which the animal bones possessed a general association with the underworld and were used to contact the dead. Indeed, the animal bones may have stood in for human remains, as many animal bones, such as ribs, look similar to their human counterparts. PGM

---

169. Frankfurter, "Fetus magic and sorcery fears in Roman Egypt," 54. On Malinowski's coefficient of weirdness, see above, ch. 1, n. 1.

170. Dynastic Egypt closely associated red with aggressive, harmful magic; the names of enemies on execration texts were written in red ink. Ritner, *The mechanics of ancient Egyptian magical practice,* 147.

171. I.e. PGM IV.52–85; PGM IV.1928–2005; PGM VII.300a-310; PDM xiv.772–804.

156   Materia Magica

IV.2006–2125, entitled Pitys' spell of attraction, suggests that the power of the dead may have been harnessed without human remains. The spell asks the practitioner to place the hide of an ass that has been decorated with various symbols beneath a corpse, but includes an interesting caveat, to "go quickly to where (someone) lies buried or where something has been discarded, if you do (not) have a buried body." The phrase "where something has been discarded" (ὅπου τι ἀπορέριπται), offers a second space in which the rite might occur and may refer to an area that has been used for the disposal of garbage. Indeed, in this alternative iteration, the corpse does not play an instrumental role— necromancy is possible in a cemetery or even at the town's trash heaps. A comparable substitution might be envisioned with regard to the animal bones, where artifacts associated with death, and likewise acquired from an area used for the disposal of trash, stand in for human remains. This also may reflect contemporary transformations in ritual practices, when simpler miniaturized rites, performed in the home, replaced or supplemented complex spells that took place in the temple.[172]

When human remains appear in the instructional texts, there are strong indications that these were used for compulsion, to force the dead to do the will of the commissioner, but when we encounter animal bones, the function of these objects is not as clear-cut. Earlier and later instances of magical practice employ faunal remains for aggressive spells, intended to curse or compel a vic- tim. Among the recently discovered artifacts from the temple of Anna Perenna in Rome, six poppets made of organic materials, each discovered within a round lead box, were formed around small slivers of bone that had also been inscribed, presumably with curses or elements of curses.[173] As the innermost feature around which the poppets were constructed, the bone fragments were ritually significant, since this material would not have been visible once the figurines had been created. The designs painted on the Karanis bones in red ochre may have endowed these objects with ritual potency, permitting them to be used for an aggressive rite.

---

172. Faraone, "Necromancy goes underground," 267–68; Smith, "Trading places," 13–28; F. Graf, "Magic and divination," in *The world of ancient magic,* ed. D. R. Jordan, H. Montgomery, and E. Thomassen (Bergen: Norwegian Institute at Athens, 1999), 291–92; Faraone, "The collapse of celestial and chthonic realms in a Late Antique 'Apollonian invocation' (*PGM* I 262–347)," 218–19.

173. Piranomonte, "Religion and magic at Rome: The fountain of Anna Perenna," 205–7; Bailliot, *Magie et sortilèges dans l'Antiquité romaine,* 99–100. The investigators suggest that these slivers are derived from animals, but the size of the fragments may preclude determining whether they come from humans or other mammals. On the fountain of Anna Perenna, see above, ch. 1, n. 125.

Identifying the Remains of Magic in the Village of Karanis 157

Some of the bones, most notably the animal skulls, must have been recognizable as belonging to domesticated fauna. This may suggest that they were used for contemporary problems with livestock and animal husbandry. The line pattern, which can be related to the Chnoubis symbol, is associated with health and protection. So, too, the dot pattern perhaps may be related to well-being, either by representing the appearance of healthy, living animals with spots or, conversely, sickly animals that are afflicted with boils, pustules, or other physical defects. Connecting these decorative patterns with ancient husbandry is a more difficult proposition. The Egyptian evidence for rituals involving livestock is quite limited, and protecting herds is not a concern expressed in the magical papyri. Numerous magical texts, such as the Horus cippi, are related to providing protection from the animals of the desert, but none of these creatures—the scorpion, the snake, or the crocodile—is present in the corpus.[174] Farther afield, the Roman agronomists report on a variety of rites that were used to protect herds; most often, these relied on offerings to divinities and ritual purification, and show no similarities with our rite.[175] Columella reports an unusual rite that he attributes to Bolus of Mendes: if a flock of sheep is sick, the pastoralist should bury one animal upside-down at the gate to the pen and drive the other sheep over it. In this way, illness will be drawn from the diseased animals into the dead one.[176] Something similar to this could be occurring with the bones, where disease was drawn from sick animals. A much later tradition may point to the appeal of this sort of idea. Although significantly removed from the Karanis bones in both time and tradition, the Pardoner's tale from Chaucer's *Canterbury Tales* provides a striking parallel. The Pardoner claims to possess a sheep bone from a Jew that has magical powers. If the bone is washed in the water from a well, animals that drink from the water will be cured of stings and worms; sheep drinking the water will be cured of pox or other ailments.[177]

Conversely, the bones may have been intended to cause disease or illness in the animal targets. This sort of aggressive magic may look back to Pharaonic traditions. We find representations of domesticated animals among the finds

---

174. On protection from the animals of the desert, see L. Keimer, "L'horreur des égyptiens pour les démons du désert," *Bulletin de l'institut d'Égypte* 26 (1944). For a later Coptic example, see Frankfurter, "The binding of antelopes: A Coptic frieze and its Egyptian religious context."

175. B. Ager, "Roman agricultural magic" (PhD diss., University of Michigan, 2010), 178.

176. Columella 7.5.17; Ager, "Roman agricultural magic," 194.

177. G. Chaucer, *Canterbury Tales.* ed. A. K. Hieatt and C. Hieatt (New York: Bantam Books, 1964), 341. I am grateful to Thomas Moser of the University of Maryland for pointing out this later parallel.

of a New Kingdom execration ritual enacted at a southern border fort of Mirgissa. The deposit consisted of three separate pits, included 197 inscribed red ceramic vessels, 437 uninscribed red vessels, 346 mud figurines, 3 figurines in limestone, the head of a fourth figurine, and the remains of a human sacrifice.[178] The ceramic vessels were shattered prior to being placed in the pit, and approximately one-third of the vessels had been inscribed with the names of enemies of the Egyptian state.[179] The fragments of inscribed and uninscribed pots were regularly interspersed with seven layers of mud figurines, with each layer including a specific corpus of items: a headless and bound torso, a severed head or foot, a blinded eye, six or seven models of reed boats, a domesticated animal, a reptile, twelve geese in flight and a number of unidentified objects. The human figures or body parts clearly represent the Nubians, who would have been ritually killed or destroyed in the sacrifice; the same holds true for their herds (the domesticated animals) and means of transport (the boats). An inscription of Sesostris III (1837–1818 BCE) from Semna records that the outposts were built "to prevent any Nubian from passing it downstream or overland or by boat, (also) any herds of Nubians."[180]

As at Mirgissa, the discovery of a large number of bones together at Karanis may point to some form of execration or aggressive rite. Some of the drawings on the bones may have been intended to transform defleshed bones into more recognizable animals by adding depictions of spots or fur, symbolized by the dots and the undulating lines. The red ochre, with its overtones of execration, would have been used to curse the animal targets of the spell. The bones, which would have connected the practitioner to the underworld and the power of the dead, would have been created and employed in this space, acting against the victims of the curse from afar. While this reading of the objects accounts for the choice of color as well as the use of the bones, it is harder to find a motive that would lead a practitioner to employ such an elaborate spell: would jealousy of another's herds warrant the decoration of eighty-four animal bones?

In any reading of these strange objects, however, we must also account for the other contexts in which painted bones were discovered. The large find at the

---

178. A. Vila, "Un dépôt de textes d'envoûtement au Moyen Empire" *JS* 3, no. 3 (1963); for a full discussion, see Ritner, *The mechanics of ancient Egyptian magical practice,* 153–80.

179. This is likely related to the ritual of the "Breaking of the Red Pots" found in the Pyramid Text 244; see J. van Dijk, "Zerbrechen der roten Töpfe," in *LÄ*, ed. W. Helck, E. Otto, and W. Westendorf (Wiesbaden: Otto Harrassowitz, 1986); J. Dieleman, "Zerbrechen der roten Töpfe," in *LÄ*.

180. Trans. S. A. H. Gardiner, *Egypt of the pharaohs* (Oxford: Clarendon Press, 1961), 135.

Identifying the Remains of Magic in the Village of Karanis 159

outskirts of town was not the sole instance of this spell, although it may be the primary location of enactment or the initial point from which the other painted bones derived. Few of these other bones were retained or photographed, so we must assume that the decoration and types of bones were sufficiently similar to suggest creation by the same practitioner. The prevalence of this form of magic in the town suggests a small-scale operation by one of the residents or by an itinerant practitioner. The majority of the other finds derive from domestic contexts, although two painted bones and a painted piece of plaster were discovered in structure 161, which is located on the eastern side of the mound, near structure 165 (plate 11). The courtyard of structure 161 was excavated in 1928, and uncovered an animal pen and two feeding troughs, suggesting that animals were resident here along with their human owners. This lends support for reading the bones as related to the safety and well-being of animals. The other domestic contexts may have served a similar function, as livestock frequently shared space within their owners. Although one should not discount the possibility of aggressive spells and counter-spells, all facilitated by the same local expert, it also seems more likely that protective or helpful magic would have been widely dispersed in the town. One might reconstruct that a ritual specialist worked on the outskirts of town, creating helpful or protective spells, perhaps over a period of time, which would account for the varied color and preservation of the bones found in 262 and 265. This practitioner may have sold or distributed his or her products among the villagers, who would have employed the bones in their own homes.

The painted bones from Karanis arguably can be assigned to the sphere of ritual, even though there is no precise parallel for their decoration or for a similar find of animal bones among contemporary magical documents. The material evidence may be the residue of a single ritual event that occurred once in this space, or the artifacts may point to multiple iterations at the site. In suggesting a function for the objects, we cannot know with certainty which Egyptian traditions were most likely to give rise to these specific artifacts. In other words, was it most important that these objects were bones, so that animal bones could stand in for human bones? Or, alternatively, should we view the fact that these artifacts derived from domesticated livestock as the determinative factor for their use? If so, then the bones may relate to local concerns about animal health or, conversely, aggressive acts undertaken by one herdsman against another. Based on our current knowledge of magical practice in Egypt, we cannot supply definitive answers to these questions. What is most important to note, however, is that it is only through archaeological inquiry that we can begin to construct this example of local ritual practice. Without the archaeological data to demonstrate that these objects were found together, as well as information related to their placement on the site, the Karanis bones would be merely curiosities.

Contextual Magic at Karanis

The contextual study of magic at Karanis allows us to investigate individual archaeological deposits and determine whether these units may preserve traces of magical activity. This analysis begins with the individual artifact. Objects may inform us through an inscription that they were used in a rite. Conversely, similarities between the item and either the written record of spells, preserved in the PGM, or other contemporary artifacts can suggest a magical function. More important, we may also find magic in the circumstances under which the item was deposited—was it found in a pit, or in a grave, or in some other space that is indicative of ritual activity? Our initial identification is only that—a first assessment of the manufactured item that is often based on our own reading of an item's "weirdness." We must see the artifact or its depositional context as odd or unusual in order to notice it among the many items of household refuse that populate a site. From this point, we can use comparative evidence, drawn from a broad range of documents and artifacts discovered in Egypt, in order to determine whether a given find was employed within a rite and, perhaps, to draw out the probable function of the ritual.

Identifying magic as an archaeological feature requires that we pursue a fine-tuned analysis. By positioning artifacts and groups of artifacts within their immediate depositional circumstances, we can understand how a practitioner may have used a given item in a ritual, and this same context can also point us to other artifacts that were employed in the rite. Depositional context can illuminate where and how an item was manufactured, employed, or consumed, permitting us to piece together elements of a ritual enactment. The context of the mud figurine permits us to associate the pins with the image of the woman and to reconstruct a more complex and nuanced ritual that involves piercing, burning, and placing the items in a significant space.

We lack this vital data when analyzing objects that appear on the art market. Magical items sold at auction have been removed illicitly from their

Identifying the Remains of Magic in the Village of Karanis 161

original findspots, and the absence of reliable information related to depositional context or even the village of discovery renders many of these artifacts archaeologically worthless. These curios are more appropriate for antiquarian display, perhaps adding one more example to a list of figurines associated with a love spell such as PGM IV.296–466 but telling us little about where these spells were undertaken, or under what temporal and geographic circumstances a spell book was consulted. Even more disturbing and challenging are questions of forgery, as items that lack precise archaeological provenance might be the products of modern, rather than ancient, hands. But the fear of forgery, too, has its dangers, as it limits our acceptance of what sorts of unprovenanced artifacts can be recognized as magical. We will be able to accept only those artifacts that fit our text-based expectations of what magic should look like. Indeed, it is only through investigating appropriately excavated sites and contexts that we can comprehend accurately the form and function of the material remains of magic.

Contextual analysis can permit us to understand the physical documents that we possess as artifacts, potentially investigable through archaeological modes of inquiry. Although many of the documents purporting to record spell instructions have been emended and compiled, the papyri that we possess are products of specific times and places, deposited in precise locations, and with exact periods of use. The documents provide evidence of their employment, through traces of damage, repair, wear, or even recycling. The archaeological study of magic must contextualize both the ritual manuals and the residue of ritual production. Furthermore, papyri, like other artifacts, may have had a limited area of circulation, and the practitioners who employed these texts often operated in a certain locality; the texts perhaps can be related to artifacts produced in their vicinity. Only by systematically viewing both texts and objects as products of the same culture can it be possible to understand the process of doing ritual or its place in society.

At Karanis analysis of individual archaeological contexts suggests that rituals utilized for personal ends may have occurred over the entirety of the site, both in the village proper, but also in peripheral zones. The painted bones, created and deposited in an abandoned insula, utilized material gathered from the desert. This space may have been selected because of its efficacy as an uninhabited area or a place where things are discarded. Gemellus reports that he was attacked outside of the village, in his land at Kerkesoucha. This incident was witnessed by a variety of individuals, including the village elders, making it a public display. Its spatial location was tied to the conflict between Gemellus and Julius, because Julius wished to remove grain (and perhaps make a claim on the land), he threw the *brephos* at Gemellus in the latter's fields.

Magic could also occur within the densely occupied areas of the village. Both the figurine and the inscribed ostracon derive from inhabited areas. In these cases, rituals were enacted within living spaces in order to achieve a desired effect—the location was tied to the outcome of the spell. The figurine may have been placed beneath the residence of the commissioner to aggressively ensure the affection of his or her recalcitrant lover. Such a rite may have occurred in secret, without the knowledge of the beloved. The ritual that involved the ostracon likely was concerned with the protection of the grain in structure C165; there is little reason to believe that this event would have been hidden. Late Antique legal documents that ban the practice of magic provide exceptions for the protection of agricultural produce, suggesting that this area of ritual enactment was viewed as acceptable and traditional, even if ritual methods similar to aggressive spells were employed.[181] We cannot be certain where Sarapion's fever amulet was created, but it seems most likely that he carried it with him, and that he was protected by it in his daily activities. Archaeological data can allow us to pinpoint where magic was employed, suggesting that some forms of ritual expression may have been hidden, secret, or marginal. Both aggressive and protective acts, however, also were enacted on the public stage, where they were visible to the community.

Accurately mapping all occurrences of magic on the site encounters a number of insurmountable gaps, as sebbakhin mining in the early twentieth century destroyed the center of the settlement. The hole in the center of the site is metaphorically equivalent to the challenges that are encountered in reconstructing magic using excavation records created in the early part of the last century. Frequently, we are left at the mercy of insufficient data. As a field, archaeology attempts to wring meaning from silent objects, and it struggles against the absence of data that could validate a hypothesis. Lacking inscriptional evidence or firsthand accounts of material remains, we must infer meaning from the artifacts that are preserved. This becomes more difficult when the excavators—often through insufficient knowledge of stratigraphy or formation processes—do not provide clear indicators of where items were found,

---

181. On the legal allowances for agriculture, see above, ch. 1, n. 53.

Identifying the Remains of Magic in the Village of Karanis 163

or records of the precise circumstances of discovery. The standards in contemporary excavation are much higher, but excavators should remain aware of the fragility of archaeological deposits of magic, as ritual enactments may not be easily identified in the field. Only through careful study of the material remains, together with a detailed unpacking of their archaeological contexts, will it be possible to identify the traces of magic that practitioners may have wished to keep hidden.

Finding magic at the site can prompt further questions about the production of ritual technologies in the local environment. The artifacts from Karanis reveal the presence of both literate magic, likely performed by a ritual expert who may have consulted magical texts, and rites that did not rely on or employ writing. Both the fever amulet and the inscribed potsherd may have been created through the use of an instructional handbook. The amulet follows a set format and incorporates speech that is typical for such artifacts—the invocation of various angels is followed by a request that these spirits will protect or heal the possessor from a variety of ills. Although no identical copy of this spell exists, parallels between this text and other fever amulets suggest that the Karanis artifact was inscribed by an individual who either consulted a model or did not require a model because they were sufficiently familiar with the names of angels and the form that the request should take. Likewise, the ostracon from House 165 can be interpreted as an abbreviated synopsis of a spell procedure that was likely copied from a handbook and employed at this location. The lines of text on the sherd suggest the ritual that was to be undertaken: words were to be spoken or written, and images of a woman and child created or manipulated.

The two inscribed artifacts from Karanis can be dated to the late third or early fourth century based on paleography. The magical ostracon related to grain processing was likely copied from a spell book that may have been in the possession of a wandering ritual professional. The religious identity of this ritual expert cannot be adequately determined from the artifacts or the texts that were written upon them. The language of the ostracon is imprecise, as the preserved instructions require the creation of an image of a mother and child without specifying whether Isis and Horus or Mary and Jesus were intended. This brief instructional text would have been appropriate for either a Christian or pagan patron, and could have been employed by a ritual practitioner trained in either tradition. In this period, Christian holy men, sometimes associated

with monasteries or with Coptic scriptoria, were competing with pagan practitioners, offering similar services and using comparable spells.[182] The text of
the fever amulet suggests that it was created for a Jewish or, more likely, a
Christian patron. Even if we can suggest that the fever amulet was composed
for a Christian, it is entirely possible that the practitioner was a pagan. These
two objects strongly call for further study of the early history of Christianity
at the site and point to the complicated nature of magical practice at the end of
the third and the beginning of the fourth centuries, when the religious needs of
local residents continued unabated, but religion itself was in flux.

In addition to these instances of literate, learned magic, we also can identify two archaeological contexts that lack texts, and, in fact, show no evidence
that the practitioner referred to a model or spell book in the creation of the
artifacts. Gemellus' complaint positions magic in this way: Julius is accused
of having thrown an object at the blind victim, but the petition does not mention a spoken incantation or a physical text. The absence of writing on an artifact does not preclude the consultation of a written recipe, nor does it imply
that the practitioner was illiterate. In the painted bones, however, we find a
desire to write, as many of the markings appear to mimic Greek letters or the
kharaktêres, well-known magical symbols. The practitioner was either unable
or unwilling to transcribe intelligible script on the bones. In the deposit discovered under house 165, the small image of the woman lacks a written text.
Based on comparison with other love spells found in the magical papyri, we
would expect an inscription that would associate the representation with the
victim. Although we should not read too much into the absence of texts, the
artifacts could suggest that illiterate individuals, or perhaps members of the
laity, were responsible for the production of these artifacts.

At Karanis, it may be possible to envision a distinction between magic
that was written, and likely the product of learned priests, and practices that
lacked intelligible text, instead relying solely on objects and perhaps spoken
spells. There is some evidence from Egypt that individuals not associated with
the temple possessed a rudimentary knowledge of what appropriate rituals
and magical symbols should look like. In a Coptic letter from Kellis, a man

---

182. Frankfurter, *Religion in Roman Egypt,* 257–58; Frankfurter, "Ritual expertise in Roman
Egypt and the problem of the category 'magician,'" 129. See, for example J. van der Vliet,
"A Coptic *Charitesion* (P. Gieben Copt. 1)," *ZPE* 153 (2005). As noted above, the ostracon is
likely pagan, but one cannot completely rule out the possibility that "woman, child" refers to
Mary and Jesus.

Identifying the Remains of Magic in the Village of Karanis 165

named Vales replies to an initial letter from another man named Psais, in which Psais had asked for a specific spell. Vales is unable to locate the requested document—he says that it was written on a small fragment—but sends Psais another charm, which he believes will also work. It is clear from the document that Vales has copied the magical formula that he includes from another source.[183] The small fragment of papyrus to which Vales refers is likely an enacted spell, perhaps an amulet that he possesses, rather than a spell book or model text; Vales may have commissioned a ritual act that he is now sending to Psais for reuse. Psais is unwilling to create a rite on the spot but will rely on a trusted, efficacious template, even if he does not have access to priestly collections of ritual recipes. While this is not an example of ritual activity performed by illiterate individuals, the letter from Kellis does indicate that laypersons may have possessed a general familiarity with the effective mechanisms of magic. Often, this magical knowledge may have derived from access to magical objects; belief in the efficacy of words or objects of power may have led laypersons to replicate symbols, incantations, or even artifacts in the hope that these would be as potent as the ones created by professionals. This knowledge may have been necessary at a time when a priest or other member of the temple personnel was not available.

Variation between literate and illiterate magic also may be associated with differences in gender. Scholars of the Renaissance have proposed a distinction between written spells, which were typically the purview of male practitioners, and unwritten magic, often practiced by women and passed down through oral traditions.[184] Male, literate friars and other churchmen, who were often itinerant specialists, possessed books of magic that they consulted in the performance of rituals to aid common people. In contrast, females in small villages engaged in a variety of nonliterate rites that resulted in healing or erotic attraction.[185] In Late Renaissance Italy, women in the village of Latisana practiced magic that relied on materials, such as cords or farm implements, to bind or unbind lovers or to heal illnesses. This ritual format, which employed specific gestures, such as the sign of the cross, was passed down through casual edu-

---

183. *P.Kell.Copt.* 35, discussion at P. A. Mirecki, I. Gardner, and A. Alcock, "Magical spell, Manichaean letter," in *Emerging from darkness: Manichaean studies at the end of the 20th century,* ed. P. A. Mirecki and J. BeDuhn (New York: Brill, 1997), 9–10.

184. Faraone, *Ancient Greek love magic,* 120 and n. 81. I am grateful to C. Faraone for suggesting this reading of the uninscribed objects.

185. This distinction was not always so clear-cut along gender lines, as women were occasionally active in learned magic in addition to rites not associated with texts.

166   Materia Magica

cation, often in families.[186] A similarly gendered distinction between literate magic, represented by the fever amulet or the spell instructions, and ritual practice that relied exclusively on objects, may be possible at Karanis, even though there is little evidence for it. The techniques that produced the bones and the small figurine likely were similar to the procedures undertaken by male priests and practitioners who employed model texts similar to the PGM, but such methods may have been appropriated by female members of the community. Indeed, our ability to recognize magic largely has depended—up to now—on the presence of texts produced by literate individuals, who were often scribes or priests, and therefore likely male. Finding magic that has been produced by unlettered individuals opens up new territory for interpretation. It will be necessary to consider whether female magic possessed distinctive features that might be recognizable in the archaeological record.

In the end, what is most striking about the ritual objects from Karanis is the evident variation from the rites described in the spell books or from other examples of enacted magic known from Roman Egypt. The figurine discovered beneath house 165, for example, is recognized as magical based on comparable rites that are known from the region, but the act of burning a small image is unparalleled. Spells from PGM XXXVI, the formulary from the Fayum, include rites aimed at enflaming the beloved, but none require the creation of an image. Likewise, the attachment holes evident on the lead sheet from Hawara suggest that it once included small figurines, but the text of the *defixio* does not refer to burning or fire. The Karanis mud doll seems to blend these traditions together, employing a figurine of a woman meant to represent the target of the spell, but burning the image to compel the love of the victim. A local practitioner, or even a layperson, may have adapted trusted and well-known magical mechanisms from multiple sources in the performance of this particular rite, perhaps imagining that the result would be doubly efficacious. The painted bones similarly demonstrate an adaptation of the symbols and signs of magical practice into a local rite. By inscribing the animal bones with designs and figures that recall, but do not precisely reproduce, the signs

---

186. Female magic: G. Ruggiero, *Binding passions: Tales of magic, marriage, and power at the end of the Renaissance* (New York: Oxford University Press, 1993), 166–74. Male magic: ibid., 93–94, 199–206. Compare M. H. Sánchez Ortega, "Sorcery and eroticism in love magic," in *Cultural encounters: The impact of the Inquisition in Spain and the New World*, ed. M. E. Perry and A. J. Cruz (Berkeley: University of California Press, 1991), 58–59; J. A. Pitt-Rivers, *The fate of Shechem or, the politics of sex: Essays in the anthropology of the Mediterranean* (Cambridge: Cambridge University Press, 1977), 76.

Identifying the Remains of Magic in the Village of Karanis 167

known from the papyri and gems, the practitioner reveals a familiarity with ritual enactments. Indeed, this apparent lack of expertise and imprecise replication of magical signs may argue for a ritual enactment that took place outside of the literate, priestly milieu. A similar loose adaptation of magical ideas may have resulted in the performance witnessed by Gemellus, attested in the petition with which this chapter began. Gemellus complains of a strange incident in which assailants threw a *brephos* at him, an act that has been characterized as magical despite the absence of parallels for this use of a fetus. We may find it difficult to assign this incident to the realm of magic, but Gemellus clearly understands the act of throwing the *brephos* to be an aggressive provocation, and he describes the effects of the *brephos* in magical terms. The *brephos,* like the painted bones, is unusual, a strange kind of magic attested only (it seems) at one small village.

Karanis, however, was not an anomaly. Rather, it seems to have been a typical village, situated in the ethnically and culturally diverse Fayum, and inhabited by a mixture of veterans, Egyptians, and Greek and Roman settlers who were making a living in agriculture. Like other elements of life at the site, the ritual practices that we have identified should be seen as typical of a small community. In general, however, our expectations for what village-level ritual should look like have relied on a reading of the magical papyri as a sort of "field guide" to Egyptian magic. In this way, text—both that preserved in the papyrus documents and the text on the artifact—dictates and circumscribes what should be identified as magical, much as we might match a bird seen in the wild with an image drawn by Audubon. Divergences from the magical papyri are viewed as variations that require explanation. But the magical papyri do not form an authoritative manual, as each papyrus roll or sheet was in use at a specific place. The antiquities market and the shortsightedness of early excavation have robbed most documents of a geographic association. Moreover, we possess only a fraction of the papyri that were likely in use, making it impossible to employ the texts as our sole guide to locating the physical traces of magic in diverse areas. The texts of the PGM can best suggest a general, big-picture framework within which local traditions developed and were implemented. To find local forms of magic, we must rely on archaeological evidence, a data source that can be associated with a specific town, village, or region.

Archaeology provides a crucial element in our investigation of how rituals were enacted at a given locality, as the material remains of ritual acts can tell a distinct story about how a rite was undertaken at a particular time and place. This, in turn, can allow us to relate these ritual acts back to the residents of the towns, villages, and cities in which magic is being practiced, and to investigate how local individuals view these rites, who is responsible for these ritual acts, and for what purpose the rites are being enacted. For Amathous, Cyprus, and Empúries, Spain, as at Karanis, archaeological evidence and its physical context offer clear opportunities to expand our understanding of ritual practice at the local level.

Chapter 4

Practitioners and Craft at Amathous, Cyprus

Finding Magic Rituals without the Magical Papyri

Egypt's rich documentary record is the result of a dry desert environment that has allowed for the preservation of papyri and other organic materials. The rest of the Mediterranean is wetter, resulting in the loss of comparable written records. Some form of ritual manuals likely existed in many locations; the practitioners at Amathous relied on a prototype for the creation of magical artifacts at the site, and model texts were likely in use from such diverse locations as Athens, Carthage, Hadrumentum, Rome, and Cnidus.[1] We only know of the existence of these models through inscriptions on archaeological artifacts, where scribal errors or multiple copies point to the consultation of a formulary. That these manuals were similar or identical to the Egyptian texts of the Greek Magical Papyri is much less likely. The magical papyri were the products of extensive redaction and compilation by the priestly class in Egypt and blended local and foreign traditions, tailored for the desires of both tourists and residents. Despite incorporating spells and magical incantations that can be attributed to Greece or the Near East, the PGM instructions are most similar to earlier Egyptian ritual practices.

While archaeological remains at Karanis could be identified as magical with reference to the spells of the papyri, we lack access to a similar ritual framework as we turn to other locations. The details provided by the magical papyri allowed us to sketch a general view of what magic might look like, and to place examples of practice within a culture-specific ritual framework. Without this data, the process of finding magic becomes more difficult. It is still possible to rely on the markers of magic outlined in chapters 1 and 2, but

---

1. For a listing of the large caches of tablets associated with formularies, see above, p. 2, n. 4.

169

170   Materia Magica

the body of comparative material that can be used to accurately identify rituals from archaeological remains alone is significantly constrained. Commonplace magical items such as curse tablets or amulets remain accessible and recognizable, but it is a greater challenge to move beyond these classes of inscribed artifacts, particularly in the absence of detailed excavation records. Therefore, the remainder of this book will investigate objects that can be identified as magical through the presence of texts. Still, the contextual investigation of artifacts, their inscriptions, and archaeological context has much to contribute to our understanding of ancient ritual and its place in the local community. These are the same sources that were employed to understand ritual at Karanis, and such data also can be used to document local forms of ritual engagement elsewhere in the Mediterranean.

Cyprus lies to the north of Egypt and near the southern coast of Asia Minor. In the late nineteenth century, locals who were digging a well near the modern village of Agios Tychonas discovered a hoard of over two hundred lead and approximately thirty selenite (a translucent, crystallized form of gypsum) tablets at the bottom of a disused shaft. The lead tablets had been rolled into small tubes; the selenite tablets, which were originally rectangular or square, were broken into many small chips. The tablets were soon sold to the British Museum, Wilhelm Froehner, and, perhaps, to other private individuals.[2] Most of the artifacts are inscribed with a variation on one spell, a curse that invokes various underworld divinities to bind and punish a victim.[3] One of the tablets, *DT* 22 (BM 1891,4–18.1, plate 20) reads:

---

2. Wilhelm Froehner, an assistant curator at the Louvre, bequeathed his collection of antiquities to the Cabinet des Médailles in Paris. His collection was acquired over many years through various contacts, and the pieces derive from an extensive number of places of origin. L. Robert, *Collection Froehner,* vol. 1, Inscriptions Grecques (Paris: Editions des Bibliotheques Nationales, 1936), ii.

3. The tablets have been published in numerous collections since their *editio princeps,* and further examples have been associated with the cache: L. MacDonald, "Inscriptions relating to sorcery in Cyprus," *Proceedings of the Society of Biblical Archaeology* 13 (1891); *DT* nos. 22–37; Wünsch, "Neue Fluchtafeln," nos. 10, 11, 12; Robert, *Collection Froehner* 106–7; T. B. Mitford, *The inscriptions of Kourion* (Philadelphia: American Philosophical Society, 1971), nos. 127–42; T. Drew-Bear, "Imprecations from Kourion," *BASP* 9 (1972); *SGD* no. 193; *CT* no. 45; P. Aupert and D. R. Jordan, "Tablettes magiques d'Amathonte," in *Art Antique de Chypre du Bronze moyen à l'époque byzantine au Cabinet des médailles* (Paris: Bibliothèque Nationale de France, 1994); D. R. Jordan, "Late feasts for ghosts," in *Ancient Greek cult practice from the epigraphical evidence,* ed. R. Hägg (Stockholm: Paul Aströms Förlag, 1994); M. d. A. López Jimeno, *Textos griegos de maleficio,* (Madrid: Akal Ediciones, 2001), nos. 273–89.

Practitioners and Craft at Amathous, Cyprus 171

Daimones, those who are under the earth, and *daimones* whoever you may be; fathers of fathers, and mothers (who are a) match (for me), you who lie here, and you who sit here, since you take men's grievous passion from their heart, take over the passion of Ariston which he has toward me, Soterianos, also called Limbaros, and his anger, and take away from him his strength and power and make him cold and speechless and breathless, cold toward me, Soterianos also called Limbaros. I invoke you by the great gods MASŌMASIMABLABOIŌ MAXAMŌ EUMAZŌ ENDENEKOPTOURA MELOPHTHEMARAR AKOU RASRŌEEKAMADŌR MACHTHOU-DOURAS KITHŌRASA KĒPHOZŌN goddess ACHTHAMODOIRALAR AKOU RAENT AKOU RALAR hear you all, ALAR OUECHEARMALAR KARAMEPHTHĒ SISOCHŌR ADŌNEIA of the earth CHOUCHMATHER-PHES THERMŌMASMAR ASMACHOUCHIMANOU PHILAESŌSI gods of the underworld, take over from Ariston and his son the passion and the anger they hold toward Soterianos also known as Limbaros, and hand him over to the doorkeeper in Hades MATHUREUPHRAMENOS and to the one who is appointed over the gate to Hades and the keeper of the door bolts of heaven, STERXERX ĒRĒXA, bursting forth from the earth, ARDAMACTHOUR PRISSGEU LAMPADEU. And bury him who is written upon this muzzling tablet [in a] mournful grave. I invoke you the king of the mute spirits. Hear the great name, for the great SISOCHŌR rules over you, the ruler of the gates to Hades. Of my enemy Ariston, bind and put to sleep the tongue and the passion and the anger he holds toward me, Soterianos, also called Limbaros, lest he oppose me in any matter. I invoke you, *daimones,* buried in a communal grave, violently dead, untimely dead, not properly buried, by her who bursts forth from the earth and forces back to the grave the limbs of MELIOUCHOS and MELIOUCHOS himself. I invoke you by ACHALEMORPHŌPH, who is the one god upon the earth OSOUS OISŌRNOPHRIS OUSRAPIO do whatever is written herein. O much lamented tomb and gods of the under-world, and chthonic Hekate, chthonic Hermes, Plouton, the chthonic Eirynes, and you who lie here below, untimely dead and the unnamed, EUMAZŌN, take away the speech of Ariston who is opposing me, Soterianos, also called Limbaros, MASOMACHŌ. I deposit with you this muzzling charge to make Ariston silent, and (you) give over his name to the infernal gods ALLA ALKĒ KE ALKEO LALATHANATŌ three-named Kore. These shall always carry out my wishes for me and silence Ariston the opponent of me, Soteria-nos also called Limbaros. Awaken yourself for me, you who hold the infer-

172   Materia Magica

nal kingdom of all the Eirynes, I invoke you by the gods in Hades OUCHI-TOU, the dispenser of tombs, AŌTHIŌMOS TIŌIE IŌEGOŌEIOPHRI who in the heavens rule the upper kingdom, MIŌTHILAMPS, in heaven, IAŌ and the (kingdom) under the earth SABLĒNIA IAŌ, SABLĒPHDAUBĒN THANATOPOUTŌĒR, I invoke you BATHUMIA CHTHAORŌOKORBRA ADIANAKŌ KAKIANBALE THENNAKRA. I invoke you, gods who were exposed by Kronos ABLANAIANALBA SISOPETRON take over Ariston the opponent of me, Soterianos, also called Limbranos, ŌĒANTICHERECHER BEBALLOSALAKAMĒTHĒ, and you, earthshaker, who holds the keys of Hades. Carry out for me, you . . . Provide for me also, . . . ASMIATĒNE. . . . GATHĒ MASŌMASŌSISO. . . . LIN provide . . . EISPITHTHUTHCHO . UĒ . . . ŌTHOUERRE (magic symbols) . . . AOTHOŌZUD (magical symbols) . . . UDĒSE TOIO (magical symbols) . . . [4]

With some variation, this formula appears on at least fifteen other published tablets; much of the cache, however, remains unpublished. Additional artifacts from the find employ different formulae, and one of the selenite tablets incorporates a spell text that is also known from PGM IV, a papyrus that has been provenanced to Egyptian Thebes. The Amathous tablets have been dated by paleography and letter forms to the late second or third century CE. Elements of the inscriptions support this approximate dating. Individuals named in the tablets are not called either Aurelius, a universally adopted *praenomen* that dates to the Severan period (the grant of citizenship through the *constitutio Antoniniana* under Caracalla in 212 CE), or Flavius, a similar name dated to the Constantinian period (306–337).[5] As a coherent archaeological deposit—an archive—the Amathous tablets provide evidence of a group of ritual experts working at the site. Similarities in hands, formulae, and epigraphic features suggest that the tablets were deposited over a relatively short period of time. Contextual analysis of the tablets allows us to reconstruct portions of the social environment in which these rituals were enacted. The practitioners at

---

4. Trans. from *CT* no. 45, pp. 134–36, with some modifications. The Greek text used here and on pp. 188–90 is courtesy of the Packard Humanities Institute Searchable Greek Inscriptions, (http://epigraphy.packhum.org/inscriptions/), number # PH208534.

5. Jordan, "Late feasts for ghosts," 133. On the adoption of imperial names, cf. J. G. Keenan, "The names Flavius and Aurelius as status designations in later Roman Egypt," *ZPE* 11 (1973); J. G. Keenan, "The names Flavius and Aurelius as status designations in later Roman Egypt," *ZPE* 13 (1974); J. G. Keenan, "An afterthought on the names Flavius and Aurelius," *ZPE* 53 (1983).

Amathous shared at least one spell recipe and deposited the completed objects in a single location. Some of the tablets bear witness to covert resistance to Roman authority, and the cache as a whole can allow us to investigate ritual strategies as they were employed at a single site.

Historical Background

Known for its copper and timber resources and strategic location in the Mediterranean, Cyprus has served as a center of commerce and movement from the time of its earliest Neolithic settlements up through the modern age.[6] The geographic proximity of the island to important Bronze Age and Classical states and empires ensured its early importance, and its strategic and economic primacy continued throughout the Roman period, when the island was a regular port of call for merchants and individuals traveling from east to west, and vice versa.[7] Cyprus came under the control of Rome in the Late Republic, when, in 58 BCE, it was appropriated from the Ptolemies through a law brought by P. Clodius Pulcher. Following a period of shifting control during the civil wars of the Late Republic, Augustus passed authority over the island to the Senate in 22 BCE, from which time Cyprus was a minor Senatorial province, overseen by a proconsul.

Local administration occurred through the towns and closely followed the polis-based system established under the Ptolemies.[8] Despite Cicero's letter to the local quaestor requesting special dispensation, the Cypriot people were not given extra privileges under the Romans, and no city was free from taxation.[9] Moreover, there is no evidence from the epigraphic sources of either large estates or upper-class Roman citizens on the island, suggesting that few prominent Romans settled on the island after its inclusion in the empire. Conversely, no Cypriot appears to have attained a high post in the imperial administra-

---

6. On early Cyprus, see V. Karageorghis, *Early Cyprus: Crossroads of the Mediterranean* (Los Angeles: Getty, 2002); L. Steel, *Cyprus before history: From the earliest settlers to the end of the Bronze Age* (London: Duckworth, 2004).

7. P. Horden and N. Purcell, *The corrupting sea: A study of Mediterranean history* (Malden, MA: Blackwell, 2000), 549. The coasts of both Asia Minor and Syro-Palestine are visible from the eastern portions of the island, Egypt lies only 264 miles to the south, and the port of Piraeus is 500 miles away, a relatively short distance for sea travel.

8. T. B. Mitford, "Roman Cyprus," *ANRW* II 7, no. 2 (1980): 1291.

9. Cic. *Ad Fam* XIII.48; Mitford, "Roman Cyprus," 296.

174   Materia Magica

tion. Indeed, the province is relatively anonymous due to its tranquility. Only two incidents disrupted the consistent peace of the island, which possessed no standing army beyond the guard of the provincial governor. Under Trajan, likely in 115, concurrent uprisings of Jews took place in Cyrene, Cyprus, Egypt, and Mesopotamia, perhaps associated with an annual poll tax, the *fiscus Iudaicus*. The Cypriot revolt was led by a messianic figure named Artemion; 240,000 Gentiles were killed (an unbelievable figure), and the city of Salamis was razed.[10] Following the revolt, the Jews were forbidden to set foot on the island on punishment of death, but Jews were evident on the island again by the third century CE, as we possess an inscription erected by a rabbi from that period.[11] Centuries later, under Constantine, Calocaerus, the keeper of the imperial camels, led a revolt against the empire, perhaps playing on resentments and fears brought about by the earthquake that destroyed Salamis. When Calocaerus crossed to Asia Minor, he was quickly defeated by Constantine's censor, Dalmatius.[12]

Beyond these incidents, Cyprus was quiet through much of the Roman period. As one of the twelve main cities of Cyprus and one of the four administrative districts in the Roman period, Amathous was a prominent urban center. In part, this was likely due to the city's economic vitality; the harbor, which faces south toward Egypt, was a trading center for the island in antiquity.[13] Amathous appears to have prospered during this time, as an aqueduct, possibly associated with Hadrian, led water from the northern Troodos mountains and terminated in a nymphaeum in the city center. Archaeologists associated with the French School under Pierre Aupert and with the Cyprus Department of Antiquities under the direction of Pavlos Flourentzos have excavated the agora, where much of the workings of the settlement must have occurred. A variety of buildings have been discovered in this area, including a stoa with a separate cult area and large structure of imperial date; work is ongoing.[14]

---

10. Cassius Dio *Hist. Rom.* LXVIII 32; P. W. van der Horst, "The Jews of ancient Cyprus," *Zutot* 3 (2003): 113–14; M. Goodman, "Judaea," in *The Cambridge ancient history, vol. XI: The High Empire, A.D. 70–192*, ed. A. K. Bowman, P. Garnsey, and D. Rathbone (Cambridge: Cambridge University Press, 2000), 669–70.

11. Cassius Dio *Hist. Rom.* LXVIII.32l; A. Reifenberg, "Das antike zyprische Judentum und seine Beziehungen zu Palästina," *Journal of the Palestine Oriental Society* 12 (1932): 211–12, plate. VIII.

12. T. D. Barnes, *Constantine and Eusebius* (Cambridge: Harvard University Press, 1981), 231.

13. Ptol. V. 13; G. F. Hill, *A history of Cyprus,* 4 vols. (Cambridge: Cambridge University Press, 1940), 231.

14. P. Aupert, "Amathonte hellénistique et impériale: l'apport des travaux récents," *Cahiers du Centre Études Cypriotes* 39 (2009); P. Flourentzos, "Chronique des fouilles et décou-

Recent work has articulated a sanctuary of the Egyptian god Bes, dating to the second century BCE, that was located in a prominent position in the agora. A colossal statue of the god Bes, now in Istanbul, likely derives from this location.[15] The agora also has yielded evidence for two Roman period temples, although it is not clear to whom these structures were dedicated.[16] Beyond the confines of the agora, a cultic installation dedicated to Aphrodite was located outside of the north gate of the city, attesting to the important role of religious acitivity in this area.[17]

To the north, east, and west of the city lay a large number of tombs. At the time of A. H. Smith's excavations in 1893, the tombs known to the north of the site were still some distance, about a half a mile, from the modern village of Agios Tychonas.[18] It is likely that enterprising locals discovered the cache of tablets near these tombs. More will be said of this archaeological context below.

The Amathous artifacts are of particular interest because the ancient sources document a distinctive form of magic on the island. Following a lengthy discussion of magic among the Persians and the education of Greeks in foreign rites, Pliny the Elder states

There is yet another branch of magic, derived from Moses, Jannes, Lotapes and the Jews, but living many thousand years after Zoroaster. So much more recent is the branch in Cyprus. In the time too of Alexander the Great, no slight addition was made to the influence of the profession by a second Osthanes, who, honoured by his attendance on Alexander, travelled certainly without the slightest doubt all over the world.[19]

---

vertes archéologiques à Chypre en 2003 et 2004," *BCH* 128–29 (2004–5): 1661; P. Aupert et al., "Rapport sur les travaux de l'école Française d'Athènes en 2003 et 2004: Amathone: Agora," *BCH* 127 (2003): 534; P. Aupert et al., "Rapport sur les travaux de l'école Française d'Athènes en 2003 et 2004: Amathone: Agora," *BCH* 128–29 (2004–5): 1036. Annual reports of the excavations at Amathous are published in *Bulletin de Correspondance Hellenique.*

15. Aupert, "Amathonte hellénistique et impériale: l'apport des travaux récents," 30–31; A. Hermary, "Amathonte classique et hellenistique: la question du Bès colossal de l'agora," in *From Evagoras I to the Ptolemies: Transition from the Classical to the Hellenistic Period in Cyprus. Proceedings of the International Archaeological Conference, Nicosia 29–30 November 2002,* ed. P. Flourentzos (Nicosia: Department of Antiquities, 2007).

16. Aupert, "Amathonte hellénistique et impériale: l'apport des travaux récents," 38–39.

17. Ibid., 35–36.

18. A. S. Murray, A. H. Smith, and H. B. Walters, *Excavations in Cyprus* (London: Trustees of the British Museum, 1900), 91 and plan, p. 88.

19. Pliny *HN* XXX.2.11. Trans. W. H. S. Jones, in Loeb Classical Library, 285.

Pliny goes on to discuss magical practice among the Italic tribes and among the Gauls. His reference to Cyprus is brief—the island was known for magic, and this form of ritual practice should be distinguished from that of the Persian Magi, the Jews, and the peoples of other geographical regions. The association between Cypriot magic and the Jews is somewhat problematic. The text does not provide a clear break between Cypriot and Jewish magic, and Pliny tells us nothing about the features of Cypriot magic.[20]

Cypriot magicians appear with some frequency in our literary sources. Josephus records that Felix, procurator of Judea, engaged a friend who claimed to be a magician, a Cypriot Jew named Atomus or Simon, to win the affections of Drusilla, the sister of Agrippa, the son of the former king of Judea.[21] Josephus does not provide insight into the methods used by the magician, although Atomus may have employed an erotic binding spell.[22] In the *Acts of the Apostles,* Paul visits Cyprus and travels overland from Salamis to Paphos. There, he encountered a man named Bar-Jesus or Elymas; *Acts* provides two separate names, which may conflate different individuals. Appropriating powers often attributed to magicians, Paul caused the man to go blind for a year for perverting the order established by God.[23]

As late as the Byzantine period, magic continues to be associated with the island in Christian literature. Two saints, Cyrus and John, were said to have traveled to the town of Lapethus to counteract a curse that was troubling the doctor Theodorus. On the advice of the saints, the doctor excavated an object from beneath the threshold of his bedroom. This likely was a curse tablet.[24] The ancient sources make it clear that magic was practiced on the island throughout antiquity, but provide little information to differentiate Cypriot magic from other contemporary practices that might be found elsewhere in the Mediterranean. Although it does not represent the totality of magical activity on the island, investigating the nature of one deposit will supply some insight into workings of ritual performance in this local environment.

---

20. Dickie, *Magic and magicians in the Greco-Roman world,* 223–24. Mitford has suggested that Jewish and Cypriot magic are the same in Pliny. "The cults of Roman Cyprus," *ANRW* II 18, no. 3 (1990): 2205.
21. Joseph, *AJ* XX, 142–44.
22. *CT* n.44, p. 132. On this episode and Jewish magic, see Bohak, *Ancient Jewish magic,* 79–80.
23. *Acts of the Apostles,* 13. 4–12; A. F. Loisy, *Les actes des apôtres* (Paris: E. Nourry, 1920), 517; Nock, "Paul and the magus," 328.
24. *PG* LXXXVII 3, col. 3625.

The Archaeological Context

Reconstructing the archaeological context of the curse tablets necessitates a close reading of the limited data available in the accession reports, as well as a few educated guesses based on the appearance of the objects.[25] The foundation for this inquiry was undertaken by P. Aupert and D. Jordan, who documented the circuitous path of the tablets from Cyprus to the collections in France and Britain.[26]

A substantial number of tablets were acquired by the British Museum between 1889 and 1891. Beginning with the initial publication by Louise Mac-Donald in 1891, the tablets were erroneously attributed to Kourion. Extensive correspondence maintained by the museum and analysis of the artifacts can demonstrate that all of these objects should be associated with the village of Agios Tychonas and the ancient site of Amathous. Following the discovery of the tablets, probably in the spring of 1889, Charles Christian, a local agent of the Ottoman Bank, offered to remit a portion of the tablets to A. S. Murray, the Conservator of Greek and Roman Antiquities at the British Museum.[27] In the British Museum accession reports, this first batch of items is associated with Mari, a small village located to the southwest of Kalavassos.[28] According to a

---

25. I am deeply grateful to Thomas Kiely, curator of Cypriot antiquities at the British Museum for his assistance and discussion of the archival material.

26. P. Aupert and D. R. Jordan, "Magical inscriptions on talc tablets from Amathous," *AJA* 85, no. 2 (1981); P. Aupert, M.-C. Hellmann, and M. Amandry, *Amathonte I. Testimonia 1: Auteurs anciens, Monnayage, Voyageurs, Fouilles, Origines, Géographie* (Paris: École Française d'Athènes, 1984), no. 12, p. 104; Aupert and Jordan, "Tablettes magiques d'Amathonte."

27. Letter from C. Christian to A. S. Murray on June 18, 1889, accompanying two fragments, one lead, one in "hornblende," a field term for a mineral, which is likely a mistaken reference to a selenite tablet. GR archives *Original Letters* (incoming letters), June 18, 1889. See also the letter dated June 8, 1889 (*Original Letters* [incoming letters]), and Murray's letter to Christian, GR archives *Letter-Book* 1880–96, fol. 185, July 15, 1889. On the British Museum archives, see V. A. Tatton-Brown, "Excavations in ancient Cyprus: Original manuscripts and correspondence in the British Museum," in *Cyprus in the 19th century AD: Fact, fancy and fiction: Papers of the 22nd British Museum Classical Colloquium, December 1998*, ed. V. A. Tatton-Brown (Oxford: Oxbow, 2001).

28. There appears to have been some confusion about the findspot as early as the first offer of sale, as the letter dated from June 18, 1889 associates a Late Bronze Age cylinder seal with the site of Moni, a different town to the west of Mari in the direction of Agios Tychonas. T. Kiely suggests that Moni may refer to Maroni, which is closer to and east of Mari, as there was frequently confusion about the place-names Moni, Mari, and Maroni at the time. Personal correspondence, July 8, 2011.

letter dated June 18, 1889, some of the objects had already been distributed to other buyers, but Murray expressed interest and sent a payment of thirty-five pounds.[29] Correspondence between Capt. Gerald Handcock and Murray, and subsequently between Handcock and Murray's assistant, C. Smith, details the next part of the process. In 1890, Capt. Handcock made an additional gift to the British Museum, with the result that the museum acquired a large portion of the cache, including both lead and selenite tablets.[30]

The selenite tablets in the British Museum are associated with accessions in multiple years, but this was likely the result of the process of acquisition. Joins between tablets from the two accession numbers, the artifacts provided by Christian in 1889 and Handcock in 1891, demonstrate that all are from the same original cache. For example, British Museum tablet 1889,10–15.14A joins with tablet 1891,4–18.59 (33). According to the documentation in the British Museum archives, Charles Christian provided a small number of tablets in 1889; Gerald Handcock gave the majority of the tablets to the museum in the following year. Other tablets with less secure provenance also have been associated with the Amathous cache. Wünsch published three tablets from the British Museum on a substance that he described as talc, which are almost certainly from the same find.[31] One of the sheets even includes a phrase that Wünsch associates with the lead tablets believed at the time to be from Kourion. The lead and selenite tablets in the Froehner collection, mentioned above, are surely associated with those in the British Museum; joins between fragments of single tablets demonstrate this conclusively.[32]

The precise provenance and findspot of the tablets are more difficult to disentangle. In a letter dated July 14, 1890, Handcock reports that the tablets were "found near the site of Curium by some natives who were clearing out an ancient shaft, for the purpose of making a well. [[The leads were found]] at about 90 feet down, under a heap of human bones, and the talc had been let

---

29. Letter from C. Christian to A. S. Murray. GR archives *Original Letters* (incoming letters), Sept. 7, 1889.
30. Letter from G. Handcock to A. S. Murray, April 22, 1890. GR archives *Original Letters* (incoming letters); Letter from G. Handcock to C. Smith, June 16, 1890. GR archives *Original Letters* (incoming letters). Jordan and Aupert (68) state that this second letter was written to Arthur H. Smith, who would later lead the British Museum's expedition to Amathous between 1892 and 1893, and serve as the Keeper of the Department of Greek and Roman Antiquities from 1909 to 1925. A more likely candidate, however, is Cecil Harcourt-Smith, who was appointed curator in 1879 and followed A. S. Murray as Keeper of the Department of Greek and Roman Antiquities from 1904 to 1908.
31. Wünsch, "Neue Fluchtafeln," nos. 10–13, pp. 244–46.
32. Aupert and Jordan, "Tablettes magiques d'Amathonte," 68.

into the side of the shaft." Handcock offers to provide more detailed information about the provenance to the British Museum but states that it will take a few weeks to do so. L. Macdonald, in her 1891 *editio princeps,* related that the tablets had been "found quite recently in Cyprus at Curium, in the south-west corner of the island, not far from Paphos. The natives, digging for a well came upon them at the bottom of a disused shaft, lying under a quantity of human bones."[33] This published claim notwithstanding, the British Museum accession records present a different story. There, the location "Kourion" has been crossed out and replaced by Agios Tychonas. This correction likely took place a few years after the objects entered the collection, as it appears to be written by A. S. Murray.[34] In 1892, the year after Macdonald's publication, Cecil Smith's review of Greek archaeology corrected her provenance and provided more details regarding the discovery of the tablet. Smith reports:

> Captain Handcock, through whom [the tablets] were procured for the British Museum, has kindly furnished me with further details of the discovery, which was made by some villagers in clearing what seemed to be a large disused well. They first found a quantity of squared stones, and then rubble, under which was a great quantity of human bones, among which were some gold earrings. In the lower stratum of the bones, they first found pieces of the lead, and subsequently pieces of the inscribed talc, some pieces of which were attached to the side of the well imbedded in gypsum. Later on, they came to water, at about 40 ft. from the surface.[35]

Macdonald's erroneous provenance of the tablets appears in the literature for close to a century, until corrected by Jordan and Aupert in 1994, but I have found no references to Smith's additional information about the circumstances of the find. Smith was in a position to have knowledge of the circumstances of the find and, more important, to be aware of the correction from Kourion to Agios Tychonas. He was in correspondence with Handcock as A. S. Murray's assistant, and succeeded Murray as Keeper in 1904, before leaving to head the Victoria and Albert Museum.

The shaft of a well or a grave would have represented an entrance to the

---

33. MacDonald, "Inscriptions relating to sorcery in Cyprus," 164.

34. Aupert and Jordan suggest that this correction is in Murray's hand, indicating that he was aware of the correct provenance, although the initial purchase may have relied on incorrect information supplied by one of the sellers. "Tablettes magiques d'Amathonte," 69.

35. C. Smith, "Recent Greek archaeology and folk-lore," *Folklore* 3, no. 4 (1892): 542.

180   Materia Magica

underworld, as Greek tradition closely associates cracks or crevices in the ground with such conduits.[36] About sixty curse tablets were discovered in a well in Herod's Praetorium in Caesarea, while a group of seventeen tablets was found in a well in the Athenian Agora.[37] Similarly, bodies of water were often the favored place of deposition for large caches of lead tablets; most well known is the group of prayers for justice from Bath, England, but other deposits of inscribed lead sheets, both imprecations and prayers, are known from the fountain of Anna Perenna in Rome.[38] The appearance of the Amathous tablets in photographs taken soon after they were accessioned provides further evidence of their likely deposition in a watery environment. On a number of tablets, the surface appears to have acquired a darkened, dull black color, while other examples preserve white encrustations. These physical features are largely consistent with the decay of lead in water, and the tablets appear similar to the contemporary examples from the well in the Athenian Agora.[39] This, however, does not necessitate a reading of the shaft as a well, as disused graves may have reached the water table, or the water table may have risen over time.

Unpacking the remainder of the description presents greater challenges. We can reconstruct the basic stratigraphy from Smith's description:

1. Cut, perhaps finished stones
2. Rubble
3. Human bones, associated with earrings

---

36. On entrances to the underworld and access to the dead, see D. Ogden, *Greek and Roman necromancy* (Princeton: Princeton University Press, 2001), 25–28; Johnston, *Restless dead,* 84–86.

37. Caesarea: Burrell, "'Curse tablets' from Caesarea"; Athens: Jordan, "Defixiones from a well near the southwest corner of the Athenian Agora." Other finds of curse tablets from wells: Athens: Dipylon well: *SGD* no. 13; well near Stoa of Attalos, *NGD* no. 15; well near civic offices, *NGD* no. 17; Isthmia: *NGD* no. 26 = Isthmia Museum 2820; Delos: *SGD* no. 58; Morgantina: *SGD* nos. 118–21; Antioch: *NGD* nos. 108–12.

38. Bath: see above, ch. 2 n. 35; Rome, fountain of Anna Perenna: above, ch. 1 n. 125.

39. On the characteristics and conservation of lead, see J. M. Cronyn and W. S. Robinson, *The elements of archaeological conservation* (London: Routledge, 1990), 203–4. The darkened areas of the lead may be the result of deposition within an anaerobic environment, in which lead sulphide caused the corrosion. Furthermore, exposure to oxygen may have resulted in the appearance of salts on the surfaces of the tablets, causing the white encrustations visible in the photographs. This corrosion, unlike the discoloration of the surfaces, may have been occurred after the removal of the tablets from the anaerobic environment, if the texts were not properly treated. I am indebted to Smadar Gabrelli for her advice on lead conservation. Compare the images of the tablets published in Jordan, "Defixiones from a well near the southwest corner of the Athenian Agora."

4. Human bones mixed with a few curses
5. Rolled lead curses
6. Selenite curses, some of which were embedded in the walls of the shaft
7. Further fill, or soil (Smith suggests that there was a break between the tablets and the bottom of the well with the phrase "Later on")
8. The water table, ca. 40 ft below the modern surface

Beginning at the top, we can read the history of the shaft backward into the past. The squared stones described in Smith's report were likely the remains of the well-head or other surface material that collapsed into the shaft after it had gone out of use. Similarly, the rubble below these stones should be seen as fill, perhaps added to the well after it had ceased its primary use as a source for water, or conversely, fill that had entered a tomb shaft through any number of processes.

This termination of the use of the well, or even adding fill to a preexisting shaft, may be tied to the next-down depositional remains—the human bones. We cannot know how many humans were represented by the "great quantity of bones" related by Handcock. The description is sufficiently tantalizing to encourage fanciful reconstruction, but insufficiently complete to allow any hope of certainty. The earrings suggest that the bones are the remains of at least some adults, probably women, with a degree of social status or wealth. It seems unlikely that these represent formal burials, as Smith records the presence of multiple bodies that were placed within a preexisting shaft. The earrings, however, also make it difficult to see the deposition as occurring after the bones had been defleshed; unarticulated human bones would not have included jewelry. The deceased individuals were therefore deposited as identifiable human remains, likely soon after death. The number of bones may suggest a sudden event that required the speedy disposal of the dead, such as a battle or plague.

The curse tablets, which come next in the stratigraphic sequence, are not related to the bones above. Although Smith's report indicates that the lowest stratum of the bones was discovered with some curses mixed in, this probably resulted from the decomposition of the human remains. As the flesh and other organic materials broke down, the bones probably shifted lower into the mud at the bottom of the shaft, intermingling with the tablets. Ogden suggests that the great quantity of human bones was the result of a mass grave, and that the tablets were placed in this space because it housed the remains of individuals

182   Materia Magica

who had been killed violently, rendering the shaft appropriate for use in curses.[40] The bones, however, lie stratigraphically above the curses, indicating that they must have been interred after the curses; this mass burial could not have provided a deathly resource for the practitioner. Handcock also distinguishes between the finds of the lead sheets and those of the selenite tablets, suggesting that the selenite tablets were lower and therefore earlier than the lead ones. Although we possess more than 200 of these rolled tablets, it seems unlikely that these objects would have formed a discrete layer at the bottom of the shaft, distinct from the selenite objects. It is more likely that these objects would have been mixed together to some degree, but that the greater number of lead tablets overshadowed the selenite ones. The lead tablets may have laid over the top of the selenite ones, perhaps indicating that the selenite objects predated the lead ones or were not employed continually through the use-period of the cache. Some of the selenite objects supposedly were affixed to the walls of the shaft using gypsum, a form of plaster that covered the interior of the shaft and was sufficiently thick to allow the selenite tablets to be mounted and held in place. At least one of the selenite tablets was mounted on the walls of the shaft, as it preserves two holes for suspension (plate 21). This detail suggests that the practitioner(s) would have entered the shaft to position the tablets in this specific location.

It is not clear whether the "disused shaft" was a well, as suggested by Handcock and Smith, or a tomb, as some scholars have posited.[41] Roman-period tombs around Amathous were made up of a *dromos*, an angled shaft leading downward to a large, rectangular chamber, with each feature cut from the soft havara, the soft porous bedrock that is found throughout the island. Mounting the tablets on the interior surface would have been easier if the entrance sloped. Some of the tombs in the area were as deep as forty feet, the length of the shaft mentioned in Handcock's account; Cesnola claims to have excavated approximately one hundred tombs to the northeast of the city, many of which lay between forty and fifty-five feet beneath the surface.[42] The tablets, which often invoke "the dead lying here," may suggest that the objects came from a tomb, but this internal testimony could refer to the larger geo-

---

40. Ogden, "Binding spells," 17.
41. Aupert and Jordan, "Tablettes magiques d'Amathonte," 68; *CT*, p.132; Ogden, "Binding spells," 17.
42. L. P. d. Cesnola, C. W. King, and A. S. Murray, *Cyprus: Its ancient cities, tombs, and temples. A narrative of researches and excavations during ten years' residence in that island* (New York: Harper & Brothers, 1878), 255.

graphic situation: the area around Agios Tychonas was used as a necropolis in the Roman period.

The text may use a characteristic formulation typical of cursing, even though the tablets were not buried with specific dead individuals. An imaginary grave is attested among other tablets, the provenance of which is not in doubt. A tablet from a well in the Athenian Agora, for example, invokes a ghost, but there is no evidence that the well in question was ever used as a burial location or was believed to have been haunted.[43] There also is other evidence of vertical shafts employed for ritual purposes. A productive parallel for the use of a shaft in repeated ritual activities might be found in the oracle of Trophonius in Lebadeia in Boeotia, known in antiquity as the *katabasion,* or place of descent. According to Pausanias, individuals wishing to consult the oracle would descend a small portable ladder.[44] A feature similar to that described by Pausanias has been discovered at Mt. Hagios Ilias, consisting of a shaft two meters in diameter and four meters in depth.[45] The shaft at Amathous was significantly deeper, perhaps as much as forty feet, and it is difficult to imagine a ladder of sufficient length. In contrast, wells in antiquity often possessed footholds that were used in construction, although descending and ascending in this manner would have been a time-consuming and dangerous process. It also is possible that the locals who recovered the tablets fabricated or exaggerated the depth of the find, perhaps to prevent other would-be treasure hunters from making a similar discovery.[46] In sorting through these conflicting reports, most important in our assessment should be Handcock's testimony, via Smith, that the bottom of the shaft was filled with water. The initial identification of the shaft as a well may be based on the report of the locals who discovered the objects. These individuals would have surely distinguished between the shaft of a dromos, which would have been angled, and the vertical shaft of a well.

In many ways, it does not matter whether the shaft was a grave or a well, as we need only be concerned with how the practitioners regarded the space of deposition. For those who created and employed the tablets, this was a ritual

---

43. Jordan, "Defixiones from a well near the southwest corner of the Athenian Agora," 231–33.

44. Paus. 9.39. At the base of the shaft, which Pausanias suggests was about eight cubits or four meters deep, suppliants would be sucked into the adyton, or inner shrine, through a small opening, and there have a spiritual experience On the oracle, see Ogden, *Greek and Roman necromancy,* 80–86, who suggests that it involved incubation.

45. E. Vallas and N. Pharaclas, "Peri tou manteiou tou Trophoniou en Lebadeia," *Athens Annals of Archaeology* 2, no. 1 (1969).

46. Aupert and Jordan, "Tablettes magiques d'Amathonte," 68.

shaft, used for a specific purpose. Whatever its earlier function, the practitioners appropriated and repurposed the shaft, transforming it into a location in which it was appropriate to mount and deposit the tablets. This shaft represented a conduit to the underworld, and whether or not it was originally a tomb, the inscriptions suggest that they believed it provided access to the dead. This may have been due to its proximity to other graves or merely because the shaft was a deep hole in the ground.[47]

The Material Evidence of the Curse Tablets

It is remarkable to discover curse tablets made out of two different materials in the same archaeological context. While it is possible that practitioners at other sites may have used multiple media for inscribing curses, organic material would have decayed leaving no archaeological traces. The Amathous artifacts can provide insight into the different material forms that related curses might have taken. The use of lead for curse tablets has an extensive history in the Mediterranean and does not require explanation. Selenite—translucent or transparent crystallized gypsum—represents a significant variation from what might be considered the normal method of cursing based on surviving evidence. The mineral is common on Cyprus, and the Hellenic Mining Company extracted selenite from large beds around the area of Kalavassos in the twentieth century; smaller deposits are known from the areas around Limassol, which is near ancient Amathous.[48] These local sources would have provided a close, easily accessible supply that could be exploited for the production of the curse tablets, perhaps at little or no cost to the practitioner. The mineral is very soft and can be scored with a fingernail or a sharp implement. Like similar inscriptions on mica (or perhaps selenite) from Quseir al-Qadim on the Red Sea coast, the tablets may have been inscribed using ink; the tip of the

---

47. The difficulties that have been encountered in identifying the geographical findspot of the tablets, as well as the precise circumstances of the deposition, can all be tied to the way in which the tablets were discovered and subsequently sold. Elements of the accession report reflect initial confusion or intentional obfuscation on the part of the antiquities dealer, which resulted in the mistaken association of the tablets with the site of Kourion for more than a century. The local individuals who discovered the tablets may also have had reason to hide or divert attention from the findspot. It may have taken some time to recover all of the tablets, or to determine if other wells also contained similarly valuable treasures.

48. L. M. Bear, *The mineral resources and mining industry of Cyprus* (Nicosia: Ministry of Commerce and Industry, 1963), 149–50.

pen would have left scratches.[49] Quartz, which has an appearance similar to selenite, was sometimes used to craft magical objects, as in the case for a large crystal rod from Egypt that is inscribed with the images of various deities and magical symbols.[50]

The physical characteristics of the mineral are largely antithetical to those of lead. Selenite is light in color, frequently translucent, and fixed in shape once worked, while lead is dark, cold, and pliable. Lead could be rolled or twisted, as many of the Amathous tablets have been. Etymologically, the Greek term for selenite, *selenites* (σεληνιτής), is closely connected with the word for moon (*Selene*), a derivation that is probably due to the appearance of the stone. Within the literary and subliterary traditions, the stone was believed to have waxed and waned along with its celestial counterpart.[51] This quality may have led to the local association of the stone with supernatural powers and its use in magical practice.

One of the selenite tablets (1891,4–18.59) possesses two holes positioned approximately 1 cm apart and located in the upper left-hand corner of the object (plate 21). These holes likely were used to suspend the tablet. This evidence supports the supposition made by Smith in his article that the selenite tablets were mounted on the walls of the shaft. Although only one tablet preserves suspension holes, multiple methods of mounting the objects may have been employed. Smith also suggests that some of the tablets were impressed into plaster that lined the walls of the shaft, but visual inspection does not reveal telltale signs of this material, and later cleaning may have removed such traces. The fragmentary nature of the tablets may suggest that some may have fallen from the walls or were cast into the shaft. While the fact that some tablets were mounted suggests that they were meant to be seen, we cannot be certain that humans were the intended audience. Indeed, underworld spirits may have been the primary recipients.

Inscribed texts related to ritual performance are known from other sites and areas of the Mediterranean, where display was often intended to convey a message to both human and divine recipients. Most common is the votive object, set up in thanks for or in anticipation of divine assistance. But we do possess a

---

49. R. S. Bagnall, "Papyri and Ostraka from Quseir al-Qadim," *BASP* 23, no. 1–2 (1986): 76a, 76b, 76c, pp. 47–50. The selenite inscriptions from Quseir al-Qadim include an offering for the safety of the dedicant, another text that may be similar, and a dedication to Sabazius.

50. Brashear, *Magica Varia,* 80–81.

51. Dioscorides Pedanius, *De materia medica* 5.141.1; Oribasius, *Collectiones Medicae:* 13.191.1.

186 Materia Magica

number of curses or prayers for justice that were treated in a similar way and displayed in a temple or other sacred space. A bronze tablet, either a curse or a prayer for justice, from an unknown location in Asia Minor preserves a small nail hole in the center of its upper edge.[52] Although discovered at the bases of statues in the sanctuary precinct of Demeter, one of the fourteen prayers for justice from Cnidus has a single hole suggesting these objects also were affixed originally to the wall of the structure.[53] Likewise, a few Latin tablets have traces demonstrating that they were put on view, although they lack obvious physical markers that would indicate suspension or mounting in some way.[54] A tablet written to Divus Nodens was found unfolded in the temple of the god to whom the tablet was inscribed.[55] The act of display has important repercussions for the interpretation of the selenite tablets from Amathous, as it both implies a desire that the tablets be seen and also requires a significant outlay of effort on the part of the ritual specialist.

The practitioner appears to have treated the lead and selenite tablets differently, mounting some of the selenite tablets on the walls but rolling the lead tablets and depositing them in the bottom of the shaft feature. The lower portions of each lead tablet consistently demonstrate damage, suggesting that the tablet was rolled downward from the top; the first lines of script occupied the centermost portion of the roll. These first lines, which were protected by the remainder of the document, may have been seen as the most vital part of the tablet; this text includes the hexameter invocation to the spirits of the dead and the names of the victims and commissioners. A number of the tablets were

---

52. C. Dunant, "Sus aux voleurs! Une tablette en bronze à inscription grecque du Musée de Genève," *Museum Helveticum* 35, no. 4 (1978); Versnel, "Beyond cursing," 74.

53. For bibliography, see above, ch. 2 n. 35. Translations of three of the texts are found at *CT* no. 89, pp. 189–90. See the discussions in Versnel, "Beyond cursing," 72–73; H. S. Versnel, "ΠΕΠΡΗΜΕΝΟΣ. The Cnidian curse tablets and ordeal by fire," in *Ancient Greek cult practice from the epigraphical evidence,* ed. R. Hägg (Stockholm: Paul Aströms Förlag, 1994); Chaniotis, "Under the watchful eyes of the gods," 6–8.

54. Faraone, Garnand, and López-Ruiz discuss three tablets that were discovered in temples, or can be associated with temples. C. A. Faraone, B. Garnand, and C. López-Ruiz, "Micah's mother (Judg. 17:1–4) and a curse from Carthage (KAI 89): Canaanite precedents for Greek and Latin curses against thieves?" *JNES* 64, no. 3 (2005): 174–75. Another tablet, from the shrine at Uley, requests that the thief return the stolen good to "this shrine." The tablet, however, shows clear indications that it was rolled, suggesting that the text would not have been readable by human visitors to the sanctuary. R. Goodburn, M. W. C. Hassall, and R. S. O. Tomlin, "Roman Britain in 1978," *Britannia* 10 (1979), no. 3: 343–34.

55. Faraone, Garnand, and López-Ruiz, "Micah's mother (Judg. 17:1–4) and a curse from Carthage (KAI 89)," 172–73, no. 9. For further discussion, see Versnel, "Beyond cursing," 60.

punched through with nails, a segment of the ritual that would have followed the inscription of the text. This manipulation of the tablets is common, and similar actions are taken with regard to other tablets throughout the Mediterranean.

The relationship between the two kinds of tablets may be chronological, although it is also possible that different media were used for different kinds of rites. Smith's report indicates that selenite sheets were discovered underneath the lead tablets, which might indicate that the selenite tablets were used first, followed by the lead ones. As we will note in the succeeding section, at least three different spells were written on the tablets. The texts that are preserved on the artifacts are all aimed at the same goal—the restraint of an enemy—but there is some evidence to suggest that the lead sheets were employed for one rite, while the selenite tablets were used in a different manner.

The Inscribed Texts

More than two hundred lead tablets and thirty selenite tablets can be reconstructed from the fragments in the British Museum and the Bibliothèque Nationale. Of this sizable corpus, however, only sixteen lead and six selenite tablets have been published.[56] David Jordan has reported that the unpublished tablets, both lead and selenite, are similar to published examples, suggesting that conclusions drawn from the analysis of the published sample may be applicable to the cache as a whole.[57] All of the tablets appear to be judicial in nature, involving members of the Amathous community. In form, the tablets mention one or more of the targets by name, frequently characterizing them as enemies who had treated the commissioner unjustly. The majority of the tablets also name the commissioner, who commands various demons and deities to bind fast the victim. Magical phrases are interspersed within the invocation and call on underworld spirits and the dead. At least three separate prototypes were used in the creation of the tablets, and at least three, if not more, individuals were responsible for the lead inscriptions. Additional individuals may have inscribed the selenite tablets. This suggests the presence of a group of professional practitioners who were active in the community; the nature of this group remains an open question, one that will be discussed below.

---

56. For bibliography see this chapter, n. 3.
57. Jordan, "Late feasts for ghosts," 135.

188   Materia Magica

It seems unlikely that similarities in the inscriptions preserved on the tablets resulted from the use of boilerplates to manufacture a substantial number of partial tablets prior to their use in specific, commissioned magical acts. While the practice of mass production is known among magical texts, with some tablets showing that the main body of the text was inscribed before filling in the names of the victim, none of the Amathous examples demonstrates space that may have been intentionally left blank for the insertion of the names into the preformulated tablet.[58] Indeed, one tablet in particular, *DT* 27, curses eleven separate individuals, some with metronymics, with no indications of cramped script. Each tablet appears to have been fully inscribed at the time of its commissioning.

The tablets from Amathous demonstrate the use of at least three templates for the inscriptions written on the lead and selenite sheets. Each of the lead tablets appears to follow a single template that probably derived from a model book. I include a transcription of Audollent *DT* 22, revised by Mitford, in which Soterianos, also known as Limbaros, curses a man named Ariston. This text was translated on pp. 171–72.

[δέμονες] οἱ κατὰ γῆν κὲ δέμονες οἵτ[ινές]
[ἐσ]τε κὲ πατέρες πατέρων κὲ μητέρε[ς ἀντι]-
[ενί]ριοι οἵτινες ἐνθάδε κῖσθε κὲ οἵτινες ἐ[νθάδε]
[κ]άθεστε, θυμὸν ἀπὸ κραδίης πολυκηδέα [π]ρό[σθε λα]-
(5) βόντες, παραλάβετε τοῦ Ἀρίσστωνος τὸν θυμὸν τ[ὸν]
πρὸς ἐμὲ ἔχι τὸν Σοτηριανὸν τὸν κὲ Λίμβαρον κὲ τὴ<ν> ὀ[ρ]-
γήν, κὲ ἀφέλεσθε αὐτοῦ τὴν δύναμιν κὲ τὴν ἀλκὴν κὲ [ποι]-
[ή]σετε αὐτὸν ψυχρὸν κὲ ἄφωνον κὲ ἀπνεύμοναν, ψυχρὸν εἰς ἐμὲ τὸν Σοτηριανὸν τὸν κὲ Λίνβαρον. ὁρκίσζω
(10) [ὑ]μᾶς κατὰ τῶν μεγάλων θεῶν Μασωμασιμαβλα[βοι]-
[ω] μαμαξω Ευμαζω ενδενεκοπτουρα μελοφθημαραρ
[α]κου ρασρωεεκαμαδωρ μαχθουδουρας κιθωρασα κηφο[ζω]-
[ν] θεὰ αχθαμοδοιραλαρ ακου ραεντ ακου ραλαρ ἀκούεστε α[λ]-
[αρ] ουεχεαρμαλαρ καραμεφθη Σισοχωρ ἀδωνεία χθὼ[ν]
(15) [χ]ουχμαθερφες θερμωμασμαρ ασμαχουχιμανου φιλα[εσωσι]
[χθ]όνιοι θεοί, παραλάβετε τοῦ Ἀρίστωνος κὲ τὸν υἱὸν αὐ[τοῦ]

---

58. Compare the evidence from *CT* 14; Jordan, "Defixiones from a well near the southwest corner of the Athenian Agora," 251.

Practitioners and Craft at Amathous, Cyprus   189

[Ἀρ]ίστωναν τὸν θυμὸν κὲ τὴν ὀργὴν τὴν εἰς ἐμὲ ἔχι τὸν Σο[τηρι]-

[ανὸ]ν τὸν κὲ Λίμβαρον, κὲ παράδοτε τῷ κατ' Ἄδη θυρουρῷ

[Μ]αθυρευφραμενος κὲ τὸν ἐπὶ τοῦ πυλῶνος τοῦ Ἄ[δους]

(20) [κ]ὲ τῶν κλήθρων τοῦ οὐρανοῦ τεταγμένον Στερξερξ ηρη[ξα]

[ρη]σίχθων αρδαμαχθουρ πρισσγευ λαμπαδευ στενα[κτὰ]

[θά]ψατε τὸν προγεγραμμένον ἐπὶ τοῦδε τοῦ φιμωτι[κοῦ]

[κ]αταθέματος.

[ἐνο]ρκίζω ὑμῖν τὸν βασιλέα τῶν κωφῶν δεμόνων·

(25) [ἀκο]ύσατε τοῦ μεγάλου ὀνόματος, ἐπιτάσσι γὰρ ὑμῖν ὁ μ-

[έγ]ας Σισοχωρ ὁ ἐξάγων τοῦ Ἄδους τὰς πύλας, κὲ κατα-

[δ]ήσατε τοῦ ἀντιδίκου μου τοῦ Ἀρίσστωνος κὲ κατακο[ιμί]-

[σ]ατε τὴν γλῶσσαν τὸν θυμὸν τὴν ὀργὴν τὴν εἰς ἐμὲ ἔχι τὸν

Σοτηριανὸν τὸν κὲ Λίμβαρον ὁ Ἀρίστων, εἴνα μὴ δύνητέ μοι μη[δ]-

(30) [εν]ὶ πράγματι ἐναντιωθῆνε. ὀρκίζω ὑμᾶ<ς> δέμονες πολυάν-

δριοι κὲ βιοθάνατοι κὲ ἄωροι κὲ ἄποροι ταφῆς κατὰ τῆς ῥη[σι]-

χθόνης κατενενκάσης Μελιούχου τὰ μέλη κὲ αὐτὸν Μελιοῦχον.

ὀρκίζω ὑμᾶς κατὰ τοῦ Αχαλεμορφωφ ὅστις ἐστὶν μόνος ἐπίγι[ος θε]-

ὸς οσους οισωρνοφρις ουσραπιω ποιήσατε τὰ ἐνγεγραμμέ[να]·

(35) [τύ]νβε πανδάκρυτε κὲ χθόνιοι θεοὶ κὲ Ἑκάτη χθονία κὲ Ἑρμῆ χ[θόν]-

[ιε] {κὲ} κὲ Πλούτων κὲ Ἐρινύες ὑποχθόνιοι κὲ ὑμῖς οἱ ὧδ<ε> κάτω

κίμ[ενοι]

ἄωροι κὲ ἀνώνυμοι Ευμαζων, παραλάβετε τὰς φωνὰς το<ῦ> Ἀρίσ[τω]-

νος τοῦ πρὸς ἐμὲ τὸν Σοτηριανὸν τὸν κὲ Λίμβαρον Μασω[μα]-

χω· τὴν παραθήκην ὑμῖν πατίθομε φιμωτικὴν τοῦ Ἀρίσστω[νος]

(40) κὲ ἀνάδοτε αὐτοῦ τὸ ὄνομα τοῖς χθονίοις θεοῖς Αλλα αλκη [κὲ αλ]-

[κ]εω λαλαθανάτω τῷ τριωνύμῳ Κούρᾳ· οὗτοί μοι πάντοτε [τελιώ]-

[σ]ουσιν κὲ φιμώσουσιν τὸν ἀντίδικον ἐμοῦ τοῦ Σοτηριανο[ῦ τοῦ]

κὲ Λιμβάρου τὸν Ἀρίσστωναν· ἔγιρον δέ μοι κὲ σὺ ὁ ἔχων τὸ ὑ[πό]-

γιον βασίλιόν σε πασῶν τῶν Ἐρινύων. ὀρκίζω ὑμᾶς κατὰ [τῶν]

(45) ἐν Ἄδι θεῶν Ουχιτου τὴν τάβων δότιραν Αωθιωμος [τιωιε]-

[ι]ωεγοωεοιφρι ὁ ἐν τῷ οὐρανῷ ἔχων τὸ ἐθέριον βασίλ[ιον Μ]-

[ιω]θιλαμψ ἐν οὐρανῷ Ιαω κὲ τὸν ὑπὸ γῆν Σαβληνια Ια[ω]

Σαβληφδαυβην θανατοπουτωηρ. ὀρκίζω σε Βαθ[υμια χθ]-

αορωοκορβρα αδιανακω κακιαβαλη θεννανκρα. ὀρκ[ίσζω]

(50) [ὑμ]ᾶς τοὺς ἀ[πὸ] Κρόνου ἐκτεθέντα[ς θε]οὺς Αβλαναιαναλβα

[σ]ισοπε[τρον] παραλάβετε τὸ[ν ἀντίδικ]ον [ἐμοῦ τοῦ Σοτηριανοῦ]

[το]ῦ κὲ Λιμβάρου τὸν Ἀ[ρίσ]στωναν Ω[ηαντιχερεχερ βεβαλλοσαλ]-

190   Materia Magica

[ακα]μηθη κὲ σὺ ἡ τὰς [κ]λῖδας τοῦ [Ἄδους κατέχουσα ῥησίχθων. συν]-
[επι]τέλι δὲ ἐμοὶ κὲ σὺ Ασμιατην[ε - - - - - - - - - - - - - -]
(55) [. . .] γαθη Μασωμασωσισο[- - - - - - - - - - - - - - - -]
[. . .] λιν παρατέθεμε (vacat)
ΕΙΣΠΙΘΘΥΘΧΟ.ΥΗ [- - - - - - - - - - - - - - - - - -]
[-] ΩΘΟΥΕΡΡΕ (magical symbols) [- - - - - - - - - - - - - - - - - - -]
[- -] ΑΟΘΟΩΖΥΔ (magical symbols) Ε [- - - - - - - - - - - - - - - -]
(60) [- - -] ΥΔΗϹΕ.ΤΟΙΟ (magical symbols) [- - - - - - - - - - - - -]

The text begins with an address to a variety of spirits written in dactylic hexameter (δέμονες . . . λαβόντες, lines 1–5). This may represent a metrical invocation that was adopted from another source for use in the ritual.⁵⁹ This prelude
is followed by an identification of the target of the rite, as well as the name of
the commissioner. The invocation requests that the spirits "draw off (the victim's) power and strength, make him cold and speechless" (ll. 7–9). The underlying metaphor relates the victim to both the lead tablet and the dead, who are
likewise cold and speechless. A long series of *voces magicae* and divine names
follows, which incorporates a variety of different ethnic sounding names,
including Sisokhor and the Jewish god Adonai (l. 14). The middle of the text
is filled with multiple injunctions to underworld deities. These instructions are
detailed and mechanistic, as the text calls on the underworld forces to "bury
him who is written on this muzzling tablet in a mournful grave . . . bind down
and put to sleep the tongue and the spirit and the anger of my enemy" (ll. 22–
23; ll. 26–28).

The tablet refers to itself as "this muzzling deposit," τοῦδε τοῦ φιμωτι[κοῦ]
[κ]αταθέματος, a phrase that also appears in line 39, as a noun, φιμωτικὴν, a
muzzler, and in line 42 as a verb, φιμώσουσιν. The term indicates the purpose
of the tablet: to prevent the victim from speaking, presumably in a court of
law. The same function is given for a selenite text from the shaft that appears
to have used a different formula, one that is related to a text from the magical
papyri (on this, see below). Moreover, the word also makes appearances in
other ritual texts, most notably in the *Cyranides,* on PGM XXXVI (the formulary from the Fayum), and in some of the magical papyri from Thebes.⁶⁰

In line 34, the *voces magicae,* OSOUS OISORNOPHRIS OUSRAPIO may

_____

59. Drew-Bear, "Imprecations from Kourion," 87–88.
60. *P.Oslo* I 1, commentary on line 164, pp. 77–78; PGM XII.967; PGM IX.4; Jordan, "Late
feasts for ghosts," 143 n. 34, provides additional references.

allude to the Egyptian divinity Osiris, as the title Oisornophris is likely related to Οσορνωφρις, an epithet of Osiris commonly used in the magical papyri. Ousrapio is likely related to Serapis, the name by which Osiris most frequently was known outside Egypt.[61] This is followed by invocations to Greek deities where the text addresses "tomb, much wept, and gods of the earth, and chthonic Hekate, chthonic Hermes, Plouton, the chthonic Eirynes, and you who lie below, untimely dead" (35–37). Although none of the tablets preserves a margin at the end, the spell appears to conclude with another lengthy invocation to various underworld deities that incorporates further *voces magicae*.[62]

Beneath line 56, a horizontal line has been incised that runs the width of the tablet. The text that is inscribed beneath this line is unintelligible but seems to be a mixture of Greek letters and magical symbols, all written larger than the rest of the text on the tablet. A similar incised line is visible on tablets *DT* 23 and 37; Mitford suggests a bar should also be supplied at the end of tablet *DT* 32. Although the lower portions of many of the tablets are badly damaged, inspection of the published tablets suggests that these may be *kharaktêres,* powerful signs that had magical efficacy. The inclusion of Greek letters, which were likewise associated with ritual usefulness, supports this reading.[63] *Kharaktêres* are clearer on some of the selenite tablets and include ring letters, a symbol similar to a lightning bolt, and other signs that are paralleled in the magical papyri and on magical gems (plate 22).

The majority of the published lead tablets show little variation from this text. Even in some of the tablets where there has been significant damage, the text often adheres to the putative model. *DT* 23 preserves only fifteen lines of text, but the phrases visible on the tablet, which has been extensively damaged on the right side and at the bottom, correspond to other examples. Often, the deviation from the template consists of modification within the spelling of the *voces magicae* or instances of repetition of syllables, which suggests errors that occurred while copying from the formulary. For example, where *DT* 23 invokes the great gods Μασωμασιμαβλα [βοι] / [ω] μαμαξω Ευμαζω ενδενεκοπτουρα (ll. 10–11), *DT* 24 reads νηθιμας . . . μασωλαβεω μαμαμαξω

---

61. Jordan, "Late feasts for ghosts," 133 n. 7; on Osornophris, see Hopfner, *Griechisch-ägyptischer Offenbarungszauber.* 37–38, §157.

62. The group of sixteen tablets includes artifacts in differing states of preservation. Although none of the texts preserves a lower margin, *DT* nos. 22, 32, 35, and 37 appear to include the end of the text.

63. On the *kharaktêres* and the power of Greek letters, see the discussion above, p. 69–72, esp. 72 n. 50 with bibliography.

μαξω ενκοπτωδιτ (ll. 9–10). The copyist had elided certain words and dropped other syllables from mystical names, alterations that do not affect the translatable parts of the text; the effect of these changes on the efficacy of the tablets is unknown, but doubtful.

Three of the fifteen lead tablets demonstrate variants from the others. *DT* 25 was intended to bind the speech of Theodoros, the Roman governor, and Timon the son of Markias. The opening lines of the tablet correspond to the initial metrical section found on other examples, but this address is followed by invocations to "those having left life behind, grievous ones, restless dead, whether foreigners or locals, or helpless ones of the grave or those from the farthest points of the stars, or you wandering in the air, or those who lie below . . ." (lines 3–7, with Wünsch's additions and emendations). The magical words that follow the initial invocation vary from the other texts in the cache, but some of the phrases often include similar sounds.[64] The text breaks off after line 20, and elements of the preserved portions of the tablet suggest that there may be substantial variation from the *Vorlage*.

DT 32 disguises the names of the victims in a form of pseudoscript. In line 4 of the tablet, a number of incised, meaningless letters occur at the point where other tablets name the victim. These symbols are not a cipher, as there is no correspondence between the pseudoscript that appears in line 4 and that in lines 16, 26, 30, and 38. The symbols do not correlate with any known alphabets. Although Mitford suggests that it might be a derivative form of Latin shorthand, it is difficult to posit what purpose this could serve, or why the scribe would intersperse Latin shorthand within a Greek text.[65] Rather, as some of the symbols appear at the bottom of other documents in the cache, it seems likely that the practitioner substituted magical *kharaktêres* for the name of the victim.[66] The middle of the Greek text is sufficiently similar to other examples to permit reconstruction from the *Vorlage,* but variation in the last third of the document, after line 25, renders the conclusion of the curse problematic. The end of the document is, like three others, marked by the presence of a line; three signs that appear similar to koppas are visible beneath this incision.

DT 36 is a small fragment that contains ten lines of text and an image of a

---

64. Brashear, "The Greek magical papyri," 3440.
65. *The inscriptions of Kourion,* 271. See R. Cagnat, *Cours d'épigraphie Latine,* IV ed. (Rome: L'Erma di Bretschneider, 1964), 384.
66. The magical papyri preserve instances in which a cipher was used to disguise the meaning of the text. PGM LVII and LXXII, both from the same scroll, are written in a cryptographic script that can be deciphered. Dieleman, *Priests, tongues, and rites,* 87–96.

Practitioners and Craft at Amathous, Cyprus   193

bird to the right of the inscription. The text does not adhere to the formulary associated with the other tablets. Much of the inscription is indecipherable and may be *voces magicae* or other mystical phrases. In line 4, the text reads ποιήσατε μιση[τὸν — — —], which is likely an order to the invoked divinities that they should make the victim "hateful." Wünsch identified the drawing as a representation of a rooster based on a parallel image in CIL VIII. Suppl. 12511, 15.[67] I have not seen the tablet, but a drawing made in the British Museum Accession Records clearly shows a bird drawn alongside the text, facing upward and perpendicular to the inscription. The torso is rounded and comes to a point to indicate a tail in the lower part. The head of the bird is largely missing, although one can discern where the head meets the neck. Two legs protrude to the right of the drawing; these are incised lines that fork into what appear to be three toes. Only this tablet preserves such an image. Representations incised on curse tablets often relate to the punishment or torture that would be visited on the victim of the spell or the spirits invoked by the text. The tablets preserved from near the Porta San Sebastiano show bound charioteers as well as images of rooster-headed anguipedes. Other tablets, such as an example from Syria, may depict the victim of the spell pierced with nails or needles, and therefore bound.[68] P. Aupert has recently discovered and published a late, seventh-century tablet on lead from Amathous that depicts a human or demon, but this image is markedly different from the bird shown on the tablet from the cache.[69]

A number of magical gems preserve images of birds, most notably the falcon and the ibis. If the head and beak of the bird had been preserved on the lead tablet, these features would help to secure the identification of the species of bird. An ibis may be indicated by the prominence of the legs, which are relatively long with respect to the body. On the gems, the ibis may be pictured in connection with a small shrine that is surmounted by plants, or in association with other spirits, such as Chnoubis.[70] Notably, the ibis often is associated with Thoth, who was, for the Greeks, related to Hermes. Hermes is named in a

---

67. *DTA* xix.
68. On the tablets from Porta San Sebastiano in Rome, see the Introduction. The tablet with the individual pierced by nails is *CT* no. 5 = *SGD* no. 167. On representations in magic, see Wilburn, "Representations and images in magical practice."
69. P. Aupert, "Hélios, Adonis et magie: les trésors d'une citerne d'Amathonte," *BCH* 132, no. 1 (2008): 370–87.
70. Michel, *Die Magischen Gemmen: zu Bildern und Zauberformeln auf geschnittenen Steinen der Antike und Neuzeit*, 286–88.

number of the other lead tablets, and his association with the underworld may be the reason for including this enigmatic symbol.

Of the published selenite tablets, four of the six (*DT* 18–20 and Jordan and Aupert 1994) follow the same model, which is different from the model used in the production of most of the lead tablets; one of the other published tablets (*DT* 21) did not contain sufficient legible text to yield a transcription. The unpublished fragments in London join to other unpublished selenite chips that are housed in the Bibliothèque Nationale, as part of the Froehner Collection. These pieces can be resolved into about thirty tablets, all of which depend on the same formula.[71] Jordan and Aupert have published the most complete version of this formulary text, but their publication does not include a transcription. A photograph shows that the tablet is broken at the top and on all four sides. Their translation is as follows:

[je vous adjure] / de posséder (?) [mon adversaire] Philodémos [qu'engendra Hèdonètô et de lui ôter / son animosité] / contre moi / *signes magiques* [je vous conjure / vous que commande Sisokhôr Isokhôr [vous les descendants de Kronos . . . / . . . le grand] Eumazô et vous, les démons sourds et muets, soumettez-moi [Philodémos . . . / et livrez (?)] Philodémos aux porteurs de mot rapide / . . . aux violents (?) Dakhalavama (?) . . . / . . . et aux] infernaux Mazô Eumazô . . . / . . . mavuôn, Emoulathathaokha (?) . . . / . . . urolarnou Mélorsokhôr et / Daimonaristôn; soumettez Philodémos à . . . / (à) Adonis chtonien *formules magiques* / *formules magiques.* Je vous conjure, Sen . . . / ainsi que . . .]ther chtonien, Hermada et Plouton . . . / . . . Zavadarkthoumau et vous, les démons . . . / emparez-vous (?) / de la langue de mon adversaire Philodémos / . . . et entravez-la (?)] de liens infrangibles, afin que [je n'aie / aucune] crainte d'aucune contestation, mais que . . . / [ ] / les . . . de l'Hades; je vous conjure par les grands dieux / . . . de grand Aiôkhômakh [. . . / . . . et ne désobéissez pas . . . / *formules magiques* / soumettez Philodémos qu' / engendra Hèdonètô, fille d'Onésiphoros . . . [72]

The text of the tablet includes detailed instructions for the spirits of the underworld to bind a man named Philodemos son of Hedoneto. A few points of commonality between the lead and selenite tablets can be identified. Some of the

---

71. Jordan, "Late feasts for ghosts," 136.
72. Aupert and Jordan, "Tablettes magiques d'Amathonte," 70.

same *voces magicae* appear in both texts, as well as invocations to the spirits Sisokhor and Eumazo.[73] While aspects of the selenite inscription suggest that it is a simpler version of the one preserved on the lead tablets, certain elements are found only on the selenite tablets. For example, the invocation to spirits that are deaf and mute (l. 7) is not paralleled. This suggests that a separate template was used for the production of these objects. Further investigation must await a full publication of the selenite inscriptions.

Only a few words are repeated among two of the three tablets published by Wünsch (*DT* 18–20), but it seems likely that these also follow the formulary used for Jordan and Aupert's selenite tablet. In line 6 of *DT* 18, the tablet reads οἱ ἐπί τῷ τόπῳ. The second preserved line of *DT* 19 reads ἐ]πί τῷ τόπῳ τούτ[ῳ. This has been reconstructed as δαίμονες ἐπί τῷ τόπῳ τούτῳ, "the spirits that are in this place," although the lead tablets would suggest that we read δέμονες. Comparison between the two tablets has also permitted the reconstruction of an invocation to chthonic Hermes. *DT* 20, which only preserves two lines, includes the partially restored phrase in the second line, τοῦ καταδ[έσμου; the injunction κὲ κατα[δ]ήσατε τοῦ ἀντιδίκου appears in the template used in the production of the lead tablets.

Magical symbols are visible on Jordan and Aupert's selenite tablet, suggesting a further area of congruence between the lead and mineral tablets. The symbols include a large zeta, a number of ring letters formed by a vertical stroke with a round ball at the lower terminus, and a symbol that resembles a triangle in which the two lines along either side are extended upward, making a shape similar to an hourglass. These *kharaktêres* are larger than the Greek letters and have been integrated into the main body of the inscription. This contrasts sharply with the lead tablets, where the magical signs typically are inscribed at the bottom of the tablet, often beneath a horizontal stroke. The same symbols are shared between the lead and selenite tablets. For example, on lead tablet *DT* 32, beneath the horizontal incision, one can detect a line of three symbols, each composed of a vertical stroke surmounted by a circle. Mystical symbols also appear on other unpublished selenite tablets, but every one does not include the same series of symbols, nor are the symbols in the same order. For example, a number of the tablets include a symbol similar to an omega, with a circular curl on the left, leading to a rounded horseshoe shape that, on the right, terminates in a leftward turning curl. This symbol appears on

---

73. On the name *Sisokhor,* see M. Schwartz, "Sasm, Sesen, St. Sisinnios, Sesengen Barpharanges, and . . . 'Semanglof'" *Bulletin of the Asian Institute* 10 (1996): 256.

196   Materia Magica

Jordan and Aupert's tablet as the eighth in the series, following the defective hourglass. On another tablet, these symbols have been reversed. It is clear that the *kharaktêres* were an important component of ritual practice at Amathous, occurring across the various classes of tablets and employed for multiple iterations of the spell.

One of the selenite inscriptions, *NGD* 115, published by D. Jordan, is markedly different from the other tablets in the archive. This artifact is fragmentary, with three pieces currently in the British Museum while a fourth portion is housed in the Bibliothèque Nationale. The text of the curse tablet calls on a vast number of underworld divinities, whose names are each modified by the epithet *chthonic*. The invocation reads

Chthonic Hermes and chthonic Hekate and chthonic Zethos (?) chthonic Demeter and chthonic earth born (fem. pl.) and chthonic Acheron and chthonic "raw dead" (neut. sg.) and chthonic Thasian (s?) and chthonic heroes (?) and chthonic avengers (?) and chthonic Amphipolis (?) and chthonic Spirits and chthonic Sins and chthonic Dreams and chthonic Necessity and chthonic Oaths and chthonic Ariste (?) and chthonic Holder of Tartaros and chthonic Evil Eye and chthonic Aion (?) and chthonic (?) Heroes (?) and Paian, chthonic Demeter and chthonic Plouton and chthonic and dead Persephone and evil demons and fortunes of all men, come with mighty fate—and necessitate, accomplish this muzzling spell, lest Ariston (f.) gainsay Artemidoros, whom Timo bore, in anything (or to anyone?) but let her remain subject for the period of her life. And also muzzle Artemidoros Melasios (?) whom Gaterana (?) bore, and do not let him make an indictment to anyone concerning the cloths but let him be muzzled.[74]

Artemidoros, the son of Timo, commissioned this spell against Ariston and Artemidoros Melasios, son of Gaterana. While it is tempting to associate the protagonists of this spell with individuals known from the lead tablets, the absence of identifying features, such as metronymics, makes such identifications problematic. An Artemidoros, who is not provided with a metronymic, is the commissioner of *DT* 28, a spell directed against Aphrodisianos. Ariston, the target of this tablet, is named as a victim in *DT* 22 and as a commissioner

---

74. Trans. Jordan, "Late feasts for ghosts," 136.

Practitioners and Craft at Amathous, Cyprus 197

in *DT* 35. Alternatively, Artemidoros Melasios, the second target, could also be Artemidoros, the commissioner of *DT* 28.

Jordan has suggested that this tablet can be associated with a spell known from one of the rolls discovered at Thebes, PGM IV.1390–1495, a "love spell of attraction performed with the help of heroes or gladiators or those who have died a violent death."[75] The papyrus instructs the practitioner to go to a place where violent deaths had occurred and to intone a spell over seven bite-sized piece of bread left over from a meal, leaving these morsels for the spirits of the dead. According to the spell, the practitioner should then "pick up some polluted dirt from the place where you perform the ritual and throw it inside the house of the woman whom you desire."[76] A secondary ritual is supplied, in the unlucky event that the first fails. The instructions continue:

Then upon ashes of flax offer up dung from a black cow and say this and again pick up the polluted dirt and throw it as you have learned.
The words spoken over the offering are these:

"Chthonic Hermes and chthonic Hekate and chthonic Acheron and chthonic flesh-eaters and chthonic god and chthonic Amphiaraos and chthonic attendants and chthonic spirits and chthonic sins and chthonic dreams and chthonic oaths and chthonic Ariste and chthonic Tartaros and chthonic witchery, chthonic Charon and chthonic escorts and the dead and the daimons and souls of all men come today, Moirai and Destiny; accomplish the purpose with the help of the love spell of attraction, that you may attract to me her, NN whose mother is NN, to me NN, whose mother is NN (add the usual), because I am calling

O primal Chaos, Erebos, and you
O awful water of the Styx, O streams
O Lethe, Hades' Acherousian pool,
O Hekate and Pluto and Kore,
And chthonic Hermes, Moirai, Punishments,
Both Acheron and Aiakos, gatekeeper
Of the eternal bars, now open quickly,
O thou Key-holder, guardian, Anubis.
Send up to me the phantoms of the dead . . ."[77]

---

75. Ibid., 137.
76. Trans. E. N. O'Neil in *GMP*, 64.
77. Trans. E. N. O'Neil in *GMP*, 65–66.

198   Materia Magica

The beginning of second incantation preserved in the PGM text is nearly identical to the selenite curse tablet discovered at Amathous; the two texts invoke many of the same deities in a similar order, modifying each name with the epithet *chthonic*. Often, the differences involve slight changes in spelling; either these are common variations, or the changes result in different words that sound similar. There are, however, a number of striking divergences.[78] The Cypriot text is fuller, often naming divinities that are not present in the papyrus, and even invoking the same gods multiple times. So, in the first two lines, the selenite text calls on "Chthonic Z[ethos] and chthonic Demeter and chthonic earth-born (nymphs?)," phrases missing from the papyrus. Likewise, at lines 6–7, the Cypriot text calls on "Chthonic Demeter and chthonic Plouton and chthonic and dead Persephone," invocations that are likewise absent from the PGM text.

Perhaps the most striking difference, however, is the function of the spell. The Amathous tablet, like others in the cache, was commissioned in the realm of judicial competition. Artemidoros requests that the speech of his adversaries, Ariston and Artemidoros, the son of Gaterana, be muzzled. In contrast, the PGM spell is intended to gain the affections of the beloved. Likewise, the role of the invocation differs in each iteration. The selenite text was inscribed, while the PGM instructs the practitioner to speak the words of the spell over an offering of flax ashes and dung. This is a second recourse if an initial ritual fails, and the spell concludes with a brief *historiola* about Isis and Zeus.

Although this selenite inscription demonstrates the use of a source that is distinct from the other tablets, there are sufficient similarities to ensure all of the tablets were produced by the same workshop. One can note the persistent spelling of the term δέμονες, in contrast to the expected spelling δαίμονες. The selenite tablet also employs the same unusual term, *muzzling,* that is found in the lead spells. In line 11, the tablet refers to itself as a τὸ φιμωτικόν; one can compare the use of τοῦ φιμωτι[κοῦ] at line 22 on the lead tablet cited above, *DT* 27. As well, the invocation to the chthonic deities on this tablet precedes the main focus of the spell. This pattern is similar to that found on the lead tablets, where the spell text begins with a formalized invocation in dactylic hexameter. The lead tablets also incorporate a series of invocations to chthonic deities, albeit in the second half of the written spell (ll. 35–36 in the spell quoted above). While the order of names varies slightly, the lead tablets' injunction

---

78. Jordan has provided an interlinear transcription of the two texts, clearly demonstrating both the parallels and the differences. "Late feasts for ghosts," 141.

for assistance from chthonic Hekate, chthonic Hermes, chthonic Plouton, and chthonic Eirynes certainly echoes the opening of the selenite spell. Indeed, the function of these verse or semiverse invocations—to invoke the spirits of the dead—is similar, a correspondence that was noted as early as 1891 by Albrecht Dieterich, as Jordan attests in his publication.[79] For both this tablet and the lead texts, the practitioner may have adopted a hymn or invocation that was known from another source, bending it to the service of the magical act. The relationship between this selenite inscription and its relative in the PGM corpus invites further reflection.

Jordan has suggested that the invocation employed in both this selenite tablet and the PGM spell derives from rites for tending the dead.[80] The Greek character of the spell is evident in both permutations. No Egyptian divinities are invoked in the Greek invocation in the PGM; rather, gods who are specifically relevant to the Hellenic world (and the Hellenic underworld) are common. Amphiarios was associated with a hero shrine and necromantic cult in northwest Attica, and this divinity does not appear in any other PGM text.[81] Although riddled with spelling mistakes and containing a number of problematic phrases that may be the result of copying errors and textual transmission, the inscription from Amathous is authoritative. It may be possible that the PGM version adapted the text from a Cypriot source. Numerous spells in PGM IV demonstrate the reorientation of ritual material from other sources for the Egyptian tourist industry, as many of the spells likely appealed to visitors to Egypt as well as local residents who desired the same sorts of ritual assistance.[82] Cyprus was well known in antiquity as the birthplace of Aphrodite; Egyptian priests with the knowledge that the invocation derived from Cyprus may have reformulated it for use in an erotic spell.[83]

---

79. "Late feasts for ghosts," 134–35.
80. Ibid., 138. On repetition in magical spells, see Versnel, "The poetics of the magical charm: An essay on the power of words," 130–35. The process of ritually sharing a portion with the dead as a means of appeasing or compelling cooperation is identifiable in other Greek contexts. One can note a similar action in a ritual text from Cyrene, where one shares a meal with a figurine of a ghost in order to appease the troublesome spirit. See above, ch. 2 nn. 6–7, 74.
81. On Amphiaraos and the hero shrine at Oropos, see J. J. Coulton, "The stoa at the Amphiareion, Oropos," *ABSA* 63 (1968); V. C. Petrakos, *The Amphiareion of Oropos* (Athens: Clio, 1995); A. Schachter, *Cults of Boiotia* (London: University of London, Institute of Classical Studies, 1981), 1:19–26; Ogden, *Greek and Roman necromancy,* 85–92.
82. Frankfurter, "The consequences of Hellenism in Late Antique Egypt," 183. On the PGM spells and tourism to Egypt, see above, ch. 2 n. 20.
83. A spell invoking Aphrodite's secret name appears at PGM IV.1265–74, but this spell is located within a different block from the spell related to the Amathous texts and likely does not derive

200   Materia Magica

Given the presence of divinities associated with cultic locations on the mainland, however, it seems unlikely that the spell originated on Cyprus. Rather, it is probable that both versions of the spell derive from a common Hellenic ancestor. Indeed, in both the selenite tablet and the PGM text, the chthonic invocation functions as a poetic unit that has been adapted for use within a larger rite. We can identify a similar process at work in the lead tablets, where the metrical invocation that begins the tablet may have been adopted from another source. Comparable adaptation and intercutting is at work in the importation and transformation of necromantic spells, such as those attributed to Pitys that adapt Greek rites involving skulls or other body parts for use in household rituals in Egypt.[84] At Amathous, we possess evidence for the compilation and recombination of religious elements within magical practice, suggesting that the practitioners on the site may have been involved in collecting and reworking the spells that were deployed in the shaft. This collation and redaction should not be surprising, as a similar process appears to have been at work among the temple priests in Egypt. Taken as a whole, the Amathous cache reveals a complex industry of copying spells onto tablets for a variety of purposes. Magical production at the site was a big business.

The Practitioners at Amathous

Clear letterforms, consistent spelling, even spacing, and the use of multiple templates all argue that professionals rather than the commissioners wrote the

---

from the same precursor. LiDonnici, "Compositional patterns in *PGM* IV (=*P.Bibl.Nat.Suppl.* gr. no. 574)," 172. There is Egyptian evidence from the New Kingdom period that may attest to an earlier incident of ritual exchange from Cyprus to Egypt. The London Medical Papyrus, dating from the New Kingdom, includes a spell that purports to be in the speech of *Keftiu*, a location that has been identified as either Cyprus or Crete. P.British Museum 10059 [38] 13, 3–7. Original publication W. Wreszinski, *Der Londoner medizinische Papyrus (Brit. Museum Nr. 10059) und der Papyrus Hearst* (Leipzig: Hinrichs, 1912), 151–52, 92. Translation in J. F. Borghouts, *Ancient Egyptian magical texts* (Leiden: Brill, 1978), no. 57. On the papyrus, see R. C. Steiner, "Northwest Semitic incantations in an Egyptian medical papyrus of the fourteenth century B.C.E," *JNES* 51, no. 3 (1992). On the identification of *Keftiu* cf. G. A. Wainwright, "Keftiu," *Journal of Egyptian Archaeology* 17, no. 1–2 (1931); F. G. Gordon, "The Keftiu spell," *Journal of Egyptian Archaeology* 18, no. 1–2 (1932); H. Goedicke, "The Canaanite illness," *Studien zur Altägyptischen Kultur* 11 (1984); Ritner, *The mechanics of ancient Egyptian magical practice,* 246, n. 1130; D. B. Redford, "The language of Keftiu: The evidence of the drawing board and the London Medical Papyrus (BM 10059) in the British Museum," *Revista del Instituto de Historia Antigua Oriental* 12–13 (2005–6).

84. Faraone, "Necromancy goes underground," 281.

Practitioners and Craft at Amathous, Cyprus   201

tablets. Cursory analysis of the unpublished tablets suggests that the same is true for the remainder of the archive. This differs from other large caches of tablets, such as those from Bath, which suggest that the commissioner was responsible for the inscription, perhaps with the assistance of the religious personnel. Hands among the Bath tablets vary greatly, and some tablets even include unintelligible scribbles that were likely the result of an illiterate suppliant.[85]

Analysis of the inscriptions suggests that multiple professionals may have been responsible for the creation of the tablets that make up the Amathous cache. The identification of hands through paleography can be a challenging enterprise, as an individual's style may change according to the medium on which he or she is writing, and his or her handwriting may alter over time. Bearing in mind these caveats, a number of scholars have suggested that the hands of multiple individuals are evident in the tablets. Two separate individuals appear to have been responsible for tablets *DT* 25 and *DT* 26; in both tablets, Alexandros curses Theodoros. Other tablets with diverse targets appear to have been written by the same individual, suggesting that a professional was involved in the creation of the artifacts. Mitford has suggested that tablets *DT* 22, 32, and 37 should all be associated with the same hand.[86] Jordan and Aupert's analysis of the selenite tablets suggests that multiple individuals also may have been responsible for these tablets.[87] In addition, we possess evidence that these individuals were likely using the same formulary, as the inscribed tablets attributed to different individuals appear to use the same set text, at least in part. This formulary may have included multiple spells that shared some features, such as the *kharaktêres,* as the evidence indicates the use of at least three separate models, two of which incorporated mystical symbols.

Briefly mentioned at the beginning of this chapter, Pliny's short discussion of Cypriot magic may prove a productive point of reference as we consider the character of magical practice at the site. There is little evidence in the content of the tablets that differentiates them as notably Cypriot. A number of the magical signs may bear some similarities to Eteo-Cypriot script, but symbols that are closer to *kharaktêres* are also evident. Evidence from other curse tablets

---

85. *Tab. Sulis,* 100. Compare the multiple hands that were also used at Mainz: Blänsdorf, "The *defixiones* from the Sanctuary of Isis and Mater Magna in Mainz," 163. Illiterate tablets: *Tab. Sulis,* nos. 112–16, commentary at p. 247.

86. Mitford is careful to describe clear variations in the hands of the tablets, noting, for example, that the letter forms of *DT* no. 27 are "angular and erratic." *The inscriptions of Kourion,* 258. Inexplicably, he states on p. 1 that they are the work of a single individual. David Jordan has stated that the tablets show the work of multiple hands. *CT* 133 b, 46.

87. Aupert and Jordan, "Tablettes magiques d'Amathonte," 67.

known from the island similarly fails to produce a distinctly Cypriot form of magical practice, although the smaller quantity of the other tablets makes the size and regularity of the Amathous corpus more striking. P. Aupert recently has discovered an additional tablet in a cistern, but it has been dated to the seventh century CE.[88] Excavations of the necropolis at Salamis by A. di Cesnola unearthed a number of lead tablets that were inscribed Cypriot syllabic script.[89] Cesnola gave three other tablets that lack precise provenance to Senator Fabretti of Turin. According to the original publication, the tablets were discovered in two graves that had been constructed one on top of the other. Zuretti provides a rough transcription of the three tablets, which were clearly curses; *voces magicae* appear scattered in the invocations.[90] The archive from Amathous is particularly striking, as it represents a corpus of tablets many times larger than the other known finds of curses from the island.

In XXX.2.11, Pliny asserts that *magices factio* is known from Cyprus. The word *factio* can be best understood as a class or group of practitioners.[91] While

---

88. On the context of the deposit, see B. Blandin and S. Fourrier, "Le dépôt archaïque du rempart Nord d'Amathonte. I. Introduction: le contexte," *BCH* 127, no. 1 (2003). On the tablet, see Aupert, "Hélios, Adonis et magie: les trésors d'une citerne d'Amathonte." I am grateful to Professor Aupert for sharing this material with me. In the depiction, the figure grasps an item in its right arm that is similar to a rough representation of an hourglass, with two triangles placed one on top of the other, so that the apices meet. Greek letters and other magical symbols decorate the torso of the figure. An inscription surrounds the main personage and appears to curse a man named Demeterios so that he is unable to have sex. The object grasped by the figure is similar to one of the symbols that appear on the selenite tablet, the hourglass shape, although on the selenite tablets, this sign lacks an upper horizontal bar. The prominent *Z* above the right shoulder of the figure can also be paralleled among the signs on the selenite artifacts. These magical symbols may have been local in nature, and perhaps continued to be important for ritual practice in the area. As well, the lead tablet was deposited in a cistern, an underground source of water. The association between water sources, particularly those beneath the surface, and the spirits of the underworld may have continued to resonate in Late Antique Amathous as it had in earlier centuries.

89. The size of Cesnola's find is not certain, and even the provenance could be questioned. Some of the inscriptions presented in his book have been identified as deriving from places other than those he provides. In addition to the three tablets given to Fabretti, Cesnola himself published one in 1884. A. P. d. Cesnola, *Salaminia (Cyprus). The history, treasures, & antiquities of Salamis in the island of Cyprus* (London: Whiting, 1884), 68–70, republished with a drawing in O. Masson, *Les inscriptions chypriotes syllabiques; recueil critique et commenté* (Paris: E. de Boccard, 1961), no. 311, pp. 13–14. The precise meaning of the text is unclear, largely because of the strange form of some of the signs, but Masson has suggested that it is a *defixio*. The use of the term ἄγος, pollution or guilt, in line 2, may suggest that the inscription is a prayer for justice.

90. C. O. Zuretti, "Iscrizioni Gnostiche di Cipro in caratteri non epichorici," *Rivista di filologia e d'istruzione classica* 20 (1892).

91. Pliny does not employ the word again within the *Natural History*, so it is not possible to compare this usage with other instances.

it seems less likely that the archive at Amathous represents a famous school or grouping of ritual specialists, it is productive to consider the implications of applying a term like *factio* to the practitioners at the site. The hands and the inscribed formulary texts suggest that a number of individuals were working together, consulting the same models, and depositing their creations within the same location. This picture diverges from our expectation that practitioners of magic were lone operators who closely guarded their methods.[92] Rather, the practitioners at Amathous may have been arranged into a formal or semiformal association. We can imagine three potential arrangements that are not mutually exclusive: a formal economic organization or *collegia,* intended to facilitate production; an informal educational group of a master and one or more apprentices; and a religious grouping perhaps affiliated with a temple or cult site that also performed private ritual functions.

During the Roman period, *collegia, societates,* and other business partnerships for tradesmen and performers are well known throughout the Mediterranean. In a letter to Trajan, Pliny the Younger complains of monetary requests by a guild of athletes, suggesting that guilds could encompass almost any group of professionals.[93] Documentary papyri from Roman Egypt provide evidence for the activities of voluntary associations of professionals within communities, and similar networks probably existed on Cyprus.[94] *Collegia* were often social groups as well as business partnerships, and many possessed elected

---

92. F. Graf, "The magician's initiation," *Helios* 21, no. 2 (1994): 166; on associations of practitioners, compare E. E. Evans-Pritchard, *Witchcraft, oracles, and magic among the Azande,* abridged with an introduction by Eva Gillies, ed. (Oxford: Clarendon Press, 1976), 205–20.

93. Pliny the Younger, *Epist.* 10.118.

94. On the guilds of Roman Egypt, see P. Venticinque, "Associations in Ptolemaic and Roman Egypt," in *Oxford handbook of economies in the classical world,* ed. A. Bresson, E. Lo Cascio, and F. Velde (Oxford: Oxford University Press, forthcoming); P. van Minnen, "Urban craftsmen in Roman Egypt," *Münstersche Beiträge zur antiken Handelsgeschichte* 6, no. 1 (1987); P. Frisch, *Zehn agonistische Papyri* (Opladen: Westdeutscher Verlag, 1986). In general on Roman period guilds, see F. M. Ausbüttel, *Untersuchungen zu den Vereinen im Westen des Römischen Reiches* (Kallmünz: M. Lassleben, 1982); J.-M. Flambard, "Éléments pour une approche financière de la mort dans les classes populaires," in *La mort, les morts et l'au-delà dans le monde romain: actes du colloque de Caen, 20–22 novembre 1985,* ed. F. Hinard (Caen: Université de Caen, 1987); J. S. Kloppenborg and S. G. Wilson, eds., *Voluntary associations in the Graeco-Roman world* (London: Routledge, 1996); N. Tran, *Les membres des associations romaines: le rang social des collegiati en Italie et en Gaules sous le haut-empire* (Rome: Ecole française de Rome, 2006); K. Verboven, "The associative order: Status and ethos among Roman businessmen in late republic and early empire," *Athenaeum* 95, no. 2 (2007); J. Liu, *Collegia centonariorum: The guilds of textile dealers in the Roman West* (Leiden: Brill, 2009).

204   Materia Magica

officials as well as a formalized vertical hierarchy.[95] Most groups in Egypt, for
which we have extensive evidence, consisted of between ten and twenty-five
members, although much larger associations are known from Rome and other
major cities.[96] There were numerous associations affiliated with craft production and trade, and groups associated with the temple appear to have included
religious professionals.[97] These associations operated as corporate identities,
loaning money and performing other collective functions. At Amathous, however, we possess no inscriptional evidence for the existence of a *collegium* of
ritual practitioners. Although we may be able to speculate about the existence
of a professional organization, further research is necessary to demonstrate
whether such an association could have existed.

It also may be possible that the group of practitioners on the island included
skilled masters and one or more apprentices who were learning the craft. Specialized training at the hands of another professional is a common method of
learning a craft, and there is some evidence that the technical skills required
for magical practice may have been passed on in this way. Comparison can be
made with enslaved African and African-American practitioners of conjure,
who appear to have been trained through apprenticeships.[98] In literary sources,
the education of the practitioner often is depicted as a peripatetic process, in
which the young acolyte travels to foreign lands (typically Egypt) to learn the
secrets of alien sorcerers, who are sometimes portrayed as peripatetic holy
men.[99] The best evidence for ritual apprenticeship derives from the Christian
Saint Cyprian of Antioch, whose *Confession* alludes to a period of study under

---

95. S. R. Joshel, *Work, identity, and legal status at Rome: A study of the occupational inscriptions,*
    1st ed. (Norman: University of Oklahoma Press, 1992), 113–22.
96. Venticinque, "Associations in Ptolemaic and Roman Egypt."
97. A. Monson, "The ethics and economics of Ptolemaic religious associations," *AncSoc* 36
    (2006): 228; A. Monson, "Private associations in the Ptolemaic Fayyum: The evidence of
    the Demotic accounts," in *New archaeological and papyrological researches on the Fayyum:
    Proceedings of the international meeting of Egyptology and papyrology, Lecce 8th–10th June
    2005,* ed. M. Capasso and P. Davoli, *Papyrologica Lupiensia 14/2005* (Galatina [Lecce]: Con-
    gedo, 2007), 184–85.
98. Wilkie, "Secret and sacred: contextualizing the artifacts of African-American magic and reli-
    gion," 85.
99. In Lucian's *Philopseudes,* the narrator, Eucrates, travels to Egypt and encounters a learned
    man named Pancrates. J. Z. Smith has suggested that these itinerant religious experts embody
    the movement away from the Egyptian temple as the center of ritual knowledge, a process that
    can be charted as early as the second century CE. *Map is not territory: Studies in the history
    of religions* (Leiden: Brill, 1978), 187; cf. P. Brown, *The world of Late Antiquity, AD 150–
    750* (New York: W. W. Norton, 1971), 102–4. On the Greek and Egyptian antecedents for the
    sorcerer's apprentice, see D. Ogden, *In search of the sorcerer's apprentice: The traditional
    tales of Lucian's "Lover of lies"* (Swansea: Classical Press of Wales, 2007), 232–48.

Practitioners and Craft at Amathous, Cyprus 205

a variety of masters.[100] Cyprian claims that he had been initiated into a variety of mysteries while a young man, learning, among other things, medicine, to converse with the dead, and how to transpose words and numbers.[101] He traveled to Egypt, Antioch, and among the Chaldaeans to train with local ritual experts.[102] A similar story is told in the autobiographical introduction to a volume on herbs, attributed to Thessalus of Tralles. Thessalus, who traveled to Egypt, eventually reached Thebes – the "real" Egypt – where he was instructed by the priests who occupied the temples.[103] This story follows in broad outline the trajectory of Egyptian priestly initiation; Thessalus appropriates Egyptian religious training to take on the guise of the magician.[104] It is notable that the acquisition of magical training often involves acquiring religious knowledge from members of local priesthoods.

The published corpus does not include any tablets that suggest the presence of an unskilled technician, such as poor penmanship, nor are there any other indications that the practitioner responsible for the creation of the tablet was not fully trained.[105] Even so, this short digression about magical training

---

100. A. D. Nock, "Hagiographica," *Journal of Theological Studies* 28, no. 112 (1927); M. P. Nilsson, "Greek mysteries in the Confession of St. Cyprian," *HThR* 40, no. 3 (1947); see most recently the discussion at R. Bailey, "The *Confession* of Cyprian of Antioch: Introduction, text and translation" (Master of Arts, McGill University, 2009), 6–8.

101. ps-Cyprian, *Conf.* 2.

102. At Antioch, he claims, he was "performing wonders like one of the ancients, and I was giving out evidence of my sorcery (γοητείας) and was known as a philosopher-magician (μάγος φιλόσοφος), since I possessed a great comprehension of the unseen world" (ps-Cyprian, *Conf.* 5.6).

103. Thessalos of Tralles, proem. 3-6 = H.-V. Friedrich, ed., *Thessalos von Tralles* (Meisenheim am Glan: Hain, 1968), 45–48. See the discussion in Smith, *Map is not territory: Studies in the history of religions,* 172–89; Fowden, *The Egyptian Hermes: A historical approach to the late pagan mind,* 162–68. Ian Moyer notes that the priests were shocked because of Thessalus' rashness in his request for secret knowledge. "Thessalos of Tralles and cultural exchange," in *Prayer, magic, and the stars in the ancient and Late Antique world,* ed. S. B. Noegel, J. T. Walker, and B. M. Wheeler (University Park: Pennsylvania State University Press, 2003), 46–51.

104. I. Moyer, "The initiation of the magician: Transition and power in Graeco-Roman ritual," in *Initiation in ancient Greek rituals and narratives: New critical perspectives,* ed. D. B. Dodd and C. A. Faraone (London: Routledge, 2003), 222–25. On initiation as part of the training of the magician, see Graf, "The magician's initiation," 161; for other educated magicians in antiquity, including Pythagoras, Plato, and Bolus of Mendes, see Diog. Laertius 8.3; Pliny *HN* XXX.9; *de virtutibus herbarum* 1–28 Fredrich; Columella, *Rust.* 7.5.17; 11.3.53. On the learned magician, see M. W. Dickie, "The learned magician and the collection and transmission of magical lore," in *The world of ancient magic,* ed. D. R. Jordan, H. Montgomery, and E. Thomassen (Bergen: Norwegian Institute at Athens, 1999).

105. On the handwriting of students and "school hands" see Cribiore, *Writing, teachers, and students in Graeco-Roman Egypt,* 102–12.

206   Materia Magica

points to an important idea: magical activity often occurs at foreign cult places, aided by local religious professionals. There is a sense from our sources that the magical production is housed within a temple. Thessalos studied alongside local priests who were also in training, suggesting that the technical skills that he acquired would have been well known among religious personnel. At Amathous, the tablets may have been produced by a group of ritual specialists who were affiliated with a temple or civic cult. As we have noted, the beginning of many of the tablets are marked by ritual invocations in dactylic hexameter that were apparently appropriated from religious liturgy. Likewise, the text on the selenite tablet that is paralleled in the magical papyri appears to have been adopted from a separate ritual that may have been performed on the Greek mainland. Analysis of other features of the tablets can expand our understanding of how and why these artifacts may have been created.

It is worth considering the important role that display appears to have played in the deposition of the selenite tablets, and a useful comparative example can be found at Cnidus, located nearby on the mainland of Asia Minor. C. T. Newton's excavations at the temple of Demeter and Kore uncovered approximately fourteen lead sheets that dedicated targets to the titular deities of the shrine.[106] The inscriptions all appear to use similar formulae and were probably written by the priests of the temple.[107] One of the tablets reads:

> I hand over to Demeter and Kore the person who has accused me of preparing poisons / spells against my husband. Having been struck by a fever, let him go up to Demeter with all of his family, and confess (his guilt). And let him not find Demeter, Kore or the gods with Demeter (to be) merciful. As for me, let it be permissible and acceptable for me to be under the same roof or involved with him in any way. And I hand over also the person who has written (charges) against me or commanded others to do so. And let him not benefit from the mercy of Demeter, Kore, or the gods with Demeter, but instead suffer afflictions with all of his family.[108]

H. S. Versnel has identified these tablets as belonging to the category of prayers for justice, inscriptions on lead or other material intended to right a wrong that has been suffered by the commissioner. The tablets, which name the plaintiff,

---

106. For bibliography, see ch. 2 n. 35.
107. Versnel, "Beyond cursing," 72.
108. Newton no. 85 = *DT* no. 4, = *CT* no. 89.3; translation *CT* no. 89, p. 190.

often claim theft, slander, or another offense, such as the reluctance to return an object that has been borrowed. The victim must redress the perceived wrong or be forced to come to temple and make public confession. The goddess, who inflicts sickness, pain, or torture on the target of the tablet, compels the responsible party to confess to their crimes.[109] Special attention is paid to making certain that the goddess does not strike the commissioner of the spell, if he or she should be in the same room as the unknown target when the goddess acts.[110]

Newton's account of the discovery of the tablets is brief, but informative:

> Close to these remains of statues (statue bases and portions of a statue of a Demeter) I found in several places portions of thin sheets of lead, broken and doubled up. On being unrolled, these sheets proved to be the tablets inscribed with imprecations, *Dirae,* in the name of Demeter, Persephone and the other infernal deities to which the *temenos* was dedicated.[111]

Although the tablets are now in a state of poor preservation, images included with Newton's original publication indicate the presence of suspension holes on a number of the tablets, and Newton suggests that the tablets likely were meant to be seen.[112] On *DT* 8, a hole is visible at the bottom of the tablet, which may have been used to attach it to another object. The tablets were distributed within a small area, and the excavators found them around the statue bases from which they had fallen. Moreover, Newton's description suggests that some tablets were folded over. Although the cursed individual would not have been able to read the inscription, this may not have been necessary. Local priests could have taken an active role in facilitating the promulgation of the complaint.[113] Display was a vital component of the tablets' efficacy, in which the intended audience may have been the gods. Human beings who were aware of the existence of the tablets may have acted on the knowledge of what the tablet said, even if the inscription could not be read.

The Cnidian tablets, like those discovered at Amathous, made use of a formulary. Moreover, the Cnidian tablets were written by professionals and were

---

109. Versnel, "Beyond cursing," 72–73; Versnel, "ΠΕΠΡΗΜΕΝΟΣ. The Cnidian curse tablets and ordeal by fire," 146; Versnel, "Writing mortals and reading gods," 52–53.
110. Versnel, "Beyond cursing," 73; Versnel, "ΠΕΠΡΗΜΕΝΟΣ. The Cnidian curse tablets and ordeal by fire," 147.
111. Newton, *A History of discoveries at Halicarnassus, Cnidus, and Branchidae,* 382.
112. Ibid., 724, but Audollent argues that the holes are not visible. *DT* cxvi.
113. Versnel, "Writing mortals and reading gods," 57, 68–72.

not inscribed by the petitioners. The discovery of the tablets in the temple precinct suggests that religious personnel were responsible for their creation. In Asia Minor, priests often played an important role in facilitating divine justice. Confession inscriptions found in Lydia and Phrygia during the first three centuries CE sometimes refer to setting up scepters, symbols of divine justice that were erected in conjunction with a ritual imprecation against an unknown culprit.[114] On a small number of the confession inscriptions, priests are shown in association with long rods, which have been interpreted as scepters.[115] The erection of the scepter presumably transferred the disagreement into the realm of the divine in order to invoke the justice of a god or gods. An inscription from Kula in Asia Minor records the fate of a woman named Tatias, who unjustly set up a scepter and deposited curses in order to proclaim her innocence. The text reads "because Ioukoundos fell into a condition of insanity and it was noised about by all that he had been put under a spell by his mother-in-law Tatias, she set up a scepter and placed curses in the temple in order to defend herself against what was being said about her."[116] As Tatias and her son Sokrates both died soon after making this complaint, her guilt was presumed by all, and her relatives were forced to remove the scepter and undo the curses that she had made. The inscription indicates that both ceremonies—the initial establishment of the curses, as well as the later rescission—were public performances, brokered by the priests.[117] In another confession inscription, the text records payment for removing the imprecation:

> In order that the oaths be annulled by the name of Mes Axiottenos (or: the oaths taken through invocation of the name of Mes Axiottenos), the person who annuls oaths shall spend the amount of 175 denarii . . . the person who annuls a curse shall pay to the sanctuary 175 denarii and then the sceptre is annulled justly.[118]

---

114. Chaniotis, "Under the watchful eyes of the gods," 13; J. H. M. Strubbe, "Cursed be he that moves my bones," in *Magika hiera,* ed. C. A. Faraone and D. Obbink (New York: Oxford University Press, 1991), 44–45; L. Robert, "Documents d'Asie Mineure XXIII-XXVIII," *BCH* 107, no. 1 (1983): 518–20.

115. Robert, "Documents d'Asie Mineure XXIII-XXVIII," 520–22; Strubbe, "Cursed be he that moves my bones," 45.

116. TAM 381; Translation *CT* no.137 p. 247. For the importance of public shame and guilt, see Versnel, "Writing mortals and reading gods," 69–72.

117. Chaniotis, "Under the watchful eyes of the gods," 11–13.

118. *BIWK* 58, translation and discussion at Chaniotis, "Under the watchful eyes of the gods," 34–35.

It is probable that the priests who operated within the temples in Asia Minor received fees and payment for setting up curses as well as their negation. The role played by priests in private imprecations calls to mind the activities of the Egyptian priests, who provided ritual expertise to both foreign tourists and local residents.

In Asia Minor, we have clear evidence that priests were engaged in creating and implementing ritual curses, often against unknown targets, for a fee. At Cnidus specifically, imprecations were written on lead tablets and displayed publicly, and the physical object served as an indicator that a wrong had been done. At least some of the selenite tablets at Amathous were mounted and displayed, even if they could neither be seen nor read. As well, the practitioners at Amathous probably were affiliated in some way, as they shared a text that was used for inscribing the curses. While it seems likely that ritual personnel were responsible for the Amathous tablets, it is difficult if not impossible to associate them with a temple. Uncertainty surrounding the precise findspot of the tablets does not allow us to situate them in a specific religious space. Kore is among the deities invoked in the Amathous tablets, but most do not mention Demeter by name, although she is invoked on the selenite tablet related to the PGM spell. The most prominent divinity at Amathous appears to have been Aphrodite, who is not mentioned in the tablets; syncretism may have led these female divinities to be associated with one another, but there is little evidence for this. Recent excavations have uncovered a sanctuary to Bes in the agora, and Egyptian divine names are included among the *voces magicae,* but there are not extensive allusions to Egyptian gods or cult practices.[119] Indeed, there is no single divinity or group of divinities that stands out among the Amathous examples, and the primary audience for the spell appears to be the dead. The social context of the tablets, inferred from the inscriptions, will provide further insight into the nature of ritual practice at the site.

The Social Context of the Tablets

Despite their length, the inscriptions on the tablets seldom provide information about the social circumstances that led the commissioners to employ the services of a ritual specialist. All of the tablets appear to have been composed

---

119. See above, n. 15.

210   Materia Magica

in the context of judicial disputes, as they frequently ask that the invoked deities restrain the speech of another individual. The inscriptions on the tablets,
which relate that the commissioner has been wronged, immediately call to
mind prayers for justice, and, as will be suggested below, the Amathous tablets
share some features with this class of ritual object.

Only two of the published tablets explicitly comment upon the cause of the
dispute. In *DT* 29, Eutyches curses Sozomenos in a dispute over θρέμματα,
slaves or the offspring of domesticated animals. *NGD* 115, the selenite tablet that incorporates the invocation to the chthonic deities, was written for a
conflict involving clothing, perhaps the theft of some article. For a few of the
other tablets, the proximate cause may be surmised with reference to the protagonists. In *DT* 31, Serapias invokes a curse against Marion, her husband; the
underlying legal action was likely motivated by a domestic dispute, perhaps
the failure to return a dowry or a separate incident related to their marriage or
divorce. The disputes that we can identify seem quite mundane, although these
cases surely must have been important for the individuals involved in defense
and prosecution. It appears that local individuals at Amathous often employed
cursing as a matter of course within judicial disputes; the size and variety of
the corpus indicates a predilection for solving conflicts in court before a magistrate, but, at the same time, having the capacity and willingness to subvert the
legal system through magical means.

Although the cause of the dispute is not listed in the case, the identity of the
commissioner and targets of *DT* 25 suggests curses could be directed against
provincial authorities. In the tablet, a man named Alexandros, also known as
Makedonios, curses Timon and Theodoros, who is named as the governor of
Cyprus: Θεοδώρῳ τῷ ἡγε[μόνι (l. 13). Theodoros is identified as the governor
of the island only on the basis of this text, and while the title *hegemon* could
relate to the Roman military, no legion is known from Amathous.[120] Like the
others in the cache, the tablet probably was commissioned in the context of
a judicial case, but here, one of the litigants is the highest authority of the
island. The tablet illustrates a conflict between Alexandros and the ruling elite
on some level, and the commissioner's response, to use magic to affect the
outcome of the case, could reflect a larger sense of dissatisfaction with a policy
or action of the provincial administration.

---

120. On the role of the procurator of the island, see Mitford, "Roman Cyprus," 1343. Theodoros
is mentioned in two other places in the text (lines 8 and 19), but in each case his position as
governor has been reconstructed within lacunae. Mitford, *The inscriptions of Kourion,* 255
and n. 4.

Practitioners and Craft at Amathous, Cyprus 211

Other tablets in the cache reveal an interlocking web of individuals employing magic against provincial authorities. Alexandros is also the commissioner of another tablet, *DT* 26, which similarly curses Theodoros. Different individuals inscribed the two tablets, but it seems likely that the same protagonists were involved. Alexandros may have felt the need to curse the governor in two separate *defixiones,* both regarding the same case, in order to double the efficacy of the spell. It seems equally likely, however, that Alexandros was in trouble with the law more than once, as Timon is not named as a victim in the second tablet. An "Alexandros" appears as the commissioner of another tablet, *DT* 27. The tablet names an assortment of individuals as targets, including Alexander Luscinus, Timon, Philodemos, Eumenes, Makarios, Demokrates, Marcus, and Metodoros Asbolios.[121] Here, too, the commissioner Alexandros identifies himself as having a second name, although this has been lost in the lacuna. Timon, an individual associated with the governor in *DT* 25, may have also been a public functionary, and the same person may be intended as a victim of this text. The final target named within the list, Metrodorus, is identified as a τραπεζίτης, either a money changer or a person in charge of a civic bank.[122] The presence of both Timon and Metrodorus may indicate that this tablet, like *DT* 25, was directed against provincial or local authorities.

In chapter 1, we briefly considered Roman prohibitions of magic and noted the frequent passage of laws banning its practice, or even the possession of magical books; offenders typically were punished with death. Magic directed at the state, particularly aggressive magic aimed at harming members of the provincial administration, clearly would have been viewed as an illegal activity, endangering both parties, the practitioners and those who employed them.[123] These proscriptions may suggest that the use of magical acts constituted resistance against Rome in the minds of the authorities. Those engaged in

---

121. The name *Makedonis* has been written beneath the name *Demokrates,* and above and to the right of the final name in the sequence, *Metrodotos.* This position might imply that Makedonis is another target, added after the scribe had moved on to the rest of the formula. Μακεδόνιον has also been reconstructed in line 32, again listed among the victims.

122. Beyond this reference, there is no evidence of a state bank associated with Cyprus. Cicero suggests that temple treasuries on Cyprus may have served a similar function to state banks. Cic. *Att.* V. 21, 12; VI. I, 7. R. Bogaert, *Banques et banquiers dans les cités grecques* (Leiden: A. W. Sijthoff, 1968), 217 and n. 449.

123. *Codex Justinian* v. 21, cf. Pharr, "The interdiction of magic in Roman law," 288. The future emperor Septimius Severus was prosecuted for the crime of consulting oracles concerning the life of the emperor. G. M. Parássoglou, "Circular from a prefect: Sileat omnibus perpetuo divinandi curiositas," in *Collectanea papyrologica: Texts published in honor of H. C. Youtie,* ed. A. E. Hanson, *Papyrologische Texte und Abhandlungen* (Bonn: Habelt, 1976), 263.

magic as practitioners and commissioners might have viewed their own activities as acts of transgression; whether these would have constituted rebellion in the minds of local residents is an open question. The limited episodes of civil unrest on Cyprus, the revolt of the Jews in the early second century, and the Late Antique uprising associated with the death of Constantine are brief deviations from the peaceful working of the colony. Magic at the site did not lead to revolt, but instead offered a means by which local individuals could act out against provincial authorities.

The tablets created a role reversal for Alexandros and many of the other commissioners, placing them in a position of power while the victim was rendered speechless, powerless, and ineffective.[124] Magic offered the residents of Amathous a perspective in which the supernatural could alter the course of events, one that stood in direct opposition to the regulated and unassailable Roman judicial system. Within an imperial regime such as that of Rome, resistance on the community level may be commonplace, appearing frequently within the typical, everyday interaction of society. Resistant acts, however, are often disguised beneath the veneer of normal public interaction.[125] Although not expressed through outright rebellion or a violent rejection of the governing elite, secretive discussions and criticism, as well as theft, slow production, and the failure to adequately pay taxes, can all be understood as indicative of dissatisfaction with those in power or with the divide between powerful provincial magistrates and local individuals.[126] Practitioners provided a means by which the unempowered within the community could improve their own social situation, case by case, and thwart the imperial system. The presence of a large number of tablets implies a community of individuals who were familiar with magic and used it in order to be victorious in court through the defeat of their enemies, to change their social position through self-empowerment, and perhaps, if the spell was effective, to better their lives. These same desires may have inspired the individuals responsible for the tablets deposited at Empúries, whose story will be told in the next chapter.

---

124. J. C. Scott, *Domination and the arts of resistance: Hidden transcripts* (New Haven: Yale University Press, 1990), 41. On the social effect of prayers for justice and cursing, see Versnel, "Writing mortals and reading gods," esp. 71–74; Chaniotis, "Under the watchful eyes of the gods," 15–21.

125. Scott, *Domination and the arts of resistance: Hidden transcripts,* 4; D. Miller, "The limits of dominance," in *Domination and resistance,* ed. D. Miller, M. Rowlands, and C. Tilley, One World Archaeology (London: Unwin Hyman, 1989), 75.

126. M. Given, *The archaeology of the colonized* (New York: Routledge, 2004), 116–31.

While certain tablets suggest that illicit activity may have been occurring at the site, other elements of the inscribed texts could imply the opposite, that these objects were products of acceptable ritual behavior as prayers for justice, a category often viewed as distinct from curses. In general, the reasons cited by the tablets suggest that the commissioner seeks redress from wrongs, a hallmark of this type of ritual activity.[127] The commissioner, who typically names himself or herself, may request that the god "muzzle the injustice" of the victim (φιμώσουσιν τὸν ἀντίδικον). The deities addressed in the texts include respectable deities, such as the Hades, Demeter and Persephone, as well as the other gods addressed by name and the epithet *chthonic*.

The list of deities, however, also includes gods and spirits commonly associated with magical practices, such as Sisokhor and Eumazo. Moreover, the dead often are invoked as the force responsible for carrying out the imprecation. Likewise, in the selenite texts, the inscriptions invoke Hermes, Pluto, and mute and silent spirits, a coded reference to the dead, alongside magical divinities. The brief tablet associated with the PGM differs from the others in the absence of a direct address to the deceased, although the text does call on the mysterious eaters of raw flesh, ὠμοφάγοι, presumably a corruption of ὠμοθα[ν]ὸν, or dying too soon.[128] The tablets make use of *voces magicae* and mystical symbols to accomplish their goals and appear to have been composed in the context of a legal dispute in anticipation of the trial.[129] The injunction that the deity should muzzle the victim is intended to prevent a future action from occurring through the medium of binding. Moreover, the victim of the spell is always named in the text (except in the anomalous tablet that employs the cipher), in contrast to many of the prayers for justice, where the perpetrator was unknown. These areas of overlap situate the Amathous texts squarely within what Versnel refers to as the "Border Area," tablets that employ elements of both prayers for justice and curses.

The treatment of the lead and selenite tablets also points us to the border area between curses and prayers for justice, as we can reconstruct two distinct forms of deposition in the shaft. Some of the selenite tablets were displayed, much in the manner of prayers for justice, as attested by suspension holes on one selenite object as well as the report provided by Captain Handcock. Many of the lead tablets preserve indications that they were pierced with some mate-

---

127. On the characteristics of prayers for justice, see the discussion in chapter 2.

128. On ὠμοφάγοι, Jordan, "Late feasts for ghosts," 141, note c.

129. Versnel, "Prayers for justice, east and west," 361–62.

rial that has not survived. A number of the unedited fragments possess small holes that are likely the remnants of this piercing; holes and associated damage are visible on some of the published tablets, most notably *DT* 24, 29, and 30. This is a common treatment for curse tablets, which typically were pierced by a nail in order to physically bind down the victim of the spell. Although Handcock's report does not specify this, it may be possible that the lead tablets, too, were mounted; the nails that pierced the tablets could have affixed them to the walls of the shaft. Given the depth of the well, however, these objects would not have been visible to most individuals, and it seems likely that only a small number of practitioners would have seen the tablets when they descended the shaft to add another one. The audience for the tablets, therefore, probably was not residents of Amathous or suppliants to a divinity, but rather divine forces and the dead. As was the case at Cnidus, where the tablets were folded and thus unreadable, it may not have been necessary for it to be read by the victim. The practitioner, or even the more informal channel of gossip, may have made the contents known.

But why display the tablets in the first place? Display would not have served a social function, as we can detect with some of the prayers for justice, particularly those at nearby Cnidus.[130] We may perhaps understand this treatment as an adoption of a mechanism that was common to both prayers for justice and other religious activities, such as the display of votive objects with the intent of influencing the divine. The structures of ritual activity that were intended to communicate with supernatural forces may have been transmitted from one context, such as a temple, to another, in this case, a repository for aggressive curses. The specialists at Amathous may have chosen to adapt and innovate within the larger framework of acceptable interaction with divine beings, posting curses and requests for aid within a space that was typically reserved for the vindictive dead. At some point, the labor-intensive work of descending the well and erecting the tablets may have been deemed unnecessary or ineffective. The lead tablets were not mounted in the same way, as they were rolled, and would have been visible only to supernatural forces.

Religious personnel were not limited to the production of prayers for justice, and other sanctuary sites in the Mediterranean provide evidence for rituals related to erotic magic or preventing an adversary from doing something. At the temple of Demeter and Kore in Acrocorinth, a corpus of eighteen tablets,

---

130. Versnel, "Writing mortals and reading gods," 57–59.

Practitioners and Craft at Amathous, Cyprus 215

as yet unpublished, was discovered, eleven of which were found beneath the floor level of a Roman structure on the site. Many of the tablets were rolled up and pierced with nails and were inscribed with a variety of purposes.[131] In the longest tablet, the (unnamed) commissioner deposits another woman, Karpime Babia, with the Fates who exact justice (*Moirai Praxidikai*), Hermes, Earth and the children of Earth, so that these divine forces might exact punishment for the insolence of Karpime. Other tablets among the archive, however, are concerned with erotic compulsion or judicial restraint, matters more appropriate for traditional curses.[132] Once the tablets have been published, we will be able to better investigate how these petitions were characterized and who was responsible for inscribing the tablets. The recently discovered lead tablets from Mainz similarly mix some features of both the traditional curse tablet, such as reversed writing and persuasive metaphors, and the prayers for justice.[133] Each tablet appears to have been inscribed by the commissioner, who often developed the text on the spot, perhaps with the assistance of the temple personnel.[134] Priests or other functionaries subsequently placed these tablets in a sacrificial fire, where many were melted beyond recognition; the tablets that we possess escaped this fate because they were protected by ash deposits at the bottom of the altar.[135] In the majority of the texts, the commissioner believes that he or she is the victim of injustice and asks that the divinity punish the perpetrator. So, in one of the tablets from Mainz, the suppliant requests that Magna Mater avenge the theft of goods from her husband, Florus,

---

131. Versnel, "Prayers for justice, east and west," 313–15; N. Bookidis and R. S. Stroud, *Demeter and Persephone in ancient Corinth* (Princeton, NJ: American School of Classical Studies at Athens, 1987), 30–31, with the translation of one text, also reprinted in *CT* p. 32 n. 92.

132. Erotic magic is named as the subject of one of the other texts in Bookidis and Stroud, *Demeter and Persephone in ancient Corinth,* 31. Versnel states that no. 5 in Stroud's forthcoming publication is a binding curse that is related to judicial proceedings. "Prayers for justice, east and west," 314.

133. Versnel, "Prayers for justice, east and west," 341–42. The Mainz tablets have been published in a number of articles: J. Blänsdorf, "The curse tablets from the Sanctuary of Isis and Mater Magna in Mainz," *MHNH* 5 (2005); J. Blänsdorf, "Die *defixionum tabellae* des Mainzer Isis- und Mater-Magna-Heiligtums," in *Instrumenta inscripta latina II: Akten des 2. Internationalen Kolloquiums, Klagenfurt, 5.-8. Mai 2005,* ed. M. Hainzmann and R. Wedenig (Klagenfurt: Geschichtsverein für Kärnten, 2008); J. Blänsdorf, "The *defixiones* from the Sanctuary of Isis and Mater Magna in Mainz," in *Magical practice in the Latin West: Papers from the international conference held at the University of Zaragoza, 30 Sept.–1 Oct. 2005,* ed. R. L. Gordon and F. Marco Simón (Leiden: Brill, 2010).

134. Blänsdorf, "The *defixiones* from the Sanctuary of Isis and Mater Magna in Mainz," 163–64.

135. Ibid., 157.

by punishing the man who defrauded her, Ulattius Severus.[136] Many of the texts are related to common forms of binding magic. Another tablet binds the lover of Narcissus, asking that she be driven out of her mind, a technique often employed in erotic spells.[137]

In the contexts such as those at Corinth and Mainz, we can detect both the prayers for justice and aggressive curses operating within the same ritual framework, one that encompasses both religious and magical means of approaching the divine. Both kinds of tablets, *defixiones* and prayers for justice, employ the same material form, and deposition in a significant place allows the tablets—and therefore, the commissioner—to contact and either entreat or compel a supernatural force. An identical pattern is at work at Amathous, where context and contextual analysis have allowed us to piece together the local form of ritual enactment. The tablets demonstrate that the commissioner believed that he or she had been wronged, as the texts make claims of injustice, but they have not been deposited in a temple.[138] Rather, professional practitioners, using formulary texts that incorporated a variety of magical words and symbols, created the tablets and, over a period of time, deposited them within a single, powerful location. These tablets, as they describe themselves, are "muzzlers," intended as preemptive strikes against judiciary opponents. Displaying the selenite tablets, which are (presumably) earlier than the folded and pierced lead sheets that overlay them, may reflect these claims to injustice. This may have drawn on traditions of display and presentation to the gods by invoking spirits related to traditional religion (Hades, Kore) and those more commonly affiliated with magical practice. This adoption of the trappings of religion is not out of line with magical practice, for, as we suggested in the introduction, magic often draws on elements of civic cult, such as sacrifice or prayer, in its performance.

Archaeological context allows us to identify an archive of curse tablets that derive from a single location. In turn, the inscriptions permit us to reconstruct

---

136. Blänsdorf, "The *defixiones* from the Sanctuary of Isis and Mater Magna in Mainz," no. 7. In other texts, we witness concerns about theft (nos. 9 and 17), the return of goods (no. 12), or fraud (no. 11).

137. Blänsdorf, "The *defixiones* from the Sanctuary of Isis and Mater Magna in Mainz," 151–52, tablet no. 5.

138. Similar claims of injustice may also be incorporated into the erotic curse tablets, which I would argue should not be classed among prayers for justice. Although a petitioner may feel wronged or jilted by a lover, and express that in the tablet, these artifacts were intended to compel and bind the recalcitrant lover until he or she does the bidding of the practitioner.

Practitioners and Craft at Amathous, Cyprus 217

a collective group of practitioners who were at work on the site, and to situate these individuals within their social environment. A large cache, as we have at Amathous, attests to the role of ritual practice in a single location over a specific period of time (even if we cannot be precisely sure about the beginning and end dates). With such a rich source of data, however, we are confronted with intransigent difficulties to establishing a coherent interpretation. The lack of publication does not allow us to sort through all of the documents and establish links and reconstruct relationships between the tablets. More important, however, illicit excavation and problematic records can easily obscure meaningful interpretations of the data. Lacking precise details of the circumstances of the find at Amathous, it is impossible to determine the exact location of the shaft in relation to other structures, such as a temple, or to fully comprehend the placement of the bones, with their telltale earrings, respective to the tablets.

The evidence that we have at our disposal indicates that all of the tablets were deposited in the same location, and physical analysis suggests that some of the tablets in the archive were displayed. This space, whether originally a well or grave shaft, was appropriated for use by the local practitioners, who gave it a new meaning as a ritual location. The tablets employ language that would have been recognized as magical—obscure names of divinities and demons and invocations to the dead are mixed with *kharaktêres* and other magical signs. Layered within this, however, are features that might be considered religious—metrical hymns and invocations to chthonic gods that likely were compiled and then deployed for use in binding spells. These hymns are foreign elements, and like their Egyptian counterparts, the practitioners at Amathous were skilled at interweaving multiple traditions to draw power from the juxtaposition of the weird, the foreign, and the mundane. The selenite tablet that replicates a text known from PGM IV results from the same processes that gave rise to the spells used on the lead tablets: the appropriation of a religious invocation for use in a binding curse. All of these epigraphic features attest to manufacture by a collective of individuals who were steeped within the magical and religious traditions of the late second or third century Mediterranean. Precise identification of the practitioners may be impossible. Comparative evidence from other sites, including those at Cnidus, Corinth, and Mainz, suggests that individuals associated with a shrine served the needs of the local population by deploying their extensive knowledge of ritual procedures in the manufacture and deposition of binding spells. This evidence urges us to rethink the performance of magic and the role played by priests and religious personnel, acting either as independent agents outside of the structure of the sanctuary or within their roles as temple functionaries.

A radically different milieu of production and consumption is found on the other side of the Mediterranean. Although excavated with greater attention to stratigraphy and context, the material from Empúries poses its own problems of interpretation. As we will see, archaeological evidence will tell one story about deposition, but that tale will diverge sharply from our expectations about the intersection of magic, family, and the treatment of the dead.

Chapter 5

Three Curses from Empúries and Their Social Implications

As in the cities and villages that have occupied our interest so far, there is substantial evidence for magical activities at the site of Empúries, situated on the eastern coast of Hispania Citerior.[1] Nine curse tablets have been discovered on the site, ranging from the fourth or third century BCE to the Roman period.[2] Of these tablets, the most striking examples—both archaeologically and

---

1. On this history of the excavations at the site, see R. Mar and J. Ruiz de Arbulo, *Ampurias Romana: Historia, Arquitectura y Arqueología* (Sabadell: Editorial AUSA, 1993), 49–102. The western portions of the Roman empire have received less attention than their eastern counterparts. A recent conference and publication is a step in addressing the discrepancy between studies of magic in the East and West: R. L. Gordon and F. Marco Simón, "Introduction," in *Magical practice in the Latin West: Papers from the international conference held at the University of Zaragoza, 30 Sept.–1 Oct. 2005*, ed. R. L. Gordon and F. Marco Simón (Leiden: Brill, 2010).

2. *SGD* nos. 133 and 135, discovered in the soil above a fourth/third century BCE necropolis. Almagro Basch, "Plomos," 287–90; republished in Almagro Basch, *Inscripciones,* nos. 19 and 20; Robert and Robert, "Bulletin Épigraphique," *Revue d'Études Grecques* 68 (1955); J. B. Curbera, "The Greek curse tablets of Emporion," *ZPE* 117 (1997).

    SGD no. 134, found in Hellenistic/Roman levels beneath a Paleochristian basilica. J. Robert and L. Robert suggest that it is a private letter. Almagro Basch, *Inscripciones* no. 21; J. Robert and L. Robert, "Bulletin Épigraphique."

    LF 2.1.1/1: Latin tablet, washed ashore. J. Mallon, *Paléographie romaine* (Madrid: Consejo Superior de Investigaciones Científicas, 1952), 68–69; Almagro Basch, "Plomos," 123; Almagro Basch, *Inscripciones,* no. 113; Solin, "Eine Neue Fluchtafel aus Ostia," no. 25; S. Mariner, "Procedimientos indirectos de datación epigráfica," in *Miscelánea arqueológica: XXV aniversario de los Cursos Internacionales de Prehistoria y Arqueología en Ampurias (1947–1971),* ed. E. Ripoll Perelló and M. Llongueras Campañà (Barcelona: Diputación Provincial de Barcelona, Instituto de Prehistoria y Arqueología, 1974), 10–12; *IRC* no. 175; J. B. Curbera, "A curse tablet from Emporiae (IRC III 175)," *ZPE* 110 (1996).

    LF 2.1.1/6: Fill of Roman House 2. Almagro Basch, *Inscripciones* no. 118; Solin, "Eine Neue Fluchtafel aus Ostia," no. 30; *IRC* no. 177.

220   Materia Magica

epigraphically—derive from a monumentalized tomb excavated in the Ballesta cemetery at Empúries, which yielded three separate but related curses. A small peribolos wall in the northern area of the cemetery zone enclosed eight cremation burials, numbered 16–23 (plate 23).

In this enclosure, cremations 21, 22, and 23 each consisted of a small coarseware pitcher; a single curse tablet had been deposited in each of the makeshift urns.[3] Each of the tablets is directed against judicial opponents that include members of the provincial administration. One of the three, tablet 2, from cremation 22 (plate 24b), reads

(Side A) Maturus, Augustan Procurator; the advocate; the legates; the legates of the Indicetani; the Indicetani;

(Side B) the Olossitani; Titus Aurelius Fulvus, Augustan Legate; Rufus, Augustan Legate

The text inscribed on the tablet indicates that it was created in the context of a judicial dispute between the commissioner, who is not named, and a variety of provincial or local authorities. There has been extensive analysis of the historical figures named in the texts, with recent treatments dating the deposi-

---

LF 2.1.1/5: Almagro Basch, *Inscripciones* no.117; Solin, "Eine Neue Fluchtafel aus Ostia," no. 29; *IRC* no. 176.

Excavations in 2002 revealed an additional tablet in the bath complex in the Roman city, but this has not yet been published.

3.   Publication history: M. Almagro Basch, "Plomos con inscripción del Museo de Ampurias," *Memorias de los Museos Arqueológicos Provinciales* 8 (1947); M. Almagro Basch, *Las necrópolis de Ampurias 2: Necrópolis romanas y necrópolis indígenas* (Barcelona: Casa Provincial de Caridad, Imprenta Escuela, 1955); M. Almagro Basch, *Las Inscripciones Ampuritanas Griegas, Ibéricas y Latinas,* vol. II (Barcelona: el Departamento de Barcelona del Instituto Rodrigo Caro de Arqueología del CSIC, 1952); N. Lamboglia, "Una nuova popolazione pirenaica: gli Olossitani," *Rivista i Studi Liguri* 25 (1959); H.-G. Pflaum, *Les carrières procuratoriennes équestres sous le Haut-Empire Romain* (Paris: P. Geuthner, 1982); *CT* no. 52; *IRC* nos. 172–74; M. Pi Vázquez, "Estudi de tres inscripcions sobre plom trobades a la necròpolis Ballesta (Empúries)," *Empúries* 54 (2005); F. Marco Simón, "Execrating the Roman power: Three *defixiones* from Emporiae (Ampurias)," in *Magical practice in the Latin West: Papers from the international conference held at the University of Zaragoza, 30 Sept.–1 Oct. 2005,* ed. R. L. Gordon and F. Marco Simón (Leiden: Brill, 2010). Simón's article critiqued the earlier version of the present chapter of my doctoral dissertation but did not address its main point—that the tablets must have been interred as part of the burial of the dead. The author argued that the tablets represented a ritual attack on the Roman authorities of the province but did not take into account my own discussion of this possibility. It is likely that we arrived at similar conclusions independently.

tion to the Flavian period. Archaeological evidence drastically enlarges the picture derived from the inscriptions, as it demonstrates that the tablets were intentionally deposited within the cinerary urns, perhaps as part of, or directly before, the inhumation of the vessels. Elsewhere in the Mediterranean, few tablets have been discovered inside a tomb—most magical artifacts appear to have been buried at some point after the completion of funerary rites, and presumably without the approval of the tomb owner, as an illicit appropriation of a burial space for nefarious purposes. Intentional inclusion has important ramifications when considered in conjunction with the texts inscribed on the tablets—curses that specifically target the provincial authorities. By juxtaposing the context of the tablets with their historical and social environments, it is possible to expand our understanding of how magic might operate as a means of resistance directed against local administrators.

Historical Background

The three curse tablets were buried in graves located in a necropolis to the north of the city. By the time of the deposition, Empúries was a well-established city, with a rich history and extensive contacts between residents and individuals familiar with traditional forms of execration. The site was founded in the sixth century by settlers from either the city of Massalia in southern Gaul or from its mother city of Phocaea on the Ionian coast.[4] Three centuries of Hellenic culture preceded the arrival of the Romans in 218 BCE, when soldiers under the command of Gnaeus Cornelius Scipio arrived at the town and successfully held it against the troops of Hannibal. Although the material under study in this chapter dates to the first century CE, the Roman presence on the site had already transformed the cultural and civic landscape to reflect Roman government and religious structures. By the end of the Julio-Claudian period, the city possessed all of the architectural hallmarks of an archetypal provincial city: an amphitheater, a forum with a Capitolium, a palaestra, and atrium houses. The presence of temples dedicated not only to the gods of the Roman pantheon but

---

4. Curbera, "The Greek curse tablets of Emporion," 90. Strabo III.4.8 attributes the foundation to the Massalians. Livy XXXIV.9.1 claims the Phocaeans. On the history of the settlement, see Mar and Ruiz de Arbulo, *Ampurias Romana: Historia, Arquitectura y Arqueología,* 323–413; B. Tang, *Delos, Carthage, Ampurias: The housing of three Mediterranean trading centres* (Rome: "L'Erma" di Bretschneider, 2005), 107–13, with extensive bibliography.

222   Materia Magica

also to Asclepius, Serapis and Isis, and the Iberian goddess Tutela suggests a close intertwining of Greek, Roman, and Iberian traditions, as well as those from the greater Mediterranean.

The cemeteries of Empúries, which lie on the south, east, and west of the ancient city, were excavated by Martin Almagro Basch in the 1940s and subsequently investigated by Martin Almagro Gorbea in the 1950s.[5] Seventeen burial areas were examined and published according to the names of the contemporary owners of each field. Early excavations likely cut across and recombined a number of ancient cemeteries that had distinct periods of use, but the divisions established by Almagro Basch have been maintained in subsequent publications.[6] The necropoleis were in use between the sixth century BCE and the fifth century CE and demonstrate a number of changes in burial practice over this period.[7] Residents of Empúries appear to have employed mortuary practices that were similar to those in contemporary use in other areas of Spain and the Roman west.[8] The preferred burial rite during the early Roman period was cremation, marking a shift from the graves found at the earlier cemetery at Las Corts, where inhumation was practiced. During the late second century CE, cremation declined and was gradually replaced by inhumation, following a trend noted elsewhere in the empire.[9]

The Ballesta necropolis, which contained the curse tablets under investigation, lies on both sides of the ancient road extending from the city to the cemetery of Las Corts, west of the urban area, and directly outside of the walls of the Roman city.[10] This cemetery was in use from the second or first century BCE

---

5. The necropoleis were published initially in M. Almagro Basch, *Las necrópolis de Ampurias I: Introducción y necrópolis griegas,* vol. III (Barcelona: Seix y Barral, 1953); M. Almagro Basch, *Las necrópolis de Ampurias II: Necrópolis romanas y necrópolis indígenas;* M. Almagro Gorbea, "Nuevas tumbas halladas en las necrópolis de Ampurias," *Ampurias* 24 (1962).

6. R. F. J. Jones, "The Roman cemeteries of Ampurias reconsidered," in *Papers in Iberian archaeology,* ed. T. F. C. Blagg, R. F. J. Jones, and S. J. Keay, BAR International Series, no.193 (Oxford: Oxford Press, 1984), 237.

7. Ibid., 237, 43.

8. See, for example, R. González Villaescusa, *El mundo funerario romano en el País Valenciano. Monumentos funerarios y sepulturas entre los siglos 1 a. de C.-7 d. de C,* (Madrid: Casa de Velázquez, 2001), passim, esp. 65–90.

9. A. Vollmer Torrubiano and A. López Borgoñoz, "Nuevas consideraciones sobre las variaciones en el ritual funerario Romano (ss. I–III d.C.)," in *Actas del XXII Congreso Nacional de Arqueología, Vigo, 1993* (Vigo: Xunta de Galicia, Consellería de Cultura, Dirección Xeral de Patrimonio Histórico e Documental, 1995). Close dating of the tombs has been problematic, as precise pottery chronologies for Catalunya have not been developed.

10. Almagro Basch, *Las necrópolis de Ampurias II: Necrópolis romanas y necrópolis indígenas,* 19.

Three Curses from Empúries and Their Social Implications   223

to the end of the second century CE. Burials include both inhumations and cremations, with the inhumations likely dating to the later period of use of the cemetery. Burials in the Ballesta cemetery were largely cremations. The ashes of the deceased were deposited in a ceramic vessel, and some form of cover was laid on top—either of ceramic, stone, or sigilata. Grave goods often were placed around the urn, although at times objects such as coins were interred directly within the cinerary vessel.[11]

In some cases, a low stone socle made of lime and mortar that presumably once supported a mud-brick wall encloses a smaller number of burials to set them apart. Funerary altars may have further monumentalized the tombs and provided a place for rituals to occur, perhaps on the anniversary of the death of the deceased or as part of larger festivals.[12]

The quantity of burials at Empúries provides sufficient data to reconstruct the basic outline of mortuary practice at the site. At Empúries, and in the Roman world in general, cremation typically occurred at a specified place within the cemeteries. Almagro Basch found evidence of an ustrinum, a central location for the burning of the bodies within one of the other necropoleis of Empúries.[13] Following the immolation of the body, the ashes were collected and placed in a cinerary urn. The size and style of the ceramic urns does not seem to bear relation to the number of other grave gifts deposited with the deceased. The more utilitarian type of vessel, such as that found in the cremation burials containing the curse tablets, is also present in Ballesta Cremation 64, where it is accompanied by three ceramic unguentaria—an unusually rich deposition at the Empúries site.[14] More elaborate cinerary urns might not be accompanied by any grave goods, such as is the case in Ballesta 49 or Ballesta 50.[15]

Grave gifts may have been deposited with the body before the cremation, during the collection of the ashes, or when the remains were interred at the grave site. Cremation 9 of the Torres cemetery contained the burned fragments of an unguentarium, a key, and a bone, suggesting that these objects were placed with the body on the pyre. Similarly, Cremations 13 and 23 in this

---

11. Ibid., 21.
12. Ibid., 22.
13. Jones, "The Roman cemeteries of Ampurias reconsidered," 245; A. Vollmer Torrubiano and A. López Borgoñoz, "Nueva aproximación a la necrópolis Romana de incineración de Les Corts (Ampurias)," in *Actas del XXIII Congreso Nacional de Arqueología, Elche, 1995* (Elche: Ajuntament d'Elx, 1996).
14. Almagro Basch, *Las necrópolis de Ampurias II: Necrópolis romanas y necrópolis indígenas,* 101.
15. Ibid., 147.

necropolis contained gold and silver rings that had been partly fused together.[16] This material would have been collected along with the ashes and deposited within the urns prior to deposition within the grave.

The Archaeological Context of the Ballesta Tablets

The Ballesta tablets were discovered in three separate vessels but interred within a single enclosure. A wall slightly separates eight cremations from other burials in the Ballesta necropolis, and Almagro Basch suggested that this was a family group. This space was specifically selected for the purpose of burying the urns that contained the tablets, as the enclosure wall almost certainly was visible at the time of deposition. Almagro Basch initially had dated the complex to the Augustan period primarily on numismatic data from the cinerary vessels. Recent work on the historical context of the tablets has settled on a Flavian date for production; F. Marco Simón has asserted that the tablets were inscribed between 75 and 78 CE.[17] As the date of the tablets was pushed downward through historical analysis, a disjunction was noted between the curses and the rest of the enclosure. Scholars have explained this discrepancy by insisting that the tablets or both the tablets and the urns were a later intrusion into the grave group. Contextual analysis of the urns, their contents, and the physical characteristics of the tablets, discussed below, indicates that the tablets were deposited in the funerary vessels near the time of burial, and that cremations 21–23 are roughly contemporary with the remainder of the enclosure.

Cremation 21 consisted of the small jug and the relatively well-preserved lead tablet, Ballesta Tablet 1 (plate 24a), which was deposited in the urn. The jug, which is 15.5 cm in height, with a mouth of 11.5 cm, possesses a small handle and is made of dark red coarse clay that has been smoothed with a lathe. The form of the vessel is very simple, and nearly identical to the vessels used in the other two cremations.

---

16. Vollmer Torrubiano and López Borgoñoz, "Nueva aproximación a la necrópolis Romana de incineración de Les Corts (Ampurias)." Not all objects deposited as grave goods were first burned with the dead. See, for example, the material from Torres 48 and 59, and Patel 22. In contrast, Torres 9 and 11 contain the remains of burned glass unguentaria.

17. Lamboglia, "Una nuova popolazione pirenaica: gli Olossitani," 155; Fabre, Mayer, and Rodà, *Inscriptions romaines de Catalogne,* 162; Marco Simón, "Execrating the Roman power: Three *defixiones* from Emporiae (Ampurias)," 399, 404–5. On the dating of the individuals who are cursed in the tablets, see ibid.

Three Curses from Empúries and Their Social Implications 225

When discussing the three lead tablets, I will refer to one face as the obverse, and the other as the reverse, although the tablets give no indication concerning the side that was inscribed first. Each side's inscription is discrete and does not continue from one side to the other. The inscriptions will be discussed at length below. The tablet from Ballesta 21 is roughly rectangular but is compressed in the middle like a bow tie. The tablet measures 5.9 by 3 cm. The upper left-hand corner is indented. On the obverse, the top preserves part of a margin and dips slightly in the center. The letters, which form a complete word, bridge this dip. The right edge of the tablet is slightly jagged, and a crease is present in the lower right-hand corner. The bottom is marked by a small lead spur, which juts out and to the right beneath the main body of the tablet. The individual inscribing the text flipped the tablet over prior to inscribing the other side. On the reverse of the tablet, the spur of lead is located at the top, and remains uninscribed. The bottom of the tablet curves in a slight arc, with either side of the tablet extending lower than the center, but a margin is preserved.

The vessel used for Cremation 22 is similar to that of Cremation 21, with a single handle, but measures 14.5 cm in height, with an opening of 11.5 cm. The urn held the cremated remains, four fragmentary nail shafts, and the lead tablet, Ballesta Tablet 2 (plate 24b). The tablet measures 5.7 cm by 6.0 cm. Tablet 2 is misshaped but remains roughly rectangular. It has suffered further decay since it was excavated. There is a greater amount of damage than Tablet 1, particularly along the top edge of the left side, and parts of some letters have been lost and others appear to be slightly distorted. The bottom of the tablet is slightly ragged, and the lower parts of a number of the letters at the right side have been lost. In the middle of the inscription, a horizontal mark suggests the end of the line, indicating that the majority of the text has been preserved. No margin is preserved at either the top or bottom.

Cremation 23 is similar to the other two deposits, if a little bit richer. As in Cremations 21 and 22, the vessel used for the ashes is a coarseware jug, measuring 14.5 cm in height, with a mouth of 11.5 cm. Within this vessel, excavators recovered a rectangular piece of bronze, 4 cm by 1.2 cm, two square nail shafts, each approximately 3.8 cm, and the lead tablet, Ballesta Tablet 3 (plate 24c). The tablet is roughly triangular in shape, with a slight curve along the top so that it resembles an overly wide pie-shaped wedge. The tablet is somewhat smaller than the others, measuring 5.2 by 4.6 cm. All sides are slightly ragged, and there is further damage along the bottom edge. A break or gouge appears on the upper-right portion of the tablet. On the obverse of the tablet, this area is inscribed, but not on the reverse. The text on the tablet follows its shape, curving around at the top of the obverse, although the letters are slightly misshaped. A margin is preserved on the right side, and although a crack is apparent in the lead, there has been no loss of letters. Damage along the bottom is limited, and although the letters appear to be faint, they can be read. A margin appears along the left side, following the edge of the tablet as it angles inward. On the reverse of the tablet, the lines of text are more difficult to make out. When inscribing this tablet, the practitioner flipped it over, as he or she did with the others. At the top of the uninscribed area, which is now on the bottom of the tablet, the tops of a number of letters are visible, suggesting that the damage here abraded or otherwise obscured letters that were initially visible.

There is limited information about the circumstances of the find, and it is productive to quote Almagro Basch's brief discussion of the context:

Otro contenía ocho urnas cincerarías con sus restos; precisamente dentro de tres de ellas aparecieron las curiosas tabulae defixionis, que describiremos en otro lugar. Tal vez se trate de una familia. Tal vez tenga un carácter mágico toda esta sepultura colectiva, como lo indicarían los plomos citados. Es un caso unico en todo el conjunto de sepulcros romanos de Ampurias que hemos excavado.[18]

In describing the complex, Almagro Basch indicates that the tablets were discovered within three of the cinerary urns. The importance of the finds as magical artifacts was noted immediately at the time of discovery, and Almagro Basch comments that this find is unique when compared to the other excavated graves from the necropolis. In the initial report, no clear distinction was noted between the three graves and the rest of the enclosure; the grave goods discovered in the three urns are similar to other cremations from the site. The archaeological data points to the likeliest scenario: the three urns with the tablets enclosed were interred in the grave group as the last burials to be added to the enclosure and were most likely part of one family or a burial collective.

A photograph taken at the time of the excavation (plate 25) shows the urns, positioned side by side, in one of the corners. The vessels have been placed close together, with the sides of two of the small jugs touching. Another, larger

---

18. Almagro Basch, *Las necrópolis de Ampurias II: Necrópolis romanas y necrópolis indígenas,* 22.

Three Curses from Empúries and Their Social Implications 227

urn is positioned along the same wall, but slightly distant from the coarseware vessels. The depth of the three urns is comparable with the other mortuary vessels in the enclosure. While the other burials are spaced farther apart relative to one another, it seems probable that a single hole was dug for the deposit of the three jugs. The three cinerary urns likely were interred in a single depositional episode. This varies from our expectations for mortuary practice, as most burials would have only included a single cremation. This does not, however, indicate that the vessels were deposited for a reason other than the disposal of the dead. In the same publication, Almagro Basch reiterates that these vessels, like the others in the tomb complex, contained the ashes of the deceased: "Esta tumba, de singular importancia, encerraba hasta 8 ocho urnas cinerarias, con sus correspondientes cenizas . . ."[19]

Nothing about the three cinerary urns or their contents marks them as different from other burials at the site, as numerous simple burials, either with a small number of grave goods or with none, are found elsewhere at Empúries. Cremation 21 contained only the tablet. In the same enclosure, Cremations 16 and 20 also contained no further material culture beyond the ashes of the deceased. These graves, like all the others at the site, may have contained perishable organic materials that have not survived.

The rectangular bronze object discovered in Cremation 23 is not sufficiently preserved to permit identification of its purpose. This object may show some signs of heat damage, suggesting that it came into contact with the pyre or with the warm ashes of the deceased. Bronze objects were frequently included within other cremations. In the Ballesta cemetery, a bronze hook was found in Cremation 4, Cremation 12 yielded a fragment of a bronze vessel, and bronze appliqués were discovered in Cremation 17.

Cremations 22 and 23 each contained multiple nails, a find that is prevalent among the burials in the Ballesta cemetery.[20] They may suggest that the body was burned upon a bier as some nails from the site show evidence of burning and are blackened or slightly misshaped.[21] Scholars also have suggested that

---

19. Ibid., 55.
20. Nails are present in Ballesta Cremations 3, 4, 7, 15, 17–18, 32, 36, 38, 46, 48, and 54. For a full list of nails associated with the cemeteries at Empúries, see S. Alfayé Villa, "Nails for the dead: A polysemic account of an ancient funerary practice," in *Magical practice in the Latin West: Papers from the international conference held at the University of Zaragoza, 30 Sept.–1 Oct. 2005*, ed. R. L. Gordon and F. Marco Simón (Leiden: Brill, 2010), 433.
21. Almagro Basch, *Las necrópolis de Ampurias II: Necrópolis romanas y necrópolis indígenas*, 100; Vollmer Torrubiano and López Borgoñoz, "Nueva aproximación a la necrópolis Romana

228   Materia Magica

nails were used for ritual purposes, either to protect the dead or to prevent the ghost of the dead individual from tormenting the living.[22] Each of the three cremations contains a different number of nails, or none at all. Here, they do not seem to have served a protective function. Curse tablets relied on the deceased individuals to carry out the binding that the practitioner desired; to prevent the dead from the tormenting the living would have been counterproductive. It remains possible that nails were used to direct the dead or prevent them from attacking the commissioner. In all likelihood, however, the nails derived from the cremation of the dead, as they are all relatively small and may have been collected along with the ashes.

The grave goods associated with the cinerary urns suggest the performance of burial rites that were typical for the site as a whole. The same is true for the repositories in which the ashes of the deceased were placed. The urns are utilitarian pieces that have been employed or reused for a funerary function, but they are not unusual for the site as a whole. Similar cinerary vessels appear in Ballesta 62 and 28. Although there were no covers on the urns of Ballesta 21, 22, and 23, lids or plates were not a necessity for proper burial, and Ballesta 62 also lacked a cover.

Comparable evidence from other burials indicates that the vessels used as cinerary urns may have been in use during the Flavian period, the date associated with the tablets. Coarseware vessels are difficult to date, as such forms can be employed for long periods of time with little alteration. Evidence from the two graves that contained nearly identical vessels, Ballesta 62 and 28, suggests that the vessels were in use from the Augustan period through the middle of the first century CE. Ballesta 62 contained ceramic unguentaria that date to the Augustan period. Ballesta 28 used a first-century CE stamped Arretine plate as a cover.[23] A glass unguentarium was also discovered in this tomb that can be

---

de incineración de Les Corts (Ampurias)," 130–31, 37 n. 17–20.

22. Alfayé Villa, "Nails for the dead: A polysemic account of an ancient funerary practice," passim, esp. 444–49. For the bibliography on apotropaic functions, see 444 n. 34; on restraining the dead, see 445 n. 39; Bailliot, *Magie et sortilèges dans l'Antiquité romaine,* 167–68.

23. Ballesta 62: Almagro Basch, *Las necrópolis de Ampurias II: Necrópolis romanas y necrópolis indígenas,* 85, see also Almagro Basch, *Las necrópolis de Ampurias II: Necrópolis romanas y necrópolis indígenas,* 252, dated by Lamboglia, "Una nuova popolazione pirenaica: gli Olossitani," 155 n. 2. Ballesta 28: Almagro Basch, *Las necrópolis de Ampurias II: Necrópolis romanas y necrópolis indígenas,* 65. This plate is signed EROS / C MEM, and dated to the Augustan or Tiberian period (10 BCE or later). On the Arretine plate, see A. Oxe, H. Comfort, and P. M. Kenrick, *Corpus vasorum Arretinorum: A catalogue of the signatures, shapes and chronology of Italian sigillata,* 2nd ed. (Bonn: Habelt, 2000), 280, no. 1145 (991).

Three Curses from Empúries and Their Social Implications 229

dated later, perhaps to the reigns of Claudius and Nero.[24] Similar one-handled jugs are preserved from other excavated areas. In the Nofre area, located a short distance to the south of the Ballesta cemetery, Cremations 3 and 4 used comparable vessels, and each contained coins datable to the Claudian period.[25]

The ceramic vessels that contained the cremations suggest a *terminus post quem* in the first century CE, between the Augustan period and Nero (~28 BCE–68 CE). This *terminus post quem,* however, is the date after which the material was deposited; the burial of the urns and the tablets could have occurred at any point, either within the use-range of the artifacts, or after this period. Our sample size is quite small for assuming a brief window of activity for these coarseware vessels. If the tablets are dated to the Flavian period, or even to Marco Simón's more precise chronology of 75–78 CE, we would move the latest attestation of the coarseware vessels down eight to ten years. There is no compelling evidence to necessitate the earlier Augustan rather than the later Flavian date; the tablets easily could be contemporary with the vessels in which they were interred.[26]

It is highly unlikely that the burials were reopened to deposit the tablets. When excavated, the vessels were in pristine condition, without breaks, chips, or damage. Furthermore, the small size of funerary urns would make them difficult to locate if a practitioner were digging years after the urns had been buried. One would expect breakage of one or more of the urns or signs of disturbance if they had been illicitly removed from the ground and subsequently reinterred.

---

24. A. Balil, "Defixiones ampuritanas," *Archivo Español de Arqueología* 37 (1964): 200.

25. Nofre 3 and 4: Almagro Basch, *Las necrópolis de Ampurias II: Necrópolis romanas y necrópolis indígenas,* 202. Sabadi 7 possessed a similar cinerary urn but few datable finds: Almagro Basch, *Las necrópolis de Ampurias II: Necrópolis romanas y necrópolis indígenas,* 252. Compare the dating of similar vessels at J. Casas et al., "Les ceràmiques comunes locals del N.E. de Catalunya," in *Ceràmica comuna romana d'època Alto-Imperial a la Península Ibèrica. Estat de la qüestió,* ed. J. Aquilué Abadías and M. Roca Roumens (Empúries: Museu d'Arqueologia de Catalunya, 1995), 115–16.

26. Balil, "Defixiones ampuritanas," 201, *contra* Marco Simón, "Execrating the Roman power: Three *defixiones* from Emporiae (Ampurias)," 405, Balil does not give a definitive date for the three urns that contain the curse tablets, but states that the placement of the tablets, either with or without the urns, is not impossible: "Creemos, por tanto, que la hipótesis de la colocación de las defixiones en época flavia, con o sin urnas, en una tumba anterior, no puede considerarse como algo arqueológicamente imposible y que es correcta su valoración prosapográfica." Balil does state that he believes the remainder of the tomb group is likely earlier, but the date derived from the associated finds is a *terminus post quem,* and deposition could have occurred at any point after the Augustan period.

230   Materia Magica

The intentional use of three separate cinerary urns also is significant, as the practitioner could have chosen to deposit the tablets within a single urn. This would have been a simpler procedure, particularly if the practitioner were attempting to evade the notice of other individuals.[27] As we noted on Cyprus, multiple *defixiones* often were deposited in the same archaeological context, whence the tablets could communicate with the spirits of the underworld; multiple conduits were not necessary. It seems most likely, then, that the three tablets were added to their respective urns before their final deposition; they may have been placed on the pyre along with the body, collected with the ashes, or placed in the urns at graveside.

Cremation requires a significant amount of heat over a long period of time to reduce the body to ash, but in the ancient period, the process did not reach a temperature that permitted all of the human remains to be completely incinerated.[28] Material from other cremations at Empúries suggests that the temperature of the funerary pyres reached between 850 and 950 degrees Celsius. Glass melts at a temperature of 1,000 degrees Celsius, and slightly misshapen unguentaria, as are found in Ballesta Cremations 8 and 19, likely resulted from exposure to heat below 1,000 degrees but above 900 degrees. Silver and gold have melting points of 960.5 and 1,063 degrees Celsius, respectively. The fused silver and gold rings found in Torres 13 and 23 demonstrate that the temperature in the ustrinum was approaching the melting point of these metals but was not so close that the nature of the artifacts was no longer recognizable.

The tablets were not placed on or with the body prior to cremation; lead melts at a temperature of 327 degrees Celsius, and the metal would have completely liquefied at the high temperature of the pyre.[29] The tablets, however, may show some signs of damage due to heat. The edges of all of the tablets appear slightly deformed. On tablet 1, slight melting may have caused the spur of lead. The triangular tablet could possess this shape because of exposure to heat; the letters all curve along the edge of the tablet, which is unusual for inscriptions. On the reverse of this tablet, the effaced letters also could be the result of this same incident. Furthermore, each of the tablets appears to have a

---

27. Johnston, *Restless dead,* 74 n. 114 and 75 n. 18.

28. On funerary pyres and cremation, see V. M. Hope, *Roman death: Dying and the dead in ancient Rome* (London: Continuum, 2009), 82–85.

29. On the melting points of the metals, see Cronyn and Robinson, *The elements of archaeological conservation,* 128, 202, 230–35. Although no scientific analysis has been performed on the tablets to determine the purity of the lead, it seems unlikely that the melting point of the metal would have increased to such a degree that it impacted the preservation of the artifacts.

slightly undulating surface, which may also be suggestive of heat. Therefore, it is likely that the tablets were placed with the remains of the deceased before the ashes had cooled completely.

Recent finds of tablets from Mainz appear to have resulted from comparable heat exposure. The Mainz tablets were found in the lower levels of ceremonial ash pits that had been used for burnt offerings. Some tablets were warped and exhibited features similar to the Empúries examples. In the same context, the excavators discovered lumps of lead that they posited had resulted from tablets that had been exposed to high heat. The excavators suggested that the legible tablets had been placed in cooler parts of the altar and were damaged but not destroyed by the heat.[30]

The evidence from the cremations suggests that the urns and their associated tablets were buried in the Flavian period. The other burials in the enclosure likely date from around the same time period, or slightly earlier. Although many of the artifacts can be dated to the Augustan period or early in the first century CE, there is also later material. A bronze *as* coin from cremation 18 depicts the bearded head of Octavian and the inscription Caesar. Divi., and on the reverse, the head of Julius Caesar facing right, with the inscription Divus. Although worn, it is comparable to Sydenham 1335, dated to 37 BCE, and minted in Italy; the extensive wear suggests that the coin was in circulation for a considerable amount of time.[31] Cremation 17 contained an *as* coin of Empúries, with the head of Athena on the obverse and Pegasus on the reverse. There is no evidence that coinage was produced in Empúries following the reign of Claudius; the coin must therefore predate Claudius but could have been in circulation for a while.[32] Numismatic evidence from two of the cremations establishes a time span from the late first century BCE, but wear on the coins may imply a later date for deposition.

Cremation 17 also contained a lamp fragment, Loescheke type II b, dated to the Augustan period. From Cremation 19, an unguentarium (no. 2) is identi-

---

30. Witteyer, "Curse tablets and voodoo dolls from Mainz: The archaeological evidence for magical practices in the Sanctuary of Isis and Magna Mater," 112–22; Blänsdorf, "The *defixiones* from the Sanctuary of Isis and Mater Magna in Mainz," 157.

31. E. A. Sydenham, *The coinage of the Roman Republic* (London: Spink and Son, 1952), 208.

32. A. Burnett, M. Amandry, and P. P. Ripollès, *Roman provincial coinage,* II vols., (London: British Museum Press, 1992), I. 106–7. City coinage in the western provinces gradually dried up over a period of twenty-five years between the reigns of Tiberius and Claudius. Spanish coinage continued until the issue of Ebusus for Claudius. Cf. the general introduction, Burnett, Amandry, and Ripollès, *Roman provincial coinage,* 1–54.

fied as Kisa Form 29; this same vessel type is associated with Tiberian/Claudian ceramics from Ballesta 8.[33] More recent analysis of the Kisa unguentaria have pushed the chronology into the Neronian or Flavian periods, or even into the second or third centuries.[34] The recent re-dating of small finds that are similar to those found in other burials in the enclosure potentially can change the dating of these burials, shifting the chronology of the enclosure into the Flavian period.

The absolute earliest date for any cremation in the enclosure is the late third quarter of the first century BCE. All of the burials almost certainly postdate this period, and the majority of the vessels and artifacts fit squarely into the early to mid-first century CE. As the complex is likely a familial or social grouping, it seems likely that it was in use over the course of several years, and perhaps as long as multiple generations. The cinerary urns are different in appearance from others in the group and possess few grave gifts, but the fortunes of families may decline over time, or other circumstances could have led to the decision to use these simple vessels. Neither the chronology of the vessel-forms nor the contents of the urns requires us to date cremations 21, 22, and 23 later than the rest of the enclosure. Moreover, the deposition of these three cremations does not appear to have disturbed earlier burials, which suggests that the individuals responsible for the interring these urns were aware of the location of other graves.

The Inscriptions and Their Historical Context

The three tablets are similar in size, and they curse the same individuals using comparable methods. In each tablet, names are given in the nominative case; none of the tablets, as best as can be determined, lists a commissioner. The paleography of the tablets indicates that the same practitioner inscribed all three. The inscriptions are exclusively written in rustic capitals, and on each, the letters *C, D,* and *Q* appear oriented properly, while letters such as *L, N,* and *S* are written backward. The *L* consistently appears with the horizontal bar joining the vertical bar at a point slightly lower than the center and resembles the Greek lambda. The *F* lacks a center bar in all occurrences. The *R* is made with two strokes; a vertical stroke is followed by a single loop and angled

---

33. Almagro Basch, *Las necrópolis de Ampurias II: Necrópolis romanas y necrópolis indígenas,* 29, 59. A. Kisa, *Das Glas im Altertume,* 3 vols. (Leipzig: Hiersemann, 1908), III. Form 29.
34. Balil, "Defixiones ampuritanas," 199; C. Isings, *Roman glass from dated finds* (Groningen: Wolters, 1957), 42 form 28a, 42.

stroke. The cross stroke of the *A* is frequently made at the bottom of the letter. These data agree with the archaeological context, which suggests a single deposition of three tablets, each in an individual cinerary urn.

Each of the three tablets is opisthographic, meaning that it should be read from right to left and from bottom to top on both sides. The use of convoluted and jumbled lettering is common among curse tablets; it was presumably intended to similarly represent the way in which a magical act would jumble the victim's agency or speech.[35] For each tablet, the practitioner appears to have inscribed one side and then flipped the tablet over vertically, as the text on one side is upside down from the text on the other. Each side is independent, and words do not cross from one side to the other. Texts and translations of the three tablets follow:

Tablet 1[36]

(Obverse)
Fulvus legatus Au
gusti, Rufus legatus
Augusti, Maturus
proqu[r]ator Augusti,
<consilium> legati, atvocati In
dicetanorum.

(Reverse)
Consilium Fulvi,
legati Olossi
tani, Campanus
Fidentinus Augus-
t[i?---]

Translation

(Obverse) Fulvus, the legate of the emperor, Rufus, the legate of the emperor, Maturus, the procurator of the emperor, the legate's (consilium) and the defenders of the Indicetani.

---

35. Ogden, "Binding spells," 29–30.

36. The text follows Marco Simón's recent readings. Ballesta Tablet 1 Obverse =Almagro (1952) 114a = Lamboglia 3a = *CT* no. 52.2b = Pi Vázquez 2b = *LF* 2.1.1/3 = Marco Simón 1a; Ballesta Tablet 2 Obverse = Almagro (1952) 114b = Lamboglia 3b = *CT* no. 52.2a = Pi Vázquez 2a = *LF* 2.1.1/3 = Marco Simón 1b.

234   Materia Magica

(Reverse) The council of the legate Fulvus, the Olossitani legates, Campanus Fidentinus, the imperial (?) . . .

Tablet 2[37]
(Obverse)
Maturus proqura
tor Augusti, consi
lium legati
legati : Indiceta
norum
Indiceta[n]orum.

(Reverse)
Olossita[ni]
Titus Aurelius
Fulvus lega
tus Augusti,
Rufus leg[atus]
[Au]gus[ti].

Translation
Obverse: Maturus, procurator of the emperor, the legate's council, the legates (representatives) of the Indicetani, of the Indicetani.

   Reverse: The Olossitani, Titus Aurelius Fulvus, legate of the emperor, Rufus, legate of the emperor

Tablet 3[38]
(Obverse)
[O]lossitani,
Sempronius
Campanus Fi
dentinus, at

---

37. Ballesta Tablet 2 Obverse = Almagro (1952) 115a = Lamboglia 1b = *CT* no. 52.1a = Pi Vázquez 1b = *LF* 2.1.1/2 = Marco Simón 2b; Ballesta Tablet 2 Reverse = Almagro (1952) 115b = Lamboglia 1a = *CT* no. 52.1b = Pi Vázquez 1a = *LF* 2.1.1/2 = Marco Simón 2a.

38. Ballesta Tablet 3 Obverse = Almagro (1952) 116b = Lamboglia 2b = *CT* no. 52.3a = Pi Vázquez 3b = *LF* 2.1.1/4 = Marco Simón 3b; Ballesta Tablet 3 Reverse = Almagro (1952) 116a = Lamboglia 2a = *CT* no. 52.3b = Pi Vázquez 3a = *LF* 2.1.1/4 = Marco Simón 3a.

versari me inique
ne in[---]nt.

(Reverse)
Fulvus legatus
Augusti, Rufus lega
tus Augusti, Matu
rus procurator
Augusti, consilium
legati atvoca
ti Indicetano
rum [Indicetano?]
rum.

Translation
(Obverse) May the Olossitani, Sempronius Campanus Fidentinus, my adversaries not (. . .) me wickedly.

(Reverse) Fulvus, legate of the emperor, Rufus, legate of the emperor, Maturus, procurator of the emperor, the legate's council, the legal representatives of the Indicetani [of the Indecatani]

Three of the named individuals that are cursed in the tablet can be associated with Roman magistrates from the province who are known from other sources. Titus Aurelius Fulvus, named on all three tablets, is probably the same individual as T. Aurelius Fulvus, consul for the second time in 85 CE, who served as the governor of Tarraconensis.[39] Rufus, who is identified in the same manner as Fulvus, is listed as a *legatus Augusti.* Syme proposed that his position was a praetorian legate, and it seems likely that he was a *legatus iuridicus,* perhaps identifiable with Q. Pomponius P.f. Rufus, who later rose to the rank of *consul suffectus* in 95 CE but was known in Tarraconenis around this period.[40]

---

39. Pflaum, *Les carrières procuratoriennes équestres sous le Haut-Empire Romain,* 97–98. T. Aurelius Fulvus is named in CIL II.6741, Tac. *Hist,* I.79, *SHA, Life of Pius.* R. Syme, "Consulates in absence," *JRS* 48, no. 1–2 (1958): 7; G. Alföldy, *Fasti Hispanienses: senatorische Rechtsbeamte und Offiziere in den spanischen Provinzen des Römischen Reiches von Augustus bis Diokletian* (Wiesbaden: F. Steiner, 1969), 19–21.

40. Syme, "Consulates in absence," 7–8; Pi Vázquez, "Estudi de tres inscripcions sobre plom trobades a la necròpolis Ballesta (Empúries)," 170; Alföldy, *Fasti Hispanienses: senatorische Rechtsbeamte und Offiziere in den spanischen Provinzen des Römischen Reiches von Augus-*

Maturus, the Augustan procurator, should be identified as Marius Maturus, known from Tacitus' histories and cited as the procurator of the Maritime Alps, who attempted to prevent the advance of Otho's troops in 69 CE.[41] It is more difficult to place Sempronius Campanus Fidentinus who is named in an imperial position in tablet 1, and listed again in tablet 3.[42] As Marco Simón notes, this name is quite rare and only attested in four instances, all but one of which occur in Hispania.[43] None of these individuals, however, can be associated with an imperial office, or with our Sempronius Campanus Fidentinus.

Articulating the precise conditions that led to the deposition of these tablets is a more complicated venture. Scholars have suggested that the tablets derive from a legal conflict between the Olossitani and the Indicetani.[44] The Olossitani inhabited an area to the west of Empúries, centered on the city of Olot.[45] The Indicetani, on the other hand, were the native Iberian inhabitants who lived around Empúries.[46] Lamboglia has proposed that Sempronius Campanus Fidentinus commissioned or deposited the tablets on behalf of the Olossitani, who were living in the neighboring area of Olot.[47] According to her reconstruction, Fidentinus, who is otherwise unknown, would have deposited vessels containing only the curse tablets within a monumental grave complex of Augustan date. As was discussed above, these three cinerary urns contained ashes, and the comparative data necessitate a funerary context for the deposition. Moreover, in most curse tablets, the commissioner seldom names himself

---

tus bis Diokletian, 21; *IRC* pp. 161–62. M. Gomez-Moreno initially identified the Augustan legate Rufus as L. Nodius Rufus, who is listed as a legate in Taraconnensis in 193 CE. *Misceláneas: historia, arte, arqueología (dispersa, emendata, addita, inédita)* (Madrid: S. Aguirre impresor, 1949), 333, citing *Corpus Inscripciones Tarraconese* 4125.

41. Pflaum, in A. Merlin, "Périodiques," *L'Année épigraphique* 1952 (1953), 42 no. 122, citing Tac. *Hist.* III.42.2–4, III.43.2; Pflaum, *Les carrières procuratoriennes équestres sous le Haut-Empire Romain,* 96–97.

42. Pflaum suggests that Sempronius Campanus Fidentinus should be read as two separate individuals, Sempronius Campanus and Fidentinus. *Les carrières procuratoriennes équestres sous le Haut-Empire Romain,* 97.

43. Marco Simón, "Execrating the Roman power: Three *defixiones* from Emporiae (Ampurias)," 406–7; I. Kajanto, *The Latin cognomina* (Helsinki: Keskuskirjapaino, 1965), 257; B. Lorincz, F. Redo, and A. Mócsy *Onomasticon provinciarum Europae latinarum* (Budapest: Archaeolingua Alapítvány, 1994), s.v. Fidentius. One attestation was found in Italy: CIL V. 143.

44. Pflaum, *Les carrières procuratoriennes équestres sous le Haut-Empire Romain,* 95–98; Balil, "Defixiones ampuritanas," 198; Solin, "Eine Neue Fluchtafel aus Ostia," 28; E. Ripoll Perelló, "Acerca de unas *tabellae defixionis* de Ampurias (Hisp. Cit.)," in *Perennitas: studi in onore di Angelo Brelich,* ed. A. Brelich (Rome: Edizioni dell'Ateneo, 1980), 416.

45. Lamboglia, "Una nuova popolazione pirenaica: gli Olossitani," 153.

46. J. Aquilé Abadías, *Empúries* (Empúries: Museu d'Arqueologia de Catalunya, 2000), 10.

47. Lamboglia, "Una nuova popolazione pirenaica: gli Olossitani," 153; *CT,* p. 142.

or herself in the inscription, which argues against reading Fidentinus as the instigator. Perhaps most important, all of the named individuals are in the same case, the nominative, suggesting that each should be understood as a target of the *defixio*.[48] The curse tablet cannot be associated with one or the other side in the imagined legal case between the Olossitani and the Indecitani, so it becomes necessary to further nuance the conflict that may have led to this ritual procedure.

This dispute may have been over an individual's land rather than communal territory. In 70 CE, Vespasian granted Latin rights to the province of Hispania, an act that may have necessitated the redistribution of land and the establishment or reorganization of urban centers, such as Aquae Calidae or Rhode, both near Empúries.[49] Fabre, Mayer, and Rodà suggest that the Roman authorities redistributed land belonging to the commissioner of the tablet to the Olossitani, thus drawing the anger of the unnamed *defigens* against the Olossitani, the Indicetani, and the imperial magistrates.[50] According to Strabo, the *Legatus Augustus Pro Praetore,* who was served by two additional legates, governed the province of Hispania Citerior. These three officials oversaw the regions of Gallaecia, Asturia, and Cantabria, as well as the area along the coast, where Empúries is located. The legates were always enumerated in the same fashion, as two Legati Augusti and one Procurator Augusti, as is found within the tablets.[51] The tablets, then, would have been commissioned in anticipation of an impending court case, perhaps one that pitted the commissioner against the Olossitani, the Indicetani, and the provincial representatives of the Roman Empire.

This reconstruction provides a compelling reading of the historical circumstances surrounding the case that the commissioner of the tablets intended to disrupt, but does not account for the striking ritual that must have accompanied their deposition. Three separate tablets were inscribed in anticipation of the case, and each mentions the same individuals. The commissioner could have chosen to either deposit one single tablet, or to name separate individuals on each lead sheet; the decision to repeat a similar curse three times, with slight

---

48. A. T. Wilburn, "Materia magica: The archaeology of magic in Roman Egypt, Cyprus, and Spain" (PhD, University of Michigan, 2005), 173 n. 46; Marco Simón, "Execrating the Roman power: Three *defixiones* from Emporiae (Ampurias)," 408.

49. Ibid.; Pliny *HN* 3.30; J. Andreu Pintado, *Edictum, municipium y lex: Hispania en época Flavia (69–96 d.C.)* (Oxford: Archaeopress, 2004), 146, 148.

50. *IRC* p. 162.

51. Lamboglia, "Una nuova popolazione pirenaica: gli Olossitani," 154.

variation, and deposit the curses in three separate funerary vessels, is significant. As we have noted, the tablets were placed within the funerary urns at the time of burial, and likely with the knowledge of those undertaking the funerary rites. The clustering of the curse tablets may indicate that some occurrence triggered the deposition, perhaps an event related to the deaths of the individuals whose remains were deposited within the urns. The imprecations inscribed on the tablets, which specifically target the imperial administration, point to an underlying current of resistance.

Curse Tablets and Deposition with the Dead

Curse tablets often made use of the dead but were seldom deposited with the remains of the deceased as part of the funerary rite. At Empúries, two Greek tablets that have been dated to the late fourth or early third century BCE were found in the soil above a contemporary necropolis, suggesting that a practitioner deposited the tablets after the completion of the burial rites. The deposition of three Ballesta tablets, either when the ashes were collected or soon thereafter, when the cinerary urn was placed within the grave, may indicate the presence and knowledge of family members or close associates of the deceased. At first glance, this appears quite unusual—that family members or associates would approve of magical activity occurring in the grave of a loved one. Analysis of the relationship between cursing and the dead suggests that a personal crisis may have led the commissioner to deposit a tablet with a family member or another known individual; in some situations, this was considered acceptable ritual behavior.

Tablets were often deposited in graves because the corpse could fulfill a specific role in carrying out a curse. Often, the dead preferred in binding rites were those who were restless—the unburied, the dead by violence, those who died before their appointed time, or those who died without marrying; these ghosts were assumed to wander the earth, unable to find peace. Three separate but not mutually exclusive mechanisms exist through which the dead can be employed in curses: (1) they may act as messengers to the underworld, (2) the practitioner may make the victim like the dead through persuasive analogy, and (3) the dead themselves may be empowered to bind the victim.[52] These

---

52. Messengers: Johnston, *Restless dead,* 74–75. Compare PGM IV.2726–35, where Hekate compels the *aoroi* to do the bidding of the practitioner. Persuasive analogy: M. W. Dickie, "Varia

Three Curses from Empúries and Their Social Implications 239

methods of implementing the dead within a curse are not mutually exclusive, and it seems that the practitioner could understand the dead as operating in different ways, even within the same tablet. In a tablet from Hadrumentum, in North Africa, the practitioner requests that underworld spirits bind the feet of a certain horse, and, in the same tablet, metaphorically compares the horses to the dead spirit, stating, "let him perish and fall, just as you lie (here) prematurely dead."[53]

It is not clear how the living regarded the exploitation of the dead for personal gain or retribution, particularly when the dead in question were deceased relatives or friends. There is substantial evidence that rituals were undertaken after the funeral to honor the dead or to protect oneself from their anger.[54] Some curse tablets, as well, appear to support this proposition. In a tablet from Olbia, on the Black Sea, the deceased must be bribed before he is willing to aid the practitioner. The tablet reads

> Just as we do not know you, so too let Eupolis and Dionysios, Makareus, Aristokrates and Demopolis, Komaios, Heragoras, at whatever lawsuit they are present, and Leptinas, Epikrates, Hestiaios, at whatever lawsuit they are present, at whatever taking of evidence (sc. they are present), let them . . . {Just as we you} And if you put a spell on them and capture them, I shall indeed honor you and shall prepare for you the best of offerings.[55]

Because it was necessary to provide compensation, Sarah Iles Johnston has suggested that the spirit would not want to perform binding magic, and in turn, that family members would not have wanted their dead to serve as conduits for magicians.[56]

Most often, the archaeological evidence suggests that curse tablets were inserted into tombs at a later date; they are typically found in the soil above a grave, where the practitioner deposited them. The Olbia tablet is addressed to

---

magica," *Tyche* 14 (1999): 61–62; Eidinow, *Oracles, curses, and risk among the ancient Greeks*, 148–50. Dead empowered to bind victims: PGM IV.296–466. Compare the address to *nekeudaimon* in a tablet published at P. J. Sijpesteijn, "Ein Herbeirufungszauber," *ZPE* 4 (1969) as well as the tablet from Pella that addresses Macron, discussed below.

53. *CT* no. 11; *DT* no. 295.
54. Johnston, *Restless dead*, 38–46.
55. *SGD* no. 173 = *SEG* 37.673; trans. D. R. Jordan, "An address to a ghost at Olbia," *Mnemosyne* 50, no. 2 (1997): 217.
56. Johnston, *Restless dead*, 74–75 and nn. 114, 118. Similar offers of gifts can be found in *DTA* no. 99; *SGD* nos. 54 and 109.

the ghost of an unknown individual, and Jordan has suggested that this spirit may have been both unnamed on the tomb and not commemorated with appropriate burial rites.[57] Tablets could also be hidden; in a tomb in Ballana, Nubia, lead tablets and a love spell written on a gold leaf were sequestered behind a number of amphorae, where they would not be visible to those entering the burial chamber.[58] Other tablets, like those discovered in the columbarium outside of the Porta Sebastiano, discussed in the Introduction, were deposited after the tomb had gone out of use. A later intrusion into a grave can be detected through stratigraphy, as the tablet may appear above the corpse or its funerary vessel, or through postdepositional disturbance, visible because the practitioner disrupted the burial as he made the deposition. In a few cases, the tablet might be added without disturbing the grave, particularly if the burial were outfitted with a tube for libations.[59]

Conversely, there also are clear instances in which the tablet was deliberately placed with the dead during the burial. In the Athenian Kerameikos, two lead tablets were each discovered in separate graves, where they had been interred with the deceased. Both were placed in the right hands of skeletons and dated by other grave goods to the fifth century.[60] The site of Crucinacum (modern Kreuznach) in Germania yielded a cinerary urn into which two separate curses had been placed, along with two coins dated to the reign of Vespasian.[61] Both tablets dedicate a series of enemies to the infernal deities, but neither tablet appears to include the same names.[62] Some scholars have sug-

---

57. Jordan, "An address to a ghost at Olbia," 216–17. Compare to the direct address to the ghost Pasianax found in Megara, *DT* nos. 43–44 = *CT* no. 131 as well as the curse found in a grave at Pella, *NGD* no. 31, discussed on pp. 241–43.

58. *SGD* no. 187; W. B. Emery and L. P. Kirwan, *The royal tombs of Ballana and Qustul* (Cairo: Government Press, 1938), Tomb 2. 74–78 with figure 35; trans. S. Eitrem 405–7, plates 107B and 116.1.

59. I.e., curse from Messana, *CT* no. 116; Tunisia: *DT* nos. 436–37; see R. Merrifield, *The archaeology of ritual and magic* (London: B. T. Batsford, 1987), 215.

60. *SGD* nos. 1 and 2; Jordan, "New archaeological evidence for the practice of magic in classical Athens"; M. d. A. López Jimeno, *Nuevas tabellae defixionis Áticas* (Amsterdam: A. M. Hakkert, 1999), nos. 1 and 2.

61. *DTA* p. 93 = *DT* nos. 96–97 = *LF* 5.1.4/3 and 5.1.4/4.

62. Other examples include (1) a tablet found at Qamadir in a Roman cemetery, where a lead tablet had been positioned by the head of one of the mummified, wrapped bodies. According to the brief report, the tablet was inscribed in Greek, and wrapped around the stylus. *SGD* no. 190; J. d. M. Johnson, "Graeco-Roman Branch (Field Report)," *Archaeological report 1911–1912* (1911/12): 14; (2) *DT* no. 258 = *LF* 11.1.1/31was discovered at in a Roman period cemetery at Carthage, buried within a glass cinerary vessel description of context, *DT* p. 288. Too little is preserved to make a secure reading of the tablet or its proximate cause.

Three Curses from Empúries and Their Social Implications   241

gested that this was clandestine activity on the part of the magician during the burial rite, as the practitioner may have slipped the tablet into the tomb without attracting the notice of the participants.[63] Alternatively, careful excavation of a freshly dug tomb may have allow the practitioner to locate the body, but finds in which the tablet was discovered in the hand of the deceased, before the onset of rigor mortis, argue against this.

A third possibility exists to explain the contemporary deposition of tablets and the dead: those undertaking the burial permitted and approved of the inclusion of the tablet. This may be supported by evidence that the practitioner or commissioner knew the deceased individual. In the tablet from Attica, discussed in chapter 2, the practitioner addresses the dead individual, Pasianax, by name. A recently discovered grave from Pella contained the partially preserved remains of an individual, including the skull and limbs; the absence of the lower torso did not allow the investigators to determine either the age or sex of the skeleton, but it was likely an adult. A tablet was discovered along the side of the right thighbone, and the excavator, I. M. Akamatis, suggested that it had either fallen from the hand of the skeleton or had been placed near the deceased at the time of burial.[64] The tablet reads

Of Thetima and Dionysophon the ritual wedding and the marriage I bind by a written spell, as well as (the marriage) of all other women (to him), both widows and maidens, but above all of Thetima; and I entrust (this spell) to Macron and to the *daimones*. And were I ever to unfold and read these words again after digging (the tablet) up, only then should Dionysophon marry, not before; may he indeed not take another woman than myself, but let me alone grow old by the side of Dionysophon and no one else. I implore you: have pity for [Phila ?], dear daimones, [for I am indeed bereft ?] of all my dear ones and adandoned. But please keep this (piece of writing) for my sake so that these events do not happen and wretched Thetima perishes miserably. [- - -] but let me become happy and blessed [- - -][65]

The text of the tablet curses the marriage of a woman named Thetima and her

---

63. Johnston, *Restless dead,* 79 and n.31; Ogden, "Binding spells," 20.
64. E. Voutiras, Διονυσοφῶντος γαμοι. *Marital life and magic in fourth century Pella* (Amsterdam: J. C. Gieben, 1998), 3.
65. Trans. Voutiras, Διονυσοφῶντος γαμοι. *Marital life and magic in fourth century Pella,* 15–16. For the Greek text and commentary, see ibid., 8–19; E. Voutiras, "Ένας διαλεκτικός κατάδεσμος από την Πέλλα," *Ελληνική Διαλεκτολογία* 3 (1992–93).

betrothed Dionysophon, so that the nuptials will not take place. Instead, the commissioner of the spell, Phila (?), will grow old with Dionysiphon. The tablet directly addresses the spirit of the dead as "Macron," which suggests that it was placed in the grave of this individual.[66] While many members of a community may have known the name of an individual that died and was being buried, the process of placing the tablet would have been more complicated. Setting the tablet in the hand of the corpse, which may have occurred in this instance, would have required the permission of those who were undertaking the burial. In many cases, the women of the family prepared the dead, readying the corpse for burial or collecting the remains after the cremation. These women would have been in a unique position to facilitate the deposition of a magical object.[67]

Contemporary deposition of the tablet and the deceased may have resulted from a variety of causes, and different communities may have had diverse societal mores regarding magic and the use of the dead. Although local variation may have existed for this practice, some overarching patterns for deposition emerge based on the inscriptions preserved on the tablets or the circumstances of the find. Determining the precise findspot of the tablet often is difficult, since early excavations may indicate that a tablet was discovered in a grave but not provide details beyond this basic provenance. Most tablets provide limited information about the source of the dispute, but some inscriptions suggest that a personal affront or plea for justice was the cause for employing magic and burying the tablet in contact with the dead individual.

Many of the curse tablets deposited with the dead only include lists of names. This brevity is typical of early *defixiones,* and those found in association with burials, like the Empúries tablets, show little variation from others in the corpus. The victims likely were the commissioner's opponents in a judicial case, although this is an assumption that often is based on the absence of other stated causes. The two tablets discovered in the Kerameikos in the hands of the corpse, for example, list only names. A lead statuette of a bound man, interred

---

66. Voutiras, *Διονυσοφῶντος γάμοι. Marital life and magic in fourth century Pella,* 18–19.

67. C. A. Faraone, "Evidence for a special female form of binding incantation?" (paper, American Philological Association Annual Meeting, San Antonio, TX, January 6–9, 2011). The dead individual may have been a criminal, or lacked family, but such corpses seldom would have received proper burial rites. See V. M. Hope, "Contempt and respect: The treatment of the corpse in ancient Rome," in *Death and disease in the ancient city,* ed. V. M. Hope and E. Marshall (New York: Routledge, 2000), 110–12, 116–20; J. Bodel, "Dealing with the dead: Undertakers, executioners and potter's fields in ancient Rome," in *Death and disease in the ancient city,* ed. V. M. Hope and E. Marshall (New York: Routledge, 2000), 128–35.

Three Curses from Empúries and Their Social Implications 243

within a coffin made of curse tablets, was also found within the Kerameikos, discovered on top of the pelvis of an adult skeleton. This object was created in the context of a court case but gives no further insight into the subject of the proceedings.[68] A tablet with unintelligible scratches and another that lists the names of enemies were each discovered in late fourth- or early third-century BCE graves at Akanthos in Thrace; the latter was discovered beneath the hand of the deceased.[69] Tablets listing names also were found at Gela, Akragas, and Messana on Sicily.[70]

When curse tablets provide additional information concerning the events that triggered a magical response, the incantation often is portrayed as a desire for just treatment or fair recompense. In the tablet from Pella, translated above, an erotic curse has been framed as if it were a prayer for justice. In the mind of Phila, the commissioner, she had been maltreated by Thetima, and the gods should see to righting this wrong.[71] The address to Macron suggests that the commissioner or practitioner knew Macron and is asking for his help; because he is dead, he is in a unique position to aid Phila (?).

---

68. *SGD* no. 9; See above, ch. 2 n. 78, for bibliography. Compare the other figurines, also placed in lead coffins, and discovered nearby: *VD* no. 6 = *NGD* nos. 11–13; Constabile, "Καταδεσμοι," 97–101.

69. *NGD* no. 42 = Trakosopoulou-Salakidou 2 = Thessaloniki Museum I.161.236ab/1989; Context: E. Trakosopoulou-Salakidou, "Κατάδεσμος από την Άκανθο," in *Γλώσσα και μαγεία. Κείμενα από την Αρχαιότητα*, ed. D. R. Jordan and A. P. Christidis (Athens: Hermes, 1997), 155. *NGD* no. 43 = Trakosopoulou-Salakidou 3 = Thessaloniki Museum I.166.22/1986. Context: Trakosopoulou-Salakidou, "Κατάδεσμοι από την Άκανθο," 158–59.

70. Gela, beneath the skeleton: *SGD* no. 90; P. Orsi, "Gela. Scavi del 1900–1905: Le necropoli del secolo V," *MonAL* 17 (1906): 472–74, fig. 336, with archaeological context shown at fig. 337; Jeffery, "Further comments on archaic Greek inscriptions," no. 13. M. Guarducci, "Nuove note di epigrafia siceliota arcaica," *Annuario della Scuola Archeologica di Atene e delle Missioni Italiane in Oriente* 21–22 (1959–60); L. H. Jeffery, *The local scripts of archaic Greece: A study of the origin of the Greek alphabet and its development from the eight to the fifth centuries B.C.*, (Oxford: Clarendon Press, 1961), 278, no. 57; M. d. A. López Jimeno, *Las tabellae defixionis de la Sicilia griega* (Amsterdam: A. M. Hakkert, 1991), 16. Names, written in the nominative and spelled backward, can be identified in the text, but the largely incomprehensible inscription provides little insight into the purpose of the curse, although it was probably a judicial imprecation. Akragas: *SGD* no. 93; M. Pandolfini, "Lamina di piombo da Agrigento (?)" *ArchClass* 27 (1975); F. Crevatin, "Alcune osservazioni linguistiche sulla lamina di piombo da Agrigento (?)," *ArchClass* 27 (1975); López Jimeno, *Las tabellae defixionis de la Sicilia griega*, no. 6. Archaeological context: Pandolfini, "Lamina di piombo da Agrigento (?)" 46 ; Messana: P. Orsi, "Messana: La necropoli romana di S. Placido e di altre scoperte avvenute nel 1910–1915," *MonAL* 24 (1916): 153–60; *SGD* no. 112, 113; López Jimeno, *Las tabellae defixionis de la Sicilia griega*, 29, 40.

71. Voutiras, *Διονυσοφῶντος γάμοι. Marital life and magic in fourth century Pella*, 37–48; Versnel, "Prayers for justice, east and west," 317–18.

244   Materia Magica

A similar pattern may be detected in other burials. At the site of Oropos, a tablet was excavated in Grave 4 above the skull of the deceased and was likely placed there during the burial.[72] The text enrolls a variety of individuals with the gods Hades and Mounogenes (Persephone), asking that the divinities bind the victims' tongues, bed, and actions, and bring the victims death and misery. Following this litany of requests, the commissioner states: "I demand that my request be heard, because I have been wronged. . . . having been wronged, and not having wronged first, I demand that what I have written down and deposited to you be accomplished."[73] As part of the curse, the commissioner of the tablet appends legal language both to suggest his innocence and to frame the conflict as one that requires divine justice.[74] A tablet from Verona, discovered within a tomb made of roof tiles, lists three names and then the phrase *Vindictam de illis fas. Vindictam,* a request for vengeance, which suggests that this may be an appeal for justice.[75]

Other tablets recovered from tombs iterate the various body parts of the victim of the spell, singling each one out for torture or punishment. At the site of Mintiurae, *DT* 190 was discovered in a tomb made from roof tiles, positioned beneath the head of the deceased individual.[76] The tablet condemns an individual named Tychene, the wife or servant of Carisus, and all of her body parts to the infernal spirits. At the close of the text, the commissioner addresses the gods: "Infernal gods, if I see her wasting away, I shall gladly make a sacrifice . . ."[77] This promise of a reciprocal gift may suggest that the commissioner believed that he or she was justified in the curse. Versnel has referred to these as anatomical curses, suggesting that they reflect a desire for retribution for some past ill that the commissioner has suffered.[78]

There are other examples of tablets contemporaneously deposited with the

---

72. *NGD* no. 23. V. C. Petrakos, *Οι επιγραφές του Ωρωπού* (Athens: Archaeologika Hetaireia, 1997) 477–79, no. 745a; Archaeological context: A. Onasoglou, "Σκάλα Ωρωπού Οδὸς 28ης Οκτωβρίου 7 (οικόπεδο Ελ. Καλογεράκη Αργ. Στρίφα)," *Archaiologikon Deltion* 44, no. B.1 (1989), 77.

73. A. Chaniotis and J. Mylonopoulos, "Epigraphic bulletin for Greek religion 1997," *Kernos* 13 (2000): 207–8, no. 296.

74. Chaniotis, "Under the watchful eyes of the gods," 8. Versnel, "Prayers for justice, east and west," 316–17.

75. A. Buonopane, "Una defixionis tabella da Verona," in *EPIGRAPHAI: Miscellanea epigraphica in onore di Lidio Gasperini,* ed. G. Paci (Tivoli [Rome]: Editrice Tipigraf, 2000), 168.

76. *DTA* praef. 27 = *DT* no. 190; H. Solin, M. Kajava, and K. Korhonen, *Analecta epigraphica 1970–1997* (Rome: Institutum Romanum Finlandiae, 1998), 291.

77. Trans. Versnel, "An essay on anatomical curses," 227.

78. Ibid., 223–40; Versnel, "Prayers for justice, east and west," 280–81.

Three Curses from Empúries and Their Social Implications 245

dead that do not fit this pattern. A curse written on a ceramic vessel discovered in a cemetery of the Roman period at Augustum Trevirorum, dated by associated coins to the Antonine period, preserves a binding spell, perhaps with an erotic purpose.[79] The inscription on the exterior of the vessel must have been completed prior to the burial of the urn; the curse cannot be a later addition to the grave. Interpreting the text, however, poses some problems. The alphabet, with letters facing backward, was inscribed on the neck of the vase; the text on the vessel appears to bind the limbs, or perhaps the sexual organ, of an individual named Dercomognus. Although Kropp has identified this tablet as a love spell, reading *artus* (line 1) as a plural accusative (limbs) may imply a specific desire to restrain the target from doing something, or to punish him.[80] At the site of Crucinacum (modern Kreuznach), excavation uncovered a glass cinerary urn that included the ashes of the deceased and three separate lead tablets.[81] Two of these texts, *DT* 101 and *DT* 102, are likely related to judicial cases, while *DT* 100 may relate to some form of competition or amorous pursuit.[82] We cannot know the precise circumstances that led to the deposition of these tablets, but the desire for retribution or a personal crisis may have prompted some individuals to employ a dead family member or acquaintance to carry out a curse.

Cursing through the dead may not have been viewed as an asocial behavior in all situations. Rather, personal circumstances may have encouraged the living to allow their deceased family members to be employed as messengers or as the agents of the practitioner. A comparable public response to magical practice may be seen in the legitimacy afforded to prayers for justice, particularly those that were placed within temples and visible to priests and other functionaries, which would not have incurred the same approbation as traditional aggressive curses.[83] Indeed, the claims of mistreatment apparent in some

---

79. *DT* no. 103; H. Lehner, "105. Trier [Thongefäss mit Graffito]," *Westdeutsche zeitschrift für geschichte und kunst: Korrespondenzblatt* (1893). The original description of the find does not specify that cremated remains were discovered within, but the presence of coins in the vessel, a common grave good, makes this likely.

80. *LF* 4.1.2/1. Gering argues against viewing *artus* as the male organ. H. Gering, "Artus fututor," *Hermes* 51, no. 4 (1916).

81. J. Klein, "Drei Römische Bleitäfelchen," in *Festschrift zum fünfzigjährigen Jubiläum des Vereins von Alterthumsfreunden im Rheinlande* (Bonn: A. Marcus, 1891) (non vidi); *DTA* pp. 28–29 = *DT* nos. 100–102.

82. *DT* no. 153.

83. Versnel, "Prayers for justice, east and west," 331. Versnel has identified prayers for justice in other depositional contexts beyond placing the artifact in a temple, including within a tomb,

of the tablets may reflect belief of the commissioner that he or she was justified in cursing the target. Kin, friends, or associates may have facilitated the deposition of a tablet in the grave of a relative because of agreement with the sentiments expressed in the execration, or because they themselves had commissioned the ritual.

The Inscriptions and Resistance to Roman Rule

The three Empúries tablets target the members of the administration—the procurator and the legates, as well as their legal representatives—for binding as part of a court case. The magistrates at Empúries had been posted to the province or appointed from the local elite in order to oversee the governance of the region. A magical attack against these persons situates the commissioner in a dispute with the Roman imperial machine, albeit one undertaken in secrecy, and likely without the knowledge of the putative victims. Family members, if they knew the contents of the tablets (which were not rolled up), also may be implicated in this ritual act. This may suggest sympathy with the commissioners who had been wronged by the targets of the tablets, or approval of the sentiments expressed in the execrations. As the tablets list only the names of the victims, it is likely that the rites surrounding the deposition included spoken spells that provided instructions for the dead or enumerated the grievances against the targets. While we cannot access such speech, if it occurred, other participants in the funeral would have heard the spoken curses.

The commissioners were not involved in an armed insurrection against the Roman authorities, but the act of cursing local administrators should be viewed as resistance to imperial control. A similar undercurrent of resistance was detected at Amathous, on Cyprus, where a commissioner targeted the governor of the island. It is productive to situate the three Ballesta tablets among other curses that are directed against administrators or representatives of the government. The known corpus of such documents is relatively small, perhaps due to the dangers associated with rebellion. Most often, curse tablets responded to private conflicts between individuals, but one of the two parties within the conflict may have been in a position of power. Magic can become a means to address this power differential, especially when the aggrieved party

---

although it must be admitted that he finds this unusual. "An essay on anatomical curses," 243. See discussion above, ch. 4 pp. 207–9.

Three Curses from Empúries and Their Social Implications 247

believes that they have no other recourse. An initial conflict with a single individual may swiftly escalate, moving from an attack targeting the local representative of imperial power up the chain of command. This may be due to the commissioner's identification of the target with the ruling regime, from whom local authority derives; in addition to taking aim at the individual, the commissioner may also pursue their superiors. Moreover, the conflict that gave rise to the production of the tablet may be associated in the mind of the commissioner with the dominance of colonial oppression. The single incident may stand for, or encompass, greater dissatisfaction with imperial rule, including anxiety over colonial control of local resources and power structures.

An escalating chain of resistance can be seen in a fourth-century BCE tablet discovered in a well outside of the Dipylon Gate in Athens. Much like the *defixiones* from Empúries, the lead tablet lists a series of names, but it specifically targets a variety of known historical figures, including Cassander, the successor of Alexander the Great who ruled Macedonia from 319 to 297, Pleistarchos, Cassander's younger brother and sometime leader of the Macedonian forces, Eupolemus, the general in charge of Cassander's forces in Greece, and Demetrius of Phalerum, who was the governor of Athens.[84] It is not completely clear how the tablet would have benefited the commissioner, although he or she was likely involved in a court case with one of the targets. The curse likely reflects broader frustration with Macedonian rule over Athens, as it not only attacks individuals who would have been present in the city but also moves to their superiors, the contemporary ruler of Greece, as well as his military commanders. Broad-based Athenian displeasure with the rule of Cassander is confirmed by the jubilant welcome given to Demetrios Poliorcetes and Antigonos when they freed Athens in 307 BCE.[85] We may be able to read larger implications into the tablet and its deposition, as the purview of the tablet could have extended beyond its immediate judicial goals. Jordan suggests that the tablet was not deposited initially in the well but was later dumped in this location; it is highly probable that it had been buried in one of the many tombs outside of the Dipylon gate.[86] While burials were always located outside of the city

---

84. *SGD* no. 14 = SEG 30. 325.2 = *CT* no. 57; Jordan, "Two inscribed lead tablets from a well in the Athenian Kerameikos." Readings in Braun, "Der Dipylon-Brunnen B1, Die Funde," 197–98, with revisions in Jordan, "Two inscribed lead tablets from a well in the Athenian Kerameikos," 230.

85. Plutarch *Dem.* 10–11; Jordan, "Two inscribed lead tablets from a well in the Athenian Kerameikos," 234.

86. Ibid., 233.

walls, the Dipylon gate marked one of the main thoroughfares into the city, the entry point through which land forces would have traveled. The tablet also may have been intended to disrupt any future military deployment into the city. Its placement recalls the deposition of potions intended to prevent the entrance of the abbot Shenoute along the road leading into the village of Plewit, discussed above in chapter 1.

In another curse, discovered outside of the walls of Rome, the commissioner targets a Roman physician named Artemidoros, assigned to the Third Praetorian Cohort.[87] The tablet was discovered accidentally near the Porta Ardeatina.[88] Demetrius, the brother of the commissioner of the tablet, had died. Following Demetrius' death, the commissioner, who is not named, wished to return to his own country, but the physician for whom he worked would not allow it. The tablet asks the spirits to "restrain the land of Italy and strike the gates of Rome, and also restrain Artemidoros the physician."[89] In response to a personal conflict, the commissioner directed his curse not only against the individual whom he views as prohibiting his return but also against the city of Rome and Italy, personifications of the geography that held him hostage. Echoing the Roman tendency to imagine places as divine personages, the commissioner confers agency on both Italy and the gates of the city. Effectively, Rome and Italy symbolize the imperial power to which the surgeon is responsible, an authority that prohibits the commissioner from returning to his own country. Here, too, the position of the tablet is important to the efficacy of the rite, as the practitioner deposited it in close proximity to the target of the spell, the city itself.

Deposition of the Ballesta tablets was a semipublic act, likely carried out in the company of witnesses. By allowing the tablets to be placed within the funerary urns, those present at the burial either instigated their creation or allowed the commissioner access to the funerary enclosure. Hidden from the Roman authorities who were cursed in the tablets, this act of ritual aggression united the participants in the funeral within a rite designed to undermine Roman rule in the local community. Moreover, the anonymity provided by the curses, which do not name the commissioner, may have provided those

---

87. *SGD* no. 129 = SEG 14.615 = *CT* no. 79; M. Guarducci, "L'Italia e Roma in una tabella defixionis greca recentemente scoperta," *BCAR* 74 (1951–52).

88. Ibid., 57. Other tablets are known from the necropolis, but these likely derive from different tombs.

89. Trans., *CT*, pp. 171–72.

Three Curses from Empúries and Their Social Implications 249

undertaking the rite with a measure of confidence when opposing the ruling regime.[90] Many of the participants, including those who collected the remains or heard a spell that was spoken in conjunction with the deposition, were well aware of what was going on.

The rite reinterpreted the cemetery outside of the city as a space in which resistance could be enacted. Separated from the administrative center of Roman power within the town, the burial area was marked off from the urban environment by the city wall. The Ballesta necropolis was located to the west of the city but was one of the cemeteries closest to the urban core. As was the case with the tablets from the Dipylon Gate and Rome, this placement may have been significant, since the burial space lay near to the putative targets of the spell, the Roman administrators. While the tablets were likely composed in response to a specific court case, the desires that they express—that the Roman administrators would be bound or somehow incapacitated—is not temporally limited. The curse would continue to affect the provincial leaders. In effect, the tablets were hidden in view, able to operate against the targets of the spell, which lay within the city wall, but protected through the secrecy of the deposit.[91]

Although the commissioner may not have believed that he or she was engaged in resistance to Roman rule, it is likely that the authorities would view such a foray with suspicion. An inscription from Tuder, in central Italy, demonstrates the Roman response to ritual attacks against the state or local administrators.[92] The inscription reads

> For salvation of the colony of Tuder, both of its city council and of its people, to Jupiter Optimus Maximus, Guardian, Keeper, because he by his own divine power has removed and vindicated the councillor's names attached to monuments by the unutterable crime of the public slave and has freed colony and citizens from fear of perils, L. Cancrius, Freedman of Clemens Primigenius, member of the six-priest colleges both of Augustus and of the Flavians first of all to be given these honors by the council has fulfilled his vow.[93]

---

90. On resistance, see Scott, *Domination and the arts of resistance: Hidden transcripts,* 4, 124, 144.

91. Ruppel et al., "Hidden in view: African spiritual spaces in North American landscapes," 324–25.

92. For an alternative interpretation of this tablet, see Marco Simón, "Execrating the Roman power: Three *defixiones* from Emporiae (Ampurias)," 414–16.

93. Trans., *CT* pp. 245–46.

The inscription records the discovery of a curse or a series of curses that targeted municipal leaders; the curses had been placed on or inside of tombs. As occurred at Empúries, the tombs outside of the city walls had been reinterpreted as a locus for insurrection.[94] The subsequent events, including the erection of a thank offering, imply that a magical crisis had been averted, although the assistance of Jupiter was necessary to locate the objects and reveal the perpetrator.[95]

A number of features in the inscription are relevant to our interpretation of the tablets from Empúries. The commemorative document insists that the god had freed the entire town, both the administrators and the townspeople, from the "fear of perils," presumably the act of magical binding. When the inscriptions were discovered and removed, this mitigated the threat. A magical attack aimed at local administrators was viewed as a danger to the municipality as a whole. In the text, local administrators—who are not named—are important to the colony because of their positions, as they embodied the government. The *defixiones* may have named each of the targets individually, as the inscription notes that multiple tablets were employed, and objects were discovered at more than a single monument, or tomb: *monumentis* is plural.[96] Alternatively, the situation may have been comparable to that at Empúries, where multiple tablets each cursed multiple targets, increasing the efficacy of the spell through repetition. Binding the councilors was viewed as a public outrage, as it threatened to upend the order embodied in the municipal leaders.

The deposition of curses has been blamed on an unnamed, and perhaps unknown, public slave. This accusation may have been correct, rather than targeting a convenient scapegoat. The absence of a name could be tied to a

---

94. The term *defixa* may mean merely "to attach," and *monumentis* could refer generally to monuments rather than tombs. Some scholars have suggested that this would imply a public display, rather than a private act of malicious magic. Luck, *Arcana mundi: Magic and the occult in the Greek and Roman worlds: A collection of ancient texts,* 90–91; *CT* p. 245; Versnel, "Beyond cursing," 63; J. M. Serrano Delgado, "Sceleratissimus seruus publicus: un episodio de la vida municipal afectando a la familia pública," in *Homenaje a José María Blázquez,* ed. J. Mangas and J. Alvar (Madrid, 1996), 333–38; Marco Simón, "Execrating the Roman power: Three *defixiones* from Emporiae (Ampurias)," 414–16. As we encountered with the Gemellus incident discussed in chapter 3, enactment in public does not preclude the possibility that a particular event is viewed as magic.

95. Marco Simón, "Execrating the Roman power: Three *defixiones* from Emporiae (Ampurias)," 416 n. 54 notes that the verb, *eruit,* likely refers to removal by digging something up, implying that the tablets had been buried beneath or within the tombs, and perhaps that the rite was hidden.

96. Serrano Delgado, "Sceleratissimus seruus publicus: un episodio de la vida municipal afectando a la familia pública," 333.

Three Curses from Empúries and Their Social Implications 251

desire to have him or her remain nameless, much as the *damnatio memoriae* effaced the names of disgraced or hated officials. A slave was largely powerless in society, but magic provided a means by which he or she could have sought redress from his or her opponents. Indeed, magical binding was viewed as a powerful force, and the inscription of Tuder suggests that only Jupiter was able to defend the town and disarm the curses. Like their counterparts at Tuder, the Ballesta tablets were concealed and therefore embodied a potent threat against the imperial regime, even though they targeted certain administrators only. Magic may have been an appropriate response for the disempowered as they faced the overwhelming force of Roman imperial rule.

The Ballesta tablets provide no concrete evidence about the occupants of the tombs in which they were interred. Unlike the curse preserved from Pella, the deceased are not addressed by name, nor is there any mention of divinities or other powers to which the inscriptions appealed. As we have noted, the contemporaneous deposition of curse tablets with the dead as part of burial was an unusual—but not unattested—occurrence. When tablets are deposited with the dead, the inscriptions often allude to a personal affront or crisis for which the assistance of the deceased is needed. Each of the three Ballesta tablets was deposited in a separate cinerary urn that corresponds to a distinct burial, and all three of these repositories were buried at the same time. No scientific analysis was conducted on the human remains discovered in the urns, so it is not possible to determine if they were young or old, male or female. It does seem likely that the dead individuals were related, as they are all buried within a single funerary enclosure and associated with a family group that was roughly contemporary. Indeed, members of the family group may have been responsible for interring these three individuals within the enclosure. This event—the death of three individuals—may be part of a crisis that precipitated the trial or the use of magic.

Unexplained, sudden, or untimely death is viewed as a tragedy, and those who are left behind struggle to make sense of their loss. In antiquity, witchcraft or sorcery often was suspected in the death of a loved one, leading the survivors to entreat a supernatural force for retribution against the offending party. Among the known corpus of inscriptions that discuss untimely death, a number of cases list conventional murder through violence as the cause. The culprit, whether known or not, is the subject of the imprecation.[97] A funerary

---

97. F. Graf, "Untimely death, witchcraft and divine vengeance: A reasoned epigraphical catalog," *ZPE* 162 (2007): 143–44. Graf includes a full catalog and discussion.

inscription from the area of Hauran, in southern Syria, states that the deceased had been "slaughtered for nothing" by a local administrator. Below the inscription, the stone has been adorned with a relief depicting a pair of raised hands, iconography that is often found in conjunction with a wish for divine retribution.[98] Graf has suggested that the survivors of the deceased approached the god for vengeance because the murderer could not be brought to trial due to his position in the local government.[99] A similar phenomenon may be at work at Empúries, where individuals responding to a personal tragedy or conflict may have lashed out against the provincial magistrates, employing supernatural force when traditional means of resistance were impossible or futile.

Regardless of the precise circumstances that surrounded the deaths of the three individuals or the complaint underlying the creation of the three tablets, the Ballesta material prompts us to reconsider how, when, and where magic might be considered an appropriate social response. By interring the tablets with the dead, and doing so as part of the burial, ritual performance moves into the public sphere, even if the public only consists of those who were present at the inhumation. As we witnessed with the forceful casting of the *brephos* at Karanis and in the display of the selenite tablets in the shaft at Amathous, magical practice was not inherently private or hidden. The success of a given rite might depend on a degree of communal knowledge that a rite has been enacted. Although performed in secret, gossip or casual conversation could have alerted a target to the fact that magic had been enacted, leading to the resolution of a problem or to satisfaction among those undertaking a curse that something had been done.

The Ballesta tablets suggest that participants might engage in a potentially illegal or dangerous ritual in situations in which they felt such activity was justified. Scholars have frequently drawn a distinction between traditional curses and prayers for justice, in which the commissioner seeks recompense for a perceived wrong. The concept of justice, however, is far from universal and is often based on personal perception. A number of the tablets that were interred with human remains assert that the commissioner had been wronged in some way. In such cases, deposition with the corpse may have been viewed as legitimate and therefore socially acceptable. Our evidence for how ancient individuals viewed the utilization of the dead is neither comprehensive nor

---

98. SEG VII.1239.
99. Graf, "Untimely death, witchcraft and divine vengeance: A reasoned epigraphical catalog," 143, 146.

indisputable. Providing gifts to the dead or entering into some form of mutually advantageous agreement may have encouraged the deceased to perform a task for the living. Much as offerings may have averted the anger of the dead, curse tablets may have been an acceptable way to put the aggression of the deceased to good use. Indeed, the dead may have had a personal interest in carrying out the curse that was deposited within the grave.

Evaluation of the archaeological context of the three tablets from Empúries alters our understanding of the social landscape in surprising ways. While the inscribed text reveals an act of resistance against the provincial magistrates, the findspot encourages us to consider those who inscribed the tablets, revealing that the commissioners likely knew the dead individuals, and indeed, that their deaths may have been part of the larger story surrounding the use of magic at the site. For the Ballesta cremations, contemporaneous burial of tablets with the dead likely was a public or semi-public enactment aimed at redressing a perceived wrong.

In the first chapter, I noted that while scholars have suggested magical practice was pervasive in antiquity, the physical evidence attesting to the performance of magic is seldom discovered through excavation. In addition to the loss of material evidence through decay, or the lack of a material component to certain magical rites, the physical remains of magic may be underrepresented because of insufficient analysis of the archaeological data. As has been argued throughout this book, the close analysis of archaeological context and local environment can hint at how and when magic was used. While this material cannot always permit definitive conclusions, archaeological data can nuance global readings of magical practice by urging us to delineate local rites and individual responses to crisis. In the final, concluding chapter, we will move outward from the three case studies at Empúries, Amathous, and Karanis to consider a number of overarching questions related to the practice of magic in the Mediterranean. Furthermore, the conclusion offers an opportunity to critique the method that has been employed in these pages and to consider how best to improve our chances of finding magic within archaeological data.

Chapter 6

The Archaeology of Magic

The archaeological evidence of magical practice at three sites in the Roman Mediterranean—Karanis, Amathous, and Empúries—reveals the rich complexity and wide distribution of ritual activity. The case studies investigated in these pages offer vignettes situated in particular times and places, permitting us to characterize some of the features of the phenomenon at each settlement. It is clear from both the literary and archaeological record that magic, as we have defined the phenomenon, could take multiple forms and serve multiple purposes. Ritual practices may employ figurines in specific poses, lead tablets that have been inscribed with names, or household implements; these may be used to harm an enemy, avenge an injustice, protect the bearer of an object, or guard against the intrusion of vermin into a storeroom. In each local community, the analysis of written evidence and comparative material suggest the forms that magic may take.

Egypt's environment has preserved abundant papyrological resources and a wealth of artifacts that can be deployed to identify the material residue of magical acts in the archaeological record. The magical papyri, which detail ritual practices in the Late Antique period, suggest a framework within which magic could be recovered, even when inscribed text or other formal indicators of magic are absent. Once artifacts have been identified as magical, attention turned to the analysis of archaeological context and deposition. These data allow us to suggest the ritual processes that produced the artifacts as well as the effects that the objects were believed to have in the world. In the case of the roughly made figurine of the woman, for example, comparison with textual sources suggested that this object was used for erotic magic. These same sources were then studied alongside the doll, which had been burned and pierced, and the findspot, the accessible basement of a house. These data suggested that the rite of burning and piercing was meant to compel the love of the target; the deposition of the figurine was intended to draw the victim to the commissioner, who lived above.

Outside of Egypt, we lack data comparable to the PGM and PDM, but the methods that we developed for identifying and analyzing the Egyptian material are transportable to other regions and settlements. In these locales, objects may declare their use as components of ritual activity through an inscription. The physical form of the artifact and its archaeological context can provide vital information for reconstructing the function of magic in its local environment. At Amathous, this analysis provided insight into the production of magic. We suggested that multiple practitioners were at work at the site, all of whom shared a formulary and used the same space for the deposition of tablets. These individuals may have been associated with a temple or other religious community. The tablets were employed as a response to perceived injustices and were displayed in a shaft, even though they were not visible to other residents. Archaeological context at Empúries likewise pointed to the enactment of a ritual and suggested that the curse tablets were deposited as part of the burial of the dead. A close reading of the three cremations that contained the tablets suggests that magic was used as a means of resistance against imperial rule and that the deaths of the three individuals may have been tied to the use of magic. In each town or village, the investigation of archaeological data also suggested some of the problems that are encountered when dealing with material evidence. At this point, it is useful to return to the issues of method with which this book began.

A Critique of the Method

Chapter 1 outlined a method through which magical practice could be identified and interpreted within the archaeological record. An artifact may hold important information about its use in ritual, data that can be revealed through a consideration of the life history of the object. Moving outward from the individual object, the methodology stressed the importance of the close analysis of archaeological context, the interlocking spatial and temporal frames within which excavators unearth artifacts that can be associated with one another. Certain spaces—particularly areas associated with a victim, or liminal areas such as the grave or a crossroads—were significant in the ritual consumption

256   Materia Magica

of magical artifacts. Considered in relation to their findspot, assemblages might be able to reveal the processes of ritual deposition. By closely investigating material remains and archaeological context, it may be possible to reconstruct a sequence of ritual events and situate magic within its social environment.

It should be noted at the outset that many of the critiques that can be articulated for the archaeological study of magic hold true for archaeology as a whole. Any investigation of material remains must address differing interpretations of mute data, as well as the problem of equifinality, where multiple processes may give rise to identical objects or assemblages.

The study of local forms of magic in antiquity must struggle constantly with the tension between our expectations of what magic should look like and the reality of magical practice in a specific community or village, which could be vastly different. Because of our temporal and cultural distances from the past, this reality is difficult if not impossible to recover. We lack the direct testimony that is the cornerstone of cultural anthropology and must rely on the inferences drawn from literature and material culture. Scholars have developed a picture of ancient practice that is grounded in the shared traits of the phenomenon, and magic often may look homogeneous because we can only identify forms of magic that fit our expectations. We can fill out a picture of local magic with reference to comparative material drawn from other, distant areas of the Mediterranean. Moreover, there is a tendency to suppose that the development of magical technologies in two separate areas resulted from the exportation of technology, rather than considering that local individuals may have invented or developed rites independently.

When we stray beyond the accepted corpora of magical items—curse tablets and gems, for example—we typically identify magic on the basis of our own assessment that an object or assemblage is weird or unusual. Reliance on Malinowski's "coefficient of weirdness" is a necessary evil.[1] Strangeness provides an initial hint that an object or group of objects may have been used for ritual purposes, and we assume that an artifact that we find unusual would have been viewed similarly by an individual in antiquity. But "weirdness" may be a product of our own distance from the events that we are attempting to reconstruct, and we must take care to test our interpretations of the material within its local context. In analyzing material from Egypt, the spell instructions can provide a rich body of comparative evidence, listing materials that were used

---

1. On Malinowski's "coefficient of weirdness," see above, ch. 1 n. 1.

in rites and how they were manipulated. By focusing on textual sources that can be associated with the region under study (in the case of the Fayum, for example, PGM XXXVI), we can minimize the potential for misidentification.[2]

If we do find magical artifacts that appear to vary from other examples, it may not be possible to determine whether this variation is restricted to this item and its specific circumstances of production, indicative of local practice, or part of a larger phenomenon. The burial of the Empúries tablets with the dead, for example, could be an isolated incident dependent on specific circumstances, or it may suggest local beliefs about the dead. Further investigation reveals that contemporaneous burial of tablets and the dead occurred in many areas of the empire, and ranges from the Greek period in Athens well into the High Empire. Given the extent of the phenomenon, we must consider whether this indicates a Mediterranean-wide practice that involved contemporaneous burial of tablets with the dead, or whether local individuals or practitioners responded to personal or family crises in similar ways.

The problems of delineating local traditions and identifying otherwise unattested forms of magic are compounded by the existence of material that lacks sufficient provenance or, worse, has been assigned false provenance by the antiquities market. The number of artifacts that are "said to be" from a given location may equal those that were discovered in controlled excavation. The absence of contextual information severely constrains an artifact's potential to tell us about the people who created it (where did they live?) or an object's ritual function (how was it deposited?). Hints within an inscribed text may suggest that an artifact has come from a specific place. An invocation to the ghost of Antioüs in the text of the curse tablet from the Louvre assemblage (plate 5) has led scholars to suggest a provenience of Antinoopolis. This is thin proof, and at times, internal references may be misleading. At Amathous, the invocation in the text to the numerous dead who "lie here" does not indicate that the tablets were deposited in a mass grave. Human bones were discovered above the tablets, but this suggests that the addition of corpses was a later event. Many of the larger questions related to the societal place of magic or the identities of the practitioners are impossible in the absence of true archaeological context.

Throughout this book, our attempts to interpret material culture have been

---

2. Even so, contexts may appear magical at first but, on further consideration and investigation of the material, are revealed to be mundane or a random accretion of occupation debris. For a discussion of some of these contexts, see Wilburn, "Materia magica: The archaeology of magic in Roman Egypt, Cyprus, and Spain," 83–87, 90–92.

258   Materia Magica

paralleled by struggles to make sense of the excavation records. The problem of insufficient or tantalizingly incomplete data about findspots and archaeological context presents the most substantial challenge to archaeological investigations. On Cyprus, the archaeological context of the tablets has been reconstructed from the account of Capt. Handcock, who acquired the cache for the British Museum. Handcock's statements, in turn, are based on the claims made by the local residents who found the tablets. This chain of informants can lead us to question whether the evidence is trustworthy or to discount some elements of the purported context. Aupert and Jordan, for example, suggested that the locals provided an inaccurate account of the depth of the shaft in order to discourage others from making a similar find. We cannot locate the shaft from whence the artifacts came, or determine where the deposit was discovered between Agios Tychonas and the ancient city center. But other evidence can help us fill in the picture and reconstruct information about the archaeological context. The presence of suspension holes on one of the selenite tablets supports Handcock's account of the find, and the tablets, considered as part of a larger cache, can help us to better understand ritual production at the site.

We are confronted with different yet equally challenging problems with the material from Karanis. Although the site was excavated in the 1920s using techniques that were scientific by contemporary standards, modern investigators have advanced far beyond these early methods. The excavators recorded finds by room, and assigned levels without regard to soil stratigraphy. This complicates attempts not only to date material from the site but also to determine which artifacts should be associated and whether a given deposit was the result of intentional actions or the accumulation of debris over time. While modern excavation carefully analyzes changes in the soil to identify a pit, or to separate different layers of occupation, all of this material might be jumbled together in the Karanis excavation diaries. Therefore, it is difficult to be certain that our reading of the excavation records is accurate, and more information about findspots and context would significantly improve our readings of the material.

The material from Karanis also is compromised by problems of absent data. Artifacts may have been left in the field and not photographed, drawn, or measured. Often, we must reconstruct part of an archaeological context based on other examples of finds rather than the artifacts that were originally discovered in a room. In the analysis of the roughly made mud figurine, only one of the three pins was retained, and it was necessary to assume that the other two pins were similar to the example that was kept.

The Archaeology of Magic 259

When an archaeological context is problematic or incomplete, it raises questions about the validity of the analysis. These are not insurmountable problems, but neither are they restricted to research on magic or the analysis of early excavations. Indeed, the study of antiquity is plagued by similar difficulties: decades for which we possess little historical data, absent or lost texts for which we know only authors or titles of works, and sources that are untrustworthy or constantly leave out the most interesting parts of the narrative. Put into perspective, the limitations of our data are endemic to the field, and the solution involves an awareness of evidential constraints as well as honesty in the presentation of data.

Great care must be taken when investigating the material remains. The scholar should take into account fully the potential shortcomings of the excavation record and consider alternative interpretations of the data, particularly the problems raised by equifinality. Presenting the full context of an excavation unit under study as part of a publication, and including references to associated finds and museum accession numbers, allow other scholars to draw their own conclusions. Moreover, a thorough analysis of the process by which material entered the soil—its deposition—can help to elucidate whether an assemblage of artifacts represents the residue of ritual activity or mere occupation debris.

The three sites investigated in this book demonstrate the importance of archaeological context to fully understanding the place of magic within a specific locality. Moreover, archaeological data can dramatically alter our understanding of magical objects by isolating previously unrecognized examples of the phenomenon and reconstructing the ritual processes that led to the creation and deposition of the material. The questions raised by this assessment of the method are not meant to undermine the conclusions that have been drawn within the pages of this work. Rather, this critique points to the potential to use archaeology to locate and interpret material culture through contemporary excavation techniques, today and in the future. We now have many more tools at our disposal: we can recover seeds and botanical remains through flotation of soil samples, we can accurately define depositional processes through stratigraphy, and we can perform complex analyses of the chemical makeup of artifacts. DNA analysis even could permit us to determine whether the three burials found in conjunction with curse tablets at Empúries were related to one another or to the other individuals in the complex.

Excavators should be aware of the potential for discovering magical objects in locations that had ritual resonance; graves and liminal spaces within the home, such as doorways, are prime suspects for finding magical behavior.

Accurate recording of finds and their contexts is essential for fully understanding the rituals that may have resulted in deposition. These data also are crucial for other scholars wishing to reanalyze excavated material. Maintaining accurate field records, including photographs, drawings, measurements, and textual descriptions is the responsibility of excavators who have been entrusted with recording cultural heritage. After all, archaeology is destruction with good record-keeping, and sites that have been excavated can only be put back together through the accounts kept by excavators. Scholars should be willing to share this information with one another. We often recognize that fieldwork is a collaborative project, but so too is the interpretation of the material that has been uncovered, and the absence of access to finds, assemblages, and findspots sharply curtails what can be done with the evidence. The methods that have been proposed in these pages are not just relevant to the study of magic but can be applied to all forms of ritual behavior. Indeed, the study of materiality opens new vistas for interpretation, significantly expanding our understanding of how to find ritual practice in the soil and interpret what we discover in its local environment.

Local Contexts and the Archaeology of Magic

Our exploration has ranged through multiple cities and villages in the Roman Empire, investigating material from the end of the first through the fourth or fifth centuries CE. This is a broad historical range, which witnessed the expansion of the Roman imperial control and its subsequent transformation into a Christian empire divided between east and west. At each site and in each time period, the material evidence of magic can tell us much about how individuals responded to problems and personal crises. Artifacts can help us look back from the product of a rite to those who manufactured and utilized these objects, allowing us to consider the professional role of the practitioner within the community. The analysis of magical practice through objects urges us to consider the vital role that material culture played in the performance of rites as well as the spread of magical technology. Thinking beyond the material discussed in this book, the completed products of magical acts, such as phylacteries and gemstones, offer an additional avenue for the dissemination of the signifiers of magic and the techniques of magical production.

The Archaeology of Magic 261

Covert Resistance and Public Magic

Ancient individuals turned to magic to solve a variety of commonplace and unusual problems, ranging from fevers and illness to conflict with authority figures. At both Amathous and Empúries, curse tablets were deployed against members of the provincial elite, suggesting that magic could be a valid tool for covert resistance against the state. The decision to employ a ritual specialist to curse local magistrates may have had a cathartic effect, allowing the commissioner to believe that he or she was taking action against a more powerful foe, but doing so without the danger associated with rebellion or revolt. The elusive nature of magic would have made detection difficult, although discovering the existence of a rite, if not the culprit, was possible, as we saw with the inscription from Tuder.

The rationale by which commissioners may have employed magic is a complicated question: did individuals choose to use magic as a response to a crisis for reasons beyond its believed efficacy? In other words, might magic have been selected for resistant acts specifically because its practice was associated with covert behavior or was viewed as antiestablishment? Historical evidence suggests that some forms of aggressive magic may have been illegal as early as the first century CE. Tacitus' account of the death of Germanicus associates cursing with attacks against the state, and by the third century, curse tablets had been grouped with poison and weaponry as punishable methods of murder. Our literary sources suggest that individuals on the borders of society, including women and foreigners, often were responsible for enacting magic. The outsider status accorded to magic and practitioners may have appealed to would-be consumers. Magical practice was subversive, or even countercultural, and in these cases, its performance was aimed at undermining the lawcourts and the local representatives of Rome.

While the use of magic for resistant acts may have played off its outsider status, the material covered in this book urges us to question whether magic was always a private undertaking or even a marginal activity. Gemellus' account of the magical attack that he suffered frames it as a public act of provocation, and the fetus was thrown in plain view of the town elders. At Karanis, the painted bones were concentrated in one area of the site, but we have evidence for their use in other areas, as well. Throughout the Mediterranean, ritual experts, who performed magic for a fee, must have been known to their clients. The material from Amathous indicates that a substantial number of community members engaged the services of these professionals, seeking out the assistance of local practitioners for a wide range of large and small crises. Likewise, at Empúries, it seems likely that some of the individuals responsible for the care of the dead either commissioned or allowed the insertion of the curse tablets. Comparative evidence indicates that concurrent deposition with the dead was not as unusual as we might believe, and our own misgivings about the use of the dead may affect our interpretation of this practice. Magic functioned as a public secret, the existence of which was known to many members of the local population but may not have been acknowledged or discussed.[3] This need not imply, however, that magic was marginal or viewed negatively by other community members.

On the other hand, some individuals, including the victim, would have been unaware of the performance of magic or uncertain of its details. Secrecy may have made the act of magic more powerful, and the removal of the tablet from the world of the living—its consumption—was integral to its effectiveness.[4] Knowing where a curse tablet was buried could permit its removal, and thus, its negation. The power of magic as a tool for social control lay not in its concealment but instead in its partial revelation. Outside of the psychological comfort it might provide to the commissioner, magic's ability to change the behavior of a victim would only be effective if the target were aware that they had been bewitched.[5] The public performance of casting a *brephos* that we witnessed at Karanis attests to the real power of magical action to affect a victim who may immediately recognize the significance of a ritual act. We do not know if Gemellus acceded to the demands of his attackers, but the act of magic was sufficiently shocking that he reported it to the authorities. A later papyrus shows that Gemellus and Julius had reached some form of resolution, since Julius appears as the tenant farmer of Gemellus in a tax receipt. In the end, magical violence may have had a positive result for the aggressor. Other methods of revelation may have contributed to the efficacy of magic in antiquity. Most communities were small, and composed of families who had lived in the same location as their direct ancestors and knew one another. We cannot

---

3. M. Taussig, *Defacement: Public secrecy and the labor of the negative* (Stanford: Stanford University Press, 1999), 50. On public secrecy and magic, see C. Nakamura, "Dedicating magic: Neo-Assyrian apotropaic figurines and the protection of Assur," *World Archaeology* 36, no. 1 (2004).

4. Taussig, *Defacement: Public secrecy and the labor of the negative,* 57–58, 143–45.

5. Versnel, "Writing mortals and reading gods," 69–72.

The Archaeology of Magic   263

discount the potential for the spread of information through informal channels such as gossip. When one deposited a curse or prayer for justice, mentioning this fact to a friend or associate could easily get back to the target of the spell.[6] The shared belief in the efficacy of magical acts as well as the widespread familiarity with the appropriate markers and symbols of practice created an environment in which magic could have effects on the real world.[7]

Practitioners and Practice

The local manifestations of ritual practice that we have identified at Amathous, Empúries, and Karanis also can allow us to move backward from material evidence to the individual or individuals who created and manipulated the artifacts. At Karanis, literate individuals were responsible for two artifacts associated with ritual practice, the inscribed potsherd and the fever amulet. The fever amulet demonstrates mistakes in copying that suggest manufacture through the use of a model, while the ostracon likely preserves an abbreviated version of a spell intended to be used on-site. The practitioner may have been an Egyptian priest, a wandering practitioner for hire, or a ritual specialist who was attached to the nascent Christian community in the village. In any case, this individual had access to a spell text removed from the temple or church, or one that was a private possession. While a practitioner may have been affiliated with a religious institution, it remains unclear whether they were acting in their official role as a priest or performing magical rites on the side, as a supplement to their official duties.

The archive of lead and selenite tablets from Amathous likewise attests to the presence of a group of practitioners who shared similar formulae, likely contained within a spell book, and a single space for ritual deposition. Evidence from nearby Cnidus suggests that ritual specialists affiliated with a temple were responsible for the production of prayers for justice that employed similar formulae; this pattern is also apparent at other sanctuary sites in the Roman world. At the Sanctuary of Isis and Magna Mater at Mainz, the inscriptions preserved on the tablets suggest that the suppliant wrote the tablet; the absence of complex formulae and magical signs argues for an absence of production by professionals, but this may be due to production before these signs

---

6. D. Cohen, *Law, sexuality, and society: The enforcement of morals in classical Athens* (New York: Cambridge University Press, 1991), 48–51.
7. Bailliot, *Magie et sortilèges dans l'Antiquité romaine*, 173–77.

were widely known.[8] The suppliants were surely aided by the priests in the temple, as the majority of the tablets subsequently were deposited in a ritual fire that lay in the back in the sanctuary.[9] At Amathous, as at Cnidus and Mainz, specialists who may have been associated with a temple were responsible for the ritual deposition or display of documents intended to communicate with the divine. The distinction that has been drawn between aggressive curse tablets and prayers for justice may not extend in all cases to either the practitioners, who could have been the same individuals, or the practice, as these individuals may have employed comparable ritual techniques for divergent motives. If the same individuals performed both acceptable forms of ritual as well as disreputable practices, it may be inappropriate to associate magic solely with the margins of society. Rather, the enactment of aggressive as well as beneficial magic may have been part of the fabric of life within a town or village.

Objects and Magical Technology in the Mediterranean

The appearance of a similar invocation at Amathous and at Egyptian Thebes points to the complexity that underlies the exchange of magical knowledge from place to place. The correspondence between the two texts reminds us that the shared vocabulary of magic, including signs, symbols, and divine names, always was received within the local environment and integrated into local traditions.[10] Conventional wisdom has suggested that the second century CE marked the era in which magical practice throughout the Mediterranean began to look surprisingly similar. Identifying these parallels, however, does not explain the means by which such similarities arose. Scholars have posited that magical knowledge may have been spread through the publication and dissemination of spell books or other formularies.[11] Most examples of artifacts that were created with reference to an Egyptian instructional manual, however, derive from Egypt, suggesting that ritual techniques may have circulated within the province, but seldom outside of it.[12] Moreover, individuals may have car-

---

8. Blänsdorf, "The *defixiones* from the Sanctuary of Isis and Mater Magna in Mainz," 163–64.
9. Ibid., 157; Witteyer, "Curse tablets and voodoo dolls from Mainz: The archaeological evidence for magical practices in the Sanctuary of Isis and Magna Mater," 116–23.
10. G. Bohak, *Ancient Jewish magic,* 230.
11. On handbooks, Introduction, n. 4.
12. Brashear, "The Greek Magical Papyri: An introduction and survey; annotated bibliography (1928–1994)," 3417 n. 156 provides a list of these objects; others are cited at Jordan, "Inscribed lead tablets from the games in the sanctuary of Poseidon," 123–25; Jordan, "Magia

The Archaeology of Magic 265

ried magical knowledge with them, as itinerant practitioners plied their trade in the major cities of the empire. Artifacts offer an important means by which magical technology may have been transmitted, as objects were portable and would have allowed both laypersons and professionals access to enacted—and potentially efficacious—forms of magic.

In addition to the formularies that we possess on papyrus from Egypt, we have substantial evidence from Amathous that practitioners were using multiple model-texts for the production of many of the 200 tablets discovered at the site. Comparable use of spell books can also be surmised from tablets in Athens, Isthmia, Rome, Hadrumentum, and Carthage. Handbooks also appear to be a familiar trope in literature. Arignotus, a character in Lucian's *Philopseudes,* claimed possession of Egyptian books of magic that he employed to rid a house in Corinth of a troublesome ghost. Paul, preaching in the city of Ephesus, performed exorcisms in the name of Jesus; the townspeople were so amazed that they burned all of their spell books, worth, according to the author of *Acts,* more than fifty thousand pieces of silver.[13] There is also evidence for elite interest in magic that may have included the acquisition of spell books or instructional texts.[14] It is difficult to separate literary imagination from reality, as some of the tales of spell books may have been the fanciful creations of authors. The character of these spell books, however, is less clear, and it is uncertain what sorts of materials they may have included, for what audience these works were created, and how these books were distributed.

---

nilotica sulle rive del Tevere," 698–700. A *defixio* that is ascribed to Rome, *DT* 188, dated to the fourth century CE, is related closely to *P.Iand.* 87 (PGM LVIII), a papyrus fragment of unknown provenance, and similar words and phrases allowed the editor of the PGM text to fill lacunae by using the curse tablet. D. Jordan has recently questioned the provenance of this artifact, showing that the earliest records relating to its acquisition are unclear about the origin of the *defixio.* Kaibel's initial publication, which attributes the tablet to the Vatican, may be in error. Jordan suggests that the tablet should be associated with acquisitions made from the Douce collection in 1875, for which the provenance is not known; other pieces that came from the Douce collection included a number of magical gems, including some inscribed with the name Abrasax. "Magia nilotica sulle rive del Tevere," 707–9. The tablet could have come as easily from Egypt as from Rome.

13. Lucian, *Philopseudes,* 30–31. Ephesus: Acts of the Apostles 19:19. Cf. Betz, *The Greek magical papyri in translation,* xli; Faraone, *Ancient Greek love magic,* 33. Suetonius (Aug. 31.1) records that Augustus ordered the burning of more than 2,000 books of prophecy (*fatidicorum librorum Graeci Latinique*), and should perhaps be understood in terms of later imperial edicts forbidding prophecy related to the emperor. Pharr, "The interdiction of magic in Roman law," 280.

14. Dickie, "The learned magician and the collection and transmission of magical lore," passim, esp. 182–89.

Books, including copies of short works, would have been expensive to acquire. The majority of the inhabitants of the Roman Empire would have been illiterate or may have possessed only a passing familiarity with letters. We possess numerous copies of certain texts, such as Homer, that were used for education, but our evidence for the private possession of other works of literature is limited.[15] Roger Bagnall recently has demonstrated the prohibitive cost of books for most individuals of moderate means, suggesting that the cost of acquiring a single, unbound Christian gospel on papyrus would have amounted to approximately one-thirtieth of an annual income. Like many other goods that we consider basic necessities, such as clothing, a book would have been an expensive commodity.[16] For those practitioners who were literate, the private possession of a book produced by another individual would have been rare. Individuals may have written out instructions for their own use, perhaps copied from a communally held formulary or from a short collection of spells compiled by another, or they may have kept records of their own successful spells. A gemstone from the Black Sea inscribed with magical instructions provides some evidence of a miniature, portable handbook that likely would have served as a template for a ritual practitioner.[17] A gem such as this may have been copied from a larger work, but it is not possible to know its precise derivation. It preserves a single spell, and it seems more likely that privately owned handbooks may have contained a small number of instructional texts. Alternatively, there may have been collective ownership of formularies, perhaps associated with institutions such as temples; this may have been the kind of handbook used by practitioners at Amathous. It is difficult to imagine the large- or even small-scale publication of substantial books of magic for private ownership, as most practitioners would not have possessed the means to acquire these resources, and it is unlikely that there was a sizable market for production.

Itinerant practitioners may have shared in the transmission of magical knowledge as they moved from place to place. As our brief survey of a magician's education in chapter 4 suggested, technical knowledge may have been acquired through travel to foreign places and study with ritual specialists in

---

15. R. S. Bagnall, *Early Christian books in Egypt* (Princeton: Princeton University Press, 2009), 17; R. Cribiore, *Gymnastics of the mind: Greek education in Hellenistic and Roman Egypt* (Princeton: Princeton University Press, 2001), 140–43.

16. Bagnall, *Early Christian books in Egypt,* 62–64.

17. Faraone, "A Greek magical gemstone from the Black Sea: Amulet or miniature handbook?" 110–11.

these locales. The itinerant practitioner could have carried personal copies of spells with them in their travels, employing these documents in the sale of commoditized rituals.[18] The existence of such specialists, however, does not fully explain the distribution of magical technology unless we can also suggest that practitioners shared information rather than closely guarding their own secret techniques. This is not a far-fetched idea, as it seems probable that specialists in any field may have swapped, bartered, or sold information with one another.

Artifacts, as the finished products of magical rituals, offer an additional means by which ritual elements moved throughout the Mediterranean. Divine names, imagery, text, or symbols could be appropriated without the wholesale adoption or understanding of the ritual that produced the object. A papyrus letter written in Coptic and discovered at the oasis site of Kellis in Egypt (*P.Kell. Copt.* 35, discussed in chapter 3) hints at this sort of procedure at work. In this case, wealthy or high-status laypersons, rather than professionals, were likely exchanging ritual components, but the text suggests a practice of reverse engineering that may have been commonplace among ritual professionals as well. The private letter includes the text of a single erotic magical spell, which was sent in response to the request of one of the two correspondents.[19] Vales, who composed the letter, admits that he was unable to find the requested spell, but has sent another in its stead that "perhaps is what you need" (column 3, line 14). He promises to send the other spell, which was on a small papyrus fragment, if he is able to locate it (ll. 3/09–3/10). This small fragment of papyrus likely did not include instructions for creating a spell but rather would have been the result of a magical act undertaken for Vales' benefit at an earlier time. Indeed, Vales may be transmitting words of power from a material example of activated magic without an accompanying ritual, in effect, disseminating components of ritual technology without knowledge of the complete procedure. Professionals, too, may have gained magical knowledge from finished ritual objects; elements of technical production as well as the inscriptions and signs of magic may have been garnered from artifacts.

There is some evidence that magical objects, which were highly portable,

---

18. This may be a possible explanation for the discovery in Beirut of a gemstone related to the "Sword of Dardanos" found in PGM IV. On this gem, see R. Mouterde, *Le Glaive de Dardanos. Objets et inscriptions magiques de Syrie* (Beirut: Imprimérie Catholique, 1930), 53–64. This congruence is quite unusual; compare the comments at C. Bonner, "Magical amulets," *HThR* 39, no. 1 (1946): 50.

19. See above, ch. 3 n. 183.

may have traveled with their owners to far-flung places. Two gemstones, one from Rome and the other likely from Afghanistan, have been inscribed with strikingly similar texts, each of which appears to have been copied from a formulary.[20] The opening lines of the amulet, "the words to be spoken," suggests a mistake made by a copyist at some point in the transmission of the text, either when the formulary was being copied, or later, when the text was transferred from the formulary to the gemstone. It seems likely that the same atelier or workshop produced the gemstones; this individual would have been responsible for the same mistake on subsequent stones.[21] Rather than providing evidence of the transmission of instructional spells in spellbooks, these gemstones, which were likely dispersed through trade or travel, attest to the important role played by artifacts in carrying magical technology from place to place. Amulets were worn in visible locations on the body, and their magical symbols may have been seen or appropriated by other practitioners. Indeed, the iconography of magical gems suggests that many of the elements of the language and imagery of magic were highly visible and easily recognizable. The amulet from the Black Sea also urges us to consider the role objects may have served in the trade in magical knowledge, as it could have been exchanged or sold as an instructional text.

Our evidence for the enactment of magic in the Roman Mediterranean is derived not from texts but from the material residue of magical acts that happen to be inscribed. That artifacts played a vital role in magic is a point that also has been discussed at length by M. Bailliot, who suggests the myriad ways in which many of the symbols of magic were written into the cityscapes of the Roman world.[22] In addition to understanding the role of materiality in magic, we also must consider the ways in which the practice of magic was constructed and disseminated through these same material objects. This inherent materiality necessitates a consideration of an artifact's physical form, its provenance,

---

20. D. Jordan, "Il testo greco di una gemma magica dall' Afghanistan (?) nel Museo Pushkin, Mosca," in *Gemme gnostiche e cultura ellenistica: atti dell'incontro di studio Verona, 22–23 ottobre 1999*, ed. A. Mastrocinque (Patron: Quarto Inferiore, 2002); Jordan, "Inscribed lead tablets from the games in the sanctuary of Poseidon"; I. Pomyalovski, *Ancient curses (tabulae defixionum)* (St. Petersburg, 1873); N. I. Novosadski, "Amulet with the name Ἀκτιῶφι," *Sbornik. Moskovskogo Obshchestuva po Issledovaniyu Pamyatnikinkov Drevnosti pri Mosckovskom Arkheologischeskom Institute* 2 (1917); N. P. Rozanova, "A magical amulet in the Numismatic Collection of the Pushkin Museum," *Vestnik Drevnej Istorii* 74, no. 4 (1960).

21. Jordan, "Il testo greco di una gemma magica dall' Afghanistan (?) nel Museo Pushkin, Mosca," 68–69; compare the discussion at Bohak, *Ancient Jewish magic,* 230.

22. Bailliot, *Magie et sortilèges dans l'Antiquité romaine,* 164–78.

The Archaeology of Magic   269

and its context. Practitioners who were operating in a specific time and place created magical objects. Through ritual, the raw components of magic were transformed into artifacts and assemblages that were believed to have a tangible effect on the world, an effect that often was enacted through use or deposition in a significant location.

Coda: Back on the Via Appia

The inscriptions and drawings preserved on the San Sebastiano tablets attest to the heterogeneous nature of ritual practice in the Late Antique period. The inscriptions call on Osiris, Aphis (Apis), and Mnevis, and on many of the tablets, a horse- or ass-headed god who represents Seth is featured prominently. Illustrations of mummified individuals that represent the target of the spells provide further instances of Egyptianizing motifs.[23] Other traditions are also apparent. The tablets invoke the archangels and *kharaktêres,* both of which had long been associated with the shared body of magical knowledge in the Mediterranean. Many of the tablets also begin with invocations to the Phrygian goddess (Demeter or Cybele), Nymph Goddess (perhaps a local divinity?), and Eidoneia, which could be an alternative spelling of Adonai, a Jewish or Christian invocation.[24] It is not sufficient, however, to declare the tablets a product of this mixed tradition. Rather, we must understand these tablets as indicators of the local performance of magic, undertaken and interpreted by resident or itinerant practitioners.

The cache of tablets, which includes more than forty-five examples, derives from a single archaeological locus, a columbarium situated just outside the San Sebastiano gate in the Aurelian wall. From the brief description of the discovery, it appears that each tablet was deposited separately in an individual cinerary urn. Although some examples of magic from elsewhere in the Mediterranean suggest a preference for graves of the young or those who died before their time, the identities of these dead individuals were not important. As the complex was out of use, it is unlikely that the practitioner could have known the age or sex of the deceased. Greater significance appears to have

---

23. On these images, see Bailliot, *Magie et sortilèges dans l'Antiquité romaine,* 117–20.
24. Jordan suggests reading EIDONEIA as an adjective modifying Nymph and locating the nymph in the underworld. D. R. Jordan, "Psegmata kritikes," *Eulimene* 1, no. 2000 (2000): 130–31; Mastrocinque, "Le 'defixiones' di Porta San Sebastiano," 53.

270   Materia Magica

been attached to using separate vessels for the depositions, so that each tablet was handed over to a different ghost for the enactment of the binding spell.

Wünsch identified at least three hands among the tablets.[25] Moreover, five of the tablets were inscribed in Latin, while the remainder were written in Greek, perhaps indicating that additional individuals were engaged in magical practice. These individuals were not passing through but were probably in business in the area, as they continued to use the same space for deposition. Like the tablets from Amathous, the practitioners appear to have worked from a shared formulary, as parts of the inscriptions and many of the drawings are repeated across the tablets. The use of the formulary, however, was not rigid; there is significant variation among the tablets in the drawings as well as the arrangement of the text and illustrations, and more than one model spell appears to have been in use. Given the skill and knowledge necessary to produce the tablets, as well as the difficulty and cost associated with owning formularies, trained professionals likely were responsible for production.

Although Egyptian elements appear to dominate the tablets, it is not necessary to posit that an Egyptian priest or a practitioner who had access to Egyptian books of magic created them. Sanctuaries dedicated to Isis and Osiris outside of the Nile valley may offer a point of contact between Egyptian religious practices and the wider Mediterranean.[26] Often, the first devotees of a cult in a given locality were native Egyptians, but the priesthood was soon filled with local citizens who may have been less familiar with traditional Egyptian practices.[27] Indeed, there is little that betrays more than superficial knowledge of Egyptian

---

25. Wünsch, *Sethianische verfluchungstafeln aus Rom,* 75–76.
26. On Isis and Serapis in the Roman world, see S. A. Takács, *Isis and Sarapis in the Roman world* (Leiden: Brill, 1995); M. D. Donalson, *The cult of Isis in the Roman Empire: Isis Invicta* (Lewiston, NY: Edwin Mellen Press, 2003), 115–87; multiple contributions in L. Bricault, M. J. Versluys, and P. G. P. Meyboom, eds., *Nile into Tiber: Egypt in the Roman world: Proceedings of the IIIrd international conference of Isis studies, Leiden, May 11–14 2005* (Leiden: Brill, 2007). On the temple of Isis at Pompeii, see E. M. Moormann, "The temple of Isis at Pompeii," in *Nile into Tiber: Egypt in the Roman world: Proceedings of the IIIrd international conference of Isis studies, Leiden, May 11–14 2005*, ed. L. Bricault, M. J. Versluys, and P. G. P. Meyboom (Leiden: Brill, 2007), with relevant bibliography at n.1.
27. Apuleius' Lucius in the Metamorphosis book 11 enrolls in the cult of Isis, progressing through various religious grades. See Takács, *Isis and Sarapis in the Roman world,* 29–30, 51–56; E. M. Orlin, *Foreign cults in Rome: Creating a Roman Empire* (Oxford: Oxford University Press, 2010), 201–7. A first-century CE inscription (*CIL* 12 1263) from Rome attests to the presence of the cult in the city, where freedmen and freeborn citizens are listed as priests. On Roman interaction with foreign cults, see most recently E. S. Gruen, *Rethinking the other in antiquity* (Princeton: Princeton University Press, 2011), 346–51.

ritual in the texts, and they also include elements that can be associated with Christianity and traditional pagan cults.[28] The practitioners likely developed or modified a ritual that drew upon the *koine* of magical practice for use in the specific circumstances demanded by the clients. Almost all of the tablets appear to have been commissioned by charioteers; a suitable location along the Via Appia and near the relevant circuses was selected. The practitioners appropriated a columbarium that had gone out of use, and over time, deposited a significant number of curses within the urns that were already there. Matter records that the columbarium included a wall painting of a woman and a child, perhaps a representation of Isis and Horus.[29] This decorative motif may have impacted the decision of the practitioners to appropriate this funerary space, given the importance placed on Egyptian divinities in the texts.

The tablets from the Via Appia attest to the vibrant exchange of magical knowledge throughout the Mediterranean. The texts of the inscriptions, however, cannot allow us to fully appreciate the performance of magical rites at the site. Rather, we must understand the tablets as inscribed artifacts that entered the archaeological record through specific depositional processes. Only by analyzing the archaeological context of the tablets can we adequately reconstruct the performance of the ritual that created them and resulted in their deposition. Such careful analysis of the findspot and depositional history of archaeological material has been the mainstay of each of the three case studies explored in this book.

This book has emphasized the importance of analyzing the phenomenon of magic on a local level by placing artifacts and texts within their physical, social, and ritual contexts. Although ancient magic was often enacted within a larger tradition that dictated its form and, to a degree, potential uses, each archaeological instance of ritual practice simultaneously reflects its creator

---

28. Although there is no reason to insist on an Egyptian identity for the practitioners, Christian legend suggests that a temple to Isis likely may have been located nearby, perhaps a kilometer northwest of the San Sebastiano gate. According to the tale, Peter, on his way out of the city of Rome following his imprisonment, passed by a temple to Isis. There, a bandage fell from his leg, and a local woman discovered it the next day. The *titulus Fasciolae,* or Church of the Bandage, now Santi Nereo e Achilleo, was supposedly founded on the site of the temple of Isis. J. M. Peterson, "The identification of the titulus Fasciolae and its connection with Pope Gregory the Great," *Vigiliae Christianae* 30, no. 2 (1976): 153; M. Kretschmer, "St. Peter at Rome," *CJ* 21, no. 7 (1926): 514 n.1. Recent soundings beneath the temple, however, have not uncovered any traces of an earlier pagan cult building. M. Cecchelli, "Fasciola, Titulus" in E. M. Steinby, *Lexicon topographicum urbis Romae,* 6 vols., (Roma: Quasar, 1993), 2:241–42.

29. Matter, *Une excursion gnostique en Italie,* 29–31.

and the social space that he or she occupied. As we have seen, the contextual analysis of ritual has the potential to illuminate the lives, the concerns, and the solutions to crises that were envisioned by residents of the Roman empire. In order to undertake this analysis, it is imperative that scholars have access to archaeological data derived from scientific excavation. Artifacts that appear on the art market without provenance, or described as likely deriving from some location, are of limited value, at best. Excavators should carefully record data related to all finds and should make this information accessible; we cannot know where magic might be found, as ritual practice often appropriated spaces that had another function, such as graves or private homes. New work that has been undertaken in the past few years shows great promise. The discoveries of Late Antique curse tablets and figurines at the fountain of Anna Perenna in Rome, or the first- and second-century artifacts found at the Sanctuary of Isis and Magna Mater in Mainz, have revealed examples of ritual practices that can tell us much more about ritual performance. A wealth of archaeological data remains to be found or rediscovered, and, if viewed contextually, these finds have the potential to radically alter our understanding of ancient magical practice and its local manifestations.

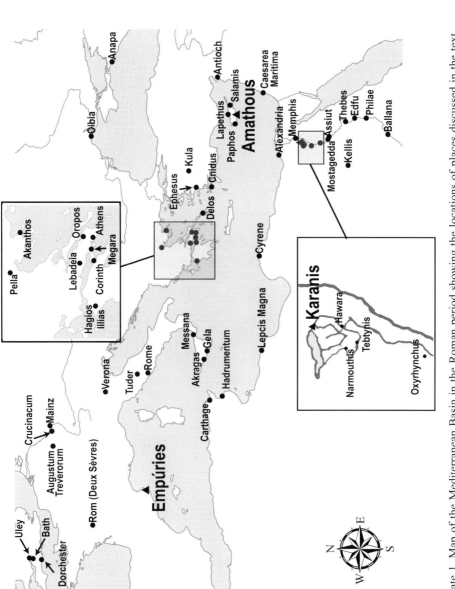

Plate 1. Map of the Mediterranean Basin in the Roman period showing the locations of places discussed in the text. Karanis, Amathous, and Empúries are indicated by triangles. (Produced by the author.)

2a

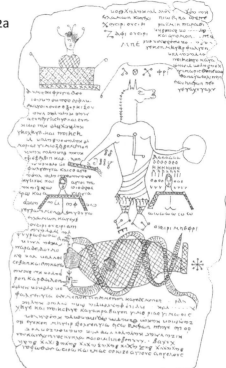

Plate 2. Line drawing (2a), photograph (2b), and schematic rendering (2c) of curse tablet from the Porta San Sebastiano on the Via Appia, Rome, third or fourth century CE, Museo Nazionale Romano, inv. n. 52202.

2a. The line drawing was made approximately forty years after discovery and shows both the obverse (top) and reverse (below). (Wünsch, *Sethianische verfluchungstafeln aus Rom* [1898], p. 16.)

2b

2b. The photograph shows the current state of the obverse of the tablet. (Courtesy of Museo Nazionale Romano.)

2c. The schematic rendering shows the placement of text on the tablet, divided into sections 1–7. The rendering is intended to accompany the translation on pp. 3–5.

2c

Plate 3. Portion of group of eighty-four animal bones and similar artifacts painted with dots, crossed lines, and undulating lines discovered at Karanis, Egypt, in Areas 262 and 265 during the 1924–25 season. (Courtesy of the Kelsey Museum of Archaeology.)

Opposite page:

Plate 5. Map showing findspots of formularies and examples of enacted or applied magic. Information based on Brashear, "The Greek Magical Papyri," 3484–85. (Produced by the author using a basemap adapted from M. Moret, *In the time of the Pharaohs* [1911], end plate.)

Plate 4. Archaeological assemblage from Middle Egypt, including, from left, a lead tablet inscribed with a curse against Ptolemais, the daughter of Aias and Horigenes, a figurine of a kneeling woman pierced with thirteen nails, and a coarseware jar that contained the two objects, third or fourth century CE. Musée du Louvre E 27145 A à C, photograph GP100334. (Courtesy of Images et Ressources Documentaires du Musée du Louvre.)

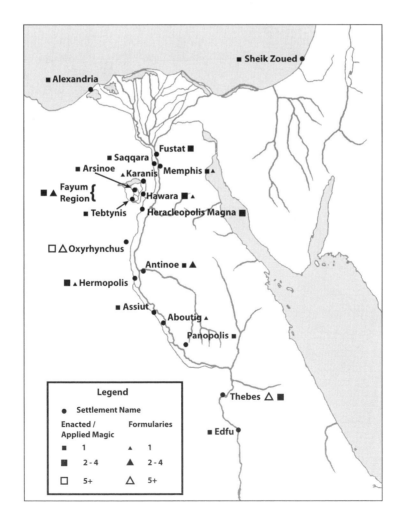

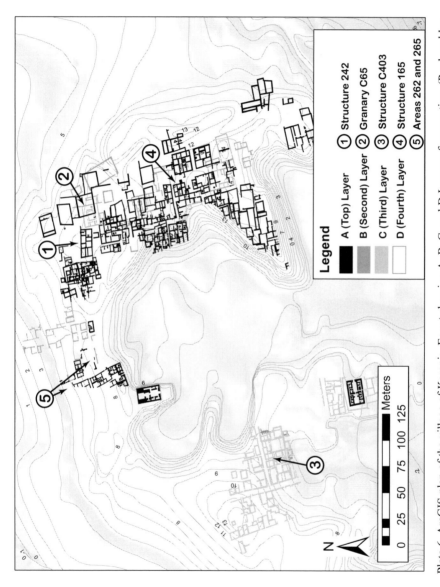

Plate 6. ArcGIS plan of the village of Karanis, Egypt showing A, B, C, and D Layers of occupation. (Produced by the author.)

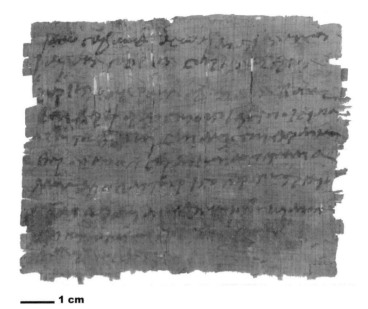

Plate 7. *P.Mich.* VIII 768, fever amulet written for a man named Sarapion, excavated at Karanis, Egypt, in unit 242*, beneath the A Layer of occupation during the 1928 season. The fever amulet has been dated to the late third or early fourth century CE. P.Mich. inv. 5302. (Courtesy of the University of Michigan Papyrus Collection.)

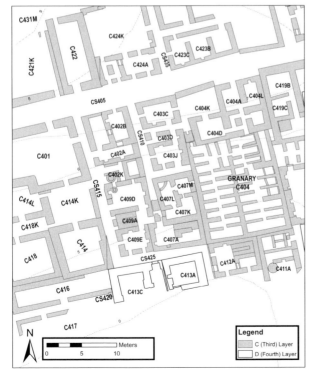

Plate 8. ArcGIS reconstruction of Karanis, Egypt, showing room C403J and surrounding buildings in the C Layer of occupation (Produced by the author.)

Plate 9. O.Mich. inv. 9883. Ostracon related to magical practice excavated at Karanis, Egypt, in structure C403, Room J, during the 1933 season. Field number 33-C403J-K. The ostracon is dated to the third or fourth century CE. It is inscribed with three lines of text: the word "image," a series of magical vowels, and "woman, child." (Courtesy of the University of Michigan Papyrus Collection.)

Plate 10. Wall painting from Karanis, Egypt, showing seated Harpocrates flanked by the god Tutu (Tithoes). Harpocrates is seated on a throne or building, and is crowned with lotus blossoms. The painting was discovered in Granary C 65, Room CF4 during the 1926 season, third or fourth century CE. K.M. Photographic Archive 5.3292. (Courtesy of the Kelsey Museum of Archaeology.)

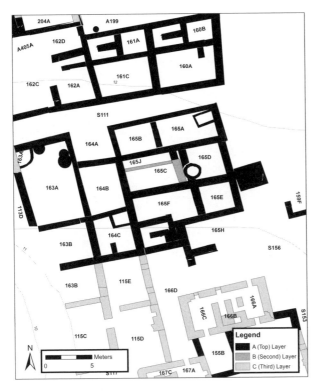

Plate 11. ArcGIS reconstruction of Karanis, Egypt, showing Structure 165 and surrounding buildings of the A Layer of occupation. (Produced by the author.)

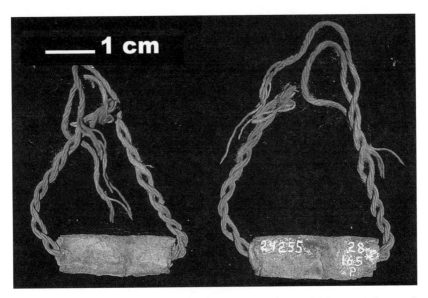

Plate 12. K.M. inv. 24255. Rolled lead sheet on suspension cord (obverse and reverse) excavated at Karanis beneath Structure 165, below the A Layer of occupation during the 1928 season. Field number 28-165*-P. The lead sheet has not been unrolled, and may be an amulet that was worn by the individual it was designed to protect. (Courtesy of the Kelsey Museum of Archaeology.)

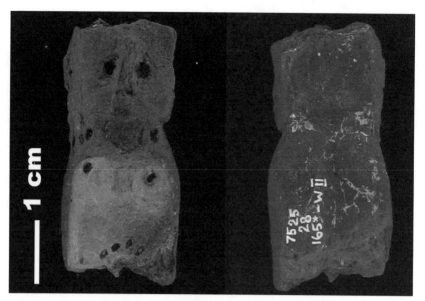

Plate 13. K.M. inv. 7525. Mud figurine (obverse and reverse) excavated at Karanis beneath Structure 165, A Layer of occupation, during the 1928 season. Field number 28-165-WII. The figurine, which is roughly shaped, is indented to indicate a head; the eyes, nose and mouth were added with a tool. The head is topped with a variety of spiky protrusions meant to indicate hair. On the torso, two pinched knobs represent breasts, and an arc of further points indicates the genitals. The figurine was burned. (Courtesy of the Kelsey Museum of Archaeology.)

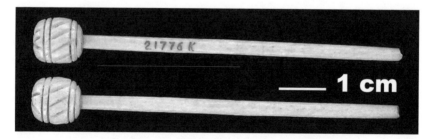

Plate 14. K.M. inv. 21776. Bone pin (obverse and reverse) excavated at Karanis beneath Structure 165, A Layer of occupation, during the 1928 season. Field number 28-165*-CII. The object likely was used as a hairpin, but subsequently was employed in a magical rite. On one end of the pin, a rounded knob has been incised with decorative lines. (Courtesy of the Kelsey Museum of Archaeology.)

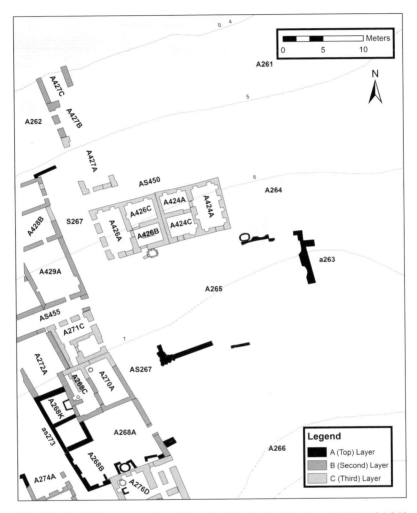

Plate 15. ArcGIS reconstruction of Karanis, Egypt, showing Areas A262 and A265 and surrounding buildings of the A Layer of occupation. (Produced by the author.)

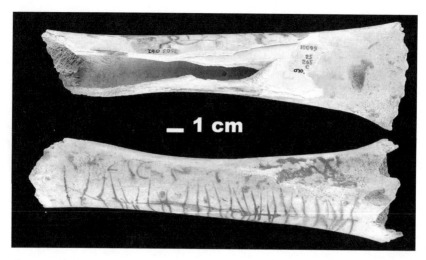

Plate 16. K.M. inv. 10099.070, joined to K.M. inv. 3503.062. Bovine femur painted with line pattern and undulating line pattern, excavated at Karanis in Area 265, A Layer of occupation, during the 1924–25 season. Field number 25-265-C. The line pattern is visible on the lower part of the bone; the upper part shows undulating lines that mimic letters. The femur demonstrates joins between bones assigned to lot 3503 and lot 10099. (Courtesy of the Kelsey Museum of Archaeology.)

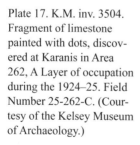

Plate 17. K.M. inv. 3504. Fragment of limestone painted with dots, discovered at Karanis in Area 262, A Layer of occupation during the 1924–25. Field Number 25-262-C. (Courtesy of the Kelsey Museum of Archaeology.)

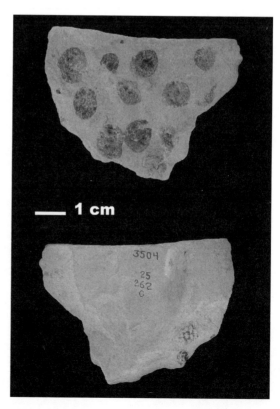

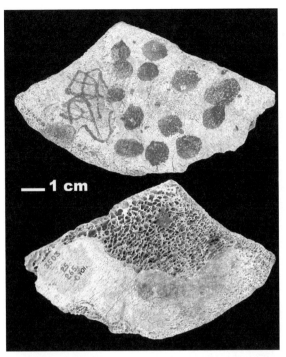

Plate 18. K.M. inv. 3503.101. Mammal inominate showing larger red dots and undulating lines discovered at Karanis in Area 265, A Layer of occupation during the 1924–25 season. Field number 25-265-C. The undulating lines may be arranged in a pattern. (Courtesy of the Kelsey Museum of Archaeology.)

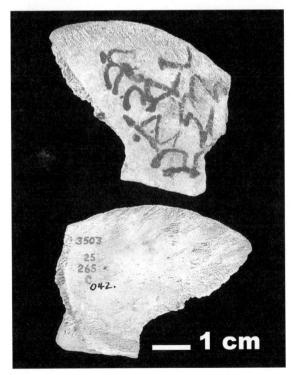

Plate 19. K.M. inv. 3503.042. Pig ramus with undulating line pattern excavated at Karanis in Area 265, A Layer of occupation, during the 1924–25 season. Field number 24-265-C. (Courtesy of the Kelsey Museum of Archaeology.)

Plate 20. BM 1891,4-18.1. Unrolled lead tablet commissioned by Soterianos, also called Limbaros, who curses Ariston. The tablet was discovered by locals at the bottom of a deep shaft near the modern village of Agios Tychonas, north of ancient Amathous, on the island of Cyprus. Magical symbols may be visible at the bottom of the tablet. (The photograph, taken by the author, appears courtesy of The Trustees of the British Museum.)

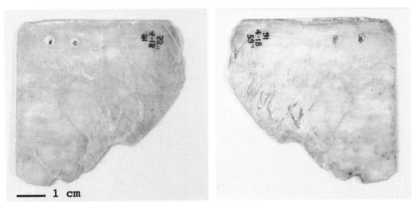

Plate 21. BM 1891,4-18.59. Selenite tablet with holes for suspension, discovered at the bottom of a deep shaft near the modern village of Agios Tychonas, north of ancient Amathous on the island of Cyprus. (The photograph by Dr. Thomas Kiely, Curator, Cyprus Digistation Project, appears courtesy of The Trustees of the British Museum.)

Plate 22. BM 1891,4-18.58. Selenite tablet discovered at the bottom of a deep shaft near the modern village of Agios Tychonas, north of ancient Amathous on the island of Cyprus. The detail shows a line of *khataktêres* at the beginning of the text, similar to other unpublished examples from the cache. (The photograph, taken by the author, appears courtesy of The Trustees of the British Museum.)

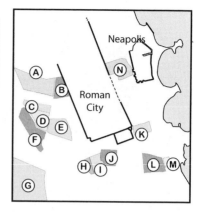

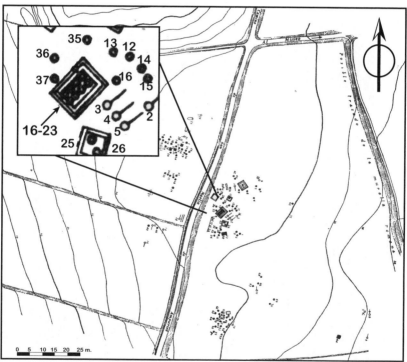

Plate 23. Top: Sketch plan of the site of Empúries, Spain, showing the locations of the necropoleis surrounding the Roman town. Bottom: Plan of the Ballesta cemetery, with an inset detail that shows the location and arrangement of Ballesta cremations 16–23. (Top image produced by the author. Bottom image adapted from Almagro Basch, *Las Necrópolis de Ampurias: Necrópolis Romanas y Necrópolis Indígenas*, [1955], pp. 13, 20.) (Bottom image ©Museu d'Arqueologia de Catalunya-Empúries.)

24a: Ballesta cremation 21. The urn is a reddish coarseware vessel with a single handle. The tablet is roughly rectangular in shape.

a

24b: Ballesta cremation 22. The urn is a reddish coarseware vessel with a single handle. The tablet is roughly rectangular in shape.

b

24c: Ballesta cremation 23. The urn is a reddish coarseware vessel with a single handle. The tablet is roughly triangular in shape.

c

Plate 24. Cremation urns and lead tablets from Ballesta cremations 21 through 23. (©Museu d'Arqueologia de Catalunya-Barcelona.)

Plate 25. In-situ photograph of Ballesta cremations 16–23, taken during excavation. Reprinted from Almagro Basch, *Las Necrópolis de Ampurias: Necrópolis Romanas y Necrópolis Indígenas*, (1955), Lam. 1, no. 2. (©Museu d'Arqueologia de Catalunya-Empúries.)

APPENDIXES

Appendix 1

The Excavations at Karanis

The University of Michigan excavated the site of Karanis between 1924 and 1935. While the final results of the excavation never were published fully, Karanis remains one of the best-documented sites from Graeco-Roman Egypt. Frequently cited as a comparative example, the importance of the village for scholars of the period can be traced to both the massive amount of material that was recovered and the clear and thorough publications, particularly of the papyri. While the excavation was scientific by contemporary standards, the methodology and recording system that were employed can appear arcane or inscrutable to modern scholars. This appendix will attempt to present my understanding of the excavation history, in the hope that it can serve as a contribution toward our collective ability to use the excavations in a considered and responsible manner.

In the nineteenth century, Karanis drew the attention of excavators who dabbled at the site, but left few substantial records. Flinders Petrie commented in 1890 that the town was likely the most important within the entire region, but his work undertook little formal exploration. Even at that early date, however, some areas of the site were damaged; a significant number of tombs to the north of the site had been looted, probably in antiquity, as is to be expected.[1] Following Petrie, Bernard Grenfell, Arthur Hunt, and D. G. Hogarth in

---

1. W. M. F. Petrie et al., *Illahun, Kahun and Gurob. 1888–90* (London: D. Nutt, 1891), 32. Hogarth, correspondence with Emily Patterson, dated January 11, 1896, reprinted in D. Montserrat, "'No papyrus and no portraits': Hogarth, Grenfell, and the first season in the Fayum, 1895–6," *BASP* 33 (1996): 149–50. Montserrat's publication includes Hogarth's excavation diaries from the 1895/6 season. These provide an intriguing glimpse into the process of early excavation, but as the finds described in the diaries cannot be linked to artifacts or architecture, and only a few references can be associated with published papyri, the field notes provide little assistance in reconstructing the seasons of digging.

1895/6 under the auspices of the Egypt Exploration Fund cleared the area of
the Southern Temple and explored some of the cemeteries located to the north
of the site; work in and among the graves was focused on a search for ancient
texts.[2] During the second expedition, in 1900, Grenfell and Hunt noted that the
center of the mound was likely the location of an agora, ringed on the east and
southeast by brick structures. Further south was an open area that was used
for garbage; this area, by the late nineteenth century, had already been a prime
spot for papyrus-hunting by locals. Neither of their two expeditions produced
spectacular results. Grenfell, Hunt, and Hogarth, in fact, report that "excavating houses proved, in short, so unproductive of the result on this site that we
did not continue long to waste energy or money upon it."[3]

These earliest explorations, although they increased scholarly and popular
interest in Graeco-Roman Egypt in general and papyri in particular, did not utilize sound methodology or keep accurate records of finds and their locations.[4]
Petrie had only given cursory attention to the site, as he was more interested in
the Pharaonic remains at nearby Illahun. Grenfell, Hunt, and Hogarth viewed
Karanis as a potential source of papyri and engaged in more extensive work.
Luckily, they left most of the site untouched, after realizing that better caches
of papyri could be discovered in garbage dumps like those at Oxyrhynchus.[5]
The site would not receive substantial archaeological attention until a quarter-
century later, when the University of Michigan began their large-scale excavations, but by then, significant damage had already occurred.

As part of an early twentieth-century government initiative to increase
agricultural production in the Fayum, local farmers and companies were
given permits to mine *sebbakh,* nitrogen-rich soil formed through the decay

---

2.   D. G. Hogarth and B. P. Grenfell, "Cities of the Faiyúm I: Karanis and Bacchias," *Egypt
     Exploration Fund Archaeological Report* (1895–96): 16; B. P. Grenfell et al., *Fayûm towns
     and their papyri* (London: Offices of the Egypt Exploration Fund, 1900), 27–35. On these
     seasons of excavation, see P. Lock, "D.G. Hogarth (1862–1927): ' . . . A Specialist in the Sci-
     ence of Archaeology,'" *ABSA* 85 (1990): 184–85; Montserrat, "'No Papyrus and no Portraits':
     Hogarth, Grenfell, and the First Season in the Fayum, 1895–6."
3.   Grenfell et al., *Fayûm towns and their papyri,* 29.
4.   Gagos, Gates, and Wilburn, "Material culture and texts of Graeco-Roman Egypt: Creating
     context, debating meaning," 177.
5.   In the 1896–97 issue of the Egypt Exploration Fund Archaeological Report, Grenfell records
     the work at Oxyrhynchus: "Since this rubbish mound proved so fruitful I proceeded to
     increase the number of workmen gradually up to 110, and, as we moved northwards over
     other parts of the site, the flow of papyri soon became a torrent, which it was difficult to cope
     with." B. P. Grenfell, "Oxyrhynchus and Its Papyri," *Egypt Exploration Fund Archaeological
     Report* (1896–97): 6–7.

Appendix 1. The Excavations at Karanis   277

of organic materials that was useful as fertilizer. Archaeological sites such as Karanis—effectively mounds of decayed organic material—were targeted as sources for *sebbakh,* leading to extensive destruction.[6] At Karanis, the mining company Daira Agnelli constructed a railway that was used to remove 200 cubic meters of *sebbakh* from the center of the mound each day; thirty years of constant mining resulted in the near total destruction of the center of the town.[7] A. E. R. Boak describes the site during the first season of excavation by the University of Michigan in 1924:

> Unfortunately, a large area in the heart of the mound, apparently the center of the town, had been cleared down to bedrock by the sebbakhin, so that it had the appearance of the crater of some extinct volcano for which the high sides of the mound supplied the rim.[8]

Despite the obvious damage, Francis W. Kelsey, a Latin professor at the University of Michigan, decided to seek a permit for excavation.

The damage to the site from *sebbakh* mining, however, would prove to be a significant challenge. The destroyed area was sizable, measuring some 2.5 hectares; most had been removed from the center of the village, where the mound was highest. The excavators speculated that this area was the portion of the site most likely to have been continuously occupied from foundation to final abandonment. Parallels with other towns from Graeco-Roman Egypt suggest that this area was the location for administrative buildings and the agora, or marketplace, where the business of the town would have taken place. The contents of these structures would have provided further evidence of the economic and political realities of town life, and excavation in this area may have uncovered a full stratigraphic sequence for occupation.

Even after the initiation of the University of Michigan's excavations, mining at the site continued. During the first season of work at the site in the winter of 1924–25, the placement of the excavation trenches was determined by the needs of the *sebbakh* mining company, Daira Agnelli, rather than the intellectual goals of the Michigan team. The mining company retained its rights to remove thousands of cubic meters of soil from the mound, and the excavators

---

6. Gazda and Wilfong, *Karanis, an Egyptian town in Roman times,* 2.
7. Boak and Peterson, *Karanis: Topographical and architectural report of excavations during the seasons 1924–28,* 2–3.
8. Ibid., 3.

278   Appendix 1. The Excavations at Karanis

were forced to dig in areas that were rich in organic debris in order to provide the daily allowance of fertilizer.[9] Excavation proceeded at an alarming pace, since the Michigan team needed to produce enough soil during the two-month excavation season to supply the company with *sebbakh* until the following season could begin. Otherwise, the mining company would have begun clearing potentially valuable areas of the village without oversight or direction.

The constraints imposed by the mining company may help explain some of the problems found in the excavation notebooks for the early seasons. Presumably because of the fast pace of excavation, Samuel Yeivin, one of the field architects, recorded that it was not until the 1927–28 season that a full sketch plan was created for the middle layer of Area A, excavated two years prior in 1924–25.[10] A number of the houses recorded for the 1924 season, including the 5000 series of buildings, presumably salvaged from areas mined by Daira Agnelli, possess no accompanying maps and cannot be accurately located on the plans.

In subsequent years, likely because of the field direction of Enoch E. Peterson and the architectural recording spearheaded by S. Yeivin and J. Terentiff, field recording became significantly more detailed. As the excavation proceeded, the field directors J. L. Starkey (1924–26) and E. E. Peterson (1926–36) developed a methodology for recording and documenting the artifacts that were discovered in the course of the investigations. Throughout the excavation, finds were associated with the architecture—houses, granaries, temples, and streets—in which they were discovered. Alternatively, if the excavated area lay between buildings or could not be associated with identifiable structures, the finds were grouped under the heading of an "area." The recording method privileged architecture as the critical factor for locating finds; this decision would have important ramifications for the chronology of the site.

Each artifact that was removed during the course of excavation was documented in the volume of the Record of Objects associated with the season it was found and listed under the heading of the appropriate architectural unit, whether a house—a general designation applied to almost all buildings—or an area. The Record of Objects also includes rudimentary descriptions of artifacts

---

9. Boak and Peterson, *Karanis: Topographical and architectural report of excavations during the seasons 1924–28*, 3.
10. S. Yeivin, "Report for the Season 1927–1928" (Ann Arbor: Kelsey Museum of Archaeology, 1928).

Appendix 1. The Excavations at Karanis   279

that were removed from the soil but left in the field or discarded in the dump piles; these objects are designated as N.T.H., or "Not Taken Home." Moreover, these volumes have been updated continuously, and each documents whether an artifact is housed in the Egyptian Museum in Cairo or the Kelsey Museum of Archaeology in Ann Arbor. Notes from the excavators are occasionally included within the Record of Objects, written in the margins beside the description of the artifact. These may provide detailed information about the circumstances of discovery or the relative findspot.

The Record of Objects is cross-referenced with the maps and plans produced over the course of the excavation. Field architects created a topographic plan of the mound as well that includes the surveying points. A master map, which shows all of the phases of the site, is complemented by maps for each of the occupation levels. Plans of excavation squares show phases of construction, reuse, and features. Finally, detailed elevations were produced for well-preserved or significant houses and administrative buildings.

The association of finds and architectural units was closely tied to the research goals of the project. According to Francis W. Kelsey, the first director of the project, the excavators intended to achieve "the reconstruction of the environment of life in the Graeco-Roman period . . . (and the) increase of exact knowledge rather than the amassing of collections."[11] These goals led the excavators to retain a much larger quantity of artifacts, including many minor household and everyday objects that were not considered artistically valuable. In this way, the excavators looked forward to modern practices of total recovery but stopped well short of that level of detail. Tied as they were to nineteenth-century notions of typologies, the excavators retained a number of examples of each artifact type, but many objects were left in the field.

The Occupation Layers

Two dates were used to establish the temporal framework for the occupation of the site. Documentary texts from Karanis and other sites in Egypt suggested that the village was first occupied during the third century BCE. At the other

---

11. Francis W. Kelsey, University of Michigan Near East Research Committee: Memorandum 14 (unpublished manuscript, Kelsey Museum of Archaeology); Gazda and Wilfong, *Karanis, an Egyptian town in Roman times,* 4.

280   Appendix 1. The Excavations at Karanis

end, the latest datable coins found on the site were from the reign of Marcian (450–457 CE).[12] These dates also proved convenient. The initial date marked the beginning of Greek presence in Egypt, following the Alexandrian conquest. The latter date placed the decline of the site in the period associated with the triumph of Christianity. For the excavators, the absence of a church or artifacts that could be associated with a Christian presence meant that the site must have gone out of use not long after the conversion of Egypt.

Along the eastern face of the central pit created by the mining company, three strata of houses were visible, each separated by a layer of sand. The excavators believed that these strata corresponded to periods of occupation and assigned a four-digit number to each structure according to its place within this schema. Houses in the top (most recent) layer on the site were given numbers between 0001 and 1000 or between 4000 and 5000, depending on whether the remains were located on the east or west side of the mound. Structures believed to be located in the "middle strata" were assigned numbers from 5000 to 6000. Letters were appended to the house number in order to designate rooms in each building, so that the Gemellus papyrus, for instance, was found in Room 5006 E 2, a subterranean storage chamber (E2) in house 5006.

The numbering system was overhauled during the 1926–27 season under E. E. Peterson. From that point onward, buildings were identified according to one of five different occupation levels, A–E, with A representing the layer below the surface; E was believed to correspond to the second and first centuries BCE.[13] Buildings were numbered consecutively in the revised system as they were unearthed. Those identified in the first season retained their original numbers, even as earlier buildings were discovered below, to which new numbers, according to the revised system, were assigned. The plans were marked with both designations to mitigate confusion.[14]

---

12. On the earliest and latest datable material, see above, chap. 3 nn. 21 and 23, respectively. Boak dates the abandonment of Karanis to the mid-fifth century. Boak and Peterson, *Karanis: Topographical and architectural report of excavations during the seasons 1924–28*, 5. This dating is echoed in B. Johnson, who created the ceramic chronology. *Pottery from Karanis: Excavations of the University of Michigan* (Ann Arbor: University of Michigan, 1981), xiii. Compare the dates given at H. Geremek, *Karanis, communauté rurale de l'Egypte romaine au IIe-IIIe siècle de notre ère,* (Wrocław: Zakład Narodowy im. Ossolinskich Wydawn. Polskiej Akademii Nauk, 1969), 34. The dating is revised in Pollard, "The chronology and economic condition of late Roman Karanis," 148–49, and new excavations have confirmed the late dating of the site.

13. Husselman, *Karanis topography and architecture*, 7–29; on the F Level near the Temple of Pnepheros and Petesouchos, see Boak, *Karanis: The temples, coin hoards, botanical and zoölogical reports, seasons 1924–31*, 29–30.

14. Thomas Landvatter, a graduate student at the University of Michigan, is also working on this problem.

Appendix 1. The Excavations at Karanis   281

As the excavators dug down through the Karanis mound, they noted variations in architectural forms and changes in house structure. Brick sizes were different, and in individual houses, alterations in the living spaces could be detected, evidence that subsequent owners changed the basic structure of a house.[15] Furthermore, at certain places over the mound, the excavators could distinguish what they believed were breaks in the occupation sequence—deep layers of sand and debris that occurred between different architectural features. The excavators noted that over time, the elevation of streets rose due to accumulation of debris and sand blown in from the desert. Houses were reconfigured to compensate for the changes in the landscape of the site; residents often abandoned lower stories and reused upper stories, at times adding on to the higher floors to increase the usable space.[16]

These data were used to suggest occupational periods along a vertical sequence for a specific house or within an insula block. Comparable patterns in occupation appeared to be evident in various parts of the site, in particular, a relatively substantial layer of sand that appeared below the second or B layer of occupation. Here, excavators believed, was evidence of a break in occupation. Collating evidence from across the mound, the Michigan excavators eventually proposed a sequence of site occupation based on architectural change and variations in elevation; each level was assigned a rough date, and excavation loci that lacked securely datable materials (i.e., coins or papyri) were assigned a date according to their place within the chronological schema. Subsequent publications have assigned the following dates to the Karanis levels:

Top Layer (A-Layer)	Late Antique to abandonment, early 4th to mid 5th
Second Layer (B-Layer)	Late Roman, early 3rd–early 4th
Late Third Layer (Late C-Layer)	Roman, c. 165–early 3rd CE
Third Layer (C-Layer)	Roman, mid 1st CE–mid 2nd or early 3rd CE
Fourth Layer (D-Layer)	Early Roman, mid-1st BCE–mid-1st CE
Fifth Layer (E-Layer)	Ptolemaic, foundation to mid 1st BCE[17]

The C-level was marked by the expansion of the urban area, and a later reduc-

---

15. Husselman, *Karanis topography and architecture,* 33.
16. Ibid., 7–8.
17. Adapted from ibid., 9, Shier, *Terracotta lamps from Karanis, Egypt,* 188–89; B. Johnson, *Pottery from Karanis: Excavations of the University of Michigan* (Ann Arbor: University of Michigan, 1981), 106–7.

282   Appendix 1. The Excavations at Karanis

tion in the size of the town (the Late C-Level) was associated with the plague of 165 CE.[18]

Often, changes in construction were evident in the architecture but not in the sand. There are numerous instances where a house may have been dated to both the C and B levels, but finds are assigned to only one level, either B or C, and no finds were listed for the other level. The reason for assignment of another level to a house is not always clear. Houses that were built side by side, in the same insula block, with shared walls, were sometimes designated as belonging to different levels, even though they were likely constructed at the same time.[19] Often, this appears to have occurred because datable material was discovered in the fill associated with one architectural phase, and the analysis of another architectural phase above necessitated that the higher fill be dated later. Moreover, the material used for dating—coins and datable papyri—did not necessarily provide accurate dates. Pottery was seldom used for dating. Despite the problems with dating the levels, the field designations that were assigned by the Karanis team have had a long life, and their rough estimates have determined the chronologies for much of the research on the site.

Assigning layers across the site had the potential to provide a rough chronology, but the Michigan team encountered a number of critical problems in their attempts to do so. The most significant was the hole in the middle of the town, which made it impossible to isolate a complete sequence for occupation. The excavators also assumed that similar patterns of construction and occupation were at work over the entirety of the village. While the sequence of layers may have been applicable to smaller areas or blocks, problems developed when it was applied to the site as a whole. This necessitated finding each of the layers in a given building and did not allow for changes that may have been specific to a structure.

Current fieldwork at the site under Willeke Wendrich is having significant success with dating and interpreting the late occupation of the village.[20] This

---

18. Husselman, *Karanis topography and architecture,* 9. Boak suggests that the Antonine plague severely reduced the population of the town. A. E. R. Boak, "Egypt and the plague of Marcus Aurelius," *Historia: Zeitschrift für Alte Geschichte* 8, no. 2 (1959): 250.

19. R. P. Stephan and A. Verhoogt, "Text and context in the archive of Tiberianus (Karanis, Egypt; 2nd Century AD)," *BASP* 42, no. 1–4 (2005): 196–97.

20. E. Cole, "Recent excavations at Karanis: Storing agricultural yield and stacking archaeological information" (paper presented at the conference "Das Fayum in Hellenismus und Kaiserzeit—Fallstudien zu multikulturellem Leben in der Antike" Bronnbach Monastery, Germany, May 4–7, 2011).

Appendix 1. The Excavations at Karanis   283

work confirms the chronology proposed by N. Pollard, who reinterpreted the ceramics recovered by the Michigan team.[21] This all suggests that the data from the earlier excavation can be rehabilitated, although it will be necessary to work upward from individual levels and houses. In the excavation of the 1920s and 1930s, all of the material discovered within the walls of a house during a particular construction phase was recorded within a single room designation and used to interpret the function and period of the room or building. While this approach does rightly associate artifacts that are found together, modern excavations rely on variations in the soil—stratigraphy—in order to differentiate between periods of use. To reconstruct the stratigraphy, if such a goal is possible, individual finds must be studied and compared to other objects from within the same building or insula.

A geographic information system (GIS) offers one avenue that can be utilized to organize the data and reanalyze the material from the site. The latest datable material from an individual unit can be used to date a room and its contents, and this material can be compared with other nearby rooms, buildings, and insula blocks. Once rooms and buildings have been dated, the GIS platform can divide and reconstitute the levels at Karanis.[22] This is a long-term project, but it has the potential to make an early twentieth-century excavation more accessible to scholars wishing to study the wealth of material that the site has to offer.

---

21. On Pollard's dating, see above, ch. 3 n. 26.
22. D. Wilburn, "Re-Mapping Karanis: Geographic Information Systems (GIS) and site analysis," in *Proceedings of the Twenty-Fifth International Congress of Papyrology, Ann Arbor 2007*, ed. T. Gagos, *American Studies in Papyrology* (2010). Katja Mueller has done productive work with GIS mapping in order to locate settlements in the Fayum. See K. Mueller, "What's your position? Using Multi-Dimensional Scaling (MDS) and Geographical Information Systems (GIS) for locating ancient settlements in the Meris of Polemon / Graeco-Roman Fayum," *Archiv für Papyrusforschung und verwandte Gebiete* 50, no. 2 (2004); K. Mueller, "Geographical Information Systems (GIS) in papyrology. Mapping fragmentation and migration flow to Hellenistic Egypt," *BASP* 42, no. 1–4 (2005).

Appendix 2

Bones from Karanis Areas 262 and 265

Lot No.	Area	Bone No.	Species	Bone Type	Joins	Side 1	Side 2
		000	Limey Chalk			Large Dots	
3503	265	001	Mammal	Rib		Lines	
3503	265	002	Mammal	Rib		Undulating Lines (Und. Lines)	
3503	265	003	Mammal	Rib		Lines	
3503	265	004	Mammal	Rib		Dots	
3503	265	005	Mammal	Rib	063	Und. Lines	
3503	265	006	Mammal	Rib		Lines	
3503	265	007	Mammal	Rib		Dots	
3503	265	008	Mammal	Rib		Lines	
3503	265	009	Mammal	Rib		Lines	
3503	265	010	Mammal	Rib		Lines	
3503	265	011	Mammal	Rib		Lines	Dots
3503	265	012	Bos/ Equus	Thoracic Vertebra		Dots	Lines
3503	265	013	Mammal	Cervical Vertebra		Und. Lines	Dots
3503	265	014	Sus	Scapula		Lines	
3503	265	015	Sus	Scapula		Lines	
3503	265	016	Sus	Scapula		Traces	Lines
3503	265	017	Sus	Scapula		Dots	Lines
3503	265	018	Sus	Scapula		Dots	Single Dot
3503	265	019	Sus	Scapula		Dots	Dots
3503	265	020	Mammal	Tibia		Lines	
3503	265	021	Sus	Tibia		Lines	Lines
3503	265	022	Mammal	Humerus		Lines	
3503	265	023	Sus	Humerus		Lines	
3503	265	024	Sus	Ulna		Lines	
3503	265	025	Equus	Ischium		Lines	
3503	265	026	Equus	Scapula		Dots	Single Dot
3503	265	027	Sus	Mandible			
3503	265	028	Canis	Mandible		Lines	
3503	265	030	Ovis/ Capra	Radius/Ulna		Lines	Dots
3503	265	031	Ovis/ Capra	Mandible	036, 067	Lines	
3503	265	032	Ovis/ Capra	Mandible		Lines	
3503	265	033	Ovis/ Capra	Mandible		Und. Lines	
3503	265	034	Ovis/ Capra	Mandible		Lines	
3503	265	035	Ovis/ Capra	Mandible	038, 064, 066	Und. Lines	
3503	265	036	Ovis/ Capra	Mandible	031, 067	Lines	

Lot No.	Area	Bone No.	Species	Bone Type	Joins	Side 1	Side 2
3503	265	037	Mammal	Mandible Ramus		Lines	
3503	265	038	Equus	Mandible	035, 064, 066	Und. Lines	
3503	265	039	Mammal	Mandible Ramus		Lines	
3503	265	040	Mammal	Mandible Ramus		Lines	
3503	265	041	Sus	Mandible Ramus		Und. Lines	
3503	265	042	Sus	Ramus		Und. Lines	
3503	265	043	Mammal	Mandible		Lines	Lines
3503	265	044	Sus	Mandible Ramus		Und. Lines	
3503	265	045	Sus	Mandible Ramus		Lines	Dot
3503	265	046	Mammal	Long Bone		Lines	Dots
3503	265	047	Mammal	Long Bone		Lines, Dots	
3503	265	048	Mammal	Long Bone		Lines	
3503	265	049	Mammal	Rib		Lines	
3503	265	050	Mammal	Long Bone		Lines	
3503	265	051	Mammal	Inominate		Lines	
3503	265	051	Mammal	Tibia		Lines	
3503	265	052	Fish	Bone		None	
3503	265	053	Mammal	Long Bone			
3503	265	054	Mammal	Long Bone		Dots	
3503	265	055	Mammal	UNID		Curvy Lines	
3503	265	056	Mammal	UNID			
3503	265	057	Mammal	Inominate		Lines	
3503	265	058	Mammal	Tibia		Lines	Dot
3503	265	059	Sus	Tibia		Large Dots	Dot
3503	265	060	Fish	Bone		Lines	
3503	265	061	Homo	Parietal	100	Dots	Blotches
3503	265	062					
3503	265	063	Mammal	Rib	005	Und. Lines	
3503	265	064	Equus	Mandible	035, 038, 066	Und. Lines	
3503	265	065	Equus	Mandible Ramus	096	Lines	Dots
3503	265	066	Equus	Mandible	038, 038, 064	Und. Lines	
3503	265	067	Ovis/ Capra	Mandible	031, 036	Lines	
10099	265	068	Bos	Mandible		Lines	Lines
10099	265	069	Mammal	Scapula		Dots	Dots
10099	265	070	Bos	Femur		Lines	
10099	265	071	Bos	Inominate		Lines	
10099	265	072	Equus	Inominate		Und. Lines	
3504	262	075	Equus	Axis		Dots	Lines
3504	262	076	Mammal	Humerus		Lines, Dots	
3504	262	077	Sus	Humerus		Line, Dots	
3504	262	078	Sus	Humerus		Dots	
3504	262	079	Sus	Mandible		Dots	
3504	262	080	Bos	Mandible		Und. Lines	
3504	262	081	Sus	Molar	093	Dots	Dots
3504	262	082	Sus	Mandible		Lines	Lines
3504	262	083	Mammal	Long Bone		Dots	Dots
3504	262	084	Mammal	Long Bone		Dots	Dots
3504	262	085	Mammal	Distal Mandible		Dots	
3504	262	086	Mammal	Shaft		Lines	
3504	262	087	Mammal	Rib		Dots	
3504	262	089	Mammal	Rib		Dots	

Lot No.	Area	Bone No.	Species	Bone Type	Joins	Side 1	Side 2
3535		088	Equus	Mandible		Dots	
3535		089	Equus	Metatarsus		Dots	
3535		090	Equus	Tibia		Dots	
3535		091	Equus	Humerus		Dots	
3535		092	Mammal	Vertebrum Centrum		Dots	Dots
3535		093	Sus	Mandible		Dots	Dots
3535		094	Sus	Mandible	081	Dots	Dots
3535		095	Sus	Mandible		Dots	1 Line
3503	265	095	Mammal	Inominate		Dots	
3504	262	096	Equus	Mandible Ramus	065	Lines	Dots
3504	262	097	Mammal	Ilium		Dots	
3503	265	098	Homo	Parietal		Lines, Dots	
3503	265	099	Homo	Parietal		Dots	Lines
3503	265	100	Homo	Parietal		Dots	Dots
3503	265	101	Mammal	Inominate		Curvy Lines and Dots	Dots
3503	265	102	Mammal	Inominate		Dots	
3503	265	103	Mammal	Mandible/ Inominate		Lines	
3503	265	104	Sus	Ilium		Lines	Stain?

Bibliography

Abt, Adam. *Die Apologie des Apuleius von Madaura und die antike Zauberei*. Gießen: A. Töpelmann, 1908.

Abusch, Tzvi. "Mesopotamian anti-witchcraft literature: Texts and studies part I: The nature of Maqlû: Its character, divisions, and calendrical setting." *JNES* 33, no. 2 (1974): 251–62.

Ager, Britta. "Roman agricultural magic." PhD diss., University of Michigan, 2010.

Alfayé Villa, Silvia. "Nails for the dead: A polysemic account of an ancient funerary practice." In *Magical practice in the Latin West: Papers from the international conference held at the University of Zaragoza, 30 Sept.–1 Oct. 2005,* edited by Richard L. Gordon and Francisco Marco Simón, 427–56. Leiden: Brill, 2010.

Alföldy, Géza. *Fasti Hispanienses: senatorische Rechtsbeamte und Offiziere in den spanischen Provinzen des Römischen Reiches von Augustus bis Diokletian*. Wiesbaden: F. Steiner, 1969.

Almagro Basch, Martín. *Las Inscripciones Ampuritanas Griegas, Ibéricas y Latinas*. Monografías Ampuritanas 2. Barcelona: el Departamento de Barcelona del Instituto Rodrigo Caro de Arqueología del CSIC, 1952.

Almagro Basch, Martín. *Las necrópolis de Ampurias I: Introducción y necrópolis griegas*. Monografías ampuritanas 3. Barcelona: Seix y Barral, 1953.

Almagro Basch, Martín. *Las necrópolis de Ampurias II: Necrópolis romanas y necrópolis indígenas,* Mongrafías ampuritanas 3. Barcelona: Casa Provincial de Caridad, Imprenta Escuela, 1955.

Almagro Basch, Martín. "Plomos con inscripción del Museo de Ampurias." *Memorias de los Museos Arqueológicos Provinciales* 8 (1947): 122–26.

Almagro Gorbea, Martín. "Nuevas tumbas halladas en las necrópolis de Ampurias." *Ampurias* 24 (1962): 225–34.

Alston, Richard. *Soldier and society in Roman Egypt: A social history*. New York: Routledge, 1995.

Altenmüller, Hartwig. "Apotropaikon." In *LÄ*, 355–58. Wiesbaden: Otto Harrassowitz, 1975.

Altenmüller, Hartwig. *Die Apotropaia und die Götter Mittelägyptens: Eine typolo-*

288   Bibliography

gische und religionsgeschichtliche Untersuchung der sog: "Zaubermesser" des Mittleren Reichs. 2 vols. Munich, 1965.

Amundsen, Leiv. "Magical text on an Oslo ostracon." *SO* 7, no. 1 (1928): 36–37.

Andreu Pintado, Javier. *Edictum, municipium y lex: Hispania en época Flavia (69–96 d.C.).* BAR international series 1293. Oxford: Archaeopress, 2004.

Andrews, Carol. *Amulets of ancient Egypt.* Austin: University of Texas Press, 1994.

Appadurai, Arjun. "Introduction: Commodities and the politics of value." In *The social life of things: Commodities in cultural perspective,* edited by Arjun Appadurai, 3–63. Cambridge: Cambridge University Press, 1986.

Aquilé Abadías, Javier. *Empúries.* Empúries: Museu d'Arqueologia de Catalunya, 2000.

Aubert, Jean-Jacques. "Threatened wombs: Aspects of ancient uterine magic." *GRBS* 30, no. 3 (1989): 421–49.

Audollent, Auguste Marie Henri. *Defixionum Tabellae.* Paris: Fontemoing, 1904.

Aune, David E. "Magic in early Christianity." *ANRW* II 23, no. 2 (1980): 1507–57.

Aupert, Pierre. "Amathonte hellénistique et impériale: l'apport des travaux récents." *Cahiers du Centre Études Cypriotes* 39 (2009): 25–48.

Aupert, Pierre. "Hélios, Adonis et magie: les trésors d'une citerne d'Amathonte." *BCH* 132, no. 1 (2008): 347–87.

Aupert, Pierre, Marie-Christine Hellmann, and Michel Amandry. *Amathonte I. Testimonia 1: Auteurs anciens, Monnayage, Voyageurs, Fouilles, Origines, Geógraphie,* Etudes chypriotes 5. Paris: École Française d'Athènes, 1984.

Aupert, Pierre, and David R. Jordan. "Magical inscriptions on talc tablets from Amathous." *AJA* 85, no. 2 (1981): 184.

Aupert, Pierre, and David R. Jordan. "Tablettes magiques d'Amathonte." In *Art Antique de Chypre du Bronze moyen à l'époque byzantine au Cabinet des médailles,* 67–71. Paris: Bibliothèque Nationale de France, 1994.

Aupert, Pierre, Jean-Paul Prête, Isabelle Tassignon, and Tony Kozelj. "Rapport sur les travaux de l'école Française d'Athènes en 2003 et 2004: Amathone: Agora." *BCH* 128–29 (2004–5): 1022–77.

Aupert, Pierre, Jean-Paul Prête, Isabelle Tassignon, Tony Kozelj, and Manuela Wurch-Kozelj. "Rapport sur les travaux de l'école Française d'Athènes en 2003 et 2004: Amathone: Agora." *BCH* 127 (2003): 526–45.

Ausbüttel, Frank M. *Untersuchungen zu den Vereinen im Westen des Römischen Reiches,* Frankfurter althistorische Studien. Heft 11. Kallmünz: M. Lassleben, 1982.

Bagnall, Roger S. *Early Christian books in Egypt.* Princeton: Princeton University Press, 2009.

Bagnall, Roger S. *Egypt in Late Antiquity.* Princeton: Princeton University Press, 1993.

Bagnall, Roger S. "Papyri and Ostraka from Quseir al-Qadim." *BASP* 23, no. 1–2 (1986): 1–60.

Bailey, Ryan. "The *Confession* of Cyprian of Antioch: Introduction, text and translation." Master of Arts, McGill University, 2009.

Bailliot, Magali. *Magie et sortilèges dans l'Antiquité romaine.* Paris: Hermann éditeurs, 2010.

Baines, John. "Practical religion and piety." *JEA* 73 (1987): 79–98.

Baines, John. "Society, morality, and religious practice." In *Religion in ancient Egypt: Gods, myths and personal practice,* edited by Byron E. Shafer, 123–99. Ithaca: Cornell University Press, 1991.

Balil, A. "Defixiones ampuritanas." *Archivo Español de Arqueología* 37 (1964): 197–201.

Barb, Alfons A. "Diva matrix." *JWarb* 16, no. 3–4 (1953): 193–238.

Barb, Alfons A. "The mermaid and the devil's grandmother." *JWarb* 29 (1966): 1–23.

Barnes, Timothy David. *Constantine and Eusebius.* Cambridge: Harvard University Press, 1981.

Barton, Carlin A. *The sorrows of the ancient Romans: The gladiator and the monster.* Princeton: Princeton University Press, 1993.

Bataille, Georges. *Theory of religion.* Translated by Robert Hurley. New York: Zone Books, 1989.

Bauman, Richard. "Verbal art as performance." *American Anthropologist* 77, no. 2 (1975): 290–311.

Bear, L. M. *The mineral resources and mining industry of Cyprus.* Nicosia: Ministry of Commerce and Industry, 1963.

Bell, Catherine M. *Ritual theory, ritual practice.* New York: Oxford University Press, 1992.

Bell, H. I. Review of *Papyri and Ostraca from Karanis* by Herbert C. Youtie and Orsamus M. Pearl. *JRS* 35 (1945): 136–40.

Belson, Janer Danforth. "The gorgoneion in Greek architecture." PhD diss., Bryn Mawr College, 1981.

Benjamin, Walter. "The work of art in the age of mechanical reproduction." In *Illuminations,* edited by Hannah Arendt, 217–51. New York: Schocken Books, 1969.

Benveniste, Émile. "Le sens du mot KOLOSSOS et les noms grecs de la statue." *Révue de philologie* 58 (1932): 118–35.

Bergman, Jan. *Ich bin Isis. Studien zum memphitischen Hintergrund der griechischen Isisaretalogien,* Acta Universitatis Upsaliensis, Historia religionum 3. Stockholm: Almqvist & Wiksell, 1968.

Bernand, André. *Sorciers grecs.* Paris: Fayard, 1991.

Bernand, Étienne. *Recueil des inscriptions grecques du Fayoum,* Bibliothèque d'étude. Leiden: Brill, 1975.

Betz, Hans Dieter. "Secrecy in the Greek magical papyri." In *Secrecy and concealment: Studies in the history of Mediterranean and Near Eastern religions,* edited by Hans G. Kippenberg and Guy G. Stroumsa, 153–75. Leiden: Brill, 1995.

Betz, Hans Dieter. *The Greek magical papyri in translation.* 2nd ed. Chicago: University of Chicago Press, 1992.

Biezunska-Malowist, I. "La famille du vétéran romain C. Iulius Niger de Karanis." *Eos* 49 (1957): 155–64.

290   Bibliography

Binford, Lewis R. "Mortuary practices: Their study and potential." In *Approaches to the social dimensions of mortuary practices,* edited by James A. Brown, 6–29. Washington, DC: Society for American Archaeology, 1971.

Blandin, Béatrice, and Sabine Fourrier. "Le dépôt archaïque du rempart Nord d'Amathonte. I. Introduction: le contexte." *BCH* 127, no. 1 (2003): 101–5.

Blänsdorf, Jürgen. "Dal segno alla scrittura. Le defixiones della fontana di Anna Perenna." *SMSR* 76 (2010): 35–64.

Blänsdorf, Jürgen. "Die *defixionum tabellae* des Mainzer Isis- und Mater-Magna-Heiligtums." In *Instrumenta inscripta latina II: Akten des 2. Internationalen Kolloquiums, Klagenfurt, 5.–8. Mai 2005,* edited by Manfred Hainzmann and Reinhold Wedenig, 47–70. Klagenfurt: Geschichtsverein für Kärnten, 2008.

Blänsdorf, Jürgen. "The curse tablets from the Sanctuary of Isis and Mater Magna in Mainz." *MHNH* 5 (2005): 11–26.

Blänsdorf, Jürgen. "The *defixiones* from the Sanctuary of Isis and Mater Magna in Mainz." In *Magical practice in the Latin West: Papers from the international conference held at the University of Zaragoza, 30 Sept.–1 Oct. 2005,* edited by Richard L. Gordon and Francisco Marco Simón, 141–90. Leiden: Brill, 2010.

Blänsdorf, Jürgen. "The texts from the Fons Annae Perennae." In *Magical practice in the Latin West: Papers from the international conference held at the University of Zaragoza, 30 Sept.–1 Oct. 2005,* edited by Richard L. Gordon and Francisco Marco Simón, 215–44. Leiden: Brill, 2010.

Blümel, Wolfgang. *Die Inschriften von Knidos.* Bonn: R. Habelt, 1992.

Boak, Arthur Edward Romilly. "Egypt and the plague of Marcus Aurelius." *Historia: Zeitschrift für Alte Geschichte* 8, no. 2 (1959): 248–50.

Boak, Arthur Edward Romilly. *Karanis: The temples, coin hoards, botanical and zoölogical reports, seasons 1924–31,* University of Michigan studies, Humanistic series vol. 30. Ann Arbor: University of Michigan Press, 1933.

Boak, Arthur Edward Romilly, and Enoch Ernest Peterson. *Karanis: Topographical and architectural report of excavations during the seasons 1924–28.* University of Michigan studies, Humanistic series vol. 25. Ann Arbor: University of Michigan Press, 1931.

Bodel, John. "Cicero's Minerva, *Penates,* and the Mother of the *Lares:* An outline of Roman domestic religion." In *Household and family religion in antiquity,* edited by John Bodel and Saul M. Olyan, 248–75. Malden, MA: Blackwell, 2008.

Bodel, John. "Dealing with the dead: Undertakers, executioners and potter's fields in ancient Rome." In *Death and disease in the ancient city,* edited by Valerie M. Hope and Eireann Marshall, 128–51. New York: Routledge, 2000.

Boedeker, Deborah. "Family matters: Domestic religion in classical Greece." In *Household and family religion in antiquity,* edited by John Bodel and Saul M. Olyan, 229–47. Malden, MA: Blackwell, 2008.

Bogaert, Raymond. *Banques et banquiers dans les cités grecques.* Leiden: A. W. Sijthoff, 1968.

Bibliography   291

Bohak, Gideon. *Ancient Jewish magic: A history.* New York: Cambridge University Press, 2008.

Bohak, Gideon. "Hebrew, Hebrew everywhere? Notes on the interpretation of *voces magicae.*" In *Prayer, magic, and the stars in the ancient and Late Antique world,* edited by Scott B. Noegel, Joel Thomas Walker, and Brannon M. Wheeler, 69–82. University Park: Pennsylvania State University Press, 2003.

Bohleke, Briant. "An oracular amuletic decree of Khonsu in the Cleveland Museum of Art." *JEA* 83 (1997): 155–67.

Bonneau, Danielle. "Un réglement de l'usage de l'eau au Ve siècle de notre ère. Commentaire de P. Haun. inv. 318." In *Hommages à la mémoire de Serge Sauneron, 1927–1976,* 3–23. Cairo: Institut français d'archéologie orientale, 1979.

Bonner, Campbell. "Magical amulets." *HThR* 39, no. 1 (1946): 25–54.

Bonner, Campbell. *Studies in magical amulets, chiefly Graeco-Egyptian.* University of Michigan studies, Humanistic series vol. 49. Ann Arbor: University of Michigan Press, 1950.

Bonner, Campbell. "Witchcraft in the lecture room of Libanius." *TAPA* 63 (1932): 34–44.

Bookidis, Nancy, and Ronald S. Stroud. *Demeter and Persephone in ancient Corinth.* Princeton, NJ: American School of Classical Studies at Athens, 1987.

Borghouts, Joris F. *Ancient Egyptian magical texts.* Leiden: Brill, 1978.

Bourdieu, Pierre. *Outline of a theory of practice.* Translated by Richard Nice. Cambridge studies in social anthropology 16. New York: Cambridge University Press, 1977.

Bourdieu, Pierre. "The Berber house or the world reversed." In *Interpretive archaeology: A reader,* edited by Julian Thomas, 493–509. New York: Leicester University Press, 2000.

Braarvig, Jens. "Magic: Reconsidering the grand dichotomy." In *The world of ancient magic: Papers from the first international Samson Eitrem seminar at the Norwegian Institute at Athens, 4–8 May 1997,* edited by David R. Jordan, Hugo Montgomery, and Einar Thomassen, 21–54. Bergen: Norwegian Institute at Athens, 1999.

Bradley, Richard. *The passage of arms: An archaeological analysis of prehistoric hoards and votive deposits.* 2nd ed. Oxford: Oxbow Books, 1998.

Brakke, David. "From temple to cell, from gods to demons: Pagan temples in the monastic topography of fourth century Egypt." In *From temple to church: Destruction and renewal of local cultic topography in Late Antiquity,* edited by Stephen Emmel, Ulrich Gotter, and Johannes Hahn, 91–112. Leiden: Brill, 2008.

Brashear, William. "768. Fever amulet." In *P.Michigan Koenen (=P.Mich. XVIII): Michigan texts published in honor of Ludwig Koenen,* edited by Ludwig Koenen, Cornelia Römer, and Traianos Gagos, 75–87. Amsterdam: Gieben, 1996.

Brashear, William. "'Botokudenphilologie' vindicated." Review of *The Greek magical papyri in translation, including the demotic spells, volume I: Texts,* by Hans Dieter Betz. *International Journal of the Classical Tradition* 5, no. 1 (1998): 66–79.

292   Bibliography

Brashear, William. "The Greek magical papyri: An introduction and survey; annotated bibliography (1928–1994)." *ANRW* II 18, no. 5 (1995): 3380–3684.

Brashear, William. "Ein neues Zauberensemble in München." *Studien zur altägyptischen Kultur* 19 (1992): 79–109.

Brashear, William. "Hocus Pocus, Verbatim." *Language Quarterly* 29, no. 1 (1992): 1–3.

Brashear, William. *Magica Varia.* Brussels: Fondation Egyptologique Reine Elisabeth, 1991.

Brashear, William. "Magical papyri: Magic in book form." In *Das Buch als magisches und als Repräsentationsobjekt,* edited by Peter Ganz, 25–57. Wiesbaden: Otto Harrassowitz, 1992.

Brashear, William. "Vier Berliner Zaubertexte." *ZPE* 17 (1975): 25–33.

Brashear, William. "Zwei Zauberformulare." *Archiv für Papyrusforschung und verwandte Gebiete* 38 (1992): 19–26.

Braun, Karin. "Der Dipylon-Brunnen B1, die Funde." *Mitteilungen des Deutschen Archäologischen Instituts, Athenische Abteilung* 85 (1970): 129–269.

Bremmer, Jan N. *Greek religion and culture, the Bible, and the ancient Near East.* Leiden: Brill, 2008.

Bremmer, Jan N. "The birth of the term 'magic.'" *ZPE* 126 (1999): 1–12.

Bremmer, Jan N., and Jan R. Veenstra, eds. *The metamorphosis of magic from Late Antiquity to the early modern period.* Vol. 1, Groningen studies in cultural change. Leuven: Peeters, 2002.

Bresciani, Edda. "Isis lactans et Horus sur les crocodiles." In *Egyptian religion: The last thousand years: Studies dedicated to the memory of Jan Quaegebeur,* edited by Willy Clarysse, Antoon Schoors, Harco Willems, and Jan Quaegebeur, 57–60. Leuven: Peeters, 1998.

Bricault, Laurent, Miguel John Versluys, and Paul G. P. Meyboom, eds. *Nile into Tiber: Egypt in the Roman world: Proceedings of the IIIrd international conference of Isis studies, Leiden, May 11–14 2005.* Leiden: Brill, 2007.

Brooten, Bernadette J. *Love between women: Early Christian responses to female homoeroticism.* The Chicago series on sexuality, history, and society. Chicago: University of Chicago Press, 1996.

Brown, James. "Charnel houses and mortuary crypts: Disposal of the dead in the Middle Woodland period." In *Hopewell archaeology: The Chillicothe conference,* edited by David S. Brose and Naomi Greber, 211–19. Kent, OH: Kent State University Press, 1979.

Brown, Peter. "Sorcery, demons and the rise of Christianity from Late Antiquity into the middle ages." In *Witchcraft: Confessions and accusations,* edited by Mary Douglas, 17–45. New York: Tavistock, 1970.

Brown, Peter. *The world of Late Antiquity, AD 150–750.* New York: W. W. Norton, 1971.

Brunton, Guy. "The oracle of Kôm el-Wist." *Annales du service des antiquités de l'Égypte* 47 (1947): 293–95.

Bibliography   293

Brunton, Guy, and Geoffrey M. Morant. *British museum expedition to middle Egypt.* London: B. Quaritch, 1937.

Bryen, Ari Z., and Andrzej Wypustek. "Gemellus' evil eyes (*P.Mich.* VI 423–424)." *GRBS* 49, no. 4 (2009): 535–55.

Buonopane, Alfredo. "Una defixionis tabella da Verona." In *EPIGRAPHAI: Miscellanea epigraphica in onore di Lidio Gasperini,* edited by Gianfranco Paci, 163–69. Tivoli (Rome): Editrice Tipigraf, 2000.

Burkert, Walter. *Die orientalisierende Epoche in der griechischen Religion und Literatur.* Heidelberg: Winter, 1984.

Burkert, Walter. "Itinerant diviners and magicians: A neglected element in cultural contacts." In *The Greek Renaissance of the eighth century B.C.: Tradition and innovation: Proceedings of the second international symposium at the Swedish Institute in Athens, 1–5 June 1981,* edited by Robin Hägg, 115–19. Stockholm: Svenska institutet i Athen, 1983.

Burnett, Andrew, Michel Amandry, and Pere P. Ripollès. *Roman provincial coinage.* 2 vols. Vol. I. London: British Museum Press, 1992.

Burrell, Barbara. "'Curse tablets' from Caesarea." *Near Eastern Archaeology* 61, no. 2 (1998): 128.

Cagnat, René. *Cours d'épigraphie Latine.* IV ed. Rome: L'Erma di Bretschneider, 1964.

Caillet, Jean-Pierre. "La transformation en église d'édifices publics et de temples à la fin de l'antiquité." In *La fin de la cité antique et le début de la cité médiévale: de la fin du IIIe siècle à l'avènement de Charlemagne: actes du colloque tenu à l'Université de Paris X-Nanterre, les 1, 2 et 3 avril 1993,* edited by Claude Lepelley, 191–211. Bari: Edipuglia, 1996.

Campbell, William Alexander. "The third season of excavation at Antioch-on-the-Orontes." *AJA* 40, no. 1 (1936): 1–10.

Capasso, Mario. "Alcuni papiri figurati magici recentemente trovati a Soknopaiou Nesos." In *New archaeological and papyrological researches on the Fayyum: Proceedings of the international meeting of Egyptology and papyrology, Lecce 8th–10th June 2005,* edited by Mario Capasso and Paola Davoli, 49–66. Galatina (Lecce): Congedo, 2007.

Casas, Josep, Pere Castanyer, Josep Maria Nolla, and Joaquim Tremoleda. "Les ceràmiques comunes locals del N.E. de Catalunya." In *Ceràmica comuna romana d'època Alto-Imperial a la Península Ibèrica. Estat de la qüestió,* edited by Javier Aquilué Abadías and Mercè Roca Roumens, 99–127. Empúries: Museu d'Arqueologia de Catalunya, 1995.

Caton-Thompson, Gertrude, and Elinor Wight Gardner. *The desert Fayum.* London: Royal Anthropological Institute of Great Britain and Ireland, 1934.

Cecchelli, Marherita. "Fasciola, Titulus." In *Lexicon topographicum urbis Romae,* 6 vols., edited by Eva Margareta Steinby, 2:241–42. Rome: Quasar, 1993.

Cesnola, Alessandro Palma di. *Salaminia (Cyprus). The history, treasures, & antiquities of Salamis in the island of Cyprus.* London: Whiting, 1884.

294   Bibliography

Cesnola, Luigi Palma di, Charles William King, and Alexander Stuart Murray. *Cyprus: Its ancient cities, tombs, and temples. A narrative of researches and excavations during ten years' residence in that island.* New York: Harper & Brothers, 1878.

Chaniotis, Angelos. "The conversion of the temple of Aphrodite at Aphrodisias in context." In *From temple to church: Destruction and renewal of local cultic topography in Late Antiquity,* edited by Stephen Emmel, Ulrich Gotter, and Johannes Hahn, 243–74. Leiden: Brill, 2008.

Chaniotis, Angelos. "Under the watchful eyes of the gods: Divine justice in Hellenistic and Roman Asia Minor." In *The Greco-Roman East: Politics, culture, society,* edited by Stephen Colvin, 1–43. New York: Cambridge University Press, 2004.

Chaniotis, Angelos, and Jannis Mylonopoulos. "Epigraphic bulletin for Greek religion 1997." *Kernos* 13 (2000): 127–237.

Chassinat, Émile, and Maxence de Rochemonteix. *Le temple d'Edfou.* Vol. 3. Paris: Leroux, 1928.

Chaucer, Geoffrey. *Canterbury Tales.* Edited and translated by A. Kent Hieatt and Constance Hieatt. New York: Bantam Books, 1964.

Cohen, David. *Law, sexuality, and society: The enforcement of morals in classical Athens.* New York: Cambridge University Press, 1991.

Cole, Emily. "Recent excavations at Karanis: Storing agricultural yield and stacking archaeological information." Lecture at the conference "Das Fayum in Hellenismus und Kaiserzeit—Fallstudien zu multikulturellem Leben in der Antike," Bronnbach Monastery, Germany, May 4–7, 2011.

Collins, Adela Y. "Numerical symbolism in Jewish and early Christian apocalyptic literature." *ANRW* II 21, no. 2 (1984): 1221–87.

Collins, Derek. *Magic in the ancient Greek world.* Malden, MA: Blackwell, 2008.

Constabile, Felice. "Defixiones dal Kerameikos di Atene, II. maledizioni processuali." *Minima epigraphica et papyrologica* 4 (2000): 17–122.

Constabile, Felice. "Καταδεσμοι." *Mitteilungen des Deutschen Archäologischen Instituts, Athenische Abteilung* 114 (1999): 87–104.

Cook, R. James. "Economy, society and irrigation at a Graeco-Roman site in Egypt: The Karanis canal system." PhD diss., University of Michigan, 2011.

Coulton, John J. "The stoa at the Amphiareion, Oropos." *ABSA* 63 (1968): 147–83.

Cramer, Frederick Henry. *Astrology in Roman law and politics.* Philadelphia: American Philosophical Society, 1954.

Crevatin, Franco. "Alcune osservazioni linguistiche sulla lamina di piombo da Agrigento (?)." *ArchClass* 27 (1975): 47–50.

Crevatin, Franco. *Gymnastics of the mind: Greek education in Hellenistic and Roman Egypt.* Princeton: Princeton University Press, 2001.

Cribiore, Raffaella. *Writing, teachers, and students in Graeco-Roman Egypt.* Atlanta: Scholars Press, 1996.

Cronyn, J. M., and Wendy S. Robinson. *The elements of archaeological conservation.* London: Routledge, 1990.

Crum, Walter E. "La magie copte: Nouveaux textes." In *Recueil d'études égyptologiques dédiées à la mémoire de Jean-François Champollion à l'occasion du centenaire de la lettre à M. Dacier relative à l'alphabet des hiéroglyphes phonétiques,* 537–44. Paris: E. Champion, 1922.

Curbera, Jaime B. "A curse tablet from Emporiae (IRC III 175)." *ZPE* 110 (1996): 292–94.

Curbera, Jaime B. "Maternal lineage in Greek magical texts." In *The world of ancient magic: Papers from the first international Samson Eitrem seminar at the Norwegian Institute at Athens, 4–8 May 1997,* edited by David R. Jordan, Hugo Montgomery, and Einar Thomassen, 195–203. Bergen: Norwegian Institute of Athens, 1999.

Curbera, Jaime B. "The Greek curse tablets of Emporion." *ZPE* 117 (1997): 90–94.

Daniel, Robert W., and Franco Maltomini. *Supplementum magicum.* Papyrologica Coloniensia 16. Opladen: Westdeutscher Verlag, 1990.

Dawson, Warren R. "Studies in medical history: (a) the origin of the herbal. (b) castoroil in antiquity." *Aegyptus* 10 (1929): 47–72.

Dawson, Warren R. "The mouse in Egyptian and later medicine." *JEA* 10, no. 2 (1924): 83–86.

De Montmollin, Olivier. *The archaeology of political structure: Settlement analysis in a classic Maya polity.* New studies in archaeology. New York: Cambridge University Press, 1989.

de Rossi, Giovanni B. "Adunanza dell'Istituto." *Bullettino dell'Istituto di Corrispondenza Archeologica* (1880): 6–9.

Deal, Michael. "Abandonment patterning at archaeological settlements." In *Archaeological concepts for the study of the cultural past,* edited by Alan P. Sullivan, 141–57. Salt Lake City: University of Utah Press, 2008.

Deal, Michael. "Household pottery disposal in the Maya highlands: An ethnoarchaeological interpretation." *Journal of Anthropological Archaeology* 4 (1985): 243–91.

Delatte, Armand. "Études sur la magie greque 5: *Akephalos Theos.*" *BCH* 38 (1914): 189–249.

Delatte, Armand, and Philippe Derchain. *Les intailles magiques gréco-égyptiennes.* Paris: Bibliothèque nationale, 1964.

Depauw, Mark. "Do mothers matter? The emergence of metronymics in early Roman Egypt." In *The language of the papyri,* edited by T. V. Evans and D. D. Obbink, 120–39. New York: Oxford University Press, 2010.

Derda, Tomasz. *Arsinoites nomos: Administration of the Fayum under Roman rule.* Juristic Papyrology. Supplement vol. 7. Warsaw: Faculty of Law and Administration of Warsaw University, 2006.

Desroches-Noblecourt, Christiane. "'Concubines du Mort' et mères de famille au Moyen Empire." *BIFAO* 53 (1953): 7–47.

Dickie, Matthew W. "Heliodorus and Plutarch on the evil eye." *CPh* 86, no. 1 (1991): 17–29.

Dickie, Matthew W. "Lo φθονος degli dei nella letteratura greca del quinto secolo avanti Christo." *A&R* 32, no. 113–25 (1987).

Dickie, Matthew W. *Magic and magicians in the Greco-Roman world.* New York: Routledge, 2001.

Dickie, Matthew W. "Magic in the Roman historians." In *Magical practice in the Latin West: Papers from the international conference held at the University of Zaragoza, 30 Sept.–1 Oct. 2005,* edited by Richard L. Gordon and Francisco Marco Simón, 79–104. Leiden: Brill, 2010.

Dickie, Matthew W. "The learned magician and the collection and transmission of magical lore." In *The world of ancient magic: Papers from the first international Samson Eitrem seminar at the Norwegian Institute at Athens, 4–8 May 1997,* edited by David R. Jordan, Hugo Montgomery and Einar Thomassen, 163–93. Bergen: Norwegian Institute at Athens, 1999.

Dickie, Matthew W. "Varia magica." *Tyche* 14 (1999): 57–76.

Dickie, Matthew W. "What is a *kolossos* and how were *kolossoi* made in the Hellenistic period?" *GRBS* 37, no. 3 (1996): 237–57.

Dickie, Matthew W. "Who practiced love-magic in classical antiquity and in the late Roman world?" *CQ* 50, no. 2 (2000): 563–83.

Dieleman, Jacco. *Priests, tongues, and rites: The London-Leiden magical manuscripts and translation in Egyptian ritual (100–300 CE).* Religions in the Graeco-Roman world 153. Leiden: Brill, 2005.

Dieleman, Jacco. "Zerbrechen der roten Töpfe." In *LÄ*, 1390–96. Wiesbaden: O. Harrassowitz, 1972–.

Dijkstra, Jitse H. F. *Philae and the end of ancient Egyptian religion: A regional study of religious transformation (298–642 CE).* Leuven: Peeters, 2008.

Dincauze, Dena Ferran. *Environmental archaeology: Principles and practice.* New York: Cambridge University Press, 2000.

Donalson, Malcolm Drew. *The cult of Isis in the Roman Empire: Isis Invicta.* Lewiston, NY: Edwin Mellen Press, 2003.

Dornseiff, Franz. *Das alphabet in mystik und magie.* Leipzig: B. G. Teubner, 1925.

Drescher, James. "A Coptic malediction." *Annales du service des Antiquités de l'Égypte* 48 (1948): 267–76.

Drew-Bear, Thomas. "Imprecations from Kourion." *BASP* 9 (1972): 85–107.

du Bourguet, Pierre. "Ensemble magique de la période romaine en Égypte." *Revue du Louvre* 25 (1975): 255–57.

Dunant, Christiane. "Sus aux voleurs! Une tablette en bronze à inscription grecque du Musée de Genève." *Museum Helveticum* 35, no. 4 (1978): 241–44.

Dunbabin, Katherine M. D., and Matthew W. Dickie. "Invidia rumpantur pectora: The iconography of phthonos/invidia in Graeco-Roman Art." *Jahrbuch für Antike und Christentum* 26 (1983): 7–37.

Dungworth, David. "Mystifying Roman nails: *Clavus annalis, defixiones* and *minkisi.*"

In *TRAC 97: Proceedings of the seventh annual theoretical Roman archaeology conference, which formed part of the second international Roman archaeology conference, University of Nottingham, April 1997,* edited by Colin Forcey, John Hawthorne, and Robert Witcher, 148–59. Oakville, CT: Oxbow Books, 1998.

Durkheim, Émile. *The elementary forms of the religious life.* Translated by Joseph Ward Swain. Free Press paperback. New York: Macmillan, 1915.

Edgar, Campbell C. "A love charm from the Fayoum." *Bulletin de la Société royale d'archéologie d'Alexandrie* 21 (1925): 42–45.

Edwards, Iorwerth E. S. *Hieratic papyri in the British Museum. Fourth series: Oracular amuletic decrees of the late New Kingdom.* 2 vols. London: Trustees of the British Museum, 1960.

Eidinow, Esther. *Oracles, curses, and risk among the ancient Greeks.* Oxford: Oxford University Press, 2007.

Eiland, Murray. "Bright stones, dark images: magic gems." *Minerva* 13, no. 6 (2002): 34–37.

Eitrem, Samson. "Kronos in der magie." In *Mélanges Bidez,* 351–60. Brussels: Secrétariat de l'Institut, 1934.

Eitrem, Samson, and Leiv Amundsen. *Papyri osloenses.* 3 vols. Oslo: Det norske videnskaps-akademi, 1925.

Emery, Walter Bryan, and Laurence Patrick Kirwan. *The royal tombs of Ballana and Qustul.* Cairo: Government Press, 1938.

Emmel, Stephen, Ulrich Gotter, and Johannes Hahn. "'From temple to church': Analyzing a Late Antique phenomenon of transformation." In *From temple to church: Destruction and renewal of local cultic topography in Late Antiquity,* edited by Stephen Emmel, Ulrich Gotter, and Johannes Hahn, 1–22. Leiden: Brill, 2008.

Enloe, James G. "Equifinality, assemblage integrity and behavioral inferences at Verberie." *Journal of Taphonomy* 2, no. 3 (2004): 147–65.

Enloe, James G. "Theory, method and the archaeological study of occupation surfaces and activities." In *Archaeological concepts for the study of the cultural past,* edited by Alan P. Sullivan, 125–40. Salt Lake City: University of Utah Press, 2008.

Evans-Pritchard, Edward E. "The morphology and function of magic." *American Anthropologist* 31, no. 4 (1929): 619–41.

Evans-Pritchard, Edward E. *Witchcraft, oracles, and magic among the Azande.* Ed. and intro. by Eva Gillies. Abridged ed. Oxford: Clarendon Press, 1976.

Fabre, Georges, Marc Mayer, and Isabel Rodà. *Inscriptions romaines de Catalogne.* Paris: Diffusion de Boccard, 1984.

Faraone, Christopher A. "Aeschylus' hymnos desmios (Eum 306) and Attic judicial curse tablets." *JHS* 105 (1985): 150–54.

Faraone, Christopher A. "The agonistic context of early Greek binding-spells." In *Magika hiera: Ancient Greek magic and religion,* edited by Christopher A. Faraone and Dirk Obbink, 3–32. New York: Oxford University Press, 1991.

298   Bibliography

Faraone, Christopher A. *Ancient Greek love magic.* Cambridge: Harvard University Press, 1999.

Faraone, Christopher A. "Binding and burying the forces of evil: The defensive use of 'voodoo' dolls in ancient Greece." *ClAnt* 10, no. 2 (1991): 165–205.

Faraone, Christopher A. "A blinding curse from the fountain of Anna Perenna in Rome." *SMSR* 76 (2010): 65–76.

Faraone, Christopher A. "The collapse of celestial and chthonic realms in a Late Antique 'Apollonian invocation' (*PGM* I 262–347)." In *Heavenly realms and earthly realities in Late Antique religions,* edited by Ra'anan S. Boustan and Annette Y. Reed, 213–32. New York: Cambridge University Press, 2004.

Faraone, Christopher A. "The ethnic origins of a Roman-era *Philtrokatadesmos* (*PGM* IV 296–434)." In *Magic and ritual in the ancient world,* edited by Paul Allan Mirecki and Marvin Meyer, 319–43. Leiden: Brill, 2002.

Faraone, Christopher A. "Evidence for a special female form of binding incantation?" American Philological Association Annual Meeting, San Antonio, TX, January 6–9, 2011.

Faraone, Christopher A. "A Greek magical gemstone from the Black Sea: Amulet or miniature handbook?" *Kernos* 23 (2010): 91–114.

Faraone, Christopher A. "Handbooks and anthologies: The collection of Greek and Egyptian incantations in late Hellenistic Egypt." *Archiv für Religionsgeschichte* 2, no. 2 (2000): 195–214.

Faraone, Christopher A. "Household religion in ancient Greece." In *Household and family religion in antiquity,* edited by John Bodel and Saul M. Olyan, 210–28. Malden, MA: Blackwell, 2008.

Faraone, Christopher A. "Kronos and the Titans as powerful ancestors: A case study of the Greek gods in later magical spells." In *The gods of ancient Greece,* edited by J. N. Bremmer and A. Erskine, 388–405. Edinburgh: Edinburgh University Press, 2010.

Faraone, Christopher A. "Molten wax, spilt wine, and mutilated animals: Sympathetic magic in Near Eastern and early Greek oath ceremonies." *JHS* 113 (1993): 60–80.

Faraone, Christopher A. "Necromancy goes underground: The disguise of skull- and corpse-divination in the Paris Magical Papyri." In *Mantikê: Studies in ancient divination,* edited by Sarah I. Johnston and Peter T. Struck, 255–82. Leiden: Brill, 2005.

Faraone, Christopher A. "Notes on four inscribed magical gemstones." *ZPE* 160 (2007): 158–59.

Faraone, Christopher A. "The 'performative future' in three Hellenistic incantations and Theocritus' second Idyll." *CPh* 90, no. 1 (1995): 1–15.

Faraone, Christopher A. "The problem of dense concentrations of data for cartographers (and chronographers) of ancient Mediterranean magic: Some illustrative case studies from the East." In *Contextos màgicos/Contesti magici,* edited by Marina Piranomonte. Rome, forthcoming.

Faraone, Christopher A. *Talismans and Trojan horses: Guardian statues in ancient Greek myth and ritual.* New York: Oxford University Press, 1992.

Faraone, Christopher A. "The wheel, the whip and other implements of torture: Erotic magic in Pindar *Pythian* 4.213–19." *Classical Journal* 89, no. 1 (1993): 1–19.

Faraone, Christopher A. "When spells worked magic." *Archaeology* 56, no. 2 (2003): 48–53.

Faraone, Christopher A., B. Garnand, and C. López-Ruiz. "Micah's mother (Judg. 17:1–4) and a curse from Carthage (KAI 89): Canaanite precedents for Greek and Latin curses against thieves?" *JNES* 64, no. 3 (2005): 161–86.

Faraone, Christopher A., and Amina Kropp. "Inversion, adversion and perversion as strategies in Latin curse-tablets." In *Magical practice in the Latin West: Papers from the international conference held at the University of Zaragoza, 30 Sept.–1 Oct. 2005,* edited by Richard L. Gordon and Francisco Marco Simón, 381–98. Leiden: Brill, 2010.

Faulkner, Raymond O. *The ancient Egyptian coffin texts: Spells 1–1185 & indexes.* Oxford: Aris & Phillips, 2004.

Fennell, Christopher C. "Conjuring boundaries: Inferring past identities from religious artifacts." *International Journal of Historical Archaeology* 4, no. 4 (2000): 281–313.

Flambard, Jean-Marc. "Éléments pour une approche financière de la mort dans les classes populaires." In *La mort, les morts et l'au-delà dans le monde romain: actes du colloque de Caen, 20–22 novembre 1985,* edited by François Hinard, 209–44. Caen: Université de Caen, 1987.

Flourentzos, Pavlos. "Chronique des fouilles et découvertes archéologiques à Chypre en 2003 et 2004." *BCH* 128–29 (2004–5): 1635–1708.

Foertmeyer, Victoria Ann. "Tourism in Graeco-Roman Egypt." PhD diss., Princeton University, 1989.

Forschia, Laurence. "La réutilization des sanctuaires paiens par les chrétiens en Grèce continentale." *Revue des études grecques* 113 (2000): 413–34.

Fowden, Garth. *The Egyptian Hermes: A historical approach to the late pagan mind.* New York: Cambridge University Press, 1986.

Fowler, Robert L. "Greek magic, Greek religion." *ICS* 20 (1995): 1–22.

Frankfurter, David. "The binding of antelopes: A Coptic frieze and its Egyptian religious context." *JNES* 63, no. 2 (2004): 97–109.

Frankfurter, David. "The consequences of Hellenism in Late Antique Egypt." *Archiv für Religionsgeschichte* 2, no. 2 (2000): 162–94.

Frankfurter, David. "Dynamics of ritual expertise in antiquity and beyond: Towards a new taxonomy of 'magicians.'" In *Magic and ritual in the ancient world,* edited by Paul Allan Mirecki and Marvin Meyer, 159–78. Leiden: Brill, 2002.

300   Bibliography

Frankfurter, David. *Elijah in Upper Egypt: The apocalypse of Elijah and early Egyptian Christianity.* Studies in antiquity and Christianity. Minneapolis: Fortress Press, 1993.

Frankfurter, David. "Fetus magic and sorcery fears in Roman Egypt." *GRBS* 46 (2006): 37–62.

Frankfurter, David. "The magic of writing and the writing of magic: The power of the word in Egyptian and Greek traditions." *Helios* 21, no. 2 (1994): 189–221.

Frankfurter, David. "Narrating power: The theory and practice of the magical historiola in ritual spells." In *Ancient magic and ritual power,* edited by Marvin W. Meyer and Paul Allan Mirecki, 457–76. New York: Brill, 1995.

Frankfurter, David. Review of *Egypt in Late Antiquity,* by Roger S. Bagnall. *BMCRev,* no. 5 (1994): 95–102.

Frankfurter, David. *Religion in Roman Egypt: Assimilation and resistance.* Princeton: Princeton University Press, 1998.

Frankfurter, David. "Ritual expertise in Roman Egypt and the problem of the category 'magician.'" In *Envisioning magic: A Princeton seminar and symposium,* edited by Peter Schäfer and Hans G. Kippenberg, 115–35. Leiden: Brill, 1997.

Frankfurter, David. "Voices, books, and dreams: The diversification of divination media in Late Antique Egypt." In *Mantikê: Studies in ancient divination,* edited by Sarah I. Johnston and Peter T. Struck, 233–54. Leiden: Brill, 2005.

Frazer, James George. *The golden bough: A study in magic and religion.* 3rd ed. New York: Collier Books, 1985.

Friedrich, Hans-Veit, ed. *Thessalos von Tralles.* Beiträge zur klassischen Philologie. Meisenheim am Glan: Hain, 1968.

Friggeri, Rosanna. *La collezione epigrafica del Museo nazionale romano alle Terme di Diocleziano.* Milan: Electa, 2001.

Frisch, Peter. *Zehn agonistische Papyri.* Abhandlungen der Rheinisch-Westfälischen Akademie der Wissenschaften. Sonderreihe Papyrologica Coloniensia. Opladen: Westdeutscher Verlag, 1986.

Gager, John G. *Curse tablets and binding spells from antiquity and the ancient world.* New York: Oxford University Press, 1992.

Gagos, Traianos, Jennifer Gates, and Andrew Wilburn. "Material culture and texts of Graeco-Roman Egypt: Creating context, debating meaning." *BASP* 42, no. 1–4 (2005): 171–88.

Gallo, Paolo. "Ostraca demotici da Medinet Madi." *EVO* 12 (1989): 99–123.

Gallo, Paolo. *Ostraca demotici e ieratici dall'archivio bilingue di Narmouthis.* Quaderni di Medinet Madi. Pisa: ETS, 1997.

Gallo, Paolo. "The wandering personnel of the temple of Narmuthis in the Faiyum and some toponyms of the Meris of Polemon." In *Life in a multi-cultural society: Egypt from Cambyses to Constantine and beyond,* edited by Janet Johnson, 119–31. Chicago: Oriental Institute of the University of Chicago, 1992.

Bibliography   301

Gardiner, Alan H. *Egypt of the pharaohs.* Oxford: Clarendon Press, 1961.

Gardiner, Alan H. "The House of Life." *Journal of Egyptian Archaeology* 24, no. 2 (1938): 157–79.

Garnsey, Peter. *Social status and legal privilege in the Roman Empire.* Oxford: Clarendon, 1970.

Gasse, Annie, and Christiane Ziegler. *Les stèles d'Horus sur les crocodiles.* Paris: Réunion des Musées Nationaux, 2004.

Gazda, Elaine K., and Terry G. Wilfong. *Karanis, an Egyptian town in Roman times: Discoveries of the University of Michigan expedition to Egypt (1924–1935),* Kelsey Museum Publication 1. Ann Arbor: Kelsey Museum of Archaeology, 2004.

Geertz, Hildred. "An anthropology of religion and magic I." *Journal of Interdisciplinary History* 6, no. 1 (1975): 71–89.

Gell, Alfred. *Art and agency: An anthropological theory.* New York: Oxford University Press, 1998.

Gell, Alfred. "The technology of enchantment and the enchantment of technology." In *Anthropology, art, and aesthetics,* edited by Jeremy Coote and Anthony Shelton, 40–66. New York: Oxford University Press, 1992.

Geremek, Hanna. *Karanis, communauté rurale de l'Egypte romaine au IIe–IIIe siècle de notre ère.* Wrocław: Zaklad Narodowy im. Ossolinskich Wydawn, 1969.

Gering, Hugo. "Artus fututor." *Hermes* 51, no. 4 (1916): 632–35.

Ghedini, Francesca. *Giulia Domna tra oriente e occidente: le fonti archeologiche.* Rome: L'Erma di Bretschneider, 1984.

Gilchrist, Roberta. "Magic for the dead? The archaeology of magic in later medieval burials." *Medieval Archaeology* 52 (2008): 119–59.

Given, Michael. *The archaeology of the colonized.* New York: Routledge, 2004.

Goedicke, Hans. "The Canaanite illness." *Studien zur Altägyptischen Kultur* 11 (1984): 91–105.

Gombrich, Ernst H. *Art and illusion: A study in the psychology of pictorial representation.* 6th ed. New York: Phaidon, 2002.

Gombrich, Ernst H. *The sense of order: A study in the psychology of decorative art.* 2nd ed. The Wrightsman lectures vol. 9. Oxford: Phaidon Press, 1984.

Gómez-Moreno, Manuel. *Misceláneas: historia, arte, arqueología (dispersa, emendata, addita, inédita).* Madrid: S. Aguirre impresor, 1949.

González Villaescusa, Ricardo. *El mundo funerario romano en el País Valenciano. Monumentos funerarios y sepulturas entre los siglos 1 a. de C.-7 d. de C.* Madrid: Casa de Velázquez, 2001.

Goodburn, R., M. W. C. Hassall, and Roger S. O. Tomlin. "Roman Britain in 1978." *Britannia* 10 (1979): 268–356.

Goodman, Martin. "Judaea." In *The Cambridge ancient history,* vol. XI: *The High Empire, A.D. 70–192,* edited by Alan K. Bowman, Peter Garnsey, and Dominic Rathbone, 664–78. Cambridge: Cambridge University Press, 2000.

Gordon, F. G. "The Keftiu spell." *JEA* 18, no. 1–2 (1932): 67–68.

Gordon, Richard L. "Aelian's peony: The location of magic in Graeco-Roman tradition." In *Comparative criticism 9,* edited by E. Shaffer, 59–95. Cambridge: Cambridge University Press, 1987.

Gordon, Richard L. "Competence and 'felicity conditions' in two sets of North African curse-tablets (DTAud nos. 275–85; 286–98)." *MHNH: revista internacional de investigación sobre magia y astrología antiguas* 5 (2005): 61–86.

Gordon, Richard L. "Imagining Greek and Roman magic." In *Witchcraft and magic in Europe: Ancient Greece and Rome,* edited by Bengt Ankarloo and Stuart Clark, 159–275. Philadelphia: University of Pennsylvania Press, 1999.

Gordon, Richard L. "Shaping the text: Innovation and authority in Graeco-Egyptian malign magic." In *Kykeon: Studies in honour of H. S. Versnel,* edited by H. F. J. Horstmanshoff, H. W. Singor, F. T. van Straten, and J. H. M. Strubbe, 69–112. Leiden: Brill, 2002.

Gordon, Richard L. "'What's in a list?' Listing in Greek and Graeco-Roman malign magical texts." In *The world of ancient magic: Papers from the first international Samson Eitrem seminar at the Norwegian Institute at Athens, 4–8 May 1997,* edited by David R. Jordan, Hugo Montgomery, and Einar Thomassen, 239–77. Bergen: Norwegian Institute at Athens, 1999.

Gordon, Richard L., and Francisco Marco Simón. "Introduction." In *Magical practice in the Latin West: Papers from the international conference held at the University of Zaragoza, 30 Sept.–1 Oct. 2005,* edited by Richard L. Gordon and Francisco Marco Simón, 1–49. Leiden: Brill, 2010.

Gosden, Chris, and Yvonne Marshall. "The cultural biography of objects." *World Archaeology* 31, no. 2 (1999): 169–78.

Gow, Andrew S. F. *Theocritus.* 2 vols. Cambridge: Cambridge University Press, 1950.

Graf, Fritz. "Magic and divination." In *The world of ancient magic: Papers from the first international Samson Eitrem seminar at the Norwegian Institute at Athens, 4–8 May 1997,* edited by David R. Jordan, Hugo Montgomery, and Einar Thomassen, 283–98. Bergen: Norwegian Institute at Athens, 1999.

Graf, Fritz. *Magic in the ancient world.* Translated by Philip Franklin. Revealing Antiquity, 10. Cambridge: Harvard University Press, 1997.

Graf, Fritz. "Prayer in magic and religious ritual." In *Magika hiera: Ancient Greek magic and religion,* edited by Christopher A. Faraone and Dirk Obbink, 188–213. New York: Oxford University Press, 1991.

Graf, Fritz. "The magician's initiation." *Helios* 21, no. 2 (1994): 161–77.

Graf, Fritz. "Theories of magic in antiquity." In *Magic and ritual in the ancient world,* edited by Paul Allan Mirecki and Marvin Meyer, 92–104. Leiden: Brill, 2002.

Graf, Fritz. "Untimely death, witchcraft and divine vengeance: A reasoned epigraphical catalog." *ZPE* 162 (2007): 139–50.

Graham, Alexander John. *Colony and mother city in ancient Greece.* 2nd ed. Chicago: Ares, 1983.

Grenfell, Bernard P. "Oxyrhynchus and its papyri." *Egypt Exploration Fund Archaeological Report* (1896–97): 1–12.

Grenfell, Bernard P., Arthur S. Hunt, D. G. Hogarth, and J. G. Milne. *Fayûm towns and their papyri.* London: Offices of the Egypt Exploration Fund, 1900.

Griffith, Francis L., and Herbert Thompson. *The Demotic magical papyrus of London and Leiden.* Milan: Istituto editoriale Cisalpino-La goliardica, 1976.

Grimes, Ronald. *Beginnings in ritual studies.* Washington, DC: University Press of America, 1982.

Grmek, Mirko D. *Diseases in the ancient Greek world.* Translated by M. Muellner and L. Muellner. Baltimore: Johns Hopkins University Press, 1989.

Gruen, Erich S. *Rethinking the other in antiquity.* Martin Classical lectures. Princeton: Princeton University Press, 2011.

Grumach, Irene. "On the history of a Coptic Figura Magica." In *Proceedings of the 12th international congress of papyrology,* edited by Deborah H. Samuel, 169–81. Toronto: A. M. Hakkert, 1970.

Guarducci, M. "L'Italia e Roma in una tabella defixionis greca recentemente scoperta." *Bulletino della Commissione Archeologica Comunale in Roma* 74 (1951–52): 57–70.

Guarducci, M. "Nuove note di epigrafia siceliota arcaica." *Annuario della Scuola Archeologica di Atene e delle Missioni Italiane in Oriente* 21–22 (1959–60): 249–78.

Haatvedt, Rolfe Alden, Enoch Ernest Peterson, and Elinor Husselman. *Coins from Karanis: The University of Michigan excavations, 1924–1935.* Ann Arbor: University of Michigan Press, 1964.

Habachi, Labib. "Finds at Kôm el-Wist." *Annales du service des Antiquités de l'Égypte* 47 (1947): 285–87.

Hansen, Nicole B. "Ancient execration magic in Coptic and Islamic Egypt." In *Magic and ritual in the ancient world,* edited by Paul Allan Mirecki and Marvin Meyer, 427–45. Leiden: Brill, 2002.

Harris, William V. *Ancient literacy.* Cambridge: Harvard University Press, 1989.

Harrison, Simon. "The commerce of cultures in Melanesia." *Man* 28, no. 1 (1993): 139–58.

Heintz, Florent. "Agonistic magic in the Late Antique circus." PhD diss., Harvard University, 1999.

Heintz, Florent. "Circus curses and their archaeological contexts." *JRA* 11 (1998): 337–42.

Hermary, Antoine. "Amathonte classique et hellenistique: la question du Bès colossal de l'agora." In *From Evagoras I to the Ptolemies: Transition from the Classical to the Hellenistic Period in Cyprus. Proceedings of the International Archaeological Conference, Nicosia 29–30 November 2002,* edited by Pavlos Flourentzos, 81–92. Nicosia: Department of Antiquities, 2007.

Hijmans, B. L. "Apuleius Orator: 'Pro se de Magia' and 'Florida.'" *ANRW* II 34, no. 2 (1994): 1708–84.

304   Bibliography

Hill, George Francis. *A history of Cyprus.* 4 vols. Cambridge: Cambridge University Press, 1940.

Hodder, Ian, and Scott Hutson. *Reading the past: Current approaches to interpretation in archaeology.* 3rd ed. Cambridge: Cambridge University Press, 2003.

Hoffman, Christopher A. "Fiat Magia." In *Magic and ritual in the ancient world,* edited by Paul Allan Mirecki and Marvin Meyer, 179–94. Leiden: Brill, 2002.

Hogarth, D. G., and Bernard P. Grenfell. "Cities of the Faiyúm I: Karanis and Bacchias." *Egypt Exploration Fund Archaeological Report* (1895–96): 14–19.

Hölbl, Günther. *A history of the Ptolemaic empire.* Translated by Tina Saavedra. London: Routledge, 2001.

Hope, Valerie M. "Contempt and respect: The treatment of the corpse in ancient Rome." In *Death and disease in the ancient city,* edited by Valerie M. Hope and Eireann Marshall, 104–27. New York: Routledge, 2000.

Hope, Valerie M. *Roman death: Dying and the dead in ancient Rome.* London: Continuum, 2009.

Hopfner, Theodor. *Griechisch-ägyptischer Offenbarungszauber. Mit einer eingehenden Darstellung des griechisch-synkretistischen Daemonenglaubens und der Voraussetzungen und Mittel des Zaubers überhaupt und der magischen Divination im besonderen.* Amsterdam: A. M. Hakkert, 1921.

Horden, Peregrine, and Nicholas Purcell. *The corrupting sea: A study of Mediterranean history.* Malden, MA: Blackwell, 2000.

Hoskins, Janet. "Agency, biography and objects." In *Handbook of material culture,* edited by Christopher Tilley, Webb Keane, Susanne Küchler, Michael Rowlands, and Patricia Spyer, 74–84. Thousand Oaks, CA: Sage, 2006.

Humphrey, John H. *Roman circuses: Arenas for chariot racing.* London: B. T. Batsford, 1986.

Hunink, Vincent. *Apuleius of Madauros: Pro se de magia (Apologia).* 2 vols. Amsterdam: Gieben, 1997.

Husselman, Elinor M. *Karanis excavations of the University of Michigan in Egypt, 1928–1935: Topography and architecture: A summary of the reports of the director, Enoch E. Peterson.* Kelsey Museum of Archaeology Studies 5. Ann Arbor: University of Michigan Press, 1979.

Husselman, Elinor M. *Papyri from Karanis, third series.* Cleveland: Case Western Reserve University Press, 1971.

Ikram, Salima. *Divine creatures: Animal mummies in ancient Egypt.* Cairo: American University in Cairo Press, 2004.

Ikram, Salima, and Aidan Dodson. *The mummy in ancient Egypt: Equipping the dead for eternity.* New York: Thames & Hudson, 1998.

Isbell, Charles D. *Corpus of the Aramaic incantation bowls.* Missoula, MT: Society of Biblical Literature and Scholars Press, 1975.

Isings, Clasina. *Roman glass from dated finds.* Groningen: Wolters, 1957.

Jameson, Michael H., David R. Jordan, and Roy Kotansky. *A "lex sacra" from Selinous,* Greek, Roman, and Byzantine Monographs, no. 11. Durham, NC, 1993.

Janowitz, Naomi. *Magic in the Roman world: Pagans, Jews, and Christians.* Religion in the first Christian centuries. New York: Routledge, 2001.

Janssen, Rosalind, and Jac. J. Janssen. *Growing up in ancient Egypt.* London: Rubicon, 1990.

Jeffery, Lilian H. "Further comments on archaic Greek inscriptions." *ABSA* 50 (1955): 67–84.

Jeffery, Lilian H. *The local scripts of archaic Greece: A study of the origin of the Greek alphabet and its development from the eighth to the fifth centuries B.C.* Oxford: Clarendon Press, 1961.

Johnson, Barbara. *Pottery from Karanis: Excavations of the University of Michigan.* Kelsey Museum of Archaeology Studies 7. Ann Arbor: University of Michigan, 1981.

Johnson, John. "Graeco-Roman Branch (Field Report)." *Archaeological report, 1911–1912* (1911–12): 12–16.

Johnson, Matthew. *Archaeological theory: An introduction.* Malden, MA: Blackwell Publishers, 1999.

Johnston, Sarah Iles. "Crossroads." *ZPE* 88 (1991): 217–24.

Johnston, Sarah Iles. *Hekate soteira: A study of Hekate's roles in the Chaldean oracles and related literature.* American classical studies no. 21. Atlanta: Scholars Press, 1990.

Johnston, Sarah Iles. *Restless dead: Encounters between the living and the dead in ancient Greece.* Berkeley: University of California Press, 1999.

Johnston, Sarah Iles. "Review: Describing the undefinable: New books on magic and old problems of definition." *HR* 43, no. 1 (2003): 50–54.

Johnston, Sarah Iles. "Sacrifice in the Greek Magical Papyri." In *Magic and ritual in the ancient world,* edited by Paul Allan Mirecki and Marvin Meyer, 344–58. Leiden: Brill, 2002.

Johnston, Sarah Iles. "The song of the Iynx: Magic and rhetoric in Pythian 4." *TAPA* 125 (1995): 177–206.

Jones, R. F. J. "The Roman cemeteries of Ampurias reconsidered." In *Papers in Iberian archaeology,* edited by T. F. C. Blagg, R. F. J. Jones, and S. J. Keay, 237–64. Oxford: Oxford University Press, 1984.

Jordan, David R. "An address to a ghost at Olbia." *Mnemosyne* 50, no. 2 (1997): 212–19.

Jordan, David R. "A love charm with verses." *ZPE* 72 (1988): 245–59.

Jordan, David R. "A survey of Greek defixiones not included in the special corpora." *GRBS* 26 (1985): 151–97.

Jordan, David R. "CIL VIII 19525 (B).2 QPVVLVA = q(uem) p(eperit) vulva." *Philologus* 120 (1976): 127–32.

Jordan, David R. "Defixiones from a well near the southwest corner of the Athenian Agora." *Hesperia* 54, no. 3 (1985): 205–55.

Jordan, David R. "Inscribed lead tablets from the games in the sanctuary of Poseidon." *Hesperia* 63, no. 1 (1994): 111–26.

Jordan, David R. "Late feasts for ghosts." In *Ancient Greek cult practice from the epigraphical evidence,* edited by Robin Hägg, 131–43. Stockholm: Paul Aströms Förlag, 1994.

Jordan, David R. "Magia nilotica sulle rive del Tevere." *Mediterraneo antico: economie, società, culture* 7, no. 2 (2004): 693–710.

Jordan, David R. "New archaeological evidence for the practice of magic in classical Athens." *Praktika tou XII Diethnous Synedriou Klasikes Archaiologias* IV (1988): 273–77.

Jordan, David R. "New defixiones from Carthage." In *The circus and a Byzantine cemetery at Carthage,* edited by J. H. Humphrey, 117–40. Ann Arbor: University of Michigan Press, 1988.

Jordan, David R. "New Greek curse tablets (1985–2000)." *GRBS* 41 (2000): 5–46.

Jordan, David R. "Notes from Carthage." *ZPE* 111 (1996): 115–23.

Jordan, David R. "Psegmata kritikes." *Eulimene* 1 (2000): 127–31.

Jordan, David R. "Il testo greco di una gemma magica dall' Afghanistan (?) nel Museo Pushkin, Mosca." In *Gemme gnostiche e cultura ellenistica: atti dell'incontro di studio Verona, 22–23 ottobre 1999,* edited by Attilio Mastrocinque, 61–68. Patron: Quarto Inferiore, 2002.

Jordan, David R. "Two inscribed lead tablets from a well in the Athenian Kerameikos." *Mitteilungen des Deutschen Archäologischen Instituts, Athenische Abteilung* 95 (1980): 225–39.

Joshel, Sandra R. *Work, identity, and legal status at Rome: A study of the occupational inscriptions.* Oklahoma series in Classical culture. Norman: University of Oklahoma Press, 1992.

Joyce, Arthur, and Sissel Johannessen. "Abandonment and the production of archaeological variability at domestic sites." In *Abandonment of settlements and regions: Ethnoarchaeological and archaeological approaches,* edited by Catherine M. Cameron and Steve A. Tomka, 138–53. Cambridge: Cambridge University Press, 1993.

Jullian, Camille. "Les fouilles de M. Blumereau à Rom (Deux Sèvres)." *Mémoires de la Société nationale des Antiquaires de France* LVIII (1897): 118–48.

Kajanto, Iiro. *The Latin cognomina.* Helsinki: Keskuskirjapaino, 1965.

Kákosy, László. *Egyptian healing statues in three Museums in Italy: Turin, Florence, Naples,* Catalogo del Museo egizio di Torino. Serie prima, Monumenti e testi v. 9. Torino: Ministero per i beni e le attività culturali, Soprintendenza al Museo delle antichità egizie, 1999.

Kákosy, László, and Ahmed M. Moussa. "A Horus stela with Meret goddesses." *Studien zur Altägyptischen Kultur* 25 (1998): 143–59.

Bibliography   307

Kambitsis, Sophie. "Une nouvelle tablette magique d'Égypte, Musée du Louvre Inv. E27145, 3e/4e siècle." *BIFAO* 76 (1976): 213–23.

Kaper, Olaf. *The Egyptian god Tutu: A study of the sphinx-god and master of demons with a corpus of monuments.* Leuven: Peters, 2003.

Karageorghis, Vassos. *Early Cyprus: Crossroads of the Mediterranean.* Los Angeles: Getty, 2002.

Karivieri, Arja. "Magic and syncretic religious culture in the East." In *Religious diversity in Late Antiquity,* edited by David M. Gwynn and Susanne Bangert, 401–34. Leiden: Brill, 2010.

Keenan, James G. "An afterthought on the names Flavius and Aurelius." *ZPE* 53 (1983): 245–50.

Keenan, James G. "Byzantine Egyptian villages." In *Egypt in the Byzantine world, 300–700,* edited by Roger S. Bagnall, 226–43. New York: Cambridge University Press, 2007.

Keenan, James G. "Deserted villages: From the ancient to the medieval Fayyūm." *BASP* 40 (2003): 119–39.

Keenan, James G. "Egypt." In *The Cambridge ancient history, vol. XIV: Late Antiquity: Empire and successors, A.D. 425–600,* edited by Averil Cameron, Bryan Ward-Perkins, and Michael Whitby, 612–37. Cambridge: Cambridge University Press, 2000.

Keenan, James G. "The names Flavius and Aurelius as status designations in later Roman Egypt." *ZPE* 11 (1973): 33–63.

Keenan, James G. "The names Flavius and Aurelius as status designations in later Roman Egypt." *ZPE* 13 (1974): 283–304.

Keimer, Ludwig. "L'horreur des égyptiens pour les démons du désert." *Bulletin de l'institut d'Égypte* 26 (1944): 135–47.

Kemp, Barry J. "How religious were the ancient Egyptians?" *CAJ* 5, no. 1 (1995): 25–54.

Kessler, Dieter. *Die heiligen Tiere und der König.* Ägypten und Altes Testament. Wiesbaden: Otto Harrassowitz, 1989.

Kippenberg, Hans G. "Magic in Roman civil discourse: Why rituals should be illegal." In *Envisioning magic: A Princeton seminar and symposium,* edited by Peter Schäfer and Hans G. Kippenberg, 137–63. Leiden: Brill, 1997.

Kisa, Anton. *Das Glas im Altertume.* 3 vols. Vol. 3. Leipzig: Hiersemann, 1908.

Klein, Josef. "Drei römische Bleitäfelchen." In *Festschrift zum fünfzigjährigen Jubiläum des Vereins von Alterthumsfreunden im Rheinlande,* 129–46; Taf VI. Bonn: A. Marcus, 1891.

Kleiner, Diana E. E. *Roman sculpture.* Yale publications in the history of art. New Haven: Yale University Press, 1992.

Kloppenborg, John S., and Stephen G. Wilson, eds. *Voluntary associations in the Graeco-Roman world.* London: Routledge, 1996.

Knox, Bernard M. W. "Silent reading in antiquity." *GRBS* 9 (1968): 421–35.

308   Bibliography

Koenig, Yvan. "La Nubie dans les textes magiques: 'l'inquiétante étrangeté.'" *Revue d'Égyptologie* 38 (1987): 105–10.

Koenig, Yvan. "Les textes d'envoûtement de Mirgissa." *Revue d'Égyptologie* 41 (1990): 101–25.

Koenig, Yvan. *Magie et magiciens dans l'Egypte ancienne.* Bibliothèque de l'Egypte ancienne. Paris: Pygmalion/Gérard Watelet, 1994.

Kopytoff, Igor. "The cultural biography of things: Commoditization as process." In *The social life of things: Commodities in cultural perspective,* edited by Arjun Appadurai, 64–91. Cambridge: Cambridge University Press, 1986.

Kotansky, Roy. *Greek magical amulets: The inscribed gold, silver, copper, and bronze "Lamellae": Text and commentary.* Sonderreihe Papyrologica Coloniensia, 22. Opladen: Westdeutscher Verlag, 1994.

Kotansky, Roy. "Incantations and prayers for salvation on inscribed Greek amulets." In *Magika hiera: Ancient Greek magic and religion,* edited by Christopher A. Faraone and Dirk Obbink, 107–37. New York: Oxford University Press, 1991.

Kotansky, Roy. "Kronos and a new magical inscription formula on a gem in the J. P. Getty Museum." *Ancient World* 3 (1980): 29–32.

Kotansky, Roy. "Two amulets in the Getty Museum." *J. Paul Getty Museum Journal* 8 (1980): 181–88.

Kotansky, Roy, and Jeffrey Spier. "The 'horned hunter' on a lost gnostic gem." *HThR* 88, no. 3 (1995): 315–37.

Kretschmer, Marguerite. "St. Peter at Rome." *CJ* 21, no. 7 (1926): 511–17.

Kroll, John H. "An archive of the Athenian cavalry." *Hesperia* 46, no. 2 (1977): 83–140.

Kropp, Amina. *Defixiones: ein aktuelles corpus lateinischer Fluchtafeln.* Speyer: Kartoffeldruck-Verlag Kai Brodersen, 2008.

Kropp, Angelicus M. *Ausgewählte koptische zaubertexte.* Brussels: Édition de la Fondation égyptologique reine Élisabeth, 1930.

Lamboglia, Nino. "Una nuova popolazione pirenaica: gli Olossitani." *Rivista i Studi Liguri* 25 (1959): 147–61.

Lee-Stecum, Parshia. "Dangerous reputations: Charioteers and magic in fourth-century Rome." *G&R* 53, no. 2 (2006): 224–34.

Lehner, H. "105. Trier [Thongefäss mit Graffito]." *Westdeutsche zeitschrift für geschichte und kunst: Korrespondenzblatt* (1893): 201–6.

Lenz, Christoph. "Carmina figurata." *RAC* 2 (1952): 910–12.

Leone, Mark P., and Gladys-Marie Fry. "Conjuring in the big house kitchen: An interpretation of African American belief systems based on the uses of archaeology and folklore sources." *Journal of American Folklore* 112, no. 445 (1999): 372–403.

Leone, Mark P., Gladys-Marie Fry, and Timothy Ruppel. "Spirit management among Americans of African descent." In *Race and the archaeology of identity,* edited by Charles E. Orser Jr., 143–57. Salt Lake City: University of Utah Press, 2001.

Bibliography   309

Levene, Dan. *A corpus of magic bowls: Incantation texts in Jewish Aramaic from Late Antiquity.* London: Kegan Paul, 2003.

Lewis, Naphtali. *Life in Egypt under Roman rule.* Oxford: Clarendon Press, 1983.

Lichtheim, Miriam. *Ancient Egyptian literature: A book of readings.* 3 vols. Berkeley: University of California Press, 1973.

LiDonnici, Lynn R. "Beans, fleawort, and the blood of a hamadryas baboon: Recipe ingredients in Greco-Roman magical materials." In *Magic and ritual in the ancient world,* edited by Paul Allan Mirecki and Marvin Meyer, 359–77. Leiden: Brill, 2002.

LiDonnici, Lynn R. "Burning for it: Erotic spells for fever and compulsion in the ancient Mediterranean world." *GRBS* 39 (1998): 63–98.

LiDonnici, Lynn R. "Compositional patterns in *PGM* IV (=*P.Bibl.Nat.Suppl.* gr. no. 574)." *BASP* 40 (2003): 141–78.

Liu, Jinyu. *Collegia centonariorum: The guilds of textile dealers in the Roman West.* Leiden: Brill, 2009.

Lloyd, Geoffrey E. R. *Magic, reason and experience.* New York: Cambridge University Press, 1979.

Lloyd, Geoffrey E. R. *Polarity and analogy: Two types of argumentation in early Greek thought.* Cambridge: Cambridge University Press, 1966.

Lock, Peter. "D. G. Hogarth (1862–1927): ' . . . A Specialist in the Science of Archaeology.'" *ABSA* 85 (1990): 175–200.

Loisy, Alfred Firmin. *Les actes des apôtres.* Paris: E. Nourry, 1920.

López Jimeno, María del Amor. *Las tabellae defixionis de la Sicilia griega.* Classical and Byzantine monographs. Amsterdam: A. M. Hakkert, 1991.

López Jimeno, María del Amor. *Nuevas tabellae defixionis Áticas.* Classical and Byzantine monographs. Amsterdam: A. M. Hakkert, 1999.

López Jimeno, María del Amor. *Textos griegos de maleficio.* Akal/clásica. Clásicos griegos. Madrid: AKAL Ediciones, 2001.

Lorincz, Barnabás, Franciscus Redo, András Mócsy. *Onomasticon provinciarum Europae latinarum.* Budapest: Archaeolingua Alapítvány, 1994.

Lucian. *Chattering courtesans and other sardonic sketches.* Translated by Keith Sidwell. London: Penguin Books, 2004.

Luck, Georg. *Arcana mundi: Magic and the occult in the Greek and Roman worlds: A collection of ancient texts.* Baltimore: Johns Hopkins University Press, 1985.

MacDonald, L. "Inscriptions relating to sorcery in Cyprus." *Proceedings of the Society of Biblical Archaeology* 13 (1891): 160–90.

MacGaffey, Wyatt. "Complexity, astonishment and power: The visual vocabulary of Kongo minkisi." *Journal of Southern African Studies* 14, no. 2 (1988): 188–203.

MacGaffey, Wyatt. "Fetishism revisited: Kongo 'nkisi' in sociological perspective." *Africa: Journal of the International African Institute* 47, no. 2 (1977): 172–84.

MacGaffey, Wyatt. "The eyes of understanding: Kongo minkisi." In *Astonishment and*

310   Bibliography

power, edited by Wyatt MacGaffey, Michael D. Harris, Sylvia H. Williams, and David C. Driskell, 21–103. Washington, DC: Smithsonian Institution Press, 1993.

MacGaffey, Wyatt, and John M. Janzen. "Nkisi figures of the Bakongo." *African Arts* 7, no. 3 (1974): 87–89.

Mack, John. "Fetish? Magic figures in central Africa." In *Fetishism: Visualising power and desire,* edited by Anthony Shelton, 53–65. London: South Bank Centre, 1995.

Malinowski, Bronislaw. *Coral gardens and their magic: A study of the methods of tilling the soil and of agricultural rites in the Trobriand Islands.* 2 vols. London: G. Allen & Unwin, 1935.

Malinowski, Bronislaw. *Magic, science and religion, and other essays.* Garden City, NY: Doubleday, 1954.

Mallon, Jean. *Paléographie romaine.* Scripturae monumenta et studia. Madrid: Consejo Superior de Investigaciones Científicas, 1952.

Malone, Caroline, David A. Barrowclough, and Simon Stoddart. "Introduction: Cult in context." In *Cult in context: Reconsidering ritual in archaeology,* edited by David A. Barrowclough and Caroline Malone, 1–7. Oxford: Oxbow, 2007.

Manniche, Lise. *An ancient Egyptian herbal.* Austin: University of Texas Press, 1989.

Mar, Ricardo, and Joaquín Ruiz de Arbulo. *Ampurias Romana: Historia, Arquitectura y Arqueología.* Sabadell: Editorial AUSA, 1993.

Marco Simón, Francisco. "Execrating the Roman power: Three *defixiones* from Emporiae (Ampurias)." In *Magical practice in the Latin West: Papers from the international conference held at the University of Zaragoza, 30 Sept.–1 Oct. 2005,* edited by Richard L. Gordon and Francisco Marco Simón, 399–423. Leiden: Brill, 2010.

Margalioth, Mordecai. *Sefer ha-Razim: A newly recovered book of magic from the Talmudic period.* Tel Aviv: Yediot Acharonot, 1966.

Mariner, Sebastián. "Procedimientos indirectos de datación epigráfica." In *Miscelánea arqueológica: XXV aniversario de los Cursos Internacionales de Prehistoria y Arqueología en Ampurias (1947–1971),* edited by Eduardo Ripoll Perelló and Miguel Llongueras Campañà, 7–12. Barcelona: Diputación Provincial de Barcelona, Instituto de Prehistoria y Arqueología, 1974.

Martinez, David G. *Michigan Papyri XVI: A Greek love charm from Egypt (P.Mich. 757),* American Studies in Papyrology. Atlanta: Scholars Press, 1991.

Masson, Olivier. *Les inscriptions chypriotes syllabiques; recueil critique et commenté.* Études chypriotes 1. Paris: E. de Boccard, 1961.

Mastrocinque, Attilio. *From Jewish magic to Gnosticism.* Studien und Texte zu Antike und Christentum 24. Tübingen: Mohr Siebeck, 2005.

Mastrocinque, Attilio. "Late Antique lamps with defixiones." *GRBS* 47 (2007): 87–99.

Mastrocinque, Attilio. "Le 'defixiones' di Porta San Sebastiano." *MHNH* 5 (2005): 45–59.

Mastrocinque, Attilio. "Le pouvoir de l'écriture dans la magie." *Cahiers Mondes Anciens* 1 (2009).

Bibliography   311

Matter, Jacques. *Une excursion gnostique en Italie*. Strasbourg: Berger-Levrault, 1852.

Mauss, Marcel. *A general theory of magic*. London: Routledge and K. Paul, 1972.

Mauss, Marcel. *The gift: The form and reason for exchange in archaic societies*. London: Routledge, 1990.

McCown, Chester C. "The Ephesia Grammata in popular belief." *TAPA* 54 (1923): 128–40.

McDaniel, Walton Brooks. "The medical and magical significance in ancient medicine of things connected with reproduction and its organs." *Journal of the History of Medicine and Allied Sciences* 3, no. 4 (1948): 525–46.

McNamee, Kathleen. "Four Michigan papyri." *ZPE* 46 (1982): 123–33.

Meiggs, Russell, and David M. Lewis, eds. *A selection of Greek historical inscriptions to the end of the fifth century B.C.* Oxford: Clarendon Press, 1969.

Merlin, Alf. "Périodiques." *L'année épigraphique* 1952 (1953): 6–64.

Merrifield, Ralph. *The archaeology of ritual and magic*. London: B. T. Batsford, 1987.

Meskell, Lynn. *Object worlds in ancient Egypt: Material biographies past and present*. New York: Berg, 2004.

Meyer, Marvin. *The magical book of Mary and the angels (P.Heid. Inv. Kopt. 685): Text, translation and commentary*. Heidelberg: Universitätsverlag C. Winter, 1996.

Meyer, Marvin, and Richard Smith, eds. *Ancient Christian magic: Coptic texts of ritual power*. San Francisco: HarperSanFrancisco, 1994.

Michel, Simone. *Bunte Steine-Dunkle Bilder: "Magische Gemmen."* Munich: Biering & Brinkmann, 2001.

Michel, Simone. *Die Magischen Gemmen: zu Bildern und Zauberformeln auf geschnittenen Steinen der Antike und Neuzeit*. Berlin: Akademie Verlag, 2004.

Michel, Simone. "(Re)Interpreting magical gems, ancient and modern." In *Officina magica: Essays on the practice of magic in antiquity*, edited by Shaul Shaked, 141–70. Leiden: Brill, 2005.

Michel, Simone, Peter Zazoff, and Hilde Zazoff. *Die magischen Gemmen im Britischen Museum*. 2 vols. London: British Museum Press, 2001.

Michl, J. "Engelnamen." *RAC* 5 (1962): 201–39.

Miller, Daniel. "Consumption." In *Handbook of material culture*, edited by Christopher Tilley, Webb Keane, Susanne Küchler, Michael Rowlands, and Patricia Spyer, 341–54. Thousand Oaks, CA: Sage, 2006.

Miller, Daniel. *Material culture and mass consumption*. Social archaeology. New York: B. Blackwell, 1987.

Miller, Daniel. "The limits of dominance." In *Domination and resistance*, edited by Daniel Miller, Michael Rowlands, and Christopher Tilley, 63–79. London: Unwin Hyman, 1989.

Miller, Patricia Cox. *The corporeal imagination: Signifying the holy in late ancient Christianity*. Philadelphia: University of Pennsylvania Press, 2009.

Mirecki, Paul Allan, Iain Gardner, and Anthony Alcock. "Magical spell, Manichaean letter." In *Emerging from darkness: Manichaean studies at the end of the 20th century,* edited by Paul Allan Mirecki and Jason BeDuhn, 1–32. New York: Brill, 1997.

Mitchell, Jon P. "Performance." In *Handbook of material culture,* edited by Christopher Tilley, Webb Keane, Susanne Küchler, Michael Rowlands, and Patricia Spyer, 384–401. Thousand Oaks, CA: Sage, 2006.

Mitchell, Jon P. "Towards an archaeology of performance." In *Cult in context: Reconsidering ritual in archaeology,* edited by David A. Barrowclough and Caroline Malone, 336–39. Oxford: Oxbow, 2007.

Mitchell, W. J. Thomas. *Picture theory: Essays on verbal and visual representation.* Chicago: University of Chicago Press, 1994.

Mitchell, W. J. Thomas. *What do pictures want? The lives and loves of images.* Chicago: University of Chicago Press, 2005.

Mitford, Terence B. "Roman Cyprus." *ANRW* II 7, no. 2 (1980): 1285–1384.

Mitford, Terence B. "The cults of Roman Cyprus." *ANRW* II 18, no. 3 (1990): 2176–2211.

Mitford, Terence B. *The inscriptions of Kourion.* Philadelphia: American Philosophical Society, 1971.

Monson, Andrew. "Private associations in the Ptolemaic Fayyum: The evidence of the Demotic accounts." In *New archaeological and papyrological researches on the Fayyum: Proceedings of the international meeting of Egyptology and papyrology, Lecce 8th–10th June 2005,* edited by Mario Capasso and Paola Davoli, 179–96. Galatina (Lecce): Congedo, 2007.

Monson, Andrew. "The ethics and economics of Ptolemaic religious associations." *AncSoc* 36 (2006): 221–38.

Montgomery, James A. *Aramaic incantation texts from Nippur.* Philadelphia: University Museum, 1913.

Montserrat, Dominic. "'No papyrus and no portraits': Hogarth, Grenfell, and the first season in the Fayum, 1895–6." *BASP* 33 (1996): 133–76.

Montserrat, Dominic. *Sex and society in Græco-Roman Egypt.* London: Kegan Paul International, 1996.

Moormann, Eric M. "The temple of Isis at Pompeii." In *Nile into Tiber: Egypt in the Roman world: Proceedings of the IIIrd international conference of Isis studies, Leiden, May 11–14 2005,* edited by Laurent Bricault, Miguel John Versluys, and Paul G. P. Meyboom, 137–54. Leiden: Brill, 2007.

Morony, Michael G. "Magic and society in late Sasanian Iraq." In *Prayer, magic, and the stars in the ancient and Late Antique world,* edited by Scott B. Noegel, Joel Thomas Walker, and Brannon M. Wheeler, 83–107. University Park: Pennsylvania State University Press, 2003.

Mouterde, René. *Le Glaive de Dardanos. Objets et inscriptions magiques de Syrie.* Mélanges de l'Université Saint-Joseph. Beirut: Imprimérie Catholique, 1930.

Bibliography   313

Moyer, Ian. "The initiation of the magician: Transition and power in Graeco-Roman ritual." In *Initiation in ancient Greek rituals and narratives: New critical perspectives*, edited by David Brooks Dodd and Christopher A. Faraone, 219–38. London: Routledge, 2003.

Moyer, Ian. "Thessalos of Tralles and cultural exchange." In *Prayer, magic, and the stars in the ancient and Late Antique world*, edited by Scott B. Noegel, Joel Thomas Walker, and Brannon M. Wheeler. University Park: Pennsylvania State University Press, 2003.

Moyer, Ian, and Jacco Dieleman. "Miniaturization and the opening of the mouth in a Greek magical text (PGM XII.270–350)." *Journal of Ancient Near Eastern Religions* 3 (2003): 47–72.

Mueller, Katja. "Geographical Information Systems (GIS) in papyrology. Mapping fragmentation and migration flow to Hellenistic Egypt." *BASP* 42, no. 1–4 (2005): 112–26.

Mueller, Katja. "What's your position? Using Multi-Dimensional Scaling (MDS) and Geographical Information Systems (GIS) for locating ancient settlements in the Meris of Polemon / Graeco-Roman Fayum." *Archiv für Papyrusforschung und verwandte Gebiete* 50, no. 2 (2004): 199–214.

Münster, Maria. *Untersuchungen zur Göttin Isis*. Münchner ägyptologische Studien. Berlin: B. Hessling, 1968.

Murray, Alexander S., Arthur H. Smith, and Henry B. Walters. *Excavations in Cyprus*. London: Trustees of the British Museum, 1900.

Nagy, Arpad. "Ancient magical gems." In *Greek magic: Ancient, medieval, and modern*, edited by John C. B. Petropoulos, 34–38. New York: Routledge, 2008.

Nakamura, Carolyn. "Dedicating magic: Neo-Assyrian apotropaic figurines and the protection of Assur." *World Archaeology* 36, no. 1 (2004): 11–25.

Newton, Charles Thomas. *A history of discoveries at Halicarnassus, Cnidus, and Branchidae*. London: Day & Son, 1863.

Nilsson, Martin P. "Greek mysteries in the Confession of St. Cyprian." *HThR* 40, no. 3 (1947): 167–76.

Nock, Arthur Darby. "Hagiographica." *Journal of Theological Studies* 28, no. 112 (1927): 409–17.

Nock, Arthur Darby. "Magical notes." *JEA* 11, no. 3–4 (1925): 154–58.

Nock, Arthur Darby. "Paul and the magus." In *Essays on religion and the ancient world*, edited by Zeph Stewart, 308–30. Cambridge: Harvard University Press, 1972.

Nock, Arthur Darby. "The lizard in magic and religion." In *Essays on religion and the ancient world*, edited by Zeph Stewart, 271–76. Cambridge: Harvard University Press, 1972.

Nordén, Fritz. *Apulejus von Madaura und das römische privatrecht*. Leipzig: B. G. Teubner, 1912.

Novosadski, N. I. "Amulet with the name Ἀκτιῶφι." *Sbornik. Moskovskogo Obshches-

314   Bibliography

tuva po Issledovaniyu Pamyatnikinkov Drevnosti pri Mosckovskom Arkheologisch-eskom Institute 2 (1917): 123–33.

O'Shea, John M. *Mortuary variability: An archaeological investigation.* Orlando: Academic Press, 1984.

Ogden, Daniel. "Binding spells: Curse tablets and voodoo dolls in the Greek and Roman worlds." In *Witchcraft and magic in Europe: Ancient Greece and Rome,* edited by Bengt Ankarloo and Stuart Clark, 1–90. Philadelphia: University of Pennsylvania Press, 1999.

Ogden, Daniel. *Greek and Roman necromancy.* Princeton: Princeton University Press, 2001.

Ogden, Daniel. *In search of the sorcerer's apprentice: The traditional tales of Lucian's "Lover of lies."* Swansea: Classical Press of Wales, 2007.

Ogden, Daniel. *Magic, witchcraft, and ghosts in the Greek and Roman worlds: A sourcebook.* Oxford: Oxford University Press, 2002.

Onasoglou, A. "Σκάλα Ωρωπού Οδὸς 28ης Οκτωβρίου 7 (οικόπεδο Ελ. Καλογεράκη Αργ. Στρίφα)." *Archaiologikon Deltion* 44, no. B.1 (1989): 76–78.

Orlin, Eric M. *Foreign cults in Rome: Creating a Roman Empire.* Oxford: Oxford University Press, 2010.

Orsi, Paolo. "Gela. Scavi del 1900–1905: Le necropoli del secolo V." *MonAL* 17 (1906): 270–536.

Orsi, Paolo. "Messana: La necropoli romana di S. Placido e di altre scoperte avvenute nel 1910–1915." *MonAL* 24 (1916): 121–218.

Osborne, Robin. "Hoards, votives, offerings: The archaeology of the dedicated object." *World Archaeology* 36, no. 1 (2004): 1–10.

Oxe, August, Howard Comfort, and Philip M. Kenrick. *Corpus vasorum Arretinorum: A catalogue of the signatures, shapes and chronology of Italian sigillata.* 2nd ed. Antiquitas. Reihe 3, Abhandlungen zur Vor- und Frühgeschichte, zur klassischen und provinzial-römischen Archäologie und zur Geschichte des Altertums Bd. 41. Bonn: Habelt, 2000.

Pandolfini, Maristella. "Lamina di piombo da Agrigento (?)." *ArchClass* 27 (1975): 46–47.

Papini, Lucia. "Domande oracolari: elenco delle attestazioni in greco ed in copto." *APapyrol* 4 (1992): 21–27.

Papini, Lucia. "Struttura e prassi delle domande oracolari in greco su papiro." In *APapyrol* 2 (1990): 11–20.

Parássoglou, George M. "Circular from a prefect: *sileat omnibus perpetuo divinandi curiositas.*" In *Collectanea papyrologica: Texts published in honor of H. C. Youtie,* edited by Ann Ellis Hanson, 261–74. Bonn: Habelt, 1976.

Parker, Robert. *Miasma: Pollution and purification in early Greek religion.* Oxford: Oxford University Press, 1983.

Parpola, Simo, and Kazuko Watanabe. *Neo-Assyrian treaties and loyalty oaths.* Helsinki: Helsinki University Press, 1988.

Bibliography 315

Peet, T. Eric, Charles Leonard Woolley, Henri Frankfort, and John D. S. Pendlebury. *The city of Akhenaten.* London: Egypt Exploration Society, 1923.

Pellegrini, Astorre. "Piccoli testi copto-sa'îdici del Museo archeologico di Firenze." *Sphinx* 10 (1906): 141–59.

Pels, Dick, Kevin Hetherington, and Frédéric Vandenberghe. "The status of the object: Performances, mediations, and techniques." *Theory, Culture and Society* 19, no. 5–6 (2002): 1–21.

Peña, J. Theodore. *Roman pottery in the archaeological record.* Cambridge: Cambridge University Press, 2007.

Perlzweig, Judith. *Lamps of the Roman period, first to seventh century after Christ.* Princeton, NJ: American School of Classical Studies at Athens, 1961.

Pestman, P. W. *The new papyrological primer.* Leiden: Brill, 1994.

Peterson, Enoch. *The architecture and topography of Karanis.* Kelsey Museum of Archaeology archives. Ann Arbor, Michigan, 1973.

Peterson, Erik. "Engel- und Damonennamen. Nomina Barbara." *Rheinisches Museum für Philologie* 75 (1926): 393–421.

Peterson, Joan M. "The identification of the titulus Fasciolae and its connection with Pope Gregory the Great." *Vigiliae Christianae* 30, no. 2 (1976): 151–58.

Petrakos, Vasileios Ch. *The Amphiareion of Oropos.* Greece monuments and museums. Athens: Clio, 1995.

Petrakos, Vasileios Ch. *Οι επιγραφές του Ωρωπού.* Βιβλιοθήκη της εν Αθήναις Αρχαιολογικής Εταιρείας 170. Athens: Archaeologika Hetaireia, 1997.

Petrie, W. M. Flinders, A. H. Sayce, Edward Lee Hicks, John Pentland Mahaffy, F. L. Griffith, and F. C. J. Spurrell. *Illahun, Kahun and Gurob. 1888–90.* London: D. Nutt, 1891.

Petropoulos, John C. B. "The erotic magical papyri." In *Proceedings of the XVIII international congress of papyrology, Athens, 25–31 May 1986,* edited by Basil G. Mandilaras, 215–22. Athens: Greek Papyrological Society, 1988.

Pflaum, Hans-Georg. *Les carrières procuratoriennes équestres sous le Haut-Empire Romain.* Bibliothèque archéologique et historique. Paris: P. Geuthner, 1982.

Pharr, Clyde. "The interdiction of magic in Roman law." *TAPA* 63 (1932): 269–95.

Philipp, Hanna. *Mira et magica: Gemmen im Ägyptischen Museum der Staatlichen Museen Preussischer Kulturbesitz, Berlin-Charlottenburg.* Mainz am Rhein: P. von Zabern, 1986.

Pi Vázquez, Marta. "Estudi de tres inscripcions sobre plom trobades a la necròpolis Ballesta (Empúries)." *Empúries* 54 (2005): 165–76.

Picard, Charles. "Le rite magique des εἴδωλα de cire brulés, attesté sur trois stèles araméennes de Sfire." *Revue archéologique* 3 (1961): 84–89.

Pinch, Geraldine. "Childbirth and female figurines at Deir el-Medina and el-'Amarna." *Orientalia* 52 (1983): 405–14.

Pinch, Geraldine. *Magic in ancient Egypt.* 1st University of Texas Press ed. Austin: University of Texas Press, 1995.

316   Bibliography

Pinch, Geraldine. *Votive offerings to Hathor.* Oxford: Griffith Institute, Ashmolean Museum, 1993.

Pintozzi, Lisa, and Naomi Norman. "The lead curse tablets from the Carthage circus." *Archaeological News* 17 (1992): 11–18.

Piranomonte, Marina. "I contenitori di piombo dalla fontana di Anna Perenna e la loro valenza magica." *SMSR* 76 (2010): 21–33.

Piranomonte, Marina. "La fontana sacra di Anna Perenna a Piazza Euclide tra religione e magia." *MHNH* 5 (2005): 87–104.

Piranomonte, Marina. "The fountain of Anna Perenna in Rome, magical ritual connected to the water." In *Atti del Convegno "Rituelle Deponierung," Mainz, April 2008,* Forthcoming.

Piranomonte, Marina. "Religion and magic at Rome: The fountain of Anna Perenna." In *Magical practice in the Latin West: Papers from the international conference held at the University of Zaragoza, 30 Sept.–1 Oct. 2005,* edited by Richard L. Gordon and Francisco Marco Simón, 191–212. Leiden: Brill, 2010.

Piranomonte, Marina. *Il santuario della musica e il bosco sacro di Anna Perenna.* Milan: Electa, 2002.

Pitt-Rivers, Julian Alfred. *The fate of Shechem or, the politics of sex: Essays in the anthropology of the Mediterranean,* Cambridge studies in social anthropology. Cambridge: Cambridge University Press, 1977.

Plassart, André. *Les sanctuaires et les cultes du Mont Cynthe.* Paris: E. de Boccard, 1928.

Pollard, Nigel. "The chronology and economic condition of late Roman Karanis: An archaeological reassessment." *JARCE* 35 (1998): 147–62.

Polotsky, Hans J. "Suriel der Trompeter." *Muséon* 49 (1936): 231–43.

Pomyalovski, I. *Ancient curses (tabulae defixionum),* Epigraphical Studies I. St. Petersburg, 1873.

Porreca, David. "Divine names: A cross-cultural comparison (Papyri Graecae Magicae, Picatrix, Munich handbook)." *Magic, Ritual, and Witchcraft* 5, no. 1 (2010): 17–29.

Porter, Bertha, and Rosalind L. B. Moss. *Topographical bibliography of ancient Egyptian hieroglyphic texts, reliefs, and paintings.* Oxford: Clarendon Press, 1927.

Posener, Georges. *Catalogue des ostraca hiératiques littéraires de Deir el Médineh.* Cairo: Institut français d'archéologie orientale, 1934.

Posener, Georges. "Les empreintes magiques de Gizeh et les morts dangereux." *Mitteilungen des Deutschen Archäologischen Instituts, Athenische Abteilung* 16 (1958): 252–70.

Preisendanz, Karl. "Ephesia grammata." *Reallexikon für Antike und Christentum* 5 (1961): 515–20.

Preisendanz, Karl. *Papyri graecae magicae: die griechischen Zauberpapyri.* 2 vols. 2nd ed., edited by Albert Henrichs. Stuttgart: B. G. Teubner, 1973–74.

Pritchard, James B. *Ancient Near Eastern texts relating to the Old Testament.* 3rd ed. Princeton: Princeton University Press, 1969.

Bibliography   317

Procopé-Walter, A. "Iao und Set." *ARW* 30 (1933): 34–69.

Rathbone, Dominic. "Towards a historical topography of the Fayum." In *Archaeological research in Roman Egypt,* edited by Donald M. Bailey, 50–56. Ann Arbor: Thomson-Shore, 1996.

Rea, J. "Aspects of the circus at Leptis Magna, appendix: The lead curse tablet." *Libya Antiqua* 9–10 (1972–73): 92–96.

Rea, John R. "P.Col. VIII 242: Caranis in the fifth century." In *Proceedings of the 20th International congress of papyrologists, Copenhagen, 23–29 August, 1992,* edited by Adam Bülow-Jacobsen, 266–72. Copenhagen: Museum Tusculanum Press, 1994.

Rea, John R. "P.Haun. III 58: Caranis in the fifth century." *ZPE* 99 (1993): 89–95.

Record of Objects, Karanis 1924–25: 10–82, XIV–XXI, 010–053, 100–344, 4001–4048, 5000–50096. Kelsey Museum of Archaeology Archives. Ann Arbor, Michigan.

Record of Objects, Karanis 1928: 102*–242*, B108-B172, CS23-CS130. Kelsey Museum of Archaeology Archives. Ann Arbor, Michigan.

Redford, Donald B. "The language of Keftiu: The evidence of the drawing board and the London Medical Papyrus (BM 10059) in the British Museum." *Revista del Instituto de Historia Antigua Oriental* 12–13 (2005–6): 149–53.

Reifenberg, Adolf. "Das antike zyprische Judentum und seine Beziehungen zu Palästina." *Journal of the Palestine Oriental Society* 12 (1932): 209–15.

Renner, Timothy. "Three new Homerica on papyrus." *HSPh* 83 (1979): 311–37.

Richards, Janet E. *Society and death in ancient Egypt: Mortuary landscapes of the Middle Kingdom.* Cambridge: Cambridge University Press, 2005.

Ridgway, Brunilde S. *The archaic style in Greek sculpture.* Princeton: Princeton University Press, 1977.

Ripoll Perelló, Eduardo. "Acerca de unas *tabellae defixionis* de Ampurias (Hisp. Cit.)." In *Perennitas: studi in onore di Angelo Brelich,* edited by Angelo Brelich, 413–16. Rome: Edizioni dell'Ateneo, 1980.

Ritner, Robert K. "Des preuves de l'existence d'une nécromancie dans l'Égypte ancienne." In *La magie en Egypte: à la recherche d'une définition: actes du colloque organisé par le Musée du Louvre, les 29 et 30 septembre 2000,* edited by Yvan Koenig, 285–304. Paris: Documentation française, Musée du Louvre, 2002.

Ritner, Robert K. "Egyptian magical practice under the Roman empire: The Demotic spells and their religious context." *ANRW* II 18, no. 5 (1995): 3333–79.

Ritner, Robert K. "Horus on the crocodiles: A juncture of religion and magic." In *Religion and philosophy in ancient Egypt,* edited by William K. Simpson, 103–16. New Haven: Yale Egyptological Seminar, 1989.

Ritner, Robert K. "Household religion in ancient Egypt." In *Household and family religion in antiquity,* edited by John Bodel and Saul M. Olyan, 171–96. Malden, MA: Blackwell, 2008.

Ritner, Robert K. *The mechanics of ancient Egyptian magical practice.* Chicago: Oriental Institute of the University of Chicago, 1993.

318 Bibliography

Rives, James B. "Magic in Roman law: The reconstruction of a crime." *ClAnt* 22, no. 2 (2003): 313–39.

Rives, James B. "Magic in the XII Tables revisited." *CQ* 52, no. 1 (2002): 270–90.

Rives, James B. "Magic, religion and law: The case of the *Lex Cornelia de sicariis et veneficiis.*" In *Religion and law in classical and Christian Rome,* edited by Clifford Ando and Jörg Rüpke, 47–67. Stuttgart: Steiner, 2006.

Rives, James B. "*Magus* and its cognates in Classical Latin." In *Magical practice in the Latin West: Papers from the international conference held at the University of Zaragoza, 30 Sept.–1 Oct. 2005,* edited by Richard L. Gordon and Francisco Marco Simón, 53–77. Leiden: Brill, 2010.

Robert, Jeanne, and Louis Robert. "Bulletin épigraphique." *Revue d'Études Grecques* 68, no. 282 (1955): 85–86.

Robert, Louis. *Collection Froehner.* Vol. 1, Inscriptions Grecques. Paris: Editions des Bibliothèques Nationales, 1936.

Robert, Louis. "Documents d'Asie Mineure XXIII–XXVIII." *BCH* 107, no. 1 (1983): 497–599.

Rochemonteix, Maxence, Emile Chassinat, Sylvie Cauville, and Didier Devauchelle. *Le temple d'Edfou.* Cairo: Institut français d'archéologie orientale du Caire, 1897.

Rodenwaldt, Gerhart. *Korkyra: archaische Bauten und Bildwerke.* Berlin: Gebr. Mann, 1939.

Rogers, Alan R. "On equifinality in faunal analysis." *American Antiquity* 65, no. 4 (2000): 709–23.

Romano, David Gilman. "A Roman circus in Corinth." *Hesperia* 74, no. 4 (2005): 585–611.

Römer, Cornelia, and Heinz J. Thissen. "Eine magische Anrufung in koptischer Sprache." *ZPE* 84 (1990): 175–81.

Rossi, Francesco. *Papyrus de Turin.* Wiesbaden: LTR Verlag, 1981.

Rowlandson, Jane, ed. *Women and society in Greek and Roman Egypt: A sourcebook.* New York: Cambridge University Press, 1998.

Rozanova, N. P. "A magical amulet in the Numismatic Collection of the Pushkin Museum." *Vestnik Drevnej Istorii* 74, no. 4 (1960): 107–8.

Ruggiero, Guido. *Binding passions: Tales of magic, marriage, and power at the end of the Renaissance.* New York: Oxford University Press, 1993.

Ruppel, Timothy, Jessica Neuwirth, Mark P. Leone, and Gladys-Marie Fry. "Hidden in view: African spiritual spaces in North American landscapes." *Antiquity* 77, no. 296 (2003): 321–35.

Ryholt, Kim. "On the contents and nature of the Tebtunis Temple Library: A status report." In *Tebtynis und Soknopaiu Nesos: Leben im römerzeitlichen Fajum* edited by Sandra Lippert and Maren Schentuleit, 141–70. Wiesbaden: Harrassowitz, 2005.

Rykwert, Joseph. *The idea of a town: The anthropology of urban form in Rome, Italy and the ancient world.* Princeton: Princeton University Press, 1976.

Sánchez Ortega, María Helena. "Sorcery and eroticism in love magic." In *Cultural*

Bibliography 319

encounters: The impact of the Inquisition in Spain and the New World, edited by Mary Elizabeth Perry and Anne J. Cruz, 58–92. Berkeley: University of California Press, 1991.

Sauneron, Serge. "Le nouveau sphinx composite du Brooklyn Museum et le rôle du dieu Toutou-Tithoès." *JNES* 19, no. 4 (1960): 269–87.

Scarborough, John. "The pharmacology of sacred plants, herbs and roots." In *Magika hiera: Ancient Greek magic and religion,* edited by Christopher A. Faraone and Dirk Obbink, 138–74. New York: Oxford University Press, 1991.

Schachter, Albert. *Cults of Boiotia.* London: University of London, Institute of Classical Studies, 1981.

Schiffer, Michael B. "Archaeological context and systemic context." *American Antiquity* 37, no. 2 (1972): 156–65.

Schiffer, Michael B. *Behavioral archaeology: First principles.* Foundations of archaeological inquiry. Salt Lake City: University of Utah Press, 1995.

Schiffer, Michael B. *Behavioral archeology.* New York: Academic Press, 1976.

Schiffer, Michael B. "Foreword." In *The archaeology of settlement abandonment in Middle America,* edited by Takeshi Inomata and Ronald W. Webb. Salt Lake City: University of Utah Press, 2003.

Schiffer, Michael B. *Formation processes of the archaeological record.* Albuquerque: University of New Mexico Press, 1987.

Schlesier, Renate. "Zauber und Neid: Zum Problem des bösen Blicks in der antiken griechischen Tradition." In *Tradition und Translation: zum Problem der interkulturellen Übersetzbarkeit religiöser Phänomene: Festschrift für Carsten Colpe zum 65. Geburtstag,* edited by Christoph Elsas and Carsten Colpe, 96–112. New York: De Gruyter, 1994.

Scholz, Hans Herbert. *Der Hund in der griechisch-römischen Magie und Religion.* Berlin: Triltsch & Huther, 1937.

Schwartz, Michael. "Sasm, Sesen, St. Sisinnios, Sesengen Barpharanges, and . . . 'Semanglof.'" *Bulletin of the Asian Institute* 10 (1996): 253–57.

Scott, James C. *Domination and the arts of resistance: Hidden transcripts.* New Haven: Yale University Press, 1990.

Scurlock, Jo Ann. *Magico-medical means of treating ghost-induced illnesses in ancient Mesopotamia.* Ancient magic and divination. Leiden: Brill / Styx, 2006.

Segal, Alan F. "Hellenistic magic: Some questions of definition." In *Studies in Gnosticism and Hellenistic religions,* edited by Roelof Van Den Broek and Maarten J. Vermaseren, 349–75. Leiden: Brill, 1981.

Sepher ha-razim = the book of the mysteries. Translated by Michael A. Morgan, Pseudepigrapha series. Chico, CA: Scholars Press, 1983.

Serrano Delgado, José M. "Sceleratissimus seruus publicus: un episodio de la vida municipal afectando a la familia pública." In *Homenaje a José María Blázquez,* edited by Julio Mangas and Jaime Alvar, 331–44. Madrid, 1996.

Seyrig, Henri. "Invidiae Medici." *Berytus* 1 (1934): 1–11.

320 Bibliography

Shaw, Ian, ed. *The Oxford history of ancient Egypt.* Oxford: Oxford University Press, 2000.

Shier, Louise Adele. *Terracotta lamps from Karanis, Egypt: Excavations of the University of Michigan.* Kelsey Museum of Archaeology Studies. Ann Arbor: University of Michigan Press, 1978.

Sijpesteijn, P. J. "Ein Herbeirufungszauber." *ZPE* 4 (1969): 187–91.

Skibo, James M., Michael W. Graves, and Miriam T. Stark, eds. *Archaeological anthropology: Perspectives on method and theory.* Tucson: University of Arizona Press, 2007.

Smith, Cecil. "Recent Greek archaeology and folk-lore." *Folklore* 3, no. 4 (1892): 529–45.

Smith, Jonathan Z. "Here, there, and anywhere." In *Relating religion: Essays in the study of religion,* edited by Jonathan Z. Smith, 323–39. Chicago: University of Chicago, 2004.

Smith, Jonathan Z. *Map is not territory: Studies in the history of religions.* Studies in Judaism in Late Antiquity. Leiden: Brill, 1978.

Smith, Jonathan Z. "Trading places." In *Ancient magic and ritual power,* edited by Marvin W. Meyer and Paul Allan Mirecki, 13–27. New York: Brill, 1995.

Smith, Morton. *Jesus the magician.* San Francisco: Harper & Row, 1978.

Solin, Heikki. "Eine neue Fluchtafel aus Ostia." *Commentationes humanarum litterarum, Societas scientiarum Fennica* 42, no. 3 (1968): 3–31.

Solin, Heikki, Mika Kajava, and Kalle Korhonen. *Analecta epigraphica 1970–1997.* Rome: Institutum Romanum Finlandiae, 1998.

Stannard, Jerry. "Medicinal plants and folk remedies in Pliny, *Historia Naturalis.*" *History and Philosophy of the Life Sciences* 4, no. 1 (1982): 3–23.

Steel, Louise. *Cyprus before history: From the earliest settlers to the end of the Bronze Age.* London: Duckworth, 2004.

Steiner, Richard C. "Northwest Semitic incantations in an Egyptian medical papyrus of the fourteenth century B.C.E." *JNES* 51, no. 3 (1992): 191–200.

Stephan, Robert P., and Arthur Verhoogt. "Text and context in the archive of Tiberianus (Karanis, Egypt; 2nd Century AD)." *BASP* 42, no. 1–4 (2005): 189–201.

Sternberg-El Hotabi, Heike. *Untersuchungen zur Überlieferungsgeschichte der Horusstelen: ein Beitrag zur Religionsgeschichte Ägyptens im 1. Jahrtausend v. Chr.* 2 vols. Wiesbaden: Harrassowitz, 1999.

Stewart, Susan. *On longing: Narratives of the miniature, the gigantic, the souvenir, the collection.* Baltimore: Johns Hopkins University Press, 1984.

Stratton, Kimberly B. *Naming the witch: Magic, ideology, & stereotype in the ancient world.* New York: Columbia University Press, 2007.

Stroud, Ronald S. *The sanctuary of Demeter and Kore: The inscriptions.* Corinth XVIII. Princeton, NJ: American School of Classical Studies at Athens, forthcoming.

Strubbe, J. H. M. "Cursed be he that moves my bones." In *Magika hiera: Ancient Greek magic and religion,* edited by Christopher A. Faraone and Dirk Obbink, 33–59. New York: Oxford University Press, 1991.

Svenbro, Jesper. *Phrasikleia: An anthropology of reading in ancient Greece.* Translated by Janet Lloyd. Ithaca: Cornell University Press, 1993.

Sydenham, Edward A. *The coinage of the Roman Republic.* London: Spink and Son, 1952.

Syme, Ronald. "Consulates in absence." *JRS* 48, no. 1–2 (1958): 1–9.

Tacitus, Cornelius. "The annals." Translated by Anthony Woodman. Indianapolis: Hackett, 2004.

Tait, W. J. "Demotic literature and Egyptian society." In *Life in a multi-cultural society: Egypt from Cambyses to Constantine and beyond,* edited by Janet H. Johnson, 303–10. Chicago: Oriental Institute, 1992.

Takács, Sarolta A. *Isis and Sarapis in the Roman world.* Religions in the Graeco-Roman world. Leiden: Brill, 1995.

Tambiah, Stanley J. "Form and meaning of magical acts: A point of view." In *Modes of thought,* edited by Robin Horton and Ruth Finnegan, 199–229. London: Faber & Faber, 1973.

Tambiah, Stanley J. "The magical power of words." *Man* 3, no. 2 (1968): 175–208.

Tang, Birgit. *Delos, Carthage, Ampurias: The housing of three Mediterranean trading centres.* Rome: "L'Erma" di Bretschneider, 2005.

Tatton-Brown, Veronica A. "Excavations in ancient Cyprus: Original manuscripts and correspondence in the British Museum." In *Cyprus in the 19th century AD: Fact, fancy and fiction: Papers of the 22nd British Museum Classical Colloquium, December 1998,* edited by Veronica A. Tatton-Brown, 168–83. Oxford: Oxbow, 2001.

Taussig, Michael. *Defacement: Public secrecy and the labor of the negative.* Stanford: Stanford University Press, 1999.

Taussig, Michael. *Mimesis and alterity: A particular history of the senses.* New York: Routledge, 1993.

Taussig, Michael. "What do drawings want?" *Culture, Theory and Critique* 50, no. 2–3 (2009): 263–74.

Thomas, Julian. *Time, culture and identity: An interpretive archaeology.* London: Routledge, 1996.

Thomas, Rosalind. *Literacy and orality in Ancient Greece.* Key themes in ancient history. Cambridge: Cambridge University Press, 1992.

Thomassen, Einar. "Is magic a subclass of ritual?" In *The world of ancient magic: Papers from the first international Samson Eitrem seminar at the Norwegian Institute at Athens, 4–8 May 1997,* edited by David R. Jordan, Hugo Montgomery, and Einar Thomassen, 55–66. Norwegian Institute at Athens: Bergen, 1999.

Thompson, Homer A. "Activities in the Athenian agora: 1959." *Hesperia* 29, no. 4 (1960): 327–68.

Thomsen, Marie-Louise. "Witchcraft and magic in ancient Mesopotamia." In *Witchcraft and magic in Europe: Biblical and pagan societies,* edited by Bengt Ankarloo and Stuart Clark, 1–95. Philadelphia: University of Pennsylvania Press, 2001.

Tilley, Christopher. *An ethnography of the Neolithic: Early prehistoric societies in*

322   Bibliography

southern Scandinavia. New studies in archaeology. Cambridge: Cambridge University Press, 1996.

Tomlin, Roger S. O. *Tabellae sulis: Roman inscribed tablets of tin and lead from the sacred spring at Bath.* Oxford: Oxford University Committee for Archaeology, 1988.

Trakosopoulou-Salakidou, Elene. "Κατάδεσμοι από την Άκανθο." In *Γλώσσα και μαγεία. Κείμενα από την Αρχαιότητα,* edited by David R. Jordan and Anastasios Ph. Christidis, 153–69. Athens: Hermes, 1997.

Tran, Nicolas. *Les membres des associations romaines: le rang social des collegiati en Italie et en Gaules sous le haut-empire.* Rome: Ecole française de Rome, 2006.

Trigger, Bruce G. *A history of archaeological thought.* 2nd ed. Cambridge: Cambridge University Press, 2006.

Trinkhaus, Kathryn Maurer. "Mortuary behavior, labor organization, and social rank." In *Regional approaches to mortuary analysis,* edited by Lane Anderson Beck, 53–75. New York: Plenum Press, 1995.

Trumpf, Jürgen. "Fluchtafel und Rachepuppe." *Mitteilungen des Deutschen Archäologischen Instituts, Athenische Abteilung* 73 (1958): 94–102.

Turner, Edith. "Liminality." In *Encyclopedia of religion,* edited by Lindsay Jones, 5460–63. Detroit: Macmillan Reference USA, 2005.

Turner, Victor. "Betwixt and between: The liminal period in rites de passage." In *Symposium on new approaches to the study of religion: Proceedings of the 1964 annual spring meeting of the American Ethnological Society,* edited by June Helm, 4–20. Seattle: University of Washington Press, 1964.

Tylor, Edward Burnett. *Primitive culture: Researches into the development of mythology, philosophy, religion, language, art, and custom.* 2 vols. London: J. Murray, 1929.

Vallas, E., and N. Pharaclas. "Peri tou manteiou tou Trophoniou en Lebadeia." *Athens Annals of Archaeology* 2, no. 1 (1969): 228–33.

van Binsbergen, Wim, and Frans Wiggermann. "Magic in history: A theoretical perspective, and its application to ancient Mesopotamia." In *Mesopotamian magic: Textual, historical and interpretive perspectives,* edited by Tzvi Abusch and Karel van der Toorn, 3–34. Groningen: Styx, 1999.

van der Horst, Pieter W. "The Jews of ancient Cyprus." *Zutot* 3 (2003): 110–20.

van der Vliet, Jacques. "A Coptic *Charitesion* (P. Gieben Copt. 1)." *ZPE* 153 (2005): 131–40.

van Dijk, Jacobus. "Zerbrechen der roten Töpfe." *LÄ,* 1389–96. Wiesbaden: Otto Harrassowitz, 1986.

van Gennep, Arnold. *The rites of passage.* Translated by Monika B. Vizedom and Gabrielle L. Caffee. Chicago: University of Chicago Press, 1960.

van Minnen, Peter. "Boorish or bookish? Literature in Egyptian villages in the Fayum in the Graeco-Roman period." *JJurP* 28 (1998): 99–184.

van Minnen, Peter. "Deserted villages: Two Late Antique town sites in Egypt." *BASP* 32, no. 1–2 (1995): 41–56.

Bibliography   323

van Minnen, Peter. "House-to-house enquiries: An interdisciplinary approach to Roman Karanis." *ZPE* 100 (1994): 227–51.

van Minnen, Peter. "Urban craftsmen in Roman Egypt." *Münstersche Beiträge zur antiken Handelsgeschichte* 6, no. 1 (1987): 31–88.

Venticinque, Philip. "Associations in Ptolemaic and Roman Egypt." In *Oxford handbook of economies in the classical world,* edited by Alain Bresson, Elio Lo Cascio, and François Velde. Oxford: Oxford University Press, forthcoming.

Verboven, Koenraad. "The associative order: Status and ethos among Roman businessmen in late republic and early empire." *Athenaeum* 95, no. 2 (2007): 861–93.

Versnel, Henk S. "Beyond cursing: The appeal for justice in judicial prayers." In *Magika hiera: Ancient Greek magic and religion,* edited by Christopher A. Faraone and Dirk Obbink, 60–106. New York: Oxford University Press, 1991.

Versnel, Henk S. "καὶ εἴ λ[οιπὸν] τῶν μερ[ῶ]ν [ἔσ]ται τοῦ σώματος ὅλ[ο]υ[. . . (. . . and any other part of the entire body there may be . . .). An essay on anatomical curses." In *Ansichten griechischer Rituale: Geburtstags-Symposium für Walter Burkert,* edited by Fritz Graf. Stuttgart: B. G. Teubner, 1998.

Versnel, Henk S. "ΚΟΛΑΣΑΙ ΤΟΥΣ ΗΜΑΣ ΤΟΙΟΥΤΟΥΣ ΗΔΕΩΣ ΒΛΕΠΟΝΤΕΣ: 'Punish those who rejoice in our misery': On curse texts and *Schadenfreude.*" In *The world of ancient magic: Papers from the first international Samson Eitrem seminar at the Norwegian Institute at Athens, 4–8 May 1997,* edited by David R. Jordan, Hugo Montgomery, and Einar Thomassen, 125–62. Bergen: Norwegian Institute at Athens, 1999.

Versnel, Henk S. "ΠΕΠΡΗΜΕΝΟΣ. The Cnidian curse tablets and ordeal by fire." In *Ancient Greek cult practice from the epigraphical evidence,* edited by Robin Hägg, 145–54. Stockholm: Paul Astroms Förlag, 1994.

Versnel, Henk S. "The poetics of the magical charm: An essay on the power of words." In *Magic and ritual in the ancient world,* edited by Paul Allan Mirecki and Marvin Meyer, 105–58. Leiden: Brill, 2002.

Versnel, Henk S. "Prayers for justice, east and west: Recent finds and publications since 1990." In *Magical practice in the Latin West: Papers from the international conference held at the University of Zaragoza, 30 Sept.–1 Oct. 2005,* edited by Richard L. Gordon and Francisco Marco Simón, 275–354. Leiden: Brill, 2010.

Versnel, Henk S. "Some reflections on the relationship magic-religion." *Numen* 38, no. 2 (1991): 177–97.

Versnel, Henk S. "Writing mortals and reading gods: Appeal to the gods as a dual strategy in social control." In *Demokratie, Recht und soziale Kontrolle im klassischen Athen,* edited by David Cohen and Elisabeth Müller-Luckner, 37–76. Munich: Oldenbourg, 2002.

Vila, André. "Un dépôt de textes d'envoûtement au Moyen Empire." *JS* 3, no. 3 (1963): 135–60.

Vogliano, Achille. "Medinet Madi. Fouilles de l'Université Royale de Milan." *CdE* 27 (1939): 87–89.

Vogliano, Achille. *Secondo rapporto degli scavi condotti dalla Missione archeologica*

324   Bibliography

d'Egitto della R. Università di Milano nella zona di Madinet Madi. Cairo: Institut français d'archéologie orientale, 1937.

Volavkova, Zdenka. "Nkisi figures of the lower Congo." *African Arts* 5, no. 2 (1972): 52–59, 84.

Vollmer Torrubiano, Anna, and Alfonso López Borgoñoz. "Nuevas consideraciones sobre las variaciones en el ritual funerario Romano (ss. I–III d.C.)." In *Actas del XXII Congreso Nacional de Arqueología, Vigo, 1993.* Vigo: Xunta de Galicia, Consellería de Cultura, Dirección Xeral de Patrimonio Histórico e Documental, 1995.

Vollmer Torrubiano, Anna, and Alfonso López Borgoñoz. "Nueva aproximación a la necrópolis Romana de incineración de Les Corts (Ampurias)." In *Actas del XXIII Congreso Nacional de Arqueología, Elche, 1995,* 373–77. Elche: Ajuntament d'Elx, 1996.

Voutiras, Emmanuel. *Διονυσοφῶντος γαμοι. Marital life and magic in fourth century Pella.* Amsterdam: J. C. Gieben, 1998.

Voutiras, Emmanuel. "Ένας διαλεκτικός κατάδεσμος από την Πέλλα." *Ελληνική Διαλεκτολογία* 3 (1992–93): 43–48.

Wainwright, G. A. "Keftiu." *JEA* 17, no. 1–2 (1931): 26–43.

Walcot, Peter. *Envy and the Greeks: A study of human behavior.* Warminster: Aris & Phillips, 1978.

Walker, William H. "Ritual technology in an extranatural world." In *Anthropological perspectives on technology,* edited by Michael B. Schiffer, 87–106. Albuquerque: University of New Mexico Press, 2001.

Walker, William H. "Where are the witches of prehistory?" *Journal of Archaeological Method and Theory* 5, no. 3 (1998): 245–308.

Walker, William H., and Lisa J. Lucero. "The depositional history of ritual and power." In *Agency in archaeology,* edited by Marcia-Anne Dobres and John E. Robb, 130–47. New York: Routledge, 2000.

Warde-Perkins, Bryan. "Re-using the Architectural Legacy of the Past, *entre idéologie et pragmatisme.*" In *The idea and ideal of the town between Late Antiquity and the Middle Ages,* edited by G. P. Brogiolo and Bryan Warde-Perkins, 225–54. Boston: Brill, 1999.

Weiner, Annette B. "From words to objects to magic: Hard words and the boundaries of social interaction." *Man* 18, no. 4 (1983): 690–709.

Westermann, William L. "Land reclamation in the Fayum under Ptolemies Philadelphus and Euergetes I." *CPh* 12, no. 4 (1917): 426–30.

Wilburn, Andrew T. "Excavating love magic at Roman Karanis." In *New archaeological and papyrological researches on the Fayyum: Proceedings of the international meeting of Egyptology and papyrology, Lecce 8th–10th June 2005,* edited by Mario Capasso and Paola Davoli, 355–70. Galatina (Lecce): Congedo, 2007.

Wilburn, Andrew T. "Materia magica: The archaeology of magic in Roman Egypt, Cyprus, and Spain." PhD, University of Michigan, 2005.

Bibliography   325

Wilburn, Andrew T. "Re-Mapping Karanis: Geographic Information Systems (GIS) and Site Analysis." In *Proceedings of the Twenty-Fifth International Congress of Papyrology, Ann Arbor 2007,* edited by Traianos Gagos, 2010.

Wilburn, Andrew T. "Representations and images in magical practice." In *The Brill guide to ancient magic,* edited by David Frankfurter and Henk S. Versnel. Leiden: Brill, forthcoming.

Wilburn, Andrew T. "A wall painting at Karanis used for architectural protection: The curious case of Harpocrates and Toutou in granary C65." In Das Fayum in Hellenismus und Kaiserzeit. Fallstudien zu multikulturellem Leben in der Antike, edited by Carolin Arlt and Martin A. Stadler, 185–97. Weisbaden: Harrassowitz, forthcoming.

Wilcken, Ulrich. *Griechische ostraka aus Aegypten und Nubien: ein Beitrag zur antiken Wirtschaftsgeschichte.* 2 vols. Leipzig: Gieseke & Devrient, 1899.

Wilfong, T. G. *Egyptian anxieties,* in preparation.

Wilfong, T. G. "Fayum, Graeco-Roman sites." In *Encyclopedia of the archaeology of ancient Egypt,* edited by Kathryn A. Bard and Steven Blake Shubert, 308–13. New York: Routledge, 1999.

Wilfong, T. G. Review of *Ein neues Archiv koptischer Ostraka* [. . .], by Hasitzka, Monika R. M. *BASP* 35, no. 1–2 (1998): 113–16.

Wilfong, T. G. "Menstrual synchrony and the 'place of women' in ancient Egypt." In *Gold of praise: Studies on ancient Egypt in honor of Edward F. Wente,* edited by Emily Teeter, John A. Larson, and Edward Frank Wente, 419–34. Chicago: Oriental Institute of the University of Chicago, 1999.

Wilfong, T. G. "'Friendship and physical desire': The discourse of female homoeroticism in fifth century CE Egypt." In *Among women: From the homosocial to the homoerotic in the ancient world,* edited by Nancy Sorkin Rabinowitz and Lisa Auanger, 304–29. Austin: University of Texas Press, 2002.

Wilkie, Laurie A. "Secret and sacred: Contextualizing the artifacts of African-American magic and religion." *Historical Archaeology* 31, no. 4 (1997): 81–106.

Willems, Harco. "The social and ritual context of a mortuary liturgy of the Middle Kingdom (*CT* Spells 30–41)." In *Social aspects of funerary culture in the Egyptian Old and Middle Kingdoms: Proceedings of the international symposium held at Leiden University, 6–7 June, 1996,* edited by Harco Willems, 253–372. Leuven: Peeters, 2001.

Winkler, John J. *The constraints of desire: The anthropology of sex and gender in ancient Greece.* New ancient world series. New York: Routledge, 1990.

Wiseman, Donald J. "The vassal-treaties of Esarhaddon." *Iraq* 20, no. 1 (1958): 1–99.

Wiseman, James. "Excavations in Corinth, the gymnasium area, 1967–1968." *Hesperia* 38, no. 1 (1969): 64–106.

Wiseman, Timothy P. "Documentation, visualization, imagination: The case of Anna Perenna's cult site." In *Imaging ancient Rome: Documentation, visualization, imagination,* edited by L. Haselberger and J. Humphrey, 51–62. Portsmouth, RI: Journal of Roman Archaeology, 2006.

Witteyer, Marion. "Curse tablets and voodoo dolls from Mainz: The archaeological evidence for magical practices in the Sanctuary of Isis and Magna Mater." *MHNH* 5 (2005): 105–23.

Woodward, Ann, Peter Leach, and Justine Bayley, eds. *The Uley shrines: Excavation of a ritual complex on West Hill, Uley, Gloucestershire, 1977–9.* London: English Heritage in association with British Museum Press, 1993.

Woodward, Peter, and Ann Woodward. "Dedicating the town: Urban foundation deposits in Roman Britain." *World Archaeology* 36, no. 1 (2004): 68–86.

Wortmann, Dierk. "Neue magische texte." *Bonner Jahrbücher* 168 (1968): 56–111.

Wreszinski, Walter. *Der Londoner medizinische Papyrus (Brit. Museum Nr. 10059) und der Papyrus Hearst.* Leipzig: J. C. Hinrichs'sche Buchhandlung, 1912.

Wünsch, Richard. *Antike fluchtafeln.* Bonn: A. Marcus und E. Weber, 1907.

Wünsch, Richard. *Defixionum Tabellae Atticae.* Inscriptiones Graecae 3.3. Berlin: G. Reimer, 1897.

Wünsch, Richard. "Neue Fluchtafeln." *Rheinisches Museum* 55 (1900): 232–71.

Wünsch, Richard. *Sethianische verfluchungstafeln aus Rom.* Leipzig: B. G. Teubner, 1898.

Yamauchi, Edwin M. *Mandaic incantation texts.* American Oriental Series. New Haven: American Oriental Society, 1967.

Yatromanolakis, Yoryis. "*Baskanos eros:* Love and the evil eye in Heliodorus' *Aethiopica.*" In *The Greek novel, AD 1–1985,* edited by Roderick Beaton, 194–204. London: Croom Helm, 1988.

Yeivin, Samuel. "Report for the Season 1927–1928." Ann Arbor, MI: Kelsey Museum of Archaeology archives. Ann Arbor, Michigan, 1928.

Youtie, Herbert C. "Ostraca from Karanis." *ZPE* 16 (1975): 272–74.

Youtie, Herbert C., and Orsamus M. Pearl. *Papyri and ostraca from Karanis.* University of Michigan studies, Humanistic series vol. 47. Ann Arbor: University of Michigan Press, 1944.

Youtie, Herbert C., and John Garrett Winter. *Papyri and ostraca from Karanis.* University of Michigan studies, Humanistic series vol. 50. Ann Arbor: University of Michigan Press, 1951.

Zauzich, Karl-Th. "Zwei Briefe von Bücherfreunden." In *The Carlsberg Papyri 3.* Copenhagen, 2000.

Zuretti, Carlo O. "Iscrizioni Gnostiche di Cipro in caratteri non epichorici." *Rivista di filologia e d'istruzione classica* 20 (1892): 1–17.

Index

Aaron, son of Tkouikira, 153
Abydos, Egypt, 99n7
Acrocorinth, Greece, 214–15
Acts of the Apostles (Paul, the Apostle), 176
Adonai, 190
Agios Tychonas, Cyprus, 170, 175, 177, 179, 183
agricultural produce
  protection of, 163
  theft of, 96–98, 126
Agrippa, Marcus Vispanius 23
Akamatis, I. M., 241
Akanthos, Thrace, 243
Alexandros (commissioner of curse tablets) 201, 210, 211, 212
Almagro Basch, Martin, 222, 223, 224, 226, 227
Almagro Gorbea, Martin, 222
altars, small, 87
Amathous, Cyprus, 9, 169–218, 255, 257, 261, 262, 263, 264, 265, 266
  archaeological context of tablets, 175, 177–84
  Aupert and Jordan (1994), tablet from Amathous, 194–96
  BM 1889,10-15.14A, 178
  BM 1891,4-18.1 = *CT* 45 =*DT* 22 = Mitford 127, 170–72, 188–91, 196, 201, Pl. 20
  BM 1891,4-18.3 = *DT* 24 = Mitford 129, 191–92
  BM 1891,4-18.4 = *DT* 25 = Mitford 130, 192, 201, 210
  BM 1891,4-18.5 = *DT* 26 = Mitford 131, 201, 211
  BM 1891,4-18.6 = *DT* 27 = Mitford 132, 188, 198, 211

  BM 1891,4-18.7 = *DT* 28 = Mitford 133, 196, 197
  BM 1891,4-18.8 = *DT* 29 = Mitford 134, 210
  BM 1891,4-18.10 = *DT* 31 = Mitford 136, 210
  BM 1891,4-18.11 = *DT* 32 = Mitford 137, 192, 195, 201
  BM 1891,4-18.15 = *DT* 35 = Mitford 140, 197
  BM 1891,4-18.16 = *DT* 36 = Mitford 141, 192–93
  BM 1891,4-18.17 = *DT* 37 = Mitford 142, 201
  BM 1891,4-18.50 (A+B) + BM 1891,4-18.59(47) + Collection Froehner inv. 9, 196–200 = *NGD* 115, 210
  BM 1891,4-18.58, Pl. 22
  BM 1891,4-18.59(1), 182, 185, Pl. 21
  BM 1891,4-18.59(33), 178
  dating of tablets, 172
  excavation of, 174–75, 217
  findspots of tablets, 178–83, 184n47, 209, 217, 258
  historical background, 174–75
  judicial disputes, 190, 192, 198, 210, 211–12, 216
  local adaptation of rituals, 214
  material evidence of tablets, 184–87
  model text (*Vorlage)* from spell manuals, 169, 188, 194, 265
  practitioners at, 200–209
  provenance of tablets, 178–79
  resistance to provincial authority, 210–12, 246
  social context of tablets, 209–18

327

Amathous, Cyprus (*continued*)
  tablets, 170–73, 177–200, 209–19, Pl. 20, Pl.
    21, Pl. 22
  texts of tablets, 187–200
Amennakhte (scribe), 60n12
Amphiarios (god), 199
Ampurias, Spain. *See* Empúries, Spain
amulets, 19, 24, 39, 65, 66, 150, 268
  child's, 130–31
  fever (*P.Mich.* XVIII 768), 109–17, 162, 263,
    Pl. 7
  use of, 48–49, 131
analogy, persuasive, 238
animals
  magic against, 158
  protection of, 157, 159
Anna Perenna (goddess), 91
  See also Fountain of Anna Perenna, Rome,
    Italy
Antigonos Monophthalmos, 247
Antinoopolis, 29n64, 257
Antinoüs, 29n64, 257
Antonine plague, 282n18
Aphis (god), 269
Aphrodite (goddess), 135, 175, 199, 209
Apolinarius Niger, Gaius, 103n17
Apology 1.3 (Apulieus), 20, 23, 56, 88
apples, throwing of, 99n7
Apulieus (Lucius Apulieus)
  Apology 1.3, 20, 23, 56, 88
  Metamorphosis, 24, 95
archangels, 110, 110n35, 269
Ares (god), 29, 30, 48, 80
Arignotus (fictional character), 265
Aristarchus (associate of Paul, the Apostle), 24
Ariston (victim of curse tablet), 171–72, 188,
    196, 198
Artemidoros (Roman physician), 248
Artemidoros, son of Timo, 196, 198
Artemidoros Melasios, son of Gaterana, 196,
  198
Artemion (revolutionary), 174
Artemis Hekate (goddess), 31
artifacts, magical, 8–9, 13, 19–20, 165
  archaeological context of, 10, 13, 30, 49–50,
    93–94, 136, 138–39, 160–69, 255–60
  burial of, 30, 40, 42, 49–50
  commoditization of, 39, 267
  deposition of, 36–37, 39, 40–53, 90, 93, 113,
    119, 132, 138–39, 140, 160, 238–46, 252,
    259, 269, 271
  discarding of/loss of, 49, 140

  distribution of, 265, 267–68
  findspots of, 31, 40–53, 104, 130, 138–39,
    162, 178–79, 271
  forgeries of, 161
  hiding of, 21, 49–50
  identification of, 22, 34, 161, 162, 166, 169–
    70, 255
  inscribed, 26, 65–74
  life-histories of, 34–40, 83, 255
  mundane, 138
  object-specific inquiry into, 35, 41
  organic (plants, animals and natural ingredi-
    ents), 10, 26, 42, 50, 55, 57, 83–89
  physical forms of, 73–74, 184–87
  provenance of, 257
  termination of, 39–40
  weird, 56, 57, 87–88, 98, 100–102, 160, 256
  writing on, 65–73, 192
Assiut, Egypt, 135–36
astrology, 23
Athenian Agora, 89, 92, 180, 182
Athenian Kerameikos, 66, 240, 242–43
Atomus (magician), 176
Audollent, Auguste Marie Henri, 1
  DT (Defixionum Tabellae). *See listings under*
    curse tablets
Augustine (Aurelius Augustinus), Saint, 18
Augustum Trevirorum, 245
Aupert, Pierre, 174, 177, 179, 193, 194–95, 201,
    202, 202n88, 258
Aurelius, Marcus, 24
Aurelius Fulvus, Titus, 220, 234, 235

Bagnall, Roger, 115, 266
Bailliot, Magali, 86, 268
BaKongo people, Central Africa, 80, 85
Balil, A., 229
Ballana, Nubia, 240
Ballesta cemetery, Empúries, Spain, 54, 220,
    222, 249
  archaeological dating of artifacts, 224, 228–
    29, 229n26, 231–32
  Ballesta Tablet 1 = *CT* 52.1 = *LF* 2.1.1/2,
    224–26, 230–31, 233–34, 236–38, Pl. 24a
  Ballesta Tablet 2 = *CT* 52.2 = *LF* 2.1.1/3, 220,
    225–26, 230–31, 234, 237–38, Pl. 24b
  Ballesta Tablet 3 = *CT* 52.3 = *LF* 2.1.1/4,
    225–26, 230–31, 234–38, Pl. 24c
  cinerary urns, 220, 223, 224, 226–27, 228–30,
    Pl. 24, Pl. 25
  Cremation 17, 231–32
  Cremation 21, 224, Pl. 24a, Pl. 25

Index   329

Cremation 22, 225, 227, Pl. 24b, Pl. 25
Cremation 23, 225, 227, Pl. 24c, Pl. 25
   deposition of curse tablets and urns at, 221, 224, 226–27, 229, 229n26
   enclosure walls, 223, 224
   excavation of, 222
   family/social burial collectives, 226, 232, 251
   findspots of tablets, 226
   grave goods, 223, 226, 228
   map of, Pl. 23
   nails, 227–28
   ustrinum, 223, 230
   See also Empúries, Spain
Bar-Jesus (magician), 176
bats, eyes of, 47, 62, 74, 87
Bes (god), 175, 209
Bibliothèque Nationale de France, Paris
   Collection Froehner, 170, 170n2, 178, 194, 196
   Collection Froehner inv. 9 + BM 1891,4-18.50 (A+B) + BM 1891,4-18.59(47) = *NGD* 115, 196–200, 210
birds, 193
   iunx, 135
BM. *See listings under* British Museum
Boak, Arthur Edward Romilly, 115, 277
body detritus, victim's. *See* materials: related/connected to victim; *ousia*
Bohak, Gideon, 14, 52n1, 55
Bolus of Mendes, 157
bones, painted, 12, 140–59, 149n152, 164, 166–67, Pl. 3, Pl. 16, Pl. 18, Pl. 19
   counting and, 145
   deposition of, 140, 141–43, 154
   human, 143, 153, 155, 181
   K.M. inv. 3492, 141
   K.M. inv. 3503, 141, Pl. 3
   K.M. inv. 3503.002, 145
   K.M. inv. 3503.004, 145
   K.M. inv. 3503.008, 145
   K.M. inv. 3503.015, 142
   K.M. inv. 3503.028, 142
   K.M. inv. 3503.038, 149n152
   K.M. inv. 3503.042, 144, Pl, 19
   K.M. inv. 3503.046, 149n152
   K.M. inv. 3503.062, 141, 144, Pl. 16
   K.M. inv. 3503.063, Pl. 16
   K.M. inv. 3503.064, 149n152
   K.M. inv. 3503.065, 141
   K.M. inv. 3503.066, 149n152
   K.M. inv. 3503.101, 143, 149, Pl. 18
   K.M. inv. 3504, 141, 142, Pl. 3, Pl. 17

   K.M. inv. 3504.081, 141
   K.M. inv. 3504.096, 141
   K.M. inv. 3535, 141, Pl. 3
   K.M. inv. 3535.93, 141
   K.M. inv. 10099, 141, Pl. 3
   K.M. inv. 10099.070, 141, 144, 149, 149n152, Pl. 16
   as medium for written spells, 151, 153–54
   pig's, 152n160
   use of, 151–60
books, possession of, 265–66
Bourdieu, Pierre, 33, 34
boustrophedon, 73
bowls, incantation, 146
Brashear, William, 110, 112, 114
brephos. See fetuses
British Museum, 170, 177, 178, 179, 194, 196
   BM 1889,10-15.14A, 178
   BM 1891,4-18.1 = *CT* 45 = *DT* 22 = Mitford 127, 170–72, 188–91, 196, 201, Pl. 20
   BM 1891,4-18.2 = *DT* 23 = Mitford 128, 191
   BM 1891,4-18.3 = *DT* 24 = Mitford 129, 191–92
   BM 1891,4-18.4 = *DT* 25 = Mitford 130, 192, 201, 210
   BM 1891,4-18.5 = *DT* 26 = Mitford 131, 201, 211
   BM 1891,4-18.6 = *DT* 27 = Mitford 132, 188, 198, 211
   BM 1891,4-18.7 = *DT* 28 = Mitford 133, 196, 197
   BM 1891,4-18.8 = *DT* 29 = Mitford 134, 210
   BM 1891,4-18.10 = *DT* 31 = Mitford 136, 210
   BM 1891,4-18.11 = *DT* 32 = Mitford 137, 192, 195, 201
   BM 1891,4-18.15 = *DT* 35 = Mitford 140, 197
   BM 1891,4-18.16 = *DT* 36 = Mitford 141, 192–93
   BM 1891,4-18.17 = *DT* 37 = Mitford 142, 201
   BM 1891,4-18.50 (A+B) + BM 1891,4-18.59(47) + Collection Froehner inv. 9, 196–200 = *NGD* 115, 210
   BM 1891,4-18.58, Pl. 22
   BM 1891,4-18.59(1), 182, 185, Pl. 21
   BM 1891,4-18.59(33), 178
Brunton, Guy, 147
Bryen, Ari Z., 99n7, 100, 103
burning, as means of erotic compulsion, 135–36, 254–55

Caesarea Praetorium, 180
Cairo Genizah, 58
Calocaerus (keeper of imperial camels), 174
Canidia (witch), 57, 87
Canterbury Tales (Chaucer), 157
carmina figurata, 65, 123, 124
Cassander, 247
Cassius Dio Cocceianus, 23
cats, sacrifice of, 86
cemeteries, 42, 54–55, 143, 249
    See also Ballesta cemetery, Empúries, Spain;
    columbaria; dead, the; graves; mortuary
    spaces
Cerberus, 152
Cesnola, Alessandro Palma di, 182, 202, 202n89
charioteers, 2, 5, 6, 39, 45, 193, 271
Chaucer, Geoffrey
    Canterbury Tales, 157
childbirth, 133
Chnoubis (god), 72, 150, 151, 157, 193
Christian, Charles, 177, 178
Christianity, 114–16, 128, 176
Cicero, Marcus Tullius, 173
ciphers, 192n66
cinerary urns, 220, 223, 224, 226–27, 228–30,
    Pl. 25
Claudius (Tiberius Claudius Nero Germanicus),
    emperor, 23–24
Cnidus, Turkey, 186, 206–7, 263
"coefficient of weirdness," 12–13, 18, 34, 56,
    57, 87, 256
Coffin texts, 30n68, 37, 151
Collection Froehner inv. *See listing under* curse
    tablets
collegia, 203–4
Collins, Derek, 79n79
columbaria, 1, 6–7, 269, 271
    See also cemeteries; dead, the; graves; mortu-
    ary spaces
Columella, Lucius Iunius Moderatus, 157
compulsion, 135, 138, 156
conception, promotion of, 132–33
conduits, magical, 43, 46, 184
conjure, 25–26, 30, 36, 55, 93
corpses, 153
cremations
    Empúries, 200, 222–23, 224, 230, Pl. 23, Pl.
    24, Pl. 25
crossroads, 44, 47, 90
Crucinacum, Germania, 240–41, 245
CT (*Curse Tablets and Binding Spells from
    Antiquity and the Ancient World*). *See list-
    ings under* curse tablets

curse tablets, 1–6, 10, 13, 20, 21, 22, 44, 55, 56,
    63, 65, 67, 67–69, 70–71, 73–74, 82, 86,
    91–90, 170, 187, 202n88, 217, 238, 245,
    250, 253
    Amathous, 170–73, 177–86, 188–93, 195–98,
    201, 209–18, Pl. 20, Pl. 21, Pl. 22
    anatomical, 244–45
    Attica, 46, 241
    Aupert and Jordan (1994), tablet from Ama-
    thous, 194–96
    Ballesta Tablet 1 = *CT* 52.1 = *LF* 2.1.1/2,
    224–26, 230–31, 233–34, 236–38, Pl. 24a
    Ballesta Tablet 2 = *CT* 52.2 = *LF* 2.1.1/3, 220,
    225–26, 230–31, 234, 237–38, Pl. 24b
    Ballesta Tablet 3 = *CT* 52.3 = *LF* 2.1.1/4,
    225–26, 230–31, 234–38, Pl. 24c
    BM 1889,10-15.14A, 178
    BM 1891,4-18.1 = *CT* 45 = *DT* 22 = Mitford
    127, 170–72, 188–91, 196, 201, Pl. 20
    BM 1891,4-18.3 = *DT* 24 = Mitford 129,
    191–92
    BM 1891,4-18.4 = *DT* 25 = Mitford 130, 192,
    201, 210
    BM 1891,4-18.5 = *DT* 26 = Mitford 131,
    201, 211
    BM 1891,4-18.6 = *DT* 27 = Mitford 132, 188,
    198, 211
    BM 1891,4-18.7 = *DT* 28 = Mitford 133,
    196, 197
    BM 1891,4-18.8 = *DT* 29 = Mitford 134, 210
    BM 1891,4-18.10 = *DT* 31 = Mitford 136,
    210
    BM 1891,4-18.11 = *DT* 32 = Mitford 137,
    192, 195, 201
    BM 1891,4-18.15 = *DT* 35 = Mitford 140,
    197
    BM 1891,4-18.16 = *DT* 36 = Mitford 141,
    192–93
    BM 1891,4-18.17 = *DT* 37 = Mitford 142,
    201
    BM 1891,4-18.50 (A+B) + BM 1891,4-
    18.59(47) + Collection Froehner inv. 9 =
    NGD 115, 196–200, 210
    BM 1891,4-18.58, Pl. 22
    BM 1891,4-18.59(1), 182, 185, Pl. 21
    BM 1891,4-18.59(33), 178
    Cnidus, 206–7, 209
    Collection Froehner inv. 9 + BM 1891,4-
    18.50 (A+B) + BM 1891,4-18.59(47) =
    NGD 115, 196–200, 210
    commissioners' names on, 187, 190, 196,
    210, 232, 236–37, 238–40
    CT 5 = *SGD* 167, 193n68

Index 331

CT 13 = *DT* 155 = Museo Nazionale Romano inv. n. 52202, 2–7, Pl. 2
CT 40 = *DTA* 107, 67
CT 42 = *DT* 60, 71
CT 45 = BM 1891,4-18.1 = *DT* 22 = Mitford 127, 170–72, 188–91, 196, 201, Pl. 20
CT 52.1 = Ballesta Tablet 1 = *LF* 2.1.1/2, 224–26, 230–31, 233–34, 236–38
CT 52.2 = Ballesta Tablet 2 = *LF* 2.1.1/3, 220, 225–26, 230–31, 234, 237–38
CT 52.3 = Ballesta Tablet 3 = *LF* 2.1.1/4, 225–26, 230–31, 234–38
CT 53 = *DT* 111–12, 63
CT 79 = *SGD* 129, 248
CT 89.3 = *DT* 4, 186, 186n53, 206–7
damaged by hair, 89
deposition of, 6, 42, 43, 45, 91–92, 180, 206, 213, 216, 220, 233, 238–46, 252, Pl. 4
display of, 185–87, 206, 207, 208, 209, 213, 217
DT 4 = *CT* 89.3, 186, 186n53, 206–7
DT 8, 207
DT 18, 194–95
DT 19, 194–95
DT 20, 195–95
DT 22 = BM 1891,4-18.1 = *CT* 45 = Mitford 127, 170–71, 188–90, 196, 201, Pl. 20
DT 23 = BM 1891,4-18.2 = Mitford 128, 191
DT 24 = BM 1891,4-18.3 = Mitford 129, 191–92, 241
DT 25 = BM 1891,4-18.4 = Mitford 130, 192, 201, 210–12
DT 26 = BM 1891,4-18.5 = Mitford 131, 201, 211
DT 27 = BM 1891,4-18.6 = Mitford 132, 188, 198, 211
DT 28 = BM 1891,4-18.7 = Mitford 133, 196, 197
DT 29 = BM 1891,4-18.8 = Mitford 134, 210, 214
DT 31 = BM 1891,4-18.10 = Mitford 136, 210, 214
DT 32 = BM 1891,4-18.11 = Mitford 137, 192, 195, 201
DT 35 = BM 1891,4-18.15 = Mitford 140, 197
DT 36 = BM 1891,4-18.16 = Mitford 141, 192–93
DT 37 = BM 1891,4-18.17 = Mitford 142, 201
DT 43–44 = *CT* 43, 46
DT 60 = *CT* 42, 71
DT 96 = *LF* 5.1.4/3, 240

DT 97 = *LF* 5.1.4/4, 240
DT 100, 245
DT 101, 245
DT 102, 245
DT 103, 245
DT 109, 74
DT 111–12 = *CT* 53, 63
DT 153, 245
DT 155 = *CT* 13 = Museo Nazionale Romano inv. n. 52202, 2–7, Pl. 2
DT 188, 265n12
DT 190, 244
DT 258 = *LF* 11.1.1/31, 240n62
DTA 67, 73
DTA 107 = *CT* 40, 67
Empúries, 220–21, 224–38, 251, 252–53, Pl. 25
exploitation of the dead and, 238–39, 245–46
false writing and, 147, 192
hidden, 240
images on, 193
inscriptions and texts on, 187–200, 220–21, 232–38, 241–42
intentional inclusion in burial space, 221, 230, 238, 240, 241–46
judicial disputes and, 209–10, 220, 237–38
lead, 184, 188
LF 2.1.1/1, 219n2
LF 2.1.1/2 = Ballesta Tablet 1 = *CT* 52.1, 224–26, 230–31, 233–34, 236–38
LF 2.1.1/3 = Ballesta Tablet 2 = *CT* 52.2, 220, 225–26, 230–31, 234, 237–38
LF 2.1.1/4 = Ballesta Tablet 3 = *CT* 52.3, 225–26, 230–31, 234–38
LF 2.1.1/6, 219n2
LF 4.1.2/1, 245
LF 11.1.1/31 = *DT* 258, 240n62
magical symbols and letters on, 191, 233, Pl. 22
Mainz, 215, 231
mass production of, 188
metaphoric congruence between object and victim in, 82
Mitford 127 = BM 1891,4-18.1 = *CT* 45 = *DT* 22, 170–72, 188–91, 196, 201, Pl. 20
Mitford 129 = BM 1891,4-18.3 = *DT* 24, 191–92
Mitford 130 = BM 1891,4-18.4 = *DT* 25, 192, 201, 210
Mitford 131 = BM 1891,4-18.5 = *DT* 26, 201, 211
Mitford 132 = BM 1891,4-18.6 = *DT* 287, 188, 198, 211

curse tablets (*continued*)
Mitford 133 = BM 1891,4-18.7 = *DT* 28, 196, 197
Mitford 134 = BM 1891,4-18.8 = *DT* 29, 210
Mitford 136 = BM 1891,4-18.10 = *DT* 31, 210
Mitford 137 = BM 1891,4-18.11 = *DT* 32, 192, 195, 201
Mitford 140 = BM 1891,4-18.15 = *DT* 35, 197
Mitford 141 = BM 1891,4-18.16 = *DT* 36, 192–93
Mitford 142 = BM 1891,4-18.17 = *DT* 37, 201
mounting of, 182, 185, 207, 214
Musée du Louvre E 27145 A, Pl. 4
Museo Nazionale Romano inv. n. 52202, = *DT* 155 = *CT* 13, 2–7, Pl. 2
NGD 23, 244
NGD 31, 240n57, 241–43
NGD 42, 243
NGD 43, 243
NGD 115 = BM 1891,4-18.50 (A+B) + BM 1891,4-18.59(47) + Collection Froehner inv. 9, 196–200, 210
Olbia, 239–40
Pella, 241–43
pierced by nails, 74, 82, 187, 213–14, 215
Porta San Sebastiano, 1–6, 269–72, Pl. 2
selenite, 184–85, 186, 194–200, Pl. 21, Pl. 22
SGD 1, 140
SGD 2, 140
SGD 9, 79, 243
SGD 14, 247
SGD 90, 243n70
SGD 93, 243n70
SGD 112, 243n70
SGD 113, 243n70
SGD 129 = *CT* 79, 248
SGD 133, 219n2
SGD 134, 219n2
SGD 135, 219n2
SGD 167 = *CT* 5, 193n68
SGD 173, 239
SGD 187, 240
SGD 190, 240n62
targeting governmental authorities, 55, 210, 220, 246–53
targets' names on, 70–71, 73, 82, 187, 190, 192, 196, 201, 213, 232, 237, 242
templates for, 188, 191
workshops for production of, 198
writing styles on, 73

Cyprian, Saint, of Antioch, 204–5
Cyprus, 10, 170
historical background, 173–76
magic associated with, 175–76, 199
Roman control of, 173–74
Cyrene, 82, 199
Cyrus, Saint, 176

Daira Agnelli, 277–78
Dalmatius the Censor (Dalmatius Flavius), 174
de Rossi, Giovanni Battista, 1n1, 7n11
dead, the
compensation given to compel magic, 239, 244, 253
disposal of, 143, 222–28
rites for tending, 199, 199n80
spirits of, 42–43, 46, 57–58, 65, 86, 136, 153–54, 155, 156, 180, 185, 190, 197, 198–99, 209, 213, 214, 216, 228, 230, 238, 243–44, 251, 270
use of in curses, 238–39
death, by unknown means, 22, 251
defixiones. See curse tablets
Delos, Greece, 44
Delphis (fictional character), 89
Demetrios I of Macedonia Poliorcetes, 247
Demetrius (brother of commissioner of a curse tablet), 248
Demetrius (silversmith), 24
Demetrius of Phalerum, 247
demons, 155
Demotic Magical Papyri (PDM). *See* Magical Papyri, Demotic (PDM)
Dercomognus (victim of curse tablet), 241, 245
Dialogues of the Courtesans 4 (Lucian, of Samosata), 89, 137
Dickie, Matthew W., 23
Dieleman, Jacco, 99n7
Dieterich, Albrecht, 199
digestion, 150
Dionysophon (victim of curse tablet), 242
Dipylon Gate, Athens, Greece, 247–48
divinities and deities, 65, 76, 85, 91, 111, 153, 170, 207, 209, 213, 214, 243
chthonic, 44, 67, 190–91, 194, 195, 196, 198–99, 213, 244
Egyptian, 85, 88, 91
Greek, 44
interactions with, 87, 208, 214
retribution through, 252
Divus Nodens, 186
Domitian (Titus Flavius Domitianus), emperor, 24

dromos, 182

Drusilla (sister of Agrippa), 176

DT (*Defixionum Tabellae*). *See listings under* curse tablets

DTA (*Defixionum Tabellae Atticae*). *See listings under* curse tablets

Durkheim, Emile, 18

Edgar, Campbell C., 31

Egypt Exploration Fund, 276

Elymas (magician), 176

Emporion, Spain. *See* Empúries, Spain

Empúries, Spain, 9, 43, 54, 219–53, 255

    archaeological context of tablets, 224–32, 253

    archaeological dating of artifacts, 224, 228–29, 229n26, 231–32

    Ballesta Tablet 1 = *CT* 52.1 = *LF* 2.1.1/2, 224–26, 230–31, 233–34, 236–38, Pl. 24a

    Ballesta Tablet 2 = *CT* 52.2 = *LF* 2.1.1/3, 220, 225–26, 230–31, 234, 237–38, Pl. 24b

    Ballesta Tablet 3 = *CT* 52.3 = *LF* 2.1.1/4, 225–26, 230–31, 234–38, Pl. 24c

    burial practices, 222, 230, 255, 257

    cemeteries, 54, 220, 222

    coins found at, 231

    deposition of urns and curse tablets at, 221, 224, 226–27, 229, 237–38, 252, Pl. 25

    excavation of, 22

    findspots of tablets, 226, 253, Pl. 25

    historical background, 221–24, 236–37

    historical context of inscriptions on tablets, 232–38

    inscriptions on tablets, 232–38

    judicial disputes, 236–38, 242, 246

    mortuary practices, 223–24, 232, 238

    resistance to provincial authorities, 220, 233–38, 246–53, 255

    social context of tablets, 245–46, 246, 252–53

    temples, 220–21

    texts of tablets, 220–21

    See also Ballesta cemetery, Empúries, Spain

envy, 100

Ephesia Grammata, 72

Ephesian letters. See *Ephesia Grammata*

equifinality, 38, 256, 259

Eumazo (god), 195, 213

Euphemia (victim of curse tablet), 135–36

Eupolemus (commander of Cassander's forces in Greece), 247

Euripides

    Hecuba, 137

Eutyches (commissioner of a curse tablet), 210

Eutyches (victim of a curse tablet), 134

evil eye, 100

exuviae. *See* materials: related/connected to victim; *ousia*

Faraone, Christopher A., 24, 42, 124, 153

Fayum, Egypt

    locations of magical artifacts, 161–62, Pl. 5

    See also Karanis, Fayum, Egypt

Febre, Georges, 237

feet, 136, 136n123

Felix (procurator of Judea), 176

fertility, 132

fetuses, 19, 96–98, 101, 167

    throwing of, 19, 96–98

figurae magicae, 119, 119n65, 148, 149, 149n150

figurines, 10, 26, 55, 56–57, 58, 74–83, 162

    binding, 28–30, 44, 48, 77–78, 79, 91, 136, 137

    buried, 30, 79, 90

    burning of, 131–39, 136n122

    creation and manipulation of, 75–78, 136–37

    dog, 62, 74, 81

    erotic, 77, 132–39

    feet of, 136, 136n123

    K.M. inv. 7525, 131–32, 135, 166, Pl. 13

    Karanis, 131–32, 135, 166, Pl. 13

    locations of, 57, 58, 91–92

    Louvre, 28–30, 77, 137, Pl. 4

    male, bound, 79

    melting of, 82–83

    Minkisi, 80–81, 85, 91

    mold made, 83

    naming of, 79

    nude, 132–33

    piercing of, 28, 77–78, 80, 136–37, Pl. 4

    sexualized, 77, 131, 132–33, 135–36, Pl. 4, Pl. 13

    woman, bound, 28–30, 48, 77–78, 80, 254, Pl. 4

    woman, burnt (K.M. inv. 7525), 131–32, 135, 166, Pl. 13

fire, association with erotic magic, 134

Firmicus Maternus, Julius, 23

fiscus Iudaicus, 174

flora, 10

Florus (husband of a commissioner of a curse tablet), 215

Flourentzos, Pavlos, 174

formularies. *See* spell manuals

Fountain of Anna Perenna, Rome, Italy, 44, 91, 156, 180, 272

Frankfurter, David, 13, 63, 64, 72, 101, 116, 128

Frazer, James, 16, 88n110

334   Index

Froehner, Wilhelm, 170, 170n2
Fry, Gladys-Marie, 25–26, 32, 36, 93

Gager, John G.
    CT (Curse Tablets and Binding Spells from
        Antiquity and the Ancient World). See list-
        ings under curse tablets
Gagos, Traianos, 117n59
Gaius (associate of Paul, the Apostle), 24
Geertz, Hildred, 14n7
Gemellus Horigenes, Gaius, also known as
    Horion, 95–98, 102, 103, 161, 164, 167,
    261, 262
    eyesight of, 95–96
gems, magical, 65, 66, 124, 146, 150, 193, 266,
    268
genitals
    female, 77, 131, Pl. 4, Pl. 13
    male, 79, 79n77
    pig, 152n160
geographic information systems (GIS), 283, Pl.
    6, Pl. 8, Pl. 11, Pl. 15
Gering, Hugo, 245n80
Germanicus (Germanicus Julius Caesar), death
    of, 45, 65, 261
ghosts, 29n64, 46, 57–58, 78, 153, 199n80,
    257, 270
    See also dead, the; supernatural
gods, foreign, power of, 18
gossip, 252, 263
Graf, Fritz, 252
grain, protection of, 119, 125–26, 162
graves, 42–43, 46, 143, 147, 259
    family/social burial collectives, 226, 232, 251
    male, 132
    mass, 181–82
    See also Ballesta cemetery, Empúries, Spain;
        cemeteries; columbaria; mortuary spaces
Great Magical Papyrus of Paris. See Magical
    Papyri, Greek (PGM): IV
Greek Magical Papyri (PGM). See Magical
    Papyri, Greek (PGM)
Grenfell, Bernard, 106, 275–76
guilds, 203

Hades (god), 244
Hadrumentum, North Africa, 239
Hagios Tychonas, Cyprus. See Agios Tychonas,
    Cyprus
hair, human, 89
hairpins, 132, 136–38, 258, Pl. 14
hairstyles, 77
Handcock, Gerald, 178–79, 182, 183, 258

Harim Conspiracy, 60n12
Harpocrates (god)
    statuettes of, 83, 127, 127n95
    wall-painting of, Pl. 10
    See also Horus (god); Horus cippi
Hauron, Syria, 252
Hawara, Egypt, 134, 166
Hekate (goddess), 44, 67, 81, 82, 86
Hellenic Mining Company, 184
Hermes (god), 67, 193–94, 195
historiolae, 66
Hogarth, D. G., 106, 275
holy men. See priests and holy men
Horace (Quintus Horatius Flaccus)
    Satires I.8, 57, 80, 87–88
Horion, son of Simourk, 103n17
horoscopes, 23
Horus (god), 119, 121, 126, 163, 271
    See also Harpocrates (god)
Horus cippi, 121–22, 127, 146
    See also Harpocrates (god); Horus (god)
humors, bodily, 134
Hunt, Arthur, 106, 275–76
husbandry, 157
Husselman, Elinor M., 109

Idyll 2 (Theocritus), 20, 57, 89
illnesses, inflicted on others, 134
images, 74–83
    creation and manipulation of, 75–77, 82–83
    formed from words, letters, and signs (see
        carmina figurate)
    imperfect representation and, 78–79, 88
    instructions for images, 119–20, 119n65, 151
    linkage between object and outcome, 81
    linkage between visual and tactile, 76
    metaphoric relationships and, 80–83
    mimesis and, 55, 76–78, 79, 82–83
    protective, 122
    representation of practitioner within, 79–80
    slippage of boundaries between thing and
        thing represented, 76–77
incantations. See inscriptions: magical; spells
Indicetani, 236–37
inscriptions
    confession, 206–8
    magical, 2–5, 10, 17, 29, 31, 55, 62–63,
        65–74, 169
    templates for, 188
Ioukoundos, son-in-law of Tatias, 208
Isis (goddess), 121–22, 126, 127, 163, 271n28

J. Paul Getty Museum, 68, 71

Jacob, son of Euphemia, 153
jars
    objects buried in, 30, 55, 220, 271
    See also Ballesta cemetery, Empúries, Spain:
        cinerary urns
Jason, 135
Jerome, Saint
    Life of Saint Hilarion the Hermit, 46
Jesus, 121, 128, 163, 164n182
Jews, uprisings of, 174
John, Saint, 176
Johnston, Sarah Iles, 239
Jordan, David R., 89, 177, 179, 194–95, 196,
        197, 198n78, 199, 201, 201n86, 247, 258
    NGD (New Greek Curse Tablets [1985–
        2000]). See listings under curse tablets
    SGD (Survey of Greek Defixiones not
        Included in the Special Corpora). See list-
        ings under curse tablets
Josephus, Flavius, 176
Julia Domna, 77
Julius, son of Iudas, 95–98, 100, 162, 164, 262
Julius Horigenes, Gaius, 95
Julius Longinus, Gaius, 103n17
Julius Niger, Gaius, 103, 103n17
Jupiter Optimus Maximus (god), 47, 95, 250

K.M. inv. *See listings under* Kelsey Museum of
        Archaeology, Ann Arbor, Michigan
Kalavassos, Cyprus, 184
Karanis, Fayum, Egypt, 9, 10, 12, 54, 94, 95–
        168, 258, 261, 262, 263, 275–86
    amulet, Pl. 12
    archaeological dating of, 107–9, 258, 279–83
    architecture, 278, 280–82
    Areas A262 and A265, 140–41, Pl. 15
    bones, human, 143
    bones, painted, 140–60, 166, 284–86, Pl. 3,
        Pl. 16, Pl. 18, Pl. 19
    coins, 112, 279
    contextual magic at, 160–68
    discovery and dating of papyri, including
        Gemellus papyri, 103n7, 280
    excavation of, 104, 106–8, 132n106, 140–41,
        275–83, Pl. 6
    excavation records of, 102–4, 107, 258, 278–79
    faunal analysis of bones, 142–43
    fertilizer mining at, 106–7, 117, 140, 162,
        277, Pl. 15
    fever amulet (*P.Mich.* XVIII 768), 109–17,
        162, 263, Pl. 7
    figurine (K.M. inv. 7525), 131–39, 162, 166,
        Pl. 13

figurines, 74, 131–39, 162
grain and granaries, 118, 125, 130, Pl. 8
hairpins, 132, 136–38, 258, Pl. 14
historical background, 105–9
K.M. inv. 3492, 141
K.M. inv. 3503, 141, Pl. 3
K.M. inv. 3503.002, 145
K.M. inv. 3503.004, 145
K.M. inv. 3503.008, 144
K.M. inv. 3503.015, 142
K.M. inv. 3503.028, 142
K.M. inv. 3503.038, 149n152
K.M. inv. 3503.042, 144, Pl, 19
K.M. inv. 3503.046, 149n152
K.M. inv. 3503.062, 141, 144, Pl. 16
K.M. inv. 3503.063, Pl. 16
K.M. inv. 3503.064, 149n152
K.M. inv. 3503.065, 141
K.M. inv. 3503.066, 149n152
K.M. inv. 3503.101, 143, 149, Pl. 18
K.M. inv. 3504, 141, 142, Pl. 3, Pl. 17
K.M. inv. 3504.081, 141
K.M. inv. 3504.096, 141
K.M. inv. 3535, 141, Pl. 3
K.M. inv. 3535.93, 141
K.M. inv. 7525, 131–39, 162, 166, Pl. 13
K.M. inv. 10099, 141, Pl. 3
K.M. inv. 10099.070, 141, 144, 149,
    149n152, Pl. 16
K.M. inv. 21776, 132, Pl. 14
K.M. inv. 24255, 130–31, Pl. 12
K.M. inv. 26980, 141
land reclamation, 105
layer designations at, 107, 112, 118, 130, 140,
    279–83, Pl. 6
lead sheet, on cord, 130–31, Pl. 12
limestone, painted, 142, Pl. 17
maps of, Pl. 6, Pl. 8, Pl. 11, Pl. 15
occupation layers at, 107, 112, 118, 130, 140,
    279–83, Pl. 6
ostraca, 20, 111–12, 113
ostracon (O.Mich. inv. 9883), 118–29, 263,
    Pl. 9
photographic archive of, 109, 130, 141–42
religious conversion to Christianity, 114–17
Structure 165, 129–32, Pl. 11
Structure 242, 11
Structure 5006, room A, storage chamber,
    103n17, 103–4
Structure C65, 126–27, Pl. 10
Structure C403, 118, 125, Pl. 8
temples, 115
variation of rites from spell manuals and

known magic, 166–67
Kardelos (victim of curse tablet), 2–5, 7
Karpime Babia (victim of curse tablet), 215
Kastor (resident of Karanis), 96n2
katadesmoi. See curse tablets
Kellis, Egypt, 101
 Coptic letter from (*P.Kell.Copt.* 35), 61n16,
  164–65, 267
Kelsey, Francis, W., 277, 279
Kelsey Museum of Archaeology, Ann Arbor,
  Michigan, 141, 146–47
 K.M. inv. 3492, 141
 K.M. inv. 3503, 141, Pl. 3
 K.M. inv. 3503.002, 145
 K.M. inv. 3503.004, 145
 K.M. inv. 3503.008, 144
 K.M. inv. 3503.015, 142
 K.M. inv. 3503.028, 142
 K.M. inv. 3503.038, 149n152
 K.M. inv. 3503.042, 144, Pl, 19
 K.M. inv. 3503.046, 149n152
 K.M. inv. 3503.062, 141, 144, Pl. 16
 K.M. inv. 3503.063, Pl. 16
 K.M. inv. 3503.064, 149n152
 K.M. inv. 3503.065, 141
 K.M. inv. 3503.066, 149n152
 K.M. inv. 3503.101, 143, 149, Pl. 18
 K.M. inv. 3504, 141, 142, Pl. 3, Pl. 17
 K.M. inv. 3504.081, 141
 K.M. inv. 3504.096, 141
 K.M. inv. 3535, 141, Pl. 3
 K.M. inv. 3535.93, 141
 K.M. inv. 7525, 131–39, 162, 166, Pl. 13
 K.M. inv. 10099, 141, Pl. 3
 K.M. inv. 10099.070, 141, 144, 149,
  149n152, Pl. 16
 K.M. inv. 21776, 132, Pl. 14
 K.M. inv. 24255, 130–31, Pl. 12
 K.M. inv. 26980, 141
Keniherkhepeshef (scribe), 60n12
kharaktêres, 5, 72, 72n50, 149, 149n150,
  149n152, 191, 192, 195–96, 201, 269,
  Pl. 22
Kiely, Thomas, 177n28
kolossoi, 78
Kore (goddess), 209
Kourion, Cyprus, 177, 179, 184
Kronos (god), 152
Kropp, Amina
 LF (Defixiones: ein aktuelles corpus latein-
  ischer Fluchtafeln). See listings under
  curse tablets

Lamboglia, Nino, 236
lamellae, 66
 gold, 68, 71
lamps, 91–92
 non-red, 91
landownership, disputes over, 96, 162, 237
Lapethus, Cyprus, 176
Latisana, Italy, 165
laws, Roman, 22
Leone, Mark, 25–26, 32, 36, 93
letterforms, mystical. *See kharaktêres*
Lex Cornelia de sicariis et veneficiis, 22
LF (Defixiones: ein aktuelles corpus lateinischer
  Fluchtafeln). See listings under curse tablets
Libanius, *Or.* I, 9–10, 47
libraries, 60n12
 Egyptian temple, 59–60
Life of Saint Hilarion the Hermit (Jerome), 46
Limassol, Cyprus, 184
limestone, painted, 142, Pl. 17
liminality, 42, 46, 255
lineage, maternal, 110, 110n37
lintels, Coptic, 128–29
London Hay 10391, 32
London Medical Papyrus, 200n83
Louvre figurine, 28–30, 77, 137, Pl. 4
lovesickness, 134
Lucian, of Samosata
 Dialogues of the Courtesans 4, 89, 137
 Philopseudes, 204n99, 265

MacDonald, Louise, 177, 179
Macron (dead individual, addressed in curse
  tablet), 241–42, 243
magic, 13–15, 256, Pl. 5
 accusations of, 20, 23, 55, 95–105
 aggressive, 45, 69, 99, 102, 133, 136, 153,
  157–58, 167, 211, 248–49, 261, 262
 apotropaic, 100–101, 228
 appropriation of, 63–64, 267
 archaeological context and, 7–8, 10, 15, 17,
  32, 40–53, 55, 93–94, 104, 128, 138–39,
  160–68, 254–72
 archaeological records of, 25–34, 57–64,
  162–63, 258, 260, 272
 binding through fetus throwing, 96–100, 101,
  262
 Cypriot, 175–76, 201–3, 212
 definitions of, 6, 9, 13–16
 documentary/textual sources of, 24–25,
  55–64, 93–94, 102, 163–64, 167, 170, 254,
  257, Pl. 5
 efficacy of, 17, 36, 41–42, 44–47, 70, 78, 88,

100, 162, 166, 211, 250, 262, 269
Egyptian, 28, 59, 64, 270
emic approach to, 14–15
empirical markers of, 19–20
enclosing, 100, 136
erotic attraction, 42n112 (*see also* magic: love)
etic approach to, 15
evidence of, 20–22, 25, 160, 169–70
exchange of, 264–71
exoticism and, 15, 17, 18
fertility, 129
fetus, 19, 96–98, 101, 167
gender and, 165–66
goals of, 8, 19, 36, 44, 66, 68, 79, 134–35, 190, 198–200
Greek and Roman concepts of, 64, 101–2
illegality of, 22–25, 162, 211–12, 252, 261
Jewish, 58–59, 176, 176n20
Late Antiquity, 1–5, 22–23, 64, 94, 117, 129, 260
local, 51–53, 63–64, 94, 101–2, 155, 159, 167–68, 169, 170, 212, 214, 255, 264, 269–71, Pl.5
love, 28–31, 42, 45, 62, 64, 70, 81, 89, 99n7, 131–39, 152, 153, 197–98, 199, 199n83
materiality of, 8, 9, 10, 11, 13, 17, 20, 25–26, 28, 36–37, 55–56, 64–93, 256, 267–69 (*see also* artifacts, magical; materials; and *specific types of objects*)
Mediterranean, 51–53, 64, 95, 264, 268, 269, 270
necromancy, 64, 153, 153n164
performance and, 17, 19, 57, 61–62, 80, 167, 217, 262, 269
political intrigue and, 23n45, 56
power and, 246–48, 249–51, 261
process of, 8, 65
public aspects of, 19, 49, 100, 104, 160–61, 162, 206, 208, 214, 248, 252, 261
punishments for practicing, 22–23, 211, 249–50
religion and, 15, 17–18, 85, 86, 128, 147, 163–64, 190, 205, 216, 217
representations in, 74–83
ritual actions and, 15, 16–18, 57, 65, 71, 79, 82–83
role of correspondences, 75
role of speech, 12, 16–17, 69–71
Roman Period, 20–25
secrecy and, 11, 15, 18, 21, 162, 246, 249, 262
society and, 18–19, 246–53

spread of, 11, 51–53, 59–61, 63–64, Pl. 5
technologies of, 256
trials of, 23
uses of, 11
vocabulary of, 51–53, 63, 264, 271
women and, 165–67
See also artifacts, magical; curse tablets; inscriptions; rituals; spell manuals; spells
Magical Papyri, Demotic (PDM), 9, 10, 26–28, 32, 52, 94, 169
xii, 45
xiv.451–58, 99n7
xiv.675–94, 33
lxi.112–27, 42, 151
Magical Papyri, Greek (PGM) 9, 10, 26–28, 32–33, 52, 61–62, 64, 84, 153, 162, 254
I.262–347, 85, 94
II.64–184, 149
III.1–164, 86
III.410–23, 38
IV.153, 172
IV.296–466, 29, 31, 48, 102, 153
IV.1390–1495, 197, 198
IV.1872–1927, 151
IV.1928–2005, 153
IV.2006–2125, 155
IV.2891–2942, 85
IV.2943–66, 47, 62, 74, 87, 88, 90, 92, 93
IV.2967–3006, 88
IV.3086–3124, 152
V.372–75, 61, 81
V.383, 61
VI.398, 98n4
VII.540–78, 91
VII.925–39, 149
VIII.407–10, 91
IX.4, 190
XII, 45
XII.967, 190n60
XVI, 89
XIXa, 135
XXXV.1–42, 149
XXXVI, 105, 119, 190
XXXVI.1–34, 148
XXXVI.69–101, 42, 134
XXXVI.102–33, 134
XXXVI.134–60, 139
XXXVI.161–77, 71
XXXVI.178–87, 149
XXXVI.231–55, 148
XXXVI.275–83, 149
LXVIII.1–20, 134
LXXVII, 148

Magical Papyri, Greek (PGM) (*continued*)
    XC.14–18, 149
    CVI.1–10, 150
magices factio, 202
magicians. *See* practitioners of magic
Magna Mater (goddess), 215
malaria, 113
Malinowski, Bronislaw, 12–13, 57
Maqlû, 133
Margalioth, Mordecai, 58
Mari, Cyprus, 177, 177n28
Marion (victim of curse tablet), 210
marriages, cursed, 241–42
Mary, Blessed Virgin, 121, 128, 163, 164n182
Mastrocinque, Attilo, 92
materia magica. *See* magic: materiality of;
    materials
materials
    categories of magical, 55, 63, 64–93
    consciousness of, 67–68
    creation of, 75–76
    forbidden, 8
    miniaturized religious, 86–87
    related/connected to victim, 10, 26, 42, 55,
        75, 84, 88–89, 88n110, 137, 255 (see also
        ousia)
    repurposed/transformed into magical objects,
        10, 26, 37–38, 43–44, 50, 55–57, 62, 65,
        88, 90–93
Matrona (victim of curse tablet), 31
Matter, Jacques, 271
Maturus, Marius, procurator of the Maritime
    Alps, 236
Mauss, Marcel, 18
Mayer, Marc, 237
Medea, 135
Mediterranean sites, discussed in text, map of,
    Pl. 1
Meroe (witch), 24
Metamorphosis (Apulieus), 24, 95
Metrodorus Asbolios (victim of curse tablet),
    211, 211n121
mimesis, 55, 76–78, 79
Mirgissa, Sudan, 158
Mitford, Terence B., 191, 192, 201, 201n86
    Mitford (*The inscriptions of Kourion*). *See*
        listings *under* curse tablets
Miysis (priest), 61
Mnesimachos (target of curse tablet), 79
Mnevis (god), 269
Montserrat, Dominic, 275n1
moon, 185

mortuary spaces, 42, 48, 222, 223, 222–24
    See also Ballesta cemetery, Empuriés, Spain;
        cemeteries; columbaria; dead, the; graves;
        tombs
Mostagedda, Egypt, 147–48
Mounogenes (goddess), 244
Mt. Hagios Ilias, Greece, 183
Mueller, Katja, 283n22
mummies
    images of, 5, 74, 269
    throwing of, 99n7
mummification, of animals, 85–86
murders, 22, 251–52, 261
Murray, A. S., 177, 178, 179
Museo Nazionale Romano inv. n. 52202. *See*
    listing *under* curse tablets

Narmouthis, Fayum, Egypt, 123–24
    ostracon (Vogliano 15), 124
Neophanes (victim of curse tablet), 46
Nero (Nero Claudius Caesar), emperor, 23, 24
Newton, Charles Thomas, 206, 207
NGD (New Greek Curse Tablets [1985–2000]).
    See listings *under* curse tablets
Nubians, 147, 158
Numantina, prosecution of, 23

O.Mich. inv. 9883, 118–29, 263, Pl. 9
oath ceremonies, 82, 83n88, 133
ochre, 140
    writing and, 143–47
Ogden, Daniel, 181–82
Olossitani, 236–37
Olot, Spain, 236
oracles, 131
Oracular Amuletic Decrees, 131
Oropos, Greece, 244
Osiris (god), 191, 269
ostraca, as mnemonic devices, 123
ousia, 62, 79, 81, 88, 137
    See also materials: related/connected to
        victim
Oxyrhynchus, Greece, 31, 89, 120, 131, 276,
    276n5

P.Chester Beatty VII, 64n21
P.Haun. III 58, 116
P.Kel.Copt. 35, 61n16, 164–65, 267
P.Köln inv. 20826, 114
P.Leiden I 384, 60
P.London-Leiden, 60
P.Mich. VI 390, 103n17

P.Mich. VI 421, 103n17
P.Mich. VI 422, 95, 97
P.Mich. VI 423–44, 95, 97
P.Mich. VI 425, 96n2
P.Mich. VI 428, 103n17
P.Mich. XVIII 768, 109–17, 162, 263, Pl. 7
P.Mich.inv. 757, 30, 31
P.Oslo I. *See* Magical Papyri, Greek (PGM):
    XXXVI
palindromes, 110, 110n36
papyri, 66–67
    Demotic, 59
    Greek, 59, 60
    See also Magical Papyri, Demotic (PDM);
        Magical Papyri, Greek (PGM); *listings for*
        individual texts
Papyri Graecae Magicae. See Magical Papyri,
    Greek (PGM)
Papyrus Harris, 64n21
Papyrus Turin 1993, 122
Parrhasius (painter), 76
Pasianax (dead individual, addressed in curse
    tablet), 46, 241
passion, enflaming of, 134–35
Paul, the Apostle, 24, 265
    Acts of the Apostles, 176, 265
Pausanias (second-century author)
    9.39, 183
PDM. *See* Magical Papyri, Demotic (PDM)
Peter, Apostle, 271n28
Peterson, Enoch E., 109, 115, 130, 278, 280
Petesouchos (elder of Karanis), 97
Petrie, Flinders, 106, 275, 276
Petropoulos, John, 70
PGM. *See* Magical Papyri, Greek (PGM)
Pherenikos (victim of curse table), 67
Phila (?) (commissioner of a curse tablet), 242,
    243
Philodemos, son of Hedoneto, 194
Philopseudes (Lucian, of Samosata), 204n99,
    265
phrases, magical. See *voces magicae*
pigs, phallus or rib of, 152n160
Pindar
    Pythian 4.213–19, 135
Pitys, King, 153
plants
    linkages within rituals, 84–85
    medicinal use of, 84
    metaphoric relationships and, 85
Plato, 39, 44, 70
    Leg. 933 a–b, 57n4

Pleistarchos (brother of Cassander), 247
Plewit, Egypt, 46, 248
Pliny the Elder (Gaius Plinius Secundus), 10, 20,
    70, 84, 99, 113
    HN XXVIII.34, 45
    HN XXX.2.11, 175, 202, 202n91
    HN XXXV.36, 76
Pliny the Younger (Gaius Plinius Caecilius
    Secundus), 203
Pollard, Nigel, 108, 283
pomegranates, throwing of, 99n7
Porta San Sebastiano, Rome, Italy, 1
    curse tablets, 1–6, 269–72, Pl. 2
portraiture, 77
Potianus (friend of Apuleius), 56
potsherds. *See* ostraca
practitioners of magic, 6, 11, 18, 21, 24, 42, 51–
    52, 89, 159, 163–65, 214, 263–64
    Amathous, 172, 182, 200–209, 217, 264
    Empúries, 232
    Cypriot, 202–3
    illiterate, 146, 147, 155, 164, 167
    itinerant, 204, 265, 266
    lay, 164, 166
    local, 51, 159, 166
    at Mainz, 263–64
    outsider status of, 261, 264
    professional, 51, 61, 159, 187, 200–209, 216,
        261–62, 263, 270
    training of, 204–6, 266–67
"prayers for justice," 68–67, 186, 206–7, 210,
    213, 215–16, 243–46, 263
Preisendanz, Karl, 26–27, 120
priests and holy men, 59–61, 104, 117, 123–24,
    263
    Asia Minor, 207–8
    Christian, 163–64
    Coptic, 61n14
    Egyptian, 205, 270
    itinerant, 204, 265
    local, 128, 270–71
    Mainz, 264
    payments to, 208–9
Psais (correspondent about a spell), 165
Ptolemais, daughter of Aias and Horigenes, 29,
    77, Pl. 4
Ptolemy II Philadelphus, 105
Ptollas (elder of Karanis), 97
pubic triangle, 132
Pudentilla, 56
puppies, sacrifice of, 63, 86
Pythian 4.213–19 (Pindar), 135

Qenherkhepshef (scribe), 60
quartz, 185
Quseir al-Qadim, Egypt, 184

red (color), Egyptian association with evil and/
  or harmful magic, 91, 155
Reese, David S., 142
refuse, 49n141, 112, 154, 155
resistance, covert, to Roman provincial authorities and Rome, 11, 173, 212, 220, 221,
  246–53, 261–63
ring-letters. See *kharaktêres*
rites, Nubian, 147
ritual manuals. *See* spell manuals
ritual pollution, 42, 101
rituals
  beneficial, 24, 91
  execration, 158, 238
  funerary, 48–49, 238
  household, 19, 24, 87, 133, 159
  locations of, 42–51, 161–62, 248, 249–50,
    259
  love inducing, 129–39, 197–98
  Mesopotamian, 133
  oral, 69–70, 198
  performance of, 27, 37–38, 57, 61–62, 70, 80,
    93, 167, 208, 252
  proximity to victim, 44–46, 255
  sanctification of, 87
Rodà, Isabel, 237
Rome, Italy
  expulsion of practitioners of magic, 23–24
  Imperial control and colonial oppression,
    246–53
  response to rituals targeting authorities,
    249–50
Rufus, Q Pomponius P.f., 235
Ruppel, Tim, 25–26

sacrifices, animal, 20, 22, 63, 84, 85
Sagana (witch), 57, 87
Salamis, Cyprus, 174, 202
Sanctuary of Isis and Magna Mater, Mainz,
    Germany
  curse tablets, 90, 133n110, 201n85, 215–16,
    231, 263–64, 272
Santi Nereo e Achilleo, Rome, Italy, 271n28
Sarapion, son of Allous, 109, 110, 113, 162
SB XVI.12593, 103n17
scepters, erection of, 208
Scipio, Gnaeus Cornelius, 221
scribes, 114
Sefire Inscription, 83n88

Selene (goddess), 98
selenite, 184–85, 186, 194–200, Pl. 21, Pl. 22
Seleucia on the Tigris, Iraq, 146–47
Sempronius Campanus Fidentinus, 236
Sepher ha-Razim, 58–59
Serapias (commissioner of a curse tablet), 210
Sesostris III, pharaoh of Egypt, 158
Seth (god), 91, 148, 155, 269
seven (number), 110n35
*SGD (Survey of Greek Defixiones not Included
    in the Special Corpora). See listings under*
    curse tablets
shafts, 182–84, 258
sheets
  lead, 8, 55, 66, 67, 68, 130–31, 186, 206–7,
    230, Pl. 12, Pl. 20
  selenite, 184–85, 186, 194–200, Pl. 21, Pl. 22
  See also curse tablets
Shenoute, Saint, 46, 248
shrines, 43
Simaetha (fictional character), 57, 89
Simón, F. Marco, 224
Sisokhor (god), 190, 195, 213
skulls
  animal, 157
  human, 24, 153
slaves, African-American, 25–26
sleeplessness, 62
Smith, Arthur H., 175, 178n30
Smith, Cecil, 178, 178n30, 179, 185, 187
Sokras (assistant to elders of Karanis), 97
Sokrates, son of Tatias, 208
sorcerers. *See* practitioners of magic
Sotas, son of Iudas, 95, 96
Soterianos, also known as Limbaros, 171, 188
Sozomenos (victim of a curse tablet), 210
spaces
  liminal, 42, 46, 255, 259
  religious, 43–44
spell manuals, 2, 25, 26–27, 29–32, 41–42, 60–
    62, 102, 124–25, 148, 161, 263, 264–66,
    268, 270
  Amathous, 170–73
  Cnidus, 206–8
  distribution of, 60–61, 161, 198–99, 264–67
  errors in copying, 114, 169, 191–92, 263, 268
  findspots of, Pl. 5
  Fayum, 105, 114–15, 124, 134, 164–65
  model texts (*Vorlagen*), 114, 148–49, 169,
    188, 194, 201, 263, 265
  reorientation of Egyptian magic in, 64, 199
  See also Magical Papyri, Demotic (PDM);
    Magical Papyri, Greek (PGM)

spells, 2–3, 10, 15, 55, 187, 263
  anti-scorpion, 122–23
  anti-witchcraft, 133
  Asia Minor, 208
  erotic, 134, 135n118, 241–42, 243, 245
  Greek, 199
  goals of, 66, 68, 170, 187, 190, 198–200
  homoerotic, 138, 138n129
  instructions for, 8, 27, 65, 118–19, 124, 128,
    134, 140, 148–49, 163, 165, 190, 194, 246,
    256–57, 266
  knowledge of, 21, 163
  language of, 12–13, 17, 59, 217
  medicinal and apotropaic, 64n21, 109–11,
    113–14, 122–23
  "muzzling," 190, 192, 198, 210, 213, 216
  negation of, 21, 40, 46–47, 133, 250–51
  oral, 69–71, 99n7, 165, 246
  protective, 122–23
  secrecy of, 21, 203
  slander, 98
  social context of, 10, 18, 172–73, 207, 245–
    46, 262
  targets of, 6, 29, 73, 129, 134, 139, 170, 269
  templates for, 27, 29, 188, 191
  written, 69–71, 73, 165, 187–200, 266
  See also Magical Papyri, Demotic (PDM);
    Magical Papyri, Greek (PGM); spell
    manuals
Starkey, J. L., 278
statuary, 76–77
  speaking, 76n67
"stereotype appropriation," 63–64
Stewart, Susan, 87
Sulla, Lucius Cornelius, 22
supernatural, 43–44, 46, 65, 179–80, 185, 212,
  216, 238, 251
  locations associated with, 43–44, 46, 179–80
  See also dead, the; ghosts
Suppl. Mag. I 49, 31, 89
Suppl. Mag. I 50, 31
Suppl. Mag. I 51, 31
Swain, George, 109
Symbols, magical, 5, 65, 72, 148–49, 150–51,
  155, 191, 194, 195–96
Syme, Ronald, 235

tablets. *See* curse tablets; sheets, lead; sheets,
  selenite
Tacitus, Cornelius
  Ann. 2.69, 45, 65, 261
Tambiah, Stanley, 16
Tatias (commissioner of rite), 208

Tebtynis Temple Library, 60
temples, 44
  Egyptian, 59–60, 206
  Sanctuary of Isis and Magna Mater, Mainz,
    Germany, 90, 133n110, 201n85, 215–16,
    231, 263–64, 272
  Temple of Demeter and Kore, Acrocorinth,
    Greece, 214–15
  Temple of Demeter and Kore, Cnidus, Tur-
    key, 206–7
  Temple of Sulis Minerva, Bath, England, 147,
    180, 201
  Temple of Zeus Hypsistos, Delos, Greece 44
Terentiff, J., 278
Thebes, Egypt, 29, 59, 60, 197, 205
Theocritus
  Idyll 2, 20, 57, 89
Theodoros (commissioner of love spell), 31
Theodoros (governor of Cyprus), 192, 201, 210,
  211
Theodorus (doctor on Cyprus), 176
Theon (commissioner of curse tablet), 135–36
Theophrastus, 84
Thessalus, of Tralles, 205
Thestylis (fictional character), 57
Thetima (victim of curse tablet), 241, 243
Thomassen, Einar, 18
Thoth (god), 193–94
Tiberius (Tiberius Julius Caesar Augustus),
  emperor, 23
Timon, son of Markus, 192, 210, 211
Tithoes. *See* Tutu (god)
tombs, 1, 182–83, 221
torture, as means of erotic compulsion, 135
tourism, Graeco-Roman, 63–64
towns and villages, rural, 95, 159, 162, 167
Trajan (Marcus Ulpius Traianus), emperor, 174
trash. *See* refuse
travel, to Egypt, 63–64, 204–5
Tuder, Italy, 47, 249–50, 261
Tutu (god)
  wall-painting of, 126–27, Pl. 10
Tylor, Edward, 16

Ulattius Severus (victim of curse tablet), 216

Vales (correspondent about a spell), 165, 267
Vassal Treaties of Esarhaddon, 83n88
vermin, protection against, 125–26
Versnel, Henk, 17n19, 68, 206, 244
Vespasian (Titus Flavius Vespasianus), emperor,
  23, 24, 237
Via Appia, Rome, Italy, 1

Vigna Marini, Rome, Italy, 1, 6
Vitellius, Aulus (Aulus Vitellius Germanicus
    Augustus), emperor, 23, 24
voces magicae, 71–72, 110, 120, 123, 124, 190–
    91, 193, 194
Vogliano 15 (ostracon), 124
votives, 185
vowels, Greek, 5, 72, 120, 123

wands, magic, 152
water, 43, 44
    as deposition location, 180
    empowered, through pouring on writing, 70,
    121
water pipes, 8, 66
wells, 43, 179–80
Wendrich, Willeke, 108, 282
witches. *See* practitioners of magic

writing
    Egyptians and, 70
    false, 146–47, 192
    Greeks and, 69–70
    mimicked, 143, 146, 164
    power of, 65–66, 69–73, 146
    sacred, 72
Wünsch, Richard, 1, 7, 178, 193, 195, 270
    DTA (Defixionum Tabellae Atticae). See list-
    ings under curse tablets
Wypustek, Andrzej, 99n7, 100, 103

XII Tables, 22, 126

Yeivin, Samuel, 278

Zenas, 96, 97
Zeuxis, of Heraclea (painter), 76
Zuretti, Carlo O., 202